CONSPIRACY, CALAMITY AND COVER-UP

THE WOODEN DOVE

"It came to me in a nightmare, Hermann—my secret weapon against the Allies for next year's campaign."

CONSPIRACY, CALAMITY AND COVER-UP

THE TRUTH BEHIND THE HESS FLIGHT TO SCOTLAND, MAY 10TH 1941

JOHN HARRIS AND
RICHARD WILBOURN

First published by Uniform
an imprint of the Unicorn Publishing Group LLP, 2023
Charleston Studio
Meadow Business Centre
Lewes BN8 5RW

www.unicornpublishing.org

10 9 8 7 6 5 4 3 2 1

ISBN 978-1-914414-97-8

Cover design by Matt Carr
Typeset by Vivian Head

All photographs from the author's collection unless stated otherwise.
The author would like to thank Toby Chance for allowing us to publish the pictures on pages 114 and 115.

Printed in Malta by Gutenberg Press Ltd

DEDICATION

'First the truth is ridiculed. Then it meets outrage.
Then it is said to have been obvious all along.'
Arthur Schopenhauer[1]

During the week ending 18 October 2020, John Harris had an untypically unpleasant exchange of correspondence with Sir Richard J. Evans, nominally one of the foremost British historians. Sir Richard had just published a book on Nazi Conspiracies, *The Hitler Conspiracies: The Third Reich and the Paranoid Imagination* and Harris and Wilbourn were clearly in the firing line (for those interested, see his Chapter 4) The main hypothesis was that conspiracy theories are no more than 'fake news', citing the USA with The Donald. All very dangerous, etc, etc. The following week Sir Richard, fronting his new book's publicity drive, enjoyed a BBC Radio 4 interview in which he basically said the same thing.

He told Harris he would only communicate with us if we first critiqued Chapter 4 of his new book. This we did in the form of five detailed pages, and then that was it. No debate. Nothing.

Presumably he had got from us what he wanted.

Somewhat surprisingly, in his Chapter 4, Sir Richard had made some silly, sloppy errors of fact. The Duke of Kent (1902–42) was stated as being killed in an air training accident, when in fact the flying boat in which he was travelling crashed into a hillside, and once pointed out, things became quite unpleasant. We have no issue whatsoever with criticism if it furthers the debate and is at least factually accurate, but to land a few cheap shots without even bothering to explain why we are wrong is disappointing and unfair to say the least. Almost uniquely, Sir Richard appears to believe the Hitler communique to the German nation of 13 May 1941, which of course described Hess flying unaided and under a delusion.

His chosen interpretation alone is incredible, but that is of course his prerogative. Presumably, being Knighted and a Cambridge professor, he must know far more than us, but in this case we suspect that he (or, more likely, his paid researchers) were too busy criticising us for a cheap shot literary effect to have time enough to take too much notice of the actual facts of the Hess case. In the early new year of 2021, John Harris discovered that in 2013 the Leverhulme Trust had funded Sir Richard to the tune of some £1.5 million[2] to research 'conspiracy and democracy'. It is these authors' contention that Sir Richard and his team have themselves ill served democracy by simply decrying and disparaging the dissenters. The Hess affair, unfortunately for Sir Richard, is very much a conspiracy and we just hope that he and his undoubted brain have not been 'bought' to try and cover up that fact. Why not be radical and instead state the facts, that surely he must know, interpret them for us dullards and then let the readers decide for themselves? Just think how daring that approach might be.

This thankfully untypical episode has just made us more determined to carry on and prove Sir Richard and his ilk wrong. It also makes us question who writes history if inconvenient facts are just disregarded by the 'Great and the Good' in favour of some easy recognisable dialogue that actually makes little sense. In addition, the discovery of the £1.5 million funding seems to pose different questions. In the past we have often wondered how 'victor's history' might possibly distort the real truth; now we are seemingly also targets for 'academic history', funded by third parties, all presumably with their own agendas. The former is at least more understandable as to motive.

However, the real issue with Sir Richard's hypothesis is that he simply chose the wrong subject for his Chapter 4. We of course agree that there has been much nonsense written about certain aspects of the Nazi period and, in particular, Hess and his flight, but sadly for Sir Richard, the Hess flight is a conspiracy. Our approach, not being superior Oxbridge historians, has always been to allow our readers the choice of what they believe. If we then continue to write rubbish, presumably no-one will buy our books. We willingly take that risk. However, we have never written anything that we do not believe to be true or accurate at the time of writing. (Nor have we, unlike other Hess 'historians', inserted documentation into any archive in support of our beliefs).

Consequently, we would now dedicate this book to Sir Richard and his team, in the hope (forlorn, probably) that they take the time to learn the facts of the Hess case *before* coming to judge others who have at least attempted to do so to the best of their abilities (and budgets). Lastly, we should state clearly that we have self-funded both our own research over many years and the many accompanying beers. The beer tabs alone would probably amount to £1.5 million.

Cheers, Sir Richard.

HELPFUL DEFINITIONS[3]

Conspiracy – A secret plan to commit a crime or do harm: a plot. (From Latin conspicuus)

Conspiracy theory – An explanation for an event that invokes a conspiracy by sinister and powerful groups, often political in motivation, when other explanations are more probable.

Calamity – An event causing great and often sudden damage or distress, a disaster. (From Latin calamitas)

Cover up – To completely cover or conceal.

Fake News – False or misleading information presented as news. The term was first used in the 1890s.

Truth – The quality or state of being true.

---

[1] Arthur Schopenhauer was an influence on Rudolf Hess – see Eugene Bird, *The Loneliest Man in the World*, Sphere, London, 1974.

[2] 'In 2013 I applied for and was awarded a Leverhulme Programme Grant on "Conspiracy and Democracy". The total sum awarded for the 5-year programme was £1,584,611.' (Prof. Sir Richard Evans's website).

[3] *The Oxford Compact English Dictionary*, OUP, Oxford, 1996.

INTRODUCTION

In late January 1942, Winston Churchill was again in trouble. On the 27th he reported to the House of Commons, having recently returned from the USA:

> 'We have had a great deal of bad news lately from the Far East, and I think it highly probable, for reasons which I shall presently explain, that we shall have a great deal more. Wrapped up in this bad news will be many tales of blunders and shortcomings, both in foresight and action. No one will pretend for a moment that disasters like these occur without there having been faults and shortcomings. I see all this rolling towards us like the waves in a storm, and that is another reason why I require a formal, solemn Vote of Confidence from the House of Commons, which hitherto in this struggle has never flinched.'

In short, Churchill had seen fit to hold a vote of confidence; ostensibly so as to provide a sign of a unified nation to the various Allies that had joined Britain in their fight against the Axis powers.

As Churchill had openly confessed, the war was not going well and privately had admitted that,

> 'The bulk of the Tories hated him, that he had done all he could and would be happy to yield to another.'[4]

Although the self-analysis and doubt were perhaps uncharacteristic, he then went on to say in the House of Commons:

> 'We have also to remember how oddly foreigners view our country and its way of doing things. When Rudolf Hess flew over here some months ago, he firmly believed that he had only to gain access to certain circles in this country for what he described as "the Churchill clique" to be thrown out of power and for a government to be set up with which Hitler could negotiate a magnanimous peace. The only importance attaching to the opinions of Hess is the fact that he was fresh from the atmosphere of Hitler's intimate table. But, Sir, I can assure you that since I have been back in this country, I have had anxious inquiries from a dozen

countries, and reports of enemy propaganda in a score of countries, all turning upon the point whether His Majesty's present Government is to be dismissed from power or not.'

This brief, yet deliberate mention is surely the key to understanding the Hess affair. This was the first time that Churchill had given any particular mention on the matter; the Scottish air crash had already taken place some eight months earlier. He had, of course, been quizzed in the House previously (13 May 19 May and 10 June) but had always managed to bat away the questioners.

However, now, when he was looking for personal support, he saw fit to refer to 'certain circles' as being the political target of the Hess flight. Was this again a ploy to challenge the self-same 'certain circle' to finally 'put up or shut up?' Churchill had previously employed a very similar tactic on 7 May 1941, just three days before the Hess flight.

This book seeks to first identify those 'certain circles' and secondly to ascertain if they were real or a mere figment of the imagination of the British Secret Services. Who were they and how could the Churchill clique be 'thrown out of power'?

We are also interested by Churchill's use of the word 'dismissed'. In wartime, general elections are not allowed and so the general public cannot vote an incumbent out of power. There is only one person who can 'dismiss' a sitting prime minister…

Incidentally, Winston Churchill won the Vote of Confidence by 464 to 1. By way of pure coincidence, the only dissenter was James Maxton, MP for Bridgeton, Glasgow, his constituency being less than 16 miles away from the Hess crash site.

---

[4] Anthony Eden, *The Reckoning*, Cassell, London, 1965.

CONTENTS

ACKNOWLEDGEMENTS

Since the 1990s we have made a nuisance of ourselves to many. In particular, and with specific reference to this book, we would like to thank the following for their continued tolerance:

Andrew Rosthorn and Spike Hodbod, for continued, support and very welcome Lobster reviews.

William and Barnaby Blacker, in connection with their grandfather, Stewart Blacker.

Aurelia Borenius and her late father, Lars, for insight on Tancred Borenius.

Persis Bower, for information on Francis Richard Christian Cecil Fletcher (1903–51).

Frances Box of Steeple, in connection with Stewart Blacker.

Helen and Annie Cara, for diagrams, correspondence and file management.

Dennis Coryell, our Washington, DC research assistance.

Edgar Dahl in Giessen, Germany for translation, good company and liaison.

John Darbyshire, for ATC expertise concerning the Sikorski flight to Prestwick.

Wolf Hess jnr, for the new information concerning the DNA and calligraphy tests.

Dr Esther-Julia Howell, at the Institut für Zeitgeschichte, Munich

Prof. Sir Richard J. Evans, for a renewal and reinvigoration of our cussed determination.

Thomas Dunskus, in Germany, for encouragement, accommodation, wine and introductions. Sadly, Thomas, who was brought up in the ruins of post-war Berlin, has recently died.

Norman Foster in Duxford, for ATC expertise concerning the Sikorski flight to Prestwick.

Andreas Gerl, at the Allgäu, Germany, for the important new information concerning Prof. Franz Seraph Gerl, his grandfather.

Nick Gilder, at RAF Henlow Signals Museum.

Glyn Gowans, for encouragement and support and checking notes referring to Prince George, the Duke of Kent.

Barbara Graham, for forwarding the previously unpublished notes of Dr Gibson-Graham.

Trevor Hearing, at Bournemouth University, for the 'Northumbrian photograph' information.

David Horry, in Shanghai, aka. John Quarrington, for providing a completely new interpretation, some of which we suspect is not without foundation.

Peter Lowe, in Hertfordshire, for information concerning Gulla Pfeffer.

Margaret Morrell, in Ayrshire, for help in 'eliminating Turnberry from our enquiries'. Margaret has recently published the definitive history of RAF Turnberry and should be congratulated accordingly.

Matthew Hogan Research Services, Washington, DC, for reference to the 1943 Mercury article.

Dominic Hunger, at the University of Basle Library, for reference to Burckhardt.

Inga Kemp, at the Orcadian, Orkney Islands.

Jan Kozdra, our Polish researcher, translator and friend from Wroclaw.

Guido Koller, at the Swiss Archives, Berne, for reference to the Hess family papers.

Ramona Lampard, our editor and the eraser of many inverted commas.

Brian Luff and Geoff Butler, at the Farnborough Air Sciences Trust, for reference to the post-crash analysis.

Tony Noble, of JEMA Publications.

Emily Oldfield, at the British Red Cross Museum, London.

Prof. John Martin, at Leicester de Montfort University, for reading and support.

Sarah MacLean and Yvonne Nicoll, at the Orkney Islands Archives.

Stuart Mclean, in Australia, for supplying the 'Hess flight plan'.

Peter Padfield, for his continued encouragement and support. Peter sadly died in March 2022, aged 89. Since his death we have been working with his son, Guy to find a fitting repository for his archival material which is typically detailed, meticulous and relevant.

Anthony Pilcher and Charlotte Studholme, for some clarification on William Spelman Pilcher.

Christian Pöpken, State Archivist, Giessen.

Prof. Anita Prazmowska, for information regarding the Polish government in exile.

Elaine Richards, at Radio Society of Great Britain, for reference to Beadnell Towers.

Kristina Ranki, at the Mannerheim Museum, Helsinki.

Piotr Rossa, at Wroclaw University, for reference to the Rackiewicz Diaries.

Dr Thomas Rütten, at Newcastle University, for assistance in connection with Prof. Gerl at Gailenberg.

Joan Schenkar, in New York and Paris, for further insight into Dolly Wilde and Tancred Borenius.

Sir Thomas Shakespeare, for assistance in connection with Prof. Gerl at Gailenberg.

General Bernd Schwipper, for an excellent meeting, Christmas 2017, and accommodating us royally.

Mr and Mrs Small, in Stromness, Orkney Islands

Tony Stott, aka. Ford Perfect and Anton Another, specialist in all matters Hess.

Dr A. Suchitz, at the Polish Institute and Sikorski Museum, London, for reference to Roman Battaglia, President Raczkiewicz and General Sikorski.

Wasyl Sydorenko, at the University of Toronto Library, for identification assistance in connection with Battaglia.

Eero Teerikangas, in France, for further Borenius information.

The Polish Hearth Club, London for making us very welcome whenever we were invited to attend.

Paulus Thomson, at the Anglo-Finnish Society, London, for allowing us to bring the memory of Tancred Borenius to the wider Finnish community.

Hugh Watson, in Ayr, for information concerning his father, H.D. Watson, who chauffeured Sikorski across Glasgow on 11 May 1941.

Wing Commander (ret'd) D.L. Preston, for assistance in connection with the navigational aspects of the flight.

The staff of: National Archives, Kew, London; British Airways Heritage Collection, Harmondsworth; British Newspaper Archive; Bundesarchiv, Freiburg and Koblenz, Germany; Cambridge City Library, England; Cambridge Crematorium, England; The Carnegie Library, Ayr; Eton College, Windsor; Northampton Central Library; The House of Commons, London; The Holocaust Memorial Museum, Washington, DC; The Indian and Oriental Collection, London; The Imperial War Museum, Duxford and London; The International Red Cross, Geneva (in particular Daniel Palmieri); The Naval Historical Branch, Portsmouth; The Jacobite Society, London; East Kilbride Library, Scotland; Stanford University Library, California; Wiltshire Record Society; Martin Zeileis at the Zeileis Institute, Gallspach, Austria.

And lastly our two wives, Ann and Anne. It was either Hess or the golf course. We believe we chose well…

Thank you one and all.

PREFACE

Thankfully, neither Richard nor I can claim any relevant qualifications that render our opinions on the Hess affair any more credible, authoritative or believable than anyone else's. Again, thankfully, we are not academics (with the inherent danger of having to 'sing for your supper'). We are both farmers and I also run a small accountancy practice. Richard can tell you about wheat production and I know something about taxation. Consequently, we merely invite you to read our book and decide for yourself as to our findings about Hess. We should also repeat that unlike our friends the academics, we have received no financial assistance in the research and publication of this, our latest and seventh book on the subject.

However, whilst not specifically funded, we do possess a fair degree of scepticism, irony, objectivity, independence, pride and perseverance. We have been learning about and studying the affair since 1987, when Hess died, and we initially became interested simply because the whole affair and its supposed explanation at the time just did not make sense. The 1941 German communique (Hess had gone mad and had flown to the enemy) was still the accepted story and at the time was an easy story to believe, as the somewhat bizarre behaviour of Rudolf Hess at Nuremberg had simply reinforced the notion that he was truly mad and so had quite likely just flown to the enemy. QED.

Quite possibly, and even more bizarrely, it now appears that one of the leading British historians, Prof. Sir Richard Evans, still believes this to be the case.[5]

Perhaps unfortunately for our wives and, at the time, young children, we soon found out that there was an awful lot more to the story than the very convenient headline explanation. In 1992 we published our first finding.[6] Mrs Roberts, to whom Hess had been writing via Albrecht Haushofer in the autumn of 1940, was the aunt of and close relation to an early member of SOE (SO1), then based at Woburn Abbey. Much of the 1990s was then spent chasing aspects of Hess around mainland Europe, cunningly (in the male mind anyway) disguised as family holidays.

Subsequently, we have discovered and explored the role of Tancred Borenius in the affair, before analysing the actual 1941 flight in the early 2010s.

We thought (and still think) that by understanding the technical nature and character of the flight we are able to garner further understanding of what was meant to happen, as opposed to what did happen. Peter Padfield, who sadly has recently died, was very helpful to us in this regard by lending us the 'Pilot's notes' that came to him via the late Prof. A.W.B. Simpson. Our subsequent books have also introduced the political role of the Polish government in exile. This area in particular is an extremely sensitive subject and is very easy to misinterpret (a crime we suspect we may well have already committed), so we already caveat the subject appropriately. To date we have published six books as our knowledge has expanded and have made discoveries that we believe worthy of wider record and publication. If we discover that we have made errors, we are pleased to acknowledge the fact as above. Thankfully, to date it has been a rare occurrence.

This is all very well, and it has all been terrific fun, but we are still not wholly sure we are able to offer the complete solution. Back in 2015, Gordon Corera of the BBC asked us: 'Well, chaps, was it a coup or a lure?' This is now known as the 'killer question'. The honest answer in the year of the eighty-first anniversary of the flight is that we still do not know for sure. Some weeks we are sure the answer is 'coup', other weeks 'lure' as some new snippet of information comes into the reckoning. We have also thought the affair could well be a hybrid; 'lure' for some participants whilst other players might genuinely have believed a 'coup' was underway. What better way for the far from secure 1941Winston Churchill to discover who the potential British 'bad guys' (or 'certain circles') were? Let them think a coup is underway, let them eventually show their hands and then 'pull the plug', courtesy of R. Hess, Esq. Very clever indeed and probably too clever by half – if indeed this is what was actually happening. We should also say that there are certainly no shortage of potential candidates for the role of the 'bad guys', or indeed just 'guys that disagreed with the British never surrender strategy'. In spring 1941, throughout the ruling classes and aristocracy, Churchill, very understandably, had far more doubters and detractors than ardent supporters. Andrew Rosthorn has again been very helpful in demonstrating to us the role of the Labour Party in the Churchillian coalition government of 1941. It no doubt played a crucial role in preserving Churchill in power when, apart from his fine words, both he and Britain were very much 'on the ropes'.

We should also (probably) proudly concede that above all the British are masters at being devious. As a nation we have massively 'punched above our geographical weight' by being clever and devious for centuries and we are also notoriously secretive, sometimes even to matters that seemingly are not particularly or vitally important. We hope that the fact that we are still having this debate some eighty years after the event adequately illustrates the point.

A very inconvenient constitutional question also arises if some of the potential 'bad guys' also hold a constitutional position. Can one be treacherous against an incumbent government if, for instance, the protagonists are acting (or think they are acting) on behalf of and in the best interests of the monarchy? To answer that complex question, we perhaps need to return to 1689 – or even earlier. Do please remember that the British Armed Forces and Secret Services swear allegiance to the monarch, not the government, a point that Hess and his staff were also busily checking in spring 1941.[7]

We should also perhaps make clear our position to Rudolf Hess as an individual. We are not revisionist historians, as to date there has been no clear version of history in respect of the Hess affair to revise. All we are trying to do is to understand why Hess flew to Scotland in 1941. He certainly was no 'martyr to peace'. His flight was a simple act of war, as the subsequent Fuhrer Directive 32 makes clear. If Hitler had conquered Russia, Britain and her empire would have been the principal targets once again, without doubt. We are certainly not right-wing apologists in any way whatsoever.[8] We hope at least that much is abundantly clear.

There is no doubt we have discovered and learned an awful lot through this process. We may well have in our possession enough pieces of the jigsaw to be able to work out for sure what the big picture on the box itself might be (if we were the more intelligent). However, we are still not sure and so one maxim we have stuck to throughout the past thirty years is never to assume or guess. We went and saw for ourselves, stated what we discovered and will let the reader decide. This is not an easy subject to decipher.

So, this time, given the above uncertainty and caveat, we thought it might be a useful exercise to record our detailed findings and debate the various aspects and known facts of the case, in just the same way that a court process might evaluate a case. State and evaluate the evidence and come to a judgement. (Not judge first and then evaluate in hindsight, Sir Richard?)[9] We also wish to record and evaluate the handling of the affair since 1941, in the hope that we may obtain further evidence as to the original intent.

Who knows, our conclusion might then be very close to the truth? At times over the past thirty years, it has genuinely felt that we might be able to completely solve the mystery. (Usually through misplaced confidence gained by reason of our ignorance of another aspect of the affair.) Currently, we even doubt that outcome, but we have certainly narrowed down the areas of uncertainty. Whilst we think we know what we do not know, we certainly know what we do. (Sorry, Mr Rumsfeld.)

We trust the reader approves of this approach. If we manage to do this well, we hope to engage the reader into a clear debate of the various issues, so they are left in no doubt as to the current pertinent issues and uncertainties. We will also take pride in hopefully making the academics look a little daft. In a so-called democracy and a country boasting a constitutional monarchy and the 'mother of parliaments', the whole Hess affair and its overbearing secrecy is actually a disgrace, but it is of course Britain and it is of course only eighty plus years later ...

John Harris and Richard Wilbourn
Northampton and Norfolk
Spring 2022

---

[5] Correspondence between Harris and Evans, October 2020.

[6] John McBlain, *Rudolf Hess: The British Conspiracy*, JEMA, Moulton, 1992.

[7] The Gestapo interrogations of Hess staff, May 1941. (As quoted by David Irving in Appendix 1 to Hess: The Missing Years 1941–1945, Focal Point, Windsor, 2010.)

[8] Unbelievably, we have recently been so accused by Herr Jatho of Giessen.

[9] Sir Richard recently tweeted that he usually assesses a book by first looking at the Acknowledgements page. 'I still follow Carr's advice in "What is History?" to study the historian before you study the book: the first thing I turn to is the Acknowledgements page, to see where the author comes from, identify friends and mentors; then the Preface, then the notes; finally, the book itself.' 8 January 2022

CHAPTER 1
AUTHORS' NOTE

The Case for the Established History

> The NSDAP hereby announces that party comrade Hess who, due to an illness he had years ago, was not allowed to fly, succeeded in obtaining an aeroplane against the strict orders of the Führer.
>
> On Saturday evening, 10 May, Rudolf Hess took off from Augsburg. He has not returned yet. We regret to say that a letter which he left behind seems to leave no doubt that he suffered from a mental derangement, and it must be feared that he has fallen a victim of hallucinations. Under these circumstances, it is possible that party comrade Hess either jumped out of the aeroplane, or died in an accident.[1]

So, there we have it. The Deputy Führer has gone mad and flown to the enemy. All is now very clear, and we should be duly grateful for the official clarification. The following day the Nazi government chose to become even more explicit:

> On the basis of a preliminary examination of the papers which Hess left behind him, it would appear that Hess was living under the hallucination that by undertaking a personal step in connection with the Englishmen with whom he was formerly acquainted it might be possible to bring about an understanding between Germany and Britain. As has since been confirmed by a report from London, Hess parachuted from his

plane and landed near the place in Scotland which he had selected as his destination; there he was found, apparently in an injured condition.

As is well known in party circles, Hess has undergone severe physical suffering for some years. Recently he sought relief to an increasing extent in various methods practised by mesmerists and astrologers, etc. An attempt is also being made to determine to what extent these persons are responsible for bringing about the condition of mental distraction which led him to take this step. It is also conceivable that Hess was deliberately lured into the trap by a British party. The whole manner of his action, however, confirms the fact that he was suffering under hallucinations.

Hess was better acquainted than anyone else with the peace proposals which the Führer has made with such sincerity. Apparently, he had deluded himself into thinking that, by some personal sacrifice, he could prevent developments, which, in his eyes, could only end with the complete destruction of the British empire.

Judging by his own papers, Hess, whose sphere of activities was confined to the party, as is generally known, had no idea how to carry out such a step or what effect it would have.

The National Socialist Party regrets that this idealist fell prey to tragic hallucinations. The continuation of the war, which Britain forced on the German people, will not be affected at all. As the Führer declared in his last speech, it will be carried on until the men in power in Britain have been overthrown or are ready to make peace.

Unfortunately, there is a big problem with both statements. Neither are particularly helpful nor, as we hope to demonstrate, particularly true. (The second does, however, contain elements of truth.) The reality was that the Hess mission had just gone disastrously wrong and its chief protagonist wandering around lowland Scotland meeting the locals (and naturally being offered tea), was surely not meant to happen. Delightful though Renfrewshire and both the buildings are, it is surely inconceivable that Giffnock Scout Hall or the Busby Home Guard HQ were ever intended to be the planned venues for a mission of such truly historical importance.

The truth is that Hitler had to come up with an excuse for the PR disaster fast unfolding before him and quickly; not least for the benefit of his nominal trading partner Joseph Stalin, who perhaps might have quite rightly smelled an even bigger rat if he had thought that Hess was seriously entreating with the British. Luckily, Hess had already given his leader the excuse. In his last letter to his Führer, Hess had suggested that if all went wrong,

'Simply say I was crazy...'[2]

Hitler had quickly latched on to the suggestion, struggling in the meantime to formulate anything else more plausible, and rightly fearful of the onslaught of possible British propaganda. Of course, Stalin did not believe him for one moment (especially after the subsequent events of 21–22 June 1941).

The Giffnock Scout Hall

The communiques to the German people also had a second very profound implication. By essentially doing as Hess had suggested, with Hitler stating that Hess was delusional, any hope of Hess being treated as a Parlamentär had also evaporated. This aspect is more thoroughly debated in Chapter 28, but the personal impact for Hess of Hitler's very public disenfranchisement was huge and lasted for some forty-two years after the Führer's death. True Parlamentärs, of course, have some rights under international law. In desperately appeasing Stalin, Hitler had just extinguished any rights Hess may possibly have once held.

The British government was also acutely politically embarrassed. Churchill and his Polish ally Sikorski had spent the early spring of 1941 frantically courting each other – and Roosevelt (and Stalin) – and lo and behold, Hess then awkwardly gatecrashes the flirtations. What might the isolationists in America think if the potential suitors were simultaneously doing deals behind their backs? What might the Pilsudki Poles think if their sympathy really lay with Germany above Russia?

Indeed, why bother to engage at all, if the Europeans were inevitably going to make peace, or entreat, somewhat hypocritically after all their stirring words and speeches?

So, what was the collective response? Given – and because of – the immense stakes they were playing for, they all chose to lie. Hitler lied, as already described above. Churchill initially said nothing and in doing so kept everyone guessing for at least eighty years. (He later dismissed the Hess affair as inconsequential.)[3] Hess, now starting an unbeknown lifetime captivity, lied about his identity and pretended he had meant to contact the Duke of Hamilton and the flight was really a triumph (and not the disaster it actually had become). Everyone had their own very sensible reasons to lie.

Consequently, with all the main players choosing to lie about an event and even more outrageous explanations subsequently being proffered (doppelgängers, astrology, the control of Antarctic etc, aided and abetted by the falsified documentation), is it really a surprise that the real truth has remained concealed for so long? If not so serious a subject, it would be amusing to record that some historians have even sought to rely on and embellish some of the falsehoods of other historians, so as to reinforce their own flawed theories.

It is also interesting to note the duration of Hess's lies and lying. Upon arrival he lied about his identity (perhaps quite understandably, given his vulnerability). At Nuremberg he lied about the state of his mind (and in doing so avoided having to say anything about his 1941 flight). Whilst in captivity he continued to lie when seemingly there was no reason to lie. In this connection we would direct the reader to Eugene Bird's *The Loneliest Man in the World*, an account of the Hess affair from inside Spandau Prison. The book describes Hess's reluctance to discuss even basic facts, often on the pretence of 'I can't remember.' In other words, at no time after 1941 could Rudolf Hess be relied upon to tell the truth, though certainly not because he was delusional.

However, the real truth is that Rudolf Hess, in flying to Scotland, thought he was attempting to instigate a regime change and instigate/force an Anglo-German secret settlement/treaty, whilst bypassing the notoriously intransigent Churchillian government.

As we have already seen, Churchill admitted this to his Parliament in 1942.[4]

A masterstroke if it were to work … but how was it to be achieved? Was the possibility just an illusion, or for real? This is what we hope to explain (and also hopefully finally convince ourselves in the process).

No persons with a complete knowledge of the affair are still alive. Some who did may have been murdered (Karl, Albrecht and Martha Haushofer in 1945/6 and Rudolf Hess in 1987). Others, long since dead, quite sensibly just kept their mouths shut (Pintsch, Rosenberg, Fath, Cadogan, Boyle, Dansey and Borenius).

These sad, but inevitable, facts have certainly made ascertaining the truth the more difficult, if for no other reason than through the need to distil fact from the ever-increasing volumes of speculation, fiction and the fraudulent documentation.[5]

We started our work back in the early 1990s and are pleased to report that whilst certainly not a fast process, we have continued to add and accumulate to our knowledge over the years without having to amend our basic interpretation along the way. New details have come to light, but our basic premise and interpretation have thankfully remained unchanged. At no time did we, or have we, set out to be sensationalist. The conclusions reached in this book, whilst quite possibly sensational, have been based on the accumulation of a large amount of data amassed over a long period of time. The conclusions are based on the result of a process, largely tedious, sometimes exciting, rather than part of any pre-ordained or sponsored objective or explanation.

---

[1] Wulf Schwarzwaller, *Rudolf Hess: The Deputy*, Quartet, London, 1988.

[2] Ilse Hess, *Prisoner of Peace*, Briton Publishing Co., London, 1954. Copies of this document have yet to see the light of day.

[3] Churchill downplayed the affair in his history of World War 2, published between 1948 and 1953.

[4] *Hansard*, 27 January 1942.

[5] *The Guardian*, 4 May 2008. The twenty-nine fakes behind a rewriting of history.

BRIEF BIOGRAPHICAL DETAIL

We do not wish to hinder or shroud the new information that we have discovered by the repetition of the same old biographical facts and details that a score of other works have previously relied upon and presented. For instance, if the reader wishes to learn about the finer details of Hess's early life, then we would refer him or her to the host of other, more valid works.

Most of these known facts are accepted as such. In this book we have attempted to debate the new knowledge to the reader wishing to ascertain the true motives and motivations behind the extraordinary flight.

However, in order to place some events into context, we do need to provide this brief chronology of the life Rudolf Hess up to 31 August 1940, the specific starting point for our more detailed evidence:

26 April 1894 Rudolf Hess born in Ibrahimieh, Alexandria, Egypt. Hess's parents were import/ export agents, trading as Hess & Co. Hess's father is often described as being a dominant individual in both business and family matters. Hess, by his own admission, was a 'mummy's boy'.

1900 Hess enters the German Protestant School in Alexandria. Leaves shortly after entrance and is tutored at home.

1908 Hess travels to Germany and continues his education at the Protestant Educational Institute at Bad Godesberg.

1911 Hess enters the École Supérieure de Commerce in Neuchatel, Switzerland. He then undertakes a commercial apprenticeship in Hamburg and is on leave from Hamburg when the First World War commences.

The first twenty years of his life were therefore dominated by his father's not unnatural wish for Hess to continue the family business that Hess's grandfather had founded in 1865. Hess had already shown signs of an impending rebellion against this wish when the onset of the First World War gave him the viable excuse he needed.

1914–17 Hess fights as an infantryman.

July 1917 Hess is shot in the lung. He recuperates in Germany at the family estate.

Spring 1918 Hess learns to fly in a Fokker D.VII.

13 December 1918 Lieutenant Rudolf Hess is discharged from active service and travels to Munich.

1919 Hess becomes embroiled in the political chaos enveloping Munich. He joins the Thule Society, becoming an active agitator.

1920 Hess enters Munich University and meets Prof. Karl Haushofer. In May 1920 he also meets Ilse Pröhl, his future wife.

May 1921 Hess meets Hitler for the first time.

8/9 November 1923 The Munich Beer Hall putsch takes place and fails. Hess escapes to Austria.

April 1924 Hitler, and subsequently Hess, are sentenced to imprisonment in Landsberg. The two men use their time to write Mein Kampf. Frequent visitors are Karl Haushofer and Ilse Pröhl. They are released in January 1925.

27 December 1927 Rudolf Hess marries Ilse Pröhl. Witnesses to the wedding are Adolf Hitler and Karl Haushofer.

1932 Hess wins second prize in the 'Round the Zugspitze' aeronautical race.

30 January 1933 Adolf Hitler becomes Chancellor.

21 April 1933 Adolf Hitler makes Rudolf Hess Deputy Führer of the NSDAP.

3 October 1933 Hess takes control of the Auslands Organisation.

1934 Hess wins first prize in the 'Round the Zugspitze' aeronautical race.

Mid-1930s First public accounts of Hess's medical issues. First record of the use of alternative medicines.

1933–38 Hess wholly engaged in NSDAP policy, amongst which he co-signs a series of anti-Semitic decrees in 1935.

1938 Hess signs necessary decrees for the Anschluss.

1938 Wolf Rüdiger Hess is born. Rudolf Hess is now aged forty-four.

March 1939 Britain and France commit to 'lend all support in their power' to Poland 'in the event of any action that threatened Polish independence'.

23 August 1939 Molotov-Ribbentrop Pact signed, together with its secret protocol.

25 August 1939 The Agreement of Mutual Assistance between the United Kingdom and Poland is signed.

3 September 1939 The Second World War begins as a consequence of the German invasion of Poland.

10 May 1940 Germany invades the Low Countries and France.

22 June 1940 Hess attends the Armistice ceremony with Hitler at Compiègne, France. He is told of the intention to invade Russia.

31 August 1940 Munich, Bavaria, Germany.

CHAPTER 2
31 AUGUST 1940 – THE GENESIS

'No sacrifice should have been too great in winning England's friendship ...'
Adolf Hitler, *Mein Kampf* (first published 18 July 1925, Munich)

August 1940 was 'unusually dry' according to Volume 57, number 8 of the British Monthly Weather Report of the Meteorological Office, then priced at 1s.

The exceptional weather had certainly assisted the Nazi war machine in its so far relentless *blitzkrieg* across Europe. Germany had not yet been at war for a year, but had already conquered Poland, Norway, Denmark, the Low Countries and France. The British Expeditionary Force had been forced to flee mainland Europe back to its island base and each day Hermann Göring's Luftwaffe was relentlessly pounding British airfields in an incessant attempt to gain air superiority prior to the invasion that would then surely follow.

The fine weather also meant there was to be little rest for the RAF, who could not rely on poor flying conditions for any respite. On 24 August, the Luftwaffe had bombed Central London, whether by mistake or not, leading to a reprisal raid on Berlin the following evening. The stakes had risen again. As Göring had stated in his policy note a few days earlier:

> To sum up: we have reached the decisive period of the air war against England. The vital task is to turn all means at our disposal to the defeat of the enemy Air Force. Our first aim is the destruction of the enemy's fighters. If they no longer take the air, we shall attack them on the ground, or force them into battle by directing bomber attacks against targets within the range of our fighters. At the same time, and on a growing scale, we must continue our activities against the ground organisation of the enemy bomber units. Surprise attacks on the enemy aircraft industry must be made by day and by night. Once the enemy Air Force has been annihilated, our attacks will be directed as ordered against other vital targets.

However, and perhaps somewhat typical of Göring, the reality was somewhat different to the rhetoric. By 31 August 1940 the Battle of Britain was fast becoming a position of stalemate. The Luftwaffe could no longer replace the aircraft it lost quickly enough and could only count on around 50 per cent of its original air fleet. Equally, the RAF was on its knees and could barely raise enough aircraft to defend the attacks on its air bases.[1] The British also knew of the German position and its various logistical problems through early Ultra intelligence.[2]

Adolf Hitler was in Berlin on 31 August, and at 1.15pm met Franz Halder and the Chiefs of Staff at the Reich Chancellery. At the previous meeting, a month earlier, on 31 July, he had stated: 'If results of air warfare are unsatisfactory, invasion preparations will be stopped.'

A month later, the eventual military result was certainly still not as yet clear. The outcome and any subsequent decision as to invasion could not yet be assessed with any degree of certainty.[3]

Hitler had also emphasised the importance of weather 'against which human effort is unavailing.'[4] The Germans were under obvious pressure. If an invasion of Britain was to be launched, this had to take place before the 'unusually dry' weather reverted to its seasonal norm. It is, however, also quite possible and probable that Hitler was merely looking for a suitable and expedient excuse; an uncontrollable factor to blame for a decision he really did not wish to make anyway.

As Peter Fleming states succinctly in *Invasion 1940*: 'Throughout the summer of 1940, as far as Great Britain was concerned, Hitler was trying to do two things at once. He planned for an invasion, but he never ceased to dream of a capitulation.'

By August 1940, Rudolf Hess, his deputy, was a purely political and administrative animal. He had no formal military position as such and played no direct role in the massive military machine created by Nazi Germany. Some have therefore written him off in importance as clearly, in times of war, the military and its personnel gain an obvious ascendancy and priority.

However, this supposition we believe wholly inaccurate and misleading, particularly in a dictatorial system, where the Duce or Führer values loyalty almost to the exclusion of any other attribute.

In his political role of Stellvertreter, or deputy, Rudolf Hess could still aim to assist in Hitler's 'twin track' strategy. He certainly had the contacts, infrastructure and means to at least instigate an examination into the likelihood of a British capitulation – not a military capitulation, that would be down to Hermann Göring, Erich Raeder, Walther von Brauchitsch and the forces under their control, but a political capitulation, fermented and distilled from within the British establishment itself. Hitler had already tried this tactic once before by attempting to kidnap the Duke of Windsor in Portugal. It was only when the Duke and Duchess had finally sailed for the Bahamas in early August 1940 that the Operation Willi was cancelled.[5]

Moreover, through his years of contact with his Führer, Hess was confident and knew that the second option was certainly the one that Hitler preferred. We would refer the reader to this chapter's opening quotation that Hitler had dictated to Rudolf Hess, his then secretary and editor, whilst in Landsberg prison, some fifteen years earlier.

So, on 31 August 1940 Hess decided to actively start and pursue the process that was to lead to his flying to Scotland some eight and a half months later.

When in captivity years later, Hess related how he first gleaned the idea of a flight to Britain shortly after the fall of France but, again, perhaps because of the 'unusually dry' weather, he chose to meet his old Munich University professor, Karl Haushofer (1869–1946) and agreed to walk together in the Grünwald Forest, just to the south of Munich, on 31 August 1940. The meeting appears to have started in the late afternoon/early evening and carried on into the early hours of the morning. It had assumed some urgency

The Hess haus at Harlaching, Munich

on account of Hess having been told at Compiègne that a Russian invasion by Germany was now very much a possibility.

At the time, Rudolf Hess lived in the south-central part of Munich at 48, Harthauserstrasse, Harlaching. The Haushofer family owned a small estate in Pähl, the Hartschimmellhof, and a further alpine house/ski chalet in Partnach-Alm, near Garmisch-Partenkirchen.

The meeting venue therefore appears to have been 'halfway' between the two men's respective houses, albeit perhaps slightly closer for Hess. Both would have to have travelled to meet. Neither was 'visiting' the other, with perhaps any implied implication of deference. Two old friends had simply decided to meet. They had known each other for at least twenty years by this time, but Karl Haushofer's influence had been on the wane with Adolf Hitler since 1938 when the two men had argued at the christening of Wolf Hess, Rudolf's only child. Haushofer, apart from being Hess's tutor, had also been a significant influence on both Hitler and Hess in the early Munich days of the NSDAP and has been credited for the adoption of the later NSDAP Lebensraum policy.

The August meeting and its subsequent action points were recorded for posterity by detailed correspondence, which survives, passing between Hess and the two Haushofers, Karl and his son Albrecht (1903–45). These letters, or copies thereof, later found their way into the German Foreign Office and were duly seized, along with 400 tons of other correspondence at the end of the war. The archives had initially been moved by the Nazis to a number of locations in the Harz Mountains and then in 1946–7, the United States, United Kingdom and French governments pledged themselves to publish the papers, 'on the basis of the highest scholarly objectivity'.

We were initially surprised that these papers 'surfaced' so early in the process and so looked into the procedures that allowed their release into the public arena. We doubted that the British in isolation would have sanctioned their release in 1947, unless of course they told a story the British were comfortable with (they have released precious little else of import). The 1947 editorial committee apparently consisted of twenty-two persons who conducted their business free from government interference. We can only assume that it was the editorial independence that allowed this correspondence trail to emerge quite so early after the event, but even so it still took a number of years before they were quoted in the early Hess research, such as that which took place.

The trail evidenced by the letters, minutes and notes directly link Hess to the Duke of Hamilton via the Haushofers (and Mrs V. Roberts, see

Chapter 6) and it has certainly been the case that much of our research over the past twenty-five years has been facilitated by simply following this trail backwards. Had these letters not been published, for whatever reason, discovering the truth would have been very much more difficult. The 'solo flight' theory may even have been partially believable, as without these letters there would be no visible hand of British Intelligence whatsoever. Everything else follows on, but we now believe that these documents were released as early as 1947 so as to hide the true rationale (but not some of the details) behind the flight and to set the post war explanation (as Nuremberg had provided no further clarification whatsoever). They also paint the Duke of Hamilton as an unwitting player, which is also quite possible. In other words, yet again a convenient explanation, but one that contradicts the earlier account of Hess, delusional, stealing a plane and flying to the enemy.

However, the fact is that the correspondence has survived, is available and has been published. The first letter is that from Karl Haushofer to his son Albrecht, relaying the details of the Hess meeting in the Grünwald Forest, on 31 August 1940. The references are those of the original German Foreign Office. They subsequently were reproduced under the Documents on German Foreign Policy 1918–1945 Series D, volume 9. Series D deals with the period 1937–45.

C109/C002185-87
Dr Karl Haushofer to Dr Albrecht Haushofer

Munich, 3 September 1940

Dearest Albrecht: Cordial thanks for your letter of the 29th from the Hotel Imperial in Vienna. I had almost a vague premonition that you might be there.

If you composed your birthday letter to me in the air raid cellar, I could have reciprocated this kind service on the night of the 1st and 2nd because I promised your mother when I left the mountain cabin to go down when the alarm sounded and consequently spent 1½ hours in exercise and gymnastics.

For, as with you, everything has changed with us too. Through Lisa's sudden departure, which you witnessed, mother's trip to the Hart became unnecessary. Because her stomach and knee both took a turn for the worse, she remained at the Alpine cabin and, only because everything was so arranged, let me go down to the valley alone from the 31st to the 3rd. But I was rewarded, for it brought me a meeting with Tomo from 5.00 o'clock in the afternoon until 2.00 o' clock in the morning, which included a 3-hour walk in the Grünwalder Forest, at which we conversed a good deal about serious matters. I have really got to tell you about a part of it now.

As you know, everything is so prepared for a very hard and severe attack on the island in question that the highest-ranking person only has to press a button to set it off. But before this decision, which is perhaps inevitable, the thought once more occurs as to whether there is really no way of stopping something which would have such infinitely momentous consequences. There is a line of reasoning in connection with this which I must absolutely pass on to you because it was obviously communicated to me with this intention. Do you, too, see no way in which such possibilities could be discussed at a third place with a middleman, possibly the old Ian Hamilton or the other Hamilton.

I replied to these suggestions that there would perhaps have been an excellent opportunity for this in Lisbon at the Centennial, if, instead of harmless figureheads, it had been possible to send well-disguised political persons there. In this connection, it seems to me a stroke of fate that our old friends, Missis (sic) V.R., evidently, though after long delay, finally found a way of sending a note with cordial and gracious words of good wishes not only for your mother, but also for Heinz and me and added the address.

Address your reply to: Miss V Roberts, c/o Post box 506, Lisbon, Portugal. I have the feeling that no good possibility should be overlooked; at least should be well considered.

In respect of this letter, we would make the following observations:

- As can be seen, this letter from father to son records his meeting with Rudolf Hess. By this time, the seventy-one-year-old Karl Haushofer had virtually retired. 'Tomo' was the Haushofer family nickname for Hess, being a derivation of the Japanese for 'friend' (*tomodachi*). As described, Karl Haushofer had left his wife at the Alpine chalet to travel first to Pähl and then onwards to the meeting.
- Albrecht Haushofer had been in Vienna at a meeting between the

Foreign Ministers of Hungary and Rumania and von Ribbentrop and Ciano, the Italian Foreign Minister. Albrecht at the time was on the payroll of the German Foreign Office, under the auspices of von Ribbentrop. Any work he did for Hess was essentially by reason of his Father's friendship, not through the 'Dienstelle Ribbentrop', the Nazi Foreign Office.

- The letter certainly appears to be more of an order than a request, but also appears to be quiet as to what is hoped to be achieved from the mooted discussions. We can only presume that the Haushofer's hope that Sir Ian Hamilton or the 'other' Hamilton (the 14th Duke) were in a position to influence events outside the normal government channels. Interestingly, by inference, it therefore appears to rule out any approach through *official* channels.
- The Duke of Kent had travelled to Lisbon in June 1940, and it is interesting in light of future events that he seems to have been dismissed at this stage as a 'harmless figurehead'. Winston Churchill had controlled the travel arrangements so that the Duke did not meet his elder brother, the Duke of Windsor, who had fled Paris in May.
- However, the most fascinating part of this letter is that dealing with Mrs V. Roberts. Following the 1941 flight, MI5 travelled to Cambridge to interview the then seventy-seven-year-old widow, who was then living at 10 Wilberforce Road, Cambridge.
- However, MI5 concluded in their later report that the letter (dated 26 July 1940) was innocently sent, by Mrs Roberts, who had sought to maintain her longstanding friendship with Martha Haushofer, Karl's wife. She had recently discovered that during wartime, correspondence was still possible through the Thomas Cook postal system.
- We are far from surprised that this earlier letter has yet to surface. It may of course be that it was not considered important enough to be retained, or it may still be in the private Haushofer family archive in Bavaria (but this was 'weeded' by the British in 1946). One certainly would not expect it to appear in the captured German Foreign Office records, as there would be no reason for it to be there if it merely records the good wishes of one elderly British lady to an elderly German woman. We do, however, believe it extremely important, as it may well make clear precisely where Mrs Roberts was located at

the time of her sending it to Martha, viz. Cambridge, England and not Lisbon, Portugal.

- Psychologically, as a result of the meeting, there is also much going on. Karl Haushofer's friendship with Rudolf Hess had already extended over twenty years, going back to Hess's time in Munich in the early 1920s. At this time, Hess and his friend Adolf Hitler had spent much time in Haushofer's company and when the two young men were imprisoned in Landsberg prison following the failed 1923 Putsch, it was Karl Haushofer who would weekly make the 100-km round trip from his estate at Pähl to visit the two men. The two men in their mid-twenties must surely have been impressed by the land-owning, erudite Prussian with his enticing mixture of wealth and intellect.

Why did Haushofer do this? Perhaps he saw the future of Germany in the hands of Hess, Hitler and the nascent NSDAP, and this was his way of influencing the same. There has been detailed debate as to the extent of the influence Haushofer actually exerted, but it is undeniable that some influence was exerted and was duly blended with other sources so as to produce the turgid *Mein Kampf*, the literary project extant whilst the two men were imprisoned.

Later on, the elderly Haushofer's influence was to wane, particularly with Hitler, and as already stated, the two men had badly argued in late 1938 at Wolf Hess's christening in Munich, when Haushofer challenged Hitler's foreign policy which by that time was starting to follow a more radical agenda. Karl Haushofer had been in virtual retirement since that time; he was in his seventies and so there must have been a degree of flattery to be asked to voice his opinion once again. Equally, it is now recorded and known that Hess had met Mrs Roberts in the 1930s when she was travelling in Europe, so the idea of a suggested contact may even have come from Hess, with Haushofer just supplying the current contact details.

The justification for the detailed recording was to also protect the Haushofer family. Under the Nazi racial laws (that Hess had sanctioned in late 1935), Karl's wife, Martha, and their two boys were designated 'mischlinge', and as such the family were potentially very vulnerable, particularly to any enemies of Hess. Albrecht had already been given specific protection by Hess in the form of a German blood certificate.

Therefore, we see the walk in the Grünwald Forest as very much the genesis of the Hess flight. In 1941, when in British captivity, Hess told Lord Simon that he first had an idea for a flight as early as June 1940, during the French campaign.[6]

Be that as it may, it took him until 31 August 1940 to instigate the early stages of such a notion. In our opinion, it was this meeting that directly led to the sensational flight 252 days later.

---

[1] Wolfgang Paul, *Herman Göring: Hitler's Paladin or Puppet?*, Arms and Armour, London, 1998

[2] Peter Wescombe, *Bletchley Park and the Luftwaffe*, Bletchley Park Trust, Report Number 8, September 2009.

[3] *The Halder War Diary*, Presidio, Novarto, CA, 1988, p. 242.

[4] Peter Fleming, *Invasion 1940*, Rupert Hart-Davis, London, 1957.

[5] See John Costello, *Ten Days that Saved the West*, Bantam Press, London, 1991.

[6] Peter Raina, *A Daring Venture*, Peter Lang, Berne, 2014.

CONSPIRACY

CHAPTER 3

THE THOMAS COOK POSTAL SYSTEM

The reason for subsequent confusion?

Chapter 2 ended with Karl Haushofer essentially telling his son Albrecht to reply to their old friend Mary Violet Roberts at PO Box 506, Lisbon. (Mrs Roberts had first contacted Martha Haushofer through the same system in July 1940.) Given that it was this correspondence that subsequently alerted British Intelligence to the fact that the Haushofers (and therefore, indirectly, Hess) were trying to establish contact with non-governmental channels within Britain, we feel it important to precisely understand the system that the parties had used to communicate and also to analyse their motives for doing so.

In this connection we can only highly recommend the reader to Charles R. Entwistle's *Undercover Addresses of World War II* (Chavril Press). First published in 1992 Chavril Press of Abernethy, Scotland, it details the means by which postal services operated during the time of war, in particular between belligerent nations. Essentially, it now appears to us that Mrs Roberts originally did nothing else other than make use of the services legally open to her (and anyone else) after the outbreak of war. Indeed, this was also the conclusion that MI5 eventually came to following their visit to Mrs Roberts in mid-May 1941.[1]

The British government felt it only right and proper that families and friends could continue to correspond during periods of war. However, so as to avoid accusations of collaboration, rather than use the GPO, the company of Thomas Cook Limited was used. Cook's were already providing a similar service to the Canadian government.[2]

In January 1940 a service commenced, based in what was then neutral Holland.

Obviously, the events of May 1940 had made Holland far from neutral and so from June 1940[3] the service moved to the still very neutral Lisbon, which at that time was becoming known as 'the gateway to Europe' for that very reason. The first 'clipper' service from the USA had taken place in May 1939, using the new Boeing 314 flying boat.[4]

Thomas Cook subsequently used the PO Box number 506 to pass literally millions of letters between the UK and friends and family in Germany and occupied Europe. Eventually, inhabitants of the Channel Island and prisoners of war would become the most common users. Thomas Cook even placed advertisements in The Times to promote the service.[5]

However, along with the service naturally came a strict series of rules. Whilst not illegal to correspond with persons abroad, all such letters would be subject to the scrutiny of the censor. That was made clear to the users of the service by large stickers being affixed to the envelopes being used.

The specific rules pertaining to the service were:

1) Communications must be clearly written (without erasures) and should not exceed two sides of a normal sheet of notepaper. Only one letter may be placed in one envelope.
2) Letters and envelopes must omit the sender's address. They must refer only to matters of personal interest.
   - Mention of a letter received from or written to enemy or enemy occupied territory is not permitted.
   - No reference may be made of any town (other than Lisbon), village, locality, ship or journey. No indication may be made that the writer is not in Portugal.
3) Each letter must be placed in an open unstamped envelope, fully inscribed to the addressee, who should be asked to address any reply to your full name, care of Post Office Box, 506, LISBON, Portugal. Poste Restante addresses are not permitted.
4) The open envelope containing the letter should be placed in an outer stamped envelope and sent to THOS COOK & SON LTD, Berkley Street, Piccadilly, London W1 together with a memorandum plainly written in BLOCK LETTERS containing the name and full address of the sender.
5) The communication to THOS COOK & SON LTD must enclose a postal order value 2s which fee will cover the postage of one envelope containing one communication to the neutral country, also of a reply (if any) from the neutral country to Messrs Cook's Head Office in London. An additional fee is payable for airmail.[6]

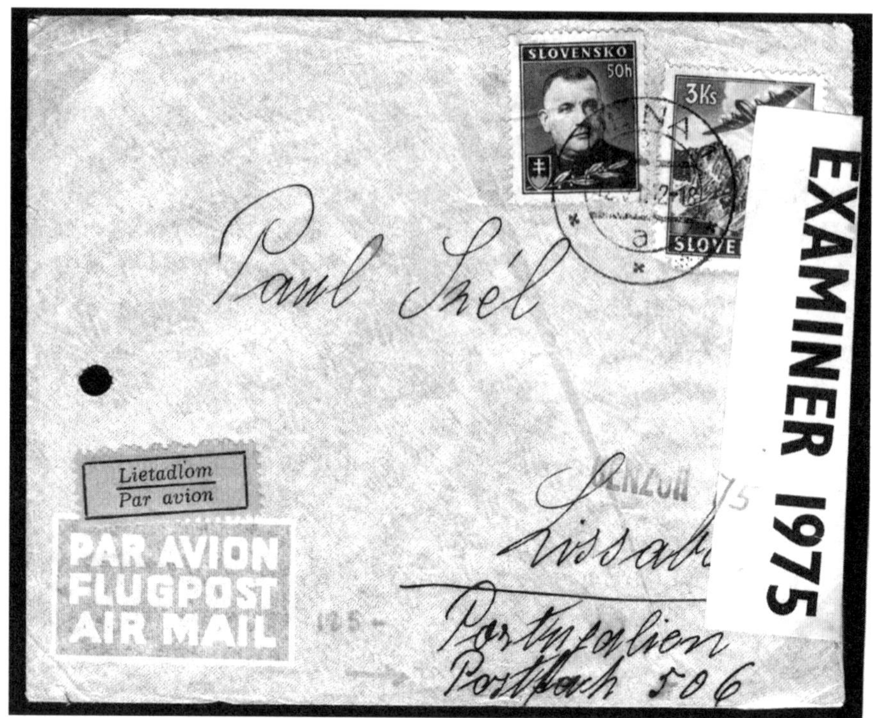

A typical PO Box 506 letter – note the proof from the censor

We believe this document exactly explains the following in our story:

- Mrs Roberts wished to communicate with her old friends the Haushofers.
- She could only write in a personal manner.
- She follows the instructions, pays her 2s and the letter is sent. She probably posts the outer envelope in Cambridge, addressed to Thos. Cook, London.
- She cannot give an address (on the actual letter), other than the return address in Lisbon.
- This may explain the impression given that she was actually in Lisbon, an impression that her German friends the Haushofers, apparently believed.
- We should not *perhaps* be too surprised at their ignorance; the service had only just started in Lisbon (June 1940).
- It may well be that the 'long delay' that Karl Haushofer refers to was

> simply occasioned by the fact that Mrs Roberts did not pay the extra money for airmail (we will shortly learn that she was of Scottish blood!).

We now do not believe that the above sequence of events infers intelligence involvement in any way. The reason that the letters were to be left open was so that the censor could be involved before despatch. It was therefore almost an inevitability that any 'dubious letters' would be found out and (at the least) returned to the sender.

This is precisely what happened to the Haushofer letter of 23 September. An Auslands agent, (an agent of the Foreign branch of the Nazi Party) posted the reply back to PO Box 506, Lisbon (apparently the postman was Hess's brother, Alfred who worked in the Auslands Organisation in Berlin) but the letter was censored by the British censor and retained. Realistically, it never stood a chance, and one explanation is that that the Haushofers did not wholly understand the system. They thought Mrs Roberts was in Lisbon, simply *because of the rules of the system*. See the above, rule 2.

We also suspect that Mary Roberts sent a further letter, as there is (or was) an envelope in the Bundesarchiv, Koblenz, dated 6 May 1941.[7] We have been unable to locate this envelope to date.

However, we now do not believe that the first Roberts letter was anything other than friendly greetings, simply because they could not be; the censor would have stopped the letter and that would have been the end of the matter. If Mrs Roberts was really taking part in an intelligence-inspired international intrigue, would she really choose to rely on the Thomas Cook service?

It is quite right to say that we do not know for sure, because the originating letter has yet to surface. The letter does not feature on the archive microfilms, but it may still possibly reside in the Haushofer private archive in Germany. What has to be the case is that it cannot be deemed to be contentious, or the censor would never have allowed its initial passage. Moreover, it did not need to be contentious if the purpose was purely to renew acquaintance.

In the very early days of our research, John Harris interviewed a member of Mrs Roberts's family in London, who confirmed that she had definitely not left Britain during the war. Harris was obviously keen to establish if indeed this was the case, as another author had recently asserted that the old lady was residing in Portugal.

The late Peter Allen, the father of fellow and equally controversial Hess author Martin Allen, had made the same flawed assumption as it appears Karl

Haushofer had in his 1983 work *Crown and Swastika*. He too made the case that Mrs Roberts was residing in Lisbon. This we now know is wholly untrue, but in so doing had helped Mr Allen in the telling of his own particular and unique interpretation of the story, at that time in trying to deal with the Duke of Windsor and his passage to the Bahamas.

Lastly, as far as the system of transmission is concerned, MI5, not surprisingly, also took an interest in Mrs Roberts and why she was sending letters to Germany. Eventually, on 14 May 1941, obviously in response to the events of three nights earlier, a Captain Hughes interviewed Mrs Roberts, safely at home in Cambridge.

Captain Hughes reported that the September letter was a continuation of a frequent pre-war correspondence and she had been told about the Cook mail service by a friend of hers. She also denied any knowledge of the Duke of Hamilton.[8] The first fact we are very willing to believe as we have established that the Roberts and Haushofers had been friends since before the First World War.[9]

Consequently, it would appear that the original letter from Mary Roberts to Martha Haushofer was sent in good faith and friendship, simply using a newly instigated service. That also appears to be the conclusion MI5 reached. Similarly, it is most likely that Karl Haushofer initially also saw the letter for what it was and merely told his son of the Lisbon address in the letter as reproduced in Chapter 2, *probably without any further indications as to the 'rules of the postal system'*.

With thanks to Tony Stott, he makes the point that British agents abroad did not necessarily trouble about a cover address but just wrote to somebody they knew, or had invented, being certain that their communications would first come to the censor and hence be routed to the proper department of intelligence. We now wonder if this is why Haushofer acted as he did.

So far and so good, but thereafter we feel the sequence of events and the apparent understanding of the participants certainly require further enquiry.

---

1 MI5 files KV2/1684.
2 Commenced 25 November 1939. Charles Entwistle to authors, 13th October 1999.
3 Ibid.
4 Clipperflying boats.com
5 Charles Entwistle to authors, 13 October 1999.
6 The British Postal Museum, London.
7 Rainer Schmidt, *Botengang Eines Toren?*, Econ, Düsseldorf, 1997.
8 TNA KV2/1684 and KV2/1685.
9 John Harris, *Rudolf Hess: The British Illusion of Peace*, JEMA, Moulton, 2010.

CHAPTER 4

THE LETTER IS DELIVERED

(And the Haushofer alibi is established)

The previous chapter dealt with the means of communication that Albrecht Haushofer had chosen to use in his attempt to reach the Duke of Hamilton, his pre-war friend. We now question whether this attempt was ever going to succeed, given the apparent misunderstanding of the necessary process. We also question whether this misunderstanding was a deliberate act.

In any event, Albrecht Haushofer meticulously recorded his every action, presumably as a defence against any future attack. It is also interesting to note what is not recorded:

- Why precisely did the Haushofers think Mrs Roberts was in Lisbon?
- Was it their misunderstanding of the Cook system? Had Karl merely passed on Thomas Cook's address and not that of Mrs Roberts?
- How (and where?) was Mrs Roberts to send the letter on to the Duke of Hamilton?
- Did Haushofer/Mrs Roberts know where the duke was stationed? If so, how?

The charade had begun.

C109/C002179-202
Dr Albrecht Haushofer to his parents

Berlin, 19 September 1940

Dear Parents: I am sending you enclosed herewith some important documents:

First T's Letter to Father,

Secondly, my answer to T. which has already been sent and, I hope, has your subsequent approval.

Thirdly, the draft of a letter to D,[1] *which I will keep to myself and not show to anyone else. I request that you examine it to see whether it might involve any danger for the woman who may transmit it.*[2] *I really believe that it sounds harmless enough. I have inserted the reference to the 'authorities' over there purposely as a safeguard for the transmitter and recipient. So I should like to have your honest opinion and any corrections. Fourthly a report of what I said on the 8th in G,*[3] *as an accounting before history (save till the last).*[4]

The whole thing is a fool's errand, but we cannot do anything about that.[5] *According to our latest reports the treaties of union between the Empire and the United States are about to be signed.*[6]

Best wishes,
Albrecht

Enclosure 1
(Letter from Rudolf Hess to Karl Haushofer)

Dear Friend: Albrecht brought me your letter, which at the beginning, besides containing official information, alluded to our walk together on the last day of August, which I too recall with so much pleasure.

Albrecht will have told you about our conversation, which beside volkdeutsch[7] *matters, above all touched upon the other matter, which is so close to the hearts of us both. I reconsidered the latter carefully once more and have arrived at the following conclusion:*

Under no circumstance must we disregard the contact or allow it to die aborning. I consider it best that you or Albrecht write to the old lady, who is a friend of your family, suggesting that she try to ask Albrecht's friend whether he would be prepared if necessary to come to the neutral territory in which she resides,[8] *or at any rate has an address through which she can be reached,*[9] *just to talk with Albrecht.*

If he could not do this just now, he might, in any case, send word through her where he expected to be in the near future. Possibly a neutral acquaintance, who had some business to attend to over there anyway, might look him up and make some communication with him, using you or Albrecht as reference.

This person probably would not care to have to inquire as to his whereabouts only after he got there or to make futile trips. You thought that by knowing about his whereabouts had no military significance at all; if necessary, you would also pledge yourselves not to make use of it with regard to any quarter that might profit from it.

What the neutral would have to transmit would be of such great importance that his having made known his whereabouts would be by comparison insignificant.

The prerequisite naturally was that the inquiry in question and the reply would not go through official channels, for you would not in any case want to cause your friends over there any trouble.

It would be best to have the letter to the old lady with whom you are acquainted delivered through a confidential agent of the AO to the address that is known to you. For this purpose Albrecht would have to speak to Bohle[10] *or my brother. At the same time the lady would have to be given the address of this agent in L – or if the latter does not live there permanently, to which the reply can in turn be delivered.*

As for the neutral[11] *I have in mind, I would like to speak to you orally about it some time. There is no hurry about this since, in any case there would first have to be a reply receiving her from over there. Meanwhile, lets both keep our fingers crossed. Should success be the fate of the enterprise, the oracle given to you with regard to the month of August would yet be fulfilled, since the name of the young friend and the old lady friend of your family occurred to you during our quiet walk on the last day of that month.*[12]

With best regards to you and Martha.
Yours, as ever,
R(udolf) H(ess)

Can be reached by telephone through: Linz – Gallspach A.[13]

Enclosure 2
TOP SECRET

My Dear Herr Hess: Your letter of the 10th reached me yesterday after a delay caused by the antiquated postal service of Partnach-Alm.[14] *I again gave a thorough study to the possibilities discussed therein and request – before taking the steps proposed – that you yourself examine once more the thoughts set forth below.*

I have in the meantime been thinking of the technical route by which a message from me must travel before it can reach the Duke of H(amilton). With your help, delivery to Lisbon can of course be assured without difficulty.[15] *About the rest of the route we do not know. Foreign control must be taken into account; the letter must therefore in no case be composed in such a way that it will simply be seized and destroyed or that it will directly endanger the woman transmitting it or the ultimate recipient.*[16]

In view of my close personal relations and intimate acquaintance with Douglas H(amilton) I can write a few lines to him (which should be enclosed with the letter to Mrs R., without any indication of place and without a full name – an A. would suffice for signature)[17] *in such a way that he alone will recognise that behind my wish*[18] *to see him in Lisbon there is something more serious than a personal whim. All the rest, however, seems to be extremely hazardous and detrimental to the success of the letter.*

Let us suppose that the case were reversed: an old lady in Germany receives a letter from an unknown source abroad, with a request to forward a message whose recipient is asked to disclose to an unknown foreigner where he will be staying for a certain period – and this recipient were a high officer in the air force (of course I do not know exactly what position H. holds at the moment; judging from his past I can conceive of only three things; he is an active air force general, or he directs the air defence of an important part of Scotland, or he has a responsible position in the Air Ministry).[19]

I do not think that you need much imagination to picture to yourself the faces that Canaris or Heydrich would make and the smirk with which they would consider any offer of 'security' or 'confidence' in such a letter if a subordinate should submit such a case to them. They would not merely make faces, you may be certain! The measures would come quite automatically – and neither the old lady nor the air force officer would have an easy time of it! In England it is no different.

Now another thing. Here too I would ask you to picture the situation in reserve. Let us assume that I received such a letter from one of my English friends. I would quite naturally report the matter to the highest German authorities I could contact, as soon as I had realised the import it might have and would ask for instructions on what I should do myself (at that, I am a civilian and H. is an officer).

If it should be decided that I was to comply with the wish for a meeting with my friend, I would then be most anxious to get my instructions if not from the Führer himself, at least from a person who receives them directly and at the same time has the gift of transmitting the finest and lightest nuances – an art which has been mastered by you yourself but not by all Reich Ministers. In addition, I should very urgently request that my action be fully covered – vis-à-vis other high authorities of my own country-uninformed or unfavourable.[20]

It is not any different with H. He cannot fly to Lisbon – any more than I can! – unless he is given leave, that is unless at least Air Minister Sinclair and Foreign Minister Halifax know about it.[21] *If, however, he receives permission to reply or to go, there is no need of indicating any place in England; if he does not receive it, then any attempt through a neutral mediator would also have little success.*[22]

In this case the technical problem of contacting H. is the least of the difficulties. A neutral who knows England and can move about in England – presumably there would be little sense in entrusting anyone else with such a mission – will be able to find the first peer of Scotland very quickly as long as conditions in the Isle are still halfway in order. (At the time of a successful invasion all the possibilities we are discussing here would be pointless anyway.)

My proposal is therefore as follows:

> *Through the old friend I will write a letter to H. – in a form that will incriminate no one but will be understandable to the recipient – with the proposal for a meeting in Lisbon. If nothing comes of that, it will be possible (if the military situation leaves enough time for it), assuming that a suitable intermediary is available, to make a second attempt through a neutral going to England, who might be given a personal message to take along. With respect to this possibility, I must add, however, that H. is extremely reserved – as many English are towards anyone they do not know personally. Since the entire Anglo-German problem after all springs from a most profound crisis in mutual confidence, this would not be immaterial.*[23]

Please excuse the length of this letter; I merely wished to explain the situation to you fully.

I already tried to explain to you not long ago that, for reasons I gave, the possibilities of successful efforts at a settlement between the Führer and the British upper class seem to me – to my extreme regret – infinitesimally small.[24]

Nevertheless, I should not want to close this letter without pointing out once more that I still think there would be a somewhat greater chance of success in going through Ambassador Lothian in Washington or Sir Samuel Hoare[25] *in Madrid rather than through my friend H.*[26] *To be sure, they are-politically speaking – more inaccessible.*[27]

Would you send me a line or give me a telephone call with final instructions? If necessary, will you also inform your brother in advance?[28] *Presumably I will then have to discuss with him the forwarding of the letter to Lisbon and the arrangement for a cover address for the reply in L(isbon).*

With cordial greetings and best wishes for your health.[29]

Yours, etc

A(lbrecht) H(aushofer)

Enclosure 3

Draft letter to D.H.[30]

My Dear D... Even if this letter has only a slight chance of reaching you – there is a chance and I want to make use of it.

First of all, to give you a sign of unaltered and unalterable personal attachment. I do hope you have been spared in all this ordeal, and I hope the same is true of your brothers. I heard of your father's deliverance from long suffering; and I heard that your brother-in-law Northumberland lost his life near Dunkerque. I need hardly tell you, how I feel about all that …

Now there is one thing more. If you remember some of my last communications before the war started you will realise that there is a certain significance in the fact that I am, at present, able to ask you whether there is the slightest chance of our meeting and having a talk somewhere on the outskirts of Europe, perhaps in Portugal. There are some things I could tell you, that might make it worthwhile for you to try a short trip to Lisbon – if you could make your authorities understand so much that they would give you leave. As to myself – I could reach Lisbon any time (without any kind of difficulty) within a few days after receiving news from you. If there is an answer to this letter, please address it to...[31]

C109/C002203
Dr Albrecht Haushofer to Rudolf Hess

23 September 1940

My dear Herr Hess: In accordance with your last telephone call, I got in touch with your brother immediately. Everything went off well, and I can now report that the mission has been accomplished to the extent that the letter you desired was written and dispatched this morning. It is to be hoped that it will be more efficacious than sober judgement would indicate.
Yours, Etc
H(aushofer)

C109/C002204-05
Dr Albrecht Haushofer to Dr Karl Haushofer

Berlin, 23 September 1940

Dear Father: I am enclosing the copy of a short letter of serious contents, which perhaps had better be kept by you than by me. I have now made it clear enough that in the action involved I did not take the initiative ...

Now to the English matters. I am convinced, as before, that there is not the slightest prospect of peace; and so I don't have the least faith in the possibility about which you know. However, I also believe that I could not have refused my services any longer. You know that for myself I do not see any possibility of any satisfying activity in the future ...
Best regards to both of you.
Albrecht

That appears to be the end of the exchange of letters. A few things emerge:

- Hess clearly believes Mrs Roberts is in Lisbon. He can only have gained that impression from the Haushofers, although it will be remembered that Hess had actually been introduced to Mrs Roberts before the war.

- The most difficult aspect here is why the Haushofers were quite happy to convey the fact that Mrs Roberts was based in Lisbon. They knew she was in her seventies, they knew her son had been killed, so quite why they thought she had moved to Lisbon in the middle of a war really deserves some further consideration. If the letter that Mrs Roberts sent to the Haushofers came through the Thomas Cook system, as is likely, then that might have been the source of the misinformation.
- We are also amazed that the Haushofers/Hess ever thought the letter would reach Mrs Roberts without being censored. If we assume that Hess and the Haushofers genuinely thought that Mrs Roberts was in Lisbon, surely the issue would remain as to how she was then going to forward the letter to Hamilton, without attracting the attention of the censor?
- The more we have considered this letter exchange, the odder it seems. First, the inordinate amount of detail we presume was a defence mechanism should anything go wrong – Albrecht in particular was detailing what he thought an unsound idea (but still went along with it) and secondly, any rational analysis must surely conclude that the proposed letter would never have got through the censor. Mrs Roberts's originating letter got through the censor because it was uncontentious. By contrast, a letter to the Duke of Hamilton (certainly not difficult to ascertain his identity), a serving wartime officer, suggesting a meeting in Lisbon was hardly likely to be passed off without comment.
- Indeed, we now must consider whether attracting the censor's attention was even part of the idea? It would appear from the chain that whilst Hess knew in general terms what Albrecht was to write, he did not actually get to see the draft itself. From MI5 file KV1684, it is now clear that the letter was simply addressed PO Box 506, Lisbon. Thomas Cook forwarded the unaddressed letter (apart from Mrs Roberts's name) to London, for them to address.[32]

The draft does seem to give the game away completely; it certainly is not written in such a way that, '*will incriminate no-one but will be understandable to the recipient*' (as per Albrecht's suggestion).

It appears to us that the letter was obvious as to the sender and obviously also implicates Mrs Roberts too.

The key here seems to be contained in the letter to his father that Albrecht sent on completion of the letter. He wrote, '*I have now made it clear enough that in the action involved I did not take the initiative*.'

Absolutely true. Albrecht was acting on the plan that was hatched by his father and Hess in the Grünwald forest, on 30/31 August 1940.

However, had he then played his part in such a manner to ensure failure, in that the letter was almost certain to be stopped by the censor? There must have been a better choice of words, or were they all genuinely ignorant? That we now very much doubt …

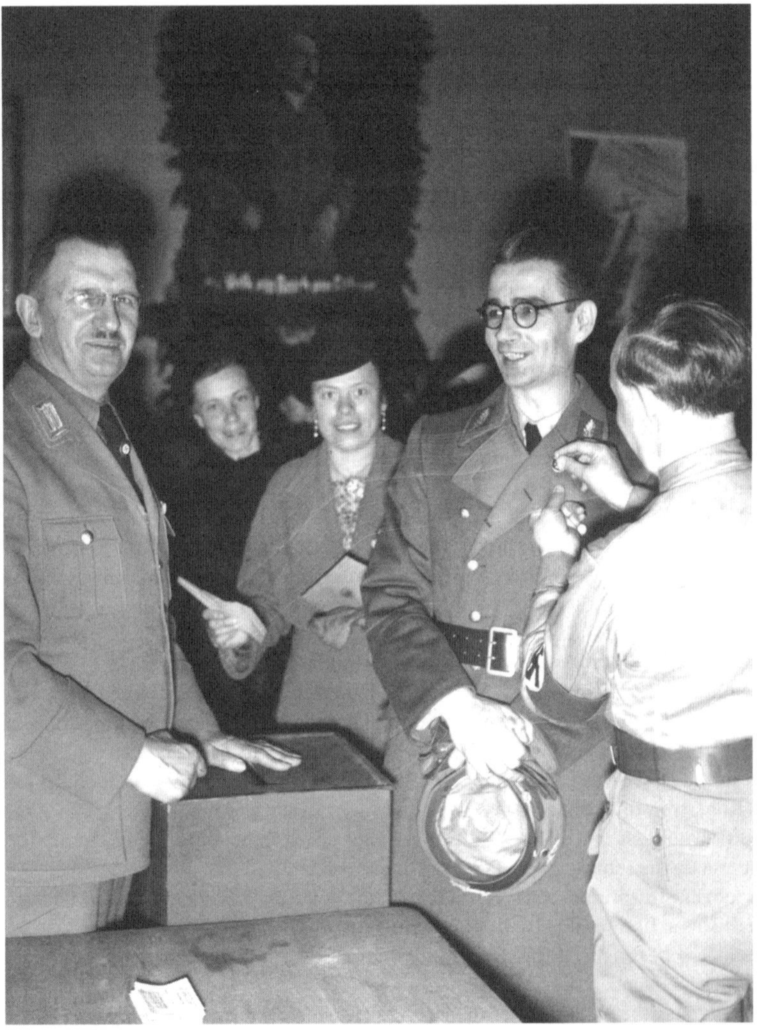

Alfred Hess (centre right), the appointed postman

[1] The Duke of Hamilton.
[2] Mrs Roberts in Cambridge, England.
[3] Bad Godesberg on the Rhine.
[4] The memorandum already analysed.
[5] A summary of the reservations already expressed to Rudolf Hess, albeit in more stringent terms. It is an interesting point to debate how Albrecht Haushofer was able to come to this conclusion in September 1940. It is certainly not clear to these authors, although clearly there had not been the British feelers at that time. They were to come in the spring of 1941.
[6] Some evidence exists to support this suggestion of an overarching political union, but it may possibly be a reference to the early stages of what became the lend lease agreement of March 1941.
[7] The affairs of ethnic Germans abroad.
[8] This is important. Hess was clearly of the opinion that Mrs Roberts was in Portugal, presumably as advised by the Haushofers.
[9] Presumably this is PO Box 506. The Germans appeared to be unaware that this was the Thomas Cook Office.
[10] Ernst Bohle – Head of the Auslands Organisation (AO). Friend of Hess, enemy of Ribbentrop. Alfred, Hess's brother also worked for the AO, based in Berlin.
[11] This appears to be an alternative to the Portugal meeting, or the next stage of the process.
[12] This appears to confirm that Haushofer at least was referring to 'an oracle' for some form of guidance.
[13] These authors have long wondered why Hess was at Gallspach, a small village in Upper Austria. Consequently, they travelled there in January 2015. The principle building in the village is that of the Zeileis Institute, a centre for alternative medicines. Established in the 1920s, we subsequently wrote to the Institute, who confirmed to us that Rudolf Hess had taken two treatments there: one in September 1940, the second 'two weeks before the flight' in May 1941. The treatment was based on high voltage electricity. Please refer to Chapter 13.
[14] Partnach-Alm is a small mountainside community, near Garmisch-Partenkirchen in the German Alps. Having travelled there in January 2015, the authors are quite prepared to accept this statement. In the winter it is virtually inaccessible by car.
[15] This again is interesting. The point is that the letter did not in itself have to be delivered to Lisbon any more than Mrs Roberts's originating message had to be hand delivered to London from Cambridge. This infers a seemingly remarkable German ignorance of the system.
[16] That is exactly what did happen!
[17] Evidence of the closeness of the Haushofer/Hamilton relationship.
[18] We think this is the first time a Haushofer/Hamilton meeting was mooted. However, what is important is that when Haushofer writes to Hamilton, the letter is far from subtle, and any well-educated censor would would have been able to determine its sender!
[19] This appears to be remarkably prescient. We have never learned what instructions were sent to Mrs Roberts in this connection, which again seems very odd.
[20] Effectively an assurance of safety. This was not unreasonable at all, and Hamilton was to request exactly the same degree of assurance in April 1941.
[21] This obviously assumes that Hamilton would have to ask for permission to travel to Portugal. This action would also implicate his superiors.
[22] A realistic assessment. If the letter route does not work, then chances are neither will the neutral intermediary.
[23] This reiterates the 'neutral intermediary' route, which is now developing into a 3rd party, who may not even know the Duke of Hamilton.

[24] A fairly blunt assessment.
[25] This approach was also put in place in the spring of 1941.
[26] A return to the 'official channels' again?
[27] This is key to the Hess affair. Haushofer was suggesting an approach to serving government ministers as being preferable but recognised that they were more politically inaccessible. That is why the Hamilton approach was being detailed.
[28] Presumably Alfred Hess, so as to deliver the letter to Lisbon.
[29] A request for the final approval.
[30] The Duke of Hamilton.
[31] A simple letter requesting a meeting. However, surely any censor would see it for what it is? How on earth was this ever going to get through a censor?
[32] NRA - KV1684, MC5v, Terminal Mails.

CHAPTER 5

ALBRECHT HAUSHOFER'S MEMORANDUM OF 15 SEPTEMBER 1940

A progress report to self?

Chapter 4 dealt with the recording of the delivery process of the letter from Albrecht Haushofer to the Duke of Hamilton, posted initially to Mary Roberts. The letter was finally sent, dated 23 September 1940.

A week earlier, whilst the air battles raged over London from dawn to dusk on what was to become known as 'Battle of Britain' day, Albrecht Haushofer was back in Berlin, making a detailed note of what was discussed between himself and Rudolf Hess at Bad Gallspach, in upper Austria, a week earlier on 8 September.

C109/C002190-04
Memorandum by Dr Albrecht Haushofer
Berlin, 15 September 1940

TOP SECRET
ARE THERE STILL POSSIBILITIES OF A GERMAN-ENGLISH PEACE?

On September 8, I was summoned to Bad G.[1] *to report to the Deputy of the Führer on the subject discussed in this memorandum.*[2] *The conversation which the two of us had alone lasted 2 hours. I had the opportunity to speak in all frankness.*

I was immediately asked about the possibilities of making known to persons of importance in England Hitler's serious desire for peace. It was quite clear that the continuance of the war was suicidal for the white race.[3] *Even with complete success in Europe, Germany was not in a position to take over inheritance of the Empire. The Führer had not wanted to see the Empire destroyed and did not want it even today. Was there not somebody in England who was ready for peace?*[4]

First, I asked for permission to discuss fundamental things. It was necessary to realise that not only Jews and Freemasons, but practically all Englishmen who mattered, regarded a treaty signed by the Führer as a worthless scrap of paper. To the question as to why this was so, I referred to the 10-year term of our Polish Treaty to the Non-Aggression Pact with Denmark signed only a year ago to the 'final' frontier demarcation of Munich. What guarantee did England have that a new treaty would not be broken again at once if it suited us? It must be realised that, even in the Anglo-Saxon world, the Führer was regarded as Satan's representative on earth and had to be fought.

If the worse came to the worst, the English would rather transfer their whole Empire bit by bit to the Americans than sign a peace that left to National Socialist Germany the mastery of Europe. The present war I am convinced, shows that Europe has become too small for its previous anarchic form of existence; it is only through close German-English co-operation that it can achieve a true federative order (based by no means merely on the police rule of a single power), while maintaining a part of its world position and having security against Soviet Russian Eurasia. France was smashed, probably for a long time to come, and we have opportunity currently to observe what Italy is capable of accomplishing. As long, however, as German-English rivalry existed, and in so far as both sides thought in terms of security, the lessons of this war was this: Every German had to tell himself: we have no security as long as provision is not made that the Atlantic gateways of Europe from Gibraltar to Narvik are free of any possible blockade.[5] *That is: there must be no English fleet. Every Englishman, must, however, under the same conditions, argue we have no security as long as anywhere within a radius of 2,000 kilometres from London there is a plane that we do not control. That is: there must be no German air force.*

There is only one way out of this dilemma: friendship intensified to fusion, with a joint fleet, a joint air force, and joint defence of possessions in the world – just what the English are now about to conclude with the United States.[6]

Here I was interrupted and asked why, indeed, the English were prepared to seek such a relationship with America and not with us. My reply was: because Roosevelt is a man and represents a Weltanschauung and a way of life that the Englishman thinks he understands, to which he can become accustomed, even where it does not seem to be to his liking. Perhaps he fools himself – but, at any rate that is what he believes.

A man like Churchill – himself half-American – is convinced of it. Hitler however seems to the Englishman the incarnation of what he hates that he has fought against for centuries – this feeling grips the workers no less than the plutocrats.[7]

In fact, I am of the opinion that those Englishmen who have property to lose, that is, precisely the portions of the so-called plutocracy that count, are those who would be readiest to talk peace.[8]

But even they regard a peace only as an armistice. I was compelled to express these things so strongly because I ought not – precisely because of my long experience in attempting to effect a settlement with England in the past and my numerous English friendships – to make it appear that I seriously believe in the possibility of a settlement between Adolf Hitler and England in the present stage of development. I was thereupon asked whether I was not of the opinion that feelers had perhaps not been successful because the right language had not been used. I replied that, to be sure, if certain persons, whom we both knew well, were meant by this statement, then certainly the wrong language had been used.[9] *But at the present stage this had little significance. I was then asked directly why all Englishmen were so opposed to Herr v. R(ibbentrop). I conceded, that, in the eyes of the English, Herr v. R., like some other personages, played, to be sure, the same role as did Duff Cooper, Eden and Churchill in the eyes of the Germans. In the case of Herr v. R., there was also the conviction, precisely in the view of Englishmen who were formerly friendly to Germany that – from completely biased motives – he had informed the Führer wrongly about England and that he personally bore an unusually large share of the responsibility for the outbreak of war.*

But I again stressed the fact that the rejection of peace feelers by England was today due not so much to persons as to the fundamental outlook mentioned above.[10]

Nevertheless, I was asked to name those whom I thought might be reached as possible contacts.[11]

I mentioned among diplomats, Minister O'Malley in Budapest, the former head of the Southeastern Department of the Foreign Office, a clever person in the higher echelons of officialdom, but perhaps without influence precisely because of his former friendliness toward Germany; Sir Samuel Hoare, who is half-shelved and half on the watch in Madrid, whom I do not know well personally, but to whom I can at any time open a personal path; as the most promising, the Washington Ambassador

Lothian,[12] with whom I have had close personal connections for years, who as a member of the highest aristocracy and at the same time as person of very independent mind, is perhaps best in a position to undertake a bold step-provided that he could be convinced that even a bad and uncertain peace would be better than the continuance of the war – a conviction at which he will only arrive if he convinces himself in Washington that English hopes of America are not realisable.

Whether or not this is so could only be judged in Washington itself; from Germany not at all. As the final possibility I then mentioned that of a personal meeting on neutral soil with the closet of my English friends, the young Duke of Hamilton, who has access at all times to all important persons in London, even to Churchill and the King.[13] I stressed in this case the inevitable difficulty of making a contact and again repeated my conviction of the improbability of its succeeding – whatever approach we took.

The upshot of the conversation was H's statement that he would consider the whole matter thoroughly once more and send me word in case I was to take steps. For this extremely ticklish case, and in the event that I might possibly have to make a trip alone – I asked for very precise directives from the highest authority.[14] From the whole conversation I had the strong impression that it was not conducted without the prior knowledge of the Führer, and that I probably would not hear any more about the matter unless a new understanding had been reached between him and his Deputy.[15]

On the personal side of the conversation, I must say that – despite the fact that I felt bound to say usually hard things – it ended in great friendliness, even cordiality. I spent the night in Bad G, and the next morning still had the opportunity, on a walk together in the presence of the Chief Adjutant, to bring up all the volksdeutsch questions from the resettlement in all parts of Europe to the difficulties as to personnel in the central offices in Berlin – which resulted in H's direct intervention.
A (lbrecht) H(aushofer)

This comprehensive memorandum is, in our view, an excellent resumé of the actual Anglo-German thought processes prevalent in September 1940. What it does not do, however, is to present any ideas of the mechanics as to how a peace might be achieved. It is difficult to see from the above how a meeting would achieve anything worthwhile, other than the British censor being alerted to a peace initiative from Germany via Lisbon.

We also suspect Albrecht and Hess already realised that a negotiated peace between governments was an unattainable goal whilst Hitler was in power. We also suspect that Haushofer already knew the letter would fail, as he surely knew that Mrs Roberts was in Cambridge, England and not Lisbon, Portugal.

Nonetheless, they posted the letter and waited for a response …

---

[1] Bad Godesberg on the Rhine.

[2] This is a record of the start of Albrecht's direct involvement with Rudolf Hess in the affair.

[3] Apparently, an observation made by Haushofer to Hess.

[4] We are absolutely sure the answer to this question is 'yes'. The more relevant question is 'how?'

[5] The fear of the blockade is a theme, almost an obsession. It was this that brought Germany to her knees in 1918.

[6] On 3 September 1940, the British and US governments had concluded an agreement for fifty destroyers in exchange for the US acquisition of bases in the Caribbean. The British also agreed not to scuttle the fleet in the event of invasion.

[7] The mistrust of Hitler is absolutely correct in our estimation.

[8] Ditto.

[9] This is a reflection of the criticism of the German Foreign Office and von Ribbentrop in particular.

[10] In other words, no peace possible whilst Hitler was the leader.

[11] We are not sure about this. Yes, of course there were some pro-German politicians, but how was peace to be effected, especially given the above issues?

[12] Lord Lothian died in December 1940, ending the connection.

[13] This statement has often been quoted as evidence of Haushofer's and Hess's naivety. On the contrary, in our view it is actually wholly correct from a constitutional point of view.

[14] Somewhat ironically, so as not to be accused of treachery later on. Haushofer was executed in April 1945.

[15] Clearly Hess and Hitler had been debating the issue. The official line is that Hess was acting alone.

CHAPTER 6
SO, WHO WAS MRS ROBERTS?
(And was there more to her than met the eye?)

Chapters 4 and 5 have described the process that culminated in Albrecht Haushofer writing to his old family friend Mary Violet Roberts on 23 September 1940, in the hope that she might then forward an enclosed letter on to the Duke of Hamilton. This chapter now describes Mary Violet Roberts, who she was and why she plays a significant role in the Hess affair.

After describing the Anglo-German relationship in August 1940, the prospect of a Russian invasion and the immense stakes that the major players were playing for, it may seem somewhat odd to then dedicate a chapter to a lady who in 1940 was already seventy-six years of age and particularly enjoyed walking her Scottie dog and bottling gooseberries.[1]

However, the more we consider the non-participatory role that Mrs Roberts played, the more convinced we become that she is, in fact, the key to understanding the Hess affair, simply because her involvement was perceived by the Germans as being wholly non-governmental (indeed it is hard to conceive anyone more non-governmental, or so they may have thought …).

Hess and Haushofer tried to use Mrs Roberts precisely because she was so non-governmental. Logically, it was their attempt to negotiate a peace *outside* the usual government channels. Had they wanted to negotiate directly with the British government, then there certainly would not have been the need for the drama of letters and flights to Scotland, and so on. That is why God had created diplomats (even Joachim von Ribbentrop), albeit diplomats that had failed in this instance.

No, we now believe that the existence of the correspondence involving Mrs Roberts is the certain evidence that Hess and Haushofer were trying to reach persons outside the government (or possibly even some dissenters within it), persons who, nonetheless, they believed, were apparently quite capable of instigating the changes that Hess desperately sought.

So, let us now discover precisely who Mrs Roberts[2] was and why she became embroiled in the Hess affair. In many ways she was an ideal, but very unlikely, intermediary.

Mrs Roberts was the starting point for our initial interest in the Hess affair back in the early 1990s. David Irving stated that Mrs Roberts was the daughter-in-law of Field Marshal Lord Roberts.[3] Quickly, we had found out this to be impossible. Lord Roberts's unmarried son, Frederick, was killed at Colenso in 1899. So, who was the Haushofer and Hess's Mrs Roberts?

Mary Violet Roberts was born on 5 September 1864 in Ferozepore, India and was baptised on 25th of the same month.[4] Her father was Patrick Maxwell, at that time a Captain in the Bengal Staff Corps. Patrick had joined the Bengal Army as a cadet on 31 January 1845[5] and had progressed to the rank of Captain, late of the 37th Native Infantry and Deputy Commissioner in the Punjab at Googaira. Mary's mother was Louisa Sarah Maxwell, née Bell, originating from Tasmania. They had married in 1853.

When looking at Patrick Maxwell's cadet papers we could not help but notice that his father, William, had to give his consent to his son following a career in the army. William was described as, 'William Maxwell, Merchant of Dargavel, Glasgow'. Dargavel is no more than 20 miles from where Hess crashed and has an obvious similarity to Dungavel, the so called 'Hess target'. Another coincidence.

Looking backwards further still, we discovered that William Maxwell had married Mary Campbell of Possil Park, which in 1834 was described thus: 'It [Possil House] was then far away from the noise and smoke of the city and

Dargavel House, Bishopton

stood among fine old trees. With its beautiful gardens, its grassy slopes, and its lear lake, Possil formed as delightful and retired a country residence as any in the county.'[6]

Clearly, here was a family of some substance. Next, we looked at Dargavel House, the ancestral home of Mary Violet Roberts.

Dargavel House, in Bishopton,[7] is again of a similar standing. Dating from *c.*1580, the house is still standing, though currently entombed in the 2,500-acre estate of the former Bishopton Royal Ordnance factory. Once the largest in Europe and so secret that it did not appear on OS maps, the site has now been decommissioned and at the time of writing is awaiting planning permission so that it can be re-developed as houses. The old house is now deep inside this secret area, apparently again much altered.[8]

Again, clear evidence of wealth and status. Further 'googling' revealed that the Maxwells seem to originate back to Caerlaverock Castle,[9] in Dumfriesshire *c.*1270.

Clearly the Maxwells were well connected and indeed appeared to be an even older family than the Hamiltons. We should not, therefore, be too surprised to learn that in 1638, Elizabeth, the daughter of James Maxwell, married William, 2nd Duke of Hamilton.[10] We have yet to discover if this family link was perpetuated through to the 1930s. Quite honestly, we doubt it, but, at times, in the Hess case it seems anything is possible. We have found no evidence of any other link between the Roberts family and the Duke of Hamilton, save their common friendship with the Haushofers. We have also singularly failed in our attempts to obtain a photograph of Mrs Roberts.

However, returning to India in 1864, the Maxwell family were only eight years away from returning to England and in 1872 Patrick retired to Bath, Wiltshire, England, with the rank of Major General. They lived in a large house at 19 Pulteney Road.[11] Mary therefore spent her formative years in the west of England. She also had a brother, Louis. General Maxwell spent his retirement writing books, such as Pribbles and Prabbles, published in 1906.[12]

In the late 1880s, Mary began her courtship of the senior maths teacher at the nearby Bath College, or vice-versa.[13] Herbert Ainslie Roberts was only marginally older than Mary, being born in the February of 1864. Academically gifted, Herbert had attended Gonville and Caius College, Cambridge, graduating in 1887.

Herbert's elder brother, Ernest, was also exceptionally academically gifted, becoming the Master of Gonville and Caius from 1903 to 1912.[14]

Mary and Herbert married in 1894 and moved to Cambridge in 1898, Herbert initially becoming a mathematical coach. The couple were not poor, Mary being the principal beneficiary of her father's will when he died in July 1906. In addition to a specific bequest, Patrick also gave his daughter the proceeds of a marriage settlement that had been settled in 1853, when he married Louisa.

By the time of his father-in-law's death in 1906, Herbert had become secretary to the recently formed (1899) Cambridge Appointments Board. It was this position that was to earn Herbert his reputation,[15/16] so much so, that on his death in 1932 it was summarised: 'It is hardly too much to say that Roberts achieved the greatest bit of constructive work of a not strictly academic character done in Cambridge by a single individual in the last 25 years.'[17]

The Roberts were becoming comfortable and in 1912/13 commissioned the then fashionable Mackay Baillie Scott to design and build a 'Sussex style farmhouse of Mock Tudor design'. Baillie Scott had also studied earlier in his career in Bath, and it is fair to say that it is a lovely house and still stands to this day. Originally designated 33 Storey's Way, it is now renumbered to 48.

However, of far more relevance to this story is that around this time the Roberts family became acquainted with the Haushofer family, a friendship that certainly lasted for the next forty years at least. How the two families met we are still not sure (even after thirty years of trying to find out) but we do know that:

- Herbert Roberts was secretary to the Cambridge Appointments Board, the Indian Civil Service Studies Board and the Foreign Service Students Committee. They may therefore have met through his work.
- Ernest Roberts may have introduced them through his important position at Gonville and Caius.
- In 1899,[18] Karl Haushofer had travelled to England and had met Joseph Chamberlain. This appears to coincide with the visit of Kaiser Wilhelm to England in a British-inspired attempt to improve relations.
- On 14 August 1925, Mary and Herbert met Albrecht Haushofer. The diary entry reads: 'Die Bekanntschaft mit der Familie R. datierte aus der Vorkriegszeit.'[19]
- What is not helpful is Martin Allen's unsourced assertion that the two families met when Karl Haushofer addressed the Cambridge 'Foreign Science Students Committee' in 1898. First, we do not think there

has ever been such a committee (we have certainly seen no reference to it) and secondly, even if he meant the 'Foreign Service Students Committee', that particular body was not formed until 1905.[20]

However, Martin Allen notwithstanding, our assertion remains that the friendship was certainly longstanding and durable. It also transcended the generations.

Karl and Martha Haushofer had two boys, Albrecht and Heinz; Herbert and Mary had one son, Patrick. Albrecht was born in 1903, Patrick Roberts in 1895.

Not surprisingly, given the family backgrounds, both sets of children were also extremely academic. Patrick went to Eton aged thirteen, and then to Trinity College Cambridge before joining the Foreign Service in 1919. His naturally proud aunt, Mrs Ernest Stewart Roberts, describes his progress: '… [Patrick] went to Eton as a scholar, and was a most brilliant one – winning almost every possible distinction, including the Newcastle and finishing with one of the best Scholarships at Trinity, Cambridge'.[21]

Similarly, Albrecht spent his formative years in Munich and graduated in history and geography from the university in 1924, aged twenty-one. Heinz studied as an agronomist.

48 Storey's Way, Cambridge

The Haushofer archives in Koblenz also detail various meetings with the younger Roberts, who was rapidly progressing through the diplomatic ranks. In chronological order:

11.6.1925: Patrick Roberts zum Mittagessen, tee u. abend essen.
14.8.1925: Mr & Mrs Roberts viel bei mir Roberts mit Albrecht um ½ I fort.
Patrick obviously met his parents and their German friends prior to his leaving the Berlin Embassy for Warsaw (he started there on 15 August 1925).

Later on, the family's meetings are less documented, and we were very grateful to Andrea Schroder Haushofer in Munich who provided us with a copy of the visitors' book at the family estate, Hartschimmelhof. The Roberts visits are recorded, but the book appeared to have been perhaps written in hindsight. All the entries are in the same handwriting, the same colour ink and it just seem to be to have been done after the event.

Nevertheless, the Roberts are recorded as having visited the Haushofers in 1925 and 1926. In 1932, Herbert Ainslie Roberts died, and in 1934 the Haushofers visited London, Cambridge and Oxford. In 1936, Albrecht visited the UK alone.[22]

By 1936, the two families' friendship had essentially passed down from Herbert and Mary/ Karl and Martha to the two sons' generation. By 1936, Karl Haushofer was sixty-seven. Mary Roberts was seventy-two and living with her high-achieving son, Patrick, in Athens, Greece, whilst he was working at the British Embassy. Patrick was, by that time, chargé d'affaires in Athens.

However, in 1937 Mary Roberts's world was completely shattered. Five years after the death of her husband, Patrick was involved in a car crash at Ekali, some 20 km north of central Athens and died shortly afterwards. Mary came back to England and was next recorded as living in London with her nephew, Walter Roberts,[23] at 36 Queen's Gate, Kensington when her son's probate was granted in 1938. Eventually, she returned broken-hearted to Wilberforce Road in Cambridge, having downsized from the larger Storey's Way property.

We suspect none of the family members anticipated the roles they were about to play in world history, particularly Mary Violet Roberts, who was then far more worried as to how she might keep her Cambridge lawn cut and tidy.

[1] Letters to the authors from a family friend.
[2] Until 1994 her identity was unknown.
[3] David Irving, *Hess: The Missing Years 1941–1945*, Focal Point, Windsor, 2010.
[4] Bengal Baptisms, Vol. 109, Folio 59.
[5] British Library l/Mil/9/209, Oriental and India Office Collection.
[6] The Old Country Houses of the Glasgow Gentry, Strathclyde University.
[7] www.maxwellsociety.com.
[8] Ibid.
[9] The only triangular castle in Scotland.
[10] www.maxwellsociety.com.
[11] It now forms part of a hotel.
[12] Patrick Maxwell, *Pribbles and Prabbles*, Skeffington, London, 1906.
[13] Bath College was founded in what is now the Bath Spa Hotel. It existed as a school from 1879 to 1909. The headmaster was T.W. Dunn, who was a close friend of the Roberts family whilst at Swineshead, Lincolnshire.
[14] See Mrs E.S. Roberts, *Sherbourne, Oxford and Cambridge*, Martin Hopkinson Limited, 1934.
[15] Apparently, before its formation, students were very much left to their own devices when pursuing their particular careers.
[16] Cambridge University Library hold the papers of the Appointments Board.
[17] Quoted from Vice Chancellor of Cambridge University 1932.
[18] Between 21September and 6 November 1899.
[19] Haushofer correspondence, volume 2, page 453.
[20] www.venn.csi.cam.ac.uk/acad/lists
[21] Mrs E.S. Roberts, *Sherbourne, Oxford and Cambridge*, Martin Hopkinson Limited, London.
[22] Haushofer archives, Koblenz Bundesarchiv.
[23] Walter Roberts was the son of Mr and Mrs Ernest Roberts. Ernest had been Master of Gonville and Caius from 1903 to 1912. After a career in the Egyptian civil service, he became a stockbroker, working for Silverston & Co. in the City of London.

CHAPTER 7
INTO THE LION'S DEN

No real surprise – the letter is intercepted

The previous chapters record the instigation and sending of the letter from Albrecht Haushofer to the seventy-six-year-old Mary Violet Roberts, via the wartime Thomas Cook mail system. MI5 Files KV2/1684 and 1685 make reasonably clear the initial sequence of events upon the receipt of the Haushofer letter in England.

A 'Terminal Mails' report dated 2 November 1940 states that the letter had arrived in the United Kingdom from Lisbon. The censor is unsure as to the identity of 'AH', but according to the report, the letter is asking for the recipient, Mrs Roberts, to forward it to the Duke of Hamilton at the House of Lords, London, an action that almost must have been guaranteed to bring the document to the censor's attention.

If this was the intent, it certainly worked. The censor passed the letter, or copies thereof, to the following organisations:

1) MI5
2) The Foreign Office
3) The IRB

We know this because the letter is so marked. We will take the recorded reaction of each organisation in turn.

MI5

Once again, file KV2/1684 makes it reasonably clear that MI5 and the Twenty (XX) committee did not instigate any ruse or scheme against the receipt of the letter, possibly more due to their own dithering rather than as a result of any formal policy decision. Following the paper trail gives the following timeline:

15.11.1940 MI5 – 'I have been unable to identify Dr AH.' Mrs Roberts had also yet to be traced.

17.11.1940 MI5 identifies AH as Albrecht Haushofer. 'Before we decide whether to send it on or not you will probably want to find out what the Foreign Office are doing about the copy which was sent to them.'

20.11.1940 Letter from Air Ministry: 'We of course have no objection to your office contacting him [The Duke of Hamilton]'.

22.11.1940 MI5 to MI6 requesting agreement to forward the letter, 'provided you do not object'.

22.11.1940 MI5 to MI6: 'It would appear not to be a matter of espionage, but one of peace propaganda.'

22.11.1940 MI5 mistaken identity of Mrs Roberts (indicating they still do not yet recognise her).

29.11.1940 MI5 correctly identifies Mrs Roberts as being in Cambridge.

07.12.1940 Two postal warrants (to inspect all post) – Mrs Roberts and Minero Silricola lda (the suggested return address for the Haushofer/Roberts/Hamilton letter)'

07.12.1940 MI6 (Hopkinson) to MI5 (Sseillito): 'We have not done anything about it ourselves and we have no objection to the letter being allowed to go onto its destination.'

26.12.1940 Note to state that Minero Silricola lda (the suggested return address of the Haushofer letter) is a German controlled company engaged in the purchase of mineral ores for Germany. (It, too, was based in Lisbon.)

11.01.1941 File note (Mondi): 'The delays have been lamentable. Boyle wants SIS and us to run him [Hamilton].'

11.01.1941 Guy Liddell's diary: 'A German named Karl Haushofer … has written to the Duke of Hamilton. We have approached Archie Boyle who is prepared to send Hamilton on some mission to Lisbon.'

13.01.1941 File note (White): 'I think this is worth proceeding with.'

20.01.1941 File note (Robertson): discussed with Mr White and Captain Masterman. Not a case for B2a.

20.01.1941 File note (Robertson): saw Boyle – not a case for the double cross section. Suggests that Hamilton is asked to write in reply.

22.01.1941 MI5 to Air Ministry (Stammers) asking Stammers to ascertain if the Duke of Hamilton would go to Portugal as the Haushofer letter suggests.

11.3.1941 MI5 to Air Ministry: 'Whether you have had an opportunity yet

	of interviewing the Duke of Hamilton concerning the matter I wrote to you on 22nd January.'
11.3.1941	Hamilton interviewed by Stammers.
11.3.1941	Written statement of the Duke of Hamilton: 'I know Albrecht Haushofer … I do not recollect, but I cannot say with any certainty, anything of a Mrs Roberts connected with AH, nor can I recall meeting Mrs V George.'[1]
23.03.1941	MI5 to Major C. Dixon Cambridge, asking if he has learned anything of Mrs Roberts.
25.03.1941	MI5 to Air Ministry (Stammers) thanking him 'for the trouble you have taken…'
07.04.1941	MI5 to Air Ministry (Boyle): 'Could you arrange for the Duke of Hamilton to be sent on a mission to Lisbon…'Suggests that the excuse be given that Hamilton's original reply was lost.

(New File KV2/1685)

06.04.1941	Hamilton to Air Ministry, explaining why he has not sent the 1939 letter from Haushofer.
15.04.1941	Air Ministry to MI5, sending a copy of the above letter.
22.04.1941	File note (Robertson): 'Discussed with B. who said he had been making enquiries … as to what action, if any they had taken in connection with the letter… No information was available…'
25.04.1941	MI5 (Robertson) interviewed Hamilton. Advised Hamilton to go to Lisbon and then write to Haushofer.
26.04.1941	Hamilton to Air Ministry: 'I am prepared to go.'
03.05.1941	Air Ministry to MI5: 'Archie is apprehensive that action … might well be misunderstood … The proposal is in abeyance.'
13.5.1941	File note summarising the above.

POINTS OF NOTE FROM THE ABOVE MI5 FILES

1. Whilst the Haushofer letter to Hamilton is copied onto the file,[2] the Albrecht Haushofer to Violet Roberts letter is not. Mrs Roberts, when later interviewed, makes the point that it was the first time Albrecht Haushofer had written to her. It was, of course, usually his mother who corresponded with her.

2. Given the above, we cannot readily explain why there was such a

delay in identifying Mrs Roberts in Cambridge and can only presume that the letter from Lisbon did not contain a forwarding address. Indeed, initially MI5 even wrongly identified Mrs Roberts as residing in Wembley (apparently from the phonebook). This was in fact the Mrs V. George that the Duke of Hamilton stated he did not know. Why this should be the case or even necessary we cannot conceive, except that the letter merely was addressed to PO Box 506 – without any forwarding address. As required. In other words, the Haushofers and Alfred Hess both apparently assumed that Mrs Roberts was in Lisbon, simply as a result of the Thomas Cook postal system. (The Haushofer personnel file seems to confirm this – Thomas Cook actually identified Mrs Roberts from *their* records.)[3]

3. MI5 then appear to dither as to response. Understandably, they have to identify who they are dealing with, but then a counter-approach appears to be on, then off, then on again until finally the Air Ministry appear to finally scupper the plans on 3 May 1941. Is this because the Air Ministry are aware of other schemes already in place? *Or* is it because they realised that the Haushofers had incorrectly used the Thomas Cook system and so any reply would theoretically have been impossible, if in the meanwhile the Haushofers had realised their mistake? It now appears that they (the Haushofers) sent the letter to PO Box 506 believing that Mrs Roberts was indeed residing at that address, rather than a mere forwarding address. This is potentially very important as it would rule out dummy forged communications as a viable option. No one should be able to reply to a letter that should not have been delivered!

4. This does now seem to be the most likely explanation, though is surely most odd.

5. In a similar vein, MI5 twice question MI6 as to whether there are any other schemes taking place. We can understand the need to ask, but twice? The reply from Hopkinson on 7.12.1940 seems pretty clear: 'We have not done anything about it ourselves ...'

6. The original letter was apparently lost from the MI5 file and

Hamilton apparently never saw it, despite MI6 giving permission for MI5 to do so. Was this because it was being used elsewhere and was Hamilton's ignorance of the letter deliberate, having been told of it by a different intelligence agency? Hugh Trevor-Roper, in 'Flight from Reality',[4] makes the point that it is also quite likely that the Duke of Hamilton was under surveillance by MI5 on account of his pre-war, pro-German activities. This would, however, quite possibly explain why the letter was not forwarded to the duke.

7. Archie Boyle, RAF intelligence, is wholly informed and appraised by MI5, at the very latest on 11 January 1941. We now believe Mr Boyle knew all about this letter a lot earlier than 11 January 1941. Please note the file says, 'Boyle wants SIS and us to run him…'

CONCLUSION

Despite careful consideration and twice seeming to try to instigate initial steps towards its implementation, MI5, or its sub-committee the XX committee, did not appear to 'run' the Duke of Hamilton in connection with a response to the letter of 23 September 1940. Largely, we suspect, because they could not be seen to be answering a letter they should never have received. We also consider in Chapter 27 whether Albrecht Haushofer was actually a British agent and, if so, that too may well explain why no further action was taken. They knew the letter was the action of an agent and so no further action was deemed necessary.

However, it may well be the case that MI5 did not know that fact either, as MI6 was the responsible body for overseas operations. MI5 had based its reactions wholly on a censor's report. One would have thought perhaps that it might have wondered why the envelope had not been addressed to an English address? There appears to be no record of MI5 ascertaining its mistake or even wondering why it had not been given the address. Equally, if Hugh Trevor-Roper was correct and the Duke of Hamilton was under surveillance, it may well be that the Duke was thus rendered as unsuitable for such a role. What is also clear is that the Duke of Hamilton was wholly aware of the letter of 23 September 1940 (since mid-March 1941 at the latest) and was waiting for the prospect of further engagement when Hess flew into Scotland on 10 May 1941.

We also wonder if Albrecht Haushofer had made quite such an honest mistake. He refers to the unlikelihood of success. This may quite possibly be by reason of the fact that he knew the letter was not even correctly addressed. It appears that he had enlisted the help of Alfred Hess, Rudolf's younger brother who was deputy head of the Auslands Organisation, so it may be that it was the younger Hess who made the mistake – not Haushofer. Alfred Hess was also based in Berlin at the time, working in the Auslands Organisation. Haushofer throughout is keen to be seen to be documenting his actions and thought processes (a full memorandum on how to post a letter and yet it is still flawed in implementation!).

Indeed, Albrecht seems to us to have recorded his actions largely so that he could not then be blamed. In his letter of 23 September to his father he wrote, 'I have now made it clear enough that in the action involved I did not take the initiative…'

So, any later independent review would presumably exonerate Albrecht from 'taking the lead', which may have been very important to him in any later deadly atmosphere seeking to lay blame. Albrecht also wrote in the same letter that he could not delay his involvement in the matter any longer, which again infers a reluctance to get involved in the Deputy Führer's scheming.

However, lastly and perhaps of most relevance, surely the Haushofer family must have wondered quite why their old friend had moved to Lisbon? She was, after all, seventy-six years old and whilst they knew her to be a seasoned traveller when younger, to travel to the Iberian Peninsula in the middle of a European war must surely have raised questions in their minds? Armed with that knowledge, did they not at least consider the possibility of a trap?

THE FOREIGN OFFICE/MI6

The second copy of the censor's report travelled to the Foreign Office, but in contrast to the release of MI5 files 1684/1685, there has been no similar release from MI6. This should perhaps come as no surprise. However, the same MI5 files also deal with Albrecht Haushofer, under the old personnel record of PF 54592. From this file the curtains are drawn a little on the activities of MI6 in connection with Haushofer. Again, most of the activity stems from the receipt of the September 1940 letter.

The whole question of MI6 and file-keeping was brought into focus in early 2014 when a 'MI6 Hess file' somewhat bizarrely came up for auction in the United States.

Lot 171 of Alexander Historical Auctions, Chesapeake City (Guide price $200,000–$300,000) appears to be a genuine MI6 file of documentation prepared by Rudolf Hess following his capture at Eaglesham. Tellingly, the part of the file that gives its reference has been torn off. According to the auctioneers, the file had come to the States from Europe, allegedly from Sir Maurice Oldfield, the former head of MI6 who had taken/stolen the file from archive to prevent its destruction. The German Bundesarchiv had apparently then tested the file for authenticity and had attested to its provenance. The file failed to sell, but its contents will be referred to later in this work.(See appendix 4).

Given the above issue, we were far from surprised, but a little staggered, when Keith Jeffery's history of MI6[5] (when first published) failed to even mention the Hess affair in passing. Further correspondence between these authors and Keith resulted in an admission that there was some incidental information, and the paperback version of the book included a postscript to that effect.

Consequently, the only evidence that we can draw on is that part of the PF54592 file that pertains to Haushofer. However, we can state that we certainly cannot trace and follow the receipt of the letter into MI6 from the censor's department in the way we have been able to in respect of MI5.

This may of course be precisely the case, as Peter Padfield quotes Ursula Laack-Michel[6] who stated that on 12 November 1940 Albrecht Haushofer had written to his mother, 'From L [Lisbon] nothing.'

This should not perhaps be too surprising as MI5/MI6 did not appear to identify Mrs Roberts until 29 November! Neither should it appear too much of a surprise, as the despatch of the letter had been dealt with in such a way that it should never have reached Cambridge, England.

However, to then accept that the letter was merely filed away and forgotten by MI6 (as Keith Jeffery would like us to believe), would be, in our opinion, a quite significant mistake. We now extrapolate the PF54592 Haushofer file as follows:

1940. Censor's report. This also forwarded the 23 September 1940 letter as follows:

- To MI 12 for MI5 – original letter
- To FO (MI6) – photostat
- To IRB (SOE) – photostat

The comment is made, 'letter forwarded from Cook's office in Lisbon. Mrs V Roberts address being filled in Cook's office – Berkeley Street, London.'

This in itself is a revelation. It confirms as we suspected that the address was not supplied by the Germans when they wrote to Mrs Roberts, PO Box 506. So, Thomas Cook then forwarded the letter to London who, in turn, supplied the address of Mrs Roberts. This begs the question as to why on earth it was necessary for MI5 to pretend that it did not know who Mrs Roberts was, taking until 29 November to mark the file, given that her address was on the original letter, already marked up by Cook.

17.11.1940	Note from B22 to DyB, (viz.Department B22 to Deputy of B dept) demonstrating that they know AH is Albrecht Haushofer, though not who Mrs Roberts is, believing her to be in Wembley. Given that the 'Terminal Mails' clearly states that Cooks addressed the envelope in London, why is this charade necessary, unless the original has been lost (or sent somewhere else)?
22.11.1940	Note from B10e to B6, attaching a report giving Mrs Roberts's address as 10 Wilberforce Road, Cambridge (the correct one, dated 29.11.1940).
30.11.1940	Note from Cowgill (MI6) to Sillitoe MI5: 'We have no record of the address in Lisbon, or of Mrs V. Roberts.'
7.12.1940	Hopkinson (MI6) to Sillitoe (MI5): 'We have not done anything about it ourselves…'

There is then a travel permit, stamped 23 June 1938, showing Albrecht Haushofer's entry into Britain from the Hook of Holland. This was obtained for the purpose of comparing his signature with that of the photostat letter of 23 September 1940. On this occasion, he was listed as staying at 34 Tufton Court, London. We believe this to be the London address of the Duke of Hamilton.

26.12.1940	Letter to Sillitoe (MI5), explaining the suggested return address of the letter.
22.1.1941	Letter from T.A. Robertson to F.G. Stammers of the Air Ministry, asking that he interview the Duke of Hamilton. The point is made that 'the original letter (of 23.9.1940) has been lost.'
11.3.1941	Letter from TA Robertson to Stammers of the Air

	Ministry: 'have you yet had the opportunity of interviewing the Duke of Hamilton?'
11.3.1941	Statement from the Duke of Hamilton as interviewed by Stammers on 11March 1941.
19.3.1941	Stammers to Robertson, enclosing the statement with an apology that the Duke has not yet forwarded a copy of the 1939 letter from Haushofer, posted when Haushofer was cruising off the Norwegian coast.
23.3.1941	Marriott (B2a) to Major Dixon at Cambridge, chasing information on Mrs Roberts.
24.3.1941	Marriott to T.A. Robertson: 'This case seems to have been allowed to go to sleep for no particular reason…'
25.3.1941	T.A. Robertson to Stammers: 'The duke should make a trip to Lisbon…'
28.3.1941	Stammers to T.A. Robertson. Note saying that Stammers has chased the Duke for the 1939 letter.
6.4.1941	Hamilton to Stammers. Apologising for not sending the letter and asking to show it personally to him when next in London, 'within the next three weeks.'
7.4.1941	Robertson to Archie Boyle at the Air Ministry: 'Can you arrange for Hamilton to be sent on a mission to Lisbon? Suggests that an early reply was lost in transit'.
9.4.1941	Boyle to T.A. Robertson. Passes the ball back to Robertson: 'I will take no further action until you have seen the Duke…'
15.4.1941	Stammers to Robertson. Sending a copy of the Duke's letter of 6 April.
22.4.1941	File note. T.A. Robertson: 'Apparently although enquiries were made in the Prime Minister's department no information on this subject was available'. The Duke of Hamilton's brother had told Blackford at the Air Ministry that the Duke had 'been to see the Prime Minister about the affair'.

This note is particularly interesting as it begs the question as to when Hamilton met the Prime Minister 'about this affair'. The comment may have pertained to the 1939 letter, but if not, it infers that Hamilton knows about the 23 September 1940 letter and had discussed it with Churchill. This is not clear.

28.4.1941	Hamilton to Blackford. Agrees to go to Lisbon but must explain why he is answering the letter after a delay of seven months. Asks why the letter was withheld from him.
29.4.1941	T.A. Robertson – file note concerning his meeting of 25.4.1941 between himself, Blackford and the Duke of Hamilton. Hamilton agrees in principle to go to Lisbon, subject to being given time to think it through. T.A. Robertson asks when Hamilton had been to the Prime Minister's department and the answer is following the receipt of the 1939 letter.
3.5.1941	Blackford to T.A. Robertson: 'Regard the proposal as in abeyance.' This appears to come from Air Commodore Boyle.
3.5.1941	Blackford to Hamilton, explaining the postponement. Again, cites Boyle as the decision maker as 'the motive of the discussion might well be misinterpreted.' He adds, 'Incidentally, the delay was in no way due to any fault of Air Intelligence, another department having mislaid the papers… A move of this kind … could not be made without Cabinet Authority…'
13.5.1941	File note – TA Robertson. Sinclair was at Ditchley with Churchill, and they had sent for Hamilton on the Sunday morning.

The censor's report of 2 November clearly identifies the intended recipient as being the Duke of Hamilton. Mrs Roberts had been given an address by Thomas Cook, London, but was yet to be identified and the censor, not unsurprisingly, did not identify Albrecht Haushofer solely from the given initials 'AH'.

However, the fact remains that MI6 and the Foreign Office were in 'pole position' to readily identify the correspondents. Why? The Duke of Hamilton had been essentially a pre-war British intelligence agent in Germany, with frequent trips that have been well documented in our earlier work.[7] Secondly, it was the Duke of Hamilton who had attended, in the Foreign Office in

Whitehall, a pre-war meeting with highly placed Nazi's[8] and, thirdly, it was the Duke of Hamilton who had taken the trouble to show Churchill his July 1939 letter from Albrecht Haushofer (written whilst on a Norwegian cruise), predicting that war would come very soon. It was then passed on to Halifax, Butler and Chamberlain.

We contend that the Foreign Office/MI6 would have quickly realised the significance of the letter and exactly from whom it came. By his own admission,[9] Haushofer was well known in pre-war Foreign Office circles, and we very much doubt it took MI6 two months to work out what was going on. However, whilst we note that John Maude , an MI5 officer, on 11 January notes that 'the delays have been lamentable', we do wonder if this was a consequence of the files going elsewhere in the meantime? We now believe we know where the files were and precisely under whose control.

Above all, however, we know by subsequent events that MI6, or a member of MI6, had indeed reacted to the receipt of the censor's report. We also now know that Tancred Borenius had left the UK on his travels by mid-January 1941. From the files, MI5/MI6 were still apparently dithering, but we also know Dansey had already acted by this time at a higher level to that as evidenced by the working papers of KV2/1684 and 1685. Despite the apparent uncertainty and dithering, we now know from other sources that other actions had already been taken in response at a higher level, or plane, than those responsible for the above files.

SOE

As we have seen above, the third copy of the censor's report was sent to the IRB. The acronym stands for the Inter Services Research Board, which in late 1940 was a cover name for the newly formed Special Operations Executive, then led by the Labour MP Hugh Dalton.

In Hess: The British Conspiracy, John Harris had discovered that the Mrs Roberts in Chapter 6 was the aunt of Walter Stewart Roberts, a pre-war stockbroker who had joined SOE and was based at Woburn, Bedfordshire as part of its 'Black propaganda' department – SO1.

Back in 1992, Harris had (not totally recklessly) thus leapt to the conclusion that it was this department that had then masterminded a forged exchange of letters that was to eventually lead to the May 1941 flight. Indeed, there was even some supporting evidence. Edvard Beneš, the leader of the Czech government in exile, had even supposedly reported to his British liaison,

Robert Bruce Lockhart that he had seen forged MI6 letters, passing to and from Hess.

What is also significant in this story is that Bruce Lockhart was, later in the war, the head of the Political Warfare executive, whose staff came mainly from SO1. In other words, he was well placed to know what was going on himself, without the need to be told.

Fuelling Harris's increasingly suspicious mind was the fact that on 10 May 1941, the morning of the flight, Eden and Dalton were both at Woburn Abbey for a meeting of SO1. Moreover, given the unique skill sets possessed by those present at Woburn (forgery, printing, fluency in German, personal acquaintances, vivid imaginations and an intimate knowledge of the German mind), it is also very easy to imagine that the potential task in hand would have been one very easy to achieve. In particular, the journalist Denis Sefton Delmer had arrived in Woburn in the spring of 1941, having been in Lisbon in late 1940. Delmer certainly had the necessary skill set and knew Hess prior to the war when stationed in Berlin for the *Daily Express*.[10]

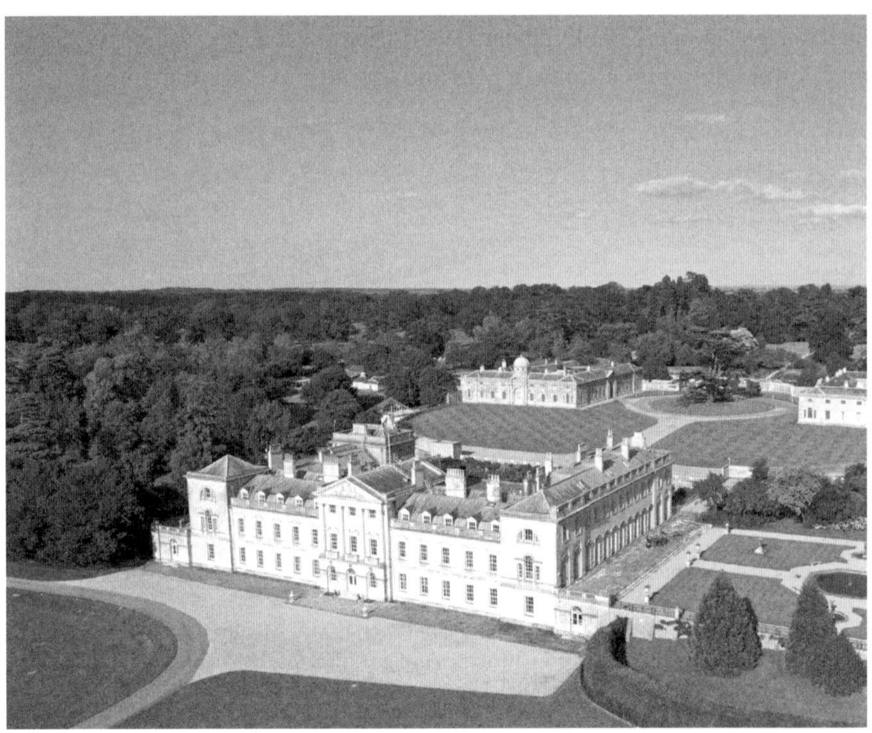

Woburn Abbey

They also potentially had the knowledge of precisely who Mrs Roberts was – because they had her nephew serving in their department as their 'finance clerk'. The Walter Stewart Roberts with whom Mrs Roberts lived on her return from Greece in the late 1930s was recruited from his stockbroking firm to become the finance officer of the newly formed SO1. That of course does not prove that the Hess affair was in anyway related to SOE /SO1. We already made that mistake, some twenty years ago.

However, in just the same manner as MI6, little relevant details have been provided by way of file release, apart from the minutes of the Saturday morning meeting of 10 May 1941.

When our second book was published in 1999, M.R.D. Foot, the eminent intelligence historian attacked the premise in the *Daily Telegraph*, saying that Harris was 'building on sand'. At the time we thought this a little presumptive, as Foot did not produce any specific evidence in support of his belief.

However, as we have learned more of the subject and in particular the role of Tancred Borenius in the affair, we also believe that whilst it is quite possible and likely that whilst SO1 played a supporting role, the major facilitator and controller was one Claude Edward Marjoribanks Dansey, the deputy head and power behind the throne in MI6 and founder 'W' Board member.

---

[1] Mrs. V. George, of Wembley Middlesex, was the name given by MI5 as being the intended recipient of the letter. This was, at the least, a clear mistake as the correct addressee had been detailed on the original letter.

[2] National Records, Kew, PF54592.

[3] KV2/1684, B10e to B6, 29.11.1940.

[4] David Stafford (ed.), *Flight from Reality*, Pimlico, London, 2002.

[5] Keith Jeffery, *MI6: The History of the Secret Intelligence Service 1909–1949*, Bloomsbury, London, 2010.

[6] Ursula Laack-Michel, Albrecht Haushofer und der National-Sozialismus, Klett, Stuttgart, 1974.

[7] John Harris, *Rudolf Hess: The British Illusion of Peace*, JEMA, Moulton, 2010.

[8] On 9 June 1939, Hamilton was present at the Foreign Office to attend a meeting with Halifax, Vansittart, Louis Greig, General von Reichenau and Prince Adolf zu Mecklenburg.

[9] 12 May 1941: Haushofer wrote his report of the Hess mission for Adolf Hitler at Berchtesgaden.

[10] The authors have a photograph of a pre-war Berlin reception featuring Hess and Delmer.

CHAPTER 8

THE STATE AND STRUCTURE OF BRITISH INTELLIGENCE – NOVEMBER 1940

What really happened to the letter?

There now appears to be a void in the timeline to our story.

The Haushofer/Roberts letter was delivered to the British Secret Services by the censor on 2 November 1940. It then apparently took MI5 until 29 November 1940 to ascertain precisely who Mrs Roberts was.

The letter had duly been intercepted and passed to MI5, MI6 and SOE. From the declassified MI5 files, it would appear that MI5 took no further action, once it had realised the parties involved. Please refer to Chapter 7.

MI5 was also a new member of the Joint Intelligence Committee, a Whitehall Committee that was originally a solely military creation, with only the various intelligence arms being recently admitted. In 1935, the then Major General John Dill wrote to the Secretary of the Committee of Imperial Defence, Sir Maurice Hankey: '… we find an increasing tendency for certain specific aspects intelligence to develop, in which two or more separate departments are equally interested, with the danger that uneconomical duplication in the collection and recording of such intelligence is tending to increase'.

Consequently, by late 1940 the Committee had been bolstered by the addition of MI5 and MI6 (though notably not SOE). Whether it is the case that the Haushofer letter was discussed in this forum is not clear, as much documentation has been destroyed. What this forum does do, however, is to potentially make the necessary interplay between intelligence and the necessary practical military capability quite possible.

MI6 and SOE have yet to fully release their files, if indeed any relevant files still exist. When Prof. Keith Jeffery published his authorised history of MI6[1] in 2010, we were absolutely staggered to discover that there was no mention of the Hess affair, as by that time information had been passed to us linking the MI6 second-in-command directly to the affair. Consequently, and suitably puzzled, we duly attended the splendid book launch held appropriately at Bletchley Park on 21 November 2010. Sir John Scarlett and Prof. Jeffery presented their work and then took questions.

Harris bravely stood up and asked if the lack of mention of the Hess affair was because it was not an MI6 operation, or was it because agents' names could still be deemed to be compromised?

Keith Jeffery fobbed off the question, though John Scarlett made the point that, 'secrets which still prejudice relations with other nations would have to remain a secret'.

A similar statement had been made in 1992, when Douglas Hurd, then Foreign Secretary, caveated some Hess papers release with the phrase, 'There are certain records which still pose a threat to national security.'

In later, more helpful, correspondence, Jeffery did admit to there being some files on Hess but repeated his view that there was no evidence that MI6 was engaged in a sting operation. We felt we had to learn more about what MI6 and MI5 were trying to achieve in late 1940/41.

In the excellent *Strategic Deception in the Second World War* by Michael Howard,[2] the point is well made that in late 1940 the major British objective of intelligence had to be defensive in nature. Britain was on its knees. Offensive intelligence and military operations were realistically years way, so the major defensive intelligence question was whether intelligence should be based on painting a picture of impregnability, or alternatively possibly alluding to weaknesses in certain areas to entice the enemy into the making of wrong moves?

A meeting of MI5 and the Director of Military Intelligence on 10 September 1940 decided on the former, a message that certainly resonated with the political messages coming from Downing Street at the time.[3] The major aim at that time had to be to prevent or deter an invasion, by any means available, and the intelligence policy had to reflect that aim. As Duško Popov, the double agent, later described: 'The technique of deception consisted of truth when it was judged it would do no harm, or when the benefits outweighed the detriments, half-truths which would be misleading, or falsehoods about conditions the Germans couldn't check.'[4]

It is interesting to note that whilst British Intelligence as a whole was in the process of necessary reform, the question of deception had been debated as early as 29 September 1939, when Admiral John Godfrey had distributed what became known as the 'Trout memo',[5] an inter- service paper giving suggestions and examples as to ideas of deceptive behaviour. The author gave fifty-six examples of such ideas and summarised by, 'The trout fisherman casts patiently all day. He frequently changes his venue and his lures. If he has frightened a fish, he may give the water a rest for half an hour, but his main endeavour, viz. to attract fish by something that he sends out from his boat, is incessant.'

Indeed, one of the rare intelligence successes in the autumn of 1940 had been the instigation, control and slow expansion of the double-cross system, to which Popov, aka. Tricycle, was a recent recruit. In truth, the British had yet to realise how successful they had become in capturing and turning German agents against their masters. The problem was fast becoming one of how to obtain enough 'traffic' from the services so as to render them relevant and so retain their relevance. These agents were a potentially very effective way of communicating with the enemy in such a way that the British could also even influence the subject of the message.

However, by its very nature, it then becomes very difficult to decide what the truth actually is and what part is fiction in connection with intelligence matters, though it is now reasonably well documented that one of the first double agents was Arthur Owens (1899–1957), code name SNOW.

SNOW had been recruited before the outbreak of war on account of his business of selling batteries for ships. As such he had contacts with both the Kriegsmarine and the Royal Navy. He was no lover of the English on account of his fervent Welsh Nationalism, something that no doubt gave him additional credibility in the eyes of the Abwehr, his German masters. Through Snow and his assistant, MI5 was able to obtain the identities of further German agents. Michael Howard estimates the number of agents being run at six in the summer of 1940. MI5 did not yet realise that this amounted to the total number of all German agents then operating in the United Kingdom.

In trying to assess whether these agents were potentially able to feedback information (real and false) to enable Hess to fly to Scotland, we need to look at the composition of the six agents at the time and to see whether it was likely that they had sufficient powers of reliable communication. At the time, most of the communication that took place was via the long winded and laborious methods of letters and secret ink. Radio sets, in general, came later in the war. It appears to us that the double agents operating in late 1940/41 were:

SNOW	based mainly in Wales
RAINBOW	provider of commercial and aviation information
SUMMER	finished as an agent in January 1941

BISCUIT	recruited by SNOW
TATE	a radio transmitter; mainly military movements
GANDER	only a transmitter, no means of receipt
GIRAFFE	petered out
SPANEHL	petered out

Probably the most famous double agent of the Second World War, GARBO had not yet started to construct his network of fictional agents, but we note for future reference that his MI6 handler was Tomás Harris, formerly a wealthy art dealer, specialising in Spanish art. He was known to Tancred Borenius, as was the other infamous MI6 art expert and Soviet spy, Anthony Blunt.

We trust the reader can see that it is unlikely that any of the above agents could or would be used in passing false information at a sufficient level of detail or speed to interest or influence Rudolf Hess in Munich and Berlin. Most were being controlled on the German side by the Abwehr in Hamburg or Berlin, usually via Lisbon, so there were at least two more hurdles in communication terms before the Deputy Führer could receive any information, even were it found to be of relevance.

However, TRICYCLE and GELATINE may be of more interest.

One of the more colourful agents of this period was Duško Popov, a wealthy Yugoslavian who was recruited as a double agent in late 1940. In his autobiography, *Spy/Counterspy*,[6] he tells of spending the period between Christmas and the New Year of 1940 with Stewart Menzies at his brother's house in Surrey. (Popov eventually became Godfather to 'C''s nephew.)[7]

Whilst earlier being recruited for the Abwehr, Popov, then in Rome, had met his German handler, who told him: 'I was told that Rudolf Hess is saying that some high personalities in the UK are seeking contact with Germany. As Deputy Führer, Hess has his own intelligence organisation, the Verbindungstab, which must have picked up that gossip. But it could come from other sources too. The Abwehr is in touch with some supposedly powerful Welsh Nationalist groups, and in those circles, there is talk of Lloyd George coming back as Prime Minister and negotiating for peace.'

This is fascinating, as it demonstrates that as early as the summer of 1940, MI5, through SNOW was already sending messages of apparent false hope to the Germans. However, the military situation did justify the sentiment. The common denominator of Welsh Nationalism is just too much of a coincidence for SNOW not to be involved.

Popov continued: 'The idea was to give Hitler what he hoped to hear, namely that certain elements in Britain were prepared to come to terms with him. The Germans believed that the Blitz was undermining English morale to the point of collapse and many politicians thought it was high time to overthrow Churchill and his 'clique' and negotiate a peace. From the way this misinformation was given to me, I have my doubts that Winston Churchill was fully informed about Intelligence's political description of England.'

Popov was at the time being cultivated as a double agent so as to be able to appear credible to his German handler, then based in Estoril, near Lisbon. On 5 June 1941 (obviously after the Hess flight), Popov met Victor Cavendish-Bentinck, the recently appointed chairman of the Joint Intelligence Committee. Cavendish-Bentinck later reported to Popov's British handler: 'I was much struck by his statement that his employers (the Germans) genuinely do believe that possibilities of Fifth Column activities exist among British subjects and that there are important elements in this country who long for the conclusion of peace and would gladly work against Churchill with this object in view… When he was recounting this I am quite certain your friend (Popov) was really telling the truth and this was the point on which his employers are most anxious to obtain information.'[8]

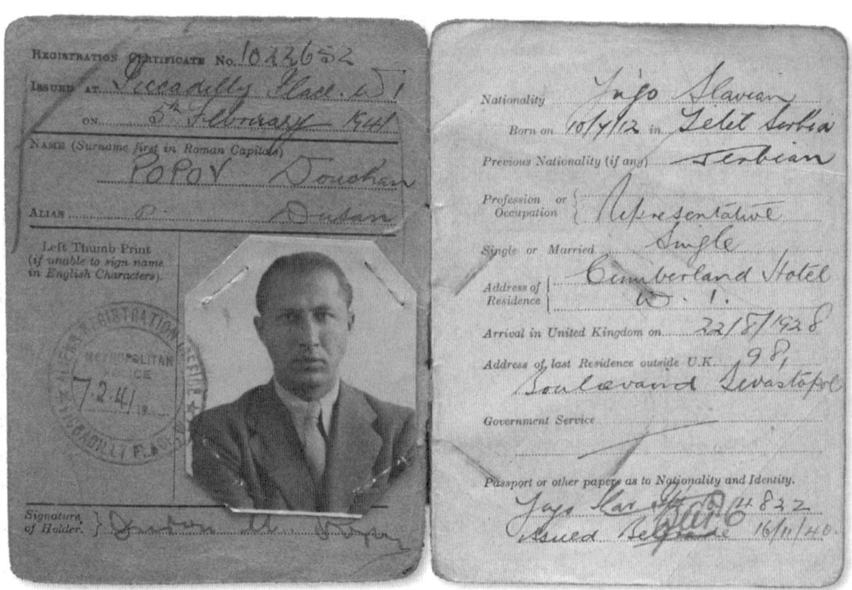

Registration Certificate No. 1023652

Issued at Piccadilly Place W1

on 5th February 1941

Name (Surname first in Roman Capitals) POPOV Douchan

Alias Dusan

Left Thumb Print (if unable to sign name in English Characters).

Signature of Holder.

Nationality Yugo Slavian

Born on 10/7/12 in Telet Serbia

Previous Nationality (if any) Serbian

Profession or Occupation Representative

Single or Married Single

Address of Residence Cumberland Hotel W. 1.

Arrival in United Kingdom on 22/8/1928

Address of last Residence outside U.K. 98, Boulevard Sevastopol

Government Service

Passport or other papers as to Nationality and Identity.

Duško Popov, aka Tricycle

So, is this conclusive proof that Hess was deliberately being fed misinformation by the MI5 double agents? No, we cannot assert that as yet, but we do believe it demonstrates that the double-cross system was certainly feeding general misinformation back through a system that reached the highest echelons of the Nazi state. Much of it was pure gossip and innuendo certainly, but nonetheless it was very much what the Germans wished to hear. It was also virtually all the British could do. As Michael Howard confirms, the adoption of a totally defensive intelligence strategy.

However, there is still a little more to learn in connection with GELATINE. Gelatine was, by all accounts an extremely attractive Austrian, real name Fredericke (Friedel) Gaertner, who had come to England in 1936 with her equally attractive sister, Alice (Liesel). Friedel had been married and divorced prior to her arrival in England.

Once again, in a bizarre Hess coincidence, the sisters were born in a small Austrian village, Roitham, about 8 miles from Gallspach, a village that will feature later in this book. The girls' maiden names were Stottinger and there are still families in the Roitham area bearing that name today.

In an additional and very bizarre coincidence, Alice had met and married Ian Graham Menzies, the brother of Stewart who was head of MI6 at the time. Consequently, the somewhat odd and unique position had arisen in that the sister-in-law of 'C', the Head of the British MI6, was in fact a German double agent.

Friedel was in turn introduced to TRICYCLE and duly, and perhaps inevitably, embarked on an affair. Her file, KV2/1276 makes it pretty clear that at the time under review, in espionage terms, she was still attempting to establish her credentials with her Portuguese-based German handler and was not in a position to pass high-grade intelligence.

By contrast, TRICYCLE's file, KV2/845 makes it clear that in the spring of 1941 he was very active (in more ways than perhaps just the obvious). Soon after the Christmas break, he was flown to Lisbon, on 2 January and his diary entries report that he travelled extensively through Britain on his return, including a week in Scotland, from 15 to 23 February. We do not doubt that he would have passed on the negative intelligence that presumably the Germans wished to hear. As has been recounted already, his German handler was based in Portugal and some of his information was passed on orally at first hand. He returned to Estoril on 15 March 1941. On 30 April, Popov flew back to Whitchurch, England. However, and yet again, we must conclude that despite the fact that TRICYCLE and GELATINE were operating at a much more enhanced social level than the majority (if not all) of the other agents, we do not believe that either would have been able to even give the impression of having the ability to pass detailed information quickly enough to enable persons in Germany to act in a way that Hess did on 10 May. It is a superficially attractive notion, but the reality of the agents' positions in Britain would simply not allow it to succeed or succeed quickly enough. Above all else, it should be remembered that Popov was an Abwehr agent, with no direct reporting responsibility back to Hess. His line of communication was ultimately to Canaris. So, to conclude this chapter we should state that in late 1940 the double-cross organisation was in the early development stage. SNOW had shown the potential of the system, but he was initially under the auspices and control of MI5. The growing constraint was obtaining the source evidence, the permittable facts and the credible lies, and so in January 1941 the Twenty Committee (XX) was formed to provide a more comprehensive and dedicated service and to cope with the growing number of agents. However, apart from general misinformation we do not believe the committee was further involved in the Hess affair. It is interesting to note that the Duke of Hamilton's proposed involvement in the suggested trip to Lisbon was being managed by the Twenty Committee, so it was obviously aware of the Haushofer/Roberts communication, presumably through MI5 when it finally realised who it was dealing with.

The much more likely explanation as to who was driving the response to the letter was that Stewart Menzies and Claude Dansey were doing it themselves, possibly as part of their involvement with the 'W' Board, but equally it is quite possible that it was a solo affair, just the two of them, with help when required.

Interestingly, Stewart Menzies is quoted as telling Popov/TRICYCLE at Christmas 1940 that, 'I am handling this matter myself ... all information that you pick up is to come to me directly with no intermediary.'[9]

Therefore, if Menzies was handling Popov directly (in this case in connection with Canaris) we see no reason why his

Archie Boyle

deputy, Dansey, would not be handling Borenius and even Albrecht Haushofer (see Chapter 27) in just the same way. We certainly know that Dansey was briefing Borenius before his mission to Geneva in late January 1941.

The 'W' Board had been constituted in Whitehall in September 1940 and the first minutes apparently record that it was formed to 'co-ordinate the dissemination of false information'.

This is precisely what Menzies, Dansey and Borenius (once recruited), were doing in January 1941, whether under the auspices of the board or not. The XX was also formed in January 1941 as a subsidiary of the 'W' Board, largely to cope with the growing number of turned agents and to take responsibility for the day-to-day management of the agents. The 'W' Board still dealt with overall approach.

What is quite clear from the agents' files is the detailed analysis by the British handlers of every nuance, move and implication of the agents' every position. At the very least this was a very costly exercise in terms of time and in some cases even had to be intricately co-ordinated within groups of agents, such as existed between TRICYCLE and GELATINE.

The 'W' Board comprised of:

Admiral Godfrey – Naval Intelligence
Major General F.H.N. Davidson – Army Intelligence
Air Commodore A.R. Boyle – Air Intelligence
Guy Liddell – MI5
Stewart Menzies – MI6
Ewen Montagu – Secretary, RNVR (later of The Man that Never Was fame)
Sir Findlater Stewart (born in Largs, on the Ayrshire coast, virtually on the later Hess flighpath.) – Chairman

Note that there was no representative from the recently formed SOE, which well illustrates their place in the intelligence 'pecking order' at that time.

Somewhat mysteriously, perhaps, Sir Michael Howard stated: 'It reported to no one and was responsible to no one. The 'W' Board would have to do some "odd things" of the kind that it was the job of the Directors of Intelligence to authorise on their own responsibility.' It was essentially a creation of the intelligence community by the intelligence community and was therefore beyond political influence or control.

It would appear to us that the 'W' Board was certainly in a position to operate and carry out the Hess deception. This is because:

- We know for sure that Dansey was involved through his briefing Borenius.
- We know that Boyle was involved (and being referred to) throughout his spring dealings with Hamilton and Blackford.
- There is the necessary access across the three services. Thus, the later necessary aeronautical knowledge could be facilitated, in particular, through Boyle. Why for instance did Hess precisely target the west coast of Scotland?
- At the very latest MI5/MI6 were aware of the Haushofer letter and the players by mid-November 1940. The timings appear to fit.
- It may explain the MI6/Keith Jeffery statement regarding their Hess involvement. Technically they were not involved – if necessary, it could be fobbed off as either a 'W' Board or even a 'Finnish initiative', by reason of Borenius' previous diplomatic forays. Is this perhaps where the files went? To the 'W' Board?
- Montagu and his assistant Charles Cholmondeley certainly had the fertile minds sufficient to manage and run such a ruse.
- The Trout Memorandum had already set the tone for British deception and Godfrey, its nominal author, was a member of the 'W' Board.
- The principle of the 'W' Board, to disseminate false information (and thus buy time), is exactly what the Hess mission was all about.
- There is currently a distinct lack of information and files pertaining to the 'W' Board. J.C. Masterman in *The Double Cross System: The Classic Account of World War Two Spy-Masters*, cannot even bring himself to name the initial attendees. At the National Archives, Kew there appears to be only one late file released, in 1945 (KV 4/70).

We are now satisfied that the Borenius mission may well have been a 'W' Board reaction to the Haushofer letter, but the Guy Liddell (of MI5) diaries do appear to demonstrate that whilst he was not personally involved, he did know of the receipt of the Haushofer letter. This too may have been by reason of his membership of the 'W' Board. He also became involved later with the management of the German internees, Maas and Semmelbauer, who were to act as German witnesses to later Hess meetings with British officials.

It was possibly at this time that a reply to the Haushofer letter was not a plausible response and so the Borenius/Burckhardt/von Hassell/Haushofer/Hess channel was considered, instigated, opened and developed. It would appear that Liddell was not involved in this initiative.

On an operational level, MI6, and its leaders in particular, had been heavily criticised in the early stages of the war. They had completely lost their 'passport control' system with the May 1940 invasions, they had been criticised for not forewarning of the Norwegian invasion, the earlier Venlo incident in late 1939 had become a costly fiasco and so they were now perhaps looking for an opportunity for redemption. The receipt of the Haushofer letter gave them just that opportunity, but exactly how were they to best 'play' the opportunity?

Furthermore, this was surely a far more subtle response to the Haushofer letter than any forged reply? For the time being, we will give the last word on this topic to Duško Popov, the playboy double agent referred to above as TRICYCLE. Famous for his languid irony, he commented in his 1974 autobiography: 'I couldn't help wondering how much our planted reports of low morale might have influenced Hess – and even Hitler. It would be interesting, I speculated, if British Intelligence had unwittingly inspired the Hess incident.'[10]

AIR INTELLIGENCE

Throughout the eighty years following the Hess flight of 10 May 1941, the role of British Air Intelligence in the affair has been studiously concealed and remains firmly concealed. A very firmly closed box. We have seen no released files in relation to their activities and whilst the authorised MI6 historian was open enough to state that there were no MI6 Hess files, RAF Intelligence, by contrast, has released nothing, which is of course its prerogative, given the rules currently extant in Britain concerning the release of intelligence papers. Of course, it might be the case that there are no RAF Intelligence files, but given that the Deputy Führer of Germany had just flown through British airspace, would it not be extraordinary if no files were opened, made or retained? It is also extraordinary that despite the 'no parley' instructions from Churchill, Archie Boyle was quite prepared to send the Duke of Hamilton to 'somewhere' in the late spring of 1941 (and the Duke had agreed to go).

We know the key players; we have already seen in this chapter that Archie Boyle sat on the 'W' Board. We know that Air Intelligence's Fred Winterbotham played a senior role within the Ultra Intelligence system, so clearly Air

Intelligence was represented at the highest levels of the Secret Services. We also know that one of the four Hamilton brothers, George, was the Fighter Command's Chief Intelligence Officer, reporting to Air Chief Marshal Dowding.

Fred Winterbotham

And yet nothing. Surely it would be reasonable to expect a report on the Hess flight? A report on how Hess managed to get to where he did perhaps? What equipment did he use? Why did he fly at all? Where was he heading? Why Scotland? If Fred Winterbotham felt confident enough in 1974 to tell the Ultra secret, surely, they must be able to tell of their involvement in the Hess affair; particularly if it were truly the solo act of a madman.

Frustratingly, and via a bit of digging, we know that of course these issues were addressed. Andrew Rosthorn's excellent article in the July 2014 *Tribune* makes it clear that the RAF ordered its instrument maker, David Mitchell, to the railway sidings at Carluke to examine the crashed plane. 'Mitch' removed the 'blind flying panel', made a wooden box for it and despatched it to RAE Farnborough.[11]

There is more evidence of involvement. Peter Padfield also states that he had received letters from Squadron Leader 'Tim' Woodman (though probably not on 24 June 1941 as stated) inferring an internal review had been carried out. Ironically, the Royal Observer Corps who tracked Hess diligently across lowland Scotland did produce a detailed report into the affair and has released it into the public arena (AIR 16/1266). This presumably proves that the ROC was *not* involved in the Hess affair, save of course for its excellent reporting of the flight itself.

The continued silence just seems odd.

It seems even odder when one considers the pre-war history of Air Intelligence. We can draw on at least two sources toexplain our scepticism. The first is the book, *The Game of the Foxes* by Ladislas Farago[12] and the second the recently digitised Rosenberg diaries now held by the United States Holocaust Memorial Museum in Washington. The diaries have only recently 'surfaced' after being stolen at the time of the Nuremberg Trials in 1945/6. Both sources, however, paint exactly the same picture.

Alfred Rosenberg (1893–1946) was an early member of the Nazi Party and initially the editor of the *Volkischer Beobachter*, the flagship Nazi Party newspaper. After 1933 Rosenberg, who was seen as influential within the party (and close to Hess), became influential in foreign policy matters and naturally the relationship with Britain soon came to dominate his thinking. His diary entry for 14 May 1934 is interesting, as he records the fact that 'Captain Bartlett' of the Bristol Aircraft Company was in Berlin trying to sell 'the new, still secret engine'. This we take to be the new supercharged 1,000 horsepower 'Pegasus' engine which had then only just come on to the market.

According to Farago, Bartlett had been introduced to Rosenberg by Fred Winterbotham of British Air Intelligence. In turn, Rosenberg used a fellow Balt, Bill de Ropp (1886–1973) as his liaison man(Rosenberg was born in Estonia, de Ropp, Lithuania) and so the Winterbotham–de Ropp–Rosenberg channel had begun.

The fact of the matter is that the British Aeronautical Industry was playing its part in the creation of the Luftwaffe, despite the Versailles Treaty and despite the fact that less than ten years later the technology was to be turned against its supplier, in just the same way as the Argentinians and Iraqis were to do forty to fifty years later. It would appear that times and ethics do not much change when money is involved.

However, the supply of war materiel and technology was only part of the task that Rosenberg had in mind. Winterbotham and de Ropp were both feted in Germany. Consequently, Winterbotham met both Hess and Hitler at this time, and de Ropp, in particular, came to be a trusted adviser to Hitler, even though he had fought with the British Wiltshire Regiment and the Royal Flying Corps in the First World War. De Ropp subsequently moved into Berlin, living on the Kurfürstendamm and entertaining in grand style.

Clearly, Winterbotham and de Ropp were playing a dangerous game. Whilst facilitating trade they were also obtaining intelligence, but their methodology of alluding to British cooperation could easily be misconstrued.

It was.

Rosenberg's diary entry for 11 July 1934 comments: 'The young generation of the British Air Force is working against this old pre-war psychosis and requests us to deal only directly with its General Staff, without the British Foreign Office, without the German Embassy in London.'

Again, in September of the same year: 'Bartlett from the Bristol plants has been here in recent days. The Air Force want to support our aviation without the Foreign Office being told about it…'

How much of these British sentiments were real and how much simply 'good for business' is difficult to precisely ascertain, but the Rosenberg–de Ropp–Rosenberg channel was not yet finished.

In January 1935, de Ropp was summoned to London to meet an 'adviser to the King'. Rosenberg reported that the two men were to meet in a club. The meeting duly took place, on 20 January and the 'adviser' who turned up was Prince George, the Duke of Kent.

The duke apparently reported that, 'they have resigned themselves about German rearmament, but it is important to have precise knowledge of the mentality of the leading figures'.

Interestingly, Farago does not go into any particular level of detail about the meeting, just reporting that Rosenberg was so elated upon hearing the identity of the 'adviser' that he rushed to the Chancellery to tell Hitler. The meeting apparently carried on through the night and ended at dawn.

This meeting, which places the Duke of Kent firmly in the 'young generation of the British Air Force' is further corroborated by Winterbotham himself in the first edition of Secret and Personal, his 1969 autobiography. However, we understand that the mention of the meeting was deleted from the subsequent editions, for whatever reason.

What is also pertinent is that Winterbotham records that King George V had expressed concern about the poor intelligence on Germany from the established sources. Hence, he had asked his son, George, to apply to the Air Ministry, which was clearly seen as having at least better information and intelligence to hand. That seems to be the major driver behind the meeting.

Thereafter, there appears to be the illusion given to Rosenberg that the British Foreign Office and 'a small clique in the War Office repeatedly spoiled all reasonable attempts at a German – English rapprochement'.[13] Somewhat mysteriously, Rosenberg records on 15 March 1935 that, 'everything turns on Phillip Sassoon'.[14]

Philip Sassoon was a brilliantly connected, immensely wealthy member of the Rothschild family, described as 'the outrageously camp millionaire aesthete'.[15] He was also the Under-Secretary of State for Air, from 1924–9 and 1931–7. In 1937 he was appointed the First Commissioner of Works and Public Buildings, which perhaps does not seem quite so exciting? Was this as a result of whatever was happening in the Air Ministry during the period? Sassoon died from complications following influenza in June 1939.

The rest of the decade is described by Winterbotham in his book as a series of interesting visits to Germany but also of an increasing sense of German frustration. Despite their best endeavours with Winterbotham and de Ropp (who by this time had met virtually all the leading German hierarchy) and despite sharing many German secrets and information, the rapprochement had not happened. The two men had not given too much away, but in turn had become a trusted source of intelligence to the British authorities and, it would appear, the royal family. Winterbotham summed up his pre-war work thus: 'Mainly I felt I had been able, through close contact with the top boys and with the great help of Bill de Ropp, to obtain a fairly accurate impression of what was shortly going to hit us, and how.'[16]

Therefore, it appears to us to be reasonable to conclude that pre-war Air Intelligence had indeed done its job and in so doing had perhaps planted some false seeds of hope for the Germans that were perhaps not wholly without foundation in the mid 1930s. It is also noteworthy to conclude that both Winterbotham and de Ropp appear to have been genuinely liked at the highest levels of Nazi society. At the same time, it would appear that the British royal family had also established links with Air Intelligence, appearing to trust their information above some other sources.

At the onset of war, de Ropp moved to Switzerland, we think to Montreux. This is not necessarily the end of his participation in the affair.[17]

Fred Winterbotham (left) and Bill de Ropp on the Baltic coast

It is also interesting to note that whilst Keith Jeffery discounted MI6 as playing a part in the Hess affair,[18] he devoted considerable space to Bill de Ropp and details his pre-war contacts within Germany. In 1938, Woolacombe, his handler estimated that '70% of SIS's German political intelligence came from one very good source, de Ropp.'

However, apart from the mention that de Ropp had moved to Switzerland (per Farago) and Claude Dansey in 1944 noting that 'all de Ropp represented now was a vehicle for Nazi propaganda', we currently have not the slightest idea what de Ropp was doing, particularly in the period under review 1940–41.

Conclusions to date

- We know for sure that Claude Dansey was involved in sending Borenius to Geneva in January 1941.
- We believe this was a direct response to the Haushofer letter of 23 September 1940.
- We do not believe the fledgling intelligence and counterintelligence systems (the XX committee, in particular) were yet developed enough to provide a plausible and alternative channel of communication.
- However, the Hess affair now is beginning to appear to use a separate and unique channel, very much under the control (at least, even if not in their name) of the 'W' Board members, or their operatives. The initial response to the Haushofer letter was certainly a Dansey response.
- Eventually, Air Intelligence would have to become involved, so as to facilitate the aeronautical aspects, but at present this involvement is not yet understood, or proven, and has certainly not been disclosed by any official release.
- The Winterbotham–de Ropp–Rosenberg communication channel certainly needs further work. It appears that de Ropp spent the war in Switzerland, though Farago notes that 'several times during the war he was summoned to Berlin by Hitler for consultations'. Rosenberg was the last Nazi leader to meet Hess prior to his flight on 10 May 1941. The two men had met for lunch.
- No Air Intelligence files have yet been released, despite us knowing that Air Intelligence had been involved in at least the post-crash analysis.
- Archie Boyle, Head of Air Intelligence, was a member of the 'W' Board.

- Boyle was certainly being referred to for guidance regarding the response to the Haushofer 23 September 1940 letter, and he was active in managing a response in the spring of 1941. We know this from the MI5 files.
- By contrast to the other, more laboured, means of communication, Air Intelligence appears to have developed a streamlined and effective channel direct to the highest strata of the Nazi government.

---

[1] Keith Jeffery, *MI6: The History of the Secret Intelligence Service 1909–1949*, Bloomsbury, London 2010.

[2] Michael Howard, *Strategic Deception in the Second World War*, Norton, London 1990.

[3] Churchill's broadcast to France on 21 October 1940: 'We are waiting for the invasion. So are the fishes…'

[4] Duško Popov, *Spy/Counterspy*, Grosset and Dunlap, New York, 1974.

[5] ADM 478/233.

[6] Duško Popov, *Spy/Counterspy*, Grosset and Dunlap, New York, 1974.

[7] The house was called Dassett, and is just outside Woking.

[8] Russell Miller, *Codename Tricycle: The True Story of the Second World War's Most Extraordinary Double Agent*, Pimlico, London, 2005.

[9] Anthony Cave Brown, C: *The Secret Life of Sir Stewart Graham Menzies, Spymaster to Winston Churchill*, Macmillan, New York, 1987.

[10] Duško Popov, *Spy/Counterspy*, Grosset and Dunlap, New York, 1974.

[11] Andrew Rosthorn, Tribune, July 2014.

[12] Ladislas Farago, *The Game of the Foxes*, Hodder & Stoughton, London, 1971.

[13] Rosenberg diary, 14 March 1935.

[14] Rosenberg diary, United States Holocaust Memorial Museum.

[15] Micheal Bloch, *The Guardian*, 16 May 2015.

[16] Fred Winterbotham, *Secret and Personal*, William Kimber, London, 1969.

[17] Bill de Ropp died in Peterchurch, Herefordshire in 1973, after moving to his daughter's house. His daughter was the local midwife, dying in 1988.

[18] See pages 79 and 80.

CHAPTER 9

CHANNELS OF INTELLIGENCE AVAILABLE TO RUDOLF HESS – NOVEMBER 1940

Clearly, men in positions such as Rudolf Hess were adept at reacting to intelligence they regularly received as part of their role. However, with the more exalted their position came perhaps the greater the sense of isolation and mistrust, particularly in a dictatorship. It now appears to us that in the autumn of 1940 Hess was quite ignorant in terms of reliable and verified intelligence, particularly that emanating from foreign countries not already under German control – partly through history, partly because of the way the hierarchy of the NSDAP was arranged and partly through internal rows and jealousies within that hierarchy. Perhaps that is why in late August 1940 he had felt the need to revert to his former tutor (and his son) from his Munich University days. For Hess, there was little viable alternative when trying to assess the possibility of such a mission.

By reason of his position as the Deputy Führer of the NSDAP, Hess still had access to other sources of intelligence from outside Germany, simply because they reported directly to him and had done so for some time. We will analyse the effectiveness of these organisations in this chapter (and debate the relevance of a two new communication channels that we have recently discovered), but whether these sources in isolation were sufficiently reliable as a basis to mount a single-handed peace mission must be highly doubtful. Hess flew for a variety of reasons and most likely he, too, was being targeted via a few channels as part of the British 'defensive intelligence strategy'.

Consequently, in addition to the September 1940 Hess/Haushofer initiative, which was very much based on an informal arrangement founded on his longstanding friendship with Karl Haushofer (and which has been known about for a long time), we now list the other influences and sources of information that were potentially available to Hess in late 1940 to 1941.

We should also say that in general terms, the Nazi intelligence machinery was certainly not as developed, sophisticated or unified as the British, which had of course existed for centuries across the empire, albeit within in some different manifestations and structures. The Nazi Party had always been quite rightly suspicious of the reputation of the British Secret Services and after the First World War had in part developed the 'stab in the back' explanatory theory, whereby it was believed that the British intelligence agencies had exerted a disproportionate influence over the eventual outcome of that war.

However, in 1940 Rudolf Hess's access to intelligence came through five channels:

a) The Auslands Organisation/Ernst Bohle

At the cessation of hostilities in May 1945, Ernst Bohle, the former leader of the Auslands Organisation, gave himself up to the 3rd Battalion of the 16th US Infantry at Falkenau, Saxony on 23 May 1945. Since November 1943 he had been living at nearby Bad Schandau, making the commute into Berlin each week for three or four days. Upon his personal surrender he was eventually taken to the Central Continental Prisoner of War Camp Number 32, more commonly known as 'Ashcan', where the US Army held some eighty prominent Nazi's prior to interrogation and, if applicable, their later trial.

Ernst Bohle (1903–60)

Bohle was kept at the camp which had previously been the Palace Hotel at Mondorf-les-Bains, Luxembourg. From there, he was taken to the Military Intelligence Service Center at Oberursel for detailed interrogation, first on 26 July 1945 and then from 5–9 September 1945.

Bohle was deemed important enough for this treatment and interrogation on account of his being the former leader of the Auslands Organisation, which had been based in the Wilmersdorf sector of Berlin. At its peak he had been in charge of some 600 persons, although towards the end of the war part of the offices and records had been relocated to Bad Schandau and Schloss Ortenhaus, near Komtau in Czechoslovakia. On 14 April 1945, orders had been received to destroy the archives.

Until his flight in May 1941, Rudolf Hess was the Head of the Auslands Organisation and his younger brother Alfred had in turn been Bohle's deputy. Bohle had been appointed as Secretary of State and Chief of the Foreign Organisation in the German Foreign Office on 31 January 1937 and had been seen in some quarters as Hess's protégé. Consequently, each American interrogation team was naturally interested in what Bohle might say about his former chief's flight.

The interrogation leaders were:

26 July: Captain Harry K. Lennon

5–9 September: Bruce Lannes Smith, Harold Deutsch and W. Wendell Blancke, with Harry N. Howard attending.

All of the above were eminently well qualified to conduct such an interview and post-war all became distinguished diplomats and academics. It is perhaps appropriate to add that none were British with perhaps vested interests to protect.

What is perhaps not surprising is that Bohle appeared to consistently give the same version of events when questioned over the Hess affair. The interviews were conveniently conducted and recorded in English (Bohle was born in Bradford, England in 1903 and brought up in England and Cape Town). The Hess affair was described as follows:

> In October 1940 Hess asked him to come to his office at 21.30 for a special purpose. There Hess pledged him to strictest secrecy. He wanted Bohle to translate a letter into English which he was preparing for the

> Duke of Hamilton. Source (Bohle) got the impression that Hess was preparing to meet the Duke in Switzerland and did not reveal to him his intention to fly to England. Over a period of 3 months, he was called several times to Hess's office where he translated and typed the documents page by page…

In January 1941, about the time the letter was completed, there was talk of war with Russia...

This version of events was repeated twice to the interrogation team. We would emphasise:

1. Bohle was being asked to prepare a letter for the Duke, *not* translate a response from the Duke, viz. a reply to the Haushofer letter of 23 September 1940. It was precisely this document that was discovered at the Eaglesham crash site in 'the wee burn' on Sunday 11 May 1941. It has, of course, subsequently disappeared.
2. The process appears to have taken three months, ending in January 1941. Presumably the duration of the task reflects the quantity of translation required. Consider also that in January 1941 Hess had only very recently acquired his Bf110, VJ+OQ.
3. The work was clearly conducted in Berlin. Hess maintained an office on the Wilhelmstrasse.
4. As we shall see, the duration taken was quite possibly a reflection of the fact that Hess kept his time in the capital to a minimum.
5. We would also pose the question as to why Bohle was used for this task and not Albrecht Haushofer, who had already participated in the initial postal approach. Was it that Bohle would simply translate what he was being given, whereas Haushofer was more likely to try and influence the author? Indeed, did Rudolf Hess wholly trust Albrecht Haushofer? Or was it perhaps that Bohle was providing the script whilst Haushofer was arranging its delivery? Was Hess keeping the two men apart deliberately, even though both were based in Berlin at the time?
6. The 'letter' was commenced in October, very much a continuation of the train of thought evidenced by the Haushofer/Hess letter of 23 September. When the letter was starting to be drafted in October 1940, the original letter had not yet reached London and the censor.

64 Wilhelmstrasse, Berlin

Again, there is no evidence whatsoever from this interrogation of any forged British reply to the Haushofer letter. Instead, as to be expected, we are yet again seeing evidence of the meticulous nature of Hess in action. He chose Bohle, a close colleague, to perform the task and as has been already noted, Bohle was fluent in both oral and written English. Hess seems to be dividing the duties between Haushofer and Bohle.

Bohle was interrogated further. Prior to the Nuremberg Trials he was again questioned on 25 October 1945 in Nuremberg by Lieutenant J.B. Martin, in order to 'fill in' any holes in the earlier work. No further mention of the Hess affair was made.

We shall return to the Nuremberg Trials in Chapter 24, but it seems to us that the they provided an ideal and obvious opportunity for Hess to explain the finer details of the flight, ably supported by Bohle and perhaps Leitgen, his Berlin-based adjutant, as witnesses.

So, despite concentrated interrogation Ernst Bohle was consistent in his assertion that he translated documents for *transmission* by Rudolf Hess, rather than any received by Rudolf Hess.

What is also significant to us is Bohle's description of the relationship between the Auslands Organisation and the German Foreign Office. Von Ribbentrop eventually came to despise Bohle and was clear in his view that it was he who should control the AO, not Hess, or later, after May 1941, Bormann.

In Britain, further to Section 18b of Defence Regulations Act 1939, much of the German community had been rounded up and sent to internment camps up and down the country. Indeed, Messrs Semmelbauer and Maass, who Hess called upon to witness his interview with Sir John Simon in June 1941, had been arrested by this time and placed in Huyton camp, in Liverpool. The point being that in Britain, the Auslands Organisation had been effectively neutered as an active intelligence gathering medium. Many of its potential participants were already under British government control.

b) The Verbindungstab

'Verbindungstab' literally means 'connecting rod', but in the context of our story, we will translate it as 'liaison offices'. Based primarily in Munich, it was the link, or 'rod', between the party (Hess as designated leader since 1933) and the State.

By 1938 it employed over 460 employees in Munich and a further five in Berlin. Primarily it was the means by which Hess was able to keep in touch with and influence virtually all walks of Nazi life. It was divided into ten departments.

1. Administration of the Office
2. Party affairs
3. State affairs
4. Economics
5. Pfeffer (Secret Service)
6. Agriculture
7. Foreign Press
8. Führer
9. Foreign Political
10. Dienstelle Ribbentrop[1]

It was through this organisation that Hess was able to theoretically keep in touch with events that affected all aspects of State government, but again there was no liaison with any military organisations. Adolf Hitler was of course, by 1940, both Reichsführer and head of all German armed forces.

The important point here is that these were liaison roles. Again, whilst there were persons reporting to the Deputy Führer on a regular basis (when they were not at loggerheads), there was no obvious means of communicating with parties in Britain, in a timely manner, except possibly for Hess's private secret service, the 'Pfeffer Buro' (department 5 above).

c) The remnants of the Pfeffer Buro/Jahnke organisations

A Major Forrest, writing to a Captain Walmsley on 22 May 1945, summarised the Jahnke Buro as follows: 'Jahnke as you will see, ran a separate intelligence service to the Abwehr and SD for some time before and immediately after the outbreak of war and we are therefore very interested in his little organisation.'

It has to be said that the 'interest' is perhaps at first glance a little difficult to fathom. The National Archives released Jahnke's file under KV2/755. This appears to be an MI5 file and incorporates the former personnel file PF 37755.

The file was first opened in August 1912 and remarkably there are papers dated 1968,[2] some fifty-six years later. Clearly, British Intelligence had been interested in Herr Jahnke for a considerable period of time. Most of the interest is quite easy to fathom; Jahnke was an effective saboteur in the First World War. At the time he was based in the US, having emigrated from Germany at the age of seventeen. Having been approached by the German naval attaché in San Francisco, he then conducted various acts of sabotage against British interests in the United States. When the US entered the war, he then focused his attention against US interests and moved on to Mexico. In the mid- to late 1930s, Jahnke appears to have established his own intelligence agency, based at 26 Sedanstrasse, Steglitz, where he kept his own 'registry' in the basement. This house was apparently bombed and destroyed in 1943. A reading of Walter Schellenberg's memoirs makes plain that Jahnke was very much involved with some of the more important intelligence operations, and he seemed to go in and out of favour with Heydrich in particular. Even in the late 1930s there appeared to be doubts as to his true allegiance and Schellenberg relates how Heydrich had placed Jahnke under house arrest for three months on account of doubtful behaviour when the Tukhachevsky incident was being played out in 1937.[3]

We suspect that the truth of the matter is that Jahnke's main motivation was money, and he would report and work for whoever had the largest chequebook. Most of the reports on Jahnke state that 'he had become a rich man etc etc'. However, the main reason for British interest in 1945 was the suspicion that he was also working for the Russians and had been for some while.

Nominally, at least, at the time under review, Jahnke was attached to the Pfeffer Buro, part of the Verbindungstab. This organisation was based at 64 Wilhelmstrasse, Berlin. Hess's official office.

The MI5 file, KV2/755 is useful in that MI5 prepared a report in the early summer of 1941, detailing the organisation of the Jahnke intelligence agency as known at that time in connection with British affairs. The superficial impression is that it really could not have been a major intelligence threat at all, because:

- MI5 knew all its operatives and had dealt with them accordingly
- of the scale of the organisation – the report only lists four to five agents
- the 'agents' were not operating at a particularly high level.

However, we have recently discovered further evidence that would certainly justify the additional attention given to the Pfeffer/Jahnke channel. This involves one 'Harold' Fletcher.

We had previously learned that one of the agents, a 'Harold' Fletcher, had worked in the Foreign Office in the late 1930s and had passed information and documents back to Berlin. Fletcher had apparently travelled to Berlin in 1935 with his wife and had been introduced to Rudolf Hess.[4]

This information came from Peter Padfield, who we assume had read the diaries of Guy Liddell (which had been published in 2005 and edited by Nigel West).[5] Peter had also called Fletcher 'Harold', as described by Nigel West on page 74, 1 April 1940.

We too have read the diaries and just to be absolutely clear, Guy Liddell, the MI5 Director of Counter Espionage does not refer to Fletcher as 'Harold'. That is down to Nigel West, who calls him 'Harold Fletcher a Cambridge mathematician' in an editor's note to the diary. We now firmly believe that Nigel (and hence Peter, too) have the wrong man completely, though perhaps quite understandably as there are some common links.

We have now researched Mr Harold Fletcher, as follows:

- Harold Malcolm Dudley Fletcher was born in North Sunderland, Northumberland in 1907. His father, Mark, was a member of the clergy, having originated from Manchester. Fletcher junior duly attended Marlborough College (who gave scholarships to the sons of the clergy) and read mathematics at Cambridge alongside Gordon Welchman, the mathematician and subsequently one of the leading codebreakers at Bletchley Park.
- Indeed, it was Gordon Welchman, one of the leading members of the 'outstanding team'[6] of codebreakers at Bletchley Park that had recruited Harold and tells us that 'he was the top mathematician in the college entrance exams in 1925'.[7]
- In 1936, Harold is recorded as living at 12, Tithe Walk, Mill Hill, London.
- Harold then reports for duty in August 1941. Apparently, according to Welchman, 'I asked him to join me at Bletchley in early 1940, but at that time his occupation was reserved.'
- Harold reported for duty because 'his occupation had become unreserved' on 1 August 1941. It appears that he was assigned a military role as a cover for his previous activities, whatever they were?

This is really quite extraordinary, if true. In the late 1930s, according to Nigel West and Peter Padfield, Harold Fletcher was in all sorts of trouble. Espionage, blackmail and, we suspect, consequently most likely marital too.

In 1941, he was transferred to the most guarded, most secret operation in Britain, if not the world at the time! Moreover, from reading Welchman's book it is certainly not clear that he knew of Harold's recent past.

This raises all sorts of questions. Harold, we know, went on to have a successful time at Bletchley and was responsible for the management of the Bombe production. ('Fletcher was the man primarily responsible for establishing standard procedures for using the bombes.')[8] After the war he stayed in what has become GCHQ and worked in the Far East, most likely, we believe, Singapore. In 1957 he was awarded the OBE for (perhaps somewhat ironically, if he is a spy?) communications. He died in 1985 in Charlton Close, Cheltenham.

We trust the reader can now understand the interest in Harold Malcolm Dudley Fletcher.

His MI5 file has yet to surface, and we doubt his name would have become known (albeit by mistake) were it not for the Liddell diaries release in 2005.

However. We now firmly believe that Harold is not our man at all and instead we should all be looking at one Francis Richard Christian Cecil Fletcher (1903–51) whose biography is much more difficult to ascertain, though more exciting too. He was helpfully described by one of our correspondents as being 'more Johnny English than James Bond'.

In this connection we really must thank Peter Lowe and Martin Comer for their assistance in this matter. Both men are currently trying to understand the motives of Gulla Pfeffer, the apparent temptress and central character in this part of the mystery and in doing so have both come across 'Fletcher'.

- Francis Richard Christian Cecil Fletcher worked at the Foreign Office as a translator. He appears as a late addition to the 1938 German section,[9] although he had been there since the mid 1920s. Adding to the confusion is the fact that he was also variously known as 'Frank' and 'Jim'.
- His troubles started in the mid 1930s. He met a rather exotic German lady named Gulla Pfeffer (1897–1967) who was at the time residing in London after travelling through Africa, following her apparent calling as an anthropologist. In 1929 she had published *Die weisse Mah: Allein bei Urvolkern und Menschenfressern* and at the time was working on a dissertation based on the Nigerian Djafun tribe.
- Born the illegitimate daughter of an actress, she had been adopted at the age of eight by an Emil Passburg. She had already married once, on 5 July 1919 in Berlin, to a forester called Emil Ludwig Pfeffer. In 1922 she gave birth to a son. The name given on her marriage certificate was Melida Auguste Johanna Passburg.
- She was also a close friend of John Leslie Carlin (1897–1976), a well-known English journalist who had travelled with Pfeffer whilst in Africa. He recounted the adventure in his book *Gulla: The Tramp*.[10] Carlin travelled widely, but when in London lived at 1 Park Walk, Chelsea with his wife and mother.[11]
- We can only presume that Fletcher and Pfeffer then embarked on an affair, because when subsequently interrogated in 1939, Pfeffer admitted to blackmailing Fletcher.
- However, as previously related, the couple (Fletcher and Pfeffer) travelled to Germany and meet Pfeffer's relations, including 'the notorious Captain Pfeffer of the German Secret Service'.[12]

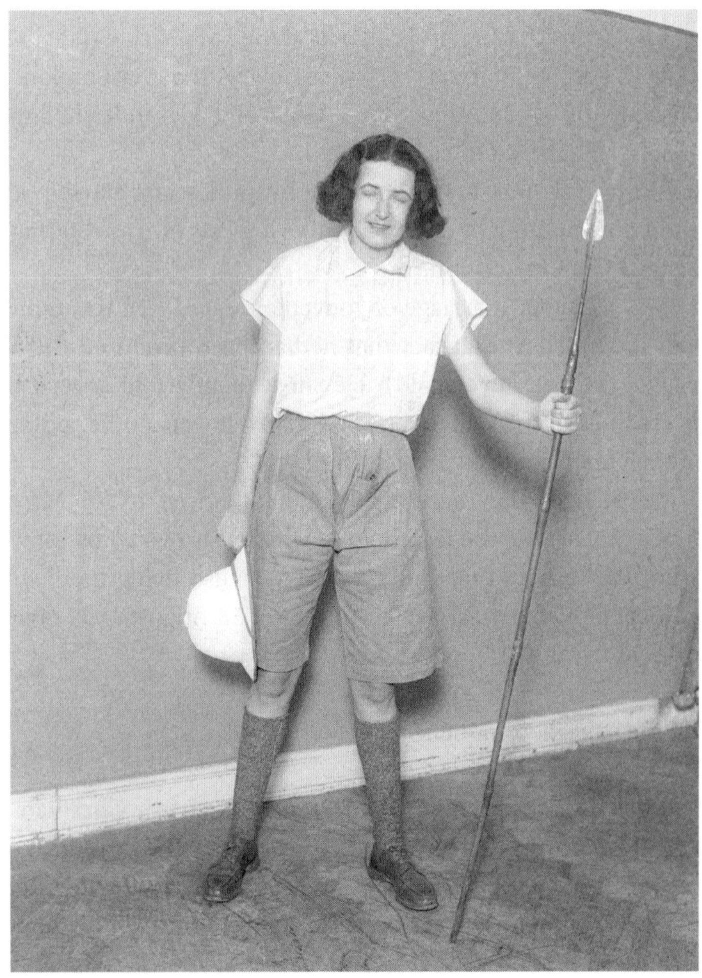

Gulla Pfeffer, the German temptress (Das Bundesarchiv)

- Fortunately, Fletcher had been sensible enough to 'alert his department prior to travel'. He had previously informed Admiral Sinclair of his invitation. As well as Captain Pfeffer, who was a relative of Gulla's first husband Emil, they apparently met Rudolf Hess, although only for 15 minutes.[13]
- In July 1939 the story continues. War was becoming imminent and Gulla Pfeffer, for whatever reason, did not wish to return to Germany and so decided to marry for the second time. We have been told that the reason for the reluctance is that she was now an anti-Nazi and has

a good academic career and contacts at the LSE. Nicholas, her teenage son from her first marriage, was also now with her in London.

- Consequently, on 28 August 1939, Gulla and Alexander Kell married at Chelsea Registry Office, London.
- Alexander Kell was a ship's purser by profession, having recently returned from India by ship. The ship's log lists him as residing at the Overseas Club in London.
- This was a blatant marriage of convenience and Kell was quite open about it, as well as that fact that he had been promised £10 for the escapade (it was never paid). He subsequently told special branch officers Buckell and Gill that he had hoped to get another purser's job and then apply for a divorce.
- By the time of the marriage, Kell had moved to 16 Margaretta Terrace in Chelsea, the leasehold of which was owned by John Leslie Carlin. We suspect that Gulla Pfeffer was also living there with her son. Certainly, the marriage certificate of 28 August 1939 gives both parties as living at that address.

However, the story does not end there.

- Thereafter, the role of Harold/Francis Richard Christian Cecil Fletcher becomes less clear. In the spring of 1940 Guy Liddell of MI5 Counter Espionage became tasked with ascertaining further details in connection with the leakage of British SIS reports and documentation to Jahnke and, somewhat bizarrely, copies of Ambassador Kennedy's telegrams to President Roosevelt. In September 1939, Francis Fletcher and his wife were recorded as living at 16 Lionel Mansions, Hammersmith. Francis was born on 27 September 1903, his first wife, Mary Isabel, on 27 October 1900.
- On 22 February 1940, Liddell records that 'Fletcher is at least the Foreign office contact who was in touch with Kurt Jahnke'.
- By this time, Gulla Pfeffer, despite her arranged marriage in late August 1939, had been interned and was in Port Erin, on the Isle of Man. Initially she was held at HMP Islington and was recorded as being there on the 29 September 1939 register. Fletcher then tried to gain her release; once by suggesting she was harmless and the second time by suggesting that she might be a 'useful double-cross agent'.[14]

Kell, her recently introduced husband, also tried the same, but to no avail.

- A day later, a high-level meeting was called to discuss Fletcher. The attendees included 'C' of MI6. Apparently,[15] Fletcher 'likes to imagine himself as a cloak and dagger man' and 'has never been very content with his ordinary cipher work'. An incident in 1938 was recounted when he was threatened with the sack if he repeated a particular indiscretion. The outcome of the meeting was the finding that he had certainly met Jahnke and Captain Pfeffer, and that further work was required to check his true motives.
- Later on, in April 1940, John Carlin was interviewed, not by MI5, but by Richman Stops of MI6. It is recorded that 'Carlin seems to know more than he is prepared to say. He intimated that he distrusted Fletcher… He was obviously very agitated.' Carlin only knew Fletcher through Gulla Pfeffer, so again we do wonder precisely what he knew. The obvious question of why MI6 had become involved also bears scrutiny, save that MI5 and MI6 counter-intelligence had to an extent merged.
- The last mention of Fletcher in the Liddell/MI5 diaries is dated 1 April 1940, where it is recorded that he was going to France for an eleven-day cycling holiday and had already left the country. Had that not been the case and Fletcher was still in England, Liddell was going to assign two girls to follow him. Clearly, he was still very much under suspicion (by MI5 at least) at that time. We then have a void for just over a year to May 1941 when Liddell reported on the arrival of Rudolf Hess as 'today's sensational news'.
- On 18 May, a week later, in a conversation with Henry Hopkinson of the Foreign Office, Liddell stated: 'I told him about the Gulla Pfeffer letter and the importance of the Innere Dienst. I thought that Pfeffer's letter might possibly give us the opening we wanted.' This is certainly important, as we have no idea what the 'Pfeffer letter' said, or to whom it was addressed. Moreover, what was the 'opening' referred to?

So, before the Hess flight it appears clear that 'Fletcher' had been used by the German Secret Service, or more specifically Gulla Pfeffer, as the remnant of the Jahnke Buro, to pass SIS documents to the Germans. The extent of his activities and true allegiance still appears to be somewhat unclear.

MI5 continued to monitor Fletcher and in 1942 had asked Valentine Vivian of MI6 (counter espionage) to give his opinion on the case. The reply came back: 'I am rather reluctant to open the matter again with Fletcher. He is, I understand, far gone with TB … he has always been rather apt to live in a world of his own imagination.'

Not very helpful or forthcoming. Fletcher died in Devon in 1951, after having married Mary Denby (1921–2007) in 1946.

It appears obvious that Liddell of MI5 did not know for sure what was going on (certainly as late as spring 1940), but that of course does not necessarily mean that others did not. Being English, Harold/Francis Fletcher did not play a part in the XX committee of 'turned agents', but again, that does not mean that he was not passing information to the Jahnke Buro that was being 'spoon fed' by others. In fear of repetition, we duplicate the conclusion reached by Popov:

> 'I couldn't help wondering how much our planted reports of low morale might have influenced Hess – and even Hitler. It would be interesting, I speculated, if British Intelligence had unwittingly inspired the Hess incident.'[16]

This may well have been the role assigned in part to Fletcher, but it should be remembered that Gulla Pfeffer had been interned at the start of the war in September 1939 and had 'fallen out with' John Carlin in 1940. Consequently, we do wonder how much of value was being passed?

According to the report, it appears that the following others were also 'Jahnke' agents:

- Frederico Stallforth (1887–1960), more of an intermediary than agent, a US businessman
- Erich von Salzmann (1876–1941), a journalist who left Britain on 11 August 1939.

Hardly the means of instigating a coup, or even communicating the prospect of a coup. In any event, apart from whatever Mr Fletcher may have or may not have been doing, by the spring of 1941 the Jahnke organisation had virtually ceased to exist, at least in Britain. The agents had either left or had been interned. Hess would surely not have been able to obtain or communicate meaningful and relevant information from this source. Moreover, the information was coming (via Fletcher) from the Foreign Office, not the non-governmental channels that Hess was seeking to rely upon.

On 23 August 1945, Walter Schellenberg, the head of Amt.V1 of the RHSA was interrogated concerning Jahnke, who by this time had disappeared, presumed dead. Schellenberg recollected: 'Jahnke had wanted to avert a war with England and had used every conceivable means to bring an English Intelligence man to Hitler, through Hess and Himmler.' Quite what, when and to whom this refers to is unclear. If by 'intelligence man' Francis Fletcher is referenced, we would remind the reader of the earlier comparison to Johnny English.

However, there is no doubt that Jahnke's proximity to Hess brought him under suspicion of involvement in the affair. Ladislas Farago states that Hitler 'dropped' him after the flight and certainly MI6 retained an interest in him well into the war. He was also recorded (like de Ropp) as visiting Switzerland frequently during the conflict.

The conclusion must remain that there is currently insufficient evidence to either categorically link or dismiss the Jahnke/Pfeffer Buro from the Hess affair entirely, and he may well have also been simultaneously reporting back to Russian Intelligence and British intelligence.[17]

Once again, the absence of files and indeed mention or confusion of the Fletcher name can only raise questions as to why that might be the case. There is certainly more yet to learn.

d) Contact with other Reich Ministers

In any conventional organisation basic intelligence would be shared between the participators at the higher levels of the structure. Board and cabinet meetings are held with precisely that purpose in mind, so that the raw intelligence, strategy and policy can be shared between those responsible for its dissemination.

Nazi Germany in 1941 was somewhat different. The 'Führer Princip' meant that orders were relayed down from the top without the ability to question. There were not cabinet meetings in the British understanding of the term; broad intended actions were relayed down, some in writing, some not, and those immediately beneath were then left to implement. There was no open forum for debate or question. The Reichstag was just used as a public relations machine for the Führer.

Consequently, the Reichsleiters implemented their own policies and interpretations of what they believed the Führer wished, or alternatively, in some cases, was most profitable to themselves. Often there would be two people who thought they were responsible for the same desired outcome and so conflict and misunderstanding would break out. In the Deputy Führer's office, Martin Bormann was slowly imposing his modus operandi to the exclusion of any input by his immediate superior Rudolf Hess. Hess was normally quite happy to acquiesce, as we believe that by this time he simply did not enjoy his role. There was growing evidence that Hess was being partially bypassed by those lower down the structure in favour of Bormann with whom they were the more likely to communicate. This is perhaps only a natural reaction.[18]

At a lower level there was already open conflict between Bohle and von Ribbentrop over the implementation of Nazi policy in occupied Holland.

Von Ribbentrop and Hess had also quarrelled. Goebbels delighted in furthering the rumour that Hess was impotent. Göring called him a 'Piesel'(a 'pee'). Clearly there would be little cooperation and sharing of information from these quarters. Bormann, Hess's deputy, merely kept working and kept his head down, though was undoubtedly aware of some impending action as the daily weather reports that Hess had requested from Schmidt in Holland were also being sent to Bormann.

Consequently, it could be said that information was being imparted to others from Hess, but Hess was certainly not part of any meaningful exchange of information from his so-called colleagues; with possibly one exception.

Much has been made by other writers of the fact that Alfred Rosenberg visited Hess for lunch on 10 May 1941, just hours before the flight to Scotland. Some have speculated that Hess told Rosenberg of his intentions and that Rosenberg somehow alerted the RAF of the flight through his longstanding connection with Baron de Ropp. This relationship has been detailed in Chapter 8. Whilst we believe this quite possible, there are some issues that require further explanation.

Since writing *Rudolf Hess: A New Technical Analysis of the Hess Flight, May 1941*, the Alfred Rosenberg diaries have been found in the US and are now published on the United States Holocaust Memorial Museum web site. A new book has just been published, based on these diaries, *The Political Diary of Alfred Rosenberg and the Onset of the Holocaust* by Jürgen Matthaeus and Frank Bajohr.[19]

In the diary, Rosenberg makes it clear that Hess had asked him to attend the luncheon appointment at Harlaching and had flown him from Berlin in his own plane. He was also accompanied by Alfred Meyer (1891–1945), a Gauleiter, and soon to be responsible with Rosenberg for the Eastern regions, once conquered. Ostensibly, the lunch was to discuss the implementation of Nazi Party in those areas.

Alfred Rosenberg and Alfred Meyer, Hess's luncheon guests on 10 May 1941

However, as Rosenberg makes clear in the diary, Hess was noted as being ill and paying particular attention to Buz, his son. He also states that Hess told him of 'an overriding matter' that he could not get out of his head:

> *'Als ich nun noch einige andre Fragen anschneiden wollte, sagte Hess, er bäte mich, doch nur das Wichtigste zu behandeln, ein Gedanke beschäftige ihn derartig, dass er von der Erörterung minder notwendiger Dinge absehen müsse. Dies war ziemlich leidenschaftlich ausgesprochen, doch konnte ich auch nicht ahnen, was er auszuführen gedachte.'* ('When I wanted to bring up a few other questions, Hess said that he would ask me to only deal with the most important things, one thought preoccupied him so much that he had to refrain from discussing less important things. This was said quite passionately, but I had no idea what he intended to do.')

Consequently, if we are to believe the diary, which we suspect was written in a way not to later incriminate the writer, Hess called Rosenberg to Munich only to tell him that he did not wish to discuss details of the Eastern occupation as he had other things on his mind!

A nonsense. Hess was clearly telling Rosenberg what he was about to do and why, partly through self-preservation and self-justification and partly as a way of letting Hitler know that he had gone. (Rosenberg went to the Obersalzberg immediately after his Munich luncheon appointment. Hitler was already in residence at his mountain retreat.)

Once again, the Deputy Führer had imparted, rather than imbibed intelligence. Rosenberg was one of the oldest Nazi Party members being present in the early days when Hess was also at his height of influence. Hitler, Rosenberg and Hess were seen as being the intellectual drivers of the movement. That is why Rosenberg was flown to Munich by Hess. Like him, by 1941 Rosenberg was also a purely political animal, with no direct military responsibility.

e) Prof. Franz Seraph Gerl

This very interesting channel of communication has been known to us in outline for a long time, though we have been typically slow in realising its significance and have only recently started to drill down into the detail. Apologies. We hope the reader will understand our excitement in discovering the following.

Walter Schellenberg (1910–52) had ended the war as the Nazi Head of Foreign Intelligence, having served his apprenticeship under Heydrich and Himmler. As such he was well placed to know the details of most of the Nazi Intelligence operations carried out throughout the war. At Nuremberg he was sentenced to six years imprisonment, but only served two on account of his deteriorating health. He died in 1952.

Whilst at Nuremberg, Schellenberg, like others, chose to write his memoirs, which eventually appeared as *The Labyrinth*, albeit much later, in 1956.[20] Given that it was published four years after the author's death, he was not able to defend the allegations of exaggeration, but exaggerated or not, it brought our attention to 'Prof. G-----' (the full name was not printed at the time, presumably because the professor was still alive). Specifically, Schellenberg had written: 'Our secret information showed that for some years Hess had been influenced by agents of the British Secret Service and their German collaborators, and that this influence played a large part in his decision to fly to Scotland. This was true, more particularly of a Prof. G-----, a gland specialist in Upper Bavaria.'

Regretfully, we had previously left the information at that. We had discovered the Prof. G----- was Prof. Gerl, but apart from that had done no more. Typically, David Irving had also beaten us to Gerl, even quoting some letters passing between Hess and his friend.[21]

However, we had yet to discover enough information to justify the conclusion that Schellenberg had made in 1946. There had to be more to be learned and our conclusion has certainly now changed. We started by trying to contact any family member and eventually managed to track down Andreas Gerl, the doctor's grandson, who was helpful and cautious in equal measure. Sir Tom Shakespeare, the academic,[22] and grandson of Sir Geoffrey Shakespeare (1893–1980), the Liberal politician in the 1930s and '40s (and Gerl patient), had also described the previous generation of the Gerl family as being cautious, and this trait appears to have filtered down to the next generation, quite understandably. Once we had made contact, detailed correspondence followed, first repeating what we had discussed with Tom Shakespeare, but then, once we gained a degree of mutual trust, further information started to flow. Some of which is quite shocking. We now record in precis the key information that we have gleaned or so far been told.

Franz Gerl was an enterprising Bavarian, and after the First World War had established a medical practice in the Allgäu, specialising in problems of the thyroid gland. His reputation thus established, he attempted to expand his practice by travelling to London with a view to establishing 'Interclinic', an international medical association. During the 1930s there are numerous records of his travelling to the United States and Canada, presumably to further expand the same aims and objectives.

However, he had struck lucky. In the 1920s he had met Eleanor Mary Calthrop (née Chance), a very well-connected widow who lived at 21 Clareville Grove, Kensington, London. Mrs Calthrop had been unlucky in marriage, her husband dying less than four months after their marriage in 1917. Later she had gone to Dr Gerl for treatment and the couple had become close friends.[23]

Coming from the well-known Chance textile family of Carlisle, she soon started to arrange introductions for the 'great and the good' to meet the doctor, when in London, who would then suggest a trip to the Allgäu for further treatment. Mrs Calthrop would also become a regular traveller, eventually having commissioned her own furniture for the pension in which she stayed in Bad Oberdorf. This furniture was the subject of a specific legacy in her 1974 will.[24] She was also a keen mountaineer and the family relate how she had conquered the Matterhorn.[25] We have been sent copies of documents

The Chance boys with Dr Gerl

Our Lodgings at Hindelang

Anthony and Jeremy with Daddy

showing that she had been in trouble with the German authorities, having contravened the currency regulations in 1936. She was also a member of the Anglo-German Fellowship.

However, business was good and Dr Gerl duly asked his accountant, Georg Ehlert, to build a children's sanatorium, the Ehlert Kinderlandschulheim. This was duly completed in a modernist style and from 1933 to 1938 many English children visited for reasons in part medical, in part international relations. The sanatorium was eventually demolished in 1976.

A relative of Mrs Calthrop's, Roger Chance,[26] became the Press Attaché to the British Embassy in Berlin in 1938 and his two boys were tutored in Bavaria and even had the honour of having their tonsils removed by the good doctor.[27]

The Gerl family has shown us photographs of many tweed-attired, middle-aged English ladies speaking and meeting with the doctor, who all no doubt agreed was a good chap and jolly good at his job. The list of attendees to the Allgäu was growing, both in its number and stature. There is a very good account of a visit to the Allgäu made by Sir Tom Shakespeare in the early 2000s, trying to trace his grandfather's trips to the practice in the 1930s.

We have also been advised of the identity of some of the other attendees, for example, Pamela Baldwin, the daughter of Stanley, the then Prime Minister. The Baldwins themselves were even rumoured to have visited as part of their annual exodus to Aix-les-Bains in the Auvergne.

However, Dr Gerl also had a star attraction for his British visitors and patients. Rudolf Hess, the Deputy Führer had also established a weekend retreat in the Allgäu. That changed everything. The Gerl family describe the ensuing history as follows:

> My grandfather's hometown is Hindelang. Today it is called Bad Hindelang. Hindelang consists of several districts. These are Hindelang, Vorderhindelang, Hinterstein, Bad Oberdorf, Oberjoch and the district of Gailenberg, which is about 170m above Hindelang. All together are also called Ostrachtal.
>
> Rudolf Hess knew Hindelang before 1933. He accompanied his wife, who underwent goitre surgery with my grandfather. From then on, he chose Hindelang as his holiday home. First, he rented a house in Vorderhindelang called 'Herrgottswinkel'. Between 1934 and 1936 he moved his holiday home to 'Haus Bürgle' in Bad Oberdorf.
>
> Neither Hess nor Gerl themselves have ever lived in Gailenberg. My grandfather bought two adjacent houses there around 1935, because he wanted to build a hospital there with a splendid view of the Ostrachtal but was unable to do so by the end of the war. Rudolf Hess's fondest wish was to acquire a house on the Gailenberg as well, to be able to do the same as Hitler on the Obersalzberg. His plan was also to turn Hindelang into a national park. My grandfather tried to find him a house on the Gailenberg but did not succeed until the end of the war. It was not until long after the war in 1970 that the Hess family was able to acquire a house on the Gailenberg itself through an intermediary named Christian Grebe, who was engaged by my grandfather. This house had previously been owned by the painter Christian Modersohn (son of Otto Modersohn, also a famous landscape artist) until 1955. However, Ilse Hess had been living with Grebe in exchange for rent since 1955. Due to the Allied restrictions, the Hess family had previously not been allowed to acquire the house for themselves.
>
> Thus, no meetings with Nazi greats or other personalities have ever taken place on the Gailenberg. Such meetings took place either

> at Hess's place (in Munich) or very occasionally at my grandfather's. Larger meetings were usually moved to Hotel Alpenhof or Hotel Prinz Luitpoldbad. Both hotels were situated on the road to Oberjoch, also with a splendid panoramic view over the Ostrachtal.

Consequently, we have been sent photographs of various photographs of Rudolf Hess and his sister with the good doctor and the various tweed-suited and pearled ladies, presumably of English origin. We now have an image of the Hess equivalent to Berchtesgaden. No ostentation, equally beautiful and Dr Gerl aiding the host and supplying the required visitors.

In earlier books we speculated that Hess had not troubled to build a house on the Obersalzberg, as his relationship with Hitler was secure enough that he did not need to. Now we realise the explanation was far simpler. He had a similar, though far more modest, and alternative location of his own. The Allgäu is to the southwest of Munich, Obersalzberg is to the southeast.

As the decade passed, the guests increased in status. Thomas Jones, the Deputy Secretary to the Cabinet describes Gerl visiting London to treat the wife of Lord Brand of Eydon. He quotes Gerl: 'He is a friend of Hess, and he brings the same message, viz, that Hitler does not want war but peace.'[28] Later, in 1936 Jones describes a trip with Lloyd George to Germany, meeting Hess and travelling with him to inspect newly built autobahns. Roger Chance was also shown the same sights.

Obviously, Hess was not in the Allgäu all the time, but certainly weekends were regularly spent there so that Ilse and Rudolf Hess could indulge their love of the outdoor life; walking and skiing in particular.

The channel to Hess was obvious. Mrs Calthrop in London, Dr Gerl and then (if deemed influential enough) an introduction to the Hess family. As stated above, Ilse spent her days post-1943 in the Allgäu and her daughter-in-law Andrea still lives there today.

So, is this the channel that we have been looking for and that as described by Walter Schellenberg?

We do not yet think so in toto. Whilst the personnel are undoubtedly correct and in situ, Dr Gerl was under Gestapo surveillance in the latter part of the decade (so much so that his brother Fritz was later used in part as a surrogate post-box) and after 1939 all communication between Hess and Gerl was apparently oral rather than written. We find it hard to conceive that a viable, reliable channel could be maintained, but now have little doubt that channels and links from the highest strata of British society were being actively maintained, certainly at least before the war.

Thinking that perhaps the two families had somehow combined their efforts in regard to the British, we have also ascertained that the Gerls and the Haushofers, whilst known to each other, did not mix or communicate. The Haushofer estate was at Pähl, just to the south of Munich. Hess seems to have compartmentalised his life and so Hindelang and Dr Gerl and Eleanor Calthrop were kept separate and apart from his many other commitments.

However, after the 1941 flight, Albrecht Haushofer and Fritz Gerl were both simultaneously interrogated. One of the few times the two men met. At the end of the war, Franz Gerl underwent a de-Nazification programme, and this was aided by references from the pre-war UK patients. He died in 1956. Haushofer was murdered in 1945.

Andreas Gerl and John Harris have made a further startling discovery. We have now studied various pre-war photographs of Lady Elizabeth Ivy Percy and are convinced that she, too, had visited Franz Gerl in the Allgäu and was pictured with the Deputy Führer. These photographs are potentially very important, as Lady Elizabeth Percy married the Marquis of Clydesdale in 1937, who in 1940 duly inherited his father's title of the 14th Duke of Hamilton.

The newly married Clydesdales

So, whilst it may well be indeed true that the Marquis/Duke had not met Rudolf Hess pre-war, we now believe it almost certain that his wife Elizabeth had, via Franz Gerl. Quite what this discovery means in the context of the Hess flight is quite honestly anyone's guess at this stage. At the very least it demonstrates a linkage between Hess and the Hamilton wider family.

In March 2021, Andreas Gerl made a further important disclosure. He stated that Stewart Blacker, the organiser of the 1933 Houston expedition to Everest, had also visited the Hindelang. Blacker was the navigator/photographer who accompanied Douglas Douglas-Hamilton in his Westland PV3, whilst making the famous flight over the world's highest mountain.

This is bringing the Hess affair very close to home indeed. In 1941, Hamilton was prepared to go to court to refute the allegation that he knew Hess.[29] What now appears to be the case is that Harry Pollitt, the defendant in the action (and secretary to the British Communist Party) had picked the wrong family member. When accusing the Duke of knowing Rudolf Hess before the war, he should have chosen perhaps the Duchess of Hamilton or, alternatively, Stewart Blacker, Hamilton's leader and fellow flyer some eight years previously in Nepal.

Stewart Blacker

When we then learned that Stewart Blacker had married Doris Peel, the wealthy heiress to a linoleum empire and owner in 1941 of Hendersyde Park, near Kelso, our imaginations temporarily began to run wild. Years previously, Richard Wilbourn and I had sat in a car in a layby just down the road from the Peel Estate, speculating as to whether Kelso Racecourse might be a viable Hess landing ground. That had been in the early 2000s. Kelso is heavily marked on the Hess flight map at Lennoxlove House, Haddington.

It does seem to us that the Hamiltons seem to be memorable in what they do not reveal in connection to Hess, rather than what they do. We discovered that they owned Prestwick airfield through Scottish Aviation Limited. We learned of the friendship between David Macintyre, who was taken to identify Hess in May 1941, and now we have learned that the Duchess of Hamilton and Stewart Blacker were at the least patients of Hess's best friend in the Allgäu and quite likely acquaintances of the Deputy Führer!

We are not leaping to conclusions yet, but we are beginning to understand why Walter Schellenberg decided to write what he did. Blacker, through his weapon design work was well known in intelligence circles and his immediate boss in 1939/40 was John Charles Francis Holland (1897–1956), later to become a leading light in SOE alongside Colin Gubbins. Yet again, Holland was a keen aviator and was quoted as saying in 1938, 'Splendid, I shall research on subversive war.'[30]

A further Gerl revelation has been shared with us. After Hess had made his flight in 1941, Martin Bormann made the shocking allegation that one of Dr Gerl's assistants was father to Wolf Hess. This was printed in the press under the headline:

Bormann über Hess Menschliche Hintergrunde und Enthfillungen[31]

Not pleasant, but coming from Bormann probably not too surprising either. We make no comment on the veracity or otherwise of the allegation.

So, in conclusion, it is now easy to see why Schellenberg took an interest in Gerl and his patients and British connections. We are however struggling currently to see how a 1941 peace mission could be arranged through this channel, given the need for viable and secure communication.

OTHER POSSIBLE CHANNELS

Bishop George Bell

George Bell (1883–1958) was a prominent Anglican bishop who was involved with the international aspects of the Church of England in the interwar years. Obviously concerned by the Nazi attacks on the German church, he quickly gained allies such as Dietrich Bonhoeffer, a Lutheran pastor, who in turn informed Bell as to what was really going on in Nazi Germany. He publicly denounced the imprisonment of Martin Niemöller in Sachsenhausen in 1938 and arranged for some ninety members of German Pastor families to emigrate to England.

On 20 September 1935, Bell had travelled to Germany, where he met Rudolf and Ilse Hess at their home in Munich ('a nice house with a garden'). Andrew Chandler, Bell's biographer describes their relationship thus: 'Frau Hess, who spoke English, evidently enjoyed the visiting Bishop rather more than her husband. This new connection came to very little beyond a smattering of letters now and then, in which Bell pressed for advantages and Hess pretended not to notice.'[32]

Hess also made the point that Rosenberg's views were of a personal nature and did not represent those of the State. Ilse Hess asked the bishop to write to Hess, and he left just before Adolf Hitler arrived at the house to discuss foreign policy matters.

What is also interesting about this visit is that the bishop had been chaperoned by Dr Gerl, and Bell had been to Hindelang before making the Munich visit. In other words, he appears to be another visitor from the Calthrop–Gerl–Hindelang–Hess school of diplomacy. Bell wrote to Hess just before Christmas 1935.

In 1936 Bell again travelled to Germany and in December to Berlin, where quite bizarrely he appears to have been chaperoned this time by 'Baron von der Ropp', who we know already was a resident of Berlin at the time. A small world indeed.

General Sir Ian Standish Monteith Hamilton (1853–1947)

Ian Hamilton was unlikely to have played an active part in the Hess affair, simply because of his age. As one can calculate, in 1941 he was already eighty-eight years of age.

However.

Ian Hamilton had spent most of his life fighting for king and queen. Aided by his wife, Jean, he had climbed to near the top of the British Army and could, for instance, count the Churchills as personal friends. His one black mark (also appearing on Churchill's list of black marks) proved to be the Gallipoli campaign of 1915, after which he never held high command again.

In the 1920s and '30s his outlook to war changed. Rather than fight, he saw rapprochement as the way to prevent further wars and in 1928 he formed the Anglo-German Association (it was disbanded in 1936).

There are also pictures of an animated Hamilton at Berchtesgaden with Hitler, sitting in front of the huge Gobelin tapestries. That meeting was later, in 1938, when he was the head of the Scottish section of the British Legion. It was during that trip that he also met Rudolf Hess.

When Hess was enquiring of Karl Haushofer in August 1940 (see Chapter 2), he specifically asked if Hamilton might be contacted as a conduit, so we suspect that Haushofer also knew Hamilton. What is clear, however, is that both Hess and Haushofer knew of and were aware of the 'old' Hamilton in 1940.[33]

There are some further coincidences. Ian Hamilton was the tenant of Lennoxlove House during the 1930s, the same house that was later acquired by the Duke of Hamilton in the late 1940s. In May 1941, Ian Hamilton was living at Blair Drummond and was apparently incapacitated by flu.

It is unlikely that Hess would have entrusted the British end of a coup attempt to an eighty-eight-year-old former general.

Ilse Hess (1900–95)

As we are both personally aware, it is a brave man indeed who continually disregards the 'advice' of his wife. Rudolf Hess was no different, particularly as Ilse Minna Berta Anna Carola Pröhl was very much a political animal herself. Unlike most of the Nazi wives, Ilse was never afraid to offer a political opinion and this apparent outspokenness had got her into hot water in the past.[34]

Her father, a doctor, had been killed in the First World War[35] and her mother subsequently married the curator of the famous Bremen Art Museum, Carl Horn. Rather than follow her mother, Ilse travelled south and met Hess whilst both were students at Munich University.

Thereafter, their relationship mirrored that of the nascent Nazi Party. They married in 1927 with Hitler and Karl Haushofer as witnesses. Consequently, with this unique provenance, they (at least) saw themselves as 'keepers of the Nazi flame' and much later Ilse reminded her husband, 'never to sell our birth right as idealists for the sake of external things'.[36]

Ilse Hess and Wolf with Hitler

Inevitably, this long-held provenance fermented jealousy amongst the other Nazi leaders. After the flight in 1941, even Joseph Goebbels, who previously had appreciated Hess, made the case that, 'Professor Haushofer and Hess's wife were the evil geniuses in this affair… I'd like to give a good thrashing to that wife of his!'[37]

We do not believe that Goebbels's analysis was wholly correct or accurate in this instance. Clearly Ilse was influential, clearly was she was an important part of the Gerl/Hess circle in the 1930s Hindelang, but we have seen nothing further. At the least, to be instrumental in her husband's mission would have required communication channels of her own and we have seen no such evidence.

f) The Anglo-German Fellowship

This essentially big business-based (and funded) organisation was formed by E.W.D. Tennant in the mid 1930s to promote Anglo-German (note: not necessarily Anglo-Nazi) fellowship and goodwill. At its height in around late 1938 it could count on some 900 of the British 'great and the good', together with a smattering of the usual suspect lunatics and extremists. It had already been infiltrated by MI5 and one H.A.R. Philby was listed as a member, presumably to keep an eye on the organisation on behalf of the Russians.

It also had a German subsidiary, the Deutsch-Englische Gesellschaft (DEG), based in Berlin. In terms of relevance to our research the following are listed as being members in 1937:

Mrs Eleanor Calthrop
Lord David Douglas-Hamilton
Lord Malcolm Douglas-Hamilton
Dr Karl Haushofer, university professor
Hautmann v. Pfeffer, Verbindungsstab – Berlin
Graf Scherwin, Berlin[38]

Clearly, a common membership does not infer any subsequent action whatsoever. However, how many coincidences are necessary before a pattern may be seen to be emerging?

In conclusion, we believe that Hess had turned to the Haushofers for help and support in late 1940 because realistically it was the only option open to him at a sufficiently high diplomatic level that could have produced a prospect of success, without involving others who could potentially dissuade or just gossip. Realistically, there was little real alternative, apart perhaps from the Rosenberg–de Ropp–Winterbotham channel. Even this had changed, though, with de Ropp having apparently moved from central Berlin to Montreux at the onset of the war.

Even more precariously, perhaps, we have devoted a later chapter querying Albrecht Haushofer's true agenda (see Chapter 27) and it should also be reported that Karl Haushofer was also under surveillance by a senior Russian agent, Richard Sorge. Sorge had come to know Haushofer in Berlin through his cover as a journalist for *Geopolitik*, a well-respected magazine that had willingly and enthusiastically expounded the views of Karl Haushofer in the 1930s.[39]

Consequently, even Hess's trust in the senior Haushofer, whilst we are sure was well placed, may well have been reported further afield than was perhaps anticipated. Sorge was in Japan in 1940/41, so was not directly party to the lead up to the flight, but by that time Schellenberg, as head of RHSA overseas, was having doubts as to the true allegiance of Kurt Jahnke, who had denied knowledge of Sorge's activities, despite Schellenberg having evidence to the contrary.

The hazy picture is becoming increasingly clear. Hess was surrounded by a Nazi Party and State Intelligence system that by 1940/41 had either been 'turned' by the British to give misleading information or neutered by way of the internment of its likely participants. It was little wonder that Hess had turned back to the Haushofers, but unbeknown to all concerned, even Father Karl had unwittingly been in contact with a Russian agent and Albrecht's loyalties were no longer in complete accord with those of either his father, Adolf Hitler or Rudolf Hess. Not an auspicious start for a secretive peace mission. Could Hess truly trust anyone?

---

1 Acts of the Party Chancellery of the NSDAP – Helmut Heiber.

2 Extracted for file PF 37755 from PF 600561.

3 Walter Schellenberg, *Hitler's Secret Service: Memoirs*, Pyramid, New York, 1958.

4 Peter Padfield, *Hess, Hitler and Churchill: The Real Turning Point of the Second World War*, Icon, London, 2013.

5 *The Guy Liddell Diaries, Vol. 1 1939–1942*, Routledge, London, 2005.

6 Gordon Welchman, *The Hut 6 Story: Breaking the Enigma Codes*, M&M Baldwin, Shropshire, 2018.

7 Trinity College, Cambridge.

8 Gordon Welchman, *The Hut 6 Story: Breaking the Enigma Codes*, M&M Baldwin, Shropshire, 2018.

9 HW3/82.

10 John Leslie Carlin, *Gulla: the Tramp: An Ethnological Indiscretion*, Cape, London, 1940.

11 The September 1939 Register.

12 *The Guy Liddell Diaries, Vol. 1 1939–1942*, Routledge, London, 2005, entry 18 February 1940.

13 Email correspondence from Lowe to Harris, August 2021.

14 Ibid.

15 Ibid.

16 Duško Popov, *Spy/Counterspy*, Grosset and Dunlap, New York, 1974.

17 In an interview with Sir Maurice Oldfield, Oldfield alluded to the fact that Jahnke was indeed an agent of the KGB.

18 Dietrich Orlow, *The Nazi Party 1919–1945: A Complete History*, Enigma, New York, 2008.

19 Jürgen Matthaeus and Frank Bajohr, *The Political Diary of Alfred Rosenberg and the Onset of the Holocaust*, Rowman & Littlefield, London, 2015.

20 Walter Schellenberg, *The Labyrinth: Memoirs of Walter Schellenberg, Hitler's Chief of Counterintelligence*, De Capo Press, 1956.

[21] David Irving, *Hess: The Missing Years 1941–1945*, Focal Point, Windsor, 2010.
[22] Sir Thomas Shakespeare is Professor of Disability research at the University of East Anglia.
[23] Please see ancestry.com – Franz Seraph Gerl.
[24] www.gov.uk – Find a Will
[25] Letter to John Harris, January 2021.
[26] Sir Roger Chance (1893–1987).
[27] Correspondence from John Harris to Andreas Gerl, autumn/winter 2020.
[28] Thomas Jones, *A Diary with Letters*, Oxford University Press, London, 1954.
[29] Hamilton threatened Harry Pollitt, the leader of the British Communist Party.
[30] M.R.D. Foot, *SOE: Special Operations Executive 1940–46*, Manchester University, 1970.
[31] Andreas Gerl to John Harris, November 2020.
[32] Andrew Chandler, *Brethren in Adversity: Bishop George Bell, the Church of England and the Crisis of German Protestantism, 1933–39*, Boydell and Brewer, Woodbridge, 1997.
[33] See Chapter 2, the Haushofer/Hess correspondence.
[34] 'Ilse's unapologetic intellectualism clashed with Hitler's archaic view that women should not hold political opinions, and even if they did, they should keep their mouth shut.' James Wyllie, *Nazi Wives*, The History Press, Stroud, 2019.
[35] Gottlieb Friedrich Emil Karl Pröhl (1868–1917). Was killed on the western front whilst serving in the German Army.
[36] Ilse Hess, *Prisoner of Peace*, Briton Publishing Co., London, 1954.
[37] Joseph Goebbels, *The Goebbels Diaries*, Hamish Hamilton, London, 1948.
[38] Membership list as part of the 2018 thesis of Charles Spicer, MA.
[39] Walter Schellenberg, *Hitler's Secret Service: Memoirs*, Pyramid, New York, 1958.

CHAPTER 10

THE PUBLIC FACADE AND THE PRIVATE ANXIETIES – LATE 1940/EARLY 1941

The elephant(s) in the room in early 1941 were simply representing the fact that *prima facie*, Germany would not be able to make peace with Britain whilst Winston Churchill was in power and, similarly, Britain would not make peace with a Germany led by Adolf Hitler.

What is more, both countries and their respective populations knew that absolutely to be the case. It was what both leaders would consistently reiterate – so it had to be true.

Any potential 'non-governmental' peace treaty between the two countries in 1941 would therefore likely have to incorporate or initiate at least one change of leader. A further and very high hurdle indeed for any potential instigator or challenger to have to plan, jump or circumvent.

A war poster depicting Churchill as a British bulldog

Elephant in the room 1 – The intransigence of Winston Spencer Churchill

It was precisely because Rudolf Hess recognised this fact that he had instructed Albrecht Haushofer to contact the Duke of Hamilton in September 1940 rather than the British Foreign Office. He knew that any official peace overture to the British government would be batted away in just the same way as those both previous and numerous. He needed to ascertain if there was an alternative to Churchill, his government and policy.

This period of the war perhaps demonstrates Churchill either at his bravest – as subsequent history has demonstrated – or quite possibly at his most stupid, illogical, and stubborn, if judged by the conditions prevalent at the time. Until the Ultra 'goose' gave him the gift of the 'golden egg' of the knowledge of Barbarossa, he was either brave or stupid enough to maintain a position which logically and probably in military terms, too, was in doubt as to whether it was sustainable, or indeed should even be sustained. The Chiefs of Staff had continually warned him, 'If German forces got a firm footing in Britain our land forces would be insufficient and our conclusion is that *prima facie*, Germany has most of the cards.'[1]

Moreover, the Joint Intelligence Committee (JIC) was still predicting that the Germans' next major offensive would be against the United Kingdom (even as late as spring 1941) and, 'the suggestion that Hitler might move eastwards was seemingly never envisaged'.[2]

We must, however, question whether this conclusion was made with the benefit of Ultra Intelligence, as it is not wholly clear when the JIC started to benefit from it. Even if the JIC had benefitted from Ultra, it was of course only the case that Hitler was preparing for invasion, it *could* always have been a deception.

At the time Germany was certainly attempting to bomb Britain into submission, whilst ever increasing the U-boat menace. Britain was not able to counterattack. Her's was a wholly defensive position, and the invasion threat must have appeared both very logical and very real indeed, particularly to those (most of the British population) who did not share Ultra Intelligence.

Churchill did, however, have the tried and tested skills and expertise of British Intelligence on his side, which at the very least could maintain or open channels for future eventualities, should the need arise. Thankfully, there were still enough Germans who doubted the Nazi regime to make this communication possible, viable and desirable. Overtly, the Churchill policy manifested itself in support for Russia, even though they were still nominally in alliance with Nazi Germany at the time. Covertly, was a door was being left open should it appear that Stalin might end up on the Channel coast? That was surely a common sense position – keeping one's options open, as long as the military position allowed that luxury. Germany knew that a British invasion would be a bloody affair, so why try to invade if a peace was attainable as surely it must eventually become?

The British perception of Hitler had already been accurately described to Hess by Albrecht Haushofer in September 1940 (see pages 35-36).

Ever since Churchill had been brave/stupid enough in May 1940 to assume the premiership, he had not for one moment (in public at least) shown any sign of weakness, any sign of being ready to talk of peace. Privately, we now know that each day he woke up, 'with dread in his heart'. With the benefit of hindsight, we also know that this was Churchill's defining moment. As events transpired, he ended up on the winning side; equally, it could quite easily have been his bloodied and dead body that was found inside or outside of whatever citadel he chose to make his last stand. Respectfully, it should be said that when making his decision to grasp the poisoned chalice of the premiership in May 1940, the outcome was probably more weighted in favour of the latter outcome. Is that why Halifax chose to decline the leadership? Was his choice just down to a matter of physical courage?

Moreover, we believe that Churchill's stance was one wholly of conviction, not just that of a politician 'waiting for something else to come up'. He knew the stakes that were at risk; his life and personal survival being just one component.

The conviction of the ultimate success has become Churchill's lasting memorial, largely communicated by the series of extraordinary addresses to the nation throughout the period under review.

13 May 1940: House of Commons – *'Blood, Toil, Tears and Sweat'*.

19 May 1940: BBC – *'Be ye men of valour'*.

4 June 1940: House of Commons – *'We shall fight on the beaches'*.

18 June 1940: House of Commons – *'Their finest hour'*.

14 July 1940: BBC – *'War of the unknown warriors'*.

20 August 1940: House of Commons – *'The few'*.

9 February 1941: BBC – *'Give us the tools'*.

These addresses have passed into history as epitomising Churchill's defiance towards the Nazis at their most powerful. *Hansard* also records his defiance on a more regular basis in the House of Commons. We really believe that Churchill was being wholly sincere when he spoke of 'taking one with you' (a German) should an invasion attempt ever have been mounted.[3]

Consequently, we genuinely believe that no government led by Churchill would ever have made a peace with Nazi Germany. Albrecht Haushofer appeared to have shared the same view. The intransigence was neither play-acting nor posturing.

It should also be said that the defiance was also a pragmatic political tool. It enabled Churchill to carry most of the British public with him throughout the war, his approval rating never falling below 78 per cent.[4] It also proved invaluable as a part of Churchill's strategy of wooing the United States. The isolationists were certainly not going to support a Britain contemplating peace. Why would they? Similarly, would the displaced Poles, French, Dutch and Belgians have come to Britain if they thought a peace was in the making?

What also makes Churchill's defiance the more remarkable is the fact that at the same time as delivering these magnificent orations, he was in an increasingly bitter battle with members of his own Conservative party.

In a particularly shameful history, those members of the Tory Party who had supported Neville Chamberlain whilst leader now turned on their new leader. Never mind that the country was facing its greatest crisis since 1066, Winston Churchill had toppled their hero. Some apparently felt they could not yet support Churchill out of a twisted sense of loyalty to Chamberlain and his memory.

Paul Einzig, the political correspondent of the *Financial Times* recorded: 'For nearly two months after the advent of Churchill the overwhelming majority of Tory backbenchers, whatever their inner feelings may have been, gave no outward evidence of their support for him. Indeed, on many occasions they went out of their way to demonstrate their unwillingness to do so.' He concluded that this attitude had led, 'Many influential Americans to the conclusion that the Tory majority was not behind Churchill in his determination to fight on against heavy odds.'

Andrew Roberts deals with this particular period of Tory self-interest and history very well in his *Eminent Churchillians*[5] and makes the surprising and even now quite shocking observation that after Churchill had delivered his early parliamentary masterpieces many of the Tory MPs just sat silent and still.

It was only after the sinking of the French fleet at Oran in July 1940 that the mood changed, in Parliament at least, but still the doubters remained. Whatever Churchill did, he was pilloried. Was it therefore really any surprise that he slowly moved the leading Chamberlainite supporters away from the war cabinet (and eventually the country)? This is surely only a natural reaction, but one guaranteed to garner yet more resentment within the party, especially when the designated replacements such as Bracken and Beaverbrook were certainly never going to appeal to the remaining Chamberlainites.

Whilst the defining Battle of Britain was raging, Hore-Belisha wrote of the continuing strife, 'The Tory party in the House were not interested in the War, were afraid for their possessions and of the rise of Labour … they might one day bring peace terms upon us, and David Margesson would get his legions into the Lobby in favour of it even though the country was dead against it.'[6]

And this is the crux of the Hess affair: an understanding of how it might be possible to get rid of Churchill by a powerful minority, one which normally would be expected to be his keenest supporters. Jonathan Pile in *Churchill's Secret Enemy*[7] provides a detailed study of the role of Joseph Ball, the Chamberlainite MI5 officer, in his persistent and dogged attempt to undermine Churchill and what was seen as his warmongering throughout the late 1930s.

So when Hess was speaking to Karl Haushofer at the end of August 1940, these were precisely the same thoughts many Tories were sharing, something that Haushofer had recognised and understood, but in August 1940 that was all. That was why the letter to Hamilton had only suggested 'talks'; he did not know at that time how to progress matters further. That came much later.

It is also why Hess wrote to a non-governmental official. The official approaches, diplomatic and military were not having the desired effect.

Unfortunately for Hess, during the period from August 1940 to May 1941 Churchill's political position did not materially worsen. It was consistently awful throughout, its nadirs merely ebbing and flowing with the various military successes and failures. Moreover, the winter of 1940 was meteorologically unusually bleak, which fortunately made military adventures the more difficult and belated when they did eventually commence. Meanwhile, Mr Micawber Churchill, isolated from most of his political caste, was just hanging on. However, unlike virtually all others, he of course had the good inkling and knowledge through Bletchley Park that 'something will indeed turn up'.

Elephant in the room 2 – The duplicity of Adolf Hitler

The second Elephant in the room related directly to the Führer, Adolf Hitler.

Hitler's dilemma, 1941

As Albrecht Haushofer recognised (and openly told Hess), Hitler was recognised by many in Britain as the devil incarnate, a view shared across the political spectrum.[8] Most of those in Britain wanting a peace overtly wanted a peace with the 'Good Germans', but not with a Germany led by a raving madman who had consistently broken his word, most notably at Munich. In those circles, Hitler, rather than Germany, was seen as the problem. It should also be stated that this impression was perhaps more widespread amongst the middle and working classes. We have an unfortunate suspicion that many in the upper classes would have made a pact with the devil, and certainly with Hitler, if it meant their estates and possessions remained secure.

At the highest social strata, Édouard Daladier, the former French Prime Minister, famously wrote of the then British Queen, 'She was an excessively ambitious young woman who would be ready to sacrifice every other country in the world so that she may remain Queen.'[9]

It should also be remembered that it was Chamberlain who had gone to war with Hitler on account of the Polish invasion and the mutual assistance agreement that had been breached in the process. The irony then became that in 1940 many Tories would not support Churchill, who had never made a secret of his wish to fight.

The issue was the more difficult in that whilst the British were making the removal of Hitler a precondition of any talks in Germany, there was little active resistance against Hitler in 1940–41, simply because it was winning the war. Why remove a winning leader, however awful.

However, not all Germans supported the Nazi's and *The History of the German Resistance 1933–1945* is a very thick book, indeed, with some 849 pages.[10] Unfortunately however, whilst undoubtedly passive resistance, disagreement and opposition were present throughout, the sad fact remains that it was only really galvanised at times of impending military action (1938–39/41) or later in the war when it became obvious that Germany would eventually lose (1943–4). The most obvious example of such conversion was Claus von Stauffenberg, who placed the briefcase bomb on 20 July 1944. He only actively resisted after 1943, when the outcome of the war was becoming more obvious. That is not being disrespectful and of course some early resisters lost their lives too.

Why was this? Surely the military could have removed Hitler, as was eventually planned in 1944. Some have ascribed the fact of the oath to the Führer as being sacrosanct; others that Hitler always managed to get his retaliation in first (Ernst Röhm, murdered in 1934, Werner von Blomberg/Werner von Fritsch forced to resign in 1938); and yet others that the German psyche simply does not allow for such action.

Consequently, in late 1940/early 1941, unless someone like Georg Elser had managed to 'get through' employing a solo, 'Day of the Jackal' type approach, there seemed to be little chance for a real organised internal movement. In May 1941, Hoffman records an assassination attempt was planned in Paris, whereby Hitler was to be shot by two designated officers, and Ulrich-Wilhelm Graf Schwerin (1902–44) had somewhat vaguely 'pledged to throw a bomb'. However, Hitler decided not to go to Paris (presumably to mark the first anniversary of the invasion), so the attempt yet again fell by the wayside (we know that Hitler was at the Berghof on 10 May). We should also record that Graf Schwerin was a pre-war member of the Anglo- German fellowship.

Georg Elser (1903–45)

Hitler is supposed to have withstood more than twenty assassination attempts. Is this good security or conversely a sign of a lack of conviction? It is of course fair to say that history is littered with the bodies of assassins who then met a bloody end for their troubles.

So, during the period under our review it must be said that solo attempt notwithstanding, it was very unlikely that Hitler would have been eliminated from within. Moreover, even if he were, would his absence have led to a change in policy/strategy sufficient for the peacemakers in Britain? We would think this very unlikely. Hess certainly would have been aware of this too, but he must surely have wondered if it was the case that Britain would not entreat with a Hitlerian government if there was really no other viable option? Beggars perhaps sometimes cannot be choosers.

Adding to the complications was the fact that others in the Nazi hierarchy were having the same thoughts. Hess had been told that Britain would not entreat with a Hitler-led Germany. Consequently, Heinrich Himmler had also started to enquire if Britain might entreat with a Himmler-led Germany?

Paul Stauffer in *Sechs furchtbare Jahre*[11] (six wasted years) records that in March, or early April 1941, Carl Burckhardt of the International Red Cross was approached by a 'Vertrauensmann von Himmler', a confidant of Himmler, asking specifically if Britain would make peace with a Himmler-led Germany?

Given his later behaviour in April 1945, one can only presume that Himmler would have gone further, selfishly, and certainly in his best interests, had a positive response been forthcoming. The 'confidant' was possibly Carl Langbehn, a lawyer working predominantly at the time for the Krupp and Messerschmitt corporations in the Ruhr, Augsburg and Regensburg.

Tragically for Langbehn,[12] he had met Himmler through being parents at the same school in Bavaria. Fate decreed that Heinrich was at home at one of his daughter's birthdays parties when the two men met. The Allen Dulles papers, expertly edited by David Irving, describe how Langbehn used this connection to help his former Jewish tutor at Göttingen University.

Langbehn seemed to almost revel in the danger this liaison placed him in. He believed that the way to overthrow the regime was from within through fermenting internal strife. This aim also ran in accord with what he was being told from external sources; any coup had to be seen from coming within Germany. The German people would not carry or sustain a coup attempt that had clear foreign involvement.

Albrecht Haushofer knew Langbehn well through the fledgling resistance participators and it fair to compare the Langbehn/Himmler initiative with the Hess/Haushofer initiative. Both parties were hoping for the same result, though the means to be employed was certainly different. However, ultimately Langbehn was to push his luck too far. There is absolutely no doubt that Himmler was interested in a Western peace. In 1943 it was becoming obvious that Germany could no longer win the war and so the strategy evolved to the best compromise. Langbehn travelled to Switzerland to meet Allan Dulles and was arrested in late September, after his return. Himmler was therefore placed in the position of having not to be seen to be party to such treachery, whilst previously covertly supporting his man. His logical but brutal solution was simply to imprison Langbehn, torture and kill him, though of course, first cutting off his genitals. Obviously, dead and castrated men cannot incriminate.

This horrible story relates to 1943-44. In the spring of 1941, Germany had yet to invade Russia, though the spectre of such an act was again seemingly awakening the need to do something. Ulrich von Hassell, the former German Ambassador to Italy, and in spring 1941 a member of the resistance, summarises the position both well and accurately,[13]

> This insanity (Barbarossa) is being defended on two grounds:
> 1. The necessity to occupy the Ukraine
> 2. The need to defeat the potential allies' of our enemies as a precaution.
>
> The real results will be:
> 1. The cutting off of imports from Russia, since it will be a long time before the Ukraine becomes useful.
> 2. A new and unprecedented strain on war material and energies.
> 3. A complete encirclement deliberately arranged.

The Germans were also mindful of the growing influence of the United States, and again later in 1941 the same themes re-emerge in a memorandum to President Roosevelt, from William J.Donovan, his then emissary to Britain.[14]

> The Germans were being told by the Americans that:
> 1. It would not be enough for Hitler and Göring to 'disappear or resign'.
> 2. A treaty with a post-coup Germany led by the army would be possible.

3. A constitutional monarchy on the English model would be a suitable replacement.

Therefore, in the spring of 1941 a lot of people recognised and understood the 'elephants in the room' and were openly discussing them and alternatives to them, most notably with Carl Burckhardt of the International Red Cross in Geneva. It is little wonder that he was starting to think that he could hold the power to broker a peace.

Unfortunately, for those still wishing for peace on both sides of the Channel, the 'opposition' had at no time come up with a viable plan to remove either Churchill or Hitler. Haushofer had told Hess of the distrust of Hitler by the British in the September 1940 correspondence (if he was in any doubt) and there is a line of thought that might suggest that in flying and ascertaining the actual position with regards to a Western peace, Hess was in part safeguarding his master. If a peace was delivered, Hitler's position would be safe; if a peace was denied, Hitler's continued presence was no longer a pre-condition and so, once again, he would be safe, at least for the time being.

Either way, the twin elephants were still firmly in the room.

---

[1] Anthony Eden, *The Reckoning*, Cassell, London, 1965, p. 182.

[2] Michael S. Goodman, *The Official History of the Joint Intelligence Committee*, Routledge, Abingdon, 2014.

[3] Churchill had debated the use of the phrase 'you can take one with you' in the event of an invasion, in particular in connection with the use of sticky grenades.

[4] However, even this statistic is misleading. Churchill enjoyed an 83% approval rating eight weeks before losing the 1945 election. (*The Guardian*, 19 April 2010).

[5] Andrew Roberts, *Eminent Churchillians*, Phoenix, London, 1994.

[6] Ibid.

[7] Jonathan Pile, *Churchill's Secret Enemy*, Create Space, Sheffield, 2012.

[8] James Douglas-Hamilton, *Motive for a Mission: The Story Behind Hess's Flight to Britain*, Macmillan, London, 1971.

[9] A diary entry following the 1938 Royal visit to France.

[10] Peter Hoffman, *The History of the German Resistance 1933–1945,* MIT Press, Cambridge, USA, 1977.

[11] Paul Stauffer, *Sechs furchtbare Jahre*, Neue Zürcher Zeitung, Zurich, 1998.

[12] Langbehn was executed in Berlin following the 1944 uprising. He had been arrested in 1943 following a mission to talk peace with the Americans. See Princeton University, Seely Mudd library, box 37, file 1.

[13] 2 March 1941.

[14] Roosevelt Library, Hyde Park, New York.

CHAPTER 11
TANCRED BORENIUS

The previous chapters have described the receipt of the Haushofer letter by the British Secret Services in late 1940 and the intelligence available to the key decision-makers at the time. We now move on to describe how the letters were countered in January 1941 by the utilisation of a most unconventional agent. James Bond he certainly was not …

Introduction

Since completing the ground-breaking *Rudolf Hess: The British Illusion of Peace*[1] in 2010, we have continued our research in respect of Tancred Borenius, who we now believe to have played the fundamental role in the Hess affair. Taking our initial findings as a base point, we now provide important additional evidence, some of which we find quite shocking. In 2017 we were delighted to be invited to a reception at the Finnish Embassy in London and address the convention celebrating the unveiling of the 'blue plaque' marking Borenius's London residence at nearby 28 Kensington Gate.

We first came across Borenius through the diaries of Ulrich von Hassell,[2] which were published in carefully edited form as early as 1948.[3] This was to demonstrate to the recently victorious peoples of the Western Alliance that not all Germans were pro-Nazi and pro-Hitler. The diaries were seen as being part of the post-war healing process; a process made more relevant given the alternative threat then starting to emanate from beyond the Iron Curtain. Upon reading the diaries, it is quite clear that many within Nazi Germany saw disaster as an inevitability, in some cases as early as 1937–8.

His January 1941 entry records that Carl Burckhardt had 'looked me up in Geneva' (on the 30th) to tell him that 'very recently' a Tancred Borenius had come to him to explain, 'apparently on behalf of English officials, that a reasonable peace could still be concluded'. The use of the word 'apparently' we find intriguing. In this context it surely means 'giving the appearance of … but'. Surely Borenius was either 'on behalf of English officials' or not. The very use of the word, we believe, means that the author had doubts as to its true application, presumably at the time the diaries were written. It also begs the obvious question, 'Who precisely were the English Officials?'[4]

We now believe that this visit was the real catalyst for the Hess flight, not the earlier 'Roberts's letter', as the Germans would surely have anticipated that any 'ghosted reply' back to Lisbon would have been caught by the censor. Haushofer had also recorded the fact that no reply had been received by early November 1940 (though that too seems all rather convenient).[5]

That realisation may perhaps explain the messing about by the security services upon receipt of the letter. Moreover, a direct approach was both necessary and vital. It was really the only way that a non-governmental peace approach could be securely and viably communicated in time of war. We also believe that the Borenius trip certainly followed on from the receipt of the Haushofer letter by the censor but, again, logically that letter should never have reached its target, so any response as a result should have raised immense suspicion within the Hess circle (*unless of course those within the circle were also part of the illusion*). In plain words, does the non-reply to the Haushofer letter indicate that Haushofer knew full well the outcome of the letter before it was sent? Hence the over-detailed recording of the delivery process.

What is also of particular note is that the 1948 edition of the von Hassell diaries describe Tancred Borenius thus: 'He has very intimate connections with----------------' (deliberately left blank)

However, the 2011 edition is much more forthcoming by disclosing: 'He has very intimate connections with the Royal House (principally the Queen).'

This raises the question as to who Tancred Borenius was appearing to represent? Was he even appearing to be an emissary of the British Royal family in the early stages of a world war? Was he just a part-time Finnish diplomat coming out of retirement?

Why (and how) should a Finnish art historian become involved in the Hess affair? Just how many 'hats' was he in fact wearing?

Given the importance and relevance of these questions, we were absolutely hooked and had to learn more about the Finnish art historian/diplomat/potential representative of the British royal family. This area of research has been amongst some of the most interesting and rewarding.

The usual curriculum vitae

In due course we hope to be able to answer all the above issues and questions, but we will initially present his usual curriculum vitae, which is impressive. This first appeared in our 2010 *Rudolf Hess: The British Illusion of Peace.*

> Carl Tancred Borenius was born in Wiborg, in what was then Eastern Finland, in 1885. [Authors – this is part of the Carelian isthmus]
> Date born: 1885
> Place born: Viipuri [a.k.a. Wiborg], Finland, modern Vyborg, Russia.
> Date died: 1948
> Place died: Coombe Bissett (near Salisbury), Wiltshire, United Kingdom.
> [Authors – This came from his official biography; the truth is however considerably more shocking].
>
> Italian Renaissance scholar, dealer and art magazine editor. Borenius was the son of Carl Borenius, a member of the Finnish Diet. Borenius was educated at the Swedish Lyceum before Helsinki University (Helsingfors), then Berlin and Rome. In Helsinki, he studied under Johan Jakob Tikkanen. After receiving his PhD in Helsingfors in 1909, he moved to London where he published a version of his dissertation, *Painters of Vincenza* (1909). The same year he married Anne-Marie Rüneberg, granddaughter of the Finnish poet J.L. Rüneberg. Roger Fry became a close friend, providing him entré into the art circles of London. An updated 1912 edition of *The History of Painting in North Italy* by Joseph Archer Crowe and Giovanni Battista Cavalcaselle bore notes by Borenius. In 1914 he was appointed lecturer at University

THE
BURLINGTON
MAGAZINE
for Connoisseurs
Illustrated & Published Monthly

APRIL, 1941

RE-DISTRIBUTING THE ART OF THE PAST

THE PAINTED HALL IN HEIDEGGER'S HOUSE AT RICHMOND—I.
BY EDWARD CROFT MURRAY

GENEALOGICAL WINDOWS AT CANTERBURY CATHEDRAL—II.
BY L. C. EVETTS

ON THE ARTISTIC EDUCATION OF BOTTICELLI
BY JACQUES MESNIL

SHORTER NOTICES ON AN UNPUBLISHED PICTURE BY COROT (THOMAS BODKIN): THE HALO: A FURTHER ENQUIRY INTO ITS ORIGIN (E. H. RAMSDEN); A SWISS EXHIBITION OF ASIATIC ART; ENGLISH WATER-COLOURS AND PENCIL DRAWINGS (A. P. OPPE) AND VICISSITUDES OF TWO FAMOUS PICTURES

REVIEWS BY R. WITTKOWER, HERBERT READ, A. F. KENDRICK AND OTHERS

OBITUARIES CORRESPONDENCE FORTHCOMING SALES

The April 1941 'Burlington Magazine'

College, London, in the position vacated by Fry. When Finland achieved independence, he acted as secretary of the diplomatic mission (1918) and later as representative of Finland in London (1919). From 1922–47 he was Durning-Lawrence Professor at the College. It was during this period that he published his major books. Although initially an historian of Italian art, Borenius also became an expert of the art of his adopted country. His methodology employed significant connoisseurship. He helped found the *Apollo* magazine in 1925, to which he often contributed. Borenius' opinion on art was highly valued in England; he was advisor to the Earl of Harewood's art collection and, in 1924, Sotheby's auction house. Together with E.W. Tristram he published *English Medieval Painting* in 1929. In 1932 he became active in archaeology by launching the dig at Clarendon Palace (Salisbury). Borenius played an influential role in two scholarly art journals. After admission to the Burlington Fine Arts Club, he contributed many articles to the *Burlington Magazine*, acting as its editor between 1940–45. By then Borenius was no longer considered reliable on attributions at Sotheby's (and considered himself too grand to do the work of cataloguing) and was replaced in 1945 by Hans Gronau. Among his book editing duties, in addition to the *History of Painting in Italy*, he assisted with the volume *On Art and Connoisseurship* (1942) by Walter Friedlaender. He died after a long illness. His students included Enriqueta Harris [Frankfort].

This is very much the 'official obituary/curriculum vitae'. It is only when one delves beneath the above that Tancred really comes alive. It appears to these authors that he was a brilliant man whose story has remained uniquely hidden for the past 70+ years.

We are not prone to exaggeration, we hope, but it is not overstating his role in the affair to say that without it, the 1941 invasion of Britain would have been certainly the more likely. Perhaps not an inevitability, but certainly the more likely. If nothing else, it is to be hoped that by continuing our research, we should be able to at least recognise and understand the role that this unique individual played.

Beyond the CV

In early 1941, Borenius was, in communication terms, (and highlighting a theme throughout this book) non-British governmental. Whilst he lived in Britain and had done so for some while, he was relying on direct contact and as such was also out of direct control, (MI6 or Finnish) or at least the illusion of such direct governmental control. Once abroad, he could not be censored and because of his Finnish passport could presumably travel a little more easily than some through then occupied Europe. He could at least in principle say what he wanted to say. He was the ideal and almost in a unique position to be the messenger to the 'neutral intermediary' (Burckhardt) that Hess was suggesting in his letter to the Haushofers in September 1940. We simply had to find out more about Borenius and go 'beyond' the standard biography.

We were and continue to be very lucky in this area of research.

Whilst researching his 1999 book, John Harris had trawled through the Salisbury area (where Borenius had died) telephone book and had spoken to Borenius's son, Lars Ulrich, known as Peter.[6] Lars was then a distinguished, retired lawyer.

His father's wartime trip had caused some (post-event) amusement in the

Borenius household on two accounts: first, that he had been asked to deliver a 'book' to Switzerland, disguised as a novel, and secondly, that he had been given a poison pill the size of a golf ball. After Switzerland, Harris was told that he had been intending to travel to Italy but was refused entry.

The family had thought it amusing and ironic that Borenius would most likely choke on the oversize pill way before the supposed poison would take its effect, should the need for its use ever be necessary.

Lars also told Harris that he had been given the book by a 'Claude Dansey', prior to his departure. Upon its delivery there was much relief.

We must confess to not really grasping the significance of the last statement as at the time (2008–09) we were in the process of getting too carried away with the Mrs Roberts/SO1/Battaglia line of thought.

Had we been perhaps a little more alert and knowledgeable, we would of course have soon realised that Claude Dansey was the then Deputy Head of MI6, which, as we have seen, was in the process of rebuilding credibility following the loss of it 'passport office' system of intelligence at the outbreak of the Second World War.[7] There was naturally a severe difficulty in communicating with Switzerland securely. Indeed, Keith Jeffery, in the official history of MI6 states: 'Cypher telegrams could still be sent, but SIS had one-time pads for this, which as Switzerland became more isolated, came to be in very short supply, as getting material into the country was as difficult as getting it out.'[8]

We can only therefore presume that the Borenius 'book' was actually a MI6 'one time pad', the then preferred method of cryptology. There was no given or pre-set code, each one was 'one time' only, hence the name. In other words, Borenius, apart from his other duties, authorised or not, was giving MI6 the means of ongoing secure communication with the Swiss station.

A decade later, after finding the original notes, we spoke to Tancred's granddaughter, Aurelia, concerning her grandfather. She too was very kind and added further to our knowledge of her intriguing ancestor.

The usual CV reproduced above certainly does not do justice to Tancred Borenius. His granddaughter made the point that he was extremely well-connected, a brilliant raconteur, but endearingly wholly impracticable; he could not drive, for instance. Osbert Lancaster, in a *Daily Mail* cartoon, characteristically portrayed him as a rather plump eccentric. It also appears to us that, above all, he thoroughly enjoyed mixing with, cultivating and advising the upper classes and beyond. The usual CV makes the point that he became art advisor to the Harewood Family, (Viscount Lascelles, 6th Earl of Harewood had of course married Princess Mary, the only sister to Princes David, Albert, Henry, John and George in 1922), but this certainly does not appear to be his only commission to the rich and famous of 1930s England. We also now have the intriguing connection to the Queen, via the von Hassell diary.

Queen Mary and Tancred Borenius at the opera May 1939

When writing the chapter on Borenius for Rudolf Hess: *A New Technical Analysis of the Hess Flight, May 1941,*[9] we had made a mistake which we now freely admit. At the time, we were feeling very smug in noticing the amendment to the von Hassell diaries as between the 1948 and 2011 versions, and assumed that the reference to the Queen was in respect of Queen Elizabeth, later becoming in 1953, the Queen Mother.

We were quite willing to believe this identification, as the former Elizabeth Bowes-Lyon had indeed already demonstrated her early dislike of Winston Churchill, particularly following the 1936 abdication. As such, the story or theory (real or imagined) of a possible royal coup, led by the King and Queen, aided and abetted by Borenius as messenger, would possibly seem quite credible, if told convincingly. Particularly as the interests of Britain, Finland and Germany were possibly all moving into alignment.

We have also recently learned that Borenius enjoyed a prominent position in the funeral cortège of George V in 1935.

However, as the standard CV amply demonstrates, Borenius was a prolific networker and his work had produced results in his working rapidly upwards through the then British social strata. He acted for the Methuen Family[10] of Corsham Court in north Wiltshire, and the National Portrait Gallery holds photographs of Borenius with Philip and Ottoline Morrell,[11] prominent members of the 'Bloomsbury Set'. He catalogued the porcelain collection of Frederick Leverton Harris[12] and occasionally acted as a dealer, buying and selling works of art for the rich and formerly rich. On 8 December 1927, *The Times* noted that Borenius had acquired a picture for £350. As his success grew, he was also gaining enemies. For instance, Kenneth Clark and Borenius often disagreed, as the two men were professional rivals, often vying for the same roles and responsibilities.

We have already seen how Borenius advised Viscount Lascelles, though it is perhaps fair to say that as the 1930s reached their climax, the 'quality' of Borenius's appointments book had also dramatically increased.

Borenius had long been cultivating royal connections; in 1922 he sent the Duke and Duchess of York a copy of his latest book, *Travels in Italy*, as a wedding present.

In 1936, Prince George, the Duke of Kent and Princess Marina visited Wiltshire, stopping at Wilton House over the weekend of 11/12 July. On the Saturday it was recorded that the couple met Tancred Borenius in Salisbury Close. At the time, Tancred oversaw an archaeological excavation of Clarendon Place, the former royal hunting lodge.

A fortnight later, he was presented to the King, this time in a diplomatic capacity. Aurelia Borenius told John Harris that as he got older, he not unnaturally rediscovered his political energy, largely on account of what was happening in Eastern Europe. (In 1939 Borenius's sister had to flee the family home in Wiborg to escape the invading Russians during the Winter War.)

In February 1937, he attended a reception at Hyde Park Hotel to commemorate the centenary of Alexander Pushkin's death. Samuel Hoare was in the Chair.

On 7 December 1937, the Duke of Kent was the principal guest at the Anglo-Finnish Society. Tancred replied to the Duke's toast. In 1940, he was recorded as a member of the Executive Committee. Later, after the Hess flight, on 23 September 1941 he addressed the Royal Institute for International Affairs at Chatham House on the subject of 'The Eastern Frontier of Finland and the East Carelian Situation'.[13] It will be remembered that Albrecht Haushofer had also addressed the same institute in 1937 and that Carelia was Tancred's home region. In May 1939, he attended a reception at the Swedish legation. Baron Knut Bonde was also recorded as an attendee.

A year later we suspect Tancred briefly returned to the art world. On 19 May 1940, nine days after the German invasion of the Low Countries, there was a major art sale in London. The Duke of Kent bought 'The Altieri Claudes', two classical Italian paintings painted by Claude Lorraine in the late 17 century. The Duke paid £3,990 and £840, respectively, for the two paintings that had been previously sold for £6,090 and £1,785 in 1884. We suspect the proximity of the German Wehrmacht to London may have had an inevitably depressing effect on the 1940 prices.[14]

We do not know for sure that Borenius was involved in the purchase, but given that the two men were well acquainted by this time and the pictures were full square in Borenius's sphere of expertise, it is certainly not inconceivable that he was in some way involved. (In 1947, when the Duke's executors sold the pictures, a healthy profit was achieved.)

However, to retrace our steps, our further research now points to the identity of 'The Queen' not being Queen Elizabeth, but her mother-in-law, Queen Mary, whose husband King George V had died in January 1936, thus sparking the abdication crisis later that year.

A perusal of local Yorkshire newspapers would indicate that in the middle years of the 1930s Queen Mary would typically travel to Yorkshire in the late summer to visit and stay with her daughter, Princess Mary, who lived with her husband Viscount Lascelles at Goldsborough Hall, near Knaresborough. When the 5th Earl Harewood had died in 1929, the couple then very slowly decamped to the ancestral home at Harewood House, further down the A1.

Typically, whilst on holiday, the Queen would then make scavenging forays in and around the area for antiques, usually accompanied by her daughter, and of obvious relevant interest to our story, Tancred Borenius.[15]

There is also a record in 1939 of Borenius travelling 'on a diplomatic passport and measures being taken to guard his luggage' on account of his taking the King's collection of Leonardo da Vinci sketches to an exhibition in Milan. In 1939 these were valued at some £50,000.[16]

In May 1939 Borenius is recorded as accompanying Queen Mary to the Royal Opera and joining with her in the royal box.[17]

Consequently, we would now be confident that if anyone, in 1941, Borenius would be representing the Queen Mary, whose somewhat strident views were well known. She had previously opined that Britain had 'backed the wrong horse' in the First World War.

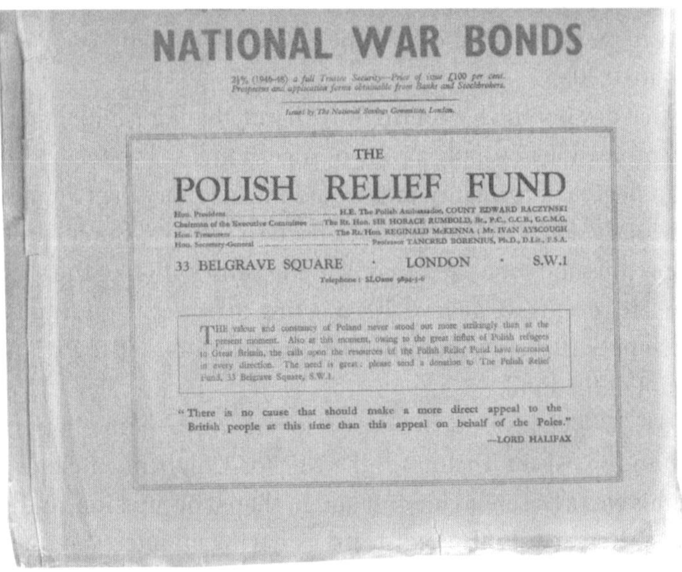

NATIONAL WAR BONDS

2½% (1946–48) a full Trustee Security—Price of issue £100 per cent.
Prospectus and application forms obtainable from Banks and Stockbrokers.

Issued by The National Savings Committee, London.

THE

POLISH RELIEF FUND

Hon. President .... H.E. The Polish Ambassador, COUNT EDWARD RACZYNSKI
Chairman of the Executive Committee .... The Rt. Hon. SIR HORACE RUMBOLD, Bt., P.C., G.C.B., G.C.M.G.
Hon. Treasurers .... The Rt. Hon. REGINALD McKENNA ; Mr. IVAN AYSCOUGH
Hon. Secretary-General .... Professor TANCRED BORENIUS, Ph.D., D.Litt., F.S.A.

33 BELGRAVE SQUARE · LONDON · S.W.1

Telephone: SLOane 9894-5-6

THE valour and constancy of Poland never stood out more strikingly than at the present moment. Also at this moment, owing to the great influx of Polish refugees to Great Britain, the calls upon the resources of the Polish Relief Fund have increased in every direction. The need is great: please send a donation to The Polish Relief Fund, 33 Belgrave Square, S.W.1.

"There is no cause that should make a more direct appeal to the British people at this time than this appeal on behalf of the Poles."
—LORD HALIFAX

Inside page of the April 1941 'Burlington Magazine'

The Polish Relief Fund

Tancred Borenius's sister had married into a Polish family, and given his dislike of all things Russian, at the outbreak of the Second World War, he became the willing Hon. Secretary General to the Polish Relief Fund. The headquarters were in London and on 1 May 1940 the British College of Nursing magazine recorded Tancred Borenius bidding farewell to a group of Canadian Poles embarking on a foreign mission.

This organisation was clearly substantial. The British government had contributed £100,000 in clothing and other forms of relief. It was through this organisation that Borenius came to meet and know General Sikorski. It must also say something about Borenius that the Hon. Secretary General of the Polish Relief Fund was a Finn rather than a Pole.

Since 2010 we have also researched the Polish Relief Fund and discovered that the organisation met weekly in the early stages of the war at 33 Belgrave Square, London. The records are currently maintained at the London Metropolitan Archives, under reference A/FWA/C/G/08/002.

We have recently ascertained from the University of Basel, Switzerland, that Borenius as secretary to the fund arranged to meet Carl Burckhardt, then a senior member of the International Red Cross during Burckhardt's October 1939 visit to London.

The two men met at the St James's Club, Piccadilly on Wednesday 4 October at 10.30am.

Later that day Borenius wrote to Burckhardt, thanking him for meeting and typically promising to supply a copy of Algernon Cecil's book on Metternich. There is a degree of formality that would indicate that the two men had not met previously. On 11 October, once back in Geneva, Burckhardt wrote to thank Borenius and requested a copy of the constitution of the society

Given later events we believe this meeting to be very significant.

In December 1939, two months later, Borenius travelled to Paris, seemingly on account of the fund.[18,19]

In 1941, 33 Belgrave Square was also the 'town' home/house of Victor Cazalet (and his sister Thelma),[20] the MP for Chippenham since 1924. We suspect this was a leasehold interest and in shared occupation, as the Institute for Psychic Research is also registered as having an interest at the property. Like Borenius, Cazalet was also extremely well-connected and in 1940 had become the liaison officer to General Władysław Sikorski, the Polish Prime Minister and Commander in Chief.

Cazalet had acquired the house in 1936 from a Mr Maurice Ruffer, a banker, who had recently died in Brighton.

The minute book of the Polish Relief Fund is also extremely well maintained and records:

27.11.1940: a film show was held at the Dorchester (Cazalet was a Director). Lady Diana Cooper was hostess.

15.1.1941: 'The Hon. Secretary [Borenius] reported that he would be absent abroad on Finnish government business for the next 3-4 weeks. He asked therefore to be excused from attendance at meetings.'

29.1.1941: Borenius absent

19.2.1941: Borenius absent

26.2.1941: Borenius absent

12.3.1941: Borenius present. 'The Hon. Secretary General had just returned to Great Britain after an absence abroad on Finnish Government business. He reported on the work of the Red Cross at

Geneva for Polish prisoners and on the condition of Polish internees, especially in Switzerland and the Pyrenees.'

Thereafter he was an ever present, until 11 June meeting where he was again recorded as absent. So, there is yet more proof of the Borenius Geneva meeting. We now have three independent sources: the Polish Relief Fund minute book, the von Hassell diaries and the personal family recollection. It would also now appear to be the case that Borenius was in London throughout May 1941.

However, he was out of the country for at least fifty days.

Finnish Government Business?

We should also record that the rationale Borenius used to his fellow committee members was not that he was embarking on an MI6 mission, but that he was travelling on Finnish Government Business.

Whilst we doubt this explanation, as Finland had of course its own Foreign Office and government departments, it is plausible in that Borenius had certainly kept his links with his home country. The two explanations are not exclusive. He was described by the Finns as 'our man in England' and in 1940 had even found the time to write a biography of Field Marshal Gustaf Mannerheim, the wartime leader of the country. The biography lists a few occasions where the two men had met. He also had the very vested interest in the country, in that much of his family still resided there, albeit worryingly in the Carelian isthmus, the nearest part of Finland to Leningrad and the Russian border.[21]

There may also be another connection. The 1935 *Who's Who* records that following the First World War, Borenius was 'Secretary to the Diplomatic Mission notifying the independence of Finland to Great Britain, France, Belgium, Spain, Italy and the Holy See'. He was also the 'Temporary Diplomatic Representative of Finland in England 1919'. What this meant in practice is hard to discern, but presumably on account of his work in this area he had been awarded honours in the following orders:

- Knight Commander of the Order of St Gregory the Great (a Catholic order)
- Commander of the Order of the White Rose of Finland
- Knight of the Order of the Fleur de Lis
- The Legion of Honour and Order of Saints Mauritius and Lazarus

He was certainly well decorated for his actions in the aftermath of the First World War, whatever they may have been.

So, what had made Borenius agree to travel to Geneva? Simplistically, we believe that in part the answer was probably financial. Keith Jeffery, in the history of MI6, records that couriers were operating based on 'Two journeys and retire for life'.[22]

From what scant evidence there is, Borenius would appear always to be very conscious of money. Perhaps that is why he came to England in 1909? However, one of the more bizarre roles he played was as guardian to Dolly Wilde (1895–1941), Oscar Wilde's wayward niece who seemed pretty set on conducting her life in such a way to ensure that she followed her uncle's early demise. Joan Schenkar, Dolly's biographer, has been very kind to us in sharing her papers on Borenius, whom she describes as 'adroit as a seal and just as slippery'.

Tancred was thus described by Viva King: 'Borenius was a tall, fat Finn, who had brought his family to live in England. His face was brown and his eyes round and black, which gave him a seal like appearance. As adroit as a seal, he had to juggle with the precarious business of picture dealing and needed all his wits and charm to counterbalance a reputation for sharp practice – something which many successful dealers have to contend with. He was criticised for the collection of pictures he bought for Lord Harewood. "So that is the man who robbed my cousin Harry," exclaimed Helen Maclagan (née Lascelles) when I mentioned him.'

In correspondence passing between Joan Schenkar and John Harris in 2014, Schenkar does question who was subsidising who? Was Dolly Wilde being subsidised by Tancred, or was it the other way around on account of the £2000 estate that Tancred was administering on behalf of Dolly's late mother? Schenkar wisely does not express an opinion, but it is something of a truism that in times of war, fine art and its dealings are not perhaps the most lucrative of occupations.[23]

However, the vital question here is 'who approached who'? Did Tancred really decide to travel to Geneva on Finnish business and then was 'hijacked' by MI6 to take their code book, or was Tancred first approached by a group of 'British Officials' to travel to Geneva and then MI6 used him to convey the code book?

In short, did the MI6 briefing cover both aspects of the mission, or was Borenius essentially 'off-piste' when talking of potential British peace moves?

Was he being used because he knew the 'British Officials' and therefore was seen as a convincing stooge, or was it the case that he *had been approached by the British Officials to talk peace*? This question appears to be key to the whole affair and indeed appears to be unclear in the mind of Burckhardt. Who precisely was he dealing with?

Jacobite revolution?

In perhaps one of the more unusual directions that our research has taken us, it is perhaps now relevant to discuss the loss of the English throne by James II in 1685 and the subsequent exile of the Stuart dynasty. (!)

When researching the life of Tancred Borenius, we came across a copy of *The Jacobite* magazine, dated 10 June 1931. This was printed and distributed in New Zealand. We were not a little surprised to discover that on 29 January 1931, at a meeting of The Order of the White Rose, held at the Old Cock Tavern, Fleet Street, London, Tancred Borenius was present as Treasurer of the Society.

Given that we suspected that Hess was being told of a coup d'état on his arrival, these facts were simply irresistible, but again, most probably irrelevant. Borenius, who we later discovered to have been described as 'the principal Legitimist' in 1940, was seemingly involved in an organisation whose main objectives presumably were the restoration of the Stuart family to the throne of England. Notably, there also appeared to be significant links to the Polish and Swedish thrones.

John Harris duly wrote to one of the leading authorities (bizarrely, no permission was granted to give an attribution), as to whether any archives exist/existed as to the Order of the White Rose and the following reply came back:

> For reasons which will become apparent below, it is most unlikely that the Royal Stuart Society has ever held any records or archives of the Order of the White Rose. I, at least, am unaware of any.
>
> The 1886 Cycle of the Order of the White Rose was founded in 1886 by a group of active and distinguished Legitimists. It was responsible for organising the important Jacobite Exhibition in 1889. It always had a strong artistic and intellectual component: one of its earlier members was James MacNeill Whistler. Like so many other Legitimist organisations it came to an end in 1914. It became impossible to voice support for the Jacobite "Duke of Cornwall" who was none other than

Crown Prince Rupprecht of Bavaria, Field Marshal in an army which was at war with this country.

Tancred Borenius was a man of great stature in his time. There is a good article on him in the *Dictionary of National Biography.* A Swedish Finn, he came to England in 1906 and put the history of art on the British academic map. He represented Finland diplomatically in London in 1919 when Finland was seeking international recognition. He was Sotheby's adviser on old master prints from 1923 until 1945. At the beginning of the Second World War, he took the lead in appealing for aid for the populations of Finland and Poland. The Times Digital Archive indicates a very wide range of activities, including accompanying Queen Mary on her annual antiquarian expeditions around Yorkshire. He wrote a very sympathetic obituary of Don Alfonso Carlos de Bourbon for The Times (30 September 1936).

Tancred Borenius was appointed one of the three Vice-Presidents of the Royal Stuart Society on 10 June 1926, after its foundation. Unfortunately, only three years later there occurred the first split in the Society after the then Governor-General, Captain Wheatly-Crowe,[24] had made certain unilateral changes to the Society's Constitution. Some of the Society's leading members, including Borenius, left in protest and founded a reconstituted version of the Order of the White Rose (the 1929 Cycle). Borenius was Treasurer. It lasted until 1940. It held at least one of its dinners (29 January 1931) at the Old Cock Tavern, Fleet Street. It was a Legitimist, Monarchist, pro-Stuart organisation. I suppose that having arrived in London in 1906, Borenius could have become a member of the 1886 Cycle, but I have never seen his name mentioned in that connection.

Borenius was awarded the Order of the White Rose of Finland in 1930 in recognition of his services to that state. That, of course, is not to be confused with the Order in which Mr Harris is interested.

We carried on with our research. Apparently, the Stuart crown passed down the generations and the 'legitimate' claimant to the throne of the United Kingdom in 1940/41 was Prince Rupert, (Rupprecht) Duke of Bavaria. He lived in the various Wittelsbach residences, in and around Munich. He was decidedly anti-Nazi and had also written to Captain Wheatly-Crowe refuting any claims made in his name.

So, we hope the reader can understand our surprise at this turn of events.

However, is it relevant to the debate? Initially we thought probably not, but it does clearly demonstrate a keen sense of the constitutional history of Britain that we now believe to be central to the Hess affair.

We should therefore perhaps record at this juncture that in 2021, whilst the Hanoverian succession places HRH Prince Charles as the Duke of Cornwall, under the Jacobite interpretation the Duke of Cornwall in 1941 was a German living in Munich. Tancred would have known this.

International Art Historians

It is of course quite possible that Tancred was notionally also working for the Finnish government, both alongside and with Claude Dansey of MI6. As already detailed, we now know that Borenius had met Burckhardt in London in October 1939 and as such were already acquainted. We have also seen reference to the fact that Burckhardt knew Karl Haushofer, but to date have been unable to prove for sure.

The 'godfather' of European art history had been Jacob Burckhardt (1818–97), a forebear of Carl Jacob Burckhardt. His principal student was Heinrich Wölfflin (1864–1945). When Jacob Burckhardt died in 1897, Wölfflin took over the Professorship of Art at Basel University. In the first two decades of the twentieth century, he also taught at the Universities of Berlin and Munich, at the same time as the Haushofer family members were also in attendance.

Carl Burckhardt, Tancred's host, was obviously directly related to Jacob Burckhardt and their Swiss dynasty and was, in turn, taught by Wölfflin.

In just the same way as Tancred had been 'taken in' and made welcome by Roger Fry, once Tancred had become established, he too returned the compliment to various European art historians looking for a new life, or more typically those escaping Nazi Germany. Most notably, Nikolaus Pevsner, when applying to the Academic Assistance Council in England in 1933, had obtained a glowing reference from Tancred Borenius. Pevsner was a former student of the University of Göttingen and would later arrange for Borenius to lecture (in an academic gown) at his former alma mater.[25]

Similarly, the letters of Bronislaw Malinowski and Elsie Masson[26] again exemplify the hospitable nature of the Borenius family: 'He stayed in the Borenius's empty flat in Knightsbridge… He came to the Borenius's flat afterwards…'[27]

Joan Schenkar, at one of their meetings, made the point to John Harris that Tancred, above all else, was fun. Intelligent, a prolific linguist, but fun.

That must surely explain the vast number of connections and friendships that have been put on record and quite possibly a large number that have not. We should also record the fact that two of MI6 most infamous agents, Anthony Blunt and Tomás Harris were also art historians and dealers in their 'day jobs'. Both were known to Borenius. The astute reader will no doubt have spotted that the 'official' CV mentions Enriqueta Harris. This was Tomás Harris's sister, who in turn also became a famous art historian.

So, we trust the above now explains why Tancred Borenius, the brilliantly well-connected art historian volunteered to take a 'one time' message code book to Geneva. Claude Dansey was formerly based in Switzerland and had only returned to Britain after the outbreak of the war. We also need to consider the route employed.

Travel arrangements and MI6

Switzerland is obviously landlocked and after the fall of France and the Low Countries in May 1940, could only be reached from the UK via Vichy France, Spain, Portugal and then a precarious air trip to Britain. The famous film star Leslie Howard was killed when his DC3 from Lisbon to Whitchurch, near Bristol was shot down by a Junkers 88 over the Bay of Biscay in 1943.

This was precisely the route that the British Red Cross used to pass messages to its HQ in Geneva for onward transmission to the various POW camps. The records of the British Red Cross reveal that from July to December 1940, 610,643 parcels were collected and 566,777 were shipped to Geneva for distribution. The process was not without problems and in May 1941 two ships were detained in Marseilles harbour,[28] with permission to unload denied. Mr Stanley Adams was seconded from Messrs. Thomas Cook to alleviate the bottleneck.

So, from the records of the Polish Relief Fund we know that Tancred Borenius was absent from 16 January 1941 to 11 March 1941 at the very longest. A period of fifty-four days.

From the diaries of Kay Foley, wife of Frank, the MI6 Passport Officer in pre-war Berlin, we now know that Frank Foley flew to Lisbon on 17 January 1941, a Friday. This is certainly within the possible leave of absence that Borenius had forewarned the Polish Relief Fund. It would appear to us that the most likely explanation was simply that Foley was accompanying Borenius on the first stage of the journey. Commentators have suggested that he was checking on the possibility of reacting to the Haushofer wish for a meeting. We believe the truth to be much more mundane; he was just ensuring Borenius got to Geneva. Foley eventually returned to Britain on 31 January 1941, a fortnight later, presumably happy that by that time Borenius had at least got to Geneva. (We know that Burckhardt had met with Borenius around this time.)

We have tried to research further into the wartime BOAC/KLM service from Whitchurch to Sintra (Lisbon), but without too much success. There are apparently no passenger lists and the guest books at the Grand Hotel, Bristol, which acted as an unofficial waiting room, are again long gone. We have belatedly discovered that Ian Fleming had also been in Lisbon and Spain for a month, returning to England around 12 March 12. (He was apparently attached to the American, Colonel Donovan.)[29]

Finland

Before then going on to consider the implications of what Borenius was recorded as saying to Burckhardt, it is important to put into context the growing tensions and alignment of interests between Finland, Germany and, to a lesser extent, Britain and Russia.

As has already been recorded, Borenius was a Finn, born in Wiborg (German) – Viborg in Russian and Viipuri in Finnish – in 1885. Wiborg is the largest city on the Carelian Isthmus, a border province with Russia. St Petersburg/Leningrad is only some 130 kms (80 miles) away. Rather like Poland, because of its proximity to larger states, throughout its history it had been under alternative control of Sweden and Russia, although since 1917 it had been an independent country and seen as a somewhat model social democracy by its Western allies.

We also obtained a copy of the extremely detailed *Field Marshal Mannerheim*, the 1940 biography of the Finnish leader that Tancred Borenius somehow found time to write and publish.[30] This work makes it reasonably clear that Borenius knew Mannerheim quite well, as since January 1918 he had been representing Finland in various diplomatic missions, and Mannerheim, who travelled frequently, would meet Borenius whenever in London. The book records visits in 1918, 1919 and twice in 1936. Mannerheim consistently gave a good impression to most that he met.

Consequently, the Winter War of November 1939 to March 1940 had attracted widespread coverage and support in the west, as during the time of the phoney war, it was one of their few active armed conflicts.[31] Britain supported Finland with munitions, as Britain was at the time Finland's largest trading partner. Germany remained neutral, though ever mindful of the need for their supply of Swedish iron ore to be maintained and not threatened. So, as late as spring 1940, Britain was actively and militarily supporting nation states in conflict with Soviet Russia.

The Winter War eventually turned into a bloody stalemate, with the Finns heavily outnumbered but with the Russians suffering disastrous losses due to the savage weather and the absence of thousands of trained officers killed by Stalin in the paranoid Red Army purges. In March 1940, the Peace of Moscow was brokered, with Finland ceding Wiborg and the Isthmus to Russia. The Carelian Isthmus was in turn evacuated with many, over 70,000 persons (including Tancred Borenius's sister) being forced to move to western Finland. They had lost virtually everything.

When Germany then invaded Russia in June 1941, the Continuation War began, being as the name implies a continuation of the Winter War. This time however, Germany was very interested, having the vested interest that the Russians did not block the supply of the vitally important Swedish iron ore. So it was that General Mannerheim, without ever overtly and explicitly backing Hitler, sought an alliance to prevent a full Russian invasion.

The British, by this time were of course allies of Russia, so somewhat bizarrely declared war on Finland in late 1941 (despite backing them six months earlier) and in so doing deported all Finns from Britain, except for the Borenius family who, we understand, remained in situ throughout. Eventually, at the end of the war, the Carelian Isthmus was still lost to Russia, in whose ownership it belongs to this day as part of the 'Leningrad Oblast'.

It is precisely for the above reasons that Tancred Borenius chose to address Chatham House on the Eastern Carelian situation in late 1941.[32]

It seems to us that in late January 1941, whilst the 1940 treaty was perhaps somewhat still tenuously still in place, Tancred had every reason to ask for and promote an Anglo-German peace. Britain supplied arms, including Bristol Blenheim light bombers, to Finland in the Winter War. Finland was an important trading partner. Although the invading Soviet Union had concluded the Molotov-Ribbentrop Pact with Germany on 23 August 1939, the Soviet invasion of Finland threatened Germany's vital iron ore supplies from Sweden.

Tancred believed in January 1941 that an Anglo-German peace would be the ideal solution, as far as Finland was concerned. Is that another reason why he chose to travel to Geneva? There was really no need for bluff or illusion in that respect – it was 100 per cent the truth.

The discussion

The above history of Finland is relevant to the Hess case because Tancred Borenius, the January 1941 carrier of peace to Carl Burckhardt, was a Finn by birth. He had also informed the Polish Relief Fund in London that he was going away on 'Finnish Government Business' in January 1941, not 'British Government Business'. Both statements therefore require further explanation.

Finland was important to Britain on several counts. She was Finland's largest trading partner and was strategically important as a bulwark against Soviet expansion. In 1939, the Winter War had pitched Finland against Russia, and Britain had readily supplied the Finns with war materiel. A year later, the picture was becoming far more difficult and complicated.

The question of the re-militarisation of the Åland Islands in 1938 had brought into sharp focus the various sensibilities at play in the strategic area. The relationship between Finland and Russia was at least clear; they had despised each other for centuries. Britain did not wish Russia to strengthen her grip on the Baltic and so had supported Finland. Germany had done the same, but not so openly, as from August 1939 Germany was cynically in a trade and political agreement with Russia.

Winston Churchill, from early in 1941 was quite aware of the German intentions to invade Russia (and hence not so Britain) and therefore also had to be mindful of potential future alliances when deciding on the varying levels of support to Finland. Consequently, even though Britain and Germany were at war with each other, they both had vital interests in supporting Finland against the Soviet Union. It is strange but true that when Tancred Borenius travelled by way of Portugal to Switzerland in early 1941, after Finland had finally lost the Winter War, he would have been aware from his own diplomacy after the First World War that an Anglo-German accord might actually be good for defeated Finland.

Eventually, as we now know, the Continuation War meant that Germany supported Finland, with Finland somewhat reluctantly acknowledging the German support. Britain eventually declared war on Finland in late 1941, with all Finns being deported from Britain; except for the Borenius family who remained in situ in London.[33]

Consequently, whilst we have no doubt whatsoever that Borenius had a lot more to impart to Burckhardt than simply Finnish policy, there is no doubt that in January 1941, as far as Tancred Borenius was concerned, an Anglo-German peace accord would selfishly be an ideal solution. His home state/province of Carelia had been lost to the Russians because of the first Winter War and the only realistic means of recovery was through a joint Anglo-German force.

It may also be relevant to record that at the time in question one of the leading lights in the 'Northern Department' of the British Foreign Office was Daniel Lascelles,[34] a son of the 4th Earl of Harewood, at whose ancestral house Tancred Borenius had spent some Yorkshire summers in the mid to late 1930s.

The record of what was said to Burckhardt comes to the modern-day reader through the diary entry of Ulrich von Hassell. Certainly, he does not mention 'Finnish Government Business' in his report of the late January 1941 meeting. (Neither does Victor Cazalet when recording his subsequent dinner with Borenius and Sikorski, following Borenius's return to Britain in March 1941.)

We should make the point that we are about to quote from the 2011 version of the Ulrich von Hassell diary, as the 1947 version had previously been censored.[35]

Von Hassell states: 'Very recently, the Finnish Art Historian, Professor Borenius, who has lived in London for many years, came to him to explain, apparently at the behest of British officials, that a reasonable peace could still be concluded. He has very intimate connections with the royal house (principally the Queen) and is personally convinced that sentiment in the British Cabinet is favourable. Of course, Eden's succession to Halifax was a handicap; there is however a lot of opposition to Eden's stance.'

We would make the following points:

- *apparently at the behest of British officials:* What precisely does this mean? Governmental or not? If von Hassell meant 'on behalf of the Government', surely he would have said that. The use of the word 'official' ('stellen') we take to mean or interpret as being a part of the British Establishment, though not necessarily the government.
- *(principally the Queen):* As has been explained, this reference is to Queen Mary, not Queen Elizabeth. As has already been described, Tancred Borenius was very close to the former Queen and her son-in-law's family, the Earl of Harewood.
- *is personally convinced that sentiment in the British Cabinet is favourable:* This may or may not be the case. It would appear to us that

> in January 1941, with Halifax newly installed in Washington there would not be an overriding Cabinet sentiment to make or broker a peace. Elsewhere, in the country perhaps, but not at Cabinet level.

Von Hassell continued: 'In reply to Burckhardt's questions Borenius had said: Holland and Belgium must be restored; Denmark to remain in the sphere of German influence; Poland (minus the former German provinces) to be resurrected for reasons of prestige, "because the Poles fought so bravely for Britain". Otherwise, no special interest in the east (not even Czechoslovakia). Former German colonies to Germany. The British Empire to remain otherwise unshorn. Britain has no special passion for France.'

We would comment as follows: This appears to be largely the 'stock' peace offer that was being floated in late 1940/41. We would, however, highlight the wish to 'resurrect' Poland. At that stage in the war the Poles had largely fought for Poland, rather than Britain, and since mid-1940 had done little else but establish themselves militarily in Scotland and politically in London. There was, however, the 1939 Anglo-Polish military alliance that had theoretically at least been responsible for the outbreak of the Second World War, simply by reason of its eventual transgression. Again, it is unlikely that Hitler would ever have agreed to that part of the proposal concerning Poland, given the much needed for Polish territory to launch and facilitate the eastern offensive.

Von Hassell concluded by stating that in the meeting (and this was his personal view as well) that there was still a 'great reluctance' to make peace with Hitler. 'The main reason is that his word cannot be believed. The British Consul General also told Carl Burckhardt that in no event could peace be made with Hitler.'

We would comment as follows: Again, the 'Hitler factor' was the oft-cited reason for the failure of peace negotiations to proceed. Perhaps the more important comment is 'The British Consul General *also* told…' In other words, the British Consul/government had *also* used that pretext, so it appears to us that this approach was not on behalf of the British Government, else why make the comment? It seems that there are two bodies at play here: the British government and the 'body' that Tancred Borenius was representing or appearing to represent.

So, the 'Finnish Government Business' that Tancred Borenius had used as the justification for non-attendance at the Polish Relief Fund was nothing of the sort. We know that MI6 had briefed him before setting off, so the vitally important question to understand was (and still is) who precisely was he representing, or purporting to represent?

For the reasons we have stated we do not think that Borenius purported to represent the British government, despite having been briefed for his mission by the deputy chief of MI6.

What is also very clear is the fact that any discussions concerning Finland had not been recorded and Borenius had not been representing Finland in these discussions. He was clearly representing a British 'body'. Presumably the 'British officials' (or *stellen*) to whom von Hassell refers.

We now believe the 'Finnish Government Business' was no more than a convenient excuse to allow Borenius out of Britain without overtly involving the British governmental services. Once again, as far as Dansey and MI6 was concerned, it made the Borenius mission deniable. If things went wrong there is little doubt that Borenius would have been on 'Finnish Government Business' when biting on his cyanide capsule (as also provided by Mr Dansey).

The return (via Italy?)

In conversation with John Harris, Lars Borenius inferred that his father had tried to return to Britain via Italy but had been refused entry. This did seem to be a bit of a mystery at the time, but we believe that Prof. Keith Jeffery, in his history of MI6 has perhaps unwittingly provided us the explanation. By way of potential counter reference, the Ciano diaries are silent during this period as the diarist had joined his air group in Bari.[36]

Bernard Berenson (1865–1959), Tancred's long-time sparring partner in matters of art history attribution, was spending a relatively comfortable war near Florence at Villa I Tatti, so we assumed it perhaps was Berenson who Borenius was trying to reach. However, Berenson does not record any visit from Borenius, or indeed a cancelled visit. On page 308 of his history of MI6, Prof. Jeffery gives us the clue as to why Borenius might wish to reach Berenson. He describes the paucity of intelligence coming from Germany after the Munich crisis and quotes a source bemoaning the fact that there were only two 'solid sources': De Ropp (who we have detailed in Chapter 7) and 'a high-status Baltic German with social connections across Europe, who was run from London by Dick Ellis and was described as 'first class'. He was 'based in Italy'.

Simple research into Berenson would indicate that he was indeed the man that Jeffery was describing. Interestingly, he was also a friend of Natalie Barney and Romaine Brooks, part of the lesbian circle frequented by Dolly

Wilde, to whom Tancred acted as guardian.

Whatever the case and whether the MI6 agent Berenson was the intended destination, we do know that by 12 March 1941 he was back presiding over the Polish Relief Fund at 33 Belgrave Square, London in his capacity of Secretary General. The Hess flight was now less than two months away. Time was fast running out.

The tragedy ensues

As we have seen, Tancred Borenius returned to London in late February/ early March 1941 after the vitally important return mission to Geneva. We will never know for sure precisely what was said between Borenius and Burckhardt, and only have the von Hassell account as evidence. As we shall see later in this work, Carl Burckhardt was meticulous in trying to cover his tracks when deemed necessary.

Tancred had clearly not used the poison pill that he had been given and so life, such as it was, continued. His wayward charge, Dolly Wilde, died shortly after his return on 10 April 1941 from an almost inevitable overdose of paraldehyde. For her, it was at last a successful suicide attempt. She was buried at Kensal Green Cemetery. She was only forty-five years of age.

In late 1941, Borenius addressed Chatham House. He was still editor of the *Burlington Magazine*, but Sotheby's began to use him less, as they thought him unreliable. He lost the editorship of the *Burlington* in 1945.

We suspect that eventually the family 'downsized', moving away from his flat in London (28 Kensington Gate, W8) to Coombe Bissett, a village near Salisbury, where he had bought Stocks Bridge Cottage (later to be renamed 'Carelia') some years previously.[37] This was also close to his former interest of Clarendon Palace, only some 6 miles away.

However, for whatever reason, Tancred Borenius was then adjudged insane, to the extent that he was admitted to St Andrew's Nursing Home, Northampton (at the time and to this day) one of the leading psychiatric hospitals in the country. Living in Northamptonshire, John Harris was fully aware of the reputation of the hospital, very much being the Priory of its day. Famous patients allegedly included Elizabeth Taylor, Malcolm Arnold the composer and John Clare the poet. He was admitted on 22 April 1947, following a reception order under the 1890 Lunacy Act, dated 1 April 1946. Sadly, this appears to infer that he was admitted against his will, after being certified by two independent medical practitioners.

St Andrew's, Northampton, the leading British hospital for the mentally ill

However, presumably because his treatment was not working (or it was costing too much) and he was away from the family home, a request was made in March 1948 to transfer him to Laverstock House, very close to Coombe Bissett. In allowing the transfer, a 'special report' under section 38 of the 1890 Act was prepared.[38]

In it, Dr G, Craishe reported that, 'He is suffering from melancholia (chronic). He is very depressed, gloomy, pessimistic, and apprehensive. He is suspicious of all those around him and complain of them regarding him with scorn and contempt. He is in constant fear of impending disaster. He is defective in habits and very untidy and slovenly in dress.'

His bodily condition is as follows: 'He is in impaired health, feeble and tottery, but fairly nourished. He has severe valvular heart disease and some oedema of the feet and ankles … I hereby certify that he is still of unsound mind and is a proper person to be detained under care and treatment.'

Consequently, in March 1948 Tancred, now clearly very ill, was brought to Laverstock House, near Salisbury. He died on 2 September 1948 of a cerebral embolism and valvular heart disease. His son, Lars, who was then corresponding from 4 Pump Court, Temple, EC4, registered the death on 6 September. It should be recorded that Tancred's granddaughter, Aurelia, has corresponded with the authors suggesting that Tancred was also suffering from early-stage Alzheimer's disease.

His will left his entire Estate to his wife, Anne-Marie, who in turn paid Estate Duty of £1,135 on an Estate valued at £14,865. This equates to around £550,000 in current terms (2021).

Tancred was buried in Coombe Bissett churchyard, and his wife eventually joined him there in 1976.

CONCLUSION

Above all else this part of the story is extremely sad. That such an intelligent, self-made man should have ended his days in compulsory seclusion from society was tragic and not completely unlike the cruel fate of Rudolf Hess.

We also have absolutely no doubt that when he travelled to Switzerland in January 1941, Borenius played two roles of truly international importance. The first was the delivery role of the 'one time pads' which allowed vital intelligence to flow in and out of Switzerland. Given the importance of the 'Lucy Ring',[39] the importance of keeping this channel of communication open cannot be understated.

The second role was that of the supposed bringer of peace, a role he was absolutely convinced of, given his vested interest in all matters Finland. He was quite possibly trying to save both Finland and Britain simultaneously, or at least that was what he thought he was doing. Through his connections he was also wholly aware of the distrust of Churchill in the upper classes, but von Hassell hits upon the biggest hurdle when he records the fact that the British working man and middle classes were full square behind their Prime Minister, aided and abetted by a powerful government propaganda department.

We have no doubt Tancred would have been convincing. It is far easier to argue and debate if you have right and truth on your side, or at least believe that to be the case. We also have no doubt that when Tancred left Carl Burckhardt in January 1941, the very circumspect Swiss intellectual would have recognised the opportunity to bring the conflict to an end and at the same time enhance his own reputation. But how?

Moreover, had the role assigned to Tancred Borenius really come to an end?

---

[1] John Harris, *Rudolf Hess: The British Illusion of Peace*, JEMA, Moulton 2010.

[2] Former German Ambassador to Rome.

[3] *The Diaries of Ulrich von Hassell* – Hamish Hamilton, London, 1948.

[4] In the German 'stellen'.
[5] Albrecht reported to his mother in a letter.
[6] Died 27 July 2006.
[7] The passport office system was wiped out when Europe was overrun by the Nazis.
[8] Keith Jeffery, *MI6: The History of the Secret Intelligence Service 1909–1949*, Bloomsbury, London 2010.
[9] John Harris and Richard Wilbourn, *Rudolf Hess: A New Technical Analysis of the Hess Flight, May 1941*, The History Press, Stroud, 2014.
[10] The publishers.
[11] Ottoline Morrell was a prominent member of the Bloomsbury Group. Philip Morrell was a Liberal politician. As a result of this association, Borenius met artists such as Roger Fry, Augustus John, Bertrand Russell, Clive Bell and Henry Lamb. Ottoline Morrell was also cousin to Elizabeth Bowes-Lyon.
[12] Frederick Leverton Harris was a Member of Parliament and benefactor to the Fitzwilliam Museum.
[13] RIIA 8/758.
[14] Coincidentally, the pictures were sold by R.B. Brassey, who formerly used to live at Cottesbrooke Hall, Northamptonshire, the village in which John Harris resides.
[15] *Aberdeen Journal*, 18 September 1937. Trip to Harrogate. *Western Daily Press* 7 September 1936. Attends Harewood Church service. *Yorkshire Evening Post.* 14 September 1938, visits Sherriff Hutton Park.
[16] *Lancashire Evening Post*, Tuesday 9 May 1939.
[17] *Illustrated London News*, 6 May 1939.
[18] FN UB Basel, NL 110:BII 46d:56
[19] *Edinburgh Evening News*, 6 December 1939.
[20] *Glasgow Herald*, 4 August 1939, wedding of Thelma Cazalet.
[21] The Borenius family home in Coombe Bissett is now called 'Carelia'.
[22] Keith Jeffery, *MI6: The History of the Secret Intelligence Service 1909–1949*, Bloomsbury, London, 2010.
[23] Unless, of course, one can benefit in the same way as the German dealers who abetted the Nazi looting across Europe.
[24] Captain Henry Stuart Wheatly-Crowe (1882–1967) (often rendered Wheatley-Crowe) was a Commander of the Order of the Crown of Thorns. (An order dedicated to the preservation of the Christian ideology.)
[25] Susie Harries, *Nikolaus Pevsner: The Life*, Chatto & Windus, London, 2011.
[26] Helena Wayne (ed.), *The Story of a Marriage*, Routledge, London and New York, 1995.
[27] Ibid.
[28] Red Cross Archives, London, 15 December 2014.
[29] Maud Russell, *A Constant Heart*, The Dovecote Press, Wimborne, 2017.
[30] Tancred Borenius, *Field Marshal Mannerheim*, Hutchinson, April 1940.
[31] See Sir Walter Citrine, *My Finnish Diary*, Penguin, London, March 1940.
[32] 23 September 1941.
[33] Email to John Harris from Eero Terrikangas, 23 March 2015.
[34] Craig Gerrard, *The Foreign Office and Finland 1938–1940*, Frank Cass, Abington, 2005.
[35] *The Ulrich von Hassell Diaries*, Frontline, Barnsley, 2011.
[36] *Ciano's Diary 1937–1943*, Phoenix Press, London (1947–2002).
[37] He was recorded as already living in Coombe Bissett in the 1935 *Who's Who.*
[38] Avon and Wiltshire NHS Trust Archives, Chippenham Wiltshire, Reference A1 /565/1.
[39] The Lucy Ring was a controversial British intelligence operation based in Switzerland, used to forward intelligence to Soviet Russia.

CHAPTER 12

THE BRITISH CONSTITUTION – SPRING 1941

The WARRANT to Collonel FRANCIS HACKER &c. for BEHEADING of K. CHARLES the First
At the high Court of Justice for the Tryinge and Judginge off Charles Steuart
King off England January XXIXth Anno Dom. 1648.

Whereas Charles Steuart King of England is and Standeth convicted attaynted and condemned of High Treason and other high Crimes And Sentence upon Saturday last was pronounced against him by this Court to be put to death by the severinge of his head from his body Of which Sentence execution yet remayneth to be done These are therefore to will and require you to see the said Sentence executed In the open Streets before Whitehall upon the morrow being the thirtieth Day off this instante month off January between the hours off Tenn in the morninge and five in the afternoone off the same Day will full effect And for soe doing this shall be your Sufficient Warrant And these are to require All Officers and Souldiers and other the good People of this Nation of England to be assistynge unto you in this Service Given under our Hands and Seales. ——

A View of the Place and Manner of K. CHARLES the First's Execution.

By its very nature, the British constitution is constantly changing. It has for ever been the case and if we are looking at and trying to interpret the events of 1941 and put them into context, it is important to find a reliable reference point as close to that date as possible. It clearly is no use trying to draw deep conclusions from comparisons between our contemporary twenty-first-century constitutional practice, or equally that pertaining to say, 1640 or 1689.

Consequently, for the purposes of this chapter, we have drawn heavily on *The Constitutional History of Modern Britain 1485–1937* by Prof. D.L. Keir (1895–1973), which was published in 1938 by Adam and Charles Black of Soho Square, London.

As has already been stated, Rudolf Hess had spent some time in the spring of 1941 acquiring books on the British Constitution and this book is hopefully one of the contenders for such selection.[1]

Whilst writing the tome, Keir was a fellow of University College, Oxford and later, in 1939, moved to Queens, Belfast where he remained until 1949.

Written in the days before academic sponsorship (!) the book is fascinating and easy to read. It records and analyses the constant ebbing and flowing of the relationship between the monarch and Parliament. At times the monarchy is politically in the ascendant. At other times, having overstepped the mark (1649–60), there is no monarchy.

When David Keir was writing his 568 pages, the abdication crisis would have been fresh in his mind, which in constitutional terms was a victory for Parliament. Baldwin had dislodged a king that was very 'off piste' and various allegiances and battlelines had been drawn as a consequence. Moreover, Winston Churchill had openly backed the King, a fact that neither the next incumbent nor his wife could easily forget or forgive.

However, in the context of the Hess affair, there are some specific provisions that we consider relevant and, though rarely used have evolved over time. As a later commentator reminds us, 'Rules and powers which are part of the common law do not merely become extinct through lack of use.'[2]

This is because much of the British constitution (whilst famously not specifically written) has typically been based on common law and precedent. An action which is followed by a balancing Act. Consequently, early monarchical excesses were followed by the Magna Carta in 1215 and the Commonwealth of 1649, the subsequent Restoration by the 1689 Bill of Rights and so on…

In case the reader is tempted to think this is all old hat and how archaic, it was only in 1948 that the medieval right of a peer to be tried by his peers was abolished. The first such trial had been in 1499. Four sections of the 1215 Magna Carta are still extant law today.

It really is all about relative control and the great thing is that the classic British compromise usually provides an apt balance and check where necessary. Charles I got his comeuppance in 1649 and equally the population was not impressed with the replacement (1649–60) and so we reverted back to type. Equally impressively, Queen Victoria actively squabbled with and replaced ministers in the latter part of her reign, hopefully for the best for the country. David Keir highlights her dislike of William Gladstone and her attempt of replacing him as Prime Minister in 1880, despite the inconvenience of him having just won the general election.

She tried the same ploy in 1892 on the back of the Home Rule for Ireland issue.

The point being made is that monarchical involvement in such political matters was far from uncommon and that was a mere fifty years before the Hess flight, where it could be argued matters were far graver in 1941 than 1892 or 1880. There is nothing new here whatsoever. Indeed, David Keir concedes: 'Her [Queen Victoria's] political bias cannot be denied. Yet, judged by the appropriate constitutional standards, her use of the prerogative was by no means indefensible.'

We then move on to a very relevant privilege of the monarch, that of the dissolution of Parliament. (It will be remembered that this privilege was being mooted as recently as 2019 in the context of forcing an outcome to the wretched Brexit debate. An item far more similar in import to those issues of 1940/41 – the future of Europe and Britain's role within it.)

Queen Victoria was quite aware of the power and in 1846 had described it as, 'A most valuable and powerful instrument in the hands of the Crown, but one which ought not to be used except in extreme cases and with a certainty of success.'

This is the crux of the Hess case. In 1941, given Churchill's apparent support in the 'country', could Hess even count on the necessary monarchical support? Was there a sufficient 'certainty of success' for this card to be played? More fundamentally, did the monarchy even know about what Hess was planning and his required role? What was the precise level of monarchical knowledge?

Those issues will be debated in a further chapter. What is patently clear, however, is that these rules explain precisely why Hess was not (and never had been) targeting the incumbent government. He already knew its response. He was targeting the monarchy in the hope that the King would action his prerogative. A monarchy who we suspect, in 1941, was thoroughly cheesed off with Churchill, though, oddly, not necessarily with his Parliament. Having withstood and endured an extended bombing campaign from September 1940 through the long cold winter of 1940, the British circumstances were certainly 'extreme' enough to warrant such careful consideration.

As David Keir concludes, 'The action of the King must be raised above the conflict of the parties and aim at the national interest for which his is the final responsibility. His prerogative, however circumscribed by conventions, must always retain its historic character as a residue of discretionary authority to be employed for the public good. It is the last resource provided by the Constitution to guarantee its own working.'

This is the fundamental question, and one could argue that King George

VI did not need Rudolf Hess (or anyone else) to make the decision to invoke his prerogative.

However, Hess's arrival would no doubt crystallise the issue, particularly if the Duke of Hamilton (and other dukes?) duly turned up at Windsor seeking an audience to discuss matters of the 'Public Weal' (the public good). What to do with Hess physically would also be deserving of serious consideration, as Peter Fleming had brilliantly predicted in his 1940 *A Flying Visit*.

Moreover, there are further constitutional 'niceties' that make Hess's task the easier. These explain precisely why Hess chose to fly to Scotland and not Hendon, for instance, or some other airfield in England near to the seat of parliamentary government.

These niceties, we believe, precede even the Magna Carta. They involve the privileges accorded to dukes and clearly merit further explanation.

A duke is, of course, a part of the overall control process. William the Conqueror, having recently invaded Britain, could not be in two places at the same time and so delegated his power in absentia to subordinates. This delegation was formalised by Edward III in 1337 when he created the first dukedom; that of Cornwall for his son, Edward, the Black Prince, who sadly predeceased his father (so the dukedom had to be later recreated.)

The word 'duke' came from the French *duc*, which in turn came from the Latin *dux*. Again, we should not be surprised by the French derivation. Parliament was still being opened in the French language, a direct throwback to 1066. A duke was, and is, a physical representation of the monarch.

The relevance of this history lesson is simply to state that as a consequence of necessary delegation of power, the dukes established a right of access to the monarch (not surprisingly, given the more brutal times of the Middle Ages). They were also given a freedom from arrest to reinforce and ease the same right of access to the monarch. Really, no more than a common sense precaution. At present we have been unable to ascertain precisely when this privilege was first recognised. Blackstone cites the case of Hugh Spencer, father, and son, who attempted to prevent … the great men of the realm … to speak to the King.[3] Interestingly, this was in the reign of Edward II, before the first dukedom had been created. Nevertheless, by 1765 the Constitutional historian, William Blackstone, was confident enough to write: 'It is usually looked upon to be the right of each particular peer of the realm to demand an audience of the King and to lay before him, with decency and respect, such matters as he shall judge of importance to the public weal.'[4]

Surely one could make the case that the future of a country and staving off an invasion was within the definition of the public weal? Consequently, we would now make the case that Hess knew exactly what he was doing in seemingly targeting the Duke of Hamilton:

- Hamilton was not a member of the Churchill government.
- Hamilton had a *right* of access to the monarch and could not be arrested in the process.
- The monarch has a duty to consider the public weal and all that entails.
- Conveniently, Hamilton was also in effective control of that part of Scottish air space through which Hess chose to fly.
- Hamilton had also made his thoughts as to the war patently obvious in his letter to *The Times* in October 1939.
- Hamilton's wife and his aeronautical friend Stewart Blacker had been telling Dr Gerl (and Hess) the same thing since the mid 1930s.

So. Why fly anywhere else? All he had to do was land, meet the Duke and be taken to the King!

Oh dear… What could possibly go wrong?

In 2021 this all perhaps sounds very archaic and unlikely. We now suspect that in 1941 this was precisely what Hess was seeking to achieve, or perhaps an amended version of the same. (Hess lands, Hamilton goes to the King/Churchill with Hess hidden in Scotland, pressure put on Churchill.) Constitutionally at least, it was quite possible.

It also appears that the government was worried enough to order the movement of the Scottish Crown jewels – the Honours of Scotland – following Hess's arrival. They had been hidden in Edinburgh Castle at the start of the war but were re-hidden, albeit still within the castle.[5]

Whilst debating the constitutional aspects of the affair, we should also briefly consider the constitutional relationship between England and Scotland. Since the Acts of Union in 1707, in theory at least Scotland and England were united.

However, the Union was fraught from the onset and that has persisted to today, for sundry and diverse reasons, from the Darien Gap project of the 1690s through 1745 to North Sea oil of the 1970s. During the period under review, the 1930–40s, the impetus was towards a form of romantic Scottish Nationalism, with the SNP having been founded in 1934 from an amalgamation of earlier groupings.

Arthur Donaldson (1901–69), an early leader, was arrested in early May 1941, a week before the Hess flight, at his pig farm in Lugton, Ayrshire. He was taken to Glasgow and interned in Barlinnie Prison for some six weeks on account of his 'subversive activities'. Quite what these were is not yet wholly clear, but there were rumours of a 'cache of weapons' having been found.[6]

However, Scottish nationalism has always been plagued by comparisons to Scottish socialism, or even Scottish communism in the early days. Because much of the working classes were engaged in the primary industries, they were seen as candidates for conversion to socialism at least. Hence the legend of Red Clydeside had come about after the First World War.

In the 1930s though, the truth was that the Scottish socialist movement was split and had not yet presented a cogent, united case.

That having been said, the British government in London was always mindful of the fact that Scottish nationalism might follow in the footsteps of Irish nationalism, which following much spilling of blood had finally succeeded (at least in part) in 1923.

The difference, however, was that the Union of England and Scotland was at least in theory consensual, whereas the Irish was not and never had been. Consequently, any 'uncoupling' of Scotland would have to be done, again in theory at least, democratically. The King's prerogative would not work in that instance, unless again he adjudged it in the best interests of the Public Weal.

Consequently, we trust the reader can see the difficulties here. Constitutionally, the monarch, as Blackstone states, 'The supreme executive power of these kingdoms is vested by our laws in a single person, the King or Queen.'[7]

In 2021 (or 1941), it is quite easy to see why that point is missed. The emphasis is always on the delegated powers of Parliament. But be in no doubt. If the monarch is confident enough to exercise his or her prerogative, then constitutionally, that is the law of the land.

How the people might choose to react is of course their choice, a factor that the monarch obviously needs to consider when deciding.

In case the reader is thinking that 'Blackstone was 1765, Hess was 1941, there is a long time in between', please find a *Guardian* article of 2003 which seeks to clarify the position at that time. This was in response to Tony Blair (or nominally the Queen) taking Britain to war in Iraq, without the assent of Parliament. The Queen was quite entitled to do so:

Mystery lifted on Queen's powers: Great British political riddle solved as scope of the royal prerogative is revealed for the first time

One of the last great riddles of the British political system was solved yesterday when the powers wielded by the government in the name of the monarchy were set down on paper for the first time.

The 'veil of mystery' surrounding the royal prerogative was lifted when a list of them was published in a move intended to encourage greater transparency.

The prerogative, which includes the power to declare war, is handed from monarchs to ministers and allows them to take action without the backing of Parliament.

In a move intended to encourage greater accountability, the Commons public administration committee (PAC) published a list of the little-understood powers which it persuaded Sir Hayden Phillips, permanent secretary to the Department of Constitutional Affairs, to supply.

'Over the years when people have asked the government to say what prerogative powers there are, they have always refused to do so,' said the committee's chairman, Labour MP Tony Wright.

'It tells us largely what we know, but it is a small victory to have the government say at least what it thinks they are.'

The PAC wants Parliament to be given a say in how the powers are used. Although MPs were given a vote on the war in Iraq, there is no obligation on the government to let them have a say.

The powers include those that allow governments to regulate the civil service, issue passports, make treaties, appoint and remove ministers and grant honours.

They also include the prerogative of mercy, which is no longer used to save condemned men from the scaffold but can be exercised to remedy miscarriages of justice which are not put right by the courts.

In its paper the government said new prerogative powers could not be invented and that some 'have fallen out of use altogether, probably forever', such as the power to press men into the navy. But it said there were still 'significant aspects' of domestic affairs in which the powers could be used, despite legislation.

And it accepted that the 'conduct of foreign affairs remains very reliant on the exercise of prerogative powers' and that they can 'still to some extent adapt to changed circumstances'.

It also set out ways in which Parliament and the courts have limited the powers through control of the supply of money, new laws and judicial review.

Mr Wright said: 'It should be a basic constitutional principle that ministers would be required to explain to Parliament where their powers come from and how they intend to use them.'

The committee is looking at proposals for an act which would force ministers to seek authorisation from Parliament before they exercised some of the powers, which were 'sometimes in effect powers of life and death'. These include the power to declare war.

The government said it was not possible to give a comprehensive catalogue of prerogative powers.

So there was scope for the courts to identify prerogative powers which had little previous recognition.

In a case about whether the home secretary had power to issue baton rounds to a chief constable without the consent of the police authority, the court held that the crown had a prerogative power to keep the peace within the realm.

Lord Justice Nourse commented: 'The scarcity of references in the books to the prerogative of keeping the peace within the realm does not disprove that it exists. Rather it may point to an unspoken assumption that it does.'

FULL LIST OF THOSE POWERS

Domestic Affairs

The appointment and dismissal of ministers
The summoning, prorogation and dissolution of Parliament
Royal assent to bills
The appointment and regulation of the civil service
The commissioning of officers in the armed forces
Directing the disposition of the armed forces in the UK
Appointment of Queen's Counsel
Issue and withdrawal of passports
Prerogative of mercy (used to apply in capital punishment cases; still used, e.g. to remedy errors in sentence calculation
Granting honours
Creation of corporations by Charter

Foreign Affairs
The making of treaties
Declaration of war
Deployment of armed forces overseas
Recognition of foreign states
Accreditation and reception of diplomats.

There is little doubt. Constitutionally it is plain to see what Hess was trying to do. He understood the British constitution far better than most of us today. He was never seeking to contact Parliament or Churchill – because he did not need to…

The question now changes as to when the deal Hess was seeking was negotiated. Did Hess bring a signed deal with him, or had one already been communicated?

TREACHERY AND TREASON

Whilst debating the constitution, not unnaturally during times of war, the Crown seeks to protect itself and its security from acts against it.

> Consequently, in 1940 the Treachery Act was passed following the fall of France. It covered those persons who:
>
> a. If, with intent to help the enemy, any person does, or attempts or conspires with any other person to do any act which is designed or likely to give assistance to the naval, military or air operations of the enemy, to impede such operations of His Majesty's forces, or to endanger life, he shall be guilty of felony and shall on conviction suffer death.

This was very much aimed at those persons who, for instance, parachuted into the country to wreak damage and indeed, the legislation was used on sixteen occasions to shoot or hang those so found guilty.

In addition, there were already the ancient laws of treason, that still in part remain extant today. In 1941 the Treason Act of 1351 was the relevant legislation. Amongst other crimes, those found guilty either of the below could again expect to be executed if found guilty:

- Levying war against the king in his realm; or,

- Those adhered to the king's enemies in his realm, giving them aid and comfort in his realm or elsewhere.

Sir John Simon, the Lord High Chancellor, saw the need for the new Act in 1940, as the old treason acts were obviously ancient and, 'The Treason Acts might not be applicable to persons who are not normally resident within the King's jurisdiction; and moreover, the Treason Acts are antiquated, excessively cumbrous and invested with a dignity and ceremonial that seems to us wholly inappropriate to the sort of case with which we are dealing here.'

We bring these Acts to the reader's attention as *prima facie* it demonstrates the potential risks that the participants were taking. However, in the context of the Hess case:

- Tancred Borenius, by reason of his Finnish nationality was outside the scope of the Treachery Act 1940, thus making him an ideal candidate for the actions that he took in January 1941.
- The Duke of Hamilton, had he agreed to travel to meet Haushofer as requested, could be seen to be in contravention of the Treason Act 1351, though would have had the defence of acting in the King's interests, rather than those of the government. Moreover, if guilty of allowing Hess to fly through undefended airspace, he would also be potentially guilty of transgressing the Treachery Act too. At the very least a legal minefield.

Given that Roger Casement had been executed in 1916 on account of how a comma was interpreted within the same piece of legislation, it is no wonder that the Duke took care in meeting with Eustace Percy, a senior Conservative MP, before agreeing to meet RAF Intelligence.

All the actions being described later in this book were clearly being played out with extremely high stakes attached and should be seen in that light.

---

1 David Irving, *Hess, The Missing Years 1941–1945*, Macmillan, London, 1987.
2 David Irving, *Hess, The Missing Years 1941–1945*, Macmillan, London, 1987.
3 Macmillan, London, 1987.
4 William Blackstone, *Commentaries on the Laws of England*, Clarendon Press, Oxford, 1765.
5 John Harris, *Rudolf Hess: The British Illusion of Peace*, JEMA, Moulton 2010.
6 *The Guy Liddell Diaries, Vol. 1 1939–1942*, Routledge, Oxford, 2005.
7 Ibid.

CHAPTER 13

SO, WHAT PRECISELY WAS RUDOLF HESS DOING FROM SEPTEMBER 1940 TO MAY 1941?

To try and build a picture of the lifestyle enjoyed, or perhaps more likely endured, by Hess during the above period, we have tried to recreate as best we are able the following description by way of extracting detailed information from the various sources available. In so doing we hope to illustrate what was possible and what was not.

Physical locations and family

Rudolf Hess lived at 48 Harthauserstrasse, Harlaching, Munich, with his wife, Ilse, and three-year-old son, Wolf. The house sat on a large plot in an affluent suburb of Munich, and had been substantially rebuilt in 1934/35 to provide ample residential and staff accommodation, security and garaging. Harlaching is in the south of Munich, bordered by the River Isar. Prior to moving to Harlaching, the family had lived in Borstei, Munich but the new house had been bought and financed by the 'Adolf Hitler Fund', thus spending some of the proceeds of sums raised from the sale of stamps and Hitler's turgid *Mein Kampf*.

His principal office was at the ever-expanding complex of Nazi Party buildings, centered around the 'Brown House' at 45 Briennerstrasse, Munich, being the national headquarters of the NSDAP. This was around 5 miles from his home and necessitated driving into and through central Munich. In 1943 both properties were bombed. At the end of the war, 48 Harthauserstrasse was seized by the Bavarian government (who most recently has allowed a theatre company to build rehearsal rooms there whilst their own theatre is being restored).[1] Rudolf Hess apparently had never considered the eventuality of a German defeat and so his family had to move into rented accommodation in the Allgäu, at the end of the war. In making his assessment he asked, 'How could I be of so little faith?'[2]

Post-war, the Brown House was never re-built in its former guise but is now the site of the Munich Documentation Centre, which records the history of the NSDAP in Munich. It opened in May 2015.

The Braunes Haus, Munich (U.S. National Archives)

We have recently learned that the Hess family also rented a couple of chalets in the Allgäu, at Gailenberg, near to Hindelang (see Chapter 9). There are reports of Hess helping with the construction of a ski lift there in 1938–9.[3]

As a member of the government and Deputy Führer, Hess also maintained a large office at 64 Wilhelmstrasse, Berlin. To get there from Munich, he had his own official plane, a three-engine Junkers 52, registered as D-ARET, complete with his own pilot, Kurt Schuhmann. Munich is some 300 miles from Berlin, so by air the trip from Munich Riem to the Templehof, Berlin would typically take two hours in the 'Tante Ju', but much longer by train or car. Immediately, one might consider this arrangement to be stressful. A stressful commute, before the terms 'stress' or 'commute' were really contemplated.

Hess, unlike Hitler and Göring, did not have his own train. Instead, he had a personalised carriage that would be attached to other trains to afford some degree of independence. Pintsch, his adjutant, used the carriage on the night of 10/11 May 1941 to travel from Munich to Berchtesgaden.

Despite being born in Egypt, Hess's ancestral family home since c. 1760 was at Reicholdsgrün, the family estate some 140 miles northeast of Munich. It was to here that the Hess family travelled most summers when based in Egypt in the early part of the century. It was also where Hess retreated to recuperate after being shot in 1917.

Augsburg and the Messerschmitt airfield and factory were 35 miles away from Munich to the northwest. There was a newly constructed autobahn between Munich and Augsburg, the A8.

At the time under review by this book, both Hess's mother, Klara, and father, Fritz, were still alive. Hess's younger brother, Alfred (1897–1963), worked in the Auslands Organisation in Berlin, under the auspices of Ernst Bohle. Alfred Hess was also married with a son. The brothers had a younger sister, Margarete, born in 1908. She also later married, becoming Margarete Rauch.

Berchtesgaden and the Hitler's Berghof were 100 miles away to the southeast, towards Salzburg.

Bavaria and Munich, in particular, were very much the homeland of the Nazi party, being distilled in part from the political maelstrom that followed the First World War. Eventually it became known as the 'Capital of the Movement'. From the research we have conducted, we have concluded that certainly Hitler and Hess much preferred Munich and 'the South' to Berlin and the strict Prussian connotations of 'the North'.

(It should be said, however, that it was perhaps these strict 'Prussian connotations' and the reaction thereto, that had led Berlin to be the centre of European free thought and sexual liberation in the period following the First World War.)

Consequently, it was perhaps only natural that both men would return to what were essentially their homes as frequently as was possible. An interesting book, *Munich Playground*,[4] although published in 1942, and so in part pure Allied propaganda, paints a vivid picture of Hitler, 'Whenever possible, Hitler plays hookey, romping around in his favourite Bavarian haunts, far from the prying eyes of ambassadors and Berlin correspondents.'

In a similar stylistic manner, Hess is also described, 'At the opposite extreme of pleasure-seeking Nazis, we have Hitler's deputy, Rudolf Hess. Rudolf was called a 'guter Junge' a good boy, by the German people, who know something about their leaders. His hobbies were aviation and music.[5] He was the most insipid of the Brown-Shirt leaders and had become little more than the Munich watchdog of Nazi Party Headquarters, before he broke his chain and ran away from his master.'

In addition to the hobbies that Pope lists, we would also include the 'outdoor life'. There are countless photographs of Hess on skis, Hess walking, Hess halfway up mountains, etc, and it seems to us that he was very much an active man who would not naturally enjoy a sedentary, office-bound environment.

He also enjoyed fast cars, apparently owning an early Mercedes 540K. He had privately flown an Me108 in the late 1930s, as well as his earlier competitive flights in German aviation competition.

Immediate Staff

In Munich, the immediate staff were Karlheinz Pintsch, the adjutant, who lived near Hess in Harlaching. Franz Lutz was his security officer and Walter Lippert his driver. Both lived on site at 48 Harthauserstrasse. His secretary was Hildegard Fath, who originated from Freiburg (hence her nickname of Freiburg). She remained a close friend of the family after the war.

In Berlin, Hess had another adjutant, Alfred Leitgen, a former journalist. His secretary was Ilse Hillmann, assisted by Ingebor Sperr. Miss Sperr was seconded to Munich from time to time, also working at 48 Harthauserstrasse.

Hess and Leitgen at the Olympic village, 1936 (Bundesarchiv)

Health

It is important to challenge, or even lay to rest, once and for all, the myth that Rudolf Hess was mad or delusional, as the official Nazi Party communique had subsequently declared.[6] Important, because if the Deputy Führer was truly insane, presumably logical, sensible decisions would have proven to be beyond him and, consequently, it would have been even more difficult to analyse and assess his true motives. If, however, Hess was sane, we can feel confident to continue our work.

We have already recorded that the pre-flight myth that Hess was insane was wholly self-instigated and, until Nuremberg, self-perpetuated. The letter that he had allowed Pintsch to deliver to Hitler at Obersalzberg on 11 May 1941 had supposedly said words to the effect of, 'If all else fails, simply say I had gone mad…'[7] The fact that both copies of the document are not currently in the public domain may well be significant, but we suspect not as a sign to, or evidence of, Hess's supposed insanity. Alfred Rosenberg had met with Hess just prior to his flight[8] and stated at Nuremberg, 'Hess gave no evidence of any abnormality…'[9]

The stark fact is that there is absolutely no evidence to suggest that before he made his flight, Rudolf Hess was insane. Somewhat idiosyncratic, yes; a little vain, perhaps, but insane, no. He quite capable of rational decision-making. After his arrival his demeanour may well have changed, but in this analysis we are attempting to ascertain if there is any evidence of insanity prior to 10 May 1941. The 'madness' alibi supposedly would cover why Hess chose to do what he did and allay any suspicions that the Russians might have that an Anglo-German peace was being jointly negotiated before an eastwards invasion was mounted.

We would also make the point that the British have also helped perpetuate the myth that Hess was insane on arrival in May 1941.

Shortly after his arrival, the Communist Party of Great Britain accused the Duke of Hamilton of assisting Hess in his mission. (Which might well be the case, but rather than the Duke, more likely the Duchess and Stewart Blacker.) The Duke, in order to defend his position, launched a legal action against Harry Pollitt, its secretary, and threatened to call Hess as a witness in the action. We suspect a good poker move.

PRO file AIR19/5 deals with the British Civil Service making sure this never happened. On 23 June 1941, David Margesson, the Secretary of State for War wrote somewhat strangely, 'I will see that Hess is not permitted to appear as a witness…'

On 19 June 1941, the same file records a medical report which states: 'Hess's condition has deteriorated markedly … his mental condition has now declared itself as a true psychosis … the outlook is rather gloomy.' Is this not just an early example of using mental instability to prevent court appearance, albeit in this case bizarrely not instigated by the defendant? Is it any wonder the myth has perpetuated? Both accuser and defendant had, in turn, used the same ploy: the British in 1941; Hess in 1941 and 1946.

What makes this report the more interesting is that at the same time Hess was preparing for his meeting with Sir John Simon on 9 June 1941. Peter Raina, in his book *A Daring Venture*,[10] describes the period leading to the meeting in similar terms to the medical report, but any reading of the transcript of the conversation makes it perfectly clear that Hess was lucid and without the treaty that he had brought with him (that had been found in the wee burn on May 11 1941). This is the importance of Raina's book. It makes clear that Hess was extremely lucid post-flight, even given the effect of the failure that had been brought to him.

We are obviously not qualified to comment in an expert medical sense, but during the research we have completed, we have found mention of stomach cramps from time to time, but certainly no major illness.[11] A keen interest in homeopathy[12] presumably also does not indicate insanity, though it may well have been deemed unusual in 1938. In 1934, a new hospital had been opened in Dresden, the Rudolf Hess Krankenhaus, specialising in homeopathy and the study of alternative medicines.[13] It was appropriately named, the Rudolf Hess Hospital. It should be said that alternative medicine was very much part of the zeitgeist of the age and Hess was certainly not the only Nazi leader to have demonstrated an interest.

An avid interest in aviation certainly would argue against madness, particularly at the exalted pre-war level at which Hess participated.[14]

However, Hess was clearly concerned with his health. We have already described his friendship with Prof. Franz Gerl, the specialist gland surgeon. (The Gerl family was also instrumental in looking after Ilse and Wolf Hess after the war.)

The assertion of later intelligence connivance may or may not be true of course, but it does perhaps place Hess's interest in alternative medicine in a different light. It was being used by others to communicate with him – again, outside the normal communication channels.

There is also a specific chapter later in this book dealing with Hess's

The Rudolf Hess Hospital, Dresden

'treatment' at the Zeileis centre in Gallspach, which certainly also raises wider intelligence-based concerns.

Wulf Schwarzwaller, in *Rudolf Hess: The Deputy*, gives a good example of the psychosomatic nature of Hess's plight. In 1947, an American doctor had merely given Hess pills of 'milk powder', a placebo, when Hess complained of stomach cramps. Within ten minutes the pain had eased.

However, in many ways, and certainly by comparison with his other colleagues, Hess could be seen to be reasonably well rounded. Well-educated, a fluent French speaker, together with some English (learned in his early days in Egypt), he came from a comfortable (in English terms) upper middle class background, where early family life was dominated by his father.The foundations of this very safe and secure background was destroyed by the First World War.[15] He was certainly not alone in Germany in sharing that fate.

J.R. Rees relates how he was well thought of by his staff, and one secretary had commented that, 'He was so kind and noble that one felt obliged to be the same way as much as possible.'

Given their eventual collective fate, it could also be argued that membership of the Nazi Party was an illogical act and therefore evidence of insanity. That is a poor argument. Desperate times often call for desperate actions, and as the recent Laurence Rees television programmes demonstrated[16] the German people were actively looking for a strong leadership with clear and simple principles in 1919–20. This does not make Hess and Hitler insane; political opportunists, quite possibly, but insane, no.

Once in power, Hess quickly became known as the 'conscience of the party'. Compared to the more radical members of the party, Hess sometimes acted as a moderator, but these were times in which it was indeed difficult to be a moderate. Richard Evans, in 2005, quoted Hess as offering to shoot members of the so-called 1934 Röhm putsch. J.R. Rees makes the same allegation. By contrast, David Irving makes a convincing case that Hess tried to save some of those executed.[17] In 1935 Hess was party to and signed the Nuremberg Race laws. He then proceeded on an individual basis to employ, protect and help Jews.[18] Certainly there seems to be two Hess's: one the devout Nazi, prepared to do literally anything for his Führer; the other, when off duty, the quiet, unassuming family man. One the State anti-Semite; the other a private protector of at least two Jewish family members.

Hess also appears to have a far less understanding attitude towards the Poles, who he saw as 'less sensitive to a curtailment of freedom'.[19]

However, above all, the overreaching, undeniable, inescapable fact is that Hess was loyal to Hitler. One of the earliest Nazi party members, imprisoned with Hitler in Landsberg in 1923, Hess was unquestionably loyal. This loyalty never disappeared. Even at Nuremberg, when it was quite possible he may have been executed because of his former association he declared, 'I was permitted to work for many years of my life under the greatest son whom my people have brought forth… I do not regret anything.'

Clearly, there was no repentance. When John Harris met Wolf Hess in 1995 it was clear too that this feeling of justification had passed down the generations. Again, without trying to labour the point, we do not believe that what could be construed as making a terrible mistake is evidence of insanity.

Even homosexuality has also been alleged.[20] Evidence in this somewhat sensitive area is thankfully sparse and seems based on the fact that it took ten years for Hess's marriage to produce Wolf Rüdiger in 1937, the only child. The case has already been made that Hess was not the father of Wolf and a 1943 OSS report, *The Mind of Adolf Hitler*, states quite clearly that Hess was homosexual, known as 'Fräulein Anna' in the early days of the Nazi party.[21]

Similarly, perhaps, does an interest in astrology render one insane? Alternatively, one could argue that Hess merely had a wide spectrum of interests.

It seems that Hess's behaviour was wholly typical of the times in which he was thoroughly immersed. We may well have acted in just the same way. We see him as a spirited, adventurous individual, albeit with an intelligent, thoughtful, sensitive side, hailing from a wealthy family who had been deprived their future by the British. Perhaps he was just a reflection of the times in which he lived, perhaps looking to set the agenda, do something about it, perhaps even looking to avenge. We do not understand his anti-Semitism, which publicly at least was undoubtably present.

Perhaps, quite understandably, we can see no written mention of pre-war mental illness, either in official or private documents. On arrival in Scotland in 1941, Hess was given a medical. Conducted by Lt Colonel Graham, Officer in Charge of the Medical Division at Drymen Military Hospital, he concluded that, '... he did not strike me of unsound mind...'[22]

At Nuremberg, the three Russian medical professors, Krashnushkin, Sepp and Kurshakov stated, 'Rudolf Hess, prior to his flight to England, did not suffer from any form of insanity...'[23] J.R. Rees telephoned his report to Nuremberg from London, stating, 'At the moment he is not insane in the strict sense' (19 November 1945). The Americans and French wrote in confirmation, 'Rudolf Hess is not insane at the present time in the strict sense of the word.' They also made the interesting point that, '... the existing hysterical behaviour which the defendant reveals was initiated as a defence against the circumstances in which he found himself while in England'. It seems reasonably clear to these authors that when Hess did not wish to speak or answer, the stock phrase of 'I don't remember' would be used to good effect.

The reader should also reflect on the fact that in 1941 Hess had just completed a significant, technical aeronautical flight. Was the actual outcome really that likely if the aviator was of unsound mind?

Thereafter, we are not able to express a definitive view. We are not qualified to understand or comment on the potential effect of the perception of a massive personal failure. What is the human reaction to a failure without possible redemption?

Equally, we are not able to comment on the use of drugs or their effects, or even the potential use of an electro-therapy lobotomy. There have been cases made that all these were used on Rudolf Hess – we may never know. What we do know is that he was an extremely wily character whilst in captivity and would certainly lie when he thought necessary or appropriate. At Nuremberg he was quite happy to cultivate the impression that he was mentally ill, until he chose to reveal to the court that his illness was indeed a charade. This ability to act was certainly used to good effect when necessary. It provided a powerful defence mechanism when most needed and most vulnerable.

Consequently, Hess was eventually adjudged sane to stand trial. We can only assume that indeed to be the case.[24] Whilst in Spandau, Hess showed a healthy interest in various matters, such as astronomy and the NASA space race. Moody and irritable, yes, but there again, perhaps quite understandably.

So, by way of prelude we can only assume that Hess was rational and consequently we will judge him and his actions on that basis. We now believe it wholly appropriate that we do so, particularly when judged by the standards of the times rather than trying to judge with the benefit of hindsight or alternatively, worse still, against modern day standards and ethics.

Religion

We have already commented on Hess's association with Bishop George Bell of Chichester, on account of Bell seeing Hess as a potential moderating influence with the ongoing party versus church battle in Nazi Germany. This is a complex area in which the Nazi Party was trying its hardest to reduce the influence of the Church in national affairs, and indeed saw and promoted the NSDAP as the new church. North German Protestantism was initially the target, but later the more typically southern Catholics were also targeted.

Hess as Deputy Führer of the party played a leading role in this issue and was typically consistent throughout in principle. Tellingly, at Nuremberg, with the hangman's noose awaiting most defendants (and they realised their fact), virtually all choose to regain their Christian beliefs.[25] There were only two exceptions: Hess and Rosenberg. Hess, when asked, simply said, I expect to be extremely busy preparing my defence. If I have any praying to do, I'll do it here.'[26] He remained averse to any Christian counselling, despite being visited by the priest Gerecke on a regular basis. We take this as another example of the man's conviction to a cause in which he was instrumental and believed in completely.

Astrology and Anthroposophy

Whilst it is easy to dismiss astrology as perhaps no more than a distraction, in Nazi Germany it was undoubtedly taken very seriously indeed. Joseph Goebbels saw the clear propaganda value of having the ability to prophesise and predict success, and both Rudolf Hess and Heinrich Himmler were adherents, simply through their upbringings. Hess had been a keen astrologer as a child and this interest was enhanced through his friendship with Karl Haushofer, who in turn was an early leader of the Thule Society. Whilst not strictly interested in astrology, it dealt with various racial and esoteric matters. Based again in Munich, it became an early sponsor of the NDAP.

By the late 1930s there were several retained Nazi astrologers. Those relevant to Hess were:

- Karl Ernst Krafft (1900–45) who had correctly predicted (apparently) the Munich Beerhall bomb in November 1938. It appears that he had also stated that if Britain and Germany had not made peace by June 1941, the omens would be bad for Germany.
- Ernst Schulte-Strathaus (1881–1968). Schulte-Strathaus was another character who combined his role of Chief of Art and Culture for Rudolf Hess with part-time astrological prediction. He assumed his role for Hess in 1934, based in the Brown House in Munich. He consequently got to know and work alongside Rosenberg, Ley and Bormann. It was Schulte-Strathaus who alerted Hess to the alignment of Taurus on 10 May 1941.[27]

We caveat the descriptions of these prophesies, simply because according to some (Richard Deacon in particular)[28] the British Secret Service were feeding false information back to Hess through a variety of agents and even doctored astrological pamphlets. Deacon even states, 'Fleming's (Ian as in 007) contact in Switzerland succeeded in planting on Hess an astrologer who was also a British agent.' We should say that Richard Deacon's reputation has been somewhat tarnished by a couple of articles challenging the veracity of the evidence he brought to bear.[29] However, we do know that back in the Britain MI5 had recruited their own astrologer, Louis de Wohl (1903–61), to try and imagine what his continental counterparts were telling their masters.

Obviously firm proof in this area is difficult to find, but one fact is not debatable. There is no doubt that on 10 May 1941 there certainly was an unusual astrological event, in that six planets in the sign of Taurus coincided with the full moon. We had previously relegated this occurrence to a navigational aid at best (just follow the planets and fly west) but, on further consideration, it could always be argued that is why Hess chose 10 May, rather than say two days earlier or later.

After the flight, the astrologers were rounded up under 'Aktion Hess'. Schulte-Strathaus was imprisoned; at first in Munich and later in Berlin, but again it is hard to discern how much of this was for show and how much was intended. Krafft died in January 1945 of typhus, so has not left any testimony. Schulte-Strathaus lived to a ripe old age, dying following a car crash in Munich in 1968.

Hess continued his interest in the post-war space race and followed the 1960s and 1970s NASA missions from Spandau with great interest, writing to suggest improvements to their equipment. NASA reciprocated by sending the old man photographs of the moon's surface.[30]

Rudolf Hess has also been cited as being an adherent of anthroposophy, a philosophy based on the life and work of Rudolf Steiner (1861–1925). This philosophy was championed by Hess and Walter Darré in the 1930s, and amongst its ideas are organic farming, natural medicines and hierarchy in races.

Duties

In 1933 Adolf Hitler actively withdrew from the day-to-day business of the party so as to emphasise his new role as Reich Chancellor. Consequently, Hess was henceforth authorised to make decisions on behalf of Hitler 'in all questions of party leadership'. He was duly appointed as a Minister without Portfolio, the Führer's Deputy.

As Deputy Führer he took responsibility for the NSDAP, virtually in entirety, and with it the expansion of the Nazi ideology throughout continental Europe.

His major role was taking the responsibility for party discipline and, in modern day parlance, the Human Resource issues for the regional political leaders, the 'Gauleiters'. Given the continual infighting and naked ambition of many so involved this was no easy role to perform and in many ways we suspect that Hess started to see the NDAP at its worst, in terms of raw human traits, as well as at its most successful in terms of accomplishments.

Interestingly, Ingeborg Sperr, Hess's Berlin secretary, ascribed the infighting as a major cause of Hess's medical issues, such as they were. She was quite clear that 'He was never able to assert himself against brutal men,' and 'It was due to the steady battle that he, in his position, had to wage against those things that were strange and repulsive to his noble nature that this extremely sensitive man's health was finally impaired' and 'He first suffered from insomnia and later from colic pains in the region of the gall bladder.'[31]

Naturally, as the Reich expanded to take in the conquered territories, the political control required expanded proportionately. Over the period 1933–45, the sheer scale of the expansion of the Briennerstrasse complex in Munich reflected the increase in NDAP membership and required leadership. Later, as Germany subsumed whole countries, appropriate systems of political control became major issues between the various factions in the Berlin government and the Munich party, with Hess being the ultimate arbiter.

However, the role was far more than simply that of an administrator and part-time mediator. The position also allowed for law making and interfaced frequently between party and state. The controversial Nuremberg Laws that Hess signed in 1935 stemmed from the 'Racial Policy Office', which fell under Hess's remit. He was also responsible for the subsequent implementation of the laws, with his office having to be consulted on all prospective exemptions of the ban on Aryan-Jewish mixed marriages. Typically, he refused any exemptions.[32]

In addition to the role described above, Hess also enjoyed, 'Sufficient breeding to extend a cordial welcome to the Reich's guests whom busy Adolf turned over to his Stellvertreter.'[33] The obvious examples are the visits of the Duke and Duchess of Windsor to Munich and the Obersalzberg in 1938, and the November 1940 Soviet deputation and Molotov to Berlin.

F.W. Winterbotham noted: 'I found a certain depth of character and level of intelligence which was often missing in other Nazi leaders. There was a latent sensitivity in place of the ruthless efficiency of the Goerings and the Himmlers.'[34]

In conclusion, Hess was certainly a busy man, with a busy and growing, political schedule. Constitutionally (such as it was in Nazi Germany), he held an extremely important position and had become adept at controlling and, where necessary, stunting the ambition of others and pretenders. He seemed to 'allow' the following for purposes of meaningful discussion and debate: Adolf Hitler, Ernst Bohle, Alfred Rosenberg, Ilse Hess, Ernst Schulte-Strathaus, Albrecht Haushofer, Karl Haushofer, Fritz Gerl.

It is likely in our opinion that the channel used to make Hess to decide to fly was included within the above list, or a combination of the same. A notably small list of confidants, given his position.

However, we also doubt that he was happy in his role. He had left his father's boring and staid world of commerce and trade in search of adventure and now, in 1941, some twenty-five years later, he had undoubtedly progressed in terms of career but had morphed back into the role of an administrator, simply because he was one of the few at the top of the Nazi Party that Hitler could trust. A backhanded compliment indeed. In 1939 he had asked to re-join the Luftwaffe, as had Heydrich. Hitler allowed the latter but banned Hess for a year. That year was due to expire in October 1940 and, as we can see, Hess lost no time.

Calendar

From the information in our possession, we have been able to re-create the following timetable for Hess's movements:

31 August 1940 Munich with Karl Haushofer. Meeting lasting into the early hours.

8 September 1940 Bad Godesberg, with Albrecht Haushofer.

10 September 1940 Gallspach, Austria at the Zeileis Institute.

2 October 1940 Berlin, meets Farinacci, the Italian Fascist.

8 October 1940 Berlin, intervenes in argument between Ribbentrop and the Ausland Organisation.[35]

9 October 1940 Berlin, asks Bohle to visit him at 64 Wilhelmstrasse to draft a letter to the Duke of Hamilton.[36]

14 October 1940 Berlin, meets Goebbels.[37]

15 October 1940 Berlin, takes tea with Goebbels: 'Hess makes an excellent impression on me: he is quiet, objective, frank and very confident.'[38] 'Hess's opinion on Ribbentrop is completely contemptuous.'[39]

4 November 1940 Berlin, writes to Ilse Hess, 'I firmly believe that from the flight I am about to make one of these days…'

8 November 1940 Augsburg, inspects the Bf110. Later, with Hitler at the Löwenbräukellar, Munich.

9 November 1940 Munich, remembers the fallen comrades of the 1923 failed putsch.

13 November 1940 Berlin, meets Molotov, the Russian Ambassador.

15 November 1940 Berlin, meets Goebbels: 'Hess is still incorrigibly hostile to Ribbentrop.'
23 November 1940 Berlin, meets Ion Antonescu, Romanian Prime Minister.
25 November 1940 Berlin, 'Hess is flying back to Munich. He looks very bad and is not in good health. He is such a decent fellow.'[40]
21 December 1940 Augsburg, trial flight.
24 December 1940 Addresses the German nation on 'Heiliger Abend'.

10 January 1941 Augsburg, Bf110 trial.
11 January 1941 Augsburg, Bf110 trial.
18 January 1941 Augsburg, Bf110 trial.
20 January 1941 Hanover, installing the Gauleiter.
22 January 1941 Munich, meets Anton Mussert, Dutch politician.
29 January 1941 Augsburg, Bf110 trial.
30 January 1941 Berlin, with Hitler at Sports Palace.
9 February 1941 Vienna, with Hitler youth. Then Breslau and Katowice to mark Karl Hanke's assumption of office as Gauleiter.
20 February 1941 Munich, funeral of Hermann Kriebel in the Feldherrnhalle: 'Hess makes an excellent funeral oration, which moves us all greatly.'
21–24 February 1941 With Albrecht Haushofer.
8 March 1941 Augsburg, Bf110 trial.
16 March 1941 Berlin, army inspection
20 March 1941 Berlin, exhibition of 'Planning and Aufbau in Osten'. Discussion of motion film industry with Goebbels.[41]
29 March 1941 Augsburg, Helmut Kaden begins a series of air tests in the Bf110.
12–15 April 1941 Berlin, with Albrecht Haushofer
20 April 1941 Hess makes a radio speech to mark Hitler's birthday.
20–22 April 1941 Rumours that Hess may have travelled to Spain and also met Darlan at Beauvais. Not corroborated.
26 April 1941 Munich, Hess meets Albrecht and Karl Haushofer at his home.
26/27 April 1941 Weekend at Zeileis?
30 April 1941 Munich to receive Salvadore Merino, leader of the Spanish Falange. Later trial flight from Augsburg.

1 May 1941 Augsburg factory presentations. Tells Messerschmitt technicians that final modifications are needed by 5 May.[42]

3 May 1941 Flies to Berlin from Munich Riem. Arrives 5.20pm. Meets Hitler that evening.

4 May 1941 Berlin, for Hitler's Reichstag speech at the Kroll Opera House at 6.00pm and subsequent interview with Hitler. Takes overnight train to Munich at 10.05pm.

5 May 1941 (Monday) Meets Albrecht Haushofer for lunch at Hotel Drei Mohren, Augsburg, then to airfield for trial flight at 4.00pm. Then Munich.

6 May 1941 Last of Helmut Kaden's air tests with the Bf110 at 11.20am., this time with Blumel, the radio expert.

8 May 1941 (Thursday): Berlin, attending Reichstag.[43]

9 May 1941 Letter writing, as evidenced by letter to Darré. Telephoned Dr Gerhard Klopfer in connection with the constitutional position of the King of the United Kingdom.

10 May 1941 (Saturday, 11.30am–1.00pm) Munich, lunches with Rosenberg and Meyer.

Augsburg, 5.42pm, take-off.
Eaglesham, Scotland, 11.09pm.

---

[1] The famous Gärtnerplatztheatre. In 2015 an announcement was made that the plot is to be sold.

[2] Wulf Schwarzwaller, *Rudolf Hess: The Deputy*, Quartet, London, 1988.

[3] 'Hitlers Deputy was Godfather of the Iselerlift,' Brigitte Horn.

[4] Ernest R. Pope, *Munich Playground*, WH Allen, London, 1942.

[5] Ernest Pope records that Hess attended the concerts of Sir Thomas Beecham, held in Munich in the 1930s.

[6] 13 May 1941.

[7] To the authors' knowledge this letter is not in the public domain. Ilse Hess also had a copy, but again her copy 'was lost in 1945 when nearly all my correspondence of those years went…' *Ilse Hess, Prisoner of Peace*, Briton Publishing Co., London, 1954, p. 27.

[8] The two men had lunched together on 10 May 1941.

[9] J.R. Rees, *The Case of Rudolf Hess*, Heinemann, London, 1947.

[10] Peter Raina, *A Daring Venture*, Peter Lang, Bern, 2014.

[11] Ibid – tells of a 1937 prostatitis and a general fear of cancer. Hess had also pursued alternative medicines. He brought a number of remedies with him when he landed in Scotland.

[12] Hess is often pictured as Chairman of a 1938 International Homeopathy Conference in Berlin.

[13] Post-flight it was renamed the Fürstenstrasse Hospital.
[14] Hess won the Round the Zugspitz air race in 1934. He was a close friend of Willy Messerschmitt and his director Theo Croneiss.
[15] The nature of the British occupation of Egypt which had started in 1882, changed in 1914 when Egypt became a formal protectorate of Britain.
[16] Laurence Rees, *The Nazis: A Warning from History*, BBC Television, 1979.
[17] David Irving, *Hess: The Missing Years 1941–1945*, Focal Point, Windsor, 2010.
[18] We cite the treatment of the Haushofer family. Please see *Hess: The Missing Years 1941–1945*, Focal Point, Windsor, 2010.
[19] Franz Schlegelberger to Hans Lammers, 17 April 1941. Wulf Schwarzwaller, *Rudolf Hess: The Deputy*, Quartet, London, 1988
[20] John Costello, *Ten Days that Saved the West*, Bantam Press, London, 1991.
[21] Walter Langer, *The Mind of Adolf Hitler: The Secret Wartime Report*. Basic Books, New York, 1972.
[22] Examination, 13 May 1941.
[23] J.R. Rees, appendix to *The Case of Rudolf Hess*, Heinemann, London, 1947.
[24] Report to tribunal, 20 November 1945, 'Rudolf is not insane at the present time.'
[25] F.T. Grossmith, *The Cross and the Swastika*, H.E. Walter, Worthing, 1984.
[26] Ibid.
[27] Institut für Zeitgeschichte, Munich, 4653/71 – 252089.
[28] Richard Deacon, *The British Secret Service*, Grafton, London, 1991.
[29] Leeson, Robert (ed.), *Hayek: A Collaborative Biography, Part III: Fraud, Fascism and Free Market Religion*, Routledge, Abingdon,1994.
[30] Eugene Bird, *The Loneliest Man in the World*, Sphere, London, 1974.
[31] J.R. Rees, *The Case of Rudolf Hess*, Heinemann, London, 1947.
[32] Dietrich Orlow, *The Nazi Party 1919–1945: A Complete History*, Enigma, New York, 2008.
[33] Ernest R. Pope, *Munich Playground*, WH Allen, London, 1942.
[34] Fred Winterbotham, *Secret and Personal*, William Kimber, London, 1969.
[35] *Goebbels' Diary 1939–1941*, Hamish Hamilton, London, 1982.
[36] Wolf Hess, *My Father Rudolf Hess,* WH Allen, London, 1984.
[37] Ibid.
[38] Ibid.
[39] Ibid.
[40] Ibid.
[41] Ibid.
[42] FO 4355/45.
[43] Wolf Hess, *My Father Rudolf Hess*, WH Allen, London, 1984, p. 83.

CHAPTER 14

THE ZEILEIS INSTITUTE

(Hess's guilty pleasure?)

Introduction

The previous chapter detailed known and recorded data concerning Rudolf Hess and was written to present a picture of how Hess was living in the months leading up to the flight. He seemed to have been commuting between Berlin and Munich, whilst training for his flight at Augsburg. We now wish to detail some very specific new data and evidence that we believe brings an important new perspective to the motives leading Hess to make the decision to fly.

John Costello

Prior to his untimely and somewhat unusual death in 1995, John Costello, the accomplished Second World War historian, agreed to meet John Harris at the Farmers Club, London, for supper. Always generous with his time and papers, Costello passed on two things at their meeting: first, some records concerning Hess's 1941 interviews at Mytchett Place[1] and secondly, a piece of advice that has sustained and subsequently proven invaluable.

The piece of advice was simply, 'don't assume, go and see for yourselves'. Over the years both authors have been devotees of this dictum, both in their business lives as well as in the matter of Hess research. We deferentially refer to it as the 'Costello principle' and it has certainly helped us in matters of BF110 auxiliary oil tanks, the alleged pilot's notes, Elektra and suchlike.

The January 2015 trip to Bavaria and Upper Austria

So, in January 2015, once again following the 'Costello principle', we travelled to Bavaria, first to track down the Haushofer residences at Pähl and Garmisch Partenkirchen and then, having successfully done so, we turned our attention to Gallspach, which is in Upper Austria, between Linz and Passau.

Gallspach had latently featured on our 'radar' on account of the letters that Hess had written to the Haushofers in September 1940 (see Chapter 3). By reference to Google Earth the letters had been marked as coming from what appeared to be a small and inconsequential village (see Chapters 2 to 6), beyond the German frontier. So, by adopting the core principle once again, Messrs. Harris and Wilborn duly paid a visit, wondering what on earth the Deputy Führer of Nazi Germany was doing in such a place in September 1940.

As has been described already, Hess spent most of his time in and around Munich in late 1940/ early 1941. At the same time as performing his Nazi Party duties, he was mastering the finer points of the Bf110 and its navigational systems. Like most of the Nazi elite he did not particularly enjoy Berlin and so tried to limit his time there. Gallspach is approximately 200 km (120 miles) east of Munich, so, as we duly discovered, was not an inconsequential journey to make. En route, speeding along the Austrian A1 autobahn, we joyfully speculated as to finding evidence of wartime brothels or even greater perversions.

When we eventually arrived, we were yet again shocked and not a little surprised, emotions that we have become accustomed to when dealing in matters Hess. Gallspach is indeed a small Austrian village, largely surrounded by undulating arable farming land in the Grieskirchen district of Upper Austria. Its population is usually around 1,800 persons. However, it has one very significant facility that is certainly unique to Gallspach – the Zeileis Institute.

The Zeileis Institute

We visited in late January 2015 and the large institute building appeared to be empty, but with the main doors oddly left wide open. The garden benches had been dismantled to shelter from the effects of winter and it all gave the appearance of perhaps having seen better days. We peered into the empty reception area and were again surprised to see a bust of Nikola Tesla, who we thought was vaguely related to electricity and its uses. There appeared to be no one about.

We then strolled around the village itself and remarked on the large number of hotels and guest houses, again either closed or boarded up. It was all rather reminiscent of an English coastal resort in winter, save there was not a coast, big sky, sea or slot machines. We managed to deduce that whatever went on in the Zeileis Institute, which was a very large, factory-like building, dominating the middle part of the village, persons must have travelled to Gallspach and then presumably stayed there, thus making use of the numerous hotels and guesthouses.

After a beer and coffee in probably the one establishment that appeared to be somewhat reluctantly still open, we left for Munich in the cold, late winter afternoon. However, there was clearly at lot of research work to be done concerning Gallspach.

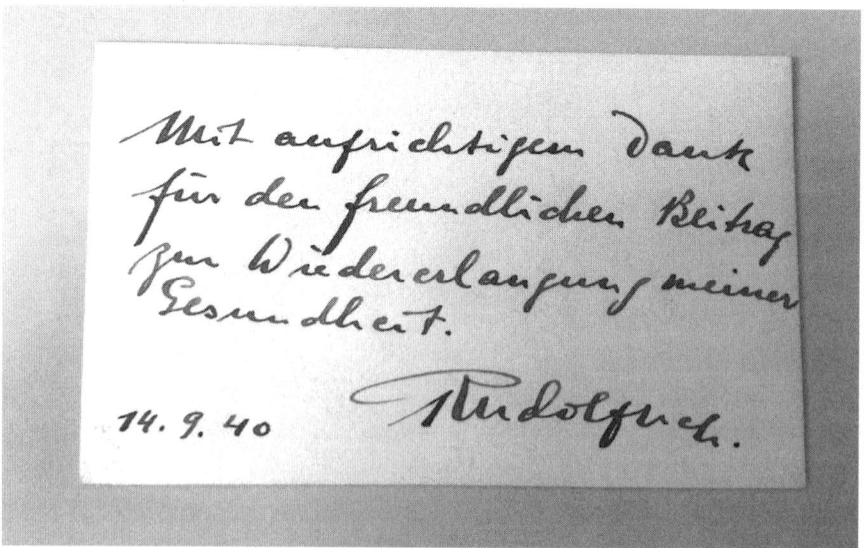

Mit aufrichtigem Dank
für den freundlichen Beitrag
zur Wiedererlangung meiner
Gesundheit.

14. 9. 40 Rudolf Heß.

The Hess compliment slip sent to the Zeileis family following the September 1940 visit (With sincere thanks for the kind contributions to the regaining of my health)

Upon our return to the UK, John Harris emailed the institute and was very pleased and grateful to receive a reply from the current owner and direct descendant of the founder, Valentin Zeileis. Martin Zeileis very helpfully advised that Rudolf Hess had indeed visited the institute twice; once in September 1940, when the Haushofer/Hess correspondence was taking place and then presumably in late April 1941, as Martin had stated that the second visit was within a fortnight of the flight of 10 May.[2] Given the uncertainty surrounding the weekend of the 20/21 April and the, did he/didn't he fly to Madrid story, we naturally became wholly hooked on this small agricultural community in upper Austria.

Martin then sent John Harris a scanned copy of a Rudolf Hess 'compliment slip', dated 14 September 1940, on which his grandfather was personally thanked by Rudolf Hess.

This seemed too incredible to be true, not an uncommon feeling in matters Hess. So, we then researched the Zeileis Institute to ascertain what was going on there and why Rudolf Hess might travel there twice, seemingly as a very satisfied customer. Once in September 1940 and once in April 1941. Perhaps, more ominously, we then discovered that we were not the only 'researchers' interested in the community, as Messrs. Himmler, Heydrich, Six and the RHSA had also prepared very detailed files.[3]

The Zeileis Institute

Valentin Zeileis (1873–1939) was above all a successful businessman. After various jobs in his youth, including a spell in the circus (and two marriages), he developed usable early electro therapy treatments, using extremely high voltages of alternating currents. This was extremely successful and profitable and in 1912 he acquired the schloss at Gallspach to conduct the treatments. By the late 1920s the demand proved so great that a specialised building was constructed; the present-day institute building that we had visited. The Zeileis family remained (and remain) in the schloss, using it as a private residence.

In addition to the schloss, the acquisition had come complete with significant agricultural property and once again Zeileis proved his financial acumen by supplying the Bols factory in the Netherlands with eggs for their production of eggnog.

Gallspach was also physically transformed with the numerous lodging and hotels being constructed solely to cater for the demand. By the mid-1930s up to 95,000 'patients' per year were being treated and accommodated in

Gallspach. The nearest equivalent today must be something like Disneyland Paris, though that is probably unfair to the efficacy of the medical processes being undertaken in Gallspach. Perhaps a 'Butlins with electrotherapy' is a closer analogy, but we certainly do not wish to disparage the Zeileis family (or their treatment), who have been very open and helpful to us.

The treatment

The treatment was essentially electrical stimulation, using the high voltage currents. Not surprisingly, perhaps, it did indeed 'unlock' some conditions and cures that had previously been either repressed or not triggered. We will discuss electroconvulsive therapy later in this book, but to the layman it certainly appears that the treatment does work in specific cases, without perhaps even the practitioners fully understanding why. It is still used on a widespread basis today.

There is no suggestion that ECT (Electroconvulsive Therapy) was performed at Gallspach, the treatment appears to be administered by the electrical current 'arcing' or 'jumping' from an insulated steel rod held by the practitioner across to the patient. By moving the rod, the area of treatment could be duly adjusted. In 2015, at the time of our visit, a spa was also offered by way of treatment.

The outcome

The saying that 'desperate people do desperate things' does come to mind. There is absolutely no doubt that the Zeileis treatment certainly helped cure and treat a great many people. Statistically, we presume that was always going to occur, given the huge numbers involved. There must also be an element of a placebo, in that some treatment, whatever it is, is better than no treatment. Either way, there is no denying the success of the enterprise as a business. The Zeileis family became rich, and the dynasty had already passed down a generation to Fritz Zeileis when his father died in 1939, aged sixty-six.

The institute under the Nazis and the Jewish aspect

Money usually fuels jealousies, and the institute has certainly suffered from various jealousies over the years. Initially they came from the established medical schools who saw the treatment as no more than 'quackery'. However, the sheer numbers of 'believers' and customers somewhat blunted their argument.

Valentin Zeileis was decidedly anti-Nazi (the Regime being bad for business), duly prohibiting the Fascist salute, and sure enough a reciprocal challenge was an inevitability. All patients were treated irrespective of race or creed, but the local Nazi party officials typically took exception to the small minded and trivial; transgressions such as a failure to display Nazi notices in the waiting rooms. Dr Holter in *30 Jahre Gallspach* (30 Years of Gallspach), written in 1956, describes his various visits to the local functionaries to 'clear up some kind of trivial friction'.[4]

Interestingly, we know that by the time under review, the Zeileis Institute had also formed the 'Bund der Zeileisfreunde e.V' (e.V = Eingetragner Verein).

Based in Ebersberg, Bavaria at 3 Rickstrasse, its 'bundesführer' or secretary was a Major Karl Schäfer. It seems that the point to the Eingetragner Verein, or 'Registered Association', was two-fold. First, it allowed some patients to pay their fees to it, thus presumably reducing the taxable profits for the Zeileis family and, secondly, it appears to have been used as a means to curry favour.

As has already been stated, the Nazis clearly coveted the money-making ability of the institute and there had been calls to nationalise it and turn it into a sanitorium for front line soldiers. The local mayor also had the somewhat odd idea that it could be beneficially converted into a 'bakery and foodstuff factory'.[5]

It now appears that the 'Bund der Zeileisfreunde e.V' also started to be used as a lobbying device, presumably to ensure its patron's independence and continuance.

Following on from Hess's stay in September 1940, on 1 October 1940, Major Schäfer wrote to Hess, promising to compile a report for him within eight days on the 'remarkable results of the radiation treatment', whilst at the same time appears to forward 1,000 Reichmarks to the Deputy Führer, for distribution 'zur verfugung gestellt' (at your discretion). 1,000 RM equated to around $400 in 1941, c,$8000 today. Whilst this is not perhaps a huge figure, we have no record as to how many times such offers were made. We have only the single record.

This offer of money is heavily underlined in the files from where it came, those of the RHSA – the Reichssicherheitshauptamt – and the Reich main security office, usually referred to as the Gestapo or SS.

Bluntly, the SS, Himmler, Heydrich and Frank Six, who was the operative responsible for the collection of the data, were quite aware that Hess was

Hess at Gallspach (The Deputy Führer, Rudolf Hess (middle) in today's Salzburger street, on the way to his lodgings, the Schützenhof

being offered money by the 'non-profit making' arm of the Zeileis Institute. Hence, we presume, the very firm underscoring of the relevant paragraphs of the letter. Frank Six (1909–75) was the SS 'English expert', having drawn up the infamous black book of those to be detained and executed in the event of a German invasion of Britain.

After the initial research, Tony Stott of the Secret Scotland website also raised an interesting point concerning the Zeileis family, who he believes were of Jewish origin. If this is indeed the case, it does seem somewhat unusual that the institute was left as unmolested as it appears to have been through the war years. We now know that Hess was being advanced monies from its e.V and one must perhaps wonder if others were so rewarded.

The research is clearly in its early stages, but it does seem to us that Hess was essentially protecting at least two Jewish families: the Haushofers and now the Zeileis. Admittedly, both were providing services to him in differing ways, but could the disclosure that the Deputy Führer was protecting Jewish families, whilst being a signatory to the 1935 Nuremberg Laws provide an embarrassment, or even a reason to be blackmailed by others? The truth is we do not yet know.

10 May 1941

It is quite probable that we would have merely discounted Gallspach as another of Hess's idiosyncrasies were it not for the events of the night of the flight and the possibility/threat of Gestapo blackmail. We now know that Karlheinz Pintsch instructed Lutz and Lippert (Hess's security officer and chauffeur) to travel to Gallspach on the night of 10 May 1941, in the Hess DKW staff car. This was after first dropping off Pintsch at Munich station so he could travel to Berchtesgaden to deliver the news to his Führer.

We presume Lutz and Lippert followed their orders, because they were duly arrested in Gallspach at 5.30am on 11 May 1941, presumably, we would estimate, the time of their arrival.

Peter Padfield has written off this odd episode as bizarre, but we now believe it important in understanding the affair. There seem to be only two possible explanations:

1. Pintsch knew what his master was trying to achieve, but he clearly did not know what Hitler had been told by Hess and others, and so was trying to protect Lutz and Lippert, or
2. Pintsch was merely controlling Lutz and Lippert and knew full well that the Gestapo would pick them up (thus being seen as being compliant in the eyes of Hitler in the uncertain aftermath of the Hess flight).

We are content that Pintsch would not have known the full extent to which Hitler was involved and was cognisant in the affair. It could well be that he anticipated Hitler 'exploding' when learning that Hess had flown and so was merely protecting his more junior staff. The far more difficult area is the inter-relationship, if any, between the RHSA and Hess. This will be discussed in a later chapter.

The obvious question in this part of the story is why on earth would Pintsch send his two colleagues to Gallspach to await developments? We are quite ready to believe that Pintsch may not have been sure of the extent of Hitler's knowledge, but the key question, even so, is why did he feel safe and secure in using Gallspach in this manner? According to Martin Zeileis, Hess only stayed there twice, once in September 1940 and once the following April. Why was this location therefore deemed quite so secure? Was it essentially a 'paid for safe house'?

Evidence of what?

We were initially quite prepared to place the Zeileis Institute in the same category as Hess's interest in homeopathy, other alternative medicines and anthroposophy that is and was well known. However, we now believe that its use as a potential safe haven' would appear to elevate its relevance and importance, particularly as it is not even in Germany.

Furthermore, given that Himmler and the RHSA were clearly monitoring it, we began to wonder if Hess was perhaps being blackmailed, or perceived the potential threat of blackmail, by reason of the 'Friends of Zeileis' organisation?

Following our 2015 visit we corresponded with Wolfgang Perr, who has written a three-part history of Gallspach and its environs. Perr believes that Hess had visited more than the two occasions that we have discovered. He put us in touch with the former mayor's son who unfortunately declined to share any knowledge he may have gleaned from his father.

---

1 Now published in 2014 by Peter Raina as *A Daring Venture*, Peter Lang, Bern.

2 Email, March 2015.

3 Instytut Pamieci Narodowej, Poland – 362/12 (also in the United States Holocaust Memorial Museum, Washington, DC).

4 Alfred Holter, *30 Jahre Gallspach*, Verlag Leitner & Co, Wels, Austria, 1956.

5 Ibid.

CHAPTER 15

POLAND

'To be defeated and not submit, is victory; to be victorious and rest on one's laurels, is defeat.'

Józef Piłsudski (1867–1935)

September 1939, rubble and ruins after the German bombing of Warsaw

This is easily the most difficult, most rewarding and most researched chapter of the book, and we sincerely hope we finally reached the correct conclusion.

One of the major findings of this book is actually to discount the active role of the Poles in the early stages of the Hess affair. That having been said, there are some truly spectacular coincidences in connection with the Polish government in exile, which would normally infer engagement, but we now firmly believe that the Poles were not at least initially involved. This certainly was not our original (and until 2019) conclusion, but we now hope to explain the sequence of our discoveries and, in particular, in Chapter 23, the explanation of the extraordinary assassination attempt that the Poles mounted on 19 May 1941.

Ultimately, we hope the reader can at least understand our thought process in this somewhat tortuous analysis. This is very important, as the invasion of Poland was of course the justification for Britain entering the Second World War.

The sad, sad history of Poland in the Second World War and its eventual fate in 1945 is well known. The history of the exiled Polish forces and their possible role in the Hess affair was first somewhat timidly explored by John Harris in his *1999 Hess: The British Conspiracy.*[1]

This book merely brought to attention the fact that Władysław Sikorski, the then head of the Polish nation in exile had landed at Prestwick Airfield on the Clyde estuary on the morning of 11 May 1941, only a matter of hours after the Deputy Führer of Germany had come to earth at Eaglesham, some 25 miles to the northeast. The first coincidence.

The second coincidence was that Harris later went on to provide the extraordinary piece of evidence that Roman Battaglia, the Polish Consular official who was first to interrogate Hess after his landing (in the unlikely setting of Busby Scout Hall) was well known to Carl Burckhardt from his time as the Head of the League of Nations delegation to Danzig, at the time of the Polish Corridor crisis. The extent of this pre-war relationship was such that Mrs Battaglia, when marooned in Angers, France in 1940, had seen fit to write to Burckhardt, asking for a loan of money.[2]

The third coincidence was that a member of Roman Battaglia's landlord's family, Keith Fairweather, was married to the daughter of Lord Runciman, who had spent much of the late 1930s trying to prevent the Sudeten crisis. As history now relates, Runciman failed, but his house, Doxford Hall,

Fa'side House, Newton Mearns

Northumberland, was virtually on the Hess flightline. In conjunction, three incredible coincidences.[3]

Surely there must be some correlation?

However, we have recently discovered what we believe to be a very important document indeed and now reproduce the same. This is the report of Roman Battaglia, the Polish consul in Glasgow to his London HQ, following his extraordinary interrogation of Rudolf Hess in what is now Giffnock Scout Hall. It reads:

Consulate of the Republic of Poland in Glasgow Glasgow, 15.5.1941

To the Minister of Foreign Affairs in London

I am honoured to communicate the following:

On the night of May 10-11, between midnight and 2 am, I served as an interpreter for the Home Guard in their dealings with a pilot, who turned out to be Rudolph Hess, in Home Guard's headquarters in Giffnock near Glasgow.

At 11.45 pm, Mr Fairweather, my host, received a call from Giffnock. He lives in Newton Mearns and serves as an intelligence officer and German interpreter for the Home Guard. He was informed that a German pilot was shot down and was held in HG [Home Guard] headquarters in Giffnock. Mr Fairweather was summoned to serve as the interpreter.

Since Mr Fairweather broke his arm and was, at that time, under the influence of a powerful dormitive, I volunteered to go in his stead. My offer was accepted, and a car was sent to pick me up.

I arrived in Giffnock shortly after midnight. I was introduced to the commander, Colonel Hardie, and begun my work.

I found myself in the following setting. A large room was crowded by over a dozen HG officers and a few civilians. All excited by the event, all were standing up.

The German pilot, a tall brunet, was sitting in a comfortable armchair. When I asked him if he had been injured, he answered that he was not, but he did suffer from lower back pain caused by the impact of the fall.

When I asked if he needed a doctor, he answered that he would not mind if they had a doctor on the premises, but overall he did not care for it.

The pilot was ordered to surrender all of his personal belongings. He took off his overalls and stood there in his elegant uniform with insignia. As he later explained, he was the captain of the Air Force.

The Home Guard had already taken his map and some other papers. He took two watches from his pocket followed by a compass, a wallet with some photographs, where I could only see children, various medication, a syringe with needles, and some ampules for injections. When asked, he said that he has problems with his liver and duodenum. He fears sudden pains during his flights. Therefore he carried all the paraphernalia with him at all times. He described other pills as sugar and concentrated nutrients.

The interrogators (the interrogation was conducted somewhat chaotically, by several people) told me to inform the pilot that all his personal belongings will be returned.

Then the pilot was asked about the purpose of his flight. He claimed that it was a special personal mission to meet with the Duke of Hamilton and headed to Duke Dungavel's residence. When asked about how he came up with such an idea, he answered that he knew the Duke personally. He met him at the Berlin Olympics. Moreover, he and the Duke share an acquaintance. This acquaintance was supposed to facilitate his meeting with the Duke. The pilot claimed that his mission is of vital importance to the RAF.

When asked if he was alone, the pilot confirmed. He gave his word. When he was informed that a burnt body was found in the fuselage and that some people saw two people jumping out of the plane, he said it was impossible, unless another plane crashed at the same time and place.

The pilot was later interrogated about where and how he flew. He answered that he took off from Augsburg around 5.45 pm /6.45 for Britain. He flew the Messerschmitt 110 and reached Scotland just before dusk. Since it was still daylight, he decided to stay in the air. He had an additional tank of gas (without which such a long journey would be impossible on a fighter plane) When above Scotland, he lost the road to Dungavel, and despite the darkness (at 10.45) he attempted to land. When he had realised that it was impossible to land, he flew higher and turned the 'plane on its back', fell out of the cockpit, and landed with his parachute.

When asked, he insisted that he carried no weapons or munitions. When he was informed that there were explosions in the burning wreck, he explained that they could have originated from three bullets on his plane. His testimony about not having any weapons was false. Police Inspector Hyslop later told me there were three machine guns on his plane.

When asked about his name, the pilot claimed it to be Alfred Horn. When, at some point, it was mentioned that he looked very similar to Rudolph Hess, he remained very calm and said that he heard that before.

The pilot claimed that he wanted to meet the Duke of Hamilton and that his map can testify to that. When I pointed out that a route could be purposefully drafted on a map to deceive, he nodded agreement.

I asked him several questions. When asked if he served in the German army during the Great War, he confirmed that he was drafted towards the end. When asked if he was a SS member, he confirmed but added that he was not in the SS anymore. When asked if he knew Gdansk, he claimed to have last visited the city in 1933. When asked about how, given the German army's discipline, he could travel without any clearance from his superiors, he answered, that he intended to explain this to the Duke of Hamilton. When asked if he was a deserter, he sharply answered 'no'.

At some point the pilot added that he flew on his initiative since because of his age (he claimed to be 47) he was forbidden to fly. Then he added that he 'showed some good sportsmanship' (*eine schone sportliche Leistung*).

Two British officers interrupted the interrogation. They asked the pilot if he flew the Messerschmitt 110 model and asked him to sign the plane's photographs, as confirmation.

Just before 2 am a high ranking officer of the Home Guard arrived to collect the pilot. He was asked if he needed to use the bathroom or if he wanted some food. He politely refused but said he was tired and asked when he could get some sleep. He was informed that it would not take longer than 30 minutes. The Home Guard officer took him and drove him to Maryhill (Glasgow suburb) barracks. The pilot left limping.

Then Colonel Hardie drove me home. He asked me if the pilot was not treated too harshly. In my opinion, he was treated too leniently.

Home Guard officers treated the pilot with great politeness as if they feared he might think he was treated harshly. Just before the pilot left, one of the officers, on his knees, helped him to put his overalls back on. The pilot remained seated for the whole time, while others were standing. I was seated right next to the pilot, on the chair's arm.

Rudolph Hess remained calm and composed. I was under the impression that he was slightly glum. He was apathetic and looked rather ill. He submitted himself willingly to all ordeals resulting from his capture and answered questions willingly.

Mr Balinski [A member of the Polish Foreign Office in Exile] asked me several questions regarding my impression of Hess and my conclusions.

After the interrogation, I came up with two hypotheses, but I consider the first to hold more merit.

My first conclusion was that the German officer flew here with a serious mission. His aims were of military and intelligence nature. He intended to land in a particular meeting place, most likely in southern Ireland. The story he came up with about the Duke of Hamilton was intended to obscure his goals and motives.

My second conclusion was that I dealt with a 'calm madman', who stole a plane to fulfil his imaginary mission.

When I heard a radio broadcast about Hess's disappearance, I realised that the pilot I helped interrogate was no other than Hess. I formulated three hypotheses.

The first was in concordance with official German and British statements that Hess acted alone and he was convinced of his mission's importance.

Second conclusion: Hess flew to G. Britain with a special mission, Hitler himself planned that.

Third conclusion – least likely – that Hess's double was sent to Britain.

I believe that based on the interrogation, we cannot draw any sound conclusions yet.

I think that it is telling that official German statements confirm Hess's initial testimony. However, his flight could not have been possible without significant assistance from the ground crew /additional gas tank.

Dr Roman Battaglia[4,5]

We have never seen this report previously and it raises some fascinating questions:

- Was the talk of a burnt body real or designed to provoke a reaction? We have certainly never seen or heard of this issue before, but we do know that the rear cockpit was not jettisoned pre -crash, as it currently resides in RAF Stafford.

- Battaglia appears to be none the wiser. It appears that he did not know the motivations behind the flight at the time of the interrogation. That of course may not be the position throughout the entire Polish government in exile, but certainly Hess's arrival appears to be a surprise to the erstwhile Polish Consul in Glasgow.

Battaglia was not the only Pole writing their views on the Hess affair. Simultaneously, in London, the Polish Ambassador to the Court of St James (Józef Lipski) penned the following report. Again, we do not believe this has been published previously.

Memorandum on Rudolph Hess's landing in Scotland on 10 May 1941

A brief bio of Rudolph Hess

(…)

Personal observations

Hess lived relatively modestly. Just like Hitler, he was a vegetarian and abstinent. Unlike other party dignitaries, he did not have much contact with foreign diplomats. But the nature of his position warranted that all foreign policy matters passed through him. He was a secretive and cunning man. I met him several times at an annual congress in Nuremberg. There, at the behest of the Nazi party, he greeted the diplomatic corps. He was believed to be Hitler's most devoted man. He bordered on divine worship in his praises for Hitler. He was believed to be the biggest party fanatic, devoted, and capable of executing Führer's every order. He was also a skilled manager.

Hess's motives

I would like to emphasise one thing. Hitler is very skilled in surprising his opponents. He employs methods previously unknown in diplomacy. Therefore, this is the most carefully and methodically planned endeavour. It is calculated to benefit Germany by influencing its enemies on a subconscious level. We cannot forget that Hitler invented a new weapon, a so-called 'fifth column'. It is aimed at weakening a given society from the inside.

At first glance, Hess's flight seems to be caused by a conflict within the Nazi party, which could cost Hess his life. Therefore, it would be a case similar to Strasser and Rohm's. We can suspect that there were some disagreements about foreign policy. Mainly regarding the plans of closer cooperation with the Soviet Union. Hess, on the other hand, proposed cooperating with Britain. Recent news seems to confirm that Hess's journey was undertaken for intelligence and diversion purposes. Hitler secured himself by formally denouncing this move, which indeed seems to be desperate. Now, we know that Hess wanted to meet the Duke of Hamilton, and he previously made some effort to contact him. This was a typical fifth column tactic, aimed to undermine Churchill's policy.

I believe that Hess flew to England with Hitler's blessing. The threat of American involvement looms over Germany. Such involvement might prolong the war and even end in German defeat. Such circumstances could have convinced Hitler to launch a new peace offensive through such a seemingly desperate move. It is aimed at the British public opinion. Even superficial German-British relations will arm the American isolationists with a powerful argument against any American involvement. Countries currently being subject to German demands like Spain and Turkey (France it seems, has already accepted German terms) could become more inclined to yield, given that the [British-German] peace seems imminent. The same applies to Russia.

Finally and most importantly, Hitler aims to sow doubt among the British public opinion to facilitate peace. I suspect that German will probe for broader Anglo-German cooperation against the Soviet Union. This will give the Germans more leeway in their dealings with Eastern European countries interested in access to Russian resources.

By observing the British press, which elevated Hess to hero status, I can see that Hitler's strategy is yielding some results. In my opinion, we should observe the effects closely [of the Hess affair] in the American, Turkish, Spanish, and Soviet public opinion. France does not matter as much, since it already agreed to German terms.

Our tactics should be aimed at explaining Hitler's motives to the British Government. We should dub Hess's flight as the arrival of 'The Chief of the Fifth Column'. We should emphasise that Hess is Hitler's most devoted man. By virtue of his office, he is responsible for the most horrible crimes committed by the Germans. We cannot forget that the party field offices, through Hess's gauleiters, were instrumental in terrorising the conquered nations. The concentration camps were designed and implemented by the national-socialist party. The same applies to the terror unleashed by the Gestapo. The whole concept of the racial struggle, persecution, and pogroms of Jews was planned in Munich's Braunes Haus and was directed by Hess.

If the British tactic of treating Hess with courtesy aims to undermine the unity of the German public opinion, it is pointless. All attention and courtesy shown to Hess are quickly used by German propaganda abroad. German propaganda adjusts its tone to circumstances. It sometimes mentions British duplicity in their attempt to extract top secret information. On other occasions, it is presented as a British weakness.

Party members who fear retaliation for their cruelty in dealing with conquered nations are further encouraged in their methods by the reverence shown to Hess.

In conclusion, I believe that the discussion of Hess and his actions should be immediately shut down. We should point out that his arrival signifies German weakness, regardless of whether this weakness stems from conflict within the Nazi party or the military situation that motivates the Reich to sue for peace.

London, 15 May 1941 *Józef Lipski, lieutenant colonel*[6]

Addendum to Memorandum of 15 May 1941

When I follow the British press's news, I have a few important points to make.

1. The first official statement of the German government claimed that Hess was a madman. In this case, all charges of treason are dismissed. In my opinion, this statement was issued in the event of Hess's death or any other event that could compromise the standing of the Nazi party.
2. The statement claimed that Hess left letters. This is a classical national-socialist tactic, used since the affair over Hindenburg's testament in 1934. The letters are used for propaganda purposes. When it turned out that Hess survived, the letters served as proof that Hess wanted to reconcile the two nations, through his meeting with the Duke of Hamilton. Such statements aim to present that there are Anglo-German relations and possible peace talks. This is used by German propaganda to boost the isolationist arguments in the US. It is also used against countries that are supposed to be subject to German demands (Russia) or political overtures (France, Spain, Turkey). Suggestions that German plans for cooperation with some British officials (Hamilton) are intended to foster suspicion and cause tensions. I am confident that if the British do not end the Hess affair, the Germans will advance new scenarios and allegations.
3. The fact that Hess did not leave Germany without Hitler's approval is confirmed by the following:

a. Hess, as confirmed by the German Foreign Office, was not removed from the Nazi party.
b. No purges followed his alleged defection. The official statement claimed that some of his adjutants were arrested because they did not follow the Chancellor's orders that forbade Hess to fly planes (in the event of a possible defection of a Nazi party boss, this statement is completely ridiculous).
c. The tone of official statements is less and less sharp. The last communique stated that Hess went to England only for a couple of days, i.e. the German public opinion is being prepared for his return.
d. Hess is replaced on his party post by his closest associate – Bormann. This stands in sharp contrast to standard practices in the event of defection of any Nazi officials. Thus far, a complete purge followed any defection. This all means that the Chancellor used all resources available to him to prevent panic in party ranks. His game is so transparent that a member of average intelligence can follow. In this way, Hitler avoids any internal trouble in the Nazi party.

Again, this makes clear that Lipski is not wholly clear as to why Hess has flown, instead, offering suggestions. However, it would be a mistake to assume that knowledge was shared throughout the Polish government in exile, simply because the Polish Government in exile was essentially split into two camps. The former Piłsudskis and those such as Sikorski, the Prime Minister, who followed a more pragmatic, pro-Russian policy.

More analysis is required:

Our research would indicate there was far more going on within the Polish government in exile than has previously been recognised. We now believe that the Polish armed forces are fundamental to truly understanding aspects of the Hess affair, the basic problem being that it appears they were wholly split – from top to bottom.

Following the fall of Poland in 1939, some 60,000 military personnel escaped their homeland, and the Polish Government was eventually re-established in Paris. After the subsequent invasion of France in 1940 it moved for a short while to Angers, before finally evacuating to London. It established its political base at the Rubens Hotel, just behind Buckingham Palace. On his arrival in Britain, General Sikorski, the newly installed Prime Minister, initially lived at Iver Lodge. This house was literally next door to The Coppins, the private estate in Buckinghamshire then belonging to HRH Prince George, the Duke of Kent. Throughout 1940 and 1941 there are countless pictures of dignitaries visiting Sikorski and reviewing troops. These were dark days indeed and any pictures of support, moral or physical, were valuable. In central London, the Duke of Kent had helped acquire a meeting place for the Poles, the Ognisko Polskie, the Polish Hearth Club, which still exists at 55 Princes Gate, SW7.

In Scotland, the Poles had quickly established a military HQ at Moncreiffe House, The Bridge of Earn, in Perthshire and from mid-July 1940, another at Eastend House, Thankerton, South Lanarkshire. On 10 May 1941, Hess flew virtually over Eastend House at around 10.45pm. Today the house is sadly a 'building at risk', although a memorial plaque does still record the period of its Polish occupation. The Poles were often billeted with locals and established bases throughout lowland Scotland at towns such as Cupar, Biggar, Douglas and Eliock.

Following Dunkirk, some 27,614 men had reached Britain, together with the nucleus of the Polish Air Force, which numbered a further 6,429 personnel. Polish naval personnel manned three destroyers and two submarines, numbering in total 1,505.[7] Sikorski had reached London on 18 June 1940. As the war carried on these numbers increased. By comparison, in 1939 the British regular army amounted to 224,000 men.

Clearly, the absorption of such large numbers of men into the Allied fighting force would have significant logistical issues, issues that were certainly not helped by serious infighting between the members of the Polish government in exile and, indeed, on occasion, even with their wartime hosts. It has recently come to our notice through the excellent Secret Scotland website that the Island of Bute was even being used as an internment camp for non-Sikorski supporters of the Polish Army. Rothesay, its principal town, was the centre of the various camps that were formed. However, slowly the Poles and their armed forces started to establish themselves, the army mainly in Scotland and the air force throughout Britain in various Polish squadrons. The Polish navy and the ships they were able to bring with them were initially based at Plymouth.

Politically, the Polish government in exile was split into two camps. Almost literally.

The Army that was slowly establishing itself in Scotland was essentially the rump of the Polish Army that had fought in September 1939 under the command of General Kazimierz Sosnkowski. Following the fall of Poland, a new leadership had been implemented, with Władysław Raczkiewicz as its President in Exile and Władysław Sikorski as Prime Minister. The French government had forced the issue and the previous President Boleslaw Wieniawa-Dlugoszowski had held the position of President for one day only. He had been made President because he was the designated successor and the previous President, Ignacy Mościcki, was interned in Rumania.

The President held one power in particular that we thought may have been relevant in the Hess affair. In April 1935, the Polish sejm had introduced the Second Polish Republic and Article 12 is very clear. The President, under clause f) 'decides on war and peace'.

Władysław Raczkiewicz, the President of Poland (Wikicommons)

At one time, we considered that Hess may have been targeting the Poles, as they too were based in lowland Scotland and any such approach may well have caused a split in the entire Western Allies, let alone further exacerbate that already present between Raczkiewicz and his Prime Minister, Sikorski. However, were this to be the case, Hess would have had to meet with the President, who we have now ascertained was spending the weekend in Sunningdale, Berkshire.

To help with the somewhat delicate integration process between the two Polish camps and the British, on 9 July 1940 Anthony Eden formally appointed Victor Cazalet as the liaison officer between the Free Poles and the British government. This appointment would eventually lead to his untimely death in 1943.[8] There were also accusations that towards the end of his appointment he had gone somewhat 'feral', being over-zealous in his role and approach in favour of the Polish.

Victor Cazalet was born into a very well-connected family of considerable means. The family had owned a villa at Cimiez near Nice, which they had loaned to Queen Victoria. Cazalet had been unhappy whilst at Eton (though not without some success) and then joined the Household Cavalry in 1915. It was at this time that he also first met Winston Churchill and as his biographer states:[9] 'It was at this moment that Victor Cazalet became one of Churchill's proteges, friends and admirers.'

After military service, which included Russia, Cazalet then attended the University of Oxford, reading history and then made his entry into politics, becoming MP for Chippenham in November 1924.

Throughout the next few years Cazalet had proven to be very able but had not perhaps advanced as it may have been expected for a man of his calibre to advance. It appeared that he chose to 'spread himself too thinly' in political terms and as Harold Nicolson had commented, 'Victor cannot see a pie without wishing to have his fingers in it. But really he does rush in where angels fear to tread and I have the feeling that his rushes are merely the roaming of a cow seeking fresh grass and getting into the flower garden.'[10]

Cazalet's 'rushes' had different consequences. Churchill and he had disagreed over India in the early 1930s and the two men had badly fallen out. Rhodes James commented: 'Their former close friendship, although repaired, was never restored.'

And so it was that Victor Cazalet was selected to be the liaison officer between the British and Polish governments. Extremely well-connected, with a wide range of knowledge and interests both at home and abroad, it was also a good appointment for Cazalet, as he commented at the time: 'Everyone very jealous, especially the War Office.'[11]

Immediately after the appointment, the late summer and autumn of 1940 were spent largely visiting troops and travelling back and forth to Scotland, where the troops were settling in well and impressing all that inspected them: 'They have taken a vow to behave superbly and they have up to date certainly fulfilled it.'

Politically, however, things were a little more testing. It was reasonably well known that Britain had never really supported an independent Poland and Churchill, 'Was not willing to allow Polish interests to impede either those of Britain or of the broader anti-German coalition…'[12]

The Poles and the British were essentially two bedfellows thrown together by their mutual distrust of Nazi-Germany and their mutual hatred of Communist Russia. The pre-war British position of tolerating Nazi Germany as long as it 'didn't get too big for its boots' because it was a better bet than Soviet Russia had failed. Like most adolescent teenagers, boundaries were being stretched and tested, both literally and metaphorically, and Poland had paid the price. The Poles had also taken to baiting the teenager, which also had not helped. However, the real problem was that the troublesome teenager had grown up into a major bully and needed stopping.

Not helping unity and cohesion was the fact that the Polish government in exile was essentially split between the pre-war members and those like Sikorski who had come back into power after the German invasion. The major common interest that remained was that both factions wished for a restoration of Poland. Sikorski could also be vain and difficult; he had already nearly been deposed through his courting of the Soviets in July 1940. In October 1940 the issue arose as to who would take strategic and operational command of the Polish army should Hitler ever invade.

Sikorski was of the opinion that it should be himself, but there was the slight difficulty of there already being a British commanding officer in Scotland; one General Carrington.

Cazalet finally appeared to obtain a commitment from Sikorski that he would not leave London without at least first obtaining Churchill's permission. However, whether this oral agreement would have actually withstood such a practical test, we suspect, is doubtful.

Throughout his life Victor Cazalet maintained a series of journals and

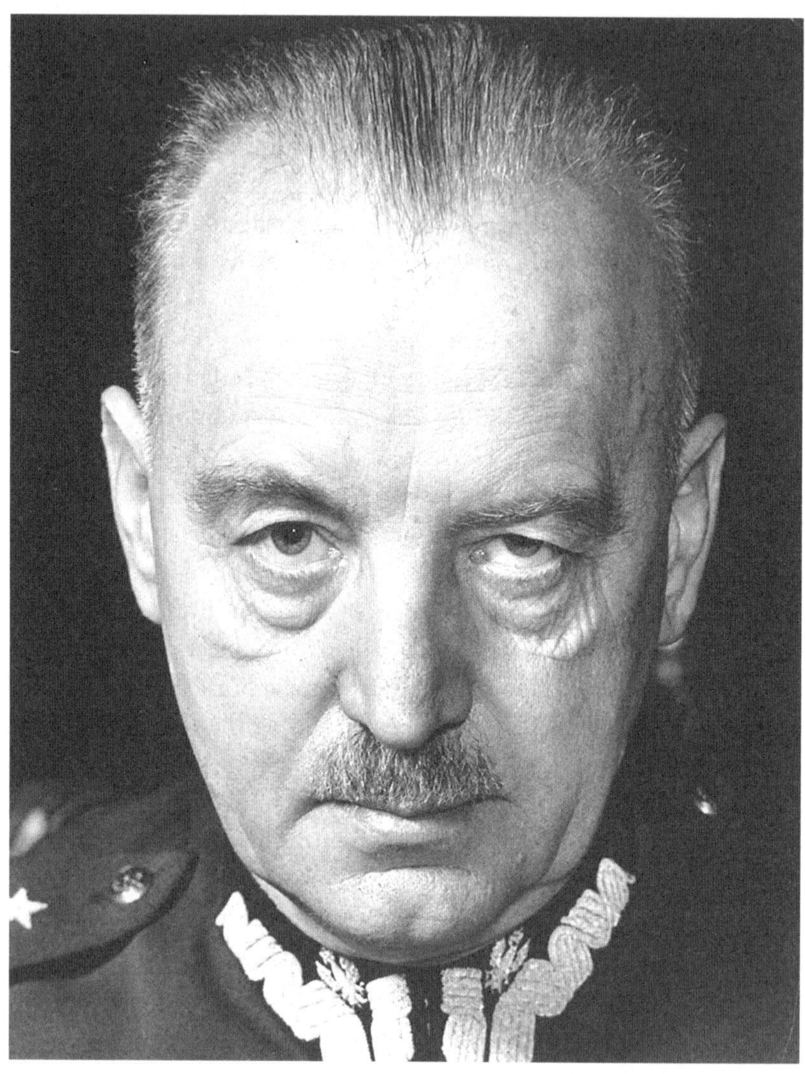

A rather sinister portrait of Władysław Sikorski (1881–1943)

scrapbooks that are currently archived at Eton College. Robert Rhodes James naturally drew heavily from this collection when writing the 1976 biography.[13]

As a result of our other findings, we saw fit to re-visit the journals to see if we could ascertain any other connections pertinent to the Hess affair which had perhaps not been extracted for the original biography. In particular, given that Victor Cazalet owned a property at 33 Belgrave Square[14] from which the Polish Relief Fund operated, we wondered if Cazalet knew Tancred Borenius. We duly travelled to Eton College in June 2015 and were not disappointed.

The winter of 1940 was noted for the heavy bombing of London and other strategic targets, together with the political exile of Lord Halifax. The Cazalet journals deal with and comment on both events as one would expect.

However, in March 1941 there were more events of relevance to the Hess affair, none of which are mentioned by Robert Rhodes James. Neither is his ownership of 33 Belgrave Square, the Cazalet home in London. (By contrast, the well documented and reported Cazalet country home was Great Swifts in Kent.)

On 5 March, Cazalet and Sikorski flew to Scotland with Louis Greig, the confidant of George VI.

On 7 March, Cazalet met the King and Queen at Glamis station. Greig 'tells me many interesting things about the present K & Q … He thinks Queen Mary is being relegated too much to background.' From the Sikorski records we learn that after a joint inspection there was a dinner and Cazalet sat opposite Greig, where presumably the two men had gossiped.

On 9 March, Cazalet travelled to Blackpool to inspect Polish troops.

On 12 March, Cazalet recorded a dinner with Weizmann.

Thereafter, Rhodes James records that, 'In mid-March Cazalet sailed to Canada with Sikorski and senior colleagues in HMS Revenge.'

Unfortunately, this statement is not completely accurate.

On 13 March 1941, the journal records 'Dinner. Borenius came in after and told us of his 7 weeks in Switzerland, France, Spain and Portugal. No sign of Germany and Italy cracking up. Switzerland completely anti-Nazi'. This dinner is not recorded in the Sikorski diaries.

This should perhaps really come as no surprise, but it does certainly prove that Tancred Borenius was known to both Victor Cazalet and Władysław Sikorski.

On 18 March 1941, further confirmation is provided by the entry, 'Lunch with Sikorski and Borenius. Full of news'. This luncheon appointment is recorded in the Sikorski diary. It was held at the Dorchester Hotel at 13.30hrs.

Thereafter, he appears to once again travel to Scotland as:

- On 22 March 1941 he records that he is at Gask (the Polish HQ) and lunches with Lady Airlie.
- On 23 March 1941 he records that he is at Drummond Castle (home to Nancy Astor's daughter) and
- On 28 March 1941 he is recorded as dining with 'Diana, Pile, Borenius,

> Tim Thomas and Duchave (?) – very good talk.' However, we are sure this date cannot be correct as by the 28th he had already left for the US.

In 1976 when Robert Rhodes James was writing the biography it is fair to say that perhaps the linkage between Tancred Borenius and Victor Cazalet was deemed perhaps not too pertinent to the then biographer. However, we are more perplexed as to why he would also inaccurately describe the departure to Canada and the US as being in mid-March when it obviously was not. HMS *Revenge* eventually left Greenock at 2400 hours on 24 March as part of convoy WS7.[15] The battleship arrived at Halifax on 1 April at 12.15pm whereupon Sikorski and Cazalet disembarked and headed on to Ottawa.

It also appears obvious to us that Sikorski would have been told by Borenius of his exploits in Switzerland and even if Borenius did not tell of his pre-trip briefing by Claude Dansey, surely the Pole must have wondered what on earth the art historian was doing, travelling to Switzerland in the middle of a war? We suspect that the more likely truth of the matter, particularly given his garrulous nature, is that Borenius would have told the assembled party precisely what he was doing and who he had met. In other words, the Poles must have at least suspected that Britain was making covert peace moves to Germany in the spring of 1941. In 1976, this probably was deemed still too sensitive for public release and knowledge, particularly with the then sole resident of Spandau still hale and hearty.

Yet again, this just seems odd to us.

However, thereafter, the facts are not in dispute. The party duly travelled to Ottawa and embarked on their PR mission, throughout the entirety of April 1941. The next issue to address is how and when to return the party to Europe from the eastern seaboard of the United States and Canada.

On 30 April 1941, Cazalet recorded (whilst in Washington, DC) that 'Sikorski getting agitated about going home. I can't help him, the planes are not ready.' By this time, Sikorski was enjoying a trip to Niagara Falls, prior to returning to New York on 2 May. He appears to have been staying at the Hotel Regis.

On 7 May 1941, Cazalet (on the way to Chicago) recorded that 'The General not gone yet, he is getting very irritable, poor man.' However, his irritation seemingly does not stop him enjoying a visit to the famous 'Rainbow Room' restaurant the following day. He appears to be killing time.

In late June 2015, John Harris visited the Public Record Office in Kew to try to ascertain the nature of the US trip and to try to discover if the trip was actually deliberately cut short. In this connection, file PREM 3/358 is very useful.

The Sikorski US trip was first mooted in a letter from the General to Churchill on 7 January 1941, when he stated, 'I also contemplate a short visit to Washington…'[16]

The diplomatic mechanics then cut in. On 19 January, Churchill tried to dissuade Sikorski,[17] but the two men met at Ditchley Park on Sunday 16 February 1941. This is corroborated in Ronald Tree's book, *When the Moon was High*.[18] It is also clearly recorded in the Sikorski diary. The meeting started at 12.45pm and the following were present: Portal, Kennedy, Duff Cooper, Lady Stanley, Gen. Davidson, Brendan Bracken, Lord Cecil, Ernest Bevin and Major Tree.

Thereafter, Anthony Bevir (the Prime Minister's private secretary and a beneficiary in Violet Roberts's will) noted that the two men met. Six days later, Roger Makins wrote to N.E. Archer, noting that, 'We presume that it would not be very long. e.g. About a fortnight…'[19]

The next we hear of the trip is on 10 March 1941, when Sikorski wrote to Churchill once more: 'There seems to be no immediate threat of invasion. I am prepared to go to the US in the first days of April.'

The alert reader will remember that shortly after this note, Sikorski met Borenius and Cazalet for lunch. His demeanour then seems to change, for he wrote on 21 March to Churchill: 'On leaving England at this moment, I am very anxious to have the certainty of getting back immediately in case of an invasion of this country.' (Or the prospect of an Anglo German peace deal perhaps? – authors.)

This wish was granted as on 27 March 1941. The Ministry of Aircraft Production send a secret cypher message to the British Air Commission, Washington, DC:

> 'General Sikorski who is on his way to America may have to return by Air from Bermuda at short notice. Please inform Powell and instruct him if necessary to give General Sikorski passage in the first available Catalina.'

On 30 March a better solution was mooted in a cable from Churchill to Sikorski: 'In the event of your willing to return urgently to this country, air route from Montreal would be preferable to that from Bermuda, journeys being more frequent, more comfortable and safer. If it should be necessary please communicate with Sir Henry Self.'

Sikorski replied to the cable on 11 April at 3.33am: 'At this grave moment my strongest wish is to be in England at your side.

Churchill's final response was reassuring: 'Do not curtail your important visit in the US. All is going well here. Churchill.'[20]

Thereafter, we have already seen that Sikorski seemingly could not wait to return, finally doing so nearly a month later. He left New York at 11.45am from the now closed Floyd Bennet airport, flying in a newly constructed Liberator Mk1 aircraft, AM916 (which was to survive the war, finally being scrapped in 1946). From New York, he flew to Gander, leaving there at 6.35pm on 10 May, some 30 minutes after Hess had taken off from Augsburg.

On 11 May he is recorded as landing at Prestwick at 11.30am. From there he travelled to Glasgow at 12.45pm and ended the day in Gask, Perthshire at Moncreiffe House. He stayed there until 19 May, when he flew to London and met Ambassador Biddle, Hugh Dalton and Colin Gubbins.

There seems to be a few oddities in this saga.

1. We are surprised that Sikorski left Britain on 24 March, apparently not knowing how (or when) he was to return. Surely, if he was really that worried, the return and its methodology would be an early consideration. It may be relevant to record that Sikorski did not learn of the Borenius mission until after the American trip had been agreed.
2. The purpose of the visit was to 'promote the recruitment of Polish man power in North America'.[21] Whilst laudable, how necessary was it at the time, given the apparent perception of the threat of German invasion?
3. Did the wish for the early return stem from the knowledge that Borenius and Cazalet had imparted at their mid-March luncheons? Was the threat an invasion or a peace settlement?
4. Why did the Ministry of Aircraft Production see the need to intervene in the travel arrangements? Presumably, because it was responsible for co-ordinating the transfer of the early Liberators across the Atlantic. Politically, Beaverbrook was no longer in charge; he had resigned on 30 April 1941.
5. Why did Sikorski and Retinger see fit to travel on what was literally

the first batch of Liberator Mk1 aircraft to cross the Atlantic? The early Liberators, with their Davis wing, were notoriously fast, but difficult aircraft to fly and suffered a high attrition. This decision just seems too risky to be true, particularly when compared to the method of outward travel. In the Ministry of Information file HS 8/329, there is a French magazine *Le Courrier de l'Air*, that was printed in London and dropped into France by the RAF, dated 19 April 1941. It shows such a Liberator and proudly exclaims, 'Les Bombardiers Americans arrivent.' This plane was one of the first six Liberators to cross the Atlantic (AM258 to AM263). They were found to be unserviceable for military use, as they did not have self-sealing fuel tanks. The next twenty planes (AM910 to AM929) started to arrive in mid-1941, the Sikorski plane being one of the first capable of military use.[22] As such, it would not have been converted for ferry work and so one can only imagine the noise and cold to which the Polish leader was subjected. A year later, National Archives file AVIA 38/70 detailed the procedure for flying dignitaries across the Atlantic. They had to give their weight, obtain a CAPOX flying suit and were then able to bring 40lbs of luggage with them. They embarked at Montreal. It really was far from comfortable, and we must again question why this route was chosen?

6. We can only presume that Sikorski was told of Hess's arrival virtually on landing. Furthermore, should any inference be drawn from the fact that he then saw fit to stay in Scotland for a week before travelling to London? It may well be that he was recovering from the ordeal of the flight, but equally that could have been achieved in Iver Lodge, his home near London.

The answers are hard to fathom. However, a perusal of the Secret Service file KV2/516[23] clearly demonstrates that all was not well in the Polish ranks. Sikorski was not initially popular with sections of the Polish Army, who preferred General Anders. Later in the war this was summarised: 'There was considerable dissatisfaction … weak method of government, love of self-glorification and neglect by too much foreign travel…'

However, Sikorski was obviously in a difficult position, not least because that whilst Churchill outwardly admired Sikorski's resilience, the British policy at that time was decidedly pro-Russian.

As Peter Stachura writes, 'The Poles were very much the subordinate power in the Western Alliance… Churchill … was not willing to allow Polish interests to impede either those of Britain, or of the broader anti-German coalition, especially following the Soviet Union's accession to it in July 1941.'[24]

Therefore, it could simply be the case that as far as Churchill was concerned, 'out of sight was out of mind'. Whilst he was abroad, Sikorski was someone else's problem and Churchill certainly had more than his fair share of those in the spring of 1941. Sikorski, however, having learned from Borenius/Cazalet in mid-March that peace overtures were being made, certainly did not wish to miss out should something happen as a result. Equally, he may have been fearful that whilst out of the country he might even have been usurped by his own fellow countrymen. They had already tried once as a result of Sikorski's policy statement towards Russia written in June 1940.[25]

However, what seems most odd is that he left Britain without seemingly a clear date for his return, particularly as it had been in planning for so long. Cazalet, by contrast, did not return until late summer, after touring the west coast of America, even meeting Charlie Chaplin en route. Furthermore, whatever Cazalet was saying certainly did not please Louis Bromfield, the famous American author, who telegraphed Winston Churchill, on 21 May 1941, advising him to withdraw Cazalet from the US on account of Cazalet's apparent appeasement: 'RESPECTFULLY ADVISE RECALL VICTOR CAZALET APPEASEMENT TALK CREATING BAD EFFECT SCHLOSS CLIVEDEN STILL STIRRING.'[26]

Cazalet, it will be remembered, had also dined with Borenius, prior to their departure across the Atlantic, so was he merely repeating what he had been told earlier in Belgravia, London? We presume that Bromfield's missive was as a result of hearing Cazalet speak – most likely in Chicago.

At the same time as the above, in what had used to be Poland, Nazi Germany was embarking on a brutal process of integrating Poland into the German Reich. More than 80 years later, it is difficult to adequately describe the scale and implications of what was essentially the extinction of a nation. The Polish Ministry of Information, part of the government in exile, now resident in London, commissioned two volumes detailing the atrocities being carried out. The first volume detailed the German invasion in 1939, the second, nicknamed the 'Black Book', detailed the transitions and absolute horrors that had been carried on in the intervening eighteen months.[27]

On 3 May 1941, Winston Churchill had delivered a radio speech to Poles throughout the world and had commented, 'The atrocities committed by Hitler upon the Poles, the ravaging of their country, the scattering of their homes, affronts to their religion, the enslavement of the man-power, exceed in severity and scale the violence perpetrated by Hitler in any other conquered land.'

We find the 'Black Book' a difficult book to read, even today. It certainly 'pulls no punches' and it is indeed hard to understand how human beings can behave in such a manner to each other. Whilst there are many other examples of Nazi brutality in all the countries they occupied, some of them can at least be explained (not understood) by the need to exaggerate, establish and retain some form of discipline and subservience. This has been seen as a throwback to the old Prussian mentality of previous centuries. However, the treatment metered out to Poland seems to have transcended this and one can only conclude that the Nazis simply wished to mechanically invade, humiliate, occupy and convert the Polish landmass into part of the Germanic state, as quickly as possible. Irrespective of any human cost.

Logistically, this awful process had to be carried out in stages as, somewhat inconveniently, Hitler had agreed to share the 1939 spoils with Stalin. Consequently, Poland was dismembered into three sections; the western part that was to be integrated into the Reich, the middle part of the country, which was to be called the 'General Government', and the eastern area, occupied by Soviet Russia (until, of course, June 1941).

The chapter headings in the 'Black Book' hopefully illustrate our point:

- Persecutions, Murders, Expulsions
- The expulsion of the Polish population from its land
- The persecution of the Jews and the Ghettoes
- Pillage and Economic Exploitation
- Struggle against the Polish spirit
- Humiliation and Degradation of the Polish nation
- The destruction of Polish culture
- The violation by the Reich of International Law
- and, lastly, Poland Fights On.

The obvious point in publication was to inform the 'free world' as to what was going on in Nazi-occupied Poland. We would normally caveat that the Polish government in exile was obviously biased, but in this case that comment is really not relevant.

This had two implications; first, it explicitly illustrated how the Nazis treated the population of occupied countries. In particular, the treatment metered out to the intelligentsia and plutocracy was given in perhaps too much detail, with the implied inference to Britons that 'it could happen here'. Particularly as Britain was accepted as being 'next on the list' and was already locked in mortal combat with the assailant.

Secondly, imagine the impact of such information on those forces currently hundreds of miles away from their loved ones in Britain in general and Scotland in particular.

Surely, the first instinct must be to do something to end the suffering; almost by any means. Ideally, we suggest, the suffering would end by the overthrow of the occupying power and a restoration of the pre-war status, or in the case of Poland, perhaps even the pre-1795 boundaries.

The added complication in the case of Poland was that Britain, its current host whilst in exile, was courting Russia, Poland's oldest enemy. The phrase 'out of the frying pan and into the fire' comes very much to mind. If a German/ Russian conflict were to break out, where would that leave Poland? History would suggest that their position would not be enhanced.

So, if a military victory was not possible (and that was certainly, without doubt, the case in spring 1941), was there a political solution, perhaps? General Sikorski had been wining and dining Tancred Borenius, so he knew that others in Britain were thinking the same and actively doing something about it. Borenius had just returned from Geneva and Burckhardt. An exchange of a Western settlement for the restoration of the Polish nation (or throne)? But how could that possibility be viably communicated? Even if possible and believed, would it really be welcomed by the incumbent in 10 Downing Street, London?

---

1 John Harris, *Hess: The British Conspiracy*, Andre Deutsch, London, 1999.

2 John Harris, *Rudolf Hess: The British Illusion of Peace*, JEMA, Moulton, 2010.

3 Margaret (Margie) Runciman married Keith Fairweather and both were killed in aeronautical accidents during the Second World War. They are buried at Dunure Cemetery on the Ayrshire coast.

4 Roman Battaglia is first described in John Harris, *Rudolf Hess: The British Illusion of Peace*, JEMA, Moulton, 2010.

5 Hoover Institution Archive (HIA), Polish Ministry of Ministry of Foreign Affairs, folder nr 4.

6 Józef Lipski was Poland's Ambassador in Berlin between 1933 and 1939.

7 Wojsko Polskie, *Barwa I Bron*, Wydawnictwo interpress, Warsaw, 1984.

[8] Cazalet was killed in a Liberator bomber, flying from Gibraltar back to Britain. It crashed shortly after take-off and all were killed apart from the pilot.
[9] Robert Rhodes James, *Victor Cazalet: A Portrait,* Hamish Hamilton, London, 1976.
[10] Ibid.
[11] Cazalet Diaries held at Eton College.
[12] P.D. Stachura, *Poland in the Twentieth Century*, Macmillan, London, 1999.
[13] Robert Rhodes James, Victor Cazalet: A Portrait, Hamish Hamilton, London, 1976.
[14] London Telephone Directory 1940, Victor and Thelma Cazalet.
[15] naval history.net
[16] PREM 3/358.
[17] PREM 3/358, 'I think it would be better for the General to stay here for the time being…'
[18] Ronald Tree, *When the Moon was High*, Macmillan, London, 1975.
[19] PREM 3/358.
[20] PREM 3/358.
[21] PREM 3/358.
[22] Edward Shacklady, *B24 Liberator*, Cerberus, Bristol, 2002.
[23] Formerly PF60518.
[24] P.D. Stachura, *Poland in the Twentieth Century*, Macmillan, London, 1999.
[25] Ibid.
[26] FO 954/29A.
[27] The Polish Ministry of Information, *The German New Order in Poland*, Hutchinson & Co., London, 1941.

CHAPTER 16
GERMANY – SPRING 1941

As the climax of the affair draws ever closer, it may be prudent to draw breath and in modern parlance, step back and look at the 'bigger picture'. To date, popular post-war Allied history and the lasting effects of wartime propaganda would suggest that in spring 1941 Nazi Germany was ruled by madmen, solely intent on world domination. The authors were raised in a post-war Europe where motion pictures such as The Battle of Britain, The Great Escape and *Where Eagles Dare* were still reinforcing the war time propaganda and post-war realities. We would respectfully suggest that in attempting to counter this somewhat populist view, little evidence of the actual wartime conditions within Germany have so far been critically analysed.

We certainly do not wish to be seen as revisionists or even worse, but further research and its subsequent evidence is slowly emerging and the conclusions perhaps becoming more certain. We believe that recent works, such as *The Taste of War* by Lizzie Collingham, in particular, are major steps forward in understanding the true motives and position of the German leaders. Consequently, we now wish to present our analysis of the conditions prevailing in Germany in 1941; the same conditions the German people were experiencing, and which Rudolf Hess was subject to, whilst making his decision whether to fly to Britain.

1) The military position

Since early 1938 Adolf Hitler had been the self-appointed head of the German Armed Forces.

At the same time, in the wake of the Blomberg/Fritsch affair, Wilhelm Keitel was appointed as the pliable head of the Oberkommando der Wehrmacht (OKW), the Hitlerian successor to the previous Ministry of War. The appointment ensured that Hitler would get his way without effective protest; personal challenge or questions were not tolerated, and Keitel rarely dissented. Albert Speer writes: 'From an honourable, solidly respectable General he [Keitel] had developed in the course of years into a servile flatterer with all the wrong instincts.'[1]

The Röhm murders and the treatment of Frisch demonstrated what happened when the 'Führerprinzip' was questioned, a principle that would hardly encourage healthy debate before precipitative action. Quite possibly this is exactly how Hitler had succeeded to date, but what would happen when times became more difficult, even more challenging? The nominal leader of the German Nation's Armed Forces had no professional experience in strategy or modern warfare, save for the bitter experiences of the 1914–18 German trenches.

As Albert Speer belatedly stated, 'Amateurishness was one of Hitler's dominant traits.'[2]

Dangerously, in early 1941, and perhaps precisely because of his unconventional, untrained behaviour, Hitler was buoyed by success; there is no doubt that he had achieved outstanding military, political and diplomatic success from the Rhineland in 1936, through Austria, Czechoslovakia, Poland, Norway, to France and the Low Countries in May 1940. In early 1941 he was as yet undefeated on the battlefield and was ready to take on his greatest challenge. He controlled a mainland Europe coast from Northern Norway to the Spanish border but equally, had yet to face a determined enemy such as the Russians, who seemingly had scant regard for the lives of their soldiers. His tactics and success may have surprised his opponents so far but was he becoming overconfident? We are not sure if Hess agreed with the Russian action; David Irving suggests that he did not.[3] Were doubts as to Hitler's military leadership a part of any reservation? If not, should they have been?

Clearly, Hitler's confidence was not without justification. In 1940, the much vaunted French army, numerically superior to the Wehrmacht, had been defeated in twenty-eight days. Much of the success to date had come from the modern strategy of blitzkrieg, a co-ordinated approach combining air power and fast moving tanks with infantry support. The equipment being manufactured obviously supported this tactic, with the Stuka and Panzer units being typical of this time. The tactic had been very successful.

However, this was all very well whilst the speed could be exploited. What Germany could not afford was to be dragged into a long, drawn-out conflict; it did not have either the resources or the appropriate equipment. In a long war, the Allies, as they eventually became, would have the time to 'out produce' the Germans; they had the overwhelming superiority in terms of production and empires of resources on which to draw. Hitler knew this and he was also aware of the huge potential of the Russian arms industry and the danger of direct American involvement and its industrial potential, in the conflict. It just had to be a short war, which in itself created its own pressures.

Franz Halder, the German Chief of Staff, was in no doubt as to importance of the decision as it was, 'Based on the need to remove Britain's last hope for continental support... Once this mission is completed, we will have a free hand, especially with air and naval arms, to bring Britain down finally.'

However, he continued, 'If we remain united and do not achieve rapid, decisive success, it is possible that the tension current in the occupied area may increase and allow Britain an intervention opportunity... The important issue is the sudden execution of the Barbarossa operation...'[4]

It therefore seems to us that the Russian invasion was actually a far more difficult decision than has been previously acknowledged. It was certainly not just based on ego. Germany definitely had the most effective and successful army in the world at the time, but against that fact was the knowledge that not only did Barbarossa have to succeed, it had to succeed rapidly.

Without rapid German success, the Allies would have time to build their production and capability, and without rapid success, Germany would be drawn into a conflict that it was not wholly prepared for in equipment terms. For example, they had already carried out the British Blitz with the wrong aircraft (a Lancaster could carry 10 tons of bombs, the German planes 2 to 3 tons). Imagine the effect had the tonnages been reversed.

There were already doubts developing about the German production methodology. The Germans spread manufacturing across a great number of companies, such as Argus, BMW and Junkers in the case of aero engines. All of which required their own logistical support and training. There was also a myriad of research projects into jet engines, rocket engines, unmanned aircraft and unmanned weapons. Were they simply too advanced and inquiring for their own good and did the diversification render a single focus impossible? Were they already spreading themselves too thinly in technological terms? In 1940, only one year into the war, Göring had decided, 'All other long range programmes are to be examined again,'[5] in part due to a shortage of raw materials. The replacement and development of the early aircraft types, now outdated, were proving difficult. The new Me210, 410 and Ju188 were proving to be unreliable in trials, and they were not even being produced with a protracted Russian campaign in mind.

Werner Baumbach summarised the weakness in this approach to production: 'In the effort to meet all the demands of the forces, even the smallest special request was fulfilled and a very large number of small lines, with idiotic sub-division, was produced. Complete confusion took the place of rational order. Everyone made everything.'

It is highly unlikely that Hess chose to make his flight for the above reasons alone. However, it is possible that in combination with concerns about military leadership and equipment, or the stated desire not to be drawn into a protracted conflict, real doubts had started to emerge in the Nazi hierarchy about German invincibility. The consequences of defeat simply did not stand scrutiny. Hess knew this. We also suspect that if he was really sure of a German victory he would not have flown to Britain – there would have been no need.

2) The British blockade of Germany, problems of raw materials and food supplies

The role of the British blockade of Germany in the First World War is reasonably well known. Imposed at the start of that war, by 1915 German imports had fallen to 55 per cent of their pre-war level and exports to 53 per cent. More controversially perhaps, and less well known, the blockade was not finally lifted until March 1919. The imposition of the same blockade in 1939 is not so well known, but its impact was certainly just as harsh.

In 1939/40, naval blockades and their effects were certainly not new but were potentially controversial in legal terms. Indeed, there is evidence that Goebbels was investigating the legal position concerning the blockade, in terms of what it might then allow the Germans to do legally in order to alleviate its impact. We quote from his diary:

> 26 February 1941 (Wed.)
> Legal judgement: not only we are not duty-bound to feed the populations of the occupied territories, but we can even requisition provisions there. An important argument in the controversy over the blockade.

Dependent upon their scope and implementation, it was not just the belligerent nations that were affected. Similarly, it was not just the militia that became affected. Women and children, young and old, rich and poor were all affected to a greater or lesser degree.

On 4 September 1939, Winston Churchill, the First Lord of the Admiralty, had instigated the British Naval Contraband Control system, a means by which every merchant vessel entering British controlled waters was subject to examination. Three European offices were established for the purpose at Weymouth, Kirkwall and Gibraltar. Essentially, the British had re-imposed the 1914–19 blockade.

Immediately, the Royal Navy went into action. British submarines were posted off the Elbe and Jade estuaries and others between Norway and the Shetland islands. The Humber Force and Home Fleet mounted regular patrols off Norway, initially hoping to intercept the Bremen, the flagship of the German merchant navy. (They failed, the Bremen eventually berthing in Murmansk.)

Between 3 and 28 September 1939, 108 merchant ships were stopped, with twenty-eight being ordered to Kirkwall for inspection. On 10 September, whilst engaged on blockade duties, HMS Triton tragically torpedoed her sister ship HMS Oxley, in the first friendly fire incident of the war. Between 11 and 16 September, the Royal Navy laid 3,000 mines off the Straits of Dover. From October 1940, the British forces were joined by the former Polish submarines, *Orzel* and *Wilk*, both having broken out from the Baltic.

The German mobilisation and the stepping up of the economy were good for business; many countries complained about the disruption to their trade and were calling the British action illegal. The blockade was very effective, especially after the intensification of early 1940 and the complaints grew as almost any cargo could be seized for assisting the German war effort.

It is our opinion that the aggressive nature of this collective action should not be underestimated. In the 1914–18 war the blockade had brought Germany to her knees, with estimates of the resultant deaths between 400,000 and 750,000. The privations of the 1916/17 'Turnip winter' are well recorded. Interestingly, in 1939 no public announcement was made, the British Navy just got on and imposed it. Similarly, its architect, Sir Frederick William Leith-Ross (1887–1967) is hardly known in Britain. The Mauritius born Civil Servant is known principally as being the brother of Harry Leith-Ross (1886–1973) the famous Impressionist painter who worked in the USA. We believe that Leith-Ross, in instigating the blockade was responsible for an act of war far more aggressive than sending the BEF to France and which would fundamentally alter the German's ability to wage war.

Germany had of course anticipated this course of action.

Hermann Göring was put in charge of the Vierjahresplan (Four Year Plan), devised to increase domestic production to meet the demands of war and reduce the dependence on imported goods. As time went on this home production failed to keep pace with demand and increasingly the plan grew to assume the products of the eastern conquests.

Frederick Leith-Ross

As Josef Goebbels, recorded:

> 29 March 1941 (Sat)
> The Ukraine is a good grain store. Once we are entrenched there, then we can hold out for a long time. With this, the Eastern and Balkan questions will finally be settled.
>
> 1 May 1941 (Thu)
> Backe [Herbert Backe, Darré's assistant at the Ministry of Agriculture] gives me report on the food situation. Meat is going to have to be cut by 100 grams per week from 2 June. The Wehrmacht is too well off and is using up too much of the available ration. Per head, three times that allowed to the civilian population. We can hope to get by so far as bread is concerned, as long as there is no problem with the harvest. Fat is still in reasonable supply. If we have to go through a third year at war, then we shall consume the last reserves of bread. But nevertheless we are better off than England in many respects. But our situation is no means rosy. I now face the question of how I am to put this over to the public. I shall wait for the most favourable moment possible and then take the announcement.
>
> 6 May 1941 (Tue)
> Backe describes the food situation. Along the same lines as his report to me a few days ago. A few extra details, which give reasons for optimism. All we need is a good harvest this year. And then, of course, we intend to be firmly established in the East.

The British declaration of war and the effective naval blockade left Germany's industrial heartland in the Ruhr vulnerable to attack and potentially starved of raw materials. Hitler had to secure his borders to the west and break the British naval stranglehold. From 1938 the Siegfried Line or Westwall fortifications were strengthened, and defensive airfields were built nearby, but now circumstances demanded attack. Hitler drove over his neighbours to secure his supplies and neutralise the chance of attack by Britain and France. In turn he could then apply his own blockade against the supply lines across the Atlantic and neutralise the British threat.

Some writers have also ascribed the Haushofer/Hitler theory of 'Lebensraum' as a natural counter to the Blockade strategy. When *Mein Kampf* was being written in Landsberg Prison in 1923, the memory of the devastating effects of blockade were fresh in Hitler and Hess's minds. If Germany were to go eastwards, no western blockade would be effective, as the necessary raw materials could be obtained without any deference to British sea power. As Hitler told Carl Burckhardt in August 1939, 'I need the Ukraine, so that no one is able to starve us again, like in the last war.'

Lizzie Collingham quotes Corni and Gies, 'Lebensraum would make Germany truly self- sufficient and immune to blockade and this would eventually enable Germany to challenge British and American hegemony.' The British geographer H.J. Mackinder had realised this as far back as 1904.

However, in May 1941 the invasion of Russia had yet to take place. Hess may well have been fearful of the consequences, but it is more likely that he would have already been mindful of the effects the British blockade was having on the German civilians and economy. Notwithstanding the effect on military production, there had already been a cut in the German bread ration by 600 grammes in July 1940. In June 1941 the meat ration was cut by 400 grammes.

By 1943–4 an ordinary German civilian was eating 40 per cent less fat, 60 per cent less meat and 20 per cent less bread than in 1939.[6]

Given our agricultural backgrounds, we find this aspect of the war very interesting indeed and are genuinely surprised that the effects of the British blockade are not wider known. In addition, Lizzie Collingham also details why the German agricultural supplies came under pressure. The blockade restricted the importation of nitrogen, an important component of artificial fertiliser, vital for increasing production.

Sure enough, so as to compensate, food was taken from the occupied countries and ordered from Hitler's allies, but it was not delivered sufficient quantity and as a consequence many in the donor countries starved. In short, by early 1941, there were signs that food supply was becoming a serious problem. Foreign labour was being imported into the Reich to work in factories and on farms; there were far more mouths to feed.

Herbert Backe was diligently calculating the effect on food demand should the planned invasion of Soviet Russia proceed. He had calmly reported that it would be likely that 4.2 million Slavs would have to starve if German troops and civilians were to be fed from the areas anticipated to be captured. It is very likely that Hess would have been aware of this eventuality.

It would therefore appear that the effect on raw materials and food when moving from a peace time economy to a wartime one had not been fully appreciated or, more likely, the terrible consequences of such an action had been chosen to be ignored and seen as part of the strategy itself. Russia continued to supply grain even on the evening before Barbarossa. Hitler's plans assumed success and his continuing strategy relied on it. Such thinking is often seen in today's business plans, when assumed future profits are counted on to carry the project forward; it does not take much for such plans to unravel. Did Hess and others have growing doubts about such strategy? Was the situation in Germany on a real knife edge?

3) The Jewish issue and knowledge of brutality to come

Some authors[7] have theorised that Hess flew to Scotland in an attempt to bring the war to an end, so as to prevent the Holocaust. They cite the fact that a German Foreign Office report had proposed Madagascar as a potential refuge and haven, but then blamed Britain and France for its failure due to their occupation of the island. The Gerhard Engel diaries[8] also quote Hitler considering Madagascar as a refuge in February 1941, but then states euphemistically, 'He had pondered on many other ideas which were not quite so nice.'

We do not believe the above and suspect that Hess, the Nazi Stellvertreter (Deputy Führer) would have simply conformed to the party line. However, Rudolf Hess the individual may have been in part conflicted; his friend Albrecht Haushofer was, for instance, half-Jewish and we have now demonstrated a link between the Jewish Zeileis Institute and Hess.

However, it is quite likely that Hess would have been uncomfortable with the knowledge of the impending brutality that Hitler saw as part of the strategy to conquer the Russian homelands. At Nuremberg, Keitel and Jodl were condemned to death, in part for their acquiescence to the Commando

Order, which dealt with the establishment of German army control in occupied Russia. The British prosecutor, G.D. Roberts, quoted from the Order: 'All resistance is [to be] punished, not by legal prosecution of the guilty, but by the occupation forces spreading such terror as is alone appropriate to eradicate every inclination to resist.'[9]

In other words, brutality was part of the strategy. The Commando Order was an order directly conveyed through and to the army. As Laurence Rees writes, 'An atmosphere was thus created in which appalling brutality was to be expected.'[10]

Himmler had told twelve SS-Gruppenführers in March 1941 that the purpose of the campaign was to reduce the indigenous population by some 30 million. Hess knew of these truly terrible plans through Rosenberg and Himmler. There are pictures of Hess and Himmler at a VOMI (Volksdeutsche Mittlestelle) conference, dated March 1941, which dealt specifically with the resettlement of Germans in occupied areas. As the 'conscience of the party', did this knowledge weigh heavily on his shoulders? Hess had signed the 1935 Nuremberg Laws and at the Nuremberg trials it was almost certain that he was aware of the atrocities committed in Poland in 1939–40, but was this a step too far? Was the brutality in Poland actually counterproductive in limiting the likelihood of a Western peace? There really was no way back should the Russians be stronger than believed.

4) The timing and decision to invade Russia

As discussed above, it is generally accepted that Hess knew of the Russian invasion prior to flying to Scotland. Eugene Bird quoted Hess as admitting as much in *The Loneliest Man in the World*. There is also the unanswered question as to whether Soviet Russia would have invaded Nazi Germany had Nazi Germany not invaded Soviet Russia? Subsequent to the publication of our *Treachery and Deception* in 2016, we were invited to Mecklenburg, Germany in December 2017 to meet and interview General Bernd Schwipper, a former GDR Airforce General. General Schwipper was a marvellous host and had devoted his post-Cold War retirement to property development and researching the above question. He published the extremely detailed *Deutschland im Visier Stalins* in 2015 and makes the case that had Hitler not invaded Russia, Russia would have moved against Germany in July 1941.

Clearly this is a controversial viewpoint, as it runs the risk of Barbarossa being seen as a preventative war, a hypothesis with which we do not agree.

However, it was undoubtedly a possibility and as such was no doubt another consideration passing through Hess's mind. He had very nearly run out of time on 10 May 1941.

The decision to invade had finally been made following the Molotov visit to Berlin in November 1940. Von Ribbentrop had told Molotov that, 'England was beaten and that it would only be a question of time before she would finally admit defeat… The axis powers, therefore, were not considering how they might win the war, but already won.'[11]

However, the proposed 'spheres of influence' were never finally agreed, nor the apportionment of the British empire 'as a gigantic world-wide estate in bankruptcy'. The proposed division as outlined in the 13 November meeting was never agreed. That directly led to Barbarossa six months later.

The invasion had been formally approved as policy on 18 December 1940, in Führer Directive 21. Originally it was timetabled for commencement on 15 May 1941. This date would allow for:

- Anticipated progress before winter.
- Anticipated progress before the wet season and the impassable muddy roads.
- Taking the vital 1941 harvest, which would be at a critical stage from June until September.

If the Soviets got the chance to harvest the grain, it would be quickly transported east; anything they could not harvest, or move could be easily destroyed by fire. If the harvest was lost, the conquered lands would yield little or nothing for a whole year. Whilst researching Josef Goebbels, we were interested to note that he made this very point in his diary entry of 11 May 1941. The Germans were very aware of the potential implications of their actions.

The planners set about their task, moving vast armies of men and machinery eastwards. The British soon realised what was happening through Ultra intelligence and told Stalin, who, unsure and mistrusting, countered by moving some divisions westward, thus heightening the German nervousness still further.

However, during the spring of 1941, the German army was already engaged in the Balkans, and this is the reason now accepted for the decision to delay the invasion until 22 June – thirty-eight days later. This delay was to have profound consequences.

Rudolf Hess would spend the winter of 1941 in Mytchett Place, just outside Aldershot, in England and so the progress of Barbarossa was out of his control and influence. Nine months earlier, in the spring of 1941, he was desperately concerned with the knowledge of the invasion and the fact that it was to take place. This was, by far, the greatest military project that Nazi Germany was to undertake, and it was almost a step into the dark. German intelligence was weak as to the size of the Soviet forces and to an extent there was no Plan B. It was very much conquer or be conquered, as subsequent events bore out. This was particularly the case as brutality was an inbuilt part of the battle plan. As we have seen already, there was the knowledge that Hitler needed a quick war. He did not have the equipment for protracted war and knew it. The order itself again demanded a quick field campaign (*einem schnellen feldzug*), the words underlined to impress the importance of the speed of the mission. Give the timetable already in place, the need for a Western peace was becoming absolutely critical.

5) Nuclear weaponry

Without wishing to state the obvious, the Second World War eventually became a race to build a usable nuclear bomb. Whichever side won the race would win the war and set the post-war agenda for the world. In the spring of 1941, an independent analysis of the respective progress made by Germany on the one side and the Allies on the other would place the Germans as clear leaders in the race.

Since the celebrated radium-barium-mesothorium-fractionation experiment of December 1938, the German chemist, Otto Hahn, was at the forefront of research into nuclear fission. However, when dealing with pure chemistry, even of such international importance, Hahn's next step had been to publish his findings in *Naturwissenschaften* on 22 December 1938. The genie had escaped from the bottle.

By the spring of 1939 the race had begun in earnest. Two German scientists, Prof. Harteck and Dr Groth had already written to the German War Office, saying, 'The newest development in nuclear physics, which, in our opinion, will probably make it possible to produce an explosive many orders of magnitude more powerful than the conventional ones…'

When war broke out in September 1939, Germany already had an office devoted to the military application of nuclear fission. The British had retaliated by merely trying to buy as much uranium as was available on the world market. 1940 saw the Germans experimenting with heavy water, D2O, as a means of inducing a chain reaction in a pile with uranium. Given the newness of the initial discovery, rapid progress was being made. However, by the spring of 1941, whilst considerable progress had been made, no real prospect of a workable bomb yet existed.

Indeed there is new research that suggests that Hitler was intent on harnessing nuclear power simply to guarantee the continued supply of electricity in order to produce sufficient rocket fuel so as to make his conventional arsenal unassailable.

Hitler knew of the research work, as presumably did Hess. The Minister of the Post Office (who was funding some of the work) had personally told him of the possibilities of making a workable bomb in the autumn of 1940. Thereafter, there was a degree of bluff. The Allies knew that the Germans were making progress but did not know precisely how much. They also knew that the Belgian uranium stockpiles had been taken as part of the May 1940 invasion and they also knew that production of heavy water had been increased at the Norsk Hydro plant in Norway. Churchill's experts assured him that the Germans were not as far advanced, because technically they could not be, but no one knew for sure. If the Germans believed they were close to having a bomb, did this underpin Hitler's confidence in winning, what was seen by many, an unwinnable war with Russia? Was this to them the 'convincer' that made all other things seem possible?

We also believe it very significant that Hitler (and Hess) chose to play on this uncertainty. When Hitler spoke to the Reichstag on 4 May 1941, just six days before the Hess flight, he spoke of, '… the scourge of modern weapons of warfare, once they were brought into action, would inevitably ravage vast territories'.

As will be described later, when Hess was in captivity, if he wanted attention he too would speak of bombs. He knew the British would want to know the reality of German nuclear production. Hess knew the reality was that, in fact, there was no nuclear bomb and possibly he may have wondered if there ever would be. Did he know or suspect that, realistically, Hitler was not holding any aces?

6) The German state, such as it was

Since 1933 Adolf Hitler had been Chancellor of Germany, his accession being the culmination of some thirteen to fourteen years of considerable struggle.

The Haigerloch Reactor, the Nazi experimental nuclear station

On 20 April 20 1941, Hitler was fifty-two years of age and was becoming acutely aware of his own mortality and position in history. He had been at the vanguard of German politics for over twenty years and quite naturally there was a younger generation beginning to emerge. Walter Schellenberg, for instance, tells of Heydrich referring to Hitler as 'the old man' and it was perhaps inevitable that after such a period of time one could expect a generational change or challenge.

To date, Hitler had been very adept at countering challenge. In 1934, Röhm was duly despatched, challenge or not, and the structure was such that there appeared to be two people for every post, both with overlapping responsibilities. The classic divide and rule. As such, it appears that there was actually little cohesion as a functioning government. Ribbentrop, for instance was the foreign minister, yet Hess had his own foreign organisation the Auslands Organisation under Gauleiter Bohle. Consequently, Bohle grew to detest Ribbentrop, and Hess subsequently fell out with Ribbentrop. Himmler also tried to dictate foreign policy, particularly later on in the war, thus too alienating Ribbentrop.

So, the government was not particularly unified and was led by a man who was beginning to come under pressure, if for no other reason than by the effluxion of time. There was almost a sense perhaps of 'if we don't invade now we will never invade'. Surely not a particularly logical reason to mount any invasion, let alone one against an enemy whose precise strength was not even clear but certainly known to be growing?

As Heinrich Müller described to Schellenberg, 'We haven't got any leaders, we do have a Leader, the Führer, but that is the beginning and the end of it. Take the mob immediately below him, and what have you got? You've got them all squabbling amongst themselves, night and day, either for the Führer's favours or about their own authority…'[12]

7) The position of the enemy

In arriving at the decision to fly to Scotland, Hess must have considered the position of the enemy. If he considered that he would have been shot on arrival, there would be little point in flying. On balance he must have considered that the enemy, or parts of the enemy, were also ready to consider peace. A treaty can only be signed by parties wishing to sign it.

From a German perspective, the following factors must have come into play:

- The Germans had failed to gain air supremacy over Britain in 1940. Any invasion would therefore be a very bloody affair.
- Despite an almost nightly attack on the cities of Britain, the 1940/41 Blitz had failed to bring the British Government to the negotiating table.
- There was little evidence of defeatism within the wider British population, and what little had manifested itself had been effectively censored.
- Churchill had made little secret of his strategy to hold out until America would enter the war. This was beginning to work with the September 1940 Destroyers for Bases Agreement and the 11 March 1941 Lend-Lease agreement being signed.
- Whilst most Americans saw these two treaties as a way of support without involvement, they were clear demonstrations as to whose side America was on, in her quest to be the 'Arsenal of Democracy'. It was also good for business. These treaties were well publicised and the Germans were certainly aware of their existence. The very real threat of a war against America was beginning to look possible; a war that rational Germans knew they could not win.
- The knowledge that a number of influential British politicians did not wish to side with America and instead saw a European Alliance against Communist Russia as a preferable option. The problem being that such politicians were not in power.

Hess's problem was two-fold in this respect. First, to make sure his approach was to the correct part of the political establishment and secondly to then ensure that it was in a position to entreat. The Churchill government had consistently made its position clear, and Hess had to make sure he was not dealing with it.

Indeed, Gerhard Engel wrote on 18 December 1940, 'I am convinced that the Führer still does not know what will happen. Distrustful of his own military leaders, uncertainty about Russian strength, disappointment over British stubbornness continue to preoccupy him.'

This was indeed the gamble. Barbarossa was everything. If, as all the Allied planners predicted, Hitler was to win a quick war against Russia then he really would be impregnable. He no longer would need to import raw materials; wheat, timber, coal, oil, they would all be under his command. He would no longer need to worry about the British Navy or its blockade; he would have all the resources he needed without having to bring them by sea. Churchill and his allies could say what they want, no doubt using fine words, but that is all they would be – impotent words. How long would it be until Germany would turn westwards once more, this time determined to crush Britain?

So. This was the moment. This was it. Literally, death or glory. May we ask what the reader would have done in the circumstance? May we momentarily be excused a little admiration for simply having the confidence to order the attack? Nothing more. Hitler was certainly vile and weird, but this was a truly brave decision, a truly historic decision. One that we believe Hess would not have taken.

---

[1] Albert Speer, *Inside the Third Reich*, Phoenix, London, 2001.

[2] Ibid.

[3] David Irving, *Hess: The Missing Years 1941–1945*, Focal Point, Windsor, 2010.

[4] *The Halder War Diary*, Presidio, Novarto, CA, 1988, 4 June 1941.

[5] Werner Baumbach, *Broken Swastika*, Robert Hale, London, 1976.

[6] Paul, Erker, *Ernährungkrise und Nachkriegsgesellschaft*, p. 24. Klett-Cotta, Stuttgart, 1995.

[7] Alfred Smith, *Hitler's Reluctant War*, Book Guild, Lewes, 2001.

[8] Gerhard Engel, *At the Heart of the Reich: The Secret Diary of Hitler's Army Adjutant*, Greenhill Books, London, 2005.

[9] James Owen, *Nuremberg: Evil on Trial*, Headline, London, 2006.

[10] Laurence Rees, *The Nazis: A Warning from History*, BBC Television, 1979.

[11] German Foreign Office Minutes, cited Chester Wilmot, *The Struggle to Europe*, Collins, London,1952

[12] Walter Schellenberg, *Hitler's Secret Service: Memoirs*, Pyramid, New York, 1958.

CHAPTER 17
SPAIN

In early 1941, the continued neutrality of Spain was nearly as important to Britain as the avoidance of a homeland invasion. The preservation of Spain's 'non-belligerent' status essentially meant that Gibraltar was secure (theoretically, at least) and with it came continued naval access to North Africa and the Eastern Mediterranean. The means to continue to both wage war and service the empire were still available to Britain.

Francisco Franco (1892–1975) (Wikicommons)

The reasons for continued Spanish 'non belligerency' during this period are complex and varied. Amongst them are:

- The shrewdness of Franco, the Spanish leader. He recognised the fact (unlike Mussolini) that it was far smarter to declare war once the outcome was reasonably certain, thus limiting the extent of any actual participation.
- Uncertainty as to potential spoils, with the Italians and Vichy France still rivals in North Africa.
- Spain had just endured three years of bitter bloodletting and the country was decimated and simply fed up with fighting.
- Britain was offering economic deals and bargains that Germany could not hope to match. The Spanish population was nearly starving and so trade deals with Britain and the United States were a far better prospect than empty promises from Germany. Any declared imposition of the British blockade did not stand contemplation.
- The continued, nagging suspicion that Britain was not yet beaten.
- The fact that Britain had a war chest available to enable the Spanish generals to be bribed so as to prevent a declaration. Foreign Office file FO1093/233 quotes the sum available of up to $10million.
- As Samuel Hoare recounts, the Spanish would far rather be led than driven. The German approach was perhaps too overt, too domineering, albeit Spain did owe the German nation over $200 million for arms supplied throughout the Civil War.

Hitler was similarly torn between the carrot and the stick. Throughout the autumn and winter of 1940/41 it was clear that Spain might enter the war at any time. However, as Mussolini discovered eventually at the cost of his life, once enjoined with Germany events were no longer wholly under your control. Franco was wise enough to understand this and so when the two dictators met at Hendaye, on the French/Spanish border on 23 October 1940, Franco's strategy was to over-demand in exchange for the promise of participation.

Franco had asked for African territory as the price for participation – a price that Hitler could not pay, as he was using this chip elsewhere with Vichy France. Consequently, each man went his own way. Hitler with no commitment for Spanish participation, Franco with no African prize. A not wholly unsatisfactory stalemate had arisen, given that Hitler was soon to wholly concentrate on the east.

The British Ambassador to Spain, Samuel Hoare's record of the period is fascinating.[1] Fascinating both for what is recorded and, in equal measure, what is not. Near the beginning of the book Hoare admits to previously being 'Chief of our Secret Service in Russia and having crossed Rasputin's path in the early years of the last war.'

As such, we believe very strongly that much that now follows should be seen in that context. The policy adopted seems virtually identical to that being adopted in Britain: keep talking about peace for long enough so as to allow Germany to potentially commit suicide by attacking Russia, or at least move the focal point sharply to the east and away from Britain. What was absolutely the case was that whilst attacking Russia, Germany would not or could not attack Spain and or Britain. That was as long as Spain would remain non-belligerent.

At Nuremberg in 1946, Göring complained that Spain should have been conquered prior to Barbarossa. With hindsight it is of course quite easy to understand why he might have thought this, were it not for Hitler's uncertainty about the Russian war machine's latent and potential capability. That is why he chose to prefer east to west in 1941, seeing Britain as effectively impotent (which of course she was at the time, peaceful or not) and Spain, whilst not an active participant, certainly was as pro-German as was then possible.

Samuel Hoare paints very much the predictable picture of rebuffing any talk of peace, 'My staff and I made it quite clear beyond a doubt that the British Government would have nothing to do with any peace negotiations and that sooner or later the British people would undoubtedly win the war.'[2] This 'stock response' had followed the strict instruction to meet peace feelers with 'absolute silence' issued by the Foreign Office on 7 February 1941.[3]

However, this appears to be not quite the complete story.

On 5 March 1941, Prince Max Hohenlohe met Hoare in Madrid, this time Hohenlohe representing von Ribbentrop. According to Hoare's memoirs, he (Hoare) duly trotted out the usual 'Britain cannot make peace until Hitler is removed…' It should also be recorded that under the Foreign Office instruction the two men should not have met at all.

However, more shocking is the disclosure that Hoare had actually reported to Hohenlohe that Churchill was not secure, he could not rely on a majority and eventually he (Hoare) would be recalled to London with the 'precise task of concluding a compromise peace'.

These vastly different comments and terms were relayed by way of telegrams from the Italian and German ambassadors to their respective Foreign Offices.

There appear to be only two alternative interpretations of Hoare's position:

1. He was doing exactly and deliberately as Tancred Borenius had already done in Geneva and was telling the truth, such as he knew it, or
2. He was lying and he knew it, but was attempting to deceive the Germans, again, simply to buy time.

There also appear to be other, more practical obstacles if one really is to believe that Hoare was in the throes of organising a coup d'état from Madrid. Communication to any potential conspirators in Britain must surely have been almost impossible and it just seems too implausible to us that this was actually taking place.

It was into this den of intrigue that Albrecht Haushofer and, by inference, Rudolf Hess then chose to enter.

Albrecht Haushofer had a student, Herbert W. Stahmer (as distinct from Heinrich Stahmer who was also a German diplomat, albeit more senior), who had been placed in the German Embassy in Madrid. According to a post-war account, Stahmer was approached by Haushofer to make contact with Hoare to discuss a basis for negotiation and to arrange a meeting of the British and German ambassadors.[4] Stahmer apparently duly opened such negotiations through the Swedish Embassy in Madrid.

This all seems a bit far-fetched to us to be true. If, as reported, Herbert Stahmer was a student of Albrecht Haushofer (who was born in 1903), it seems unlikely that Herbert was much older than perhaps twenty-five years of age in 1941. Whilst recognising that in times of war conventional rules are stretched, we would question if essentially the office junior would be in a position to influence world events in the manner described. It could well be, of course, that the approach to the Swedish Embassy was made in such a way that the age of the messenger became irrelevant, but we trust the reader can at least share our scepticism.

Thanks to Thomas Dunksus in Germany we have also recently discovered that during the Second World War the British and German embassies were literally adjacent to each other in Madrid. Communication between the two parties should not have been difficult at any level.

In support of our scepticism, Haushofer chose not to refer to the Stahmer initiative in his 12 May 1941 confessional at the Berghof and, similarly, but more understandably, Hoare did not mention any such approach in his record of the period. That is not to say it did not happen, merely that if it did, it passed unrecorded at the time. Haushofer was quite able to pick up and put down at ease the various hats he was wearing. If, as has been suggested, the Spanish approach was in support of the German resistance and not Hess in this instance, then the reason for non-recording becomes clear. One should perhaps compare and contrast the meticulous recording by Haushofer of the rationale behind sending a letter back in September 1940, with the apparent complete lack of recording when events appeared to be gathering apace some six months later.

The Haushofer/Stahmer initiative is notable for two further reasons. First, Stahmer invited Haushofer to Madrid on 10 May 1941, an action that has been seen as an escape hatch for Albrecht, and secondly, the mystery as to whether an Anglo-German meeting took place in late April 1941.

Currently, there are some Foreign Office files that cast doubt as to what was happening in Madrid over the weekend of 20–22 April 1941. Some authors have even speculated as to a meeting between Hoare and Hess. If this really was the case, surely Haushofer would have mentioned this in his memorandum to Hitler on 12 May?

We now know from Gallspach that Hess was at the Zeileis Institute in late April, 'a fortnight before the flight'.[5] Consequently, given his other movements, we suspect that this may explain where Hess was at the time. Not Madrid. Hess also later denied the accuracy of the assertion that he had travelled to Madrid, though that denial certainly should not be taken as fact.

Whether Albrecht Haushofer was in Madrid is another matter. We have absolutely no proof either way, but certainly the Madrid connection was not allowed to fall to fallow as evidenced by the subsequent invitation extended to Albrecht of 10 May.

The conclusion to this sequence of events is simply that whilst the details remain unclear, the intent is obvious. Winston Churchill had 'parachuted' Samuel Hoare, a previous Intelligence Chief in revolutionary Russia into Spain with the virtually impossible task (in June 1940) of keeping Spain out of the war. The early stages of his role were achieved with the assistance of the pro-British Foreign Minister, Juan Luis Beigbeder, but once Beigbeder was forced to resign in October 1940, Hoare adopted a very similar approach to the British mainland: pretend to talk peace (even if told officially not to by London) to anyone that will listen, in the hope that Germany will start to believe the story. If necessary, pretend to talk to the office junior at the German Embassy. Every day talking is one less day to fight, or one less day until dawn, 22 June 1941. Such was, we are sure, the story of Spain. Real or imagined.

---

[1] Samuel Hoare, *Ambassador on Special Mission*, Collins, London, 1946.

[2] Ibid.

[3] FO 371/26542.

[4] H.W. Stahmer cited Rainer Schmidt, *Botengang Eines Toren?*, Econ, Düsseldorf, 1997.

[5] Email to John Harris from the Zeileis family concerning Hess's two known visits to the Zeileis Institute.

CHAPTER 18

WESTMINSTER, LONDON, 7 MAY 1941

The House of Commons – pre 10 May 1941 (Wikicommons)

In the various books on Rudolf Hess, it is rarely mentioned that Winston Churchill could have been politically defeated quite legitimately, properly and democratically on 7 May 1941 – just three days before the Hess flight. Given that outcome, there would have been no need for any member of the German Nazi Party to fly to Scotland, or anywhere else for that matter, as the unwritten British Constitution would have come into play to eventually achieve the same ends as Hess hoped for.

We therefore believe the timing of these two events warrant further research. Was Churchill attempting to 'flush out' his opponents once and for all? Both British and German?

If the Government had lost the motion – 'That this house approves the policy of His Majesty's Government in sending help to Greece and declares its confidence that our operations in the Middle East and in all other theatres of war will be pursued by the Government with the utmost vigour' – it follows that a new Prime Minister would have been appointed, in extremis, directly by the King[1] (see Chapter 12). Presumably the new incumbent would then have followed an alternative strategy to that outlined and intimated by the motion.

Clearly, in bringing the motion at all, the stakes were quite naturally and quite properly extremely high. Churchill realised this full well and had then raised them still one notch further by making the motion one of confidence. In other words, this was his decision and not, as happened later in 1942, when as more usually, it was tabled by the opposition parties. Churchill's was a highly unusual action to take and as Lord Addison as leader of the Labour Party in the House of Lords commented, 'The form of motion which has been submitted to us by the leader of the House is not perhaps that which is altogether usual in Parliamentary Procedure.'

The nearest modern example was perhaps the occasion when John Major made a vote on the Maastricht Treaty (in 1993) a vote of confidence, knowing full well that a defeat would lead to a change of government.

This really was a high-stake decision. We checked with the House of Commons and sure enough, it was Churchill who had first brought the motion and then had 'self-elected' to make it one of confidence. He had then also amended the standing orders for the day to allow for a longer debate than originally planned. The controversial aspect of this decision was that in a time of war, there was inevitably a mixing of national and party interests to consider and indeed Lloyd George, opening the debate in the Commons on 7 May started by saying, 'I regret that this decision should take place on a motion of Confidence… what we really want is a discussion, rather than a polemical debate, which involves an issue I am not aware that anybody in the House wants raised.' Lloyd George was annoyed because Churchill, through his use of parliamentary tactics and procedure, had got his retaliation in first. Whilst there were undoubtedly many in the House uncomfortable in endorsing Churchill, to not do so could be construed as voting against the national interest, something that the vast majority of the British population were quite content they understood and in their eyes Churchill actually represented.

So, before looking at the debate in detail it may well be instructive to consider the composition of the chamber in May 1941, as it too was unusual in that it was elected in 1935, nearly six years previously.

In the November of that year, Stanley Baldwin had won a majority for the National Government with 429 seats, out of the 615 available. The Labour Party was the next largest party with 154.

In arriving at the 429 seats, 386 were Conservative seats, so Baldwin already had a clear Conservative majority, without having to rely on his other National Government allies.

Thereafter, from November 1935 to 10 May 1941, there had been 136 by-elections, with fifteen Conservatives having lost their seats to other parties, although that calculation included losing to two Independent Conservatives. Essentially, however, the arithmetic stayed roughly the same. If Churchill was to be defeated, his own party would have to turn on him en masse and jeopardise their own futures at the same time. There would also be the inherent uncertainty as to a replacement. There was no precedent for an election in wartime, so how precisely would a leader be elected and by whom?

How likely was this possible scenario?

Stanley Baldwin had fought the 1935 election on a manifesto that reaffirmed Britain's commitment to the League of Nations. It made the point that 'the actual position of our defence force is not satisfactory', but also stated that arms limitation would be as important as the manufacture of weapons. However, very sensibly, the main thrust was the continued recovery from the earlier depression and how certain sectors of industry and agriculture might benefit and be stimulated further by the continuation of a National Government.

In other words, a completely different set of circumstances. Added to which, Baldwin had retired in 1937 and Neville Chamberlain had been appointed his replacement. In 1941, Churchill, Chamberlain's recent replacement, was at the helm, having essentially grabbed the tiller. The right man in the right place at the right time perhaps, but were there enough like him? What had the previous twelve months actually achieved? Britain was still in the fight, albeit hanging on the ropes and at a terrible cost, and on no account in a position to yet strike back at Nazi Germany.

Winston Churchill had travelled to some of the areas affected by the almost incessant night-time bombing in late April 1941 and again, mindful of the parlous situation Britain found herself in, had decided to address the nation via the BBC on 27 April 1941. The power of his oratory was certainly, to date, his most potent weapon and had so far been extremely well deployed.

He first addressed the recent defeats in Greece and the decision to send British troops to assist, followed by the defeats of the Libyan Desert. However, to defeat Britain would still either require an invasion or the cutting of the maritime lifeline across the Atlantic.

That enabled him to report on and develop his true strategy, of bringing the United States into the war and, in that regard, there was definitely progress being made, almost casually remarking, 'When you come to think of it, the United States are very closely bound up with us now…' He ended with the now famous, 'But Westward, look, the land is bright.'

However, had Winston Churchill done enough this time? To date, he had used his electrifying powers of oratory to galvanise the masses, but politically, in Westminster this skill was now wearing thin, if indeed it had ever been particularly persuasive to the rump of Conservative MPs brought up and nurtured by the two very different previous leaders. The perception was gathering that there was actually very little behind the speeches, magnificent oratorical records though they may be.

Adolf Hitler had also chosen to jump on the anti-Churchill bandwagon. It will be remembered that his speech on 4 May 1941, only three days previously in Berlin, had accused Churchill of one of the greatest strategic blunders of the war, by transferring troops from Libya to Greece and stated that he was one of the most 'hopeless dabblers in strategy'.

We do wonder if this was a deliberate attack by Hitler, particularly given the knowledge of the forthcoming debate in Westminster and the fact that apparently Karl Haushofer had directly influenced the content of the speech by prompting Hess, prior to his departure to Berlin, to attend the Reichstag assembly and alter its content.

There was also a real sense of unease within the Conservative Party. Oliver Stanley, the younger brother of the Lord Derby and 'intelligence liaison' for Churchill, had visited Hugh Dalton, the combative Labour MP and recently appointed head of SOE. The meeting had taken place on 28 April, the same day as Churchill's latest BBC speech and, as Dalton recorded,

'He then began a long tirade against the Prime Minister and the foreign secretary,' which heavily criticised the leadership since May 1940. Dalton concluded that, 'I do not understand why Stanley was so rashly indiscreet to me tonight. I could, if I chose, do him great damage…'

Was Stanley 'sounding out' Dalton as to his views as to a change of government? Clearly, Dalton did not 'bite', as amongst other reasons he had just been promoted by the pugnacious subject of the Stanley tirade.

Clearly, the pressure, real or imagined was growing.

On 6 May 1941, Chips Channon recorded: 'The first day of the great Debate; and I wonder if Anthony will survive it…' Eden had been seen by some as being personally responsible for the Greek debacle and a fortnight earlier Channon had questioned whether, 'Winston is preparing to throw Eden over if the going gets too hot?'

As events transpired, events did not 'get too hot'. Despite Eden making a poor speech on the first day, 'I have never heard an important speech so badly delivered.'[2]

Lloyd George then made an equally unimpressive speech on the second day, the 7th, 'Lloyd George makes a deplorable opening speech…'[3]

Shortly after 4.00pm, Winston Churchill rose and in a 'pungent, amusing, cruel and hard-hitting' manner lashed out at Lloyd George, in particular. The climax of the attack was to liken Lloyd George to Marshal Philippe Pétain, a comment that Dalton thought 'will stick'. It did.

Channon later summarised the speech simply as, 'He tore his opponents to shreds and captivated the House.'

The result was 447 votes to 3. Lloyd George abstained and never spoke in the House of Commons again.

In summarising, Churchill also explained his rationale for making the vote one of Confidence. He stated that the Government had 'a right to know where they stand with the House of Commons and where the House of Commons stands with the Country'. He went on, 'Still more is this knowledge important for the sake of foreign nations which are balancing their policy at this time, and who ought to be left in no doubt about the stability or otherwise of this resolved and obstinate war Government.'

In other words, Churchill was sending out a clear message to both home and abroad. He and his Government were going nowhere, and he had just decisively proven that to be the case. However, behind the bravado and courage, 'The Government has been shaken and both Anthony and Winston know it.'[4]

The question that remains is how different might the eventual outcome have been had Churchill not have played the masterstroke of making the motion one of confidence? Had Churchill just saved his position and in the process staved off a constitutional political coup? Is this why Churchill knew 'the Government has been shaken?'

To Rudolf Hess, at now at home in Munich, the message the vote sent from London was unambiguous.

An alternative approach had to now take place. The British Parliament was not going to remove Churchill.

[1] This interpretation was kindly confirmed by Prof. Vernon Bogdanor in an email to John Harris dated 17 August 2015. It was agreed by convention that there should not be a General Election in wartime.

[2] 6 May 1941, *Henry 'Chips' Channon: The Diaries*, Weidenfeld & Nicolson, London, 1967.

[3] 7 May 1941, *The Political Diary of Hugh Dalton*, Jonathan Cape, London, 1986.

[4] Op. citation.

CALAMITY

CHAPTER 19
THE FLIGHT AND ITS CHARACTER

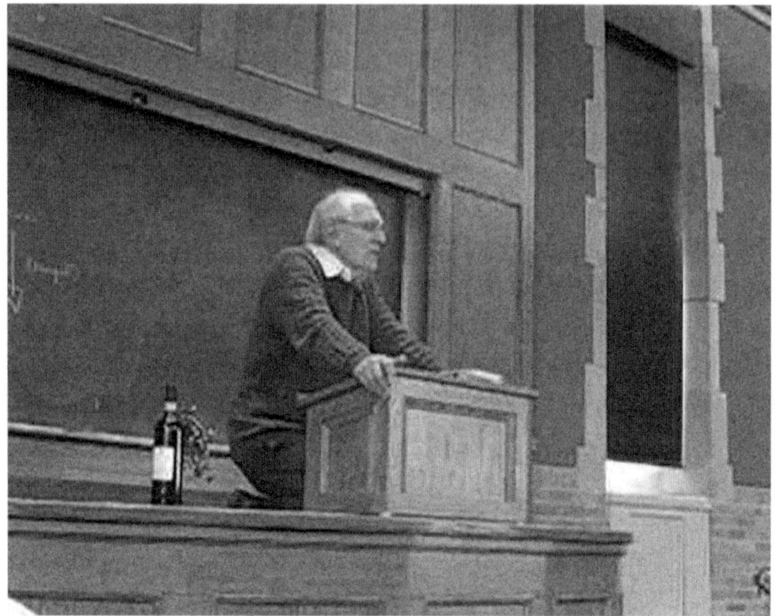

Professor A.W.B. Simpson (1931–2011)

The flight of Rudolf Hess from Augsburg, Bavaria to Eaglesham, Scotland 1745 hours to 2307 hours

As time went by, like most Hess researchers, the finer details of the flight never really quite made sense to us. It was also becoming clear that Hess was always very astute in protecting such secrets and knowledge that he wished to preserve (not in just matter aeronautical) and so we have always taken some of the details that others have chosen to accept as 'gospel' very much with a pinch of salt. Hess was certainly not stupid. On 10 May 1941 he was in charge of one of the most modern planes in the world, fitted with the most modern radio navigation system in the world and, succeed or fail, he certainly was not going to hand the latest Luftwaffe equipment and its secrets to the enemy.

In the 1980s there various books had been written questioning whether the Hess plane had the range in terms of fuel to make the journey. There had been other books stating that there were different planes used and, *in extremis*, there had been a mid-flight handover. We had studied these books carefully and were struggling, in the absence of fresh evidence, to understand what had really happened. We never believed the more outlandish theories, as 1941 wartime aviation was quite difficult enough without any further silly complications. Like all the other Hess researchers, we had superficially studied the flight map housed at Lennoxlove House that had been presented to the Hamilton family in 1941 and the supposed flight map that Hess had drawn whilst in captivity in 1942. This was published in J.R. Rees's book, *The Case of Rudolf Hess*, in 1947.[1] Apart from the aforementioned, the only other record of the flight came from the excellent Royal Observer Corps reports and records at the National Archives and the summary contained within, 'Attack Warning Red', the official history of the ROC.[2]

Then along came the pilot's notes. This was the game-changing break we were waiting for.

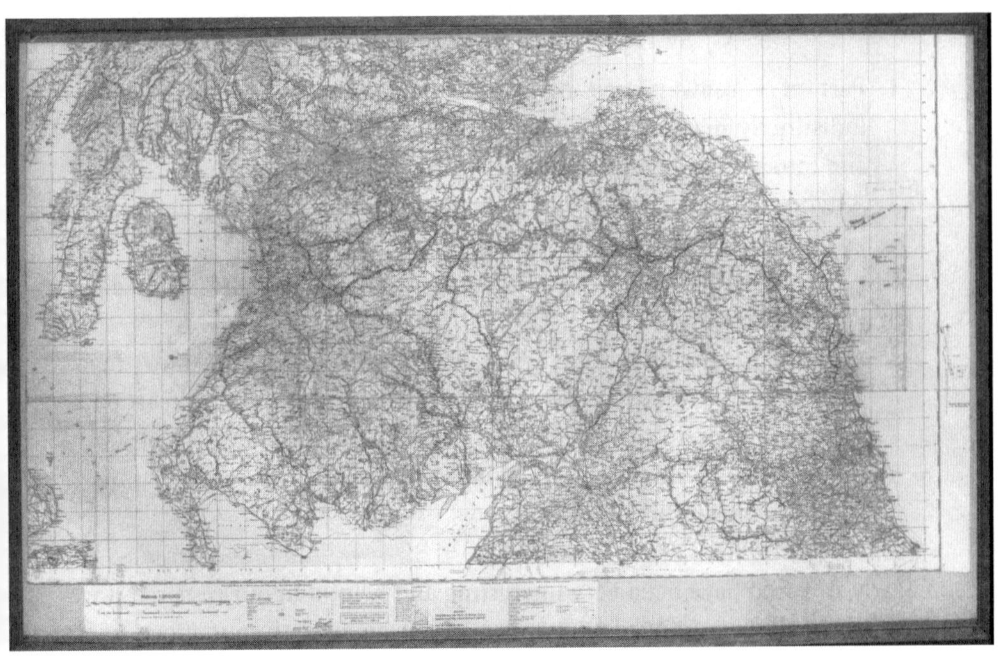

The Lennoxlove Map

The mystery of the pilot's notes and Hess's preparation for the flight

In 2008/09, whilst trying to interpret the Lennoxlove map (the map given to the Duke of Hamilton in 1941 by the RAF, purporting to come from the Hess plane) we were approached by Peter Padfield, the well-known and respected military historian, who had obtained what were claimed to be and described as copies of the flight notes of Rudolf Hess. He and his son had tried to interpret them to elicit some insight or meaning but had struggled to make any sense of them at all. He was kind enough to offer them to us for inspection.

Initially we came to the same result. They made no sense. We had pestered Peter as to the notes' provenance and he told us that they had come from a Prof. A.W.B. Simpson, a prominent human rights lawyer who had unfortunately died in 2011, aged eighty.

Again, we pestered. Prof. Simpson had apparently obtained the notes from a 'David Oliver' who had served in the RAF. Copies of the notes had been taken in the late 1950s and there were rumours that the notes had also been taken to *The Times*, at that time. 'David Oliver' had apparently at some time served at the Central Navigation School at RAF Shawbury, Shropshire. Later we were to find out from Peter that Prof. Simpson had also referred to additional documents. We were told that the documents originally included:

1. Part of a railway map of Britain, 1:1000000, which was 'very indistinctly' marked with a number of courses across Northumberland and into southern Scotland.
2. A typed document with handwritten alterations and calculations, giving details of legs and distances.
3. A sketch map of the area to the west of the Farne Islands, marked with railways and hills.
4. A two-page document, including a set of calculations to show the time taken to cover distances of 290 km, 410 km and 370 km (in order as given) at speeds of 300– 520 km/hour, in 10 km/hour intervals.
5. A handwritten document showing four calculations of the time taken for the flight, or part of it.

Clearly, it would have been very interesting and helpful to our research if we had sight of all the original documents. We have made strenuous efforts to do so but, to date, without success. We only had been given the two scrambled flight plans, which we assumed were document 5 from the above list.

However, with that paucity of detail we began our research.

First, we contacted the RAF Air Historical Branch. They did not recognise the notes. We then contacted RAF Shawbury, who referred us to the National Archives. They too denied all knowledge of the notes as did the RAF Museum, Hendon.

We then researched the history of RAF Shawbury. The following research material mainly came from *Man is Not Lost* by Group Captain Dickie Richardson. Whilst much of the book deals with early aerial navigation and its techniques, Richardson ended the war as Deputy Commander and Director of Studies for the nascent Empire Air Navigation School, newly housed at the Shropshire base.

As Richardson says, 'We decided our first aim should be to create a central repository of navigation knowledge, covering every aspect of military aviation … This prodigious mini-empire drew upon the resources of twelve specialised sections, including radar, signals and astro-nav aids, compasses, instruments, maps and charts, meteorology … a museum and finally editorial.'

It therefore seems perfectly sensible and possible that the Hess flight notes (always assuming they were indeed rescued from the crashed Hess plane) had ended up at Shawbury and were copied when the navigational school closed in the late 1950s and moved to RAF Manby, Lincolnshire, in 1963. The explanation given to us still appeared plausible. So far so good.

We then checked with David Oliver the well-known aviation editor and writer, but once again he had not heard of or seen, the flight notes. We were clearly looking for a different David Oliver.

In short, we had drawn a blank. It would then have been very easy to dismiss the notes as mumbo jumbo, or a forgery, or both, and go no further. In some ways it would have been easy – or easier – to have done so, except for one remarkable fact.

We now believe the notes to be a very poor transcript of the original Hess pre-flight planning notes, probably transcribed by someone unfamiliar with navigation and not a fluent German speaker, rather like ourselves. Some details remain unclear, but we do believe that we now largely understand the notes and their later, terrible implications to Hess.

Of most relevance, there are references contained within the notes that directly refer to and relate to the Lennoxlove map and other navigational and operational details that certainly stand up to very close scrutiny. In other words, we now believe that the Lennoxlove map and the flight notes were being drawn up at the same time. References appear on both documents that relate to each other. In 2019, in preparation for this book, we revisited the notes again and slowly, they began to become clearer.

Peter Padfield's son, Guy, had apparently transcribed the notes on to a word processor and the numbers and phrases appear to thereafter have become muddled; there seemed to be little or no order to them.

Our initial impression of these notes was that the two pages were different in their objective. The first page seems to be a chronological plan, with kilometres and other instructions. The second a series of numbers, which appear to be in terms of time.

We also contemplated that the notes were actually muddled up completely, and that some numbers might even be on the wrong page.

Then, over the summer of 2019, after more work and revision, small breakthroughs were made, and after much more head-scratching and reading around the subject, slowly the flight notes began to come together. We now present our interpretation of the notes themselves.

One sheet we believe was a 'preferred route', the other actually gives four options as to how to achieve the same goal; the flight to and across the North Sea.

We also believe that in the end, Hess did not follow exactly any of the options described in the notes. Moreover, we were very mindful that they could still be complete bunkum – but, if so, why would Hess bring notes with him that he had not used and why would Peter Padfield and his son become interested in them?

Over the summer months of 2022 we had noticed that if selected carefully, the above jumble is actually a four-column table, which is (almost) arithmetically correct. This is reproduced on the following page.

Recompilation of pilot's notes' data

II			I			
a		b	a		b	
60	verdun	60	55	?	55	
42	kuste	42	42	kuste	42	
56	b2/g/b1	77	35	b'//b	60	
31	kuste	25	31	kuste	25	
5	insele	5	5	insele	5	
194		209	168		187	
3h 15		3h 30	2h 48		3h7	
15	wind	15	15	wind	15	
3h 30		3h 45	3.03		3h 22	

As you can see, the table gives four options. The flight times appear to range from just over 3 hours to 3 hours 45 minutes.

We were initially a little apprehensive, given the use of the letter 'h' to denote hour. What little German we had would expect us to have seen an 's' for *stunde*. Was this a fake British document after all? After a little work we discovered that lower case 'h' was also used by the Germans to denote hours. We carried on.

Moving on to the figures themselves, one can see that each of the 2 columns marked I and II show similar results until after the line KUSTE, i.e. 60 and 42 and 55 and 42.

Eventually we deduced that what we were seeing was essentially two flight paths to the coast and then a variety of ways to approach the same point 'INSELE'. All four routes ended at the same point which was then 5 minutes away from the 'INSELE'.

We then drew the above diagram and suddenly much became clear. The table refers to four alternative routes of getting up the North Sea, presumably whilst being mindful of the intersecting radio beams.

The two points of entry to the North Sea appear to relate to Den Helder (a) and Borkum (b), both points being used by and shown by Hess on his 1941 plan. Furthermore, given that we had discovered at Duxford that there had been no auxiliary oil tank fitted (this discovery was documented in our 2014 work, *Rudolf Hess: A New Technical Analysis of the Hess Flight, May 1941*), we were absolutely intrigued to see that the first leg of both options appeared to have a pause; column II after 60 minutes, column I after 55 minutes.

It became apparent that Hess was actually planning to land en route, a plan that we now believe was actually a necessity rather than an option. Where he was going to land was 60 minutes away on column II and 55 minutes away on column I planning.

Clearly, we were making headway, but as yet had nothing concrete to tie these notes into any other documentary evidence. The notes were still potentially unauthenticated mumbo jumbo that we had made arithmetically correct. We moved on to the first plan, which we soon discovered, replicates exactly the plan outlined in column I – b.

This describes a flight of 55 minutes, a further 42 to the coast, then 60 minutes up the north sea, before turning inland for 25 minutes, before a final 5 minute leg to the INSELE. The first pilot note is important we believe because this also links the Lennoxlove map to the above pilot notes.

We will now move on to describe the German radio navigation systems available at the time. This, we now know is the key that provides the link between the Lennoxlove map, the pilot's notes and what actually happened on the evening of 10 May 1941.

However, during the long, dry summer of 2018, we made two new major breakthroughs. Wilbourn theorised that the notes actually start from the North German location that Hess needed to stop at en route, so as to top up the oil and fuel. We knew there was no auxiliary oil tank fitted and so this was a pre-requisite.

This made perfect sense, given that whatever route was followed subsequent to the en route stop, the distance and fuel and oil usage from Augsburg to the inflight landing airbase was actually irrelevant, as the completion of the flight would start from the same place. Wherever that might be.

In 2014, when we had last tried to solve this riddle, we speculated that the stopover might have been either at Lippstadt (in 1941 home to an operational Bf110 *geschwader*) or Göttingen, the home to the Horten brothers and their ground-breaking aeronautical research. Neither guess is correct.

As can be seen above, the pilot's notes mentioned Verdun as being the first line of the plan. We had previously struggled with this, thinking perhaps it meant Verdun in eastern France, or even Voerden in Northern Germany. Neither seemed to fit. However, by working backwards from the two North Sea entry points of Den Helder and Borkum, we alighted on the *Flugplatz* Giessen, which fitted the required timings and distances exactly. Moreover, simple 'googling' of the *Flugplatz* revealed that in 1941 the recently constructed barracks, or *Kaserne*, were named after the infamous battle of 1917. The Verdun barracks at Giessen, adjacent to the airfield, we believe, mark the starting point of the flight itself, in terms of the pilot's notes at least.

The Verdun Kaserne at Giessen (Wikicommons)

This is a major breakthrough. It then renders the subsequent work on the flight plan the more valuable, as we now know the correct starting point.

It also renders Hugh Thomas's theory that two planes were used quite possible. Hess could of course fly one Bf110 to Giessen and then refuel and reoil, or alternatively, he could fly another, different, Bf110 to Giessen and then change to a fully fuelled and oiled bf110 *werk nummer 3869* ready and waiting to complete the flight. That decision could simply be a function of available time.

If one analyses the time factor, it is generally accepted that take off from Augsburg was at 1745 hours. Giessen is some 290 km away, which is around 40 minutes in a Bf110. Therefore, Hess could have been at Giessen by say,

1830 hours, ready for take-off at around 1900 hours, prior to a 60 minute flight to the German coast at Borkum.

It does all fit, and it de-risks the flight significantly.

When we then add the fact that Hess had two close friends at Giessen by way of Dr Alfred Kaufmann (1868–1946), Hess's teacher (whilst being educated in Alexandria) and Gerhard Pfahler a clinical psychiatrist (1897–1976), it does all perhaps seem the easier to understand.

However, the notes themselves remain a mystery. Their provenance is far from secure. How they got to Brian Simpson does seem most odd, though we suspect that David Oliver lived in the Canterbury area, somewhere near the late professor.

So, we do now believe them to be wholly genuine, but almost wish we did not, given the lack of proven provenance. They do, however, link all the components together. We now know and understand the flight plan. It does also clearly demonstrate that Hess was prepared to lie to protect Nazi secrets.

The preparation continued – German navigational systems, May 1941

The Hess flight over the North Sea was clearly a challenge for the lone flier to navigate. The obvious difficulty of the task has led, over the years, to various suggestions of, for example, additional crew in the plane, to accompanying planes and greeting flights to guide the plane along its course. Many have suggested the use of radio bearings, fixed from Kastanie-Y near Kalundborg and guidance beams, like Knickebein, as possible aids to this feat. Clearly the navigation over the sea was a crucial aspect of the flight and Hess's position and direction during the journey were critical points of failure. From what we have discovered and know of Hess, this would not have been left to chance. We now seek to analyse the various, then contemporary, means of navigation available to Hess when planning his flight. Throughout this part of our research, we have received much help and assistance from the acknowledged experts in this field: Dr Phil Judkins in England, Major S.E.S. Svjegaard in Denmark and, in particular, Arthur Bauer from Diemen, Holland. We have now summarised the available navigational tools available to Hess and tried to assess what was of practical use to him.

Visual

Rudolf Hess trained as a pilot during the formative years of the First World War. Whilst, somewhat surprisingly, radio navigation systems were in existence by that time, the vast majority of flight was carried out by simple visual recognition and comparison to a map of the area. Roads, railways and canals provided early visual aids, together with woods, lakes and streams. Viaducts were often specifically marked, as they provided a cross-check between water and railways or roads, an early form of 'fix'. As we have seen, the Lennoxlove map, at first glance, provides a text book example of how to mark-up a map for a visual flight, with all the features listed above clearly marked.

Obviously, visual recognition becomes more difficult at night, or in cloud or fog. When sending the Lennoxlove map to the Hamilton family in May 1941, the Air Ministry noted that it had been marked up in accordance with the practice of the last war.

Mapping and maps

At the time of the Hess flight, the standard Luftwaffe mapping system was the 'Gradnetzmeldeverfahren' or 'Gradnetz', which had been in existence since before 1939 and with a few modifications was to last until 1943. The system enabled a common map reading system over a number of different map sizes, scales and projections. The mapping broke the world down into grid squares of diminishing scale:

- Zusatzzahlgebeit: based on the Greenwich Meridian, these sectors were bordered by every ten degrees of longitude and latitude. They were sub-divided into 100 sectors.
- Großtrapez: each of a degree of longitude and latitude and given numbers from 00 to 99. The numbering sequences were in a different order to the east or west of the Meridian. Each was separated into eight sectors of two wide and four squares tall.
- Mitteltrapez: numbered from the top left corner 1 to 8. A further division follows into nine.
- Kleintrapez: equal square divisions numbering from the top left corner. Until 1943 these were divided into four.
- Meldetrapez: numbered 1 to 4, which were again divided into four;
- Arbeitstrapez: which, again until 1943, had the descriptors lo (links oben), ro (rechts oben), lu (links unten) and ru (rechts unten).

Further details of the system can be found by searching the work of Andreas Brekken and Werner Muller.

We have seen Luftwaffe Gnomischerkarte using the Gradnetz system at the British Library. The Gnomonic projection ingeniously allows lines of bearing to be drawn as straight lines, the projection automatically adjusting for the curvature of the earth. Not surprisingly, perhaps, the German mapping industry had experienced somewhat of a renaissance after the immediate First World War decline. Staffing numbers at the Die Reichsamt für Landesaufnahme had risen from 539 in 1935 to 1,325 in 1937. So, in researching the equipment that Hess would have had at his disposal, we have purchased some original wartime maps, some of which were actually used on raids. These now appear to be quite plentiful. As usual, we have been impressed by the quality of the product, but yet again we have also been surprised at the sheer quantity of variations produced. Whilst researching this book we have acquired:

- A German Gradnetz map of continental Europe, mounted on Perspex sheets, so as to allow easy 'flipping' of the pages from one area to that adjacent: vertical or horizontal.
- A German Luftwaffe map of Great Britain showing specifically all rivers, canals and estuaries. This is described as an 'Ubersicht der Gewasser'. This clearly demonstrates the level of specific detail the Germans were capable of.
- A German Luftwaffe map of Germany (Navigationskarte in Merkator-projection) at a scale of 1; 2,000,000, showing the restricted air spaces. This, too, is a Gradnetz map, and we have acquired a black and white copy for daytime flying and a coloured chart for the night. The restricted areas clearly centre around airfields, but there are other areas marked, such as around Peenemünde, presumably to facilitate rocket testing.

  Of particular interest is the fact that the Kalundborg radio station is marked in the margin as a 'Rundfunksender' and coincidentally the map reveals it to be virtually due north of Augsburg. We now believe that in allowing Kalundborg to be marked (but certainly no other radio stations), the Reichsamt für Landesaufnahme was actually making a statement that Kalundborg was not of military importance. In February 1940, the 'Verordnung über die Veröffentlichung kartographischer Darstellung (KartVeröffVO)' was issued, stating that each map had to be assessed for its economic or military significance and, where appropriate, items 'should be omitted or falsified'. The fact that Kalundborg was allowed to remain presumably shows its assessed military value.

The point to the above observation is simply that once again the Germans appeared to have a map for every purpose and occasion. Hess had no shortage, in theory at least, of maps to choose from. That is what made his eventual choice, based on British Ordnance Survey road maps, described as being 1:250,000 (actually, slightly expanded 4 miles to the inch projections) to seem at first glance, quite so odd.

We now believe this was very clever indeed, as the maps were marked up for sophisticated radio navigation direction finding but disguised as being British Ordnance Survey road maps. It certainly appears to have fooled the British Air Ministry in May 1941.

In theory, Hess could have used such mapping and dead reckoning by watch and compass to guide his way up the North Sea, but his course and timings would then have been critical for success. To put the proposed flight into context, Charles Lindbergh had crossed the Atlantic in 1927 on a solo flight, so such an undertaking was certainly not unprecedented, but that was not in wartime, albeit navigation had certainly improved in the meanwhile. In 1941, Hess had to avoid detection by radar and interception or observation by patrolling ships and aircraft, and arrive at his destination at the right time. His heading and distance to (if the commonly accepted flight plan is considered) his turn point towards Northumberland was key to his success. Would Hess have trusted time-consuming calculation or would he have used other means, or both?

Radio Navigation and Guidance

It is easy to underestimate the degree and pace of technical development of radio and radar at the time of the flight; driven by conflict, the technology had advanced at a tremendous pace. The secret nature of much of this development does lead to some problems with the chronology of the advances and may have further strengthened the need for covert planning and later denial or misleading responses. This is a complex field in which we are not yet expert, but we are convinced that Hess would have planned the use of the technology to improve his chances of success. There is plenty of evidence to support this view, but which system would best fit the task at hand?

Radio bearings

Hess' traditional story has many references to Radio Kalundborg or *Saarbruken*. These stations have been attributed with playing particular tunes as a form of message and acting as beacons from which positions and bearing could be set. Elsewhere, alterations to his on-board radio system have been reported. We now consider that these references do form an important part of the story but that the explanation so far has been to justify their inclusion rather than to understand the underlying facts.

First, to examine the use of radio as a beacon. In order to fix a bearing on a station, Hess would have had to tune in his Bf110's loop aerial to find the 'null' sectors and so set his position by azimuth, the clockwise position measured from true north. If he could not turn the antenna, he would have had to align his plane with the radio source and read from his master compass. We know that loop aerials which could detect a bearing from a fixed position were developed later, but it is not clear if Hess would have had that equipment available at the time. It is unlikely that he would have been able to turn an antenna to find a bearing, as a shortage of space and time would have made that very difficult. The radio beacons were more commonly used for an aircraft to 'home in' on to its base.

The setting of his position by azimuth is only giving part of the information required for navigation; he would need two bearings to get a clear idea of his position. The Germans did employ various means of directing aircraft on to their target, including Knickebein. These systems were known to the British and often misdirected by the 'Beam Benders'. Not only were they not to be relied on, due to British interference, they were specifically intended for multi-crewed planes in bomber formations. Consequently, they needed some effort, skill, time, space and equipment to operate them. Additionally, and perhaps fatally for the Hess flight, they had to be switched on and directed to a target. If Hess's flight had really been covert to both sides, this would have demanded a lot of cooperation from the operators of the system and a general awareness of what was going on. Hess needed a simple to operate and low-key navigation aid.

Elektra, Sonne and Consol

In addition to the bombing systems that had been developed, there was also a Lorenz radio guidance system, fully operational, called, Elektra. This guidance system (Leitstrahl) was a development of the Lorenz blind landing system, where the approaching aircraft would receive Morse signals to mark its position to the left or right of a flight line. The landing system had been used successfully since the mid 1930s.

Dr Kramer at C.Lorenz AG (now Alcatel SEL AG), had used the interaction of three transmitting antennas to throw out lobes of signal lines on fixed bearings, each with a sequence of Morse dots or dashes to one side or the other of each of the lobes or 'beams'. In this way the plane could keep to the continuous tone, equisignal, sector to fly along a known bearing. The Germans established several of these Elektra stations which would mostly operate during the daytime; night-time conditions caused reduced accuracy from the signals. Stations included Elektra 1, Stavanger (Varhaug) and Elektra 2, originally E1 (until Stavanger was given that designation), Husum (Poppenbüll). Elektra did not identify individual equisignal lines, other than by the known fixed bearing to the transmitter, and the navigator had to know roughly where they were as a starting point.

Rather inconveniently for understanding the system, at the time of the Hess flight improvements to the Elektra system were underway and the stations were undergoing conversion to a later development of the Elektra system known as Sonne.

Sonne used the same aerials and broadcast patterns as Elektra, but importantly the signals could now carry navigational information. Instead of the dots and dashes to each side of the equisignal line, the stations now broadcast different numbers of dots and dashes between each equisignal line. The station continuously broadcast a two-minute-long signal sequence containing meticulous bearing and positional information.

First, the station broadcast its identifier call sign, then a short continuous tone to allow a bearing fix to be taken. The big difference from Elektra was that after a short pause a 60 second transmission of numbers of dots and dashes was broadcast. These Morse characters always added up to sixty, but numbers of each character varied across the distance between the equisignal lines. In between the change from dot to dash the keying merged into a short continuous tone before breaking out again into the next character. By counting the numbers of dots and dashes the navigator could further refine his position between the equisignal lines. The difficulty in counting the characters as the sequence approached the changeover from one to another could be overcome by timing the arrival of the short, combined tone with a stopwatch. The sequence lasted for 60 seconds, so every second was equivalent to one dot or dash. The whole transmission would repeat every two minutes and was repeated over all the equisignal lines in the pattern of dots into dashes or dashes into dots.

The extra information carried by Sonne became an important aid to navigation and the system became so useful that the Allies stopped attempting to bend the signals but instead made us of if under the codename Consol. It was still in use from some stations, like Stavanger, into the early 1990s. This could explain why so little of the system has been mentioned in the Hess story to date; it was still very current technology for the armed services.

In summary, the Germans had a passive radio net across the North Sea. It could have operated as a beam flying system, Elektra, which gave only rudimentary navigational information or in addition to that, the basis for a much more accurate *positioning* system, Sonne. Neither had to be 'directed' or switched on at a particular time, but, equally, both could be switched on and off if the need arose. Hess did not necessarily have to arrange for it to be active or wait until a Luftwaffe raid, and it was not being actively 'bent' by the British.

The next question is: Did Hess have the equipment training or time to use either system? If so, who would have trained him? The practical operation of Elektra and Sonne only required basic equipment, a standard Luftwaffe radio, like the FuG10 EL, a stopwatch and a map or conversion table. The only modification required to the radio was to put the EL receiver in the pilot's area of the cockpit or make the set controllable from there. Once set on a station, though, there was little to do.

The original Elektra maps are very difficult to find, but the British Library does hold some slightly later German Sonne and British Consol charts. We duly obtained a copy of the British Consol chart, as it included the station Stavanger and have seen the German Sonne Chart, Nr, 2020 Grossbritannien, Großkreise aus Sonne 5 Holland and Sonne 6 Quimper. The Luftwaffe chart showing the Stavanger station is somewhere in the British Library but has apparently been lost since 2009. The Luftwaffe map shows the Sonne equisignal lines and Morse sectors overlaid on a 1:2000000 Schiefachsiger gnomisher netzenwurf (Gnomonic projection) Gradnetz chart.

The practicality of Hess tuning the radio and counting and noting specific numbers of dots and dashes or time in seconds or referring to navigation chart does not seem likely for his flight. He was otherwise occupied.

There is, however, another more practical use of the radio beams. By employing them as waymarks, Hess could have maintained a compass bearing and then by just counting the number of equisignal lines as he approached and passed through them, have fixed his position along his course. His turn point towards Britain could then be determined. If he were to lose his position, there was little in the circumstances that either Elektra or Sonne (or any beam system for that matter) could do for him without a lot of calculation or retracing his steps. This far more simple use of the technology is exactly what we believe he used and what the pilot's notes demonstrate that he planned to use.

General aeronautical navigation

One of our relations was a serving RAF Officer with a background in navigation. We asked him some basic questions about navigation and how it was likely to have been achieved at the time of Hess flight.

Our navigator explained the dynamic nature of the problem and how knowing where you are and where you are heading is as much a product of a combination of factors as it is relying on any one particular guide.

The most basic form of navigation was, and is still, achieved by using the 'Mark I navigation device': the human eyeball. Looking for features and comparing those with a chart or a mental map is the simplest way to navigate.

An on-board compass, if correctly calibrated, will give a heading for the aircraft but varying wind speeds can allow a lot of error to creep in. The Hess Bf110 had a Siemens autopilot based on the master compass that was suspended in the rear part of the fuselage. This can be factored in when planning a flight but, even as we saw on our short flight from Carlisle (in 2012 recreating the latter part of the Hess flight), the errors can quickly magnify.

The sun, moon and stars offer known points and they have been used extensively as means of fixing a point, almost for as long as man has sought to travel. Here very good time-keeping is essential, as shown by the admiralty quest for better and better chronometers and the breakthrough invention of the Harrison Chronometer of 1761. Little help for Hess here, but the flight towards Britain was basically towards the setting sun in the west.

Accurate measurement of airspeed is important so that the flier can compare the arrival at any point with his original plan. There are references to Hess asking for the calibration of the plan's pitot tube, the device which measures airspeed.

So, we trust that we are now building the picture of how Hess was to achieve his challenging flight. He would have measured his progress along a compass bearing and from a known start point in terms of time to waypoints. In the absence of visual features over the sea, he would have used the beams emitted from a radio beacon, together with an expectation of duration obtained from a watch. At a point following the crossing through of a given number of beams, he would turn on to another known bearing and head towards the British coast.

As our RAF navigator told us, and as we would probably have worked out for ourselves, the coast of Britain is a fairly easy target to find; the difficulty is finding the correct point of entry across it. To facilitate this we were introduced to the principle of 'funnel features' and entry points. Once on a rough bearing to the coast, Hess needed some landmarks to fix his approach and hence know where he was. There are several prominent features along the Northumberland coast, from islands to castles and lighthouses. Any of these features, or a combination thereof, would have helped Hess to home in on his first major navigational landmark, the Cheviot.

This was his 'entry point', the start of his flight over Scotland and the key to his planned path. From now on such as like high points, lakes, rivers and, importantly, the railway lines along his way. Railway lines have always been a sought-after landmark; they do not move, they go from one known place to another, they are clearly not natural and with the shiny surface of the rails they will be easily observable under a wide range of visibility.

However, before moving on to the flight itself, we need to establish the precise position, frequencies and modus operandi of the two Elektra stations at Stavanger and Husum, for reasons that will become clear later in the book.

The Stavanger and Husum Elektra Stations

As the previous paragraphs make clear, by 1941 the various German radio navigational systems were developing rapidly and Elektra/Sonne had made pinpoint precision a possibility if the operator had the need, the time and the available space.

The RAF was still mainly relying on the 'traditional' astronavigation and dead reckoning, and the 1941 Butt Report made the case that British bombing accuracy (and hence, by inference, navigation) was at that time really quite inadequate. Eventually the RAF would develop the Gee, Oboe and H2S systems by way of response. This should not be too much of a surprise as by early 1941, the British, when compared to the Germans, had not completed too much bombing.

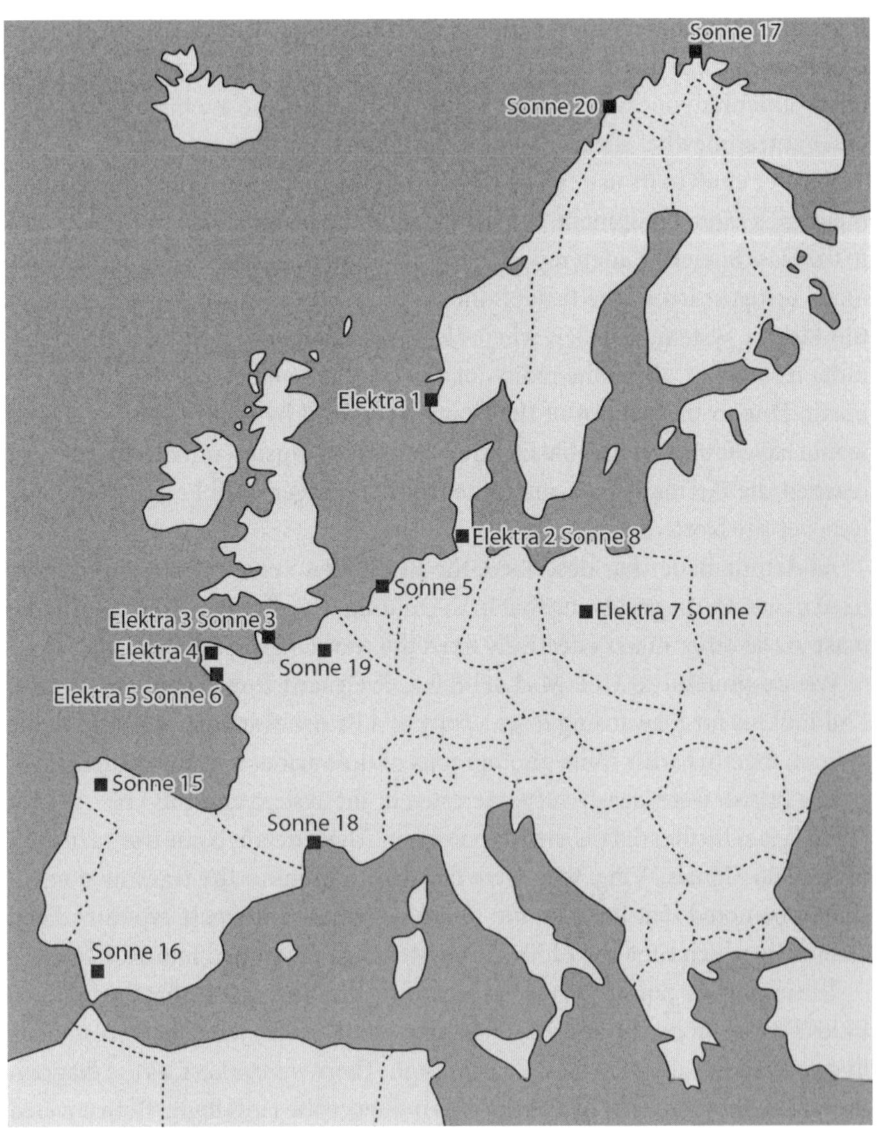

Elektra / Sonne radio navigation stations

The story of the 1940/41 Battle of the Beams is reasonably well known, and the R.V. Jones autobiography, *Most Secret War*, is an excellent telling of the story and the British response to the threat posed by the German navigational systems.

As already debated, these authors now have significant reason to believe that Hess did not use the Knickebein system. A solo pilot would have found it too difficult to operate. Instead, we are content that he attempted to use the older and somewhat simpler system, designated Elektra.

Further clues to its use can be taken from the many references made about the plane's radio equipment. In particular, in the Helmut Kaden 1989 lecture to the Hess Society, Kaden reported the details of dots, dashes and continuous tones being heard in the headphones, which we know are the signals from the Elektra system. Further, when Hess had complained to Josef Blümel, a radio technician, about the radio not working, he had been told to fly further north. Due to the pattern of the beams produced by the transmitters, Hess would have found no useable Elektra beams from Husum until he had almost reached the German coast and none from Stavanger until he was some way out over the North Sea.

As Arthur Bauer has described, the ELEKTRA system consisted of three fixed masts, the largest being that in the middle. The distance from the middle mast to the outer masts effectively fixed the wavelength of the station.

We are grateful to Col. Michaël S.E.S. Svejgaard from Denmark and Dr Phil Judkins for forwarding to us a copy of a British wartime appraisal of the system, together with some photographs of the various key components.

The British were clearly very interested in the system and PRO file AVIA 6 /12437 gives further details as to its operation. These details come from a history of RAF 80 Signals Wing, who were detailed to monitor the transmissions. It should be noted that the files and photo reconnaissance were typically dated 1943/4, by which time the ELEKTRA system had developed into SONNE.

The important points to grasp as regarding the Hess case is that the first two ELEKTRA stations, E1 and E2, Stavanger and Husum, were the two stations that covered the area that Hess flew through. There were others, as the diagram shows, but they were not in a position to influence the Hess flight. Both covered the North Sea, and both covered the Scottish Lowlands. The system was quite capable of reaching the furthest extremities of the Hess enterprise.

It is also important to note that the Elektra system did not endure too long, as it was deemed too easy to jam, usually by a process that was called 'meaconing', whereby the radio waves were distorted by the British.

The FuG10 EL (Long wave receiver)

Eventually the system was then developed into the Sonne system, which lasted throughout and beyond the war. As Bauer notes, the name was somewhat ironical, as Sonne is German for 'sun', although at night time the system was known to be less reliable in terms of accuracy.

The Lorenz FuG10 EL and Loop Aerial system

By the outbreak of the Second World War, the FuG10 (then FuG X) was a standard fitment to all Luftwaffe heavy aircraft, where it served for both radio and crew communication.

The installation was made up of modules which could be easily removed for repair or upgrade. The major components of the system were the transmitters, Sender Kurzwelle (SK) covering shortwave and the Sender Langwelle (SL) longwave, each paired with a corresponding receiver, Emfanger, EK and EL respectively.

The FuG10 EL receiver covered frequencies around 300-600 kHZ and would have been used by Hess to receive signals from the Elektra transmitters at Stavanger, operating on 297 and 319 kHZ and Husum which was operating at 481 kHZ. Clearly, both stations were well within the FuG10EL frequency range. From email correspondence with Arthur Bauer: 'Sonne and Elektra were so-called medium wave, some say long wave, systems. Operating between say roughly 300-450 kHz. The only radio necessary was thus one that covered this wave band. The Germans used then an E10L or equivalent types.'

The equipment was manufactured by Lorenz AG and the radio waves were received by the aircraft by way of a loop aerial, which was attached to the lower fuselage of the Bf110. Initially, the loop antenna would have been fixed in position, aligned with the central line of the aircraft fuselage.

The often-reproduced photograph of the Eaglesham crash site certainly shows a loop aerial just to the left of the Balkenkreuz on the remains of the fuselage. When we visited Imperial War Museum Duxford, it was obvious that the ring aerial had been fitted and then taken out of the fuselage, together with the master compass and oxygen bottle mechanisms. These items have yet to resurface from 1941. We suspect, but do not yet know, that they were taken post-haste to RAE Farnborough.

When a 'bordfunker' was employed, sitting behind the pilot, as was the norm, the loop aerial may have had the mechanism for it to be rotated, so as to point it at a particular bearing. As far as the Hess flight was concerned, this requirement would have necessitated yet more equipment to be transferred into the cockpit, and therefore we consider it highly unlikely that Hess had made arrangements for his loop aerial to be rotated. Given what we have learned about the Elektra system, this was not a requirement. He did not need the rotational function.

As part of our research, we acquired a working FuG10EL in the summer of 2012, together with a copy of its original manual from ARCHIV-HAFNER. We wanted to ascertain if there were further clues to be obtained from the machine itself, possibly by linking it back to the pilot's notes, or even the Lennoxlove map, or as events turned out, both pieces of evidence.

We were not to be disappointed. One of the features of the Fug 10 EL allows it to be pre-set with four frequencies, designated I, II, △ and □. This allows the user to readily change between radio stations, without the need for manual re-tuning; a white panel is provided next to the illuminated channel indicator for these settings to be noted in pencil.

Straightaway, we noticed that these symbols correlated to the pilots' notes and the Lennoxlove map – the blue triangles.

There was one further link that Wilbourn discovered. The pilot's notes (still of unknown provenance) give the instruction '30min v.A aufnehmen 03e1'. This we now believe should be translated as:

> 30 minutes from point A – switch on machine (FuG10EL) to setting 0 (Frequenzangleich – Fine tuning), 3 (pre-set frequency△) – Elektra Station 1 –E1 (Stavanger).

0 was the 'default' start position setting on the machine – the überlagerungswahlschalter.

In his headphones Hess could now listen for the dots, dashes and continuous tones of the Elektra system to guide his flight across the sea.

Consequently, it now appears to us that the FuG10 system was also part of the planning process that was carried out at the same time as the pilot's notes and Lennoxlove map were being prepared/marked up. There have been a number of accounts of alterations and amendments to the radio equipment to facilitate its operation from the pilot's seat of the Bf110.

We are not alone in this supposition. David Irving, in his narrative from the subsequent RSHA (Reichssicherheitshauptamt, Reich Main Security Office) interrogations, also makes mention of Elektra; he does not make any further reference to the system other than report that 'Pintsch phoned the air ministry and asked them to switch on a certain beacon…'. The name of the beacon does concur with the request to switch on the system; Elektra was probably operated as required, Sonne was constantly operational. We have to say that besides David Irving there has been little debate as to how Hess achieved his flight and got to where he went. This aspect is fundamental, because it could also explain what went wrong and cause Hess to act as he did.

On 12 February 1950, Hess wrote from Spandau to Ilse, his wife, 'Everything turned out quite otherwise than I had expected; the compass point to give me the right bearings, which I needed so badly at the decisive moment, was just the one thing missing… Before taking off I had lived in a world of … radio bearings (which afterwards failed to function)…'

Time, Sun and Moon – 10 May 1941

When writing to his wife in 1941 and 1947, Rudolf Hess made specific mention of the prevailing light conditions whilst making his flight.

- 'The North Sea was illuminated by an evening light of unearthly loveliness…'

- 'I crossed the East Coast at about 10.00pm and after sunset … at this level the visibility was surprisingly good.'
- 'On I went over level ground, skimming merrily over house tops and trees and waving greetings to men working in the fields.'
- 'The smooth sea lay beneath me as calm as a mirror, lit by the rising moon.'
- 'So, there I was … the mist barely illuminated by a full moon.'

In the first instance, so as to check that the above statements could possibly be true, we travelled to the West Coast of Scotland on 2/3 May 2009 specifically to check the prevailing light conditions at 11.09pm. We arrived at Prestwick in the early evening and waited, with pints in hand…

In 1941, sixty-eight years earlier, the United Kingdom had operated 'double summertime', which is Greenwich Mean Time,plus two hours. This action was a counter-reaction to increased traffic accidents, partly as a result of the wartime requirement to blinker vehicle headlights. This policy had been implemented as recently as 4 May 1941:

S.R. & O. 1940 No. 1883 (Emergency Powers (Defence) – Summertime)

- Long title: Order in Council amending the Defence (Summer Time) Regulations, 1939.
- Date: 24 October 1940.

This order, under the Emergency Powers (Defence) Acts, 1939 and 1940, amended the Defence (Summertime) Regulations, 1939 to make the time be one hour in advance of GMT throughout the year.

S.R. & O. 1941 No. 476 (Emergency Powers (Defence) – Summertime)

- Long title: Order in Council amending the Defence (Summertime) Regulations, 1939.
- Date: 4 April 1941.

This order, under the Emergency Powers (Defence) Acts, 1939 and 1940, amended the Defence (Summertime) Regulations, 1939 to provide for double summertime, during which period the time was two hours in advance of Greenwich Mean Time, starting on the day after the first Saturday in May and ending on the day after the second Saturday in August, both at 1.00am Greenwich Mean Time (rather than the previously used 2.00am). The time for the rest of the year remained one hour in advance of GMT. The order provided savings for certain contracts with agricultural workers and concerning the production of milk: for those purposes, the time was to be taken to be one hour in advance of GMT throughout the year, unless the parties to the contract agreed otherwise.

German time is usually one hour ahead of GMT, simply by reason of longitude. On 1 April 1940, it had adopted 'Mitteleuropäische Sommerzeit' which had the effect of adding a further hour. So, on 10 May 1941, 23.09 in Germany was 23.09 in Scotland. This fact seems to be accepted by all authors and most notably by Rudolf Hess personally. In the 1947 work *The Case of Rudolf Hess* by J.R. Rees, a map is reproduced that purports to be drawn by Hess himself and is annotated with the various times at various points. 17.45pm and 23.09pm are shown as the start and conclusion of the flight.

Clearly speed is a function of time and distance and is therefore vital in understanding the flight. Some authors have spoken of 'the missing hour', which we will analyse later, but a simple explanation of the 'missing hour' could just be a differential between the German and UK basis of time measurement. Hence the need to be absolutely sure.

We felt we needed to be in the same area as Hess, as there is also a differential between the oft-quoted 'lighting up time' in London and that pertaining to Glasgow, some 400 miles to the north. We wanted to eliminate any uncertainty and so had travelled to Ayrshire, stopping over in Prestwick.

So, at the equivalent time to 23.09 on 10 May 1941, we duly made our observation. It was dark, very dark. So dark that it would not be possible to attempt to safely land a plane without some form of runway lighting. However, on 2 May 2009 we were still a week away from the full moon and therefore noted that the prevailing light conditions as described above were without any benefit of moonlight. Public Record Office file AIR 28/40 makes the point that there was cloud cover over Prestwick in the ratio of 3:10 on 10 May 1941, and that fact should also be factored into any assessment of light conditions. Any light that there was came from the moon, low in the sky, partially obscured by clouds.

Using various on-line calculators, it is possible to ascertain the sun and moon positions at any point and time, and from this to gauge the condition of twilight. Although light levels vary from day to day, depending on the amount of sunshine reflected in the atmosphere, this is sufficient for us to get a good idea of the conditions in which Hess was flying.

From: http://planetcalc.com/874/ using the co-ordinates from Google Earth and all times at GMT +2 (BDST), the sunset times were:

Dunstanburgh Castle	55.29'05"N, 01.35'26"W	22:00:11
Dungavel	55.35'56"N, 04.07'02"W	22:10:41
Dundonald	55.35'32"N, 04.36'21"W	22:12:35
Kilmarnock	55.36'45"N, 04.26'55"W	22:12:15
West Kilbride	55.42'01"N, 04.51'27"W	22:14:06
Eaglesham ROC[4]	55.44'38"N, 04.17'37"W	22:12:04

As a cross-check,http://www.world-timedate.com/astronomy/sunrise sunset / sunrise sunset time.php?month=5&year=1941&sun param=2&city id=156 shows us that at Glasgow on the day the sunset time was 22:12:45 GMT+2, civil twilight ended there at 23:00:03, with nautical twilight ending at 00:10:19.

This introduces a time for twilight, which has an accepted description of the prevailing light conditions. Using the calculators as previously: the sunset azimuth, the bearing clockwise as taken from true north that day was around 304° and it would have moved around from 289° at an elevation of nearly 8° at 21:00 hrs. It would have been to the north of Hess's course and set for all of his Scottish flight.

The same calculators can set the state of twilight for each position along the flight. Civil twilight starts at sunset, sun elevation 0° and ends at -6°. For this exercise we can consider the end of civil twilight to mean dark.

	Sunset time	**Time of Hess pass**	**Sun elevation**
Dunstanburgh Castle	22:00	22:28	– 4.2°
Dungavel	22:10	22:45	– 4.9°
West Kilbride	22:14	22:50	– 5.0°
Kilmarnock	22:12	23:00	– 6.2°
Eaglesham	22:12	23:09	– 7.1°

As a check, this calculation method was compared with a pre-calculated result for Glasgow on another website and no significant difference was found.

It was also calculated that Hess's height would have altered the timings and light conditions. The time of sunset is one minute later for every 1.5 km of altitude, so very little change would be registered, about one minute for Hess at 5000 ft.

Some mention is also made about the full moon that had risen that night; this can also be calculated.

We can put the moonrise time, when it can first be seen over an ideal (flat) horizon, at Glasgow as 21:13:32 at an azimuth of 113.35°. This was to be a 99.02% illuminated full moon so potentially bright.

In the area around Dungavel the approximate position of the moon would be:

Time (GMT+2)	Altitude	Azimuth
21:11	0°	113° APPROX MOONRISE
22:30	8.14°	129°
22:45	9.44°	132°
22:50	10.13°	133°
22:55	10.42°	134°
23:00	11.10°	135°

So, we have a bright full moon but very low during the time of the flight and 'veering' from SEE to SE.

At that time, while it was still twilight, and with the moon at a low angle of elevation, it is doubtful that it would have of much help with visual feature recognition navigation. However, the true effect on illumination and visibility is very difficult to ascertain or appreciate.

We can probably work on him having around 30-40 minutes of useable light after sunset. It is interesting that his approach and over flight are all in a narrow time band in relation to the sunset as it progressed from east to west. Was Hess really intending to make the flight so late in the day?

He would have already been well into civil twilight as he reached Dungavel at 10.45pm. Going to the coast for bearings would have put him in what was effectively darkness on his return. Would he really have been able to find Dungavel by sight?

Conclusion

The inescapable fact is that when over Scotland, Hess was desperately chasing the light, without any realistic chance of success.

As the calculations above have shown, sunset at Dunstanburgh (on the

Dunstanburgh Castle, Northumberland, where Hess crossed the coast

east coast of England near to Embleton ROC) was at 10.00pm. Hess crossed the coast around 20 minutes later, technically towards the end of 'civilian twilight'. Already it was becoming far too dark to land a sophisticated plane such as the Bf110 without landing aids. He was already in serious trouble and would have already realised that to be the case.

By the time Hess arrived over Dungavel House at 10.40-10.45pm, sunset had been some 35 minutes previously. Hess was now technically verging towards the area of 'nautical twilight', whereby no difference between the coast and the sky could be discerned. By this time his only light source was coming from the moon, which, whilst bright, was low in the sky. This presumably must have been sufficient to allow the various ROC stations to make a positive identification of the silhouette of the Bf110. However, surely a controlled landing was certainly no longer a viable option? In reality it is questionable whether any form of unlit viable landing was now an option. We believe that by this time the flight had completely unravelled. Parachuting may now have featured in Hess's thinking for the first time, as perhaps the only option.

The secondary question must now be as to why Hess, in retrospect, was attempting to describe a situation in which he was apparently wholly in control. The reality was he was now completely reacting to events; he was certainly no longer in control of them. He was inexorably heading towards his fate. The opening quotes to this section cannot stand scrutiny by reference to the facts and once again must be seen as no more than devices to mislead the researcher from ascertaining Hess's true intentions and situation.

Parachuting

Rudolf Hess, in his 1941 letter to his wife describing the flight, makes the point that when he parachuted from the Bf110 it was indeed his first ever parachute jump. Given the meticulous detail that the other aspects of the flight had been planned and conducted, it seems most unlike Hess to not have at least considered his means of exit, if indeed parachuting was the intended method. As Hess later recounted, 'There was just one thing I had overlooked. I had never asked about how to jump; I thought it was too simple!'

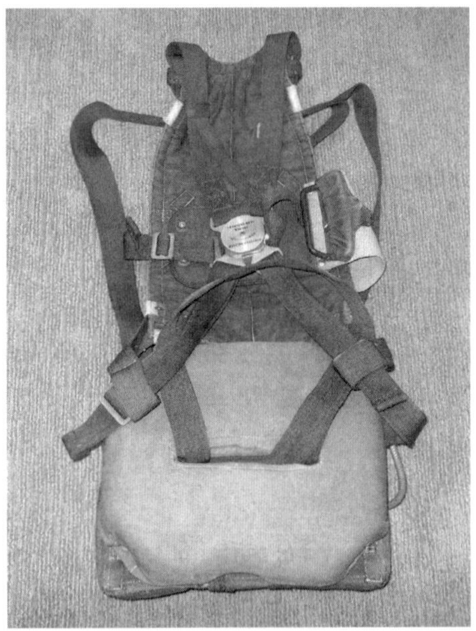

A Sitzfallschirm parachute

What Hess does not go on to say or clarify is whether he actually intended to parachute, or whether his true intention was to land conventionally, somewhere, the parachuting escapade only being an inevitable consequence of the original plan having gone wrong. Had he merely discounted asking about parachuting simply because it had never been his intention?

Some authors have asserted that it was always Hess's intention to parachute from the plane, citing the need to preserve the Bf110's secrets from the enemy (possibly interpreting an inference in the 1941 Hess letter). This notion we disagree with completely, but consider it necessary to study the evidence first.

- The parachute was an ancient device in concept but had only been developed militarily since the end of the First World War. At the onset of the Second World War, both Germany and Russia had established large-scale airborne forces. Britain, too, had a fledgling parachute regiment. Germany had used their 'Fallschirmjäger' to good effect in the Norway campaign, although their major parachute deployment was yet to come, when just ten days after the Hess flight the airborne assault on Crete was successfully undertaken. The point is that the parachute had been developed to the point that it was not necessarily seen as a means of last resort with little or no chance of salvation. An Australian aviator had escaped from a crashing plane in 1916 by parachute and since that time the science had been developed and refined.
- There were two main types of parachutes employed: the traditional 'backpack' and in the case of the pilot (such as Hess), the Luftwaffe parachute was combined with the dual role of a padded seat, a *Sitzfallschirm*. An example of such a parachute is held at the RAF Museum, Hendon. The dual use also explains the spartan appearance of the Bf110 seat – a bare metal bucket. The German and British designs were near identical on account of the German use of the ubiquitous Irving design.
- The Messerschmitt factory, typically, had also considered the issue, but perhaps it is fair to say not with the same degree of thoroughness as other parts of their design. Their instructions for exiting the Bf110 are as follows:

Fallschirmaussteig (parachute exit)
Führer (pilot)
Beobachter verständigen (inform observer)
Fahrt nach Möglichkeit verringern (fly to reduce necessity)
Nach Möglichkeit (if possible)
Netzausschalter drücken (press electrical system cut-out switch)
Zündungen ausschalten (switch off ignition system)
Brandhähne schließen (close fuel cocks)
Losschnallen (unbuckle)

Führerraumüberdachung öffnen und Flugzeug verlassen; Vorsicht vor Luftshraube und Antennenmast (open pilot's roof and leave the aircraft. Beware of the propellers and aerial mast)

This is broadly the sequence that Hess followed, as described by his 1941 letter to his wife. He describes, 'Switching off the engines and turning the propeller indicator to null and … opening the cabin roof.' It was at this point that the real problems started. The cabin roof was in three parts: a roof and the two sides. A single lever at the front of the cockpit released the roof, which hinged back to rest against the aerial. The two sides then folded down. Consequently, Hess was now sitting in the open cockpit, protected only by the armoured windscreen. The issue was that the air pressure was far too great to allow Hess to exit safely.

Eric 'Winkle' Brown, the famous British test pilot of captured aircraft, anticipated the problem in a later report, 'The pilot's cockpit was entered from the port side by means of a ladder normally accommodated entirely within the fuselage in a slot aft of the port wing trailing edge, a button aft of the wing being pressed and the ladder springing out to the extended position. The Perspex canopy over the forward seat was formed by three parts, the upper part hinging aft and the side panels folding down, and it could not be locked from the outside. I had always been intrigued to ascertain exactly how one vacated the Bf110 in an emergency as it did not look in the least simple, yet Rudolf Hess, Hitler's deputy, had apparently achieved this operation with ease after making his notorious solo night flight from Munich to the outskirts of Glasgow. Studying the problem, I had to admit that I was little the wiser and concluded that an element of luck entered into a successful bail-out from the aircraft. The cockpit upper panel could be jettisoned by unlocking it and allowing it to swing up into the airstream, but thereafter the pilot apparently had to roll on to the wing and risk getting blown back against the rather considerable empennage.'

Consequently, it must be fair to say that it is unlikely in the extreme that Hess planned to voluntarily parachute from the Bf110. There are many contemporary references to the problems of baling out of aircraft, reports often refer to 'after surviving bailing out', and 'despite managing to bail out successfully'. In 1941 this was an emergency procedure and one fraught with difficulty and danger.

According to Hess, he finally bailed out by bring the nose of the plane up to the near perpendicular and falling out backwards, just before the machine stalled and fell to earth. Hess later said that his friend, General Ritter von Greim, had told him to turn the plane over and fall out. We fail to see how this would present a solution to the problem of the air pressure.

So, if Hess is to be believed, he somewhat luckily managed to bail out and eventually fall to earth. Given his description of the ordeal and the practical difficulties involved, we cannot believe that this was what he anticipated. The procedure was too hazardous and the risk of failure too high for it to have been part of any realistic plan. If Hess had intended to land and not draw attention to his visit, his plane crashing into a Scottish field was hardly evidence of a stealthy arrival.

More evidence to call the planned parachute arrival into question is to be found in the reports of 'papers' being found at the crash site. Hess would not have left important items in his plane, he would have carried them with him.

The only point at which Hess chose to bail out of his plane was after he had missed his landing place and his mission was, to all intents and purposes, over. Again, we have to discriminate between what happened and what was intended.

Flight preparation continued – Fuel and Oil

The previous paragraphs have we hope, demonstrated that the Bf110, works number 3869, was most likely that in which Hess flew to Scotland. We now wish to become yet more precise, again in the search for performance statistics and capability.

Type

Roy Conyers Nesbit and Georges van Acker completed their 1999 research into the machine identification by carefully detecting that in certain pictures of the crash site the plane's fuselage revealed a groove running along the top, front to back. This groove carried a control cable, operated from the rear cabin, which allowed an inflatable dinghy (*Schlauchboot*) to be released from a storage area at the end of the fuselage. The fuselage was especially extended to facilitate this modification, albeit only on two types of Bf110, the D3 and E2.

In addition, the fuselage (which at the time of writing is currently on display at the Imperial War Museum, Duxford, whilst its London site is being refurbished) has a vent on the starboard side to allow fresh air to the heating

The crumpled fuselage, showing the dinghy release cable groove

system (*Kabinenheizanlage*). The heating system had been re-introduced on the E type of the Bf110.

Therefore, by a process of elimination the plane was a BF110 E 2/N. The 'N' designation is a classification of the type of Daimler Benz 601 engines used to power the machine. As well as an alphabetic-type descriptor, it also means the engine was configured and timed to run on 100 Octane, C3 fuel. The 'N' is marked on the engines (in white paint) and would have been similarly marked on the fuel fillers to avoid potentially dangerous mistakes.

Correspondence between Messerschmitt AG and the *Generalluftzeugmeister* reveals that the 601N engines were in short supply in October/November 1940, and that the supply of such engines was to be prioritised in favour of the Bf109. The Bf110 was to be fitted with the earlier (and less powerful) 601A engines. The fact that the Hess plane was fitted with 601N engines would appear to show a degree of preferment over the then current production regime. We have no evidence to infer outside influence in this decision.

Engine and carburation

Apart from the fledgling jet engines of 1940/41, the Daimler Benz 601N was one of the most modern, sophisticated and powerful engines in world aviation. The 601 was a derivative of the earlier 600 series of Daimler Benz aero engines that had been designed in the early 1930s. By late 1940 the engine had been developed to give the following power statistics:

On the ground @ 2600rpm – 1175PS. (864Kw)
At 2.1km altitude @ 2600rpm – 1270PS. (934kw)

This compared with the 1105Kw of the British Merlin XX, which had been in production since July 1940.

Both Daimler Benz and Rolls-Royce were developing their engine's output by the use of superchargers, whereby air is pressurised prior to entering the combustion chamber. The use of 100 octane fuel was also being developed. The British had found that 100 octane fuel consequently generated much higher operating temperatures and so, by way of alternative, had developed a water/glycol mix to cool the engine more efficiently. If the engines were allowed to run too lean, they would burn a hole in the engine pistons with disastrous consequences. However, there were two main differences. First, the German engine was an inverted design with remote oil sumps, and secondly, the method of carburation was different. The British (at that time) preferred a traditional carburettor, whereas the Daimler Benz company employed a state-of-the-art Robert Bosch fuel injection system (*Einspritz-Anlage*), the PZ 12 HP 110/19. The Imperial War Museum holds one of the original Hess plane fuel injectors. Eventually, the British also employed a pressurised system, but in late 1940 it was felt that the carburettor would produce a denser (and therefore more combustible) mixture. However, the Germans chose injection, one advantage being that it could operate irrespective of gravity. This difference in approach soon had practical implications. In a steep dive the Merlin powered engine would cut out, as the carburettor would empty itself by reason of g forces. (This problem was eventually remedied in part by the insertion of a disc in the fuel lines. Named after its inventor, the simple device was duly called, somewhat ironically, perhaps, 'Miss Shilling's orifice').

Therefore, it is fair to say that Rudolf Hess was making use of cutting-edge fuel technology. Whilst commonplace today, it was not until the 1970s that automobile technology utilised the direct injection system that Hess was already taking advantage of in 1941.

The relevance of this description is simply to reflect that Hess would have to know his twin engine's fuel consumption figures when calculating the amount of fuel required to fly from Germany to Scotland. The rate of fuel consumed directly reflects the performance of, and demands placed upon, the equipment detailed above.

The Bosch PZ 12 HP110/19 is essentially a carefully engineered measuring device. It receives low pressurised fuel from the lift pump and injects it at high pressure (15-20 lbs/square inch) into the combustion chamber just prior to ignition, via the injector valves. The specification is as follows:

P	–	Injection pump
Z	–	Own drive shaft
12	–	For 12-cylinder engine
H	–	Series designation
P	–	Separate suction chamber
110	–	Piston diameter (11 mm)
19	–	Mark number.

To understand the fuel consumption, one needs to first ascertain the engine revolutions required for the various stages of flight.

Aero engines are not like automobile engines; they tend to run at a more consistent rate of revolutions than the automobile engine with its typical rapid acceleration, followed by braking and deceleration. Once a plane reaches its optimum height, the pilot fixes the engine speed at its cruising speed, which is the optimal speed in terms of engine and overall plane efficiency.

Daimler Benz expressed the various engine speeds and power for the 601N as follows:

A – Start und Rotleistung – Start and warm up – 2600 rpm (1175 PS)
B – Steig und Kampfleistung – Climbing and combat power – 2400 rpm (1020 PS)
C – Dauerleistung – Maximum continuous power – 2400 rpm (970 PS) – (with reduced inlet manifold pressure)

The company also expresses at each of these engine speed a theoretical fuel consumption.

A – 215 grams per unit of power per hour
B – 210 grams per unit of power per hour
C – 205 grams per unit of power per hour

Consequently, if one now multiplies the engine power by the fuel consumption:

A – 1175 * 215 = 252 kgs per hour
B – 1020 * 210 = 214 kgs per hour
C – 970 * 205 = 198 kgs per hour

100 octane fuel weighs 6lbs per gallon
This equates to 2.72kgs per gallon, or 4.54 litres

Therefore:

A – becomes 252/2.72 *4.54 litres per hour = 420 litres *2 engines = 840 litres per hour
B – becomes 214/272 *4.54 litres per hour = 357 litres *2 engines = 714 litres per hour
C – becomes 198/272 *4.54 litres per hour = 330 litres *2 engines = 660 litres per hour

It should be remembered that these are theoretical figures, based on specific fuel consumption, which is a theoretical measurement of the use of energy. By way of further verification, we were able to obtain from the Deutsches Museum in Munich a Flugstrecken (Route planner) issued by the Luftwaffe, Rechlin. Unfortunately, this deals with the immediate predecessor of the 601N engine, the 601A.

The 601A engine was a slower revving engine, with less power and no necessity for 100 octane fuel.

However, the comparable fuel consumption figures (given in terms of litre per hour) were:

A – not given
B – 630 litres/hour
C – 660 litres/hour

It is also pertinent to note that the lift pump (which draws fuel from the aircraft tanks to the engine) has the stated maximum capacity of 750 litres/hour (*Grosste einspritzmenge*). The computed consumptions are comfortably within these limits.

Fuel tanks

The Bf110 had four fuel tanks, two each in either wing, between the cockpit and the engine. They were each covered by rubber in an attempt to make them self-sealing after enemy fire.

From this specification and from other sources we do not believe there is any contention in this basic specification:

2* 260 litres + 2* 375 litres = 1270 litres
This appears to have remained unaltered through the various types, B-G

Basic duration

We have already established that using Daimler Benz source information the fuel consumption of the DB601N not surprisingly varies with engine revolutions. If the engine is flown using 'maximum continuous power' (*Daurerleistung*), the fuel is utilised at between 600-660 litres/hour, dependent upon height. Consequently, the basic plane would typically have sufficient fuel for around two hours, if flown as fast as possible (1,270/630). The higher power/revolutions were only used for short bursts, such as when in combat and take-off.

Grosste Flugstreken

Clearly the BF110 pilot did not fly using 'maximum continuous power' at all times. The Luftwaffe technical department at Rechlin also gave figures for *Grosste Flugstreken*, which means 'longest flight plan', or essentially the 'economy mode'. Instead of 2,200 rpm, the engine would be run at much lower revolutions. Figures are given for 2,000 rpm, 1,800 rpm and 1,600 rpm, albeit at different heights. At the lower engine revolutions, consumption fell (although speed also naturally fell). At 5,000 m (approximately 15,000 ft) at 2000 rpm, the consumption fell to 470 litres/hour. At 1,600 rpm, 360 litres/hour. This appears to make perfect sense. Like any engine, the more that is demanded of it, the more fuel it consumes. Consequently, we need to see the Hess flight in terms of consumption, speed and time in order to understand what was and was not possible.

If the 1,270 litres of fuel were consumed at *Grosste Flugtreken* rates, then there was enough fuel for around three hours (1,270/400). However, if at 'maximum continuous power' the consumption was sufficient for barely two hours (1,270/660). At maximum continuous power the plane was travelling at 480 km/hr, with engine rpm at 2400 (at 5,000 m). At *grosste flugstreken* rates, the plane was travelling at between 367 and 420 km/hr, with engine rpm at 1600 (at 5,000 metres).

The use of auxiliary fuel tanks

Prima facie, this is the crux to the Hess flight, as it clearly explains what was and what was not possible. As analysed above, the basic Bf110 could fly for between two to three hours, dependent upon the method of use and the demands placed upon it. This is based on the standard specification of 1,270 litres. However, there is a considerable weight of evidence that the Hess plane was fitted with auxiliary fuel tanks, a common device to lengthen potential flight duration.

It should be stated that the use of such tanks was not ideal. Any additional weight attached to the underside of a plane would affect (a) its handling characteristics and (b) its fuel consumption, on account of the additional weight. In particular, landing with fuel tanks attached was a perilous occupation and David Irving cites the Hess plane (whilst in training) having to circle around the Augsburg airfield waiting for the fuel to be utilised before a safe landing could be contemplated.

First, we would like to study the available evidence:

Franz Halder war diary, 15 May 1941[5]

'New facts discovered (Hess) – D. Planning of Technical preparations for flight (reserve fuel tanks).'

Double Standards (2001)[6]

'The specially fitted drop tanks contained an extra 1800 litres of fuel, extending the range of the plane to a maximum of around 1560 miles (2600 kms).'

Wolf Hess (1986)[7]

'With its two reserve fuel tanks, it had a range of 4200 kilometres or 10 flying hours.'

Ilse Hess (1954)[8]

'Messerschmitt … was tricked into fitting two auxiliary tanks of 700 litres each in the wings!'

James Leasor (1962)[9]

'Messerschmitt technicians had fitted the aeroplane with a cigar-shaped auxiliary petrol tank…'

Derek Wood (1976)[10]

'Off Holy Island he jettisoned his underwing fuel tanks.'

Len Deighton (2002)[11]

'With a 900 litre tank under each wing…'

James Douglas-Hamilton/Roy Conyers Nesbit (1993)[12]

'The machine did carry two drop tanks containing a total of 396 gallons of fuel (1800 litres).'

Hugh Thomas (1979)[13]

By contrast, Hugh Thomas claims that the Hess plane that took off from Augsburg did not carry auxiliary fuel tanks (Works number 3526) and that a different plane crashed in Scotland (Works number 3869). Whilst these authors do not yet wholly subscribe to Dr Thomas's theory, we do believe that it is quite possible that the Hess plane that took off from Augsburg did not have auxiliary fuel tanks, instead they were either fitted en route or alternatively a fully fuelled and ready-to-go plane awaited Hess at Giessen. This is the more likely explanation.

These authors now believe that Rudolf Hess's subsequent actions make it absolutely clear and obvious that one of his principal concerns was to preserve Luftwaffe secrets and consequently we find it difficult to believe that Willi Messerschmitt, Willi Stoer or Helmut Kaden did not have some idea as to the true nature of Hess's mission. It would surely be unbelievable not to wonder what Hess was up to, especially given the extremely technical work that was being undertaken whilst modifying his 110 over a number of months.

Therefore, whilst we are quite content to assess the impact of all sizes of fuel tanks, we are not so ready to accept all that Helmut Kaden chose to tell Roy Conyers Nesbit. The reason for this caution will become apparent in due course.

Sizes/Types of Auxiliary Fuel tanks

The 'normal' 1,270 litre fuel loading was sufficient to sustain a two-hour combat mission (typically at the higher engine rpms), or perhaps three hours at lower engine speeds. It should also be noted that pilots typically build in a contingency, as clearly it would be unwise to have just sufficient fuel to complete a mission or task. (Modern aircraft typically plan on a variable reserve of 5 per cent of total fuel, together with a fixed reserve, sufficient to complete an additional 45-minute flight duration.)

In 1941, whilst the concern would remain the same, the methodology of computation would be at the discretion of the pilot, mindful of the nature of the flight. In researching the plane specification, we have studied a number of pictures of the various sizes of fuel tanks available. It appears to us that the following sizes were potentially available:

2 at 220 litres = 440 litres (fitted under the wings – outboard of engines – jettisonable)
2 at 900 litres = 1800 litres (fitted under the wings – outboard of engines – jettisonable)
2 at 400 litres = 800 litres (fitted under the wings – outboard of engines – jettisonable)
1 at 500 litres = 500 litres (fitted under the fuselage – non jettisonable)

In addition to the above, the Messerschmitt works also created an enclosed 'under fuselage' fuel and oil tank called the *dacklebauch* (dachshund belly), which contained 1,050 litres of fuel and 106 litres of oil. This specification is not relevant to the current debate as the option was not fitted to the Bf110 E/2.

Consequently, it would appear that at an engine rpm of 1,600-2,000 rpm the tanks are almost arranged in terms of 'additional hours flying time'. The 440 litre combination would typically support an extra hour, the 800 litre combination an extra two hours and the massive 1,800 litres an extra four to five hours. The very fitting of the tanks would infer that combat flying was not the purpose of the flight and therefore perhaps a lower fuel consumption could reasonably be assumed.

In extremis, with the 2 at 900 litres tanks fitted and filled, the Bf110 E/2N would have sufficient fuel to support seven to eight hours' flight at between a 1,600-2,000 rpm engine speed (3,070 litres/400 litres per hour). The Hess flight as described by Rudolf Hess in 1942 apparently took 5 hours 24 minutes. In other words, the flight as described in duration terms was quite possible, with auxiliary fuel tanks fitted – *as far as fuel was concerned.*

Engine oil tanks and system

As well as the necessity for fuel, the DB601N also required a powerful oil supply to ensure all moving engine parts were kept well lubricated. The German engine was a dry sump design and much larger than the comparable

Merlin (33.9 litres versus 27 litres) and as such required a powerful oil pump which was mounted between the inverted cylinder blocks.

The DB601N utilised a Graekin type ZD500 oil pump with a capacity of 55 litres per minute at 2,600 rpm. The actual consumption of oil was listed as being 5-9 litres/hour, per engine, again dependent upon engine revolutions. In order to accommodate this consumption, there was a synthetic rubber oil tank of 35 litres located behind each engine. The Hess plane oil tanks are currently at the RAF Museum reserve collection at Stafford. Arithmetically, it is therefore possible to see that each oil tank would be sufficient for just under a four-hour flight, to one of seven-hours duration, again dependent upon the nature of the engine use.

For these longer flights, a 75-litre oil reservoir could be fitted underneath the fuselage. Typically, this would be fitted at the same time as wing drop tanks. This modification/configuration was called *Rustsatzes B1* (Field modification B1). It would be carried out at the operational base, using factory supplied parts, dependent upon need. However, in Hess' case there was no field modification. The plane came straight from the factory and the E2 designation gave it the available specification. It was already fitted with the ability to carry wing tanks for fuel and to carry an additional oil tank under the fuselage. A *Schmierstoffbehalter* (oil tank) carrying 75 litres of oil. With this tank fitted, there would be ample oil for a 5 hour 24 minute flight. An additional 75 litres would effectively double the normal oil consumption to eight to nine hours. In their detailed and thorough analysis, Conyers Nesbit and van Ackers assumed this tank was fitted and indeed made reference to it being rolled around the crash site by Major Graham Donald ROC. The fitment of the tank was necessary to make their description of the Augsburg to Eaglesham flight possible.

The Bf110 E manual gave explicit instruction as to its use. A pump in the observer/gunner's compartment would be utilised to pump additional oil into the existing engine tanks in each wing. A three-way valve was available to direct the oil between the engines as desired and two minutes' pumping on the hand pump would deliver 7.5 litres of oil to an engine. As the instruction manual states, '*Nach jeder Stunde Flugzeit sind je Behalter 7,5 Liter Schmierstoff nachzumpumpen*.' (After every hour of flight time, 7.5litres of oil must be pumped into each oil tank).Once the oil tank was empty, the pump would no longer work and could be jettisoned by the release lever in the observer compartment. The oil line from the tank to the handpump would be closed by a non-return valve (*Ruckschlagventil*).

The system was theoretically present. The system was theoretically in place. There was certainly the capacity in terms of fuel and oil for the Hess plane to fly for 5 hours 24 minutes.

The Hess fuselage revelation and other Bf110 parts

At the time of writing the fuselage of the BF110 – VJ +OQ is on display at the Imperial War Museum, Duxford. It has recently been moved from Hangar 5 to the new display space by the main gate.

On 30 December 2012, the authors travelled to Duxford to study the fuselage. We were keen to see the dinghy escape mechanism and the heating system vent that would prove the plane to be an E2. This would enable us to re-check and confirm the possible flight duration and fuel consumption figures. Alongside the fuselage was the DB601 engine from the plane, with the letter 'N' clearly marked on the inverted crankcase. We requested permission to take close-up photographs but were denied access on account of some health and safety issues surrounding the exhibits. Undeterred, we took what photographs we could, and in particular we tried to ascertain where the 75-litre engine oil drop tank would be fitted under the fuselage. In order for such a flight as Hess undertook (according to his account in 1941), the oil tank would have to be fitted. Without it, there was a very real danger of engine seizure during the 5 hours 24 minutes flight. A sensible pilot would not take such a risk. Please refer to the previous section for details.

We already knew the oil tank would present a mechanical challenge. We knew it was usually jettisoned from the observer's section of the cabin (*Beobachterraum*) and we knew that the hand pump mechanism was operated from the same section of the cabin. We had assumed that alterations would have been made to enable the pilot (i.e. Hess) to manually pump the oil from the tank and then jettison it. We were visiting Duxford (so we thought) largely to confirm what we already knew. We believed we were just being thorough.

The following week witnessed dramatically increased telegraphy traffic between Northamptonshire and Norfolk. The photographs that Wilbourn had taken had cast serious doubt as to whether a drop tank had ever been fitted. The jettison device was indeed present, apparently unused, but the seemingly undeniable evidence was that the hole that would accommodate the oil feed pipe had been blanked off. The non-return valve had been covered by a brass cap, complete with wire security seal. There had never been no 75-litre oil drop tank.

Practically, without such a tank the flight duration was limited to around four hours, especially if the parts of the flight demanded high engine rpm. On a flight lasting 5 hours 24 minutes a rational decision would certainly be to fit such a tank. To not do so would be a complete gamble, especially given that the instruction manual instructs the pumping of 7.5 litres of oil per engine per hour.

As the drawings reveal, the system was that the Observer had an auxiliary pump fitted in his section of the cockpit. It was his responsibility to operate the hand pump and flow switch to ensure that the two engine oil tanks were kept at full.

This has a fundamental impact on the flight as it appears that the total duration was 5 hours 24 minutes. It would make no sense whatsoever to fit two 900 litre fuel tanks under the wings if the engines did not have sufficient oil to use the extra fuel.

Consequently, Wilbourn duly arranged to obtain supervised access to the fuselage, thus presumably circumventing the prevailing health and safety issues. This was duly achieved on 7 January 2013. We now reproduce the report of his visit, written the following day.

Richard Wilbourn
Report on visit to Duxford – 07.01.2013

Visit made to Hangar 5 to carry out a visual examination and photograph the remains of the Hess Bf110 fuselage, which had recently been moved from IWM Lambeth. This was a follow up visit to one made 30.12.2013 when the exhibit was found to be confined behind a tape with the right-hand side out of sight. Permission was given by IWM Duxford staff to make a supervised inspection all around the item. The supervision and caution were due to Health and Safety concerns, this is a working hangar, and there is considered to be a possible asbestos risk from this item.

Overall

The fuselage is still mounted on a black exhibition frame. The rear end of the item contains two rolls of a black foam material and is wrapped in a cling film which is further secured with brown parcel tape. Access to the public is generally good to the left side; it is close to the walkway and offers a good view into the front of the fuselage. One of the plane's engines is placed directly behind the exhibit.

From the side out of view to the public it is clear that the right-hand side of the plane is less complete, a large square hole had been cut, hacked, out where the side 'Balkenkreuz' cross had been removed. [This is now displayed in the RAF Museum, Hendon]

It was noticed that there is a number, painted in white, in an area under where the tail would have been. Cling film obscures some of it but 869 is clear to see, with another digit before them being behind the covering and on a more damaged part of the plane. This corresponds partially with the supposed works number for the plane 3869. A request for permission to pull back some of the film covering was denied by IWM staff, because of the concerns of possible asbestos contamination.

Forward part of fuselage

This second visit was largely undertaken to carry out a closer examination of details noticed here during the earlier visit.

The first parts of the fuselage are the damaged partial section (*Rumpfteil*) 7 and the more complete section 8. This section 8 contains a number of inspection/access panels and, from the Messerschmitt Bf110 *Handbücher Bedienungsvorschriften*, is where the auxiliary, jettisonable engine oil tank (*Rüstsatzes*, 'B1') would have been mounted.

Of particular interest was a mechanism on the inside floor of the section. This has been identified as the suspension/release system for an auxiliary oil tank (*Schloss zum Einhängen und Auslösen de Behälter*). Part of the mechanism protrudes through to the outside of the fuselage and can be seen as a tapered lever (Hebel) in a slotted hole.

A little further towards the rear of the plane is another hole through the floor, fitted with what appears to be a tapered 'rubber' grommet. This is where the suction pipe from the non-return valve (*Rückschlagventil*) would emerge and go down into the tank.

To the side of that opening is another which is fitted inside with a metal strip and shaped ferrule. This correlates with the positioning hole or guide (*Führungen*) for one of the tank struts (*Behälterabstutzung*).

To the front of the mechanism a cable attachment is showing. This cable is the release control which went forward into the crew compartment (*Seil zug für Schmierstoffbehälter abwurf*). From the arrangement of the parts of the mechanism, it appears that it is in the closed position; the lever (Hebel) under the plane is forward and close to the fuselage and the hook part of the latch, which held the attachment (*Behälteraufhängung*) in the 'Schloss' is visible. There is no significant damage apparent and other than a slight bend in the side plates behind it, the mechanism appears to be in good condition.

Behind this latch system, where the top of the non-return valve (*Rückschlagventil*) would attach to an oil line, is a blanking cap, which appears to be made of brass. There is no oil line (*Endstück der Schmierstoffleitung*) or remains of one present and the cap has the substantial remnants of a twisted wire security seal still in place.

Conclusion

The plane had the fittings and mechanism to carry an engine oil drop tank. This mechanism is still complete and in good condition. The mechanism and the area around it are largely un-damaged and show no signs of any violent detachment such as may result from crashing.

The apparatus appears to be set in the closed position. This is a cable trip release mechanism and so could not have been re-set from the crew compartment.

The oil pipe connection was not in place and the fitting is covered by a sealed blanking cap.

This leads to the conclusion that no external oil tank was fitted for this flight.

We believe there is little or no doubt. The Hess plane, 3869, did not have an auxiliary oil tank fitted. We find it inconceivable that the British, post 10.5.1941 would have stripped the crashed plane and then fitted a sealed metric blanking cap to an auxiliary oil tank fitment.

This finding has very wide and profound implications, but the most notable is that the Hess BF110 could not have realistically flown for 5 hours 24 minutes without such a tank. To repeat the argument, because it is fundamental.

Each engine's oil tank was emptying at a typical rate of 7.5 litres per hour. More when the engine was operating at the engine's higher rpm. Each tank held 35 litres. After 35/7.5 = 4 hours 40 minutes or thereabouts the sensible flight planner would expect the oil to be have been exhausted.

Without the hand pumping system an auxiliary tank the engines would overheat and seize. Rudolf Hess would have then crashed in the North Sea, or over southern Scotland, depending on when the oil ran out. The Hess mystery would then have subsequently turned into an Amelia Earhart type affair, rather than the far more important political issue it has become.

The tank release mechanism (b) as shown in the Bf110 manuals. This view shows the layout for a fuel tank application, but the details are the same for oil except that no filling pipe (d) is used. Please note the non-return valve (e); on the Hess plane this is blanked off and without any following pipe (c).

Following the above startling discovery, we were surprised to learn that there are further parts of the Hess plane still in official custody. Consequently, on 18 February 2013 we travelled to the RAF Museum, reserve collection at the MOD Stafford – area 6. Met by the very helpful Ian Alder, he showed us the 'Hess pallet' which comprised the following parts:

- The pilot's roof and side panels of the Bf110 cockpit frame – ref 408517
- Parts of the observer cockpit frame. This appeared to prove to us that there was only one person aboard the plane, as the whole of the observer cockpit frame was jettisonable. The fact that it was present would infer that it crashed with the plane unused.
- A leather/fabric tonneau cover, presumably from the rear of the observer cockpit – ref 137480.
- Two armoured plates to protect the pilot – ref 137484 and 137485.
- A retractable ladder that fitted to the fuselage to the rear of the left wing – ref 174856.
- In addition, there were two rubber coated containers – ref 137482 and 137483, embossed with the initials SB. These were described as 'fuel tanks', but we believe it far more likely that they were actually the 35 litre oil tanks (*gummigeschützter Behälter*) that sat behind each engine. The SB thus translates to *Schmierstoff Behälter*.

Consequently, at the time of writing, the following parts are available for public inspection:

IWM, Duxford – fuselage and DB601 engine
Museum of Flight, East Fortune – DB601 engine and ROC map; part of tail plane of Bf110

Lennoxlove House, Haddington – Hess maps (s?), and compass
MOD, Stafford – list as above
RAF Museum Hendon – the fuselage *balkenkreuz* and ROC map
Durham County Hall – an ROC map of the approach to Northeast England

Somewhat bizarrely perhaps, the IWM Lambeth also list further instruments from the plane, together with a pair of Hess's underpants. These authors make no claims as to the authenticity or otherwise of the latter items, though discuss their relevance in the concluding chapter.

We also have no doubt that further parts exist in and around Eaglesham, Scotland, purloined from the Baird field on the night of 10 May 1941. There is also a British Pathé newsreel (canister UN1265D) which gives a snapshot view of the fuselage (complete with *Balkenkreuz* at that time).

Whilst at Stafford we also enquired as to the provenance of some of the articles, as some were tagged 'Hess' and some 'alleged Hess'. The fact is that we do not consider there to be any particularly controversial evidence apart from the fuselage.

Apparently, the remains of the plane were initially taken to Carluke and dumped with other aircraft parts. It was then taken to either Carlisle, or Sealand, to be reassembled at an RAF maintenance unit (operated by Scottish Aviation Limited), prior to being loaded on to a Queen Mary trailer and taken south, for propaganda purposes. There are pictures of the said trailer in Oxford.

From there we understand the engines were taken to RAF Biggin Hill for storage and eventually transferred to RAF Bicester, before final transfer to Stafford. The rest of the Stafford plane came from the Newcastle upon Tyne Science Museum in 1977.

What is probably more important is what is not there. We would like to have seen:

- the cockpit for the existence of the amended radio equipment
- the wings for evidence of wing tanks
- the cockpit for the existence of oil pumps, or otherwise

It is unfortunate, but the fact remains that besides the auxiliary oil tank mechanism, there are no parts remaining on display that give any clues as to how the plane was modified to facilitate a solo peace mission.

However, we now believe that the discovery concerning the 'blanked off' oil pipe is one of the most significant in respect of the Hess flight for the past seventy years. Its implication is stark – Hess could not have flown for as long as he claimed. He may well have had enough fuel, but he did not have enough oil. The engines would have seized.

We now believe that Hess landed in Germany en route, at Giessen – because he had to. Presumably, the transfer of the oil pumping system to the pilot's cockpit was adjudged too cumbersome and Hess certainly had enough to do without the additional chore, but, more likely, he had calculated that by landing he did not need to have an auxiliary oil tank – the existing 35 litre tanks could merely be refilled. That would give him a further five hours from Giessen, more than enough time to complete the flight.

SO WHAT ACTUALLY HAPPENED?

Since the publication in March 2014 of *Rudolf Hess: A New Technical Analysis of the Hess Flight, May 1941*, further information has come to light that we now wish to bring to the reader's attention.

The general timeline/diary is agreed by virtually all Hess writers:

September 1939	–	Hitler bans Hess from flying for a year.
October 1940	–	Hess considers the ban over and starts to look for a plane.
October–December 1940	–	Hess decides on a Bf110, after being refused by other manufacturers.
January 1941–May 1941	–	Hess refines his knowledge and skill of the Bf110.
10 May 1941	–	Hess makes the flight to Scotland in Bf110 works number 3869.

The flight took nine months to prepare. The decision to fly was not taken on the spur of the moment. Comprehensive training and repetition were necessary to avoid catastrophe.

In addition, Hess obviously had a number of other responsibilities to the government, to the party and to his family.

There is, however, one more variable that perhaps has not been adequately explored and that may have had a direct bearing on the duration of training and implementation of the flight. That variable was the unusually awful weather throughout the winter and spring of 1940/41. We perhaps did not research this aspect adequately when writing *Rudolf Hess: A New Technical Analysis of the Hess Flight, May 1941* in late 2013.

In the same way that the weather had assisted in the summer, it now prevented a still more concerted campaign over the winter. The winter of 1940/41 was exceptional in weather terms. There have even been various academic treatises trying to explain why the three winters of 1939/40 and 1941 were quite so extreme, with the suggestions ranging from the effects of El Niño to a warming of the oceans due to the increased naval activity. Whatever the reason, the statistical evidence is present to explain exactly why there was not still more aerial activity. It is self-evident from the records that the Luftwaffe was deadly when over Britain, but the point is that were it not for the unusual weather patterns that winter and early spring, Rudolf Hess's flight may not have been necessary. The British could have been just pounded into submission.

In January 1941, the records tell us that Munich experienced far higher than usual snowfall and this must surely have curtailed or at the least delayed and extended the training and preparations that Hess was undertaking. Over Britain the weather was also not good, the summary of the Metrological Office monthly reports reading as such:

January 1941 Cold with frequent snow.
February 1941 Rather cold. Considerable snow.
March 1941 Rather cold. Wet in England and Wales and Northern Ireland.
April 1941 Dry, dull and rather cold.
May 1941 Unseasonably cold, particularly in the south.

The reader might justifiably be tempted to think that 'it's always cold in winter', but these summary headlines are prepared to contrast the actual results against statistical norms and averages. The evidence is there to see.

Locally to Eaglesham, Renfrewshire, the first ten days of May saw no rainfall whatsoever and, on the 10th, the Meteorological Office recorded, 'Light southwest winds, veering west later. Cloudy, some showers or occasional light rain; less cool.'

In other words, apart from the clouds, an ideal day for flying and then landing into a south-westerly wind. The crucial question now becomes 'where was Hess anticipating to land?'

Character of the Flight

When we researched the 1941 flight we tried as best we could to analyse the 'character' of the flight in order to hopefully then draw meaningful conclusions as to Hess's motives and methodology. We suggest that the following characteristics would suggest a very different flight to that usually described:

1. No auxiliary oil tank was fitted to the Hess Bf110. The fuselage, which is currently at RAF Duxford has the fitting securely blanked off with the wired brass nut. Without such an oil tank, it is unlikely that a flight lasting much over 4.5 hours could be achieved, however much fuel was on board. The Hess flight, as previously described, was 5 hours 24 minutes in total. No sensible pilot would have embarked on such a flight without an auxiliary oil tank. To not do so was a gamble that would not be taken.
2. The logical conclusion is therefore that Hess landed so as to refuel and re-oil. The flight notes given to us by Peter Padfield would also suggest this to be the case, as the notes we have discovered do not start at Augsburg but at Giessen, some 45 minutes away. This is by their reference to the Verdun barracks.
3. Hess, at no time flew the route that he described whilst in Mytchett Place. This was simply to disguise the fact that he had landed at an operational Luftwaffe base, thus inferring official connivance. This is also hinted at the 1989 lecture to The Rudolf Hess Gesellschaft ev. by Helmut Kaden, Hess's flying instructor.
4. Having refuelled and re-oiled at Giessen, Hess then headed for the North Sea on his bearing of 335 degrees. He crossed the coast in the Borkum/Wangerooge area, where coincidentally Reinhard Heydrich was stationed that night, flying his own SS insignia marked Bf109. As Peter Padfield has speculated, it is quite possible that Heydrich saw fit to accompany Hess part of the way up the North Sea, as he was essentially stationed at the start of the North Sea section of the Hess flight path. However, by reading the Heydrich flying records, it is unlikely that Hess would have been able to, or even wished to have

relied on Heydrich aeronautically. He seems to have had a constant record of scrapes and crashes throughout the war, even stupidly crashing behind Russian lines in 1941.

5. So, after a further half hour he switched on his new state of the art Elektra receiver. This would allow him to know when to 'turn left' to approach northern England at the most undefended part of the Northumbrian coast, between Seahouses and Bamburgh. Timings were also now becoming critical, as it was starting to get dark.
6. However, as he then later described to Ilse Hess, just when the radio system was critical to his mission, the system failed (or, more likely, he failed to interpret the dots and dashes being transmitted into his headset). Whilst he had a stopwatch, without the Elektra system being operational he would not know precisely when to turn or bank left.
7. Being an experienced pilot, he did not panic, but turned back to simply retrace his steps. He knew this was critical. An entry too low would put him over Newcastle, RAF Ouston and RAF Acklington; an entry too high would place him on top of the fighter stations protecting Edinburgh and Rosyth, those of RAF Drem and East Fortune.
8. Eventually, he found his bearings and felt confident enough to approach the coast from a height of 15,000 ft, crossing the coast near Chathill, near Beadnell, further south than was planned, but far enough north from the Northumbrian RAF bases. RAF Home Chain radio had already spotted the plane and had sent up a Spitfire from Acklington. As the RAF pilot, Pocock, climbed, Hess had dived and was at sea level, trying to locate his 'entry point,' the Cheviot. Having done so, by flying up the coast he then turned inland. The Cheviot was exactly due east of the newly opened bases at Prestwick, Ayr and their satellite base at RAF Dundonald.
9. From the coast he climbed to pass over the Cheviot and then remained at 4,000–5,000 feet, travelling due west. All was going well, save the radio malfunction had cost him around 40 minutes' worth of fuel and more importantly, light. It was now getting dark. Very dark indeed.
10. At St Mary's loch he slightly altered his course and headed 12 degrees to the north. He increased speed and was virtually going flat out when he passed over Eastend House and Dungavel House, both

some 4,000 feet beneath him. Hess made no attempt whatsoever to land and was now flying as fast as he had done since when he had dived to cross the Northumbrian coastline at 22.23pm.

11. At 22.34pm, Hector MacLean at Operations Room Ayr sent up William Cuddie and his gunner Hodge in a Defiant night fighter with the specific instruction 9 degrees, climb to 2,000 feet and 'Dive and Buster'. This would have put the night fighter attacking whatever might be at the end of RAF Dundonald airstrip. A truly telling order, especially as he had no idea as to where the Hess plane was headed as at 22.34pm, the Bf110 was still in the middle of Lowland Scotland. We have recently discovered a Canadian newspaper account of an

Reginan Tells Of Chasing Hess

Nazi Plane Too Fast

The story of how FO. William Cuddie, of Regina, chased Rudolf Hess, Hitler's erstwhile right-hand man and now a British prisoner of war, into Scotland last year was told in a Canadian Press cable from Scotland on Tuesday.

Fact that Flying Officer Cuddie, son of Mrs. Walter Jones, The Grenfell, Regina, was on the tail of Hess during his flight was reported some time ago, but Tuesday's story was the first to come from Cuddie himself.

Hess' Plane Faster

Flying Officer Cuddie, who trained with 120 Bomber Squadron in Regina in peacetime and went overseas to join the R.A.F. in 1939, wasn't able to catch Hess because the Nazi's Messerschmitt 110 was faster than Cuddie's Defiant.

The prairie pilot, when he read the Hess story in British papers the next day, remarked: "It would've been pretty nice cracking him down."

A fair-haired, fighter pilot of 24 with a trim red mustache, Cuddie related the story of the chase as he leaned against the ceiling-high fireplace of red sandstone in the officers' mess at a base in Scotland.

"It was just an ordinary patrol," said Cuddie, the only Canadian member of this particular R.A.F. night fighter squadron. "My gunner and I were alone on patrol and neither of us saw the Hess plane at all, unfortunately. The station kept giving us radio directions but he went into a cloud and then through the balloons."

Cuddie waited for the Nazi to come out of the cloud. Hess didn't. And the next thing Cuddie heard was an order to return to base, "because your bandit has crashed."

Kidded By "The Boys"

Next morning Cuddie heard rumors around the station that the plane he had chased was flown by Hess. "I didn't know for sure until the story of his escape appeared in the papers later that day," Cuddie said. "Some of the boys kidded me and asked why why I hadn't let off a quick squirt and claimed him."

If such a thing happened again there wouldn't be the same speed problem for the Regina flier to contend with. He is flying a twin-engine Beaufighter now instead of a Defiant and few German aircraft if any, can trim a "Beau."

Cuddie is one of those airmen who answered an R.A.F. pre-war appeal for Canadian volunteers. He crossed to Britain on a liner with eight other Canadians nearly three years ago and was one of the first British airmen to fly across the channel and over France at night, in December, 1940.

"It was the first chance I had of seeing German flak and search-lights," he said. "It wasn't very frightening, it really wasn't. You got that hollow feeling in your stomach crossing the coast, but when the lights and flak started coming up it wasn't very spectacular."

Cuddie hasn't shot down any Nazis yet.

"I've been shot at a couple of times, but I haven't been hit yet. That's good enough for now."

The Canadian report of the affair

interview with Cuddie and the comparison could not be starker. Cuddie described a 'routine patrol', whereas the reality was he was scrambled and given a precise instruction. See previous page clipping.

12. Hess was expecting to bank left just before he crossed the railway lines at Kilmaurs, just north of Kilmarnock. There was a high tower on the parish council hall as a marker and by then banking left would have precisely lined him up for a landing at Dundonald, adjacent to the Troon–Glasgow railway line. However, by this time it was too dark, and no landing was possible. Hess had run out of time. Consequently, he flew on in a straight line and descended yet again to cross the Clyde estuary at West Kilbride, in clear sight of the ROC staff. He turned due south down the Clyde, still at sea level. We now strongly suspect that he was too far to the north and essentially flying off the extremes of the flight map. He was not expecting to have crossed the coast at all and so he then turned sharply in land, thinking that he was approaching Troon, with its harbour and small island just off the coast. Dundonald airfield awaited, just behind Troon, adjacent to the railway.

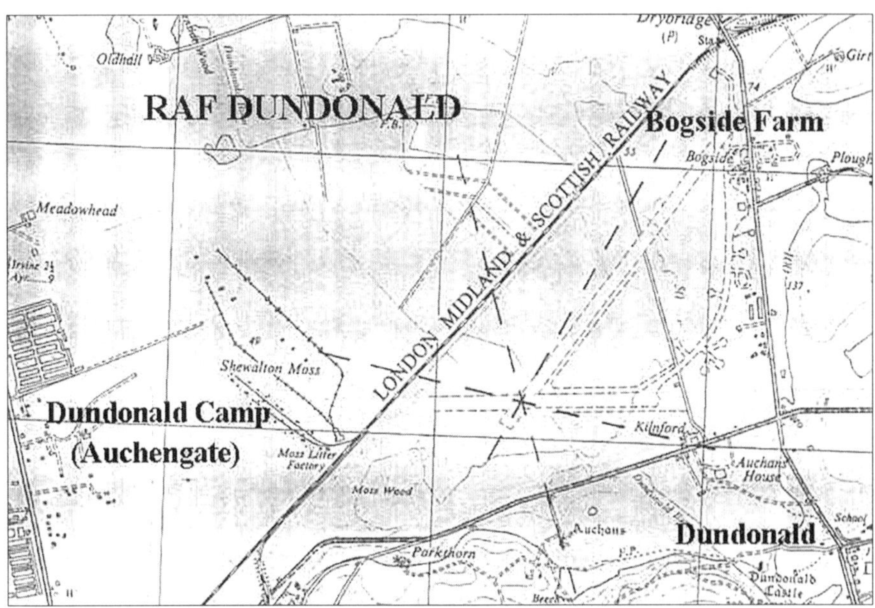

RAF Dundonald

13. However, he was further north and had just mistaken Ardrossan with its near identical harbour and small island offshore. There was no airfield! Avoiding the massively defended ICI Ardeer (although we have some reports that he actually flew between the barrage balloons), he realised his mistake and then tried to go south to rectify. He was virtually over Dundonald at this point, and we suspect that it was then that he then saw the Defiant. (Cuddie later stated that he had not seen the Hess plane.) This made him turn further inland, climbing in panic so that he could affect a parachute exit if necessary. When he managed to exit the cockpit, he left the important papers he brought with him in the plane. Hardly a planned exit, or indeed a planned parachute jump. This was not planned or rehearsed. It was a panic measure.
14. He parachuted to ground at Floors Farm, Eaglesham. The Bf110 crashes at 11.09pm. There is however considerable evidence to make the case that it was actually an attempted crash landing. We also now have some evidence to suggest that there was a second occupant in the plane, as it is surely bizarre that the plane and

ROC Irvine – where is their report?

pilot ended up in virtually the same field. It is also most odd that the plane, whilst damaged, did not appear to go vertically into the ground, instead seeming to glide to a halt (as evidenced by the robust state of the engines today). Did the second occupant try and land the plane and was killed in the process? Does this also explain the absence of any pictures of the cockpit?

15. The subsequent behaviour in and around Eaglesham is then wholly indicative of the fact that Hess was not expected or anticipated in that area. Home Guard officers with loaded pistols and fixed bayonets; confusion and a disregard for proper procedure; German baiting in the Scout Hut. The whole event looks just like an episode of Dad's Army. After things had calmed down there was a review of what should have happened by comparison to what had taken place. If what had taken place was that intended, no such review would have been necessary.
16. There was also small-scale looting. Davy McLean, the supposed hero of the hour, was busy secreting fuselage parts in the ditch for later retrieval and resale (Bonhams, New York, 2014). He also had ripped off part of a flight chart from Hess's knee, but had then hidden it for fear of retribution when the official world turned up the following morning looking for the Hess/Bohle peace proposals, which they eventually found in a ditch: 'The Police was ordered to search for a valuable document which was missing, he found it over near the wee burn in the park.'[14]
17. There were subsequent lists of what was present prepared and what had gone missing and then returned. In the melee, Hess's iron cross went missing, eventually to turn up years later when Stephen Prior (of *Double Standards* repute) acquired it in auction from the estate of a Sgt McBride-2310157, a soldier on duty that night.
18. The plane was inspected and the important pieces were taken away to Farnborough, never to reappear. The rest was then collected and taken to a Carluke scrapyard. From there it was sorted once more and placed on a Queen Mary trailer, for purposes of a nationwide propaganda tour. However, the tour was cancelled on arrival in Oxford and the various pieces distributed to museums or scrapped. We have already listed the present resting place of the various components of which we are currently aware. Subsequently, we believe the Hess plane was

The Hess plane on the Queen Mary trailer

The reconstruction at RAF Sealand (thanks to A. Rosthorn)

reconstructed as much as possible at RAF Sealand. The picture, yet again, fails to include the cockpit of the Bf110.

19. One of the stranger occurrences was the sending of the Hess map(s) to the Duke of Hamilton, as early as 21 May 1941. Two pieces of the map were then framed and now hang in Lennoxlove House. The existence of a third map is denied, despite Roy Conyers Nesbit having described it when researching his book. We do wonder if the true significance of this map and its radio markings were appreciated by RAF Intelligence. It was essentially a pre-war German copy of a British road map, marked up with very disguised, but very clear Elektra radio system markings. We also believe it clearly marks RAF Dundonald as the destination, though not surprisingly that fact is carefully disguised.

The Flight Plan!

Shortly after publication of our *Rudolf Hess: A New Technical Analysis of the Hess Flight, May 1941*, we were contacted by a former employee of John Harris who had perhaps wisely emigrated to Canada. She had been reading the international version of the Daily Express and was interested to learn that a Stuart Mclean had been trying to contact John Harris, via the letters page, in connection with matters Hess. Kindly, she had then made contact with John across the Atlantic, to ascertain if he had read the letter. Unsurprisingly, he had not.

So, after quite a lot of detective work and tracing of letters we ascertained that Mr MacLean lived in Western Australia. We duly made contact and was astonished to learn that he claimed to have the Rudolf Hess flight plan.

What made us even more more excited was the provenance of the information. Stuart's father was the younger brother of David (Davy) McLean, the Scottish ploughman who had been credited with the capture of the Deputy Führer on 10 May. Apparently, after Davy's death, the flight plan had been given to his brother and, he, in turn, had passed it down to Stuart.[15]

By this time, we were about to board the next international airliner (any international airliner!), but this was not necessary as Stuart kindly emailed the plan to us.

Apparently, Davy, far from being the benign bystander with his pitchfork,[16] had seen his opportunity and on the night had ripped the plan from Hess's thigh map holder and secreted it away. He is also credited with secreting away a slice of the Bf110 fuselage that was sold in New York for $3,000 in 2014. Further plane parts duly came up for sale at Bonhams 2015 New York sale. However, when the following morning what appeared to be the whole world had descended upon Floors Farm, he had kept his hoard very secret indeed, in particular on the Sunday morning, when the search for the 'papers in the burn' took place.

What is present is not a 'flight plan' in the strict sense. It is essentially a navigational aid that appears to give the ability to correct a position, should Hess not arrive at a given point at a given time. As we had just completed an entire book stressing how important it was that he knew when to 'turn left' over the North Sea, we were very excited by this document for three reasons:

1. It clearly reinforced the premise of our book.
2. It further validates and reinforces the authenticity of the Prof. A.W.B. Simpson 'flight notes'.
3. It specifically notes the bearing of 335 degrees as that being used.

We are naturally very grateful to Stuart Mclean, as we now feel completely satisfied with our interpretation of the 'flight notes'. The document on page 313 also clearly shows a tabulation of 'speed versus time' – exactly as the preamble to the Simpson notes describes.

We are now convinced that the 'flight notes' – whether still in the hands of the Simpson family or not, are genuine and really deserve more work on them. Peter Padfield did not really use them in his 2014 work, but they have now been validated by both our work and probably more importantly by the 'flight plan' that is certainly third-party evidence coming independently to us from some 12,000 miles away.

So, what are the conclusions that can be drawn from the flight alone? We list these as follows:

- Hess was not targeting Dungavel airfield. He may well have hoped to have eventually ended up at Dungavel House, but only after a safe landing at Dundonald. This straightaway alters the character of the flight from one previously described as a solo flight.
- Hess landed in Germany to de-risk the flight and to prevent him

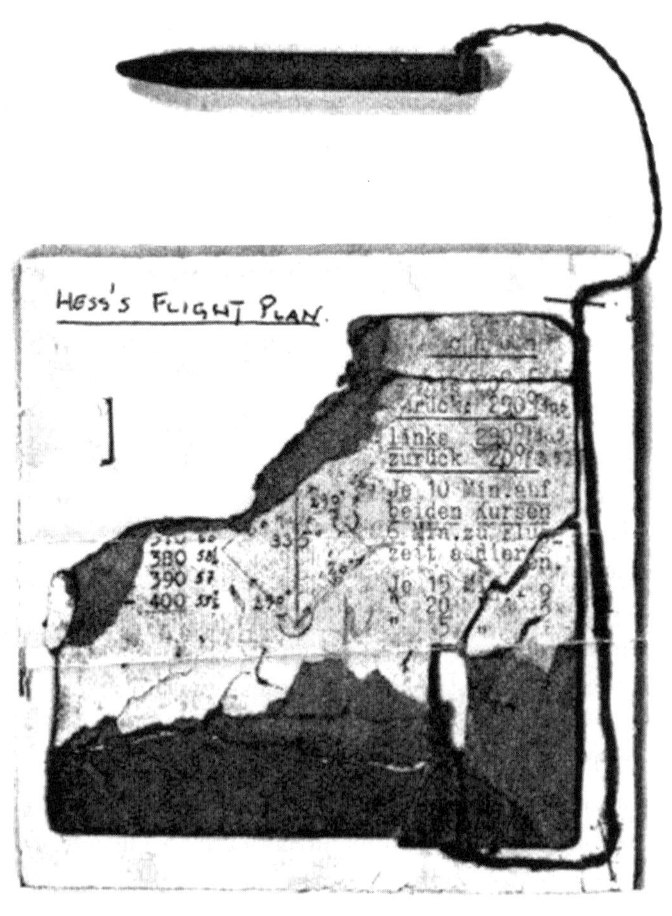

Rudolf Hess's Flight Plan

having to install and operate an auxiliary hand-cranked oil pump. This, too, alters the character of the flight, as it infers connivance with the Luftwaffe and was therefore not a 'solo mission'.

- Hess lied about the route to disguise the fact that he landed and the fact that he had on board the Elektra system, the then state of art German navigational system.
- Hess got lost and in doubling back to find his turning point lost 40 minutes. This loss of time prevented him landing in light.
- Hess was never going to land at Dungavel, else why fly past and over it at 4,000 feet? If, as some authors assert, it was to check his bearings, why then descend as if to land when approaching the Clyde?
- The true story of the RAF Defiants has yet to be told, as too the true story of RAF involvement. Hector MacLean's (the Duty Officer) version of events is at odds with the operational records held at Kew. MacLean states there were already Defiants up in the air before Cuddie and Hodge were launched. Surely the RAF must have reported on the Hess affair? If they did, the report certainly has yet to see the light of day.
- Was Hess helped in? We suspect not, simply because he was not expected as late as 20.23pm at Chatton. When the RAF realised what was happening, they appear to have tried to shoot the plane down, as evidenced by the very precise command given to Cuddie by Hector MacLean. The question is also unanswered as to how MacLean knew to vector Dundonald. This we believe very significant and was essentially a panic measure.
- The eventual outcome, an alive Hess, wandering around the Renfrewshire farming community prior to being interrogated for two hours in German by the part- time Polish Consul in Glasgow, was actually a disaster in security terms. The worst possible outcome. Certainly, a calamity.

The Hess flight plan versus actual plan

Plan

17.45hrs – Augsburg to Giessen. Leaves 17.45pm; arrives 18.20–18.30.
19.00hrs – Leaves Giessen with Bf110 wk. nr.3869. Full of fuel, 3070 litres and 2*35 oil tanks.
Takes off, heading for Borkum (370 kms).

19.54hrs – Reaches Borkum. Sets compass bearing at 335 degrees up the North Sea.

20.24hrs – 30 minutes out, switches on Elektra.

20.24hrs – Reaches Point B1.

20.54hrs – Reaches point B.

20.54hrs – Turns left 90 degrees, heading 245 degrees.

Scottish coast now 410 kms away, approximately 56 minutes away.

21.42hrs – Crosses east Scottish coast. Finds the Cheviot and then St Mary's loch. Adjusts course north by 12 degrees. When bisecting the Troon–Glasgow railway north of Kilmaurs, banks left, ready to land at Dundonald.

22.31hrs – Lands.

From Giessen: 3 hours 12 minutes. Fuel usage approximately 2,300 litres and oil usage 26 litres (per engine).

Actual

17.45hrs – Augsburg to Giessen. Leaves 17.45pm; arrives 18.20–18.30.

19.00hrs – Leaves Giessen with Bf110 wk.n3869. Full of fuel, 3070 litres and 2*35 oil tanks.

Takes off, heading for Borkum (370kms).

19.58hrs – Reaches Borkum, sets compass bearing at 335 degrees up the North Sea.

20.28hrs – 30 minutes out, switches on Elektra

20.28hrs – Reaches Point B1.

20.52hrs – Reaches point B.

20.52hrs – Turns left 90 degrees, heading 245 degrees.

Scottish coast now 410 kms away, approximately 56 minutes away.

Hess now gets into trouble. He cannot find the Husum reverse bearing and retraces his tracks.

22.23hrs – Crosses east Scottish coast (47 minutes late).

22.55hrs – Crosses west Scottish coast (48 minutes late).

23.07hrs T– Crash-lands (55 minutes late).

From Giessen: 4 hours 7 minutes. Fuel usage approximately 2,700 litres and oil usage 30 litres (per engine).

Conclusions

- Hess landed at Giessen to make the use of the auxiliary oil tank redundant.
- Hess got lost over the North Sea and the 40 minutes taken finding his bearing meant a controlled daylight landing was no longer possible.
- The evidence suggests a landing at Dundonald, not Dungavel. Please see chart extrapolated from Lennoxlove map (p. xx).
  a) The RAF reacted as if they knew Hess's eventual destination.
  b) There is a recent question as to whether there was a further person in the plane. The Battaglia report (Chapter 15) refers to a 'burnt body' in the place and there is also a MI6 report dated 23 May (FO1093/11) which mentions, 'So far nothing can be ascertained about the second occupant of the aircraft.' If true, this further demolishes the solo flight theory, but we do still wonder if two occupants were expected in a Bf110 and yet only one had been accounted for.
- The flight was meticulously planned, yet unravelled through an over-reliance on the Elektra system.

---

[1] J.R. Rees, *The Case of Rudolf Hess*, Heinemann, London, 1947.

[2] Derek Wood, *Attack Warning Red*, Macdonald and Janes, London, 1976.

[3] Werner Muller, *Ground radar systems of the Luftwaffe 1939-45*, Schiffer Publishing, Atglen, 1998

[4] Royal Observer Corps station.

[5] Franz Halder, *War Diary 1939-42*, Presidio, Novarto, 1988

[6] Picknett, Prince, Prior and Brydon, *Double Standards*, Little Brown, London, 2001

[7] Wolf Hess, *My Father Rudolf Hess*, WH Allen, London, 1986

[8] Ilse Hess, *Prisoner of Peace*, Berg:Druffel Verlag, Munich, 1954

[9] James Leasor, R*udolf Hess: The Univited Envoy*, Allen and Unwin, London, 1962

[10] Derek Wood, *Attack Warning Red*, Macdonald and Jane's, London, 1976

[11] David Stafford, *Flight from Reality*, Pimlico, London, 2002

[12] James Douglas-Hamilton, *The Ttruth About Rudolf Hess*, Mainstream, Edinburgh, 1993

[13] Hugh Thomas, *The Murder of Rudolf Hess*, Hodder and Stoughton, London, 1979

[14] John Harris, *BBC History* magazine, May 2001, citing a letter from Margaret Baird to her sister, May 1941.

[15] Davy McLean had left the Baird's farm after the war and had subsequently died, whilst living near Edinburgh.

[16] We subsequently learned that on the night Davy did not have a pitchfork. Sensing a marketing opportunity, the local agricultural merchants gave him a pitchfork so he could pose for the world's press. The pitchfork eventually ended up in Canada, at the manufacturers. This story was first told in our *Rudolf Hess: Truth at Last*, in 2019.

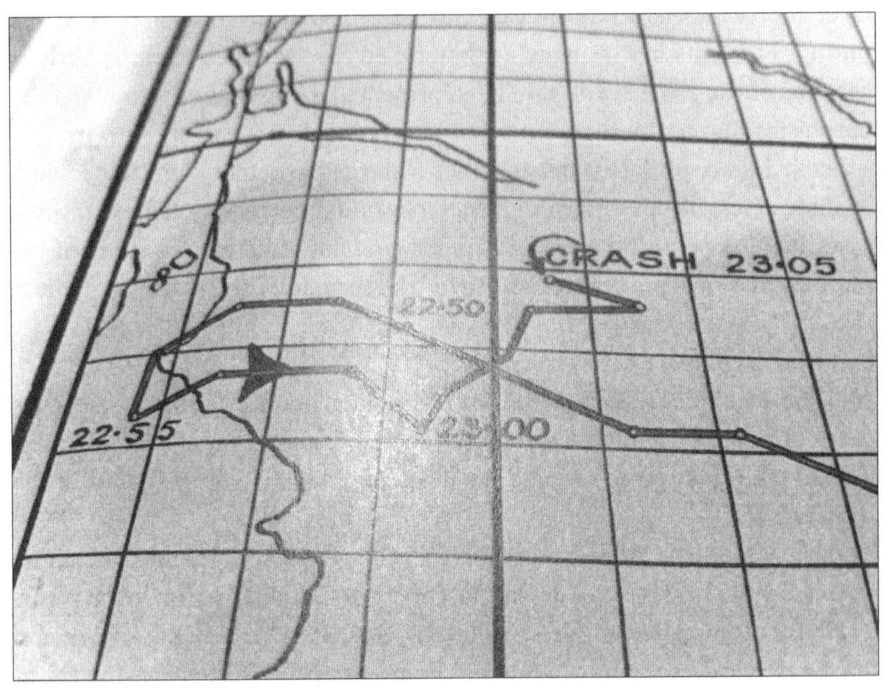

The original Royal Observer Corps recording of the climax of the Hess flight. (RAF Archives)

CHAPTER 20

GERMANY, 10–13 MAY 1941

Over the years there has appeared to be a degree of confusion as to the timings of events in Germany as they rolled towards their climax. Various versions of the same event have been presented. Consequently, to hopefully put the lead up to the flight into sharp chronological focus, we now present a detailed diary of the events, together with the particular source cited and, in some cases, the alternatives given. One should perhaps note that in some cases there seem to be two, very understandably different, versions of the same event – one 'pre-Russian captivity' the second 'post Russian captivity'.

Saturday 10 May – the day of the flight

10.00am, Munich: Hess rings Pintsch, his adjutant, requesting that he arranges for him to be taken to Augsburg airfield at 2.30pm that afternoon.[1] Hess then takes his young son and his dogs for a walk along the banks of the river Isar.[2]

12.00am, Munich: Alfred Rosenberg meets Hess for a buffet lunch at Hess's house. Hess has flown Rosenberg to Munich in his own plane. He is accompanied to Hess's house by Gauleiter Meyer.[3] Rosenberg and Meyer leave at around 2.00pm.[4] From Munich, Rosenberg travels to Berchtesgaden.[5]

2.30pm, Munich: Hess leaves his Munich home for the last time and heads for Augsburg airfield.[6] With him are Pintsch (adjutant), Lutz (security) and Lippert (chauffeur).

15.30: Helmut Kaden states that Hess 'started' his flight (there may have been some later confusion with the effect of Double Summertime).[7]

18.10pm, Augsburg Haunstetten: The Hess Bf110 takes off[8] (17.40pm according to Borman's diary).[9]

Evening, Berghof: Adolf Hitler telephones Ernst Udet to enquire if it is likely that Hess can reach Scotland in his Bf110.[10]

Early Evening, Guipavas, France: Adolf Galland receives a telephone call from Hermann Göring, instructing him to put his whole *Geschwader* (squadron) into the air at once, so as to shoot down Hess. Galland duly pays lip service by sending up two aircraft from each Gruppe (group).

After a decent interval, he ordered his pilots down.[11]

Evening, Berchtesgaden: Martin Bormann holds a drinks party at his house on the Ober Salzburg.[12]

21.00pm, Augsburg Haunstetten: Pintsch makes a call to the Air Ministry, Berlin, apparently requesting a 'radio beam'.[13] (The alternative version is simply that Pintsch drove from Augsburg to Berchtesgaden, leaving at 19.00hrs.)[14]

21.15pm, Augsburg Haunstetten: Pintsch, Piel (the airfield manager), Lutz and Lippert leave the airfield and then drop off Piel at his house in Augsburg.

21.30–21.45, Augsburg: Pintsch tells Lutz and Lippert, 'There may be trouble about what the Stellvertreter's doing. I just don't know yet. It depends whether he's successful or not. I've got a letter to take from him to the Führer. Now for your plans. This car (a Nazi party Mercedes) is far too conspicuous to use and also everyone knows whose it is. You two get some supper and put this car in the garage (at the Hess house). Pack your kit and take the small DKW out of Munich to Gallspach. We have a friend there. Wait there with him if you can, or at least in the village, if you can't, until you hear how the flight has gone, whether it's been successful or not. I'll do my best to get a message to you as soon as I have some news.'[15]

22.30–22.45, Munich station: Pintsch is dropped off by Lutz and Lippert.[16]

(23.09: Hess crashes at Eaglesham, Scotland).

24.00, Munich Station: train leaves for Berchtesgaden. Pintsch travels in Hess's railway coach.[17]

Sunday 11 May 1941 – the day of uncertainty

05.30: Lutz and Lippert duly travel to Gallspach, Austria, as instructed, and both are arrested.[18]

07.00: Pintsch arrives at Berchtesgaden.[19]

09.30, Berghof: Linge, Hitler's valet, knocks on Hitler's bedroom door to find him most unusually, already fully dressed.[20]

10.00, Berghof: Pintsch meets Hitler and hands over the letter from Hess. Todt, who had an 11.00 appointment, is made to wait.[21]

On reading the letter, Hitler is reported as commenting, '*Considering the present war situation that could be an extremely dangerous escapade*.'[22]

Lunch is then taken with, amongst others, Dietrich, Hewel and Bodenschatz. During lunch Göring arrives.[23] Pintsch is arrested after lunch and taken away.

15.30–19.30hrs, Berghof: Hitler meets Admiral Darlan, as pre-arranged. 'Everyone under the impression that Führer could not concentrate on the matter in hand.'[24] Ribbentrop also present.[25]

20.00hrs, Berghof: 'Endless talking … Jeschonnek is there too … but he knows nothing.'[26]

Monday 12 May 1941 – the first explanation

21.40hrs: German Radio (Berlin)[27] issues the following statement, 'The NSDAP hereby announces that party comrade Hess who, due to an illness he had years ago, was not allowed to fly, succeeded in obtaining an aeroplane against the strict orders of the Führer. On Saturday evening, 10th May, Rudolf Hess took off from Augsburg. He has not returned yet. We regret to say that a letter which he left behind seems to leave no doubt that he suffered from a mental derangement, and it must be feared that he has fallen a victim of hallucinations. Under these circumstances, it is possible that party comrade Hess either jumped out of the aeroplane, or died in an accident.'[28]

We know this was broadcast at 22.00hrs.[29] Apart from this, we also know that Albrecht Haushofer was summoned to the Berghof, flying there from Berlin, not to meet Hitler personally but to simply write a detailed report of his involvement, under the title, 'English Connections and the Possibility of Utilising Them'. This report will be analysed in a later chapter, but presumably was 'factored in' to the press statement that apparently Hitler had later dictated.[30] Haushofer was recorded as being devastated by the Hess flight.[31] Martin Bormann was made 'Head of the Party Chancellery'.

Ilse Hess, having been made aware of the communique, tries to speak with Hitler, but is only allowed to talk to Borman, who insists he knows nothing.

Joseph Goebbels is telephoned in Berlin and is asked to attend a meeting at the Berghof the following day. He appears to place the responsibility for the press release on to Otto Dietrich, his long-time rival.[32]

23.20hrs: the BBC announces that Hess has parachuted over Scotland and was being treated in hospital near Glasgow.

Tuesday 13 May 1941 – Reichsleiters and Gauleiters

Berghof: Hitler stays in his first-floor apartments and does not leave the house (11–14 May).

4.00pm-6.30pm,[33] Berghof: Hitler briefs the Reichsleiters and Gauleiters (60-70 men) First Bormann reads out the letters that Hess has left and then Hitler rises to comment. Hans Frank reports, 'He spoke to us in a very low, halting voice, expressing an underlying depression beyond words.'[34] And, 'It was mentioned that there had been other cases of mental illness in the Hess family.'[35]

It should be recorded that Himmler attended the above meeting.[36]

Rome: Von Ribbentrop despatched to meet Mussolini and Ciano. Dines with Ciano (and meets Mussolini the following day). Ciano records: 'The Germans want to cover themselves before Hess speaks…' and 'Von Ribbentrop repeats his slogans against England with that monotony that made Göering dub him – Germany's No.1 Parrot.'[37]

Von Ribbentrop left Rome the following day, 14 May 1941.

Conclusion

The initial reaction to the flight had been dealt with. It would appear to us that Hitler's reaction was one of concern as to the mission whilst uncertain as to outcome. The feigned 'animal noises' as described by Speer and the 'underlying depression' only came when it became apparent that Hess had not achieved what he set out to achieve. Whether over the outcome or the individual concerned, Hitler certainly put on a convincing display. The consummate actor.

---

1 James Leasor, *Rudolf Hess: The Uninvited Envoy*, George Allen and Unwin, London, 1962.

2 Peter Padfield, *Hess, Hitler and Churchill: The Real Turning Point of the Second World War*, Icon, London, 2013.

3 Rosenberg diaries, United States Holocaust Memorial Museum, Washington, DC.

4 Peter Padfield, *Hess, Hitler and Churchill: The Real Turning Point of the Second World War*, Icon, London, 2013.

5 Ibid.

6 Ibid.

7 Helmut Kaden lecture to the Rudolf Hess Gesellschaft e.v – 23 November 1989.

8 Ibid. We presume these timings come from Leasor's post-war interview of Karlheinz Pintsch.

9 Borman's Notizkalendar, National Archives, Washington, DC, T-84 EAP 105/18.

10 Armand van Ishoven, *Udet*, Paul Neff Verlag, Vienna, 1977.

11 David Baker, *Adolf Galland*, Windrow and Greene, London, 1996.

12 Jochen von Lang, *Martin Bormann: The Man Who Manipulated Hitler*, Book Club, London, 1979.

13 Ibid.

14 Wolf Hess, *My Father Rudolf Hess*, Cassell, London, 1986.

15 Ibid.

16 Ibid.

[17] Ibid.
[18] Lippert to Wolf Hess, as cited by Peter Padfield.
[19] Ibid.
[20] Peter Padfield, citing Rainer Schmidt.
[21] Ibid.
[22] Wulf Schwarzwaller, *Rudolf Hess: The Deputy*, Quartet, London, 1988.
[23] Ibid. Göring was staying at his castle at Veldenstein, near Nuremberg.
[24] Gerhard Engel, *At the Heart of the Reich: The Secret Diary of Hitler's Army Adjutant*, Greenhill Books, London, 2005.
[25] Photographic evidence of meeting at Berghof. He travelled from Fuschl castle, near Salzburg.
[26] Ibid.
[27] David Irving, *Hess: The Missing Years 1941–1945*, Focal Point, Windsor, 2010.
[28] Wulf Schwarzwaller, *Rudolf Hess: The Deputy*, Quartet, London, 1988.
[29] Peter Padfield in *Hess: The Fuehrers Disciple* (Cassell & Co., London, 1991) places the broadcast at 8.00pm.
[30] Otto Dietrich, *The Hitler I Knew*, Skyhorse Publishing, New York, 2010.
[31] James Douglas-Hamilton, *The Truth About Rudolf Hess*, Mainstream, Edinburgh, 1993. Citing Rainer Hildebrant, one of Haushofer's Berlin students.
[32] David Irving, *Goebbels: Mastermind of the Third Reich*, Parforce Ltd, London, 1996.
[33] Jochen von Lang, *Martin Bormann: The Man Who Manipulated Hitler*, Book Club, London, 1979.
[34] Peter Padfield, *Hess: The Fuehrers Disciple*, Cassell & Co., London, 1991.
[35] Wulf Schwarzwaller, *Rudolf Hess: The Deputy*, Quartet, London, 1988.
[36] Wolf Hess, *My Father Rudolf Hess*, WH Allen, London, 1986. Himmler was recorded as being in Greece on or around 7 May (his wife's diaries).
37 *Ciano's Diary 1937–1943*, Phoenix Press, London, 2002.

CHAPTER 21
BRITAIN, 10–12 MAY 1941

In a similar vein to the previous chapter, we now present a British chronology of events for the same three days, 10–12 May 1941. Again, we look to highlight any differences in the various accounts.

Saturday 10 May 1941 – the day of the flight

Morning

Ditchley Park, Oxfordshire – Churchill is apparently spending the weekend at the home of his friend Ronald Tree MP. Whilst the Luftwaffe still posed a threat, he much preferred the elegant James Gibbs house to Chequers, which was of course a more obvious target.[1]

The guest list was as follows:

Andrew Duncan (Ministry of Supply)
General Harold Franklyn (8th Corps, South of England)
Duncannon (Later Lord Bessborough)
Herschel Johnson (American liaison – First Secretary, American Embassy)
Mr and Mrs Archie Sinclair (Secretary of State for Air)
J.M. Martin (Principal Private Secretary)
Clementine Churchill (Wife)
W.A. Harriman (American liaison)
Mary Churchill (Daughter)
Freda Casa Maury/Dudley Ward (Edward VIII's former mistress)
Brendan Bracken
Alice Winn (Nancy Lancaster's sister)
The recently married, Andrew and Deborah Cavendish (arrived Sunday).
And, Winston Churchill[2]

Somewhat surprisingly, perhaps, Winston Churchill signs the visitor's book after the other visitor known to have arrived on Sunday, the Duke of Hamilton. This action will be debated later in the chapter.

The obvious comment is surely that the guest list is hardly that of a house

The James Gibbs designed hall at Ditchley Park, Enstone

party awaiting the arrival of the Deputy Führer of Germany. From the guests invited, it would appear to be more of a continuation of Churchill's policy of flirtation with America, particularly with Harriman and Johnson being present. Surely this is a clear sign that Hess was not expected by Churchill that weekend, as American house guests would be the last persons to be invited? Contrast the scene painted above with that in the White House when Osama Bin Laden was being hunted down in 2011.

The King and Queen's whereabouts cannot currently be stated with any certainty.[3] The King was in London on Friday 9 May. William Shawcross observes that they were 'probably' at Windsor.[4] We also have the King's somewhat obtuse subsequent diary entry to consider. Deborah Cadbury, in her *Princes at War* quotes the King's diary entry for 13 May: 'My Lord Steward, Hamilton, has only been appointed for a year. I had to ask Walter Buccleuch his predecessor to leave owing to his sympathy with the Nazis. Perhaps the post of Lord Steward is bewitched or is it Germanised? Hess might have landed 2 miles from Drumlanrig instead. The Prime Minister came to lunch…'

This was written on the Tuesday, after the crash on late Saturday night. The papers had released the story and Churchill by that time was in possession of the facts of the case. He would surely have shared these with the King and so the issue really becomes the sentence, 'Hess might have landed 2 miles from Drumlanrig instead'.

This is far from clear in meaning. Drumlanrig is of course one of the Duke of Buccleuch's main residences in lowland Scotland and we suspect he was there on the night of the crash with his sister Alice and her husband, HRH The Duke of Gloucester. The comment about '2 miles' could be seen to be a 'throw away' but why 2 miles? Why not 5 miles, or 1 mile?. Or, alternatively, was the King actually recording that Hess crashed 2 miles away from where he intended to land?

Dungavel House, for the record, is 18 miles away, so it would be an odd use of numbers if that were the intended suggestion, or the King might have just been muddled, but oddly there was an airstrip at Newton Mearns, which is 2 miles away. This belonged to Wallace Fairweather, whose son Keith had married Lord Runciman's daughter Margaret. To add to the coincidences, Roman Battaglia, the Polish Consul in Glasgow was their lodger. He had rushed to Giffnock Scout Hall to interrogate the German visitor.

This is all very odd. Yet again.

The airstrip was called King Henry's Knowle, and Fairweather used to fly his Avro Avian from it in the 1920s. The reader will have to make his or her mind up as we do not believe Newton Mearns to be the target. Dundonald remains the more likely.

The Fairweather Avro Avian

The Duke of Kent's whereabouts, until recently, also could not be stated with any certainty.[5]

This particular conundrum was first debated in Double Standards, way back in 2001.

The authors made the case that Prince George was waiting at the end of the runway at Dungavel House, Lanarkshire, ready to receive Rudolf Hess when he landed, complete with landing lights and telephone calls from Bowhill and the Duke of Buccleuch. Rather like 'the doppelgänger in Spandau' theory, this compelling image has almost passed into the realm as an accepted Hess fact. Consequently, any subsequent analysis has to disprove this seemingly 'given' fact.

Unfortunately, perhaps for *Double Standards* fans, we now are of the firm opinion (after twenty-five years of research) that the Duke of Kent was certainly not present at Dungavel House. This is for a number of reasons:

- No actual evidence was given in *Double Standards*, save the testimony of two ladies who have continued to remain anonymous.
- Dungavel was not where Rudolf Hess was headed, at least aeronautically, and as such any attendance would have been a pointless gesture.
- Hess would not have risked landing at such an airfield. A dead and anonymous Deputy Führer would be no use to anyone.
- Of more pertinence, we now believe we know precisely where the duke was.

First, we should say that our research has been made the more difficult on account of a total and consistent lack of cooperation from either the late duke's family, or the Royal Archives. In our early research days, our polite letters were at least acknowledged; now we do not even receive that courtesy. This approach does no one any good at all and simply reinforces any suspicions that there must be reasons to be quite so rude.

Consequently, we now wonder if the lack of cooperation was deliberately designed to obfuscate and further confuse?

In 2008, not at all happy with the Double Standards placement of the duke, we had inserted an advertisement in the *Daily Telegraph*, enquiring if any reader might know the whereabouts of the prince on 10 May 1941. The Duchess of Sunderland kindly replied, stating that the duke had stayed at Dunrobin Castle that weekend (which may well be partially correct), but for reasons that were first given in our 2010 book, *Rudolf Hess: The British Illusion of Peace*, we now doubt this.

Since 2008 we have continued to write to Kensington Palace and the Royal Archives from time to time, but with no success or engagement. However, as mentioned previously, the expansion of the internet has coincided almost precisely with our Hess research and we are now pleased to report significant progress, largely through our subscriptions to ancestry.com and britishnewspaperarchive.co.uk. We now present the new evidence we have obtained over the intervening period.

1. *Double Standards* claim that the Duke of Kent was waiting for Hess at The Kennels, a house across the B743 from the main house at Dungavel, and next to what was the airfield. We have obtained an early plan of the Hamilton Estate and ascertained that The Kennels were actually on the same side of the road as the main house, and the building to which they seem to refer is actually known as Greenhead. In other words, The Kennels were simply the kennels – not a house, but a sanctuary for the Hamilton's hounds. Not a good start.[6]
2. We have asked for further information as to the sources of the *Double Standards* information, but unfortunately two of the authors have now died (Stephen Prior and Robert Brydon). We have also ascertained from the two surviving authors that there were protracted difficulties with the publishers and so it is unlikely that any further corroborating evidence or otherwise will be produced from that source. The more we have learned, the more we understand the 'difficulties'.
3. The whole premise of landing a Bf110 on a small grass strip (even if it could be found from the air) does not stand scrutiny. Why take that risk if there were more accessible alternatives?
4. The Duke of Hamilton flew smaller aircraft onto the strip. He is recorded as owning pre-war:

   G-ABPD AW133 – De Havilland Gypsy Moth
   G- ACPK X9382 – De Havilland Leopard Moth
   G-ADVC BB812 – De Havilland Tiger Moth
   G-AELF VTA32 – Percival Pro Vega Gull

These were all much smaller and lighter aircraft. There is also a rumour that the duke crashed a slightly larger Hawker Hart at Dungavel when trying to land there in 1938. Moreover, Hector MacLean, in *Fighters in Defence*[7] tells the story of a proposed landing at Dungavel in a Hart being prevented by saying, 'If you do, it'll be your last'. He also describes Dungavel as, '… no bigger than a pocket -handkerchief, surrounded by fir trees and a nasty cross wind blowing…'

A Percival Pro Vega Gull

We would also make the obvious point that a Bf110 at approximately 7.5 tons is a far heavier machine than the Hart, which weighed in at just over a ton unladen. The comparison and implication is stark.

By way of counter, Tony Stott has made the valid point that Luftwaffe pilots were regularly landing such aircraft on grass strip,s particularly on the Eastern Front. We can of course only agree, but would counter in turn that the Hess

A Hawker Hart

flight was meticulously planned and de-risked. Why then de-risk only to risk all on a challenging, potentially suicidal landing after a five hour flight?

The Duke of Kent, we know, was in London at the start of May and had then subsequently travelled to the east coast of Scotland (we do not yet know how for sure). He was reported as follows, usually in the local newspapers (albeit belatedly) of the area:

1 May Visits Tunbridge Wells to inspect the ARP and drivers of the Regional Mobile Canteens (accompanied by Flight Lieutenant P.J. Ferguson, formerly of the Glasgow 602 squadron).
7 May Visits Fraserburgh and Peterhead. Both towns had been heavily bombed and the duke visited ARP sites and the Mission to Deep Sea Fishermen. The Earl of Caithness and Lord Saltoun were also present.
8 May Visits a demonstration of Canadian logging techniques in Nairnshire. He was dressed in the uniform of a Group Captain of the RAF.
14 May Is reported as meeting Chips Channon in London, sometime after 6.00pm: 'I had not seen him for several weeks and he has been in Scotland for a fortnight.'[8]
16 May Visits Westminster Abbey to witness the effects of the bombing raid of 10 May. (The Duke of Hamilton visits the King.)
20 May Visits YMCA London HQ.
27 May Has lunch at the Savoy as part of an ENSA function. Whilst there, the sinking of the Bismarck is announced.

All valid information, but none of which actually answers the basic question. However, as the British Newspaper Archive has expanded its coverage, more newspapers have been archived and so we duly came across an obscure article from the *Orkney Herald*, and *Weekly Advertiser* and *Gazette for the Orkney & Zetland Island*.

Dated 21 May 1941, the article gave details of a 'recent informal' visit to a 'North of Scotland' port by the duke.

Whilst not saying specifically which port, further tantalising details were given, including a visit to a Toc H house, called Halifax House.

After working Google overtime, we discovered that the named Toc H house (a Christian military relief charity founded in Northern France in 1915. Named after Talbot House, its first base was in Poperinge, Belgium. It had rapidly grown subsequently) was located on the Isle of Hoy, one of the larger Orkney Islands. In 1941 there were five such houses in and around the Orkney Islands, servicing the various needs of the adjacent and massive Scapa Flow naval base.

We felt after twenty-five years we were getting somewhere. Harris had long ago discovered pictures of the duke's trip at the Imperial War Museum, but the photographs, whilst dated May 1941, were not more accurately timed. They show the duke (dressed as a Rear Admiral) visiting HMS *Dunluce Castle*, one of a number of depot ships to the Home Fleet when stationed at the famous Scapa Flow naval base. The ship also acted as the mail collection/delivery ship for visiting ships in the Flow.[9]

However, still no fixed date. At the time of the visit, we discovered that the naval base had gained its own military newspaper called *The Orkney Blast*, which quickly gained an enviable reputation for the quality of its reporting.[10] The girls at the Orkney record office kindly emailed a copy that covered the visit. A young reporter, Gerald (Gerry) Meyer, had covered the visit of the duke, even interviewing him whilst engaged on his tour.

Gerry Meyer duly reported that he had presented the duke with issue number 17 as a memento. The visit had been reported in issue 18 of the newspaper and that was dated Friday 16 May. Logically therefore, the royal visit had to have taken place during the period Friday 9 May to Thursday 16 May. We were getting closer.

We also noted that the duke was dressed in naval uniform rather than that of the RAF, for which he had been working for some time. Whatever the duke was doing, he was theoretically at least under naval control and command. The IWM photographs clearly show his dress as naval.[11]

The final slice of luck came when Harris discovered that Gerry Meyer had gone on post-war to edit *The Orcadian*, the weekly newspaper for the Orkneys. He had enjoyed a long and distinguished career. Harris then traced his daughter and son-in-law (who still live in the Orkneys), who said they would 'have a look through his journals and diaries, which had been kept' (and were in the attic). They were as good as their word and during the week ended 6 June 2021 relayed the fact that Gerry had conducted his interview with the duke on Saturday 10 May 1941, which fitted in perfectly with what we had already established.

So, after twenty-five years of investigating, we now know where the duke was on 10 May 1941, with Dungavel and Lanarkshire now looking less likely

No. 18. PUBLISHED WEEKLY FOR H.M. FORCES — STROMNESS, FRIDAY, MAY 16, 1941 — PRICE THREEPENCE

DUKE OF KENT FINDS THE BLAST

"MOST INTERESTING"

ROYAL VISITOR MEETS OUR REPORTER ON ORKNEY VISIT

Courtesy: "Daily Mirror."

Bed and Breakfast with 54

"CLYMACS" GREET YOU LIKE AN OLD FRIEND

By Our Own Reporter

Hoy. Saturday.

I got stranded on Hoy—and those who know Hoy and its environs will know what that means! So I went along to see what the "Clymacs" could do, having heard from divers sources that they were wont to take pity on poor misguided souls who were so rash as to become stranded on Hoy—and even to be on Hoy at all.

And I was greeted like an old friend. You'd have thought that I was a personal pal of everyone in the unit, and in five or ten minutes I was fixed up with a bed with food, with a roaring fire, home comforts and an odd spot of gossip to take my mind off things.

There was little reason to wonder for long where lay the sources of this hospitality. You see, most of the unit personnel come from Glasgow, and Glasgow is noted for its warm-hearted-ness, so I'm told, and about the only two "foreigners" in the unit are York-shiremen—and well of course that means something!

But then, I'm a Yorkshireman myself.

The O.C., Major [illegible], comes from

(CONTINUED IN PAGE 4)

"I'll read this copy," he says

HIS Royal Highness the Duke of Kent, while on a visit to Orkney recently, met and talked with a representative of THE ORKNEY BLAST—Pte. Gerald G. A. Meyer (R.A.M.C.) News Editor and Chief Reporter, best known to readers as "Gem"—discussed the activities of the paper and accepted a copy.

"Gem's" account of the meeting is printed below.

It was interesting that a copy of the paper which His Royal Highness saw and took away with him, was a copy of the new BLAST—the new eight-page bright tabloid size newspaper which has succeeded the four page large size sheet.

This introduction of the Orkney troops' own newspaper to Royalty was entirely accidental and unplanned and as a result, the Duke's interest was all the more spontaneous.

CHANCE MEETING

Our representative was visiting the particular spot for a routine story for THE BLAST and was until a few minutes before the meeting, totally unaware that a Royal visitor was in the vicinity—so well had the secret of the Royal visit been kept, for obvious reasons.

The Duke, dressed in Naval uniform, was making a tour of inspection on foot when he met Gerald Meyer and asked him:

"What do you do here?"

"I am only a visitor here. I am from THE BLAST," answered Gem.

"THE BLAST! What is that?" asked the Duke.

"The troops' newspaper," was the reply. "The troops in these defences have their own weekly paper. Would you like to have a copy?"

"Yes, certainly," said the Duke, and accepted a copy which Gem produced from his haversack.

GEM'S OWN STORY

But here is Gerald Meyer's own story.

The Duke was most surprised to hear that troops in the Orkney Defences had a paper of their own, describing their activities and written by themselves.

He asked questions as to where the paper was printed, who were the editorial staff and, as any journalist might have done, asked what the circulation of the paper was. A figure was mentioned and it was explained to His Royal Highness that double that number could easily be disposed of were it not for paper rationing regulations. Once again he expressed his surprise when an estimated figure of the shadow circulation of the paper was given him.

ROYAL READER

When presented with a copy of the paper, His Royal Highness examined carefully each page, still asking me a number of questions and taking an evident interest in each of the features.

His conclusion was that THE ORKNEY BLAST was "most interesting" and "very good."

(CONTINUED IN COLUMN 2.)

(CONTINUED FROM COLUMN 3.)

The Duke of Kent then left me with his copy of THE BLAST tucked under his arm. Turning to a member of his party, he remarked smilingly: "Here, have a look at THE ORKNEY BLAST."

The copy of the paper which the Duke examined was issue No. 17, of last week, which appeared for the first time in the present tabloid size. This particular issue was fairly rich in illustrations and drawings executed by the troops.

He was most anxious to know if all the Services read the paper and was told that the Navy and Air Force had been contacted with a view to supplying them with it.

BICYCLES ARE £10 APIECE IN PARIS

"Gay City" is becoming a Nazi Garrison Town

THE BLAST'S Military Correspondent this week tells how Paris is faring under German domination; reports the "success" of Japanese parachute troops; and reveals the growth of food regulation offences in the occupied countries.

Paris is slowly but surely being turned into a German garrison town. The population have mostly returned to their homes since the armistice, but industry is almost at a standstill and large numbers of people are unemployed. The telephone system is working normally, but buses only run very occasionally and all cars are reserved for official use.

Most of the people get about on bicycles, which are being sold for £10 apiece.

Food Problem Serious

The food problem is acute and there are daily queues of people outside the shops. The famine threatens to be the worst since 1870 when the Zoo animals were killed and eaten.

When the Germans first arrived, they ate everything in sight and especially butter, with the result that all the more tasty commodities, such as butter, eggs, coffee and cheese, are now practically unobtainable.

The anti-Jew movement is growing, and some shops have notices which state that Jews will not be served. A French party movement has been started by the Germans as an attempt to foster anti-semitism. On the other hand, German soldiers are encouraged to treat the local inhabitants with the greatest courtesy.

The few amusement centres that remain cater mainly for Germans. A few cinemas are open, but only old French films and Nazi news reels are shown. The Rex Cinema, one of the largest in Paris, is reserved only for Germans, no French people being admitted.

Nazi-instructed Jap Paratroops

Reports have been received that Japanese troops have been receiving special training in parachute jumping from German instructors.

The instructions have been carried out on Hainan Island, and a large-scale exercise has recently been held in Japan proper.

At this exercise there was a very high percentage of casualties, which included twelve deaths. This shows that a high degree of training has not yet been reached by the Japanese. It is reported that 400 troops were dropped; some in sections of four, carrying machine gun parts and ammunition, and that many of the casualties were caused by these men jumping in a bunch, with the result that their parachutes failed to open. Others suffered injuries from their equipment as they landed.

Food Offences are Rife

Germany is having great difficulty in preventing offences being committed which are contrary to food regulations.

The worst place for these offences is Austria and the worst offenders are the Nazis themselves.

A common offence all over Germany and occupied countries is the illegal slaughtering of cattle. In Denmark, a number of convictions have been made against people who forged or stole coupons.

Stealing of food, proper, is assuming large proportions in Holland, while in Belgium hoarding of food and cases of illegal selling of food have steadily increased since last summer.

Two men were recently arrested in occupied France for selling 30,000 meat coupons and other ration cards.

Two probable cases of sabotage have recently been reported from Norway. In the first case, the cheese-packing department of a factory was burnt out, and in the second case a herring oil factory was destroyed at Borsa.

The Orkney Blast – dated 16.5.1941

by the minute, though obviously not yet impossible, given that the duke had the use of a RAF Anson.

We have continued to try and track the duke's movements after 10 May and are currently relying on Norman Glass's excellent *Caithness and the War, 1939–45*. Like Gerry Meyer, Norman was a reporter on the *John O'Groats Journal* and *Caithness Courier*, and as a memorial to the fallen of Caithness had post-war compiled a record of the war in that area.[12]

On 12 May 1941, he duly recorded that the Duke of Kent was at RAF Wick, accompanied by the Duchess of Sutherland who helped dispense 'tea, cakes and chocolate' from a mobile canteen and 'extended her generosity to a number of appreciative workmen who were engaged nearby'.

So, we now have the duke on the Orkneys on the Saturday and the northernmost point of mainland Scotland on Monday 12 May. However, there is now one further significant complication.

We had acquired copies of the *Alanbrooke War Diaries 1939–45* years ago, simply to ascertain where the great man was on 10 May 1941. The answer was Luton, Bedfordshire, driving tanks.

But there is yet again another major coincidence. On 13 May (the Tuesday after the Saturday night), Alanbrooke was dispatched from London at 2pm via Glasgow to … yes, you have guessed, the Orkney Islands. He arrived at Kirkwall at 8.50pm and dined with the two principal admirals, Tovey and Binney.

We will debate this trip in due course. The obvious question is: what on earth was his purpose? The diary, not surprisingly, gives little clues, instead recording his various bird-watching expeditions whilst on the islands. In fairness, he also looked at some defences, on both Orkney and Shetland.

He eventually returned to London on Friday 16 May, the same day as we believe the Duke of Kent also publicly appeared in the capital, ostensibly so as to study the effects of the previous weekend's bombing. He is recorded as visiting Westminster Abbey.

As far as we can see, Alanbrooke did not return to/had not been to the Orkneys during the Second World War, it being largely a naval concern. So, what on earth was he really doing?

In conclusion, we are still acutely aware that this may not be a complete analysis. The Duke of Kent is seemingly accounted for on 8 May, 10 May, 12 May and 14 May.

It may of course be the case that he had flown from the Orkneys on late 10 May to Dungavel or Dundonald that same afternoon/evening, and then flown back to the Orkneys/Wick/Dunrobin once the Hess mission had catastrophically unravelled. The reader must decide how likely this may have been. The Orkneys to RAF Prestwick/Ayr is around 240 miles in a straight line, around an hour and a half flight in an Avro Anson, such as the one issued to the Duke of Kent.

More research is still required in this area, though our suspicion is now that the duke did not leave the Orkney Islands over the fateful weekend because he did not need to. There may already have been suitable proxies in place in Lowland Scotland. We suspect he, too, was a guest of the admirals at Melsetter House on the Isle of Hoy.

Melsetter House, Isle of Hoy (The Victorian Web)

Richard Wilbourn has also considered the possibility of Hess flying directly to the Orkney Islands. We know from the pilot notes that he was following a course of 335 degrees from Giessen and if one plots that line past the point where he chose to turn left towards the British coast, the line does indeed put him on route to the Orkneys/Shetland Islands. Is this what was shown on the third map that was given to the Duke of Hamilton, the existence of which is now denied?

Nothing would now surprise us in connection with the Hess affair. Yet another coincidence.

Our previous trials and tribulations in trying to ascertain the above whereabouts are well detailed in *Rudolf Hess: The British Illusion of Peace*.

Other players' whereabouts continue:

Woburn Abbey, Bedfordshire: Anthony Eden and Hugh Dalton attended the regular Saturday morning SO1 meeting, starting at 12.30.[13] It would appear that Eden's attendance was planned well in advance, as Dalton mentions that it was to take place in his diary entry for 23 April 1941. Hugh Dalton was engaged in an ongoing feud with Duff Cooper at the Ministry of Information and whilst in his company was hoping to influence Eden to act as potential mediator.

Turnhouse Airfield, Edinburgh: The Duke of Hamilton was on duty that day. He had been on duty for the four previous nights. On 3 May, an Albion 2-ton truck and a Bedford 30cwt truck had left the base for the newly established RAF Ayr,[14] which was also under the control of Turnhouse.

Lowland Scotland: HRH the Duke and Duchess of Gloucester inspected troops at Hawick, 'during the weekend'. We presume they would have been staying with the Duchesses brother, the Duke of Buccleuch.

Luton: Lord Alanbrooke, Chief of Home Forces, British Army inspected the new British heavy tank (35 tons).[15]

Hemel Hempstead, Hertfordshire: Clement Atlee prepared to address a 'war week' meeting.

Montagu Norman, the controversial Governor of the Bank of England had travelled from Euston to Symington, just south of Glasgow before changing for Stobo on 2 May. He was apparently visiting his younger sister, Gertrude, at Dawyck and returned to London on 15 May.[16] Dawyck was on the Symington–Peebles railway in Lowland Scotland.

Similarly, Lord Halifax, one of the 'arch appeasers' was in Chicago, away from Washington, DC and was perhaps oddly met by Robert Menzies, the Australian Prime Minister, who was returning to the Antipodes following a four-month trip to Europe. Halifax records, 'I got back to see Menzies, who told me a good deal about Cabinet discussions in England and about his judgement on events in the Middle East.'[17]

There is no mention of Hess.

Northiam, East Sussex: Alexander Cadogan, the Permanent Under-Secretary of State for Foreign Affairs, spent a rare weekend away from the Foreign Office at his thatched cottage.[18]

Apart from the King and Queen, most of the leading players in this affair were spending what appears to be a weekend away from London. Certainly not an organised assembly, waiting for a visitor.

Afternoon

Leeds, Town Hall: Ernest Bevin prepared to give his address at 5.00pm. The hundreds who had been unable to obtain tickets would have the opportunity of hearing the speech through loudspeakers in Victoria Square.[19]

North Atlantic Ocean: General Sikorski was heading fast for Prestwick airfield, Scotland, in a Consolidated Liberator bomber, AM 916. He left Gander, in Newfoundland, at 18.35hrs (local time), some 30 minutes after Hess had left Augsburg-Haunstetten (local time). The newly built Liberator hoped to cruise at around 200 mph.

London: Ivone Kirkpatrick was working at the BBC as part of the Ministry of Information, whilst living at Cadogan Court, Chelsea.[20]

Evening

10.23pm: Hess crossed the Northumberland coast at Chatton. He found the Cheviot, his way mark and flew due west.

10.34pm: Pilot Officer William Cuddie and Rear Gunner Hodge took off from RAF Ayr in their Boulton Paul Defiant. They were given the strict instructions 'Scramble Angels two five – zero nine degrees – Dive and Buster, vector three five zero'. Once plotted, this would place the Defiant over RAF Dundonald. However, how did the RAF know that the solitary plane was headed for Dundonald? At 10.34pm it was still halfway across southern Scotland. In theory at least, it could have been heading anywhere, so why did

Hector MacLean, the Duty Officer, place Cuddie and the Defiant's Browning .303's so precisely over RAF Dundonald?

11.09pm: Hess crash-landed near Floors Farm, Eaglesham, Renfrewshire, owned by the Baird family. He was taken to the cottage occupied by the ploughman, Davy MacLean, and his mother, Annie.

11.45pm: Hess was moved to Busby Scout Hall.

Sunday 11 May 1941

12.14am: Hess moved to Giffnock Scout Hall. Interviewed by Roman Battaglia, the Polish Consul in Glasgow (see Chapter 15). David McIntyre, Hamilton's lifelong friend and head of Scottish Aviation Limited at Prestwick, was also taken to identify the airman.

02.00am: Major Graham Donald, head of Glasgow ROC, rang Hector MacLean, Senior Controller at RAF Ayr. Suggested it might well be Hess.[21] Donald then rang Hamilton at Turnhouse to say the same thing.

02.00am: Hector MacLean at Ayr rang Hamilton at Turnhouse, telling him that the pilot wished to see him.[22]

2.00–2.30am: The Duke of Hamilton left Turnhouse, telling his wife, 'I'll have to go; it's to do with the crashed plane.' According to the Duchess of Hamilton, she did not see him again until about 4.00pm that afternoon. This version, however, is directly contradicted in Mark Peel's recent The Patriotic Duke.

02.30am: Hess moved to Maryhill Barracks, Paisley. After a sleeping draught, Hess was left to sleep under guard.

Mid-morning, Ditchley: Churchill asked Nancy Tree, his hostess, if the Duke of Hamilton might spend Sunday night at Ditchley.[23] This was apparently despite any report of any communication from Hamilton at that time!

10.00am: Hamilton arrived at Maryhill Barracks to interview Hess. He was accompanied by Flight Lieutenant Benson, RAF Turnhouse's Intelligence Officer. He then travelled to Eaglesham to inspect the plane before returning to Turnhouse mid- to late afternoon.

11.30am: The Consolidated Liberator carrying General Sikorski landed at RAF Prestwick. Sikorski was taken to Glasgow, arriving at 12.15pm.[24] It seems a virtual certainty that he was straightaway informed of Hess's arrival by Roman Battaglia, but this is not recorded in the Sikorski diary. Sikorski eventually travelled to the Polish HQ at Gask, Perthshire.

15.30hrs: Hess moved to Drymen Military Hospital.

c.16.00hrs: Hamilton telephoned the Foreign Office, asking to speak to Alexander Cadogan. Cadogan was at his country cottage and John Addis, a junior official at the time, was in receipt of a frustrated roasting.

The call was then apparently interrupted by John Colville, Churchill's secretary and Hamilton asked that a car be at Northolt aerodrome 'within an hour and a half'. Colville had said that 'The Prime Minister had sent me over to the Foreign Office as he is informed that you have some interesting information.'[25]

This is where the versions of the same story begin to differ. Quite markedly.

John Colville, in his diary, placed the telephone call from Hamilton as being in the morning of 11 May, not the afternoon, and he intercepted a call being taken by a Nicholas Lawford, not John Addis.

A completely different story from Hamilton's.

However, what we suspect to be more relevant is that Colville had phoned Ditchley that morning (after breakfast) and had spoken to Winston Churchill, who had reported to him that the RAF had shot down forty-five German planes. Clearly, and far from surprisingly, Churchill whilst at Ditchley was in receipt of RAF intelligence. We suspect that Churchill was also in possession of the fact that a German pilot had crashed in Scotland who might well be Rudolf Hess. We strongly suspect that it was Churchill who told Colville and not vice versa. That is why Colville was able to ask Hamilton 'Has anyone arrived?' when he phoned that afternoon. In government circles it was already old news, but positive identification was still awaited.

The next oddity to consider is 'Why Northolt?' It would appear that Hamilton assumed that Churchill was at No. 10 Downing Street, and so asked that a car be sent for him to Northolt, on the A40 heading out of London.[26] If this were the case, then RAF Northolt would appear a logical choice for an aerodrome within distance of central London. It should be noted that VIP flights, such as Chamberlain's 1938 missions to Munich had left London from Northolt.

However, it is not clear to us the precise sequence of events thereafter. It would appear that 'someone' then phoned Ditchley and spoke to Churchill who then 'sent for him' (Hamilton). Ditchley had a fully functioning government communications suite installed in a lobby on the ground floor.

Consequently, it was only on landing at Northolt that Hamilton was told to fly on to Kidlington.[27] This task was made the more difficult as his Hawker Hurricane would not start, as an engineer had apparently flooded the already warm engine. Consequently, the last part of the journey, retracing earlier steps, was made in a Miles Magister. He landed at Kidlington and was driven to Ditchley.

As to timings, we estimate the following:

Depart Turnhouse 16.30 hours.

Cruise speed 178mph – 400 miles, therefore 2 hours 15 minutes.

Arrive Northolt 18.45 hours.

Depart Northolt 19.30 hours (Go to 'watch hut', try to restart engine, find Miles Magister).

Cruise speed 124mph – 40 miles, therefore 20 minutes.

Arrive Kidlington 19.50 hours.

Arrive Ditchley approximately 20.00hrs–20.15hrs.

The duke's arrival was reported as coinciding with the guests finishing dinner. Ronald Tree records that 'Dinner would be at 8.30'. Therefore it would appear that the above estimates are perhaps too optimistic in terms of travel time.

However, James Leasor records (after presumably interviewing the duke in the early 1960s) that he eventually told Churchill and Archibald Sinclair of the arrival of the German airman. It was then that Churchill made the notorious comment, 'Well never mind Hess for the moment, I'm going to see the Marx Brothers.'

Double Standards[28] made their own interpretation of the above comment, but we are prepared to take it at face value.

Ditchley Park had, and has, its own cinema, and the film in question was *The Marx Brothers Go West*. This had been released in December 1940 with a running time of 80 minutes. Leasor states that the film ended at midnight, which means it must have started at around 22.30.

Hamilton was then interrogated by Churchill for another two hours. In particular, he seemed concerned as to whether the airman really was Rudolf Hess or whether he was a doppelgänger, planted to cause mayhem. Hamilton made it clear that he was convinced it was the real Hess.

The men then retired to bed.

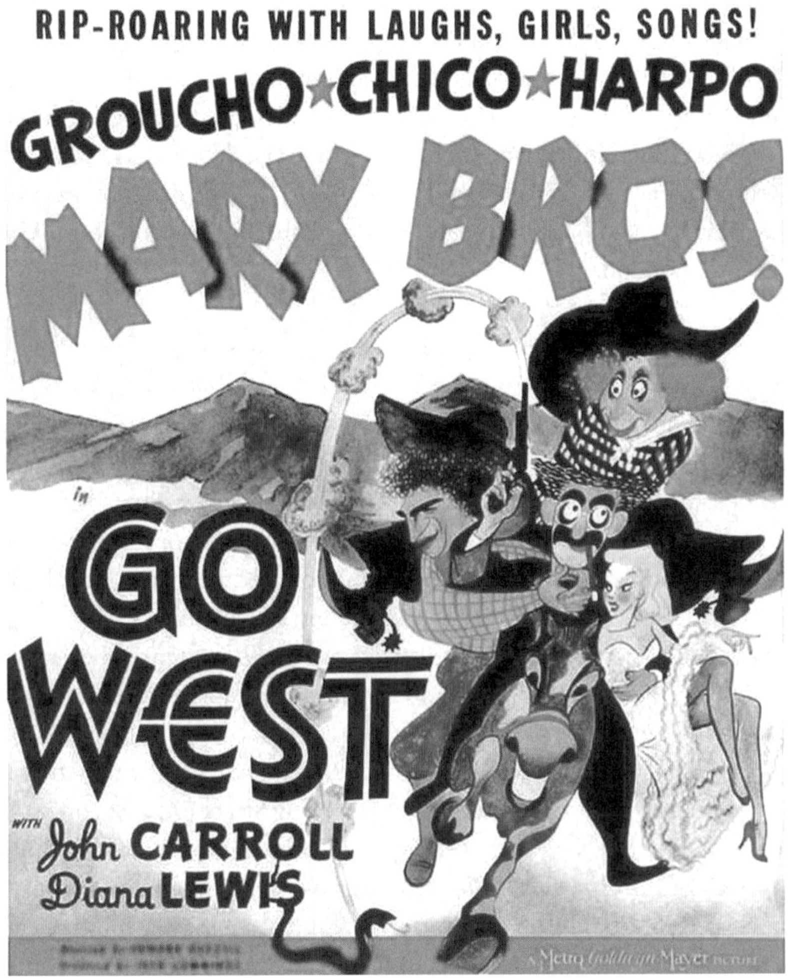

The billboard for the 'The Marx Brothers Go West'

The above chronology does therefore appear to fit, albeit perhaps not exactly. Hamilton must have left Turnhouse later than 4.30 or travelled slower than a normal cruising speed.

The reason that this version of events requires audit is simply that there is alternative evidence to suggest that Churchill was not at Ditchley when Hess actually flew in. The evidence is:

- The instruction/assumption to fly to Northolt. Why fly 80 miles past a destination only to return later? It may of course be that this was a device to safeguard Churchill's presence at Ditchley, although it seems more odd the more it is contemplated.
- The fact that Churchill signed the Ditchley visitor book that weekend after the Duke of Hamilton. This again may of course just be due to the timing of the signature. Neither does his signature follow that of his wife Clementine, who carefully records the dates 10 –12 May.
- The evidence in *A World in Your Ear: The Broadcasting of an Era*[29] by Robert Wood. This appears to place Churchill in the Central War Room, London.

We are not sure whether Churchill's location is actually the key point here. The key point is surely when he was aware of Hess's arrival. It would appear to us that the evidence appears to be that he knew far earlier than previously thought. This really should not be too much of a surprise, given the RAF personnel that descended on the Busby Scout Hut and the fact that Hamilton had a pretty good idea that Hess had arrived during the early morning of 11 May. It is very likely to our minds that the RAF had communicated the arrival to Churchill prior to any telephone call from either Hamilton or Downing Street.

We are of the opinion that the well-tried and tested sequence of events have been slightly 're-engineered' simply to give the later impression that Churchill was in blissful ignorance of Hess's arrival, instead enjoying the company of his American friends at Ditchley Park, which also was owned by an American. It is quite possible that Churchill was in Downing Street until late on 10 May, travelling to Ditchley late that evening, even after Hess had crashed. Indeed, Sefton Delmer, in *The Black Boomerang*, makes the comment that he was being chased as a potential 'identifier' on Sunday 12 May, a full day earlier than the Kirkpatrick mission detailed below. Again, this is inconsistent and would infer that the positive identification had already been made. Robert

Bruce Lockhart later made the comment that Delmer had been prevented from identifying Hess.

Monday 13 May 1941 – more identification required

Ditchley: after breakfast, Churchill and Hamilton and staff left for London in a convoy of three cars. They left[30] at approximately 9.15am.[31]

Downing Street: upon arrival, Churchill and Hamilton met Anthony Eden. According to Ivone Kirkpatrick, Churchill had telephoned Eden the previous evening. Nationally, the story had yet to break, and the Germans had yet to show their hand. Ditchley to Whitehall is approximately 73 miles and even though there are reports of speeds of up to 70mph in London, the journey must have taken 2 hours. It was now approximately 11.30am.

Foreign Office: Hamilton and Eden walked to the Foreign Office and met Ivone Kirkpatrick, who had been summoned by Alexander Cadogan. Kirkpatrick arrived at 1.15pm.[32]

15.15hrs: Eden met Kirkpatrick and the Duke of Hamilton joined them at 4.00pm.[33]

There seems to be a little confusion as to who met whom and when. It is presumed that the Foreign Office might have wished to discuss the matter without the Duke of Hamilton being present, at least initially. This was as Kirkpatrick described the situation.

Leasor, by contrast. described a Cadogan/Kirkpatrick/Hamilton meeting before the arrival of Eden from a War Cabinet meeting.

The purpose of inviting Kirkpatrick was simply to enquire if he could identify Rudolf Hess, as he had met most of the leading Nazis whilst in Berlin in the 1930s. He said he could, but 'Had one horrid moment of misgiving at the possibility of being hoaxed…'

Nonetheless, he agreed to the task and he and Hamilton flew north from Hendon, leaving just before 5.00pm. It has to be said that if Churchill had really feared Hamilton's motives, it is surely unlikely that he would have allowed him to return to Scotland?

So, the two men flew north. Kirkpatrick described it as 'our slow Flamingo aircraft'[34] (but a Flamingo was not a slow aircraft).

Hamilton, by contrast described it as a de Havilland Rapide, which is a slow aircraft and Hamilton would be more likely to correctly identify. It was more likely a Rapide, as the journey had to be broken at Catterick for refuelling. The two men landed at Turnhouse, Edinburgh at 21.40 hours; a journey of 4 hours 40 minutes to cover the 400 miles, by contrast to Hamilton's earlier Hurricane flight of 90 minutes.

As soon as they arrived, Hamilton took a call from Archie Sinclair, the Secretary of State for Air (again, by contrast, James Leasor says it was Anthony Eden) who asked if it was the real Hess and informed them that German radio had released a statement to the effect that Hess was missing. Positive Identification was now vital.

Consequently, the two men left straightaway for Buchanan Castle, some 55 miles away. Leasor describes their arrival as being 'after midnight'. After meeting the prisoner, at 1.00am Kirkpatrick was summoned to the telephone. It was Anthony Eden demanding to know if it was really Hess. Kirkpatrick confirmed that it was.

At the same time, the *Glasgow Daily Record* was just starting to distribute Tuesday 13 May's paper, with the headline – **RUDOLF HESS IN GLASGOW – OFFICIAL**. Clearly the local 'bush telegraph' had beaten the UK government. They, at least, had made up their mind.

Somewhat surprisingly, at 23.20 hours the official statement came from Downing Street, stating that Hess had crashed near Glasgow, and finished by saying that, 'an officer of the Foreign Office who was closely acquainted with Hess before the war has been sent up by aeroplane to see him in hospital'.

Whilst this was of course the case, the statement issued at 23.20 hours seems quite sure that the pilot was Rudolf Hess, yet the man sent to specifically identify him was at the time on the road between Turnhouse and Buchanan Castle. Why release the statement before the verification was complete? Did London already know it was Hess and, if so, how?

Other Reactions

The Deputy Führer of Germany had just landed in Scotland; still, more than seventy years later one of the most outstanding events of the Second World War. We now look at some of the recorded reactions:

CHIPS CHANNON

'There is an extraordinary rumour at the Foreign Office that a German

Peace envoy has arrived and that he has some connection with the Duke of Hamilton.'
(Diary, 12 May 1941)

ALEXANDER CADOGAN
'I have never been so hard pressed. Mainly due to Hess, who has taken up all my time and I am 48 hours in arrears with work.'
(Diary, 12 May 1941)

IVONE KIRKPATRICK
'The Hess episode was comedy from the beginning to the end.'
(*The Inner Circle*, Macmillan, London, 1959)

LORD ALAN BROOKE
No mention whatsoever.
(War Diaries)

THE EARL OF HALIFAX
No mention whatsoever.
(*The Fullness of Days*, Collins, London, 1957)

ERNEST BEVIN
No mention whatsoever.
(*The Life and Times of Ernest Bevin*, Heinemann, London, 1967)

However, on 15 May 1941, Bevin told a War Weapons lunch in London that he was convinced Hitler had known Hess was planning the peace mission: 'From my point of view Hess is a murderer. You can understand my feeling about him when I tell you he was the man who collected every index card of every trade union leader in Germany and every social democrat and when the time came they were either in a concentration camp or murdered. My own views on this adventure I will not express at this gathering, further than to say that I do not believe that Hitler did not know that Hess was coming to England.'

F.W. WINTERBOTHAM
'His flight to England during the war was quite in character.'
(*Secret and Personal*, William Kimber, London, 1969)

SEFTON DELMER

'What baffled me about the whole Hess episode was the astonishing reluctance of our authorities to handle his case with the realism and practicality the British normally show when faced with an opportunity of this kind.'

(*The Black Boomerang*, Secker and Warburg, London, 1962)

HUGH DALTON

'He [Ismay] and the Chiefs of Staff are delighted over Hess. The PM has been thinking and talking of nothing else, and therefore they are free, for once, to carry on the war.'

(Diary, 13 May – no published entry for 12 May).

WINSTON CHURCHILL

'I never attached any serious importance to this escapade. I knew it had no relation to the march of events.'

(*The Second World War*, (vol. 5), Cassell, London, 1964)

JOHN COLVILLE

1. 'Has somebody arrived…?'
2. 'The Hess story has, of course made everyone gape … in the Travellers (Club) at lunch time there was no other topic.'

There seems to be a common link here. Those who know what had just happened and why, tried to make light of the matter (Churchill, Kirkpatrick, Colville and Cadogan). Those who really did not know made it clear that they did not know (Channon and Delmer) and those that get told later thought it best to make no further mention (Eden, Brooke, Halifax and Bevin). Hugh Dalton's response is perhaps the only one that is somewhat ambiguous.

The national papers had no such reservations and, as can be imagined, even given the strictures of wartime reporting, had a bonanza, in general starting on 13 May. Popular culture responded. Arthur Askey on his popular *Band Waggon* programme recorded, 'Thanks for Dropping in Mr Hess', A.P. Herbert wrote the ditty, 'He is insane. He is the Dove of Peace…'

Peter Fleming must also have dusted down his unsold copies of *The Flying Visit*[35] released nearly a year earlier. Astonishingly, the story had just come true.

GF.114.27

Greys Clerihews ... No. 8

WE WONDER IF HESS
(PLEASE NOTE NEW ADDRESS)
WAS LOOKING FOR GREYS
AS HE BANKED O'ER THE BRAES

Do you buy your Greys by the jar? Half-pound glass jars of Greys are perfectly sealed and assure you of extra freshness; and the plain glass jars are perfect for kitchen use after you've finished with them.

Greys is Great

BECAUSE ONLY A PERFECT TOBACCO CAN GIVE YOU A PERFECT SMOKE

The Evening Post *[Wellington, NZ] 15 May 1941,*
Hess cigarette advertisement

[1] Chartwell Papers – 20/32: 'We hope so much that you will come to Ditchley as often as it may suit your convenience (11 November 1940).
[2] Thanks to Ditchley Park, Enstone, Oxfordshire. The above is taken from a copy of their visitors' book for the weekend.
[3] John Harris, *Rudolf Hess: The British Illusion of Peace*, JEMA, Moulton, 2010.
[4] William Shawcross, *Queen Elizabeth: The Queen Mother*, Macmillan, London, 2009.
[5] This is despite *Double Standards*, which we do not consider conclusive.
[6] Ordnance Survey 1909. Sheet 030.13.
[7] Hector MacLean, *Fighters in Defence: Memories of the Glasgow Squadron*, Squadron Prints, Glasgow, 1999.
[8] *Chips Channon Diaries, 1938–43*, Hutchinson, London, 2021.
[9] Malcolm Brown and Patricia Meehan, *Scapa Flow*, Pan, London, 1968.
[10] The newspaper was published from 1941 to 1944.
[11] IWM photographic archive – A3955 to A3960.
[12] Norman M. Glass, *Caithness and the War, 1939–45*, North of Scotland Newspapers, Wick, 1994.
[13] John Harris, *Hess: The British Conspiracy*, Andre Deutsch, London, 1999.
[14] Air 28/861.
[15] *Alanbrooke War Diaries 1939-45*, Weidenfeld & Nicolson, London, 2001.
[16] Montague Norman diaries, Bank of England, London.
[17] *Lord Halifax Diaries*, University of York, England.
[18] *Sir Alexander Cadogan Diaries*, Cassell, London, 1971.
[19] *Yorkshire Post* and *Leeds Intelligencer*, 8 May 1941.
[20] Ivone Kirkpatrick, *The Inner Circle*, Macmillan, London, 1959.
[21] Mark Peel, *The Patriotic Duke*, Thistle, Edinburgh, 2013.
[22] Ibid.
[23] Ronald Tree, *When the Moon was High*, Macmillan, London, 1975.
[24] Sikorski diary.
[25] National Archives – INF 1/912.
[26] TNA INF 1/912.
[27] James Douglas-Hamilton, *Motive for a Mission: The Story Behind Hess's Flight to Britain*, Macmillan, London, 1971.
[28] Lynn Picknett, Clive Price and Stephen Prior, *Double Standards: The Rudolf Hess Cover-Up*, Little Brown, London, 2003.
[29] Robert Wood, *A World in Your Ear: The Broadcasting of an Era*, Macmillan, London, 1979.
[30] James Douglas-Hamilton, *Motive for a Mission: The Story Behind Hess's Flight to Britain*, Macmillan, London, 1971.
[31] James Leasor, by contrast, has Churchill at Downing Street by 10.00am.
[32] *Sir Alexander Cadogan Diaries*, Cassell, London, 1971.
[33] Ibid.
[34] Ivone Kirkpatrick, *The Inner Circle*, Macmillan, London, 1959.
[35] Peter Fleming, *The Flying Visit*, Jonathan Cape, London. July 1940.

CHAPTER 22

PUSH AND PULL

By analysing the evidence presented to date and categorising the various forces at play, it is now possible to understand why the Deputy Führer of Germany decided to 'dare' on the evening of 10 May 1941 and fly to Scotland.

The Pull

There is now absolutely no doubt whatsoever that Hess was being actively 'pulled' to fly to Britain. The British, desperate to buy time so as to prevent invasion, had sent Borenius to Burckhardt in January 1941, under the pretext/cover of a Finnish Diplomatic Mission. From that initial contact, Haushofer had become involved and had also engaged with Hoare in Madrid. There is also no doubt that this contact and its progress was being relayed back to Hess (and Hitler), quite possibly after being further embellished by Haushofer. However, from his subsequent reaction it is clear that Haushofer did not expect Hess to fly to Scotland on 10 May and the conclusion is that the flight plan was not sufficiently prepared so as to be the means of completing the diplomatic mission, presumably based on what Haushofer knew at that time and had imparted to Hess.

We will discuss what Hess was being told and by whom in the concluding chapter.

What is sure is that Haushofer would not have wished for the Anglo-German settlement that Hess was attempting to broker, as that would have led to a continuation of the Hitler regime. The fact that Hess saw fit to fly to Scotland rather than England indicated that he did not anticipate dealing with the incumbent Churchill-led government.

Equally, his love of his family was an opposing and huge 'pull' that also had to be addressed when deciding to fly. From the private family papers now in Bern, there is no doubt that he was and remained extremely close to his family, both immediate and wider. The photographs of him and, in particular, his son, Wolf, in the days leading up to 10 May 1941 clearly demonstrate this. Ultimately, though, he made his decision and placed himself and his Führer over the love for his family.

Ilse Hess with their son, Wolf

Push

Similarly, there were a number of factors, that when accumulated, pushed Hess into making his action. What is clear, however, is that it was Hess's decision alone to fly. We do not believe he was being forced into any action, whether rash or not. We would cite the following:

- Throughout his life Hess had been a man of action. He had participated. He participated in the 1914–18 war, the early Munich Street fights, the 1923 Putsch, the 1934 murders. He flew planes, he liked fast cars. He was forty-seven and, rather like the exponent of the modern mid-life crisis, he craved action and excitement. However, in 1941, in the middle of a war he was stuck in an office, either in Munich or, less frequently, in Berlin. Despite being busy on important party business, we strongly suspect he was actually bored and felt unfulfilled. That is why he had asked to be released to fly for the Luftwaffe in 1939.
- He was not alone in the above. Reinhard Heydrich, despite being Himmler's deputy and literally brim full of state secrets, was still

permitted to fly in an active Luftwaffe squadron, and indeed his potential role in the actual Hess flight will be discussed later. Heydrich's flying reached the absurdly dangerous levels of him being shot down behind Russian lines in 1942. One can only conclude that this complete disregard for military discipline and common sense provides a good example of the inherent weakness of structure and control at the upper echelons of the Nazi state. One could argue that the Hess flight, nine months in gestation, is another prime example of the same weakness.

- Other writers have made the point that the more ambitious had overtaken Hess in terms of prestige. We disagree. Overtly, Bormann was perhaps closer to Hitler in terms of daily accessibility, but Hitler was never as close to Bormann in human terms as he was to Hess (and the other leaders knew it). After the flight it was a new role and title that was assigned to Bormann, not simply a duplication of his predecessor's. We see Hess in 1941 as simply a reluctant office worker who had been initially assigned the role very much on account of his strengths of unquestionable loyalty and probity. Hess was also possibly the most self-confident Nazi leader in his relationship with Hitler. Unlike other senior Nazis he did not see the need for a house at Berchtesgaden, for example. He lived in Munich, 100 miles away and had his own weekend house in the Allgaii. That was good enough.
- We also suspect that Hess's unhappiness in his role was the root cause that he wrongly addressed by treating various medical ailments, real or imagined, with various alternative medicines. Hess lived until he was ninety-three, some forty-seven years after his flight, so there clearly were no real serious issues affecting his health in 1941. His attendance at the Zeileis Institute, for example, was clearly not evidence of illness as such; it seems to us to have been a cure for a man who did not really understand himself, or what was happening to him. He was simply in the wrong job at the wrong time and felt trapped, though quite possibly did not even realise it, instead believing he was physically ill. Stress-related illness was perhaps not as understood then as it is in more modern times.
- We have already listed the issues that Hess would have been aware of in connection with the war effort. Clearly, all was not well within Nazi Germany despite the overwhelming military successes to date.

Hess would have realised that fact. Adding to his sense of frustration must have been the fact that he could actually do little about it. He was not included in any military activity as such and the one military committee on which he had been elected to serve never met. He was increasingly unhappy with the development of the monster that he had been instrumental in creating. He saw and witnessed the infighting (he was not speaking to Ribbentrop; few were) and he knew that the pressures and strains would only increase after Barbarossa.

- Barbarossa. There is no doubt that Hess knew of Barbarossa. The British also knew of Barbarossa, as did the Russians. The only real doubt was regarding the starting date. Originally scheduled for 15 May 1941, it finally started on 22 June. There was growing time pressure on Hess to free himself from his current existence. Once the invasion began it would be too late. He also had to allow sufficient time for his plans to bear fruit once in Britain. Hess knew only too well the likelihood and implications of a two-front war, though Hitler did not see Barbarossa in those terms. He saw Britain as cowed and therefore Germany had only, in effect, a single exposed front.
- We should also not forget the obvious. Yes, Britain was on the ropes militarily, but she still had her empire and she still (to be vulgar) had plenty of money accumulated over a long period of time. She eventually bought herself out of trouble and whilst we now know what eventually happened, there must have still been an element of doubt in the minds of the leading Nazis as to how Britain might react upon news of Barbarossa. It was certainly no secret that many in the ruling classes still saw Russia as a greater threat than Germany. Might she be persuaded to 'stand aside' or even call a truce? Hess's flight would, if nothing else, possibly crystallise that position. (In the end it did not. By saying nothing, the British cleverly gave nothing away, and it was perhaps only the sinking of the *Bismarck* in late May 1941 that signalled the true British intention.)
- Other Nazis. This interesting area is relatively undocumented and so we were interested to discover that the RHSA was closely monitoring the Zeileis Institute and its non-profit-making adjunct. We were also interested to learn that Himmler had sent a representative to Geneva to meet Carl Burckhardt. We also believe it significant that Carl Langbehn, Himmler's unofficial peace envoy, knew Albrecht Haushofer through

the fledging Hitler opposition. Certainly, in May 1941 it would appear to be the case that Himmler and Hess were thinking along very similar lines in terms of a Western peace; although who was to be the leader of Germany when any such peace was to be made was certainly ready for debate, at least as far as Himmler was concerned.

- In connection with the above, we have no direct evidence of blackmail by Himmler. However, we do have the RHSA files on the 'Friends of Zeileis Organisation' which indicate that Hess was in receipt of funds, albeit but not very much, and it is questionable if this would be much more of an embarrassment rather than a scandal. However, it is perhaps another source of pressure, again real or perceived. There is no doubt that the RHSA was fully aware of this financial arrangement. There is certainly more to learn of Hess's relationship with the Zeileis Institute and, in particular, we are interested to learn as to why Karlheinz Pintsch saw fit to send Lippert and Lutz to Gallspach on the night of 10 May 1941. For whatever reason, the Institute remained relatively unscathed throughout the war years, despite the threats that were issued from time to time. We now understand that the Zeileis Institute was essentially a Jewish-run organisation and therefore would also question if Hess's protection of members of Jewish families (Haushofer and Zeileis) was beginning to create problems, given his role within the Nazi state.
- Hess's knowledge of Hitler's pro-British viewpoint. One of the most telling comments Hitler made to his Gauleiters on 15 May 1941 was that when on 4 May Hess had come to Berlin to speak with his Führer, he had been insistent in his questioning as to whether Hitler still maintained his ideas as to an alliance with Britain. Clearly he was in prime position to have known Hitler's thinking back in 1924/5 when the two men formulated *Mein Kampf*, but that was of course years ago and much had occurred in the meanwhile. Hess was looking to Hitler for further justification for the action he was about to take.
- Hess's loyalty to his Führer. This is quite likely the key to the affair, perhaps the explanation is really no more complicated, hence our earlier comparison to Parsifal. Hess knew of the various peace moves and initiatives that were coming from Britain. However, there were two basic problems to overcome. First, were they real or illusory and secondly, was the removal of Adolf Hitler really a pre-condition, or

merely a preference? Realistically there was only one way to find out. Haushofer and Burckhardt could talk all they like and pass messages back and forth, but rather like in battle the infantry is always required to take the risk and stake possession of captured territory. There had to be a means of discovering whether the peace moves were real or illusory.

- Similarly, there was only one way to discover if the removal of Hitler was really necessary to obtain a peace settlement. Go and find out. Other ambitious and far more ruthless Nazis were also discovering that Hitler's removal was seemingly necessary for a Western peace (Himmler, in particular) and perhaps Hess was fearful that this knowledge might well lead to just such an action. The saying, 'live by the sword, die by the sword' might well become a self-fulfilling prophesy. Hitler's actions towards others in the past had almost provided a textbook display of such action that someone such as Himmler or Heydrich might now be prepared to take. Again, if the peace was merely illusory, this train of thought would become irrelevant and Hitler the more likely to survive. There is no doubt that Hess was fully aware of the terms of the suggested peace and the preconditions that at the time were being mooted.
- And lastly, ego. Clearly Hess had a considerable ego, albeit not as overt as other Nazi leaders. Otherwise, he would not have achieved what he had already. The mission, if successful, would surely grant Hess the same status as had been granted to Chamberlain in 1938 on his return from Munich. He had been waiting nearly nine months for the chance to make the flight and now was the time to dare.

That is why we believe Rudolf Hess chose to fly to Scotland on 10 May 1941. No single reason, certainly not a decision taken in haste, but an accumulation of reasons and rationales, some recent, some not so. Above all, though, it was Hess who made the decision – no one else. He too wished to cement his place in history. In that regard he was certainly successful.

COVER-UP

CHAPTER 23

THE POLES AND THEIR SOMEWHAT ODD ASSASSINATION ATTEMPT

We have already made the point in Chapter 15 that we originally suspected that Hess may have been targeting a section of the Polish government in exile with a view to making a separate peace with the Polish nation (or at least part of the Polish nation), hence removing the reason the British gave for their ultimatum as to war on 3 September 1939.

If successfully completed, this would have driven a wedge firmly between the various Allies assembled in Britain at the time.

However, in order to achieve this objective, under the Polish constitution the President, Wladyslaw Raczkiewicz would have to be a party to any such treaty as, under the 1935 Constitution, the choice between peace and war was his and his alone (Clause 12f).

Raczkiewicz had visited Scotland and on 17 April 1941. The *Hartlepool Northern Daily Mail* reported that the President had told 'Polish airmen at a Scottish airbase', 'I am confident of the ultimate resurrection of Poland, and I hope that by next Easter we will be able to meet again in Poland.'[1] Quite how this was to be achieved he did not say…

We have also determined that on 10 May 1941, Raczkiewicz was in Sunningdale, Berkshire, and not lowland Scotland. It appears that Edward Raczyński, the Polish Foreign Minister, was also in London, as he gave a speech to the Forum Club on Monday 12 May.[2]

We have already determined that Wladyslaw Sikorski and his advisor, Józef Retinger, were fast approaching mainland Scotland from Gander, Newfoundland in a state-of-the-art heavy bomber, a Liberator, AL916. Whilst there is some confusion as to their precise time of arrival on 11 May, there is no doubt that the Polish Prime Minister landed no more than 30 miles from where the Deputy Führer had crashed only a few hours previous.

So, far so good.

However, the first signs that all was perhaps not as portrayed come from the actions of General Kazimierz Sosnkowski (1885–1969). He, too, was in London on the night of 10 May but got caught up in the bombing raid, and in trying to disarm an incendiary bomb, seriously injured his right hand and neck. We have pictures of him in early July, still with bandages applied to both areas.

We also have a copy telegram timed at 11.47 on 11 May, informing Colonel Krubski in Glasgow that Sosnkowski was catching the overnight train to Glasgow and requesting an 'immediate operation' on arrival. Subsequent to the operation, Sosnkowski made his way to army HQ at Gask.

Clearly an important meeting was being convened at Moncreiffe House (Gask was the nearby airstrip) as we now know that Sikorski – the Prime Minister – and now Sosnkowski – the nominal head of the Polish Army – were in attendance. We can only presume that the meeting was held to discuss the arrival of Rudolf Hess, as relayed by Roman Battaglia, via the location of Giffnock Scout HQ.

Sosnkowski is important, as he was very much the head of the army in exile, and many of the soldiers present in Scotland would have favoured him as opposed to the more illustrious Sikorski.[3]

The meeting was held we presume, on Monday 12/Tuesday 13 May.

The next time we hear of the matter is on 9 June in Guy Liddell's diaries, where he calmly records: 'Certain members of the Polish forces in Scotland have been plotting to kidnap and murder Rudolf Hess. It is difficult to say how far the matter has gone but it is of course the kind of thing they might attempt to do. We are taking steps to get hold of either the commanding officer or the officers themselves and explain to them what serious harm they might do both to their own cause and to the Allied cause if they attempt to do anything of the kind. This quite apart from what might happen to themselves. I think the Poles imagine that Hess may be making peace overtures and that this will be listened to by the British Government. Nothing, of course could be further from the truth.'

On July Liddell continues: 'Some 17 Polish officers and possibly 2 British subjects had worked out a scheme to assassinate Rudolf Hess, but it seemed that the plot was due to take place on 19 May, the project may have been abandoned… The Poles seem to think that Hess may have come here to offer peace negotiations and the British government may succumb to the idea of leaving the Poles in the hands of Germany.'

The reader will recall that Hess had been moved to London on the night of 17 May and therefore we presume this is why the plot failed. However, it now appears that MI5 also had an operative within the Polish government in exile, as on 5 July Liddell again records: 'General Sir Alan Hunter knew Alfgar Hesketh-Prichard who was one of the Englishmen thought to be concerned and seems to be of an SO2 type. He attached himself to the Guards at the beginning of the war and was rather a nuisance. He could be very useful to the plotters, since he would have access to the Guard's mess at Pirbright and might find out quite a lot about Rudolf Hess. Edward Hinchley Cooke[4] was to go down to Camp Z on Monday with Coates[5] in order to acquaint the commandant with the position and study the general layout.'

Two days later on 7 May, the Polish informant, De Rema has obviously been interviewed.

> 'I saw De Rema about the Polish plot to murder Rudolf Hess … he has obviously handled the whole business with great ability and discretion. He thought however, that Alfgar Hesketh-Prichard might be interviewed, since this could be done without raising difficulties for De Rema.'[6]

This whole episode is very odd. We can quite understand the Polish motivation for the attempt on Hess's life and it was clearly in character. Equally, we are not surprised that MI5 had infiltrated the Polish exiles, and we are currently struggling to positively identify 'De Rema'.

However, what is odder still is the involvement of Alfgar Hesketh-Prichard. He came from a military family and his father, Major Hesketh Vernon Prichard (1876–1922) had written a leading book on sniping, following the First World War.

His son, Alfgar (1916–44), as to be expected, had also joined the military, serving with the Royal Fusiliers. He was later seconded to SOE and was killed in 1944 on active service in the Balkans. His body was never found.

However, it is far from clear therefore why he would become embroiled in the Hess affair and under whose instruction he was acting. We also have still to discover who the other British subject was (Liddell had mentioned two in number). Was the fledgling SOE in some way involved and if so, why?

This whole affair does seem most odd and as yet is unexplained. It does, however, explain why Mytchett Place near Aldershot was as well protected as it eventually was – not to keep Hess in seemingly, but to keep the Poles and Hesketh-Prichard out.

The Polish motives were reasonably obvious: kill Hess before he was allowed to entreat with the British Government. Sikorski would know from

Borenius of the Geneva meeting in late January and so an assassination attempt was at the least understandable. Thereafter, Hesketh-Prichard was another matter. The creation of SOE was, in part, a left-wing counter to the traditional right-wing sympathies of the Secret Services, and so was that a reason for his involvement? If so, was Hugh Dalton, the minister in charge, aware of the proposed course of action?

We currently do not know enough to even speculate as to what was really going on in this matter. So, we will not.

Alfgar Hesketh Pritchard (1916 – 1944)

[1] British newspaper archive.

[2] Edward Raczyński, *W Sojuszniczym Londynie*, London 1974.

[3] Jerzy Kirszak, *General Kazimierz Sosnkowski (1885–1969)*, Instytut Pamieci Narodowej, Warsaw, 2012.

[4] Colonel Edward Hinchley -Cooke (1894 – 1955) – MI5 Officer.

[5] Colonel Norman Coates (1890-1966) – Directorate of Prisoners of War.

[6] Guy Lidell, *Diaries*, Routledge, London 2005

CHAPTER 24
THEREAFTER AND NUREMBERG

Germany

A second German communiqué was issued on 13 May 1941:

> On the basis of a preliminary examination of the papers which Hess left behind him, it would appear that Hess was living under the hallucination that by undertaking a personal step in connection with the Englishmen with whom he was formerly acquainted it might be possible to bring about an understanding between Germany and Britain. As has since been confirmed by a report from London, Hess parachuted from his plane and landed near the place in Scotland which he had selected as his destination; there he was found, apparently in an injured condition.
>
> As is well known in Party circles, Hess has undergone severe physical suffering for some years. Recently he sought relief to an increasing extent in various methods practised by mesmerists and astrologers, etc. An attempt is also being made to determine to what extent these persons are responsible for bringing about the condition of mental distraction which led him to take this step. It is also conceivable that Hess was deliberately lured into the trap by a British party. The whole manner of his action, however, confirms the fact that he was suffering under hallucinations.
>
> Hess was better acquainted than anyone else with the peace proposals which the Führer has made with such sincerity. Apparently he had deluded himself into thinking that, by some personal sacrifice, he could prevent developments, which, in his eyes, could only end with the complete destruction of the British Empire.
>
> Judging by his own papers, Hess, whose sphere of activities was confirmed to the Party, as is generally known, had no idea how to carry out such a step or what it would have.
>
> The National Socialist Party regrets that this idealist fell a prey to tragic hallucinations. The continuation of the war, which Britain forced on the German people, will not be affected at all. As the Führer declared in his last speech, it will carried on until the men in power in Britain have been overthrown or at ready to make peace.

Looking at this statement in 2021 and knowing what we now know about Borenius and Burckhardt, it could be argued that it is actually a fair attempt at the truth. However, in 1941 it was not seen as particularly helpful. To the faithful party member, Hess appeared to still be mad, which must have raised questions about the upper echelons of the Nazi party, but he did now at least appear to have been trying to make some type of personal sacrifice. However, yet again it raised still more questions than it answered.

We would also comment that much that was contained within these 1941 statements, both German and British, has effectively set the post-war history of the affair. To the ordinary German and Briton who was busy either fighting or just trying to survive an increasingly brutal war, these statements were their only source of information. Consequently, it not too surprising, when seventy years later and the oral history of the war has passed down one or two generations, we often encounter statements such as, 'Rudolf Hess – oh yes, he was the mad one that flew to Britain, etc, etc.'

It really is no wonder that these preconceptions have endured. Why would they not? At the time most people had far more important things to worry about in their own daily lives.

After 10 May 1941, the NSDAP tried as best it could to expunge the name of Rudolf Hess. A new job title was created for Martin Bormann, who was effectively promoted to Hess's former position in terms of his administrative duties. However, Bormann was never the soulmate to Hitler in the way Hess had been. Hitler had definitely been wounded.

Bormann typically then changed his children's names. Rudolf and Ilse Hess were godparents to two of the Bormann children (and so Ilse duly became Eike and Rudolf duly became Helmut).

Hess's advisors, doctors, astrologers and colleagues were all arrested and interrogated but eventually released. Pintsch, Leitgen, Lippert and Alfred Hess were all expelled from the Nazi Party. The news of the arrests was spread near and far; the subsequent releases less so.

Ilse Hess and Wolf were allowed to remain at 48 Harthauserstrasse, Munich, though they chose to move into Lippert's, the old chauffeur's accommodation. This remained the situation until the property was bombed in 1943, when they moved to the Allgäu. Ilse Hess eventually received a pension from the state. Hess's father, mother, brother and sister were all unmolested and left alone. All died natural deaths.

By stark comparison to the 20 July 1944 bomb attempt on Hitler's life, there was no bloodbath. (It should be noted in this connection that Germany was however winning the war in 1941; in 1944 it was losing). Probably the most unfortunate was Karlheinz Pintsch, Hess's former adjutant, who was transferred to the Eastern Front and later captured, imprisoned and tortured by the Russians. He returned to Germany in 1955, literally a broken man.

Ernst Bohle was admonished by Hitler in front of the Reichsleiters and Gauleiters at the Berghof on 15 May, but then returned to work. He was also later interrogated by Heydrich. Bohle survived the war and Nuremberg, dying in Hamburg in 1960. He acted as a witness for Hess's defence at Nuremberg.

Von Ribbentrop was glad to take the opportunity to sack Albrecht Haushofer from the Foreign Office in Berlin, but as Haushofer was deemed of sufficient value in any possible future British negotiations, no further action was taken against him at the time. He was duly released in July 1941, albeit a heavily marked man. Von Hassell makes the obvious remark in his diary, in connection with German resistance, 'The flight of Hess has now shattered every possibility of advancing our cause through Haushofer.'[1]

Dr Gerl, in the Allgäu, was also arrested and taken for questioning, but subsequently released.

On the broader, populist front, the mission had drawn the inevitable wise cracks: 'New name for Hess – The Reich Emigrant Leader' and 'The thousand-year Reich has been shortened to one hundred years? Why – One zero less.'[2]

It was of course clear to most rational-thinking Germans that there was still more to the flight of the Deputy Führer than had been explained. However, the convenient fact remained that there was no rational explanation. Enough confusion had been created so as to effectively disguise the truth.

It is of course the case that Hitler was about to launch Barbarossa and so also had other, more pressing items on his personal agenda. However, the clear analysis is that initially Hitler just acted as he had to do. He behaved as though he did not know what had happened. He acted specifically for the world press consumption and as the world might expect him to do, particularly as he was hoping to launch the Russian invasion in a matter of weeks. To present any evidence or sign of foreknowledge would raise all sorts of suspicions, especially in the Kremlin, and so he desperately had to feign ignorance. There was really no other approach that would be plausible and so he chose to accept Hess's somewhat awkward suggestion to 'simply say I am mad'. The press statements did not help the cause of clarity, but they did at least put 'clear blue water' between Hitler and his deputy at a time that Hess had to been seen as acting alone.

However, the most telling subsequent observation to our minds is the comparison to the Skorzeny mission to free Mussolini in September 1943.

Hitler told Otto Skorzeny that, 'Should the mission fail, I'll just say that it was carried out by hotheads acting without orders. I will disassociate myself from them just as I did from deputy Rudolf Hess when his operation failed.'

And that is exactly what had happened. Hitler had effectively 'disassociated' himself. There was sufficient confusion surrounding the flight to make the truth uncertain. Precisely the desired outcome.

Lastly, Hitler felt the need to reassure Stalin that the Hess affair affected their relationship. Stalin of course had already made his mind up as to what the flight meant but the Führer arranged for the delivery of a letter, the authenticity of which is still questioned. We reproduce the same below.

> Dear Mr Stalin,
> I am writing this letter at the moment of having finally concluded that it will be impossible to achieve a lasting peace in Europe not for us not for future generations without the final shattering of England and her destruction as a state. As you well know, I long ago made the decision to carry out a series of military measures to achieve this goal.
>
> The closer the hour of a decisive battle, however, the larger the number of problems I face. For the mass of the German people, no war is popular, especially not a war against England, because the German people consider the English a fraternal people and war between them a tragic event. I will not conceal that I have felt the same way and have several times offered England humane peace terms, taking into consideration England's military situation. However, insulting replies to my peace proposals and the continuing expansion by the English of the field of military operations with the obvious intention of drawing the entire world into war persuade me that there is no other way out of this situation except for an invasion of the Isles and the decisive destruction of that country.
>
> ... In order to organise troops for the invasion away from the eyes of the English opponent, and in connection with the recent operations in the Balkans, a large number of my troops, about eighty divisions, are located on the borders of the Soviet Union. This possibly gave rise to the rumours now circulating of a likely military conflict between us.
>
> I assure you, on my honour as a chief of state, that this is not the case.

From my side, I also react with understanding to the fact that you cannot completely ignore these rumours and have also deployed a sufficient number of your troops on the border.

In this situation I cannot completely exclude the possibility of an accidental outbreak of armed conflict, which given the conditions created by such a concentration of troops might take on very large dimensions, making it difficult if not impossible to determine what caused it in the first place.

I want to be absolutely candid with you.

I fear that some one of my generals might deliberately embark on such a conflict in order to save England from its fate and spoil my plans.

It is a question of no more than a month.

By approximately 15–20 June I plan to begin a massive transfer of troops to the west from your borders. In connection with this, I ask you, as persuasively as possible, not to give in to any provocations that might emanate from those of my generals who might have forgotten their duty. And, it goes without saying, try not to give them any cause. If it becomes impossible to avoid provocation by some of my generals, I ask you to show restraint, to not respond but to advise me immediately of what has happened through the channel known to you. Only in this way can we attain our mutual goals, on which, it seems to me, we are clearly in agreement.

I thank you for having agreed with me on the question known to you and I ask you to forgive me for the method I have chosen for delivering this letter to you as quickly as possible.

I continue to hope for our meeting in July.

Sincerely yours,
Adolf Hitler

Britain

The position in Britain was perhaps even more convoluted. The Deputy Führer of Germany had just arrived in the country, just as Winston Churchill was apparently spending the weekend in the company of leading Americans at Ditchley Park, Oxfordshire. The only plausible strategy that Churchill had at the time was to court the US and Roosevelt, who in turn were still under significant pressure from the isolationists in Congress.

Why therefore should America come to the aid of Britain, if they in turn were contemplating negotiations with Nazi Germany? Hess's arrival, if handled badly, had the ability to completely scupper Churchill's one and only realistic diplomatic policy.

Even as far as courting America was concerned, Britain was on far from a firm footing. The 1934 Johnson Act in the US had made clear that any war materiel could only be acquired on a 'cash and carry' basis, as there were still outstanding British loans from the First World War due to America. At the same time, the American Army Chief of Staff, George C. Marshall was anticipating a British surrender after May 1940 and so was fighting the release of further weaponry to Europe.

However, there had recently been two major concessions. On 2 September 1940, a 'Destroyers for Bases' deal had been signed and this was followed by the Lend Lease Act, formulated on 17 December 1940. The latter, whilst vitally important to Britain, was actually a brilliant compromise. There were thirty countries who eventually benefitted from 'Lend Lease', certainly not just Britain. In total some $50 billion was pledged and it was a typically isolationist and pragmatic approach. Lend money to and make money from those who would then try to win the war without American lives being put at risk. Good politically, good for business.

By contrast, Churchill just wanted to 'get them in', but so far there had not been the pretext. Consequently, how he was to handle Hess would potentially be vital to the future 'special relationship' that had not as yet even been christened as such.[3] This was to manifest itself in two ways:

1. Press and Parliament statements

From reading the Cadogan diaries in particular, it is quite clear that there was an initial difference in opinion between Churchill and the Foreign Office as to how the affair should be handled. Churchill's suggestion (backed by Duff Cooper) was to respond to what Hess had said about peace, but Cadogan and Eden simply favoured saying nothing apart from the known facts, so as to leave everyone (Germans, Americans and Russians included) guessing. Cadogan's fear was that if Churchill tried to rebut peace proposals, or even acknowledge peace proposals, it would inadvertently validate the German statement of 12 May and allow the German population en masse to 'understand' the actions of *gute Rudolf*, their Deputy Führer. Instead, by saying nothing, the British, German, American and Russian populations were all kept guessing (for at least the following eighty years). A very clever strategy indeed in our view.

2. Letter to Roosevelt

Given the import of the Anglo-American relationship, it was only natural that Churchill would soon write to Roosevelt concerning the Hess affair. This he did on 17 May, the subsequent weekend to the Hess flight. In the letter, there is absolutely no explanation as to the events leading up to the flight, just a report of what Hess was reported to have said on arrival (essentially, a précised version of the Kirkpatrick conversations in Scotland).

The nearest Churchill came to reporting what happened was the sentence, 'If he is to be believed, he expected to contact members of a "peace movement" in England, which he would help to oust the present Government. If he is honest and if he is sane this is an encouraging sign of the ineptitude of the German Intelligence Services.'

This would infer that the German Intelligence Services were wrong about the 'peace movement'. Please note there is no mention of Tancred Borenius or the fact that Britain had sent the Finnish diplomat/art historian specifically to ascertain the likelihood of peace and to establish channels to facilitate the same earlier that spring. Instead, Churchill quite accurately records, 'Here we think it best to let the Press have a good run for a bit and keep the Germans guessing.'

This is where the internal and external statements come together. Let the press speculate what happened, so that the government cannot be implicated in Anglo-German peace negotiations, exactly like those that had been instigated and acted upon from January 1941.

It was no wonder that Churchill had disintegrated into a 'raging temper' when debating the response on 14 May. The response was of fundamental importance to his medium-term policy and political survival. Contrast this with the much later, 'I never attached any serious importance to this escapade,' as related in his post-war history of the Second World War. This is obviously a crass and inaccurate remark, yet again designed to obfuscate.

Thereafter, for the rest of his Hess's life the policy was one of news containment, simply to prevent the fact that Britain had approached and courted Hess in equal measure, rather than vice-versa. There were various 'flash points'. The Duke of Hamilton launched a legal action against the secretary of the Communist Party, Harry Pollitt, following the publication of a pamphlet, 'Why is Hess here?' in 1941. The Duke of Hamilton was later refused leave to travel to America in 1945, for fear of what he might say, and Stafford Cripps had to prepare a pre-agreed government statement, ready for when he travelled to meet Stalin in 1942.

Cripps was mindful as, 'I was asked to get out a note on the Hess incident of the kind that might possibly be shown to the Russians, or, if necessary, even published here.' The inference being that the note as prepared was adequate for the Russians but may not be whole truth.

The Allies won the war and chose Nuremberg as a venue to take their legal revenge. The treatment and handling of Rudolf Hess must have been a significant challenge to those responsible for safeguarding the fact that the Hess flight was in part a response to a British initiative. Whilst in Scotland, Mytchett and Abergavenny, Hess had been listened to, bugged and interrogated, but he was certainly canny enough not to have disclosed anything that should not have been disclosed. The stock phrase, 'I don't remember,' was a convenient deflector whenever the inquisitor came too close to a subject that Hess did not wish to talk about. Consequently, the thought of amnesia started to perhaps come into his mind as a more substantial future defence should the need arise. There was already a history of mental illness and suicide in the Hess family, of which both Hess and his captors would have been aware.

The British Secret Service was meanwhile carefully monitoring letters, newspapers and radio broadcasts for intelligence pertaining to the Hess affair. Most of this is currently released in TNA File KV2/34. In particular, a central department report, number 225, details reactions in overseas countries.

In Buenos Airies, for example, 'At a meeting of Nazi Officials, a message was received from the German Ambassador stating that it was neither a case of desertion, nor of misunderstanding with Hitler, nor of a break-up of the Nazi party. He said that Hess's arrival in part of Scotland was due to the furtherance of a plan which had taken an unfortunate turn as a result of the capture of Hess.'

This again we believe to be wholly true.

Subsequent Captivity and Nuremberg

Hess was moved from Scotland on 16 May, the Friday after his flight. He was first transferred to the Tower of London and thence to Mytchett Place, near Aldershot, Surrey on 20 May, arriving at 5.45pm. He was placed in the charge of Messrs Arnold-Baker, Foley and Kendrick, all very accomplished MI6 officers. (Arnold-Baker was born in Prussia, and his true identity was kept a secret for some 60 years, simply being known as Captain Barnes.)

On 26 June 1942 he was transferred to Maindiff Court, Abergavenny,

Mytchett Place

Maindiff Court, Abergavenny

a former admission clinic to the County Mental Hospital. Hess arrived at 3.45pm in the afternoon. There have been subsequent reports of threats and attempts on his life whilst at Mytchett and they are usually cited as being the reason for Hess then being moved to Wales.

Hess eventually left Wales, flying from Madley airfield near Hereford on the morning of 8 October 1945. The plane flew directly to Fürth airfield, adjacent to Nuremberg, Germany. By contrast, Major Kelley[4] details Hess's arrival in Nuremberg to be on the evening of 10 October 1945.[5]

Consequently, simple arithmetic demonstrates that Hess was held captive in Britain for four years and 151 days. During that time, he was generally treated and behaved as one might expect. He was 'bugged', he was moody, he was interviewed by two ministers, Sir John Simon and Lord Beaverbrook, his behaviour and every comment were recorded. At times he was depressed and amnesic; at other times not. He attempted suicide twice. He accused his guarders of being poisoners. He liked Frank Foley, the MI6 Passport Officer in pre-war Berlin. He disliked any guards responsible for making sudden noises.

There are several good and very detailed books which deal with this part of the story, in particular David Irving's *Hess: The Missing Years 1941–1945*.

However, we now wish to specifically address the British use of drugs on their captive.

On 7 May 1944, J.R. Rees, in *The Case of Rudolf Hess*[6] openly records the British administering the drugs Sodium Evipan and Coramine, seemingly whilst Hess was asleep.[7]

By his own admission, Hess had tried to use amnesia as a means of escape: 'After the one-and-a-half-year long pretence of having lost my memory, it had not effected the desired repatriation.'[8]

So, the British took steps to treat him with the aforementioned medicines. Seemingly with his permission. Not surprisingly, they had little effect on Hess because a) much of the amnesia was feigned and b) the drugs, Evipan and Coramine have been subsequently discredited and are now described as potentially dangerous. Sodium Evipan is now known to reduce blood pressure, but both were relatively new compounds in 1944 and at that time their full effects unknown.[9]

(Evipan was a Bayer brand narcotic and was used to euthanise in various German concentration camps.)

The major impact of the treatment, not surprisingly, appears to have reinforced Hess's distrust of all foreign substances introduced into his system (a recurring theme throughout his captivity) and one very easy to understand given a) the choice of drugs and their likelihood of success and b) Hess's well-known tendencies and preference towards alternative cures over those of conventional medicines. From the research we have undertaken, this seems to be a medical area that was still in its formative stages and Hess inadvertently became a semi-willing guinea pig in a very untried and untested area of medicine.

In the past, the authors of Double Standards and Hugh Thomas have alleged that the Hess in Maindiff Court was not the Hess that arrived in Scotland (or had taken off from Augsburg, in Thomas's case). We are afraid to say that both theories are nonsense. Complete nonsense. A careful reading of the available source evidence would demonstrate to our satisfaction that the character traits demonstrated by Hess whilst in captivity are wholly consistent with our understanding of his character prior to making his flight. Moreover, there is simply no credible evidence to support either alternative theory, save perhaps a large dose of wishful thinking. *Double Standards*' authors base their case on Hess being subsequently imprisoned in Scotland, not Wales (no evidence) and Hugh Thomas on the basis of a doppelgänger inserted somewhere between Augsburg and Eaglesham (no evidence, plus much conjecture).

In 2015, John and Ann Harris travelled to Munich to meet Wolf Hess, Wolf's son. Over a pleasant lunch in the Löwenbräukeller, Wolf Jr explained (again, in perfect English) that DNA swabs had been taken from Wunsiedel when his grandfather was exhumed in 2011 and compared to another 'family member' (we suspect Wolf Jr). The DNA matched, thus proving that the Spandau Hess was the Hess that flew in 1941. Subsequently, these findings have also come under scrutiny,[10] but we are content that they are still valid and categoric.

Churchill had placed Hess under the responsibility of MI6 in 1941, with the orders that he should be treated as a 'prisoner of war … whose ultimate fate must … be reserved for the decision of the Allied nations when the victory has been won'.[11] That time had now arrived. Surely under legal cross-examination the truth as to why Hess flew to Scotland in 1941 would become clear.

Nuremberg and Spandau

In connection with matters pertaining to Nuremberg and Rudolf Hess, much has been written. Hess arrived in the decimated city on either 8 or 10 October 1945, dependent upon who the reader chooses to believe.

On 16 October 1946, just over a year later, death sentences were carried out on those so condemned by the process, although Hermann Göring had taken his own life the night before and Martin Bormann, whilst tried in absentia, was at the time still of whereabouts unknown.

The remaining German defendants were released into the western sectors of occupied Germany or detained in Nuremberg until their eventual prison in Spandau, Berlin had been made ready. There were to be seven inmates it total, with Hess being numbered seven. After the arrangements had been made, the men were transferred to their new abode on 18 July 1947.

Hess was never to leave Berlin, dying there on 17 August 1987, just over forty years later. From 30 September 1966 to the date of his death, he was to become the sole inmate of the Prussian prison, originally designed to hold 600.

In this connection, the following works are usually cited when discussing the later period of Hess's life:

The many works on the Nuremberg Trials (*Tusa, James Owen, 'The Avalon Project'*)
Such correspondence as has been allowed to be published (Primarily from *Ilse Hess: 'Prisoner of Peace'*)
David Irving, *Hess: The Missing Years 1941–1945*, Focal Point, Windsor, 2010.
Eugene Bird, *The Loneliest Man in the World*, Sphere, London, 1976.
J.R. Rees, *The Case of Rudolf Hess*, Heinemann, London, 1947.
Desmond Zwar, *Talking to Rudolf Hess*, The History Press, Stroud, 2010.
Wolf Hess, *My Father Rudolf Hess*, WH Allen, London, 1986.

All these books are fine in their own way and tell us much about Hess during this period of captivity. Some explore his psyche, while others tell us things we would perhaps rather not know (for instance, his masturbatory habits and his reactions to wet dreams). The year-long Nuremberg Trials have been analysed, detailed and recorded for posterity. The transcripts are posted on the internet for all to see and read. Eugene Bird's book gives a good description of the conditions in Spandau. The J.R. Rees book is perhaps the most interesting in terms of detail, but there is one common denominator they all share.

Absolutely no detailed explanation is given as to why Rudolf Hess flew to Scotland in 1941.

The name 'Tancred Borenius' does not even appear in the index or text of any of the above works.

There is clearly some detail that it was assumed that Hess knew that someone wished to remain secret. When it was discovered that Eugene Bird had been talking to Hess in the late 1960s and a book was potentially in the offing, 'I was then interrogated for several hours. I was allowed to go home but placed under house arrest. My house was kept under 24-hour surveillance, my phone was tapped, and a team of officers came and made a thorough search of every room. They took away documents, letters, photographs and negatives dating back to 1934.'

Desmond Zwar, Bird's collaborator, in the meanwhile had moved away to Cairns, in Northern Australia. His wife one day had, '… walked into our large dingy cellar under the house, at Stratford, a fairly remote spot, 8 km from the city – and she had found two men there; one wearing mirror sunglasses, who spoke to her in an American accent.'

In other words, in the only potential security breach since 10 May 1941, the powers to be (CIA, in this instance) had moved extremely quickly and effectively to regain their absolute control of Rudolf Hess. The above example has been cited so as to demonstrate the seriousness with which the matter was taken in the 1970s when Hess was of course still alive.

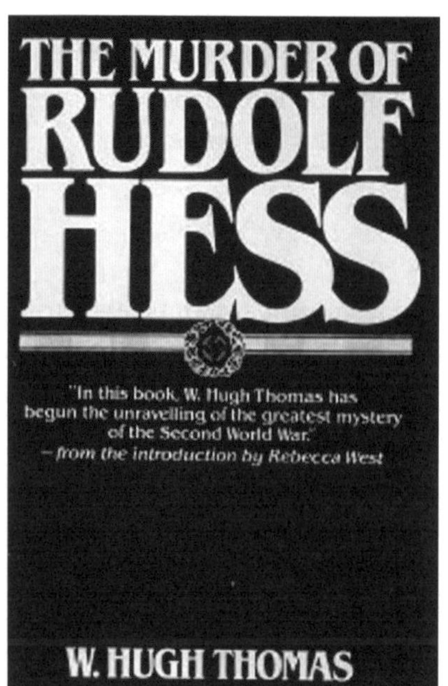

THE MURDER OF
RUDOLF
HESS
"In this book, W. Hugh Thomas has begun the unravelling of the greatest mystery of the Second World War."
– from the introduction by Rebecca West
W. HUGH THOMAS

The Hugh Thomas book

Again, in the 1970s Hugh Thomas made the doppelgänger accusation in his book, *The Murder of Rudolf Hess*. In hindsight we are not wholly sure why this was given too much credence because the medical report dated 30 May 1941 clearly records, 'He told me about the chest wound in the last war…' and the medical report at Nuremberg dated 10 November 1945 clearly states, 'Two well healed linear scars 1/8" apart are present over the sixth left rib, two inches from the lateral margin of the sternum.'

These reports both come from the

J.R. Rees book, published in 1947, well before Hugh Thomas's apparent revelations and unanticipated challenge. However, notwithstanding the available evidence, such was the public interest that a question was later asked in the House of Commons.[12]

There is also the matter of Hess's death. Was it murder or suicide? Was this ultimate sanction executed as a means of keeping Hess quiet, just as it appeared that the Russians might be prepared to allow a release, presumably as part of their Perestroika initiative or, more likely, a forced Russian cost-saving measure? We do not have a view in this regard, not having fully researched the issue. We do know, however, that the family believe the death to be a murder and have recently undertaken tests of the so-called suicide note.[13]

This document we now consider to be a forgery.

So, from 1941 to 1987 Rudolf Hess was micro-managed and micro-controlled, even quite possibly up to the point of and timing of his death. Consequently, we would now wish to concentrate on the only time since 4 May 1941,[14] that Hess once again came under the scrutiny of the public and the world in general. That time was of course his extraordinary appearance at Nuremberg, where it appeared only reasonable to hope that surely the truth must emerge.

Equally, if, as we suggest above, Hess was being totally controlled, so as to prevent the truth emerging, how would or indeed could this control manifest itself whilst under the gaze of the eyes of the world?

Nuremberg – the legal position

Looking back at Nuremberg over seventy years later, one is tempted to conclude that Rudolf Hess managed to reduce his case to a complex legal argument that had the net effect of not allowing any detailed discussion of the facts in relation to his flight, but rather encourage a descent into a detailed discussion of his mental state and possible amnesia. On one very basic, yet vital level, the strategy worked: he was not hanged.

The Nuremberg Trials were based on a set of principles enshrined in the London Charter, signed by the four participating nations in August 1945. This in turn had in the main come from the 1943 Moscow Conference that had discussed, in part, post-war reconstruction and judicial sanction. By contrast, Winston Churchill had merely suggested a summary execution of the leading Nazis without any trial. Thankfully, he was eventually persuaded otherwise.

Consequently, at Nuremberg there was an inevitable amount of hypocrisy,

The defendants at Nuremberg-L-R: Hermann Göring, Rudolf Hess and Karl Dönitz

a degree of 'law on the hoof' and certainly a dose of well intentioned 'victor's history" Nowhere was this more self-evident than in the case of Rudolf Hess. The whole Nuremberg process was based on a 'collective presentation of guilt', with films being shown of Nazi atrocities as an integral part of the prosecution. However, there were twenty-three defendants from all parts of the Nazi state and the implied inference was that each was therefore a part of what was being shown, as indeed theoretically they were. It was essentially an efficient system of 'trial en masse', law in bulk.

The individual defendant had the chance to defend himself and then make a closing statement.

However, in Rudolf Hess's case, the first issue/hurdle was whether he was fit even to stand trial. Hess's defence counsel, Dr Gunther von Rohrscheidt, was obviously alert to the possibility of absolving his client from even that necessity. Consequently, the first debate was whether Hess was even 'legally fit' to stand trial.

In the UK the law was reasonably well developed in this area. The 'Prichard case' in 1836 had implied that if the defendant was not able to understand what he was being tried for, there would instead be a 'trial of the facts', i.e. did the defendant commit the act, rather than did he know what he was doing? Was he *fit* to stand trial, rather than be *able* to stand trial? This was the proposed legal treatment for Greville Janner MP in 2016, before he inconveniently died in 2015.

We suspect that the tribunal had anticipated this line of defence and had already ordered four independent psychiatric reports. These were dated as such:

Russia and France: 17 November 1945
UK: 19 November 1945
US: 20 November 1945

Each report was clear. Hess was not insane.

However, in British legal terms this was still not enough. The reports unanimously demonstrated that Hess was *able*, a fact that was cited throughout the trial, but that in itself did not necessarily prove he was *fit*. If the trial had been held in Britain, it is most likely that the Hess trial would not have gone any further and that would have ended the matter for him. Hess would have been silenced once and for all. If so deemed and he was not able to stand trial, he would have been either incarcerated until he was deemed fit, or perhaps more likely, suffer just the same fate as Tancred Borenius and be locked away.

Given a British interpretation of the law, Hess would have at best stood trial for an 'interpretation of the facts'. If then found guilty, he would have been placed into care if deemed a danger to others. There was a long precedent in English case law, going back to 1836.

Unfortunately for von Rohrscheidt, the Tribunal was not wholly mindful of English case law. This was because a) it was not technically an English trial and b) not surprisingly, there seemed to be an overarching need for revenge and the pound of flesh and c) and most perhaps most honourably, Rudolf Hess wanted to be tried and said so.

To be blunt, Hess had been devious at best, ever since 1941. He had first feigned amnesia when he wanted to be repatriated to Switzerland during the war and saw this device to be the best method of achieving his goal. It appears that at times even he was not sure if he was amnesiac. His defence even suggested that he feigned amnesia to disguise the fact that he had actually been amnesiac, which of course was possible. In Nazi Germany and the subsequent trial, open displays of weakness were not allowed. The truth was that in Hess's mind, no one knew the full truth – quite possibly Hess included. He had foxed the experts. Completely. On 30 November he admitted that he was fit to stand trial and his memory had returned. The timing of this admission was, however, interesting. The self-admission was only made when it appeared that the von Rohrscheidt appeal was not succeeding.

> Mr President, I would like to say this: At the beginning of the trial of this afternoon's proceedings I gave my defence counsel a note that I am of the opinion that these proceedings could be shortened if one would allow me to speak myself. What I say is as follows:
>
> In order to anticipate any possibility of my being declared incapable of pleading, although I am willing to take part in the rest of the proceedings with the rest of them, I would like to give the Tribunal the following declaration, although I originally intended not to make this declaration until a later point in the proceedings:
>
> My memory is again in order. The reasons why I simulated loss of memory were tactical. In fact, it is only that my capacity for concentration is slightly reduced. But, in consequence of that, my capacity to follow the trial, my capacity to defend myself, to put questions to witnesses or even to answer questions – these, my capacities are not influenced by that.
>
> I emphasise the fact that I bear the full responsibility for everything that I have done or signed as signatory or co-signatory. My attitude, in principle, is that the Tribunal is not competent – is not affected by the statement I have just made. Hitherto in conversations with my official defence counsel I have maintained my loss of memory. He was, therefore in good faith when he asserted, I lost my memory.

However, we are not convinced that even that explanation and confession was necessarily that straightforward. As expected, the psychiatrists and the world press had a field day. It may of course be the case that Hess, although impaired, had just lied again and he had suffered amnesia and had not feigned. Who knows? The outcome of the confession was that Hess was adjudged fit to stand trial and to face the consequences of his actions. However, the 'legal water' had certainly been muddied. Interestingly, and by stark comparison, Wolf Hess certainly plays down the claim of amnesia. In his 1984 book, the amnesia is seen very much and described as a device, not an actual illness. Given the fact that the family did eventually meet Hess and were therefore in a position to judge, we believe the disparity of views to be very telling. It is almost as if the British wished it to be known that Hess was going or had gone mad. They certainly did not deter J.R. Rees from publishing his work as early as 1947 – easily the earliest book on Hess to be published.

Subsequent to the revelation on 30 November 1945, it was naturally assumed that Hess had regained normality. Accusations of his 'malingering' and 'dishonourable conduct' were actively debated amongst the other Nazi defendants, but interestingly and tellingly, there was never any debate as to whether the Rudolf Hess, who sat next to Hermann Göring, was actually the Rudolf Hess that they had all known and interacted with since the early 1920s. That was not the issue. They all knew it was Hess. There was no doubt as far as they were concerned; it was his behaviour that was causing the concern and whether indeed it was honourable.

On 5 February 1946, whilst the prosecution was presenting its evidence, to our eyes another strange occurrence took place. Mid-stream Hess changed counsel to Alfred Seidl. Gunther von Rohrscheidt had originally been allocated to Hess by the tribunal and Wolf Hess explains the change to Seidl as being due to a) Seidl was Munich-based and b) there had been no 'relationship of trust' between Hess and von Rohrscheidt. The latter explanation we can wholly understand, particularly if the client (Hess) was not even prepared to tell his counsel if he was feigning insanity or not. A not inconsiderable hurdle to the establishment of trust. However, von Rohrscheidt was also in hospital with a broken ankle. Seidl was already representing Hans Frank and had been given covertly, by an American Officer, a copy of the secret protocol of the Molotov-Ribbentrop Pact that was deadly regarding the Russian position at Nuremberg.

Clearly, Hess did care about what was happening to him, despite his protestations and behaviour. Else why bother to change counsel in the middle of a trial? It could of course be the case that von Rohrscheidt had decided that he could no longer act for a man whom he was unable to trust, but nonetheless the change does appear somewhat odd, given that it was done in the knowledge that the next stage of the process would be Hess's handling of the response to the prosecution which duly took place on the afternoon of 7 February 1946. Hess did not speak and the case for the tribunal was made by Mervyn Griffith-Jones, the junior British counsel.

Griffith-Jones made a very understandable case that Hess, given the position that he was in, knew of all the major decisions that had been made. The usual version of events was then duly supplied in connection with the flight on 10 May 1941; Hess had been flying to meet the Duke of Hamilton (it was actually stated that they *had* met at the Olympics in 1936). Thereafter, the intention was to forge a peace.

Needless to say, in the prosecution (which interestingly was originally going to be presented by the Americans) there was absolutely no mention of Burckhardt or Borenius, or the Hess initiative of September 1940. Essentially only half the truth of the affair was being presented to the court and the world at large.

After Hess's revelation that he had recovered his memory, it was assumed that all was well and he would be able to speak, but again, as the time came closer for him to defend his actions, the memory loss perhaps conveniently appeared to start to recur.

Consequently, when Alfred Seidl commenced the defence of his client on 25 March 1946, the first thing he said to the court was that Hess would not take any part in his defence personally on the basis that he did not recognise the court. Seidl reported, 'The defendant Hess contests the jurisdiction of the tribunal where other than war crimes proper are the subject of the trial.'

Seidl was, we suspect, cannier than von Rohrscheidt and it is clear from Wolf Hess that Seidl won the trust of his client through his attempt to challenge the validity of the tribunal as a whole. An echo of Hess's thinking. Indeed, Wolf Hess spends a complete chapter explaining its invalidity and precisely why the Russians, in particular, should never have played a part. This clearly appealed to the increasingly awkward Hess, who his son details making very perceptive comments and listing points of detail, by contrast to the 'growing dementia' keenly described by Rees. Seidl was probably quite aware of the impact that Hess had made already and perhaps wondered about the tribunal's appetite for hanging a man who had already made a good and convincing demonstration of the onset of insanity. Perhaps Hess did not need to say anything else and indeed, were he to do so and appear cogent, his fate would then be terminally sealed.

So, Seidl then continued the defence through the 'document pack' that each defendant had prepared in advance of their 'defence slot'. When it came to the flight and his motives, Seidl simply quoted from the Hess/Simon meeting of 10 June 1941, without of course making the point that by the time of the meeting Hess knew that his mission had failed and was simply telling Simon what he wanted to hear. It certainly did not deal with the reasons for Hess making his flight.

Thereafter, Ernst Bohle was brought in as a witness, in an attempt to prove that the Auslands Organisation, of which Hess had been the head, was a potential world-wide Fifth Column. In any event, Hess had mounted a defence and had certainly not managed to describe the true sequence of events in the lead up to his flight.

By the time the defence cases came to an end in June 1946 Hess had completely, 'Reverted to the withdrawn, apathetic state with total amnesia in which he came to Nuremberg…' According to Rees, Wolf Hess reported that his father was allowed to remain seated when he made his final statement, 'Because of his weakened state of health…'

Certainly, the letters that were published by Ilse Hess in this period show no mental deficiency, whatsoever. Indeed, most are quite intimate and touching, and written in a cogent, lucid manner. Hess also takes some important decisions for the future; most notably not to receive his family before the judgement is made.

As Hess recorded in his letter to Ilse of 31 August, 'They may tell you I have lost my reason; or at least suffer from fixed ideas. I hope you will see the humorous side of this also.'

Hess was convicted as being guilty on two of the four counts on which he was charged. He was awarded a sentence of life imprisonment, the same sentence as Walther Funk (guilty on three out of four counts) and Erich Raeder (guilty on three out of four counts).

Neither of the other two men served their life sentence. Raeder was released in September 1955 (dying in 1960) and Funk was released in May 1957 (also dying in late 1960).

There seemed little logic to the sentencing. As James Owen records,[15] 'The judges' verdicts surprised nearly everyone in court … many of the sentences were, to say the least, perplexing.'

Throughout the trial Hess had been consistent in that he would still not accept any treatment for the amnesia that he was at times claiming and at other times in equal measure denying. J.R. Rees, in his *Case of Rudolf Hess*, stipulated the drugs that he would have prescribed had Hess allowed sodium pentathlon and sodium amytal, which he described as, 'The ordinary sedative that you perhaps take on a sleepless night.'

It is perhaps as well that Rees is not prescribing today, as a review of the barbiturates concerned reveal that they are used as truth serums and, in some cases, used as lethal injections. However, if Rees is to be believed, there is no evidence that Hess ever allowed them to be used on him during the trial (Rees received an OBE shortly afterwards). It is, however, well recorded that he was administered with 5.5cc of Sodium Evipan on 7 May 1944 whilst at Maindiff.

Hess's final statement and drug use

30 August 1946 saw the defendants make their final statements. By his behaviour to date, Hess had probably done enough to cast doubt over his mental capacity. Surely the Allies would not execute a man so clearly in difficulties? However, if there was any doubt as to Hess's true state of mind, the final statement erased it. On review though, seventy-six years later, we wonder if there is actually more to it than it appears at face value? We believe it was not actually necessary for Hess to have said anything at the stage the trial had reached. What he said was interesting, but rambling, probably as he had been advised. It is transcribed below in full:

> RUDOLF HESS (Defendant): 'First of all, I should like to make a request to the High Tribunal that I may remain seated because of my state of health.
>
> THE PRESIDENT: Certainly.
>
> HESS: Some of my comrades here can confirm the fact that at the beginning of the proceedings I predicted the following:
>
> 1. That witnesses would appear who, under oath, would make untrue statements while, at the same time, these witnesses could create an absolutely reliable impression and enjoy the best possible reputation.
> 2. That it was to be reckoned with that the Court would receive affidavits containing untrue statements.
> 3. That the defendants would be astonished and surprised at some German witnesses.
> 4. That some of the defendants would act rather strangely: they would make shameless utterances about the Führer; they would incriminate their own people; they would partially incriminate each other, and falsely at that. Perhaps they would even incriminate themselves, and also wrongly.

All of these predictions have come true, and as far as the witnesses and affidavits are concerned, in dozens of cases; cases in which the unequivocal oath of the defendants stands in opposition to the sworn statements of the former.

In this connection I shall only mention the name Messersmith: Mr. Messersmith, who, for example, says that he spoke to Admiral Doenitz at a time when the latter was, to my knowledge, in the Pacific Ocean or the Indian Ocean.

I made these predictions, however, not only here at the beginning of the Trial, but had already made them months before the beginning of the Trial in England to, among others, Dr Johnston, the physician who was with me in Abergavenny.

At the same time, I put these statements down in writing, as proof. I base my predictions on some events in countries outside of Germany. In this connection I should like to emphasize now that, while I mention these incidents, I was convinced from the beginning that the governments concerned knew nothing about them. Therefore, I am not raising any accusation against these governments.

In the years 1936 to 1938 political trials were taking place in one of these countries. These were characterized by the fact that the defendants accused themselves in an astonishing way. For example, they cited great numbers of crimes which they had committed or which they claimed to have committed. At the end, when death sentences were passed upon them, they clapped in frenzied approval to the astonishment of the world.

But some foreign press correspondents reported that one had the impression that these defendants, through some means hitherto unknown, had been put into an abnormal state of mind, as a result of which they acted the way they did.

These incidents were recalled to my mind by a certain happening in England. There it was not possible for me to get the reports of the trials at that time, any more than here. However, the corresponding years of the Voelkischer Beobachter were at my disposal there. While looking through these numbers I came upon the following passage in the number of 8 March 1933.

A report from Paris dated 7 March 1938 reads as follows:

> 'The big Paris newspaper *Le Jour* made revelations about the means which were apparently used in these trials. These are rather mysterious means.'

I quote literally what the Voelkischer Beobachter reprinted from *Le Jour*:

> 'These means make it possible for the selected victims to be made to act and speak according to the orders given them.'

I emphasize and point out that this report in *Le Jour* not only says 'to make them speak according to orders given them', but also 'to make them act according to orders given them'. The latter point is of tremendous importance in connection with the actions, the hitherto inexplicable actions of the personnel in the German concentration camps, including the scientists and physicians who made these frightful and atrocious experiments on the prisoners, actions which normal human beings, especially physicians and scientists, could not possibly carry out.

But this is also of equally great significance in connection with the actions of the persons who undoubtedly gave the orders and directions for the atrocities in the concentration camps and who gave the orders for shooting prisoners of war and lynchings and other such things, up to the Führer himself.

I recall that the witness Field Marshal Milch testified here that he had the impression that the Führer was not normal mentally during the last years, and a number of my comrades here have told me, independently of each other and without having any knowledge of what I am saying here now, that during the last years the Führer's eyes and facial expression had something cruel in them, and even had a tendency towards madness. I can name the comrades in question as witnesses.

I said before that a certain incident in England caused me to think of the reports of the earlier trials. The reason was that the people around me during my imprisonment acted towards me in a peculiar and incomprehensible way, in a way which led me to conclude that these people somehow were acting in an abnormal state of mind. Some of them – these persons and people around me were changed from time to time. Some of the new ones who came to me in place of those who had been changed had strange eyes. They were glassy and like eyes in a dream. This symptom, however, lasted only a few days and then they made a completely normal impression. They could no longer be distinguished from normal human beings. Not only I alone noticed these strange eyes, but also the physician who attended me at the time, Johnston, a British Army doctor, a Scotsman.

In the spring of 1942 1 had a visitor, a visitor who quite obviously tried to provoke me and acted towards me in a strange way. This visitor also had these strange eyes. Afterwards, Dr Johnston asked me what I thought of this visitor. He told me – I told him I had the impression that for some reason or other he was not completely normal mentally, whereupon Dr Johnston did not protest, as I had expected, but agreed with me and asked me whether I had not noticed those strange eyes, these eyes with a dreamy look. Dr Johnston did not suspect that he himself had exactly the same eyes when he came to me.

The essential point, however, is that in one of the reports of the time, which must still be in the press files on the proceedings – this was in Paris, about the Moscow trial – it said that the defendants had had strange eyes. They had had glazed and dreamy eyes! I have already said that I am convinced that the governments here concerned knew nothing of these happenings. Therefore, it would not be in the interest of the British Government either if my statements about what I experienced during my imprisonment were denied publicity in any way, for that would give the impression that something was actually supposed to be concealed here, and that the British Government had actually had a finger in the pie.

On the contrary, however, I am convinced that both the Churchill Government and the present Government gave instructions that I was to be treated fairly and according to the rules of the Geneva Convention. I am conscious of the fact that what I have to say about the treatment which I received will at first glance appear incredible. Fortunately for me, however, prison guards at a very much earlier time had already treated their prisoners in a way which at first appeared absolutely incredible when the first rumours about it reached the outside world. These rumours were to the effect that prisoners had been deliberately allowed to starve to death, that ground glass, among other things, had been put in the meagre food which had been given them, that the physicians who attended the prisoners who had been taken sick in this way had added harmful substances to their medicine, which increased their sufferings and at the same time increased the number of victims. As a matter of fact, all of these rumours afterwards proved to be true. It is a historical fact that a monument was erected for 26,370 Boer women and children who died in British concentration camps, and who for the most part died of hunger. Many Englishmen at that time, among others, Lloyd George, protested strongly against these happenings in British concentration camps, and likewise an English eyewitness, Miss Emily Hopfords.

At that time the English people were confronted with an incomprehensible riddle, the same riddle which today confronts the German people with regard to the happenings in the German concentration camps. Indeed, at that time, the British Government itself was confronted with a riddle regarding the happenings in the South African concentration camps, with the same riddle which today confronts the members of the Reich Cabinet and the other defendants, here and in other trials, regarding the happenings in the German concentration camps.

Obviously, it would have been of the utmost importance if I had stated under oath what I have to say about the happenings during my own imprisonment in England. However, it was impossible for me to persuade my counsel to declare himself willing to put the proper questions to me. It was likewise impossible for me to get another counsel to agree to put these questions to me. But it is of the utmost importance that what I am saying be said under oath. Therefore, I now declare once more: I swear by God the Almighty and Omniscient, that I will speak the pure truth, that I shall leave out nothing and add nothing. I ask the High Tribunal, therefore, to consider everything which I shall say from now on as under oath. Concerning my oath, I should also like to say that I am not a churchgoer; I have no spiritual relationship with the Church, but I am a deeply religious person. I am convinced that my belief in God is stronger than that of most other people. I ask the High Tribunal to give all the more weight to everything which I declare under oath, expressly calling God as my witness.

> THE PRESIDENT [interposing]: I must draw the attention of the Defendant Hess to the fact that he has already spoken for 20 minutes, and the Tribunal has indicated to the defendants that it cannot allow them to continue to make statements of great length at this stage of the proceedings.
>
> We have to hear all the defendants. The Tribunal, therefore, hopes that the Defendant Hess will conclude his speech.
>
> HESS: Mr President, may I point out that I was taking into account the fact that I am the only defendant who, up to now, has not been able to make a statement here. For what I have to say here, I could only have said as a witness if the proper questions had been put to me. But as I have already stated …
>
> THE PRESIDENT: I do not propose to argue with the defendants. The Tribunal has made its order that the defendants shall only make short statements. The Defendant Hess had full opportunity to go into the witness box and give his evidence upon oath. He chose not to do so. He is now making a statement, and he will be treated like the other defendants and will be confined to a short statement.

HESS: Therefore, Mr President, I shall forego making the statements which I had wanted to make in connection with the things I have just said. I ask you to listen to only a few more concluding words, which are of a more general nature and have nothing to do with the things that I have just stated.

The statements which my counsel made in my name before the High Tribunal I permitted to be made for the sake of the future judgment of my people and of history. That is the only thing which matters to me. I do not defend myself against accusers to whom I deny the right to bring charges against me and my fellow-countrymen. I will not discuss accusations which concern things which are purely German matters and therefore of no concern to foreigners. I raise no protest against statements which are aimed at attacking my honour, the honour of the German people. I consider such slanderous attacks by the enemy as a proof of honour.

I was permitted to work for many years of my life under the greatest son whom my people has brought forth in its thousand-year history. Even if I could, I would not want to erase this period of time from my existence. I am happy to know that I have done my duty, to my people, my duty as a German, as a National Socialist, as a loyal follower of my Führer. I do not regret anything.

If I were to begin all over again, I would act just as I have acted, even if I knew that in the end I should meet a fiery death at the stake. No matter what human beings may do, I shall some day stand before the judgment seat of the Eternal. I shall answer to Him, and I know He will judge me innocent.

THE PRESIDENT: I call upon the Defendant Joachim von Ribbentrop.'

And so ended the last public oration that Rudolf Hess was ever to make. Thereafter he returned to subjection of the total control that had been exercised over him since the early morning of 11 May 1941.

An analysis of what he said would appear to show that he was trying to reinforce his new Counsel's approach in challenging the validity of the Tribunal itself. How could the Allies try the Germans for something similar to that which they had themselves been engaged in previously?

However, it is the analogy to the Russian show trials that warrant further analysis. In the early part of the twentieth century the compound scopoline had been used in the process of the extraction of information from criminals.

Sodium pentathol had been used in a similar way – one of the drugs that J.R. Rees had intimated that he would have used if Hess had given his permission.

Reading the diagnosis and case history that Rees so meticulously recorded in *The Case of Rudolf Hess*, one of the cited issues that Hess had to endure was constipation, a noted side effect of scopoline. We merely ask the reader to consider the premise that in making his rambling concluding statement that included religion, Russian show trials and, bizarrely, the inaccurate reference to whom we presume was meant to be Emily Hobhouse (1860–1926), we wonder if Hess was actually cleverly recording the fact that he too had been drugged, or at least suspected he had been drugged? Scopoline is often administered in powder form, just as Hess had referred to in the similarity to ground glass. Was his behaviour as a result of true amnesia or administered drugs? It is certainly not clear to us.

More importantly, however, the main reason that the finer details of the Hess flight did not emerge during the trial was that they were not in Hess's interest to reveal. He was too busy trying to paint the picture of insanity. Moreover, revealing embarrassing British secrets to the world would not presumably hold him in great stead when final sentencing was to be considered.

Consequently, that is why the truth did not emerge. Hess had embarked on a strategy of adopting insanity and so did not speak until the end of the trial when he was told to stsop talking after apparently 20 minutes. Hess's performances at Nuremberg were all about saving his skin, a feat which ultimately, he achieved.

Having done so, the priority then reverted back to making sure the flight details and their rationale were never revealed. Despite Zwar and Bird, that goal was also achieved. When Rudolf Hess died in August 1987, the name of Tancred Borenius, for instance, was still virtually unknown outside the rarefied worlds of art history and Finnish diplomacy. It was rarely, if ever, linked with that of Rudolf Hess.

---

1 *The Ulrich von Hassell Diaries*, Frontline, Barnsley, 2011 (18 May 1941).
2 Ibid.
3 First used in 1946 by Winston Churchill.
4 Douglas Kelley (1912-58). Chief psychiatrist at the Nuremberg War Trials.
5 J.R. Rees, *The Case of Rudolf Hess*, Heinemann, London, 1947.
6 Ibid.
7 Ibid.

[8] Ibid.
[9] S.C. Das, *The Influence of Sodium Evipan on the Heart and Circulation*, Department of Pharmacology, University of Edinburgh, 8 May 1941.
[10] Please see various editions of the *Lobster* magazine.
[11] TNA PREM 3 219/4.
[12] Written answer by Sir Ian Gilmour to Patrick McNair-Wilson – 23rd May 1979 as to the identity of the Spandau prisoner.
[13] John Harris/Wolf Hess meeting in Munich, 2015.
[14] Hess was last seen in his public role at the Reichstag speech in Berlin on 4 May. Thereafter he had retreated to Munich.
[15] James Owen, *Nuremberg, Evil on Trial*, Headline, London, 2006

CHAPTER 25

CARL BURCKHARDT TRIES TO CLEAR HIS NAME

At the end of the Second World War, it was not just former Nazi leaders who were on trial. Others, previously pleased to be associated with the former regime, were busy trying to destroy any incriminating evidence or prior connections. Anthony Blunt and Owen Morshead were detailed to travel to Germany specifically to pick up any British correspondence that could subsequently prove embarrassing. They headed straight for the Princes of Hesse. However, in the case of Carl Jacob Burckhardt, the diary of Ulrich von Hassell could not be much clearer:

3 February 1941

It is also significant that Prof. Carl Burckhardt, who is active in the Red Cross, looked me up in Geneva (30 January 1941) and gave me the following information for any purpose I might find for it (he was thinking primarily of [Ernst von] Weizsaeker): very recently the Finnish Art Historian, Prof. Borenius, who has lived in London for many years, came to him to explain, apparently at the behest of British Officials, that a reasonable peace could still be concluded...

(Please note, in particular, that Burckhardt 'looked' von Hassell up, i.e. he made a point of making contact, not vice versa. Please also note that Borenius is described as the 'Finnish Art Historian'.)

18 May 1941

Burckhardt told Ilse in Zurich that an agent of Himmler had approached him to enquire if Britain would perhaps make peace with Himmler instead of Hitler – new proof of the fragility of the Nazi structure.

(It would appear that the agent was Carl Langbehn, the lawyer and resistance activist, who had the misfortune to meet Heinrich Himmler at his daughter's birthday party.)[1]

Carl Burckhardt

In other words, in the spring of 1941, Carl Burckhardt was seen as the 'go to' man in terms of peace negotiation. First, by Borenius and secondly, by Himmler. This was not the first time either. In June 1940, Burckhardt had played an intermediate role between Rab Butler and Prince Hohenlohe.

There is also no doubt that Carl Jacob Burckhardt was involved in the Hess affair, certainly in so far as his role as 'first receiver' for the Borenius mission. This is without doubt, as it has been evidenced by the von Hassell diary in Germany and intimated at in the Cazalet diary and the minute book of the Polish Relief Fund in London. We also know that Albrecht Haushofer travelled to Geneva to meet Burckhardt on Monday 28 April 1941 and subsequently another meeting had been proposed in mid-May. Ulrich von Hassell's wife, Ilse, seems to have helped with the travel arrangements.

Whilst we have no reason to question his motives, although he was certainly suspected as having pro-German sympathies by the British, Burckhardt undoubtedly saw this as an opportunity to announce his arrival on the world stage, rather than merely the European.

Unfortunately, though, at the same time he was still closely connected with the International Red Cross, theoretically a non-partisan, non-political organisation, which relied greatly on those two criteria for its very existence. As the war years progressed, Burckhardt assumed greater responsibility within the organisation, eventually becoming its President from 1945 to 1948. It would perhaps be very embarrassing if later it was to become clear that in 1941 Carl Burckhardt was trying to broker a peace deal between an unbroken Germany and the West. He was also a noted anti-Communist.

Ostensibly an academic historian, he first came to international prominence as the final High Commissioner for the Free State of Danzig, from 1937 to 1 September 1939. Whilst in the virtually impossible role, (his Irish predecessor had wisely resigned), he not unnaturally came to know many of the leading personalities on both sides of the debate. His published book on the subject, *Meine Danziger Mission*, lists those that he became acquainted with, including Ribbentrop, Albert Forster and Weizsaeker on the German side, and Halifax and Duff Cooper representing Britain.

It may also be relevant to record that from 1938 he began an affair with Lady Diana Cooper, the wife of the wartime Minister of Information. In 1938 Duff Cooper was the first Lord of the Admiralty and, as such, had decided to embark on a Baltic cruise, making use of the naval yacht, *The Enchantress*.

Clearly the name of the ship had different connotations for the randy, yet discrete Swiss diplomat.

The itinerary was apparently Kiel – Gdynia – Gdansk – Helsinki – Stockholm – Copenhagen, but the cruise came to an abrupt end as the Munich crisis unfurled, with Duff Cooper eventually resigning as a consequence. However, the relationship between Diana and Burckhardt continued until late 1939, when he 'stood up' Diana in London. It was during this trip that he had met Tancred Borenius.[2]

The November 1941 visit to London

The only other time Burckhardt was recorded as being in London during the war was in November 1941, when quite extensive correspondence was entered into, supposedly to prevent him meeting persons of any particular influence. Eden was noted as having 'considerable misgivings. In view of his political ambitions and the possibility that he might put peace feelers on behalf of the Germans…'[3]

Consequently, he was chaperoned and sent off pheasant shooting, meeting Rab Butler, but no one any more senior. The discussion was apparently limited to talks 'concerning POWs' and it was recorded that Burckhardt was 'most sensible and helpful'.

However, we have managed to obtain the itinerary of the trip to London and Oxford, which lasted from 21 November to 20 December 1941. This gives a somewhat different impression.

Burckhardt stayed at the Athenaeum Club on Pall Mall and was granted an Honorary Membership. He had flown in and left via the Whitchurch–Sintra air route, and whilst he was in London he had met (amongst others):

Sir John Kennedy: Director of Military Planning (21 November)
Richard Law MP: Financial Secretary to the War Office
Lady Ampthill: Lady of Bedchamber to Queen Mary (26 November)
Sir Hans Fischer: Nobel Prize-winning scientist
Lady Churchill: (10 December)
Lord Harewood: A patron of Borenius (11 December)
Lady Granville: Former Head of Polish Relief Fund
General de Gaulle: (18 December)
Ivan Maisky: Russian Ambassador (20 December).

Surprisingly, there is no mention of Borenius. This omission will be debated in the concluding chapter of this book.

Nuremberg

It is probably fair to say that Burckhardt may have thought 'he had got away with it' by the time the Nuremberg Trials came around in late 1945. The trial started on 20 November and by that time Albrecht Haushofer, Hitler, Himmler, Heydrich, Langbehn and Ulrich von Hassell were dead. It was questionable if Hess was even fit to stand trial (so how reliable would his evidence be adjudged?) and poor Borenius, back in England, was struggling with his mental health in a Northampton sanatorium. The British government certainly would not wish to admit to early secret peace overtures, having just won the war, and so Carl Jacob Burckhardt perhaps felt a little confident of his earlier role not coming under too much scrutiny. On 1 April 1945, he had been appointed the President of the International Red Cross.

The first sign of trouble, however, came in early January 1946 when extracts of the Haushofer correspondence of September 1940 and Albrecht's report of 12 May 1941 first surfaced in America. Burckhardt's role was hinted at. In Britain, the *Western Morning News* of 8 January 1946 reported the news and the subsequent Foreign Office statement, which read, 'It may be stated at once that no person in a responsible position in this country ever took any initiative for the opening of negotiations with Germany in 1941…'

Clearly, the definition of 'a responsible position' requires further clarification. Why the need to say it? Does it not infer those persons *not in a responsible position* may have taken the initiative? Given that the government in power was now that of Clement Attlee and not that of Churchill, is this actually an admission that perhaps the action itself was not sanctioned by Churchill?

However, on 1 February 1946, the *Voix Ouvrière*, a left-wing Swiss French journal, went still further and reported on the role of Burckhardt as an intermediary between the belligerents in 1941. They, too, had picked up on the revelations from America. No sooner was the ink dry on the paper, on 4 February 1946 Burckhardt wrote very formally to Duff Cooper, who at that time was the recently appointed British Ambassador to Paris. At the time of the Hess affair, he had been the Minister of Information.

The letter made a number of unconvincing points:

1. Burckhardt did not believe the report (it came from Haushofer who had, of course, met him on 28 April 1941 in Geneva).
2. There was never any question of negotiations between anyone from the City of London (Samuel Hoare) or any other 'personalite Anglais' (Borenius was of course a Finn but had lived in London since around 1909).
3. It would be easy for the British government to say that 'someone else had done it'!
4. After returning from a trip to Berlin and Munich in August 1941, Burckhardt had made a report to David Kelly, the British Ambassador. '*C'est tout*'.
5. In November 1941, when he visited London, 'je n'ai point eu de conversation politique' (despite meeting Rab Butler and a trip to the Foreign Office). We have received a copy of the itinerary for this trip which was certainly potent in its Agenda.

Not surprisingly, Duff Cooper passed the letter on to London for a considered reply. Whilst close to Burckhardt (his wife was considerably closer), he too had seen the letter for what it was – nonsense. Burckhardt had probably done little wrong in principle, save backing the losing side. When Duff Cooper wrote to Ernest Bevin, the post-war Labour Foreign Secretary, he passed the somewhat ironic comment, 'I was not altogether astonished when I saw his name mentioned as a possible intermediary…'

More tellingly he adds, 'Nor do I see that a Swiss should be much, if at all blamed for having been willing to lend his services to the cause of peace, however much he may have misunderstood the real facts of the situation.'

This statement we think very, very important, as it surely reveals that the actual situation was not as it appeared: two belligerents wishing for a peaceful settlement. Given that at the time (1941) Duff Cooper was Minister of Information and on the night of 10 May 1941 was in the middle of the 'action' at Ditchley Park, we feel it very likely that he knew exactly what was going on and had been going on, hence being in a position to judge that Burckhardt had 'misunderstood the real facts…[4] Bevin was apparently also aware of the truth of the situation, and his precise role on the evening of 10 May 1941 remains unclear.

Needless to say, the Foreign Office made short work of the request by Duff Cooper for a question to be raised in the House of Commons so that a denial could be made. Any such denial, it was decided, 'would merely serve as fuel for a renewal of criticism'.

A comment in the file index card is also telling, 'I think M Burckhardt takes in M Duff Cooper. The former is somewhat of a "*faux bonhomme*" and is busy "trimming". We certainly should not go out of the way to defend him.'

There ends the matter. By his wartime actions and subsequent denials, Carl Burckhardt's reputation was undoubtedly damaged and he subsequently retreated back into academia, dying in 1974. In 1978, Michael Stettler, the curator of the Burckhardt archive compiled a very thick index indeed of the various documentary evidence then extant. Pages 101–104 deal solely with the issue of documents pertaining to '*Angeblichen Friendensverhanlungen* 1941'.[5] Of course he was involved, but by trying to be clever with semantics with those who knew the truth, he really did himself no favours at all. We will detail more precisely how he was involved in the concluding chapter.

---

1 Claus Langbehn, *Das Spiel des Verteidigers*, Lukas Verlag, Berlin, 2014.

2 Philip Ziegler, *Diana Cooper*, Hamish Hamilton, London, 1981.

3 Caroline Moorehead, *Dunant's Dream*, Harper Collins, London, 1998.

4 FO371/ 60508 / 664708.

5 University of Basel/Vinzel, 1978.

CHAPTER 26
A POSSIBLE COMMON DENOMINATOR?

At this stage of the debate, the real issue seems to us to be not 'Why did Hess fly?', but 'What had he been told to expect if he flew?'

Winston Churchill, writing much later stated, 'I never attached any serious importance to this escapade [as it] had no relation to the march of events.'[1]

That may well be a fair comment, given the benefit of a generous dose of hindsight, the fact that Britain had won the war and Churchill's eventual full knowledge of the Hess affair, but it does raise the obvious counter as to whether the 'march of events' to which he referred may well have been different, or indeed could have been different? That is the true conundrum. What precisely was Hess being told by Albrecht Haushofer and others?

We have addressed the issues that were 'pushing' Hess from Germany to Britain in Chapter 21. We now believe that the real reason that the mission has been shrouded in secrecy for so long is not 'Why did Hess fly?' but the details behind this second part of the conundrum. That is, what the British have kept quiet about since 1941 and have gone to extreme lengths to do so. Hence, 'What did Hess think might happen if he did?'

An Avro Anson, as used by HRH Prince George, the Duke of Kent

Ever since 1941, British Secret Service involvement has actively been denied and it is this denial that we have now chosen to question and investigate more closely. Clearly, this position is coming under ever closer scrutiny and is no longer tenable.

We have described the roles of Albrecht Haushofer and Tancred Borenius and have concluded that whilst they may or may not have been on the British Secret Service payroll, anyone who was prepared to send to the enemy detailed instructions and warnings as to their country's intentions must surely be capable of being designated as being a 'quasi agent' or 'informer' (or even a 'Finnish diplomat') at best. In earlier chapters we have also revisited the meticulously recorded September 1940 postal chain and concluded that Haushofer's actions do not altogether stand detailed scrutiny in this regard either.

Given the above, we must also at least query the truthfulness of what Haushofer was telling Hess as the climax of the flight came ever closer and wonder if what he was saying at least encouraged Hess still further, particularly if he was desperately looking for a reason and justification to fly. There is little or no doubt that Haushofer was not anticipating or expecting Hess to fly on 10 May (that is not to say he was not perhaps anticipating a later flight) and was devastated when he did, largely, we suspect, through the crystallisation of fear for his and his family's own future preservation. It is also interesting to note that whilst Hess chose Haushofer to conduct potential negotiations with Burckhardt, when it came to drafting his own peace terms he chose Ernst Bohle in Berlin rather than Haushofer. Why was Bohle deemed more suitable in this regard? It could, of course, be as simple as Bohle was better at written English (being born in England) whereas Haushofer's expertise was in the spoken word.

Equally, it could well be that in the spring of 1941, Haushofer merely relayed exactly what he was being told and Hess chose merely to rely on the false hope of peace as an excuse or justification for what was seen as his eventual recklessness. What is important is that when forced to give his interpretation of the affair on 12 May 1941, Albrecht Haushofer did mention his latest initiative via Burckhardt and Borenius (albeit not by name), thus giving the reader (Hitler) the option to latch on to that explanation as a justification for any uncharacteristic leniency. We strongly suspect that Hitler already knew of the channel and would have been suspicious had it not been mentioned.

Hess, too, could have simply latched onto this 'feeler', recognising that whilst it was not yet fully mature, it would still provide him with a plausible rationale to make the flight, safe enough and well evidenced enough to ensure protection for his family. Haushofer, in writing his report, also had to give Hitler the justification to understand that he, Haushofer, was not complicit in any venture sure to fail and that Hess, whilst well intentioned and with sufficient justification, had not relied on an obviously flawed plan of Haushofer's.

That is precisely why Haushofer had minutely detailed the sending of the letter in September 1940, so as to make clear whose initiative it had been and to record his reservations. As has already been commented, there is tellingly no similar, extant evidence detailing the spring 1941 communications.

However, on closer reading of the 12 May report that Haushofer prepared following the flight, it does make one vitally important point. It deals with the issue as to how Hess and Haushofer were able to communicate with the 'non-governmental' grouping in Britain. This has perplexed us over the years to distraction, contemplating radios, secret ink, etc, but without ever being totally convinced. In order to give sufficient encouragement to make Hess fly, there surely had to be a means of imparting relatively detailed information, both from Germany to Britain and vice versa.

Simplistically, there had to be a means of contacting Carl Burckhardt, if for no other reason to tell him that Borenius was on his way and could be expected in January 1941. This had to come from Britain. It could come from nowhere else.

Moreover, the information had to be capable of being conveyed in a reasonably speedy way and ideally without the chance of detection if the information was seen as coming from British 'non-governmental' sources.

Given that the Churchill-led Government controlled most of the means of communication, we struggled to see how any potential coup d'état or 'broad based revolution'[2] could ever be organised without a secure means of communication. Or a means of communication that, in the first instance, at least appeared to its users to be secure.

In the end, it was Albrecht Haushofer who gave both us and Hitler – if he did not already know – the answer as to how that could be achieved. It was staring us in the face.

Who knew what and when?

We have already alluded to the British knowledge that Germany was heading eastwards in spring 1941, courtesy of Bletchley Park. In the context of the Hess story, we should perhaps consider this knowledge more carefully.

In March/April 1941, the following knew of this development, or thought most likely:

Winston Churchill – through Ultra that a German/Russian invasion was likely in May; that many in his party and in the British plutocracy were baying for his blood.

Most Britons – that Germany was in an economic and military pact with Russia. Britain was being bombed nightly by the Luftwaffe. An invasion was likely. What was Churchill doing?

British MPs and plutocracy – that Germany was in an economic and military pact with Russia. Britain was being bombed nightly by the Luftwaffe. An invasion was likely. They had most to lose and were likely to lose it.

The British Joint Intelligence Committee – that a German invasion of Britain was the most likely the next step.

MI6 – a Russian invasion by Germany was likely in May. Much of the plutocracy favoured a Western peace. Borenius had gone to Geneva to deliver a code pad and to talk peace.

It could therefore be argued that in theory, at least, Churchill held all the cards.. He knew that Britain was unlikely to be invaded; he knew that a Russian invasion was at least likely. However, at that time the Ultra information was extremely closely guarded, and Churchill was paranoid that it should stay that way.

The Russian invasion was Churchill's 'get out of jail card', in both political and military terms. As, indeed, it transpired, after 22 June 1941 much of the military activity against mainland Britain ceased.

Churchill and Hitler, virtually alone, knew the future at that point in time. Churchill tried to share his unique information with Stalin, but Stalin would have none of it. He did not believe Germany would break the Molotov / von Ribbentrop pact given the sheer quantity of goods being shipped to the Reich and, equally, he did not trust the British.

Consequently, when engaged in the House of Commons on 7 May, Churchill knew that salvation was around the corner, but couldn't say so. Military analysis passed to Churchill indicated a quick German victory in Russia, but no one could be sure. It was certainly in Britain's longer-term interests to make Germany's task that much more difficult by not making any Western peace.

So, whilst a British plan promoting the 'illusion of peace' was an enticing proposition in that it gave Germany the prospect of a settlement, thus negating the need for an invasion, it was not actually necessary. Churchill knew that Germany was going east rather than west – at least for the time being.

This knowledge also put Churchill in a somewhat unique position with his political opponents. He knew that shortly many of their selfish concerns would be dissipated by the German invasion of Russia, but again, could not say so publicly (or privately). By contrast, many of his opponents knew nothing of Ultra. All they were convinced of was what they knew to be the case: that a German invasion of Britain (and the loss of all they possessed) was about to take place. Of course an Anglo-German peace should take place. It was a logical conclusion. The real enemy was, and always had been, Communism.

Churchill was also in the fortunate position of not having to do anything but survive in office until Barbarossa was unleashed. That is why the 7 May parliamentary vote was so important.

By contrast, any peace plotters were fast running out of time. Battles and invasions always took place in the spring and summer. They had to show their hand before the German invasion of Britain that they so feared would take place. They were wholly ignorant of Barbarossa. Time was fast running out for everyone – except Winston Spencer Churchill.

The Common Denominator?

Over the twenty or so years we have been researching the Hess affair, our approach has always been to drill down into the known facts so as to hopefully discover new linkages and coincidences. We would like to think that this approach has been reasonably successful, particularly in connection with our early work on Mrs Roberts (Chapter 6), Sikorski (Chapter 15), the flight (Chapter 19) and now the Zeileis Institute (Chapter 14).

However, whilst adding to the 'number of pieces in the jigsaw' we have perhaps struggled over the years to see quite what the overall picture shows. Many questions remained unanswered. Were the components linked at all?

Given the absence of any death bed revelations we began to wonder if there really was any true explanation of the affair. Clearly, there did not need to be; Hess could simply have imitated Parsifal, without any other external stimuli. That in itself was not a wholly irrational act, as it would certainly flush out the true British intention. Equally, Hess could have really acted irrationally and simply decided to fly anyway, just to escape his tedious, routine existence.

But, if that were really the case, would there have been the deafening silence of the past seventy-five years? Would Hess have continued to have been held until his death? We do not believe so and have never believed so. There had to be another factor that explains the picture as a whole; another factor that justified the subsequent treatment. We now believe we know what that factor is.

So far, this book has looked into the intelligence services, the pre-war appeasement circles and the isolated position of Churchill. In perhaps more detail we have now looked at the role of Tancred Borenius, Sikorski in the spring of 1941 and the pre-war channels between the RAF and the Luftwaffe.

There appears to us to be one (and only one) common denominator.

The common denominator is the personage of HRH Prince George, the Duke of Kent (1902–42).

We can think of no other single person who:

- knew Tancred Borenius well
- was the son of Queen Mary, also a close friend of Tancred Borenius
- was a known proponent of a negotiated peace
- was close to Sikorski. In 1972 it was suggested that George was even offered the Polish Throne, first in 1937 and then in 1940;[3] Roger Hinks in his diaries repeats this claim[4]
- was a serving member of the RAF. Indeed, when he was killed in 1942, he was the first royal to have died in action for 500 years
- knew the Duke of Hamilton and his brothers[5]
- had 'fallen out' with the King and Queen: 'The duke proceeded to abuse the King and Queen: says they are inept, ineffectual and inexpert and had no influence in Whitehall, Westminster or anywhere. They never answer letters or messages and are treacherous friends and hopelessly lazy'[6]
- was implicated in the pre-war RAF/Luftwaffe rapprochement
- had been used diplomatically previously, making use of his family ties with the Princes of Hesse and Prince Paul of Yugoslavia.

- was in Scotland on the evening of 10 May 1941
- was a member of the British Royal Family with their obvious allegiances to Germany and hatred of Communism.

This is a difficult area, in that common association does not automatically infer any involvement or activity. However, given the above connections we do believe that the Duke of Kent did have the necessary persons and authority in place to at least stage-manage the illusion of a peace negotiation, or allow his name to be used in such a fashion: Borenius to 'open the door', Haushofer, Winterbotham and Borenius to continue and develop the dialogue and the RAF intelligence connections to facilitate the flight and a landing/meeting. In this connection Hamilton might well have been no more than a knowledgeable bystander.

We repeat again that the fact that Prince George knew all the participants of course does not in itself prove any involvement. However, it does raise the question as to why the persons involved were doing what they were doing if truly operating in isolation. Was George the instigator or just an unfortunate (and uniquely) common denominator?

We doubt very much indeed whether we shall officially ever learn if Prince George was essentially orchestrating a single-handed peace mission or merely giving the illusion of such, being played by others.

It is very unlikely that Churchill would have entrusted George with the Ultra secret, given some of his wilder traits, so, as far as George was concerned, the major threat to Britain continued to come from a German invasion. It would also explain why Hess flew to Scotland, though clearly not intending to crash or parachute.

HRH Prince George, the Duke of Kent (1902–42), in RAF dress

Proof? Why none, of course. *Double Standards* places him at the end of Dungavel runway, but this we know to be untrue for reasons already well-rehearsed. If true, he would simply have witnessed an almighty air crash and the likely death of the Deputy Führer. We do however know that the Duke was a close friend of Loel Guinness, the Station Commander at Ayr and Dundonald (only 15 miles away) and so we think this the more likely landing target, but again have no concrete evidence, save that of the Lennoxlove map and pilot's notes.

However, we do remain extremely suspicious by reason of the fact that we have been deliberately denied for sure that small piece of knowledge as to Prince George's precise whereabouts. If he was at home with Princess Marina and his children at Coppins in Berkshire, then we are sure we would have been told. Why was he in the Orkneys on naval business and why was Alanbrooke despatched to the Islands, apparently to watch birds?[7] Had the real bird already flown?

So, we return to the conundrum. We think we now have most, if not all, of the jigsaw pieces, but do we now perhaps have the picture too? Is the Hess affair actually an orchestrated royal peace mission that went spectacularly wrong?

---

[1] Winston Churchill, *The Second World War (vol. 5)*, Cassell, London, 1964.
[2] A reference to the NKVD interpretation. See Chapter 26 for further details and citation.
[3] The two men had met ten times prior to the Duke's death in 1942 (*Double Standards*, p. 281).
[4] Roger Hinks diaries, 23 September 1940, 'he is personally in favour of the scheme'.
[5] The two men had documented meetings in January 1941 (*Double Standards*, p. 282).
[6] *Chips Channon Diaries*, 1938–43, Hutchinson, London, 2021 (9 January 1942).
[7] See *Rudolf Hess: The British Illusion of Peace* for details of the earlier attempts to obtain this piece of information.

CHAPTER 27

ALBRECHT HAUSHOFER – BRITISH AGENT?

The relationship between Albrecht Haushofer and his father's former student, Rudolf Hess, is obviously important in understanding the sequence of events that led to the flight on 10 May 1941, but probably not as overridingly important as other authors have previously sought to justify.[1] We are now no longer convinced that Hess flew solely on account of what Haushofer was telling him. We also suspect Hitler realised this too, as demonstrated by his later reaction to events and subsequent treatment of Albrecht and the Haushofer family.

In earlier chapters, we have already seen how Albrecht was instructed by Hess to send the letter to the Duke of Hamilton via Mrs Roberts in September 1940. The start of the affair.

We have also already seen how Albrecht then spent much of spring 1941 flitting around Europe (Geneva, Berlin, Stockholm and possibly Madrid), presumably trying to react appropriately to the Borenius initiative/mission of early 1941 and gather more information as to what was being mooted.

However, by stark contrast to the minutely detailed trail of evidence surrounding the September 1940 letter, we have no similar written evidence at all as to what the thirty-nine-year-old Foreign Office advisor was telling and relaying to the Deputy Führer, after the British/Finnish contact had been made in January 1941. Again, by stark contrast, when asked to recount to Hitler on 12 May 1941, little was actually revealed surrounding the time from January when Borenius was in Geneva to 10 May. Given the fact that the 'stakes had considerably risen' since the previous September, we do find this a little odd. Surely, if it takes detailed memorandum to record the incorrect posting of a letter in September 1940, why are the subsequent reactions to the early 1941 Borenius trip not similarly recorded?

The cynic might counter, 'because there were no reactions', but we know this is not correct. By 10 March 1941 at the very latest, and most likely much sooner, Haushofer knew about the Borenius initiative. Why no records of that initiative, which clearly had come from the top of British society?

Throughout the 1930s Albrecht had visited England. His trips to England have been well documented in our earlier works and there is no doubt that he was well connected and, moreover, *well thought of*. The Duke of Hamilton had invited him to his 1938 wedding. He had addressed Chatham House in May 1937. He was well known in government circles.

In July 1939 he had written to the Duke whilst on a cruise off Norway, forewarning the start of the war. Hamilton had visited Churchill in London to show him the letter (hardly the act of a potential revolutionary). In October 1939, Hamilton's letter to *The Times* could almost have been addressed to Haushofer.

There is nothing new here. These details have been well known for a number of years. MI5 was also naturally interested in Haushofer, maintaining a file on him, PF54592 since at least May 1937.[2]

However, what is new is the question as to whether Haushofer knew exactly what he was doing and knew that Hess was doomed to fail, but despite that fact, still carried on. Clearly, Hess desperately wanted to believe, if only to give him a plausible excuse for some relative excitement, possible prestige and a means to escape his insufferable existence. But did Haushofer emotionally fuel Hess in just the same way as his flight engineers subsequently fuelled his Bf110? Put simply, did he deliberately lead Hess astray?

Very oddly, from September 1940 to 10 May 1941 there is little surviving evidence as to communication between the two men. The correspondence and references that do exist are mainly third party, whereby the actions and reactions of Hess and Haushofer are described – most notably by Martha Haushofer, Albrecht's mother. This absence of evidence could very well be explained by the rifling of the Bavarian Haushofer archives in 1946 but, similarly, there is little surviving Haushofer/Hess correspondence in the private family papers in Berne. The next detailed piece of evidence appears to be the written explanation that Haushofer was asked to prepare and subsequently gave to Hitler at the Berghof following the flight, on 12 May. We have already seen how the previous September correspondence was in part produced to record Haushofer's actions and motives, and now in May 1941 Albrecht was theoretically writing for his life, explaining his actions since the previous autumn's letter writing.

By comparing what was written on 12 May 1941 to the now known facts, we may well be able to see precisely what Albrecht Haushofer was seeking to disguise and what he was willing to reveal. Equally, it must have been presumed that Hitler would eventually read the report and Haushofer would most likely have to second guess what Hess had told him and, equally, what he had not.

However, before analysing the report, it may be useful to repeat the Hess/Haushofer timeline such as it is known:

31 August 1940 Karl Haushofer meets Hess in the Grunwald Forest, south of Munich.
23 September 1940 the letter is sent to Lisbon, PO Box 506.
2 November 1940 Postal intercept and a 'Terminal Mail' intercept report is produced.
4 November 1940 Hess letter to wife, 'I firmly believe I will return from the flight I am about to undertake one of these days and that the flight will be crowned with success.' This is most odd indeed, as at the time Hess had neither a plane nor the ability to fly a Me110. He was, however, recorded as making an early test flight of a Bf110 on 8 November. This may have prompted the outpouring.
12 November 1940 Albrecht writes to his mother, 'From L. Nothing. It will doubtless come to nothing'. The interesting question here is whether Haushofer knew it would come to nothing because the letter should never have reached its intended recipient?
17 January 1941 Frank Foley flies to Lisbon, with, we suspect, Tancred Borenius, who had given his apologies to the Polish Relief Fund on 15 January.
29/31January 1941 Borenius meets Burckhardt in Geneva.
2–5 February 1941 Albrecht visits Stockholm. The potential reasons for this trip are myriad. At the time, the Archbishop of Stockholm was active in Anglo-German negotiations and, intriguingly, the newly appointed SOE representative at the British Legation was one Roger Hinks (1903–63), yet another well-known art historian, who had been dismissed from the British Museum for being held responsible for having the Elgin Marbles scrubbed in an attempt to clean them. We have no doubt that Hinks and Borenius would have been known to one another. Moreover, Hinks was the son of the Cambridge er well-known art historian[3], astronomer and geographer, Arthur Hinks (1873–1945), who of course was a contemporary of the Cambridge-based Roberts family.
21–24 February 1941 Haushofer meets Hess.
10 March 1941 Haushofer meets von Hassell in Berlin, at the house of Johannes Popitz.
12–15 April 1941 Haushofer with Hess in Berlin.
26 April 1941 Karl and Albrecht meets Hess. Martha records a 'remarkable event'.

28 April 1941 Albrecht meets Carl Burckhardt in Geneva.
5 May 1941 Hess meets Albrecht in Augsburg.
12 May 1941 Haushofer flies to the Berghof to explain himself.

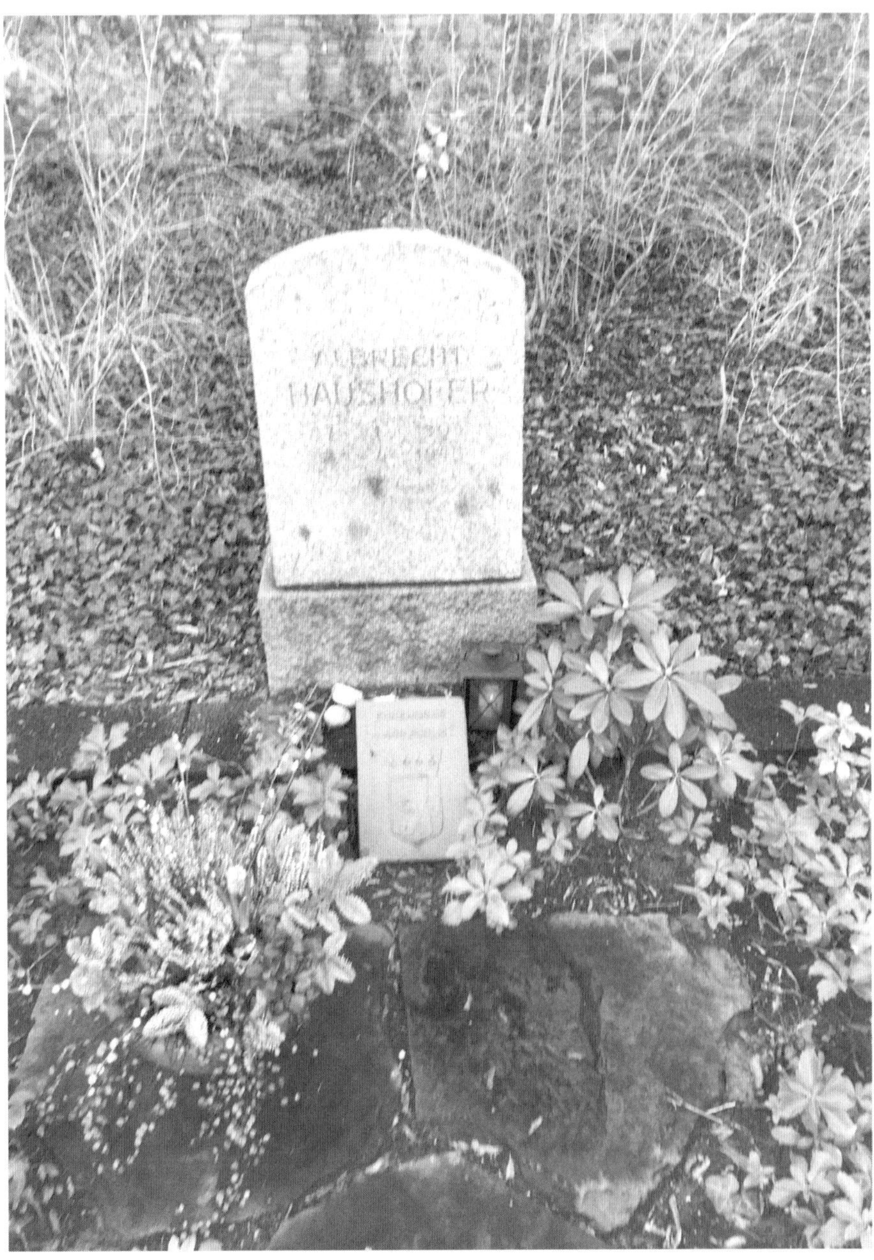

Albrecht Haushofer's grave in Berlin

Whilst it may appear that there was significant time delay between the Borenius meeting in late January and the Haushofer/Burckhardt meeting in late April, some twelve weeks later, it is clear from the above that Ulrich von Hassell was acting as a conduit between the factions. His diary entries of 16 March 1941 clearly demonstrate that Burckhardt had imparted the details of the Borenius correspondence and certainly, by no later than 10 March 1941, Haushofer also knew precisely what had been said. On 10 March, von Hassell had met Haushofer in Berlin at the residence of Johannes Popitz a fellow member of the fledgling resistance.

Ilse Hess wrote *Prisoner of Peace*[4] in 1954 and revealed many of the letters that she had written to her husband and vice versa. There is not one in which the name of Albrecht Haushofer is even mentioned. The introduction mentions Albrecht and the fact that Hess left a letter for him on his departure from Germany, but even though there are letters sent to Karl Haushofer,[5] apparently no mention is made of Albrecht, his son.

John Harris met a Hess family member in Munich in August 2015 and suggested that Rudolf Hess had realised that Albrecht had potentially double crossed him in the spring of 1941. The family member essentially agreed. It also appears that Karl Haushofer may also have realised what had taken place, as the two men had also fallen out prior to the time of Albrecht's death in 1945. His body was never returned to Bavaria, instead being buried in the Sankt Johannis-Friedhof in Berlin.

Nor are there any records of their reaction to the deaths of the senior Haushofers in 1944 and 1946.

The last record of Albrecht Haushofer's involvement in the Hess affair (apart from his Moabit Prison poems,) was the report he compiled for Adolf Hitler on the morning of 12 May 1941 at the Berghof, Berchtesgaden. Haushofer had been in Berlin on 10 May and was summoned to fly to Bavaria the following Monday morning. James Douglas-Hamilton makes the case that Haushofer was 'writing for his life'.[6] This we find perhaps a little overstated, but for certain he could not be completely sure what Hitler knew and did not know.

Hitler, by contrast, had received two long and detailed letters from Rudolf Hess on 11 May and, interestingly, according to a SHAEF Psychological Warfare Division release dated 6 May 1945, the Hess letter was accompanied by a second letter from General Karl Haushofer sharing the Hess viewpoint and then seeking to rely on a horoscope that justified the flight.[7]

Consequently, his job was to compare and contrast what Hess (and apparently Haushofer) had told him with what he was about to read from the pen of Albrecht Haushofer. On the morning of 12 May 1941 it should also be borne in mind that neither Adolf Hitler nor Albrecht Haushofer knew[8] whether Hess was alive or dead.

The report read:

English connections and the possibility of utilising them

The circle of English individuals whom I have known very well for years, and whose utilisation on behalf of a German-English understanding in the years from 1934 to 1938 was the core of my activity in England, comprises the following groups and persons:

1. A leading group of younger Conservatives (many of them Scotsmen). Among them are: the Duke of Hamilton – up to the date of his father's death, Lord Clydesdale – Conservative Member of Parliament; the Parliamentary Private Secretary of Neville Chamberlain, Lord Dunglass; the present Under Secretary of State in the Air Ministry, Balfour; the present Under Secretary of State in the Ministry of Education, Lindsay (National Labour); the present Under Secretary of State in the Ministry for Scotland, Wedderburn.

Close ties link this circle with the Court. The younger brother of the Duke of Hamilton is closely related to the present Queen through his wife; the mother-in-law of the Duke of Hamilton, the Duchess of Northumberland, is the Mistress of the Robes; her brother-in-law, Lord Eustace Percy, was several times a member of the Cabinet and is still today an influential member of the Conservative Party (especially close to former Minister Baldwin). There are close connections between this circle and important groups of the older Conservatives, as for example the Stanley family (Lord Derby, Oliver Stanley) and Astor (the last is owner of The Times). The young Astor, likewise a Member of Parliament, was Parliamentary Private Secretary to the former Foreign and Interior Minister, Sir Samuel Hoare, at present English Ambassador in Madrid.

I have known almost all of the persons mentioned for years and from close personal contact. The present Under Secretary of State of the Foreign Office, Butler, also belongs here; in spite of many of his public utterances he is not a follower of Churchill or Eden. Numerous connections lead from most of those names to Lord Halifax, to whom I likewise had personal access.

2. The so called 'Round Table' circle of younger imperialists (particularly colonial and Empire politicians), whose most important message personage was Lord Lothian.
3. A group of the 'Ministerialdirektoren' in the Foreign Office. The most important of these were Strang, the chief of the Central European Department, and O'Malley, the Chief of the South Eastern Department and afterwards Minister in Budapest.

There was hardly one of those named who was not at least occasionally in favour of a German-English understanding.

Although most of them in 1939 finally considered that war inevitable, it was nevertheless reasonable to think of these persons if one thought the moment had come for investigating the possibility of an inclination to make peace. Therefore when the Deputy of the Führer, Reich Minister Hess, asked me in the autumn of 1940 about possibilities of gaining access to possibly reasonable Englishmen, I suggested two concrete possibilities for establishing contacts. It seemed to me that the following could be considered for this:

A. Personal contact with Lothian, Hoare, or O'Malley, all three of whom were accessible in neutral countries.
B. Contact by letter with one of my friends in England. For this purpose the Duke of Hamilton was considered in the first place, since my connection with him was so firm and personal that I could suppose he would understand a letter addressed to him even if it were formulated in very veiled language.

Reich Minister Hess decided in favour of the second possibility; I wrote a letter to the Duke of Hamilton at the end of September 1940 and its despatch to Lisbon was arranged by the Deputy Führer. I did not learn that whether the letter reached the addressee. The possibilities of its being lost en route from Lisbon to England are not small, after all.

Then in April 1941 I received greetings from Switzerland from Carl Burckhardt, the former League of Nations Commissioner in Danzig and now Vice President of the International Red Cross, whom I had also known well for years. He sent the message that he had greetings to pass on to me from someone in my old circle of English friends. I should please visit him some time in Geneva. Since the possibility existed that these greetings we in connection with my letter of last autumn, I thought I should again submit the matter to the Deputy of the Führer, though with the reservation (as already last autumn) that the chances of a serious peace feeler seemed to me to be extremely slight. Reich Minister Hess decided that I should go to Geneva.

In Geneva I had a long conversation with Burckhardt on 28 April. I found him in something of a quandary between his desire to support the possibilities of a European peace and the greatest concern lest his name might somehow be involved with publicity: he expressly asked that what went on be kept strictly secret. In consideration of the discretion enjoined upon him he could only tell me the following:

> 'A few weeks ago, a person well known and respected in London, who was close to the leading Conservative and city circles, had called on him in Geneva. This person, whose name he could not give, though he could vouch for his earnestness, had in a rather long conversation expressed the wish of important English circles for an examination of the possibilities for peace; in search for possible channels my name had been mentioned.'

I for my part informed Professor Burckhardt that I had to expect the same discretion with regard to my name. Should his informant in London he will come to Switzerland once more and should he further be willing to have his name communicated to me in Berlin through confidential channels, so that the earnestness of both person and mission could be investigated in Germany, then I thought I, too, could agree to taking another trip to Geneva. Professor Burckhardt stated that he was willing to act as go-between in this manner: it would simply be communicated to England through an entirely safe channel that there was a prospect for a trusted representative from London, after he himself had given his name, to meet in Geneva a German also well known in England, who was in a position to bring such communications as there might be to the attention of the competent German authorities.

My own conversation with Professor Burckhardt furnished a number of important points regarding the substantive part of possible peace talks. (Burckhardt has not only been in England during the war – for example, he had along and detailed conversation with Halifax – but he also has frequent contact with the English observer in Geneva, Consul General Livingstone, who likewise is one of those Englishmen whom the war does not please). Burckhardt's general impression of the opinions of the more moderate groups in England can be summarised as follows:

1. The substantive English interest in the areas of eastern and south-eastern Europe (with the exception of Greece) is nominal.
2. No English government that is still capable of action will be able to renounce (the aim of) a restoration of the western European system of states.
3. The colonial question will not present any overwhelming difficulties if the German demand is limited to the old German possessions and if the Italian appetite can be curbed.

All of this, however – and this fact could not be stressed seriously enough – under the assumption, which overshadowed everything else, that a basis of personal confidence could be found between Berlin and London; and this would be as difficult to find as during the Crusades or in the Thirty Years War.

As matters stood, the consent with 'Hitlerism' was being considered by the masses of the English people, too, to be a religious war with all the fanatical psychological consequences of such an attitude. If anyone in London was inclined toward peace, then it was the indigenous portion of the plutocracy, which was able to calculate when it, along with the indigenous British tradition would be destroyed, whereas the indigenous, mainly Jewish element, had already in large part completed the jump to America and the overseas dominions. It was Burckhardt's own and deepest concern that if the war continued for a considerable length of time every possibility that the reasonable forces in England would force Churchill to make peace would disappear, since by that time the whole power to decision regarding the overseas assets of the Empire would be taken over by the Americans. Once the remainder of the indigenous English upper class had been eliminated, however, it would be impossible to talk sense to Roosevelt and his circle.

The report thus ended. Upon reading it we suspect that it basically told Hitler what Hitler already knew, and most likely had known for at least a fortnight (since the Hitler/Hess meeting in Berlin on 4 May.) There was a group wishing for peace in Britain and there had recently been an approach via Carl Burckhardt in Geneva (who Hitler also knew well and had lastly met at the Berghof in August 1939).

However, what is remarkable and important is what the report did not say. We would suggest:

- The dates are deliberately inaccurate. Haushofer implies that the 28 April was the first time he became aware of the peace feeler, whereas we suspect he was quite aware of the Borenius mission from at least 10 March, if not even earlier. 10 March was the date that Haushofer had met Ulrich von Hassell in Berlin. Understandably, Haushofer was not advertising the fact that he knew von Hassell. In other words, Haushofer was trying to make out that the peace feeler was very recent as far as he was concerned and had not had time to react to it. This, we believe, is a blatant lie.
- Similarly, we are bemused by the fact that no intermediary's name is mentioned, despite Haushofer being aware of Borenius's identity, again, since 10 March. It is clearly Borenius that is being referred to and yet no name is mentioned. This could be a device to protect Burckhardt of course, but obviously Hess had been told far more than this report suggests.
- This report, whilst based on the truth, is certainly not an invitation to Hess to fly to Britain. It simply gives the impression of a potential peace proposal in the making. Certainly not as a justification for a flight to the enemy. Just as Haushofer intended – 'it wasn't on my say so'.

The important question we suspect is to ascertain what, by contrast, Haushofer had been telling Hess in the meanwhile. We suspect it was not the same information at all. This is debated further in the final chapter.

Moabit Prison, Berlin, 2020

Karl Haushofer's post-war interviews

Albrecht Haushofer was executed amongst the rubble of Berlin on 23 April 1945. He had been incarcerated in the Moabit Prison as a result of the 20 July 1944 plot and his potential use in any last-minute peace negotiations. As the prospect of the latter disappeared, so did the necessity to keep the academic alive. We are then told that Albrecht's brother Heinz found the body on 15 May, still grasping the last sonnet he had composed. We are a little surprised that identification would prove quite that decisive given the stated twenty-two days that the body would have been exposed to the Berlin elements and assorted vermin. However, Haushofer was dead.

Albrecht's father, Karl, had spent most of the war at his Hartschimmelhof estate, to the southwest of Munich. Just before the 1944 plot he, too, had been interned, at Dachau on the northern side of Munich, having been released on 21 August 1944. His presence there was verified at the end of the war by Major Stevens, of the Venlo incident notoriety, who had also spent most of the war at the camp.

However, the war in Europe ended on 8th May 1945.

It must surely be a sign of his potential importance that less than one month later, Karl Haushofer was interviewed by the US Combined Intelligence Objectives Sub Committee. He was described as target c.28/8.82. This was reported as being the second interview – the first having been held on 4 May 1945, four days before VE day. Munich had been liberated on 30 April, virtually without resistance.

If the interviewing officer, James S. Lay Jr, thought he might be told the details behind the Hess flight, he was to be disappointed. Lay actually was told very little that he might not have known already.

He made a couple of interesting observations about Karl Haushofer:

- Hess had not told Haushofer of the impending flight (Observation number 13).
- Hess had met Hamilton, although only casually (Observation number 14).

We do not believe Karl Haushofer was telling the truth about Observation 13, since it now appears quite likely that he actually wrote a letter to Hitler that was attached to Hess's own letter.

However, the report is really very bland indeed. It reveals very little, save perhaps the realisation that he too had been taken in by the Nazi Party. He bemoans the fact that although he had been often consulted, his advice been rarely acted upon. His son is not mentioned. If the Americans were hoping that interviews such as those would reveal the truth about the events of spring 1941, they were to be disappointed. In just the same way as Albrecht had told Hitler nothing in May 1941, his father had just done the same thing to his victors. They would now have to rely on the legal process to perhaps extract the truth.

Lay's report was used as the basis of a decision as to whether or not to charge Haushofer with war crimes. In the event Haushofer did not stand trial at Nuremberg, but he did attend as part of the process designed to ascertain the mental state of Rudolf Hess. The two men last met face to face in November 1945.

On 11 March 1946 Karl and Martha Haushofer were found dead on their Hartschimmelhof estate.

According to various accounts they both drank arsenic, and Martha was found hanging from a tree. Clearly the true sequence of events will never be known, but we would like to record that the previous day they had been interviewed, this time by British agents. We would also record that for a military man the choice of arsenic as a poison just seems most odd. Arsenic poisoning is a notoriously slow death which therefore seems a bizarre choice for a suicide.

Anyway, by the time the Nuremberg Trials had reached their climax Karl, Martha and Albrecht Haushofer were all dead. None were able to appear as witnesses.

---

[1] James Douglas-Hamilton, *Motive for a Mission: The Story Behind Hess's Flight to Britain*, Macmillan, London, 1971.

[2] See KV 2 /1684.

[3] Peter Tennant, *Touchlines of War*, University of Hull Press, Hull, 1992.

[4] Ilse Hess, *Prisoner of Peace*, Briton Publishing Co., London, 1954.

[5] Ibid., Hess to Haushofer, 20 May 1942.

6 James Douglas-Hamilton, *Motive for a Mission: The Story Behind Hess's Flight to Britain*, Macmillan, London, 1971.

[7] Daniel Lerner Collection, Box 3 – 401/419, Hoover Institution Archives, Stanford University, California.

[8] Documents on German Foreign Policy, series D, vol. X11,783-7.

CHAPTER 28
PARLAMENTÄR?

Parlamentär, or flag of truce

The concept of a Parlamentär, or bearer of flag of truce, is both ancient and well understood. A messenger, usually waving a white flag approaches the enemy; sometimes to surrender, sometimes to entreat or perhaps to just relay a message. We have all seen the movies and watched the many dramatic scenarios unravel.

As civilisation has developed, it has been deemed progressive and beneficial to determine a code of behaviour that applied even in the extreme stresses of times of war. The role of a Parlamentär was quite properly considered important enough to be defined and enshrined into the law of war. One of the first attempts at such regulation was carried out by Franz Lieber, a Prussian veteran of Waterloo, who was commissioned by Abraham Lincoln to draft the code which determined how American soldiers were to behave. This early and ground-breaking code was published in 1863 and we reproduce those sections dealing with intermediaries:

1 *The bearer of a flag of truce cannot insist upon being admitted. He must always be admitted with great caution. Unnecessary frequency is carefully to be avoided.*
2 *If the bearer of a flag of truce offers himself during an engagement, he can be admitted as a very rare exception only. It is no breach of good faith to retain such flag of truce, if admitted during the engagement. Firing is not required to cease on the appearance of a flag of truce in battle.*
3 *If the bearer of a flag of truce, presenting himself during an engagement, is killed or wounded, it furnishes no ground of complaint whatever.*

These principles also formed the basis for the 1899 and 1907 Hague Conventions which sought to unify on a worldwide basis the laws and rules of war. Again, the role of a Parlamentär was discussed and we reproduce those articles dealing with the specific issue:

ARTICLE 32 An individual is considered a parlementaire who is authorized by one of the belligerents to enter into communication with the other, and who carries a white flag. He has a right to inviolability, as well as the trumpeter, bugler, or drummer, the flag-bearer, and the interpreter who may accompany him.
ARTICLE 33 The Chief to whom a flag of truce is sent is not obliged to receive it in all circumstances. He can take all steps necessary to prevent the envoy taking advantage of his mission to obtain information. In case of abuse, he has the right to detain the envoy temporarily.
ARTICLE 34 The envoy loses his rights of inviolability if it is proved beyond doubt that he has taken advantage of his privileged position to provoke or commit an act of treachery.

(Inviolability is defined as 'never to be broken, infringed, or dishonoured.')

The reader may at this juncture be wondering the relevance of these articles, drafted some thirty-four years prior to the Hess flight and already sorely tested on a practical basis by the horrendous events of 1914–18.

The relevance is explained as follows:

1) In 1985 Alfred Seidl, the Hess family lawyer, published a book claiming that his client was a Parlamentär when making his

flight in 1941.[1] The book title alone, *The Peace Denied – German's Parlamentär Rudolf Hess Must Remain Silent*, makes it quite clear what Seidl is implying. Clearly, in 1985 the onus was very much on trying to gain Hess a release, this time on legal grounds rather than perhaps the more obvious moral justification. Consequently, much of the book is based on Seidl obtaining expert opinion that Hess was of course a Parlamentär in the legal sense (he was not). Conversely, had Hess really been a Parlamentär, he should have been 'inviolate' and presumably returned to the enemy unharmed. In 1985, two years before Hess's death, this certainly had not taken place.

2) Rudolf Hess also tried the same ploy in 1941, though perhaps not in such trenchant terms. When he was in captivity in Mytchett, he wrote a letter to George VI, which has yet to see the light of day. However, a draft obtained by David Irving makes it clear that Hess was appealing to the King's 'fairness'. He does not however specifically call himself a Parlamentär but does remind the King he came 'at the risk of my life'. We have still to see the full five-page letter, so have no idea as to what was conclusively written. The J.R. Rees book, publishes a lengthy statement which is described as Hess's own statement. In the said statement Hess records twice appealing to George VI: first, at the time of the air crash via the Duke of Hamilton, and the second, very specifically, is dated as being on 13 November 1941. The second appeal ended up with Sir Alexander Hardinge, the King's Private Secretary. Where the letter currently resides is unknown. It does record, however, that Hess had 'insisted on the protection that had been promised me'. This is important because it demonstrates that Hess recognised the constitutional differences between the monarch and the British Government, and it also hints that Hess had been given some such assurances before he flew (when and how and by whom?).
3) On 20 May 1941, Winston Churchill, who very untypically had said virtually nothing about Hess following the extraordinary flight nine days earlier, chose to make one very telling comment. In answer to a Parliamentary question by R.J. Taylor, Churchill stated that, 'As far as I am at present advised, he is being treated as a prisoner of war, and will receive appropriate treatment.' Conversely, that statement made it clear that Hess was not a Parlamentär, at least as far as Churchill was concerned.

However, the supreme irony here is that Hitler, in trying to explain the flight, had essentially condemned his deputy. According to the May 1941 communique, Hess was 'delusional' and 'suffering under hallucinations'. There was certainly no talk of peace-making because there could not be. What would Stalin think if Hess was suddenly proclaimed an authorised Parlamentär by Adolf Hitler? Why might Germany be suing Britain for a settlement?

Equally, what would Roosevelt and the isolationists in America think if Hess were to be proclaimed a Parlamentär?

The Hague Convention is quite clear. The Parlamentär has to be authorised as such by one of the belligerents. In May 1941, the Germans had essentially publicly disowned Hess and the British had just stated they were treating him as a prisoner of war, a position they maintained throughout.

A convenient compromise. The Russians were baffled. Most of the British were equally baffled, though they had just inadvertently obtained a valuable bargaining chip should the need arise.

Rudolf Hess was not and could not be a Parlamentär because he failed the Hague Convention legal definition. He may even have believed he was one at the onset, even at the time of the flight, but once the German communique had been made his fate was sealed. Clearly, had all gone well and as planned, the question would have been irrelevant. As it was a near catastrophe had just taken place and Hess and Hitler were certainly no longer in control of the situation.

We should also make the point that whilst the Bf110 apparently had no weapons, we are unaware of the presence of any white flag, the traditional symbolic manifestation of the need to talk peace. That is not to say there was not one on the plane, but to date we have seen or heard no evidence of such. It might be interesting to learn if such an item is part of a Second World War collection in a house in Eaglesham or Newton Mearns. Most local houses appear to have obtained a relic of the flight.

Hess could never be a Parlamentär. Hitler had inadvertently said so himself by reason of his first hurried communique. The implications were to last a lifetime.

---

1 Alfred Seidl, *Der verweigerte Friede*, Universitas, Munich, 1985.

2 David Irving, *Hess: The Missing Years 1941–1945*, Focal Point, Windsor, 2010.

3 J.R. Rees, *The Case of Rudolf Hess*, Heinemann, London, 1947.

CHAPTER 29

WILLIAM SPELMAN PILCHER, KENNETH DE COURCY AND JAMES LONSDALE-BRYANS

The three individuals named above usually appear in most books on the Hess affair, without their supposed involvement ever being satisfactorily explained. Consequently, we have conducted the following research, if for no other reason than to finally eliminate them from our enquiries.

William Spelman Pilcher and Kenneth de Courcy

The authors are pleased to report that following some research and with the grateful assistance of Lt Colonel Pilcher's son, Anthony, the fog that previously surrounded William Spelman Pilcher is partially beginning to clear.

William Spelman Pilcher (1888–1970) was born into a family of means, the home being 21 Ennismore Gardens, London. A decorated First World War hero, Pilcher had returned to service at the beginning of the Second World War and in 1940 had been placed in charge of a training battalion of the Grenadier Guards based at Windsor Castle.

Thereafter, William Spelman Pilcher has been assigned all types of roles in the Hess affair.

Double Standards dramatically report that Pilcher had signed a letter of safe conduct for Rudolf Hess and had consequently been banished to a 'remote cottage on the Balmoral estate ... He was held there incommunicado from 1941 until his death in 1970'. Peter Padfield typically has done further research and contacted Kenneth de Courcy to try and elicit further explanation. This correspondence took place in the late 1980s before de Courcy's demise in 1999 and well before the publication of the Guy Liddell diaries in 2005. There is an amount of irony in what de Courcy told Padfield.

Kenneth de Courcy (1909–99) was an interesting individual in that he had made a lot of money in his lifetime, mainly through owning a chain of tobacco shops. Famously, he owned a Rolls Royce which had been waterproofed for potential underwater driving. In 1938 he founded a journal, which duly became the Intelligence Digest. He ended up in jail in the 1960s for financial fraud.

Consequently, he needed intelligence information simply to feed his journal and so befriended those well connected or on the periphery of government. It appears that Spelman Pilcher had been duly befriended, because the Liddell diaries record on 15 August 1941 that, 'A cousin of Toby Pilcher's who is commanding a battalion of the guard at Windsor is under arrest for communicating information obtained from an intelligence summary to Kenneth de Courcy.'

According to Anthony Pilcher, this was not the complete story. The family story is that Pilcher was attending a cocktail party at Windsor and 'spoke out of turn about Stalin and the Russians' in the earshot of the King and Queen. His remarks were reported to Churchill.

Whatever the reason, Pilcher and his family were then effectively banished to Scotland, only returning to London in 1953. However, they did not go to Balmoral, but instead were given the use of Laggan House, that belonged to Archie Grant of Carron House, Carron, Moray.

Anthony Pilcher went on to say that, 'I do not think he was banished, but it must have been a terrible time for him. His friends did stand by him, but he was not very social after that. Stewart Menzies came to stay once or twice in Scotland, so I suppose he must have been forgiven. I doubt he gave any information to de Courcy, but I think that is what Churchill accused him of

Laggan House

… my father was a great patriot, he hated the Nazis and communists in equal measure.'[1]

In 1942, the War Cabinet minutes of 13 April record that de Courcy 'was up to mischief' writing 'poisonous publications' about the Russians.

Consequently, it appears that Pilcher was sadly caught up with de Courcy, his need for newsprint and the government policy in 1941 to court Stalin, irrespective of the true feeling of many within the British establishment. Barbarossa, not peace, was now the story and as Churchill had famously remarked, 'If Hitler invaded hell, I would make at least a favourable reference to the devil in the House of Commons.'[2]

So, woe behold those like Pilcher who disagreed, especially in the presence of the King, who also needed little persuasion. That, we believe is the story of William Spelman Pilcher and Kenneth de Courcy.

Interestingly enough, in de Courcy's later *Review Of World Affairs*, volume 3,[3] it is pretty clear that de Courcy had no particular special knowledge of the Hess affair, instead merely detailing the usual possible reasons for the flight. He did suggest that, 'It is quite clear that his act, variously interpreted as it is, has increased the number of people throughout the world who do not believe that Germany has it in her power to break the British empire and thus dictate a peace.'

In conclusion, the whole affair can be seen as a consequence of a persistent journalist seeking political intelligence. However, what remains difficult to understand is the apparent punishment metered out, a punishment that was ended only once King George VI had died.

James Lonsdale-Bryans

The case of James Lonsdale-Bryans is perhaps more pertinent to our understanding of the affair, as the amateur diplomat travelled to Arosa, Switzerland in 1940, specifically to meet Ulrich von Hassell, the former German Ambassador to Italy. A year later, Albrecht Haushofer chose to make exactly the same, though unlikely, journey and chose exactly the same, though unlikely, venue.

James Lonsdale-Bryans (1893–1981) was also born into wealthy London-based family. His father, Herbert, was a famous stained-glass artist who saw fit to send young James to Eton College.

Of potential relevance to the later history, his time at Eton coincided with that of the 8th Duke of Buccleuch and Stewart Menzies.

After leaving Eton, Lonsdale-Bryans joined his father as a partner in the stained-glass business, but then spent much of the 1930s travelling the world, only returning to England from the Far East in the last week of August 1939.

Quite what James had been doing in the Far East is open to conjecture. However, upon his return to London he managed to acquire an audience with Lord Halifax and seemingly on the strength of the twenty-minute meeting, literally on the steps of the Foreign Office, he travelled to Rome, whereupon he gained the confidence of the son-in-law of von Hassell, one Detalmo Pirzio-Biroli..

Lonsdale-Bryans proudly details his travels and contacts in his *Blind Victory*, first published in 1951.[4] Subtitled *Secret Communications, Halifax–Hassell*, it details how Lonsdale-Bryans, with the permission of Lord Halifax and the sponsorship of the Duke of Buccleuch and Lord Brocket, travelled first to Rome and then to Arosa in March 1940 to meet Ulrich von Hassell.

Of later relevance, to reach Arosa, Lonsdale-Bryans travelled from Rome to Milan to Zurich and then, 'Changed into the narrow-gauge railway that climbed into the hills, reaching its mountain terminus at nine o'clock that night.'

After having met von Hassell and obtained a signed paper detailing the peace terms that he would like to see, Lonsdale-Bryans returned to London. He recorded this trip under the heading 'Government Sponsored'.

We suspect that Lonsdale-Bryans was essentially right in his description. However, he was known to Halifax on account of his 'father's uncle was Lord Grimethorpe who was an associate of Lord Halifax's father'.

We also suspect that Halifax would have seen Lonsdale-Bryans as a pest, but one where there was little downside as far as the British were concerned.

Thereafter, the second part of the book is entitled 'Government Opposed' and in it Lonsdale-Bryans describes his later travels to Lisbon and how he attempted to rekindle his contact with von Hassell. However, what is clear is that Lonsdale-Bryans was back in England in early March 1941, flying into Whitchurch, Bristol. He had failed to meet von Hassell for a second time.

What is also interesting is that there is a completely different version of Lonsdale-Bryans and his travels. This comes from MI5 and is dated 15

March 1941, a week after his return. In a report to Sir Alex Cadogan, MI5 stated that Lonsdale-Bryans has returned from Lisbon and had had dealings with a Danish citizen, Ole Erik Anderson, who worked as a courier for the Germans. It also states that Lonsdale-Bryans was not to be trusted and rather than acting as potential intermediary, was actually pro-Hitler and wanted to use a von Hassell meeting as a means to arranging a meeting with the German leader.

Sir Alex Cadogan wrote in reply to Brigadier Harker of MI5 on 7 April, stating that they could not lock up Lonsdale-Bryans because of his friendship with Lord Halifax, but requested that MI5 kept him under surveillance and checked his mail.

Consequently, we now believe that the Lonsdale-Bryans/von Hassell channel was really no more than another of a myriad of similar peace overtures in 1939/40/41. It would be amazing if there were no such moves, given the huge stakes. However, ultimately nothing came of this particular initiative, save for the details of the venue and the necessary travel arrangements for the Haushofer and von Hassell meeting on 28 April 1941.

---

1 Anthony Pilcher to John Harris, email, 14 October 2020.

2 Churchill to John Colvile, 22 June 1941.

3 *Review of World Affairs*, written and published by Kenneth de Courcy, London, April 1942.

4 James Lonsdale-Bryans *Blind Victory: Secret Communications, Halifax–Hassell*, Skeffington and Son Limited, London, 1951.

CHAPTER 30
SPANDAU

Operation Traffic, the movement of the seven former Nazi leaders from Nuremberg to Spandau, was implemented at 4.00am on 18 July 1947. At 4.00pm on 17 August 1987, some forty years and nearly a month later, Rudolf Hess was pronounced dead.

Apart from a period of hospitalisation from 24 November 1969 to 13 March 1970, and other routine check-ups, Hess did not leave the prison. Behind the scenes the four powers responsible for guarding Hess continuously bickered as to whether he might be released and what might happen when he died. With a backdrop of tense Cold War politics, that was hardly a surprise.

As regards this book, the details of the period from 1947–87 are both fascinating and irrelevant. The whole period was essentially a reflection of the aftermath of the Second World War and how the geo-politics eventually played out. Arguing over detail and an intractable desire for Hess not to be released appear to be the main principles; but there are also three issues that warrant further attention with regards to the title of this book:

1. Was the Hess in Spandau a doppelgänger?

This question first raised it head in 1969, when Hugh Thomas, a former army surgeon published *The Murder of Rudolf Hess*. The book claimed that the prisoner was not the same man as the one who had crashed at Eaglesham, as a result of some bullet scars not being present on the 'Spandau Hess'. The issue was the subject of written questions in the House of Commons in London.

However, the Rudolf Hess who was imprisoned in Spandau and died in Spandau was the same Rudolf Hess who flew to Scotland in 1941. John Harris went to Munich in 2015 to meet Wolf Hess Jr, Rudolf's grandson. Over a pleasant lunch in the Löwenbraükeller, Wolf advised that when his grandfather's body had been exhumed in 2010 from Wunsiedel, a DNA test was carried out. This proved that the family DNA was indeed present. This came as no great surprise, as there had also been a number of facial comparison and vocal comparison tests carried out in the late 1980s that concluded that Spandau's prisoner no. 7 was statistically most likely to be Rudolf Hess.

This finding effectively ends the theory of the doppelgänger, as previously peddled by both Hugh Thomas and the *Double Standards* team. It also clearly proved that Hess did not die with the Duke of Kent in 1942, also as alleged in *Double Standards*. No real surprises whatsoever, but reassuring, nonetheless. This revelation was finally confirmed in January 2019, when further details were released. Prof. Jan Cemper-Kiesslich, of the University of Salzburg, had carried out the research, but this knowledge was of course already well known to the family and (somewhat surprisingly, perhaps) to us. We should also record that we never really understood Hugh Thomas's claims. The scars on Hess's chest that he claimed were not there had been recorded in Scotland in 1941 and at Nuremberg when examined by Captain B. Hurewitz, the Prison Surgeon. This detailed report appears in J.R. Rees's *The Case of Rudolf Hess*.[1] Hugh Thomas made the case that the 'two men' had been swapped somehow during the flight, but with the Nuremberg Hess showing the scars and now the DNA evidence, this is impossible.

However, this important discovery then goes on to raise other questions. Most notably, why was the real Rudolf Hess incarcerated for the forty-six years from the day of his flight to the date of his death? From 10 May 1941 to 17 August 1987, Hess was totally controlled and was not allowed to speak publicly, with the single exception of the Nuremberg Trials, where it is most likely he was being drugged (see Chapter 24).

After the war, it was deemed obvious and necessary to make sure that Hess was not given a platform, any platform, particularly as he remained so unrepentant and spent a lot of time in the late 1940s busily planning a Fourth Reich (!), but why just Hess? Why was he singled out in this manner? After the 1966 releases, Hess was the only occupant in the huge, Prussian, Spandau Prison in Berlin. By way of direct comparison, Walther Funk was also given a life sentence at Nuremberg, yet he was released in 1957, three years before he died. Why was Hess treated so differently and, in this day and age, some might say so inhumanely?

Various explanations have been espoused. The Russians wanted to keep a foothold in Berlin and so had the excuse of tending to Hess, albeit on a rotational basis. The Russians wanted Hess to be executed at Nuremberg and when he was not, the life sentence had to mean life. Hess was, by that time, the most senior surviving Nazi in terms of rank. Meanwhile, the supporters of the now completely redundant doppelgänger theory obviously required the lifetime incarceration of their said doppelgänger (whoever he was), so as to be able to preserve and support their unlikely secret and theory.

The truth is, we are sure, far simpler. Hess was effectively silenced for ever. He was never allowed to explain his flight and the reasons for making it. Doppelgängers are, and were, a very convenient diversion. Not the only diversion.

Hess was never in a position to explain why he chose to fly to Scotland in 1941.

It was really therefore no wonder that various 'release Hess' groups were formed around the world, especially in the period from 1966 to the date of his death. Wolf Hess, his son, lobbied tirelessly and recruited some powerful allies; amongst others, Airey Neave and Sir Hartley Shawcross in the UK and in Germany, the Minister of State, Alois Mertes and Willy Brandt, the former Chancellor.

Meanwhile, in Germany, the Hilfsgemeinschaft Freiheit für Rudolf Hess had been formed in 1966.

They were never going to succeed. Rudolf Hess clearly knew too much, irrespective of his true mental state, a position later used to justify the use of the phrase 'British National Interest'. A knowledge that at the least would challenge the accepted and comfortable victor's history of the Second World War. Millions had died as a result of the Nazis and that is why Hess had remained in prison. Those deaths could never be seen to be in vain, quite properly and quite understandably.

He was never going to be released – alive, at least.

2. The suicide note – real or used previously?

At the same Munich meeting in 2015, Wolf Hess Jr informed us that calligraphy tests had been made of the supposed suicide note that was found on his grandfather's body at the time of his death in 1987. A scrap of paper had been found in one of Hess's pockets, which read:

> 'Would the Governors please send this home. Written a few minutes before my death. I thank you all my loved ones for all that you have done for me. Tell Freiburg that I was infinitely sorry that I had to behave ever since the Nuremberg Trials as if I did not know her. There remained nothing else for me, otherwise all attempts to free me would have been vain. I had looked forward to seeing her again. I have

received photographs of her as well as of all of you.
Euer Grosser'

The family had never believed that this was written at the date of death. Instead, it seemed to refer back to a specific incident in 1969 when Hess had suffered a burst ulcer and it was feared he might die. The reference to Freiburg was in respect of Hildegath Fath, his last Munich-based secretary, who he had denied knowing as part of his charade at Nuremberg in 1946 (she came from Freiburg). However, the officials had told the family that it was written using the same pen as was found on the body (but that, not surprisingly, had been destroyed post death).

Again, we were informed by Wolf Jr that the results of the tests indicated that it was not written at the time of Hess's death, as suspected all along by the family. The reader must decide why this might be so and who placed the note. The calligraphy test is surely a significant result. Why would anyone wish to fake a suicide note? That must surely tell us something?

3. Murder or suicide?

We have never concerned ourselves with the issue of Hess's death previously, simply because to our simple minds the outcome was the same whichever methodology was employed. Hess was permanently silenced.

Moreover, at the time of writing, thirty-five years after Hess's death in Spandau in August 1987, there is still no definitive, conclusive answer as to the above question either way.

The evidence currently appears to be as follows:

Suicide

The principal case for suicide was made by Tony Le Tissier, the last British Governor of Spandau, who described later (he was not even at Spandau at the time) how Hess was found slumped against the wall in his summer house, a converted porta-cabin, with a loop of electric cable around his neck. Apparently, Hess had slid down the wall, fatally tightening the loop around his neck in the process. Despite efforts to resuscitate, Hess was declared dead just after 4.00pm. The suicide note had been later found in one of his pockets.

> *Murder*
> By contrast, there is quite a lot of evidence of foul play, largely detailed by Abdallah Melaouhi, Hess's Tunisian nurse who had been with him since 1982. The evidence has been given in part on national TV and then later in written form. According to Melaouhi, when he found Hess there were two men in US Army uniforms and an American warder, Jordan, who had a long record of disliking Hess. The electric cable was still plugged into the socket and had not been used for the alleged purpose.

There are other issues to consider, such as was Hess capable of such an act of suicide? Aged ninety-three, he was riddled with arthritis, and so could he even tie the cable? Was the cable high enough to effect such an outcome? Was Hess of such a mind to take his life?

The key medical debate revolves around the horizontal bruising on Hess's neck that featured in the second autopsy. First, there was an official British autopsy and then a second, commissioned by the Hess family. The first was carried out by a Welshman, Prof. J. Malcolm Cameron (1930–2003) and the second by the German, Dr Wolfgang Spann (1921–2013) of Munich University. Both men were eminent in their field, though Cameron's reputation had been somewhat tarnished by reason of his involvement in the infamous Australian 'dingo baby' affair (he had made the case for foul play).

Prof. Cameron concluded that the cause of death was:

1. Asphyxia (due to, or as a consequence of)
2. Compression of the neck (due to, or as a consequence of)
3. Suspension.

The death was therefore not due to natural causes, according to Prof. Cameron.

Dr Spann performed his tests after Cameron (a day later) and by that time further bruising had emerged, as is apparently usual in the circumstance.

Dr Spann concluded that the cause of death was strangulation by the forceful closure of two carotid arteries. He concluded that the horizontal marks on the neck were evidence of such an action. Had hanging been employed, the marks would not be horizontal. They would taper towards the point of suspension.

The reader will have to make his or her own mind up. We doubt we will ever learn the truth. Furthermore, there are also some somewhat macabre YouTube videos which show how it is quite possible to have a horizontal line by hanging if the body initially hangs and then leans forwards at 45 degrees away from an available wall, but one must ask why Hess would attempt the deed anyway, even if physically capable? (and after forty-six years of captivity?

On the basis of the second autopsy, Hess' son Wolf, not surprisingly challenged the original death certificate which had been issued by the British Government. Somewhat bizarrely they reacted by withdrawing the certificate, so technically Rudolf Hess is not yet dead (! – amongst his many other accomplishments). The legal challenge then fizzled out, as sadly Wolf Hess had died in October 2001.

This bureaucratic issue had already been debated in the House of Commons in 1997 when Nicholas Soames, the Minister of State for the Armed Forces (and Winston Churchill's grandson) explained to Rhodri Morgan that the certificate had been wrongly issued under the Registration of Births, Deaths and Marriages (Special Provisions) Act 1957. Morgan, who has also since died (in 2017), was asking awkward questions, being brave enough to challenge the official report into Hess's death.

So, the whole issue is now a mix of contradiction, misunderstandings and the removal of evidence. On 3 September 1987, the bulldozers started to dismantle Spandau Prison, less than two weeks after Hess's death. It really is no wonder that the issue is still unresolved and those that challenge the suicide verdict should certainly not be simply discounted as mere conspiracy theorists. That is just too easy and lazy. There is evidence that Rudolf Hess was murdered and, if so, a public enquiry should be held, though more than three decades later, this is unlikely in the extreme. The BBC *Newsnight* programme conducted a televised inquiry under Olenka Friedel.

What we also find interesting, however, is to then consider who might have committed the act, and why? In the summer of 1987, the first cracks in the disintegration of the USSR were starting to manifest themselves. Mikhail Gorbachev, since 1985 the General Secretary of the Communist Party, had soon realised that he was in trouble and very much into damage limitation and decline management. Consequently, new words from Russia soon came into the Western vocabulary and consciousness, *Glasnost* and *Perestroika*. They were Russian for 'we are running out of money so please help us'. In March 1987, Margaret Thatcher had travelled to Moscow and there still remains the debate as to who was actually stopping the Hess release. His death five months later obviously rendered that debate irrelevant.

What is sure, however, is that the Russians were not on duty the day Hess died. There appears to be a mixture of American and British involvement. The suspicion must sadly remain that the British could no longer rely on the Russian veto of release and so took matters into their own hands.

As Colonel Eugene Bird, Hess's last US Commandant of Spandau Prison stated, 'Hess was murdered. I am convinced of it. The man was 93 years old. He could not even rise from a bench alone, he had to be helped up… If that man was murdered it had to be a decision taken at the highest level. I will say no more than that.'

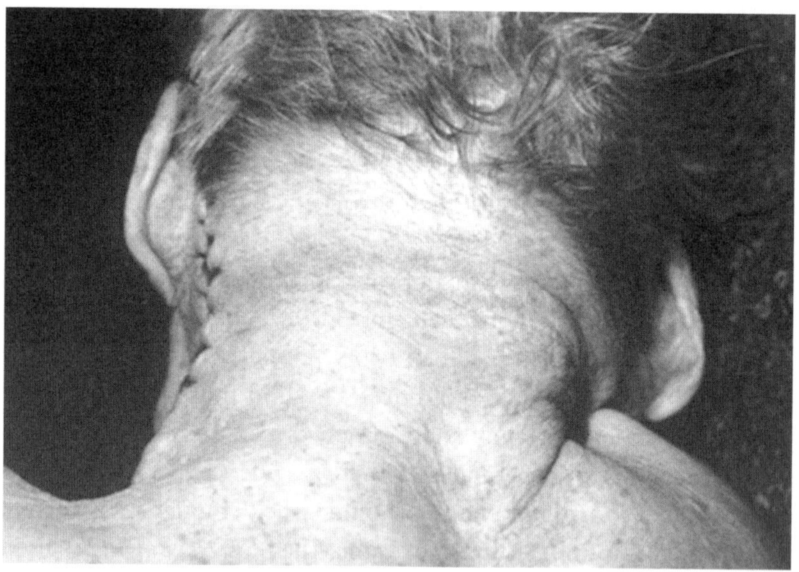

Hess autopsy – note the horizontal bruising

[1] J.R. Rees, *The Case of Rudolf Hess*, Heinemann, London, 1947 .

CHAPTER 31

CONCLUSIONS – 'A VERY HIGH PLANE'[1]

'A decision taken at the highest level'[2]

On 18 May 1941, just a week after Hess's arrival in Renfrewshire, Guy Liddell, then Director of B division of MI5 spoke to Henry Hopkinson, then private secretary to Sir Alexander Cadogan, who in turn was the Permanent Under-Secretary of State for Foreign Affairs. We presume the conversation to have taken place in London.

Liddell duly recorded that, 'I saw Henry Hopkinson and explained our point of view about Hess. He said that the matter was still on a very high plane and that Hess was not in a mood to discuss matters on our level. He told me that so far only the Duke of Hamilton and Ivone Kirkpatrick had seen him.'

This comment appears to us to be very significant. If Hess was 'not in a mood to discuss matters on our level', at just what 'level' was he anticipating operating? Liddell and Hopkinson were essentially very senior civil servants and yet a higher level still is being mooted. Just who did Hess believe he was flying to meet? At the time of the above conversation Hess was somewhere in transit between Buchanan castle, Drymen and the Tower of London and, as Liddell quite correctly records, at that point in time the two individuals mentioned above had indeed interviewed Hess whilst in Scotland. (Even though, don't forget, the Duke was nothing to do with the affair and would sue you if you insinuated otherwise.) In coming south on 17 May, Hess had also narrowly avoided the Polish assassination team headed by Alfgar Hesketh-Prichard that was intending to eliminate him two days later.

The evidence we have seen so far suggests that far from being a solo flight by a madman, the Hess flight was a well-planned German peace mission, with the clear aim of bypassing the incumbent Churchill government. (Kenneth de Courcy, see Chapter 29, at least got that part of the story correct.) During the period under review, at no time did Hess directly communicate, or attempt to communicate, with the incumbent British government. Instead, from 31 August 1940, to 11 May 1941 he tried to locate and communicate with those persons, both within and outside Britain who he thought still preferred a negotiated settlement with Nazi Germany and had presented a viable means of achieving the same.

Similarly, there is now clear evidence that despite the public 'We will fight them on the beaches...' oratory from the British government, there were alternative initiatives coming from within the British Intelligence community, which at the very least were designed to explore the true Nazi appetite for peace. Not surprisingly, given Britain's precarious military position at the time, there was not a unanimous approval of the overt governmental approach. Moreover, before becoming too judgemental, it is also vitally important to ascertain whether these overtures were real or imaginary; simply and cleverly designed by government agencies so as to buy more time and thus stave off the very real threat of an invasion.

The new information contained within this book also makes it quite plain that prior to September 1939, Hess was being supplied with good, high-grade political intelligence from a number of British and German sources (e.g. Jahnke, Haushofer, Gerl/Calthrop) all saying the same thing. An Anglo-German accord was preferable to any accommodation with Communist Russia. However, Hitler and his duplicity was still the major hurdle and persistent problem; one that was proving very difficult to overcome.

In summing up and concluding, we must therefore try to ascertain which of these channels of communication continued post-September 1939 and whether they were clear and persuasive enough to ferment and instigate the non-governmental change of political direction that many in the higher 'planes' of British society were demanding. In many people's eyes, the very future of Britain and her empire was at stake.

Consequently, in the first instance, we now cite and highlight the conclusions and new information that we have gleaned from each chapter, prior to summing up for the reader (and then allowing the reader to make their own minds up), based on the previous evidence presented.

Chapters 1–6: The Letter to Mrs Roberts

Clearly, Rudolf Hess was the instigator of this initial attempt to contact the Duke of Hamilton. At the time, late August 1940, there was no talk of negotiations, merely the wish to make contact with someone to discuss the likelihood of a peace. It appears to us that the letter (and the manner of its delivery) was always likely to be intercepted by the Censor and moreover was incorrectly addressed, thus causing additional confusion upon arrival in England. Mrs Roberts did not see the letter and the Duke apparently only got to learn of the letter in March 1941, some seven months after its despatch. It was not responded to, but its arrival did alert MI5, MI6 and SOE as to the fact that Albrecht Haushofer was trying to communicate with the Duke of Hamilton. We are also concerned by the apparent ignorance of the Thomas Cook postal system and now wonder if this was deliberate in an attempt to bring extra attention to the letter upon its receipt in Britain.

Chapters 7–8: British Intelligence

These chapters highlight the wholly defensive nature of British intelligence during the period under review. Invasion was the major threat to Britain at the time and so this was naturally the focus of attention. The chapters also highlight the creation of the 'W Board', a creation of the intelligence community themselves, with the sole objective of deception planning. Some of the officers serving on the W Board crop up throughout the analysis of the Hess affair (Dansey and Boyle, in particular) and combine the necessary communication channels and practical military knowledge required to facilitate such an enterprise. The W Board secretary was Ewen Montagu, who with his colleague Charles Cholmondeley later devised and implemented *The Man who Never Was*. The necessary nous was certainly present as any reading of Montagu's subsequent book will amply demonstrate.

Chapter 9: Channels of Intelligence Available to Rudolf Hess – November 1940

There is important new information contained within this chapter, especially in connection with the Gerl and Gulla Pfeffer communication channels which appear far more functional and operational than have been previously documented. However, these were essentially pre-war communication channels. In 1939, Pfeffer was interned and 'Fletcher' was put under close watch by MI5. Moreover, the onset of war prevented further use of the Calthrop/Gerl/Hess channel that we now know existed throughout the 1930s. Whilst fascinating, it is highly unlikely that these two routes to Hess provided him with anything other than background political information, albeit at a reasonably high level. We would also record that Lady Hamilton and Stewart Blacker were both 'patients' at the Gerl clinic in Bavaria. We suspect that Hess had also realised these channels were now concluded, by reason of his reversion to the Haushofers in August/September 1940.

Chapter 10: The Public Facade and the Private Anxieties – Late 1940/ Early 1941

This chapter can be seen as the crux of the book. Outwardly Churchill was the British Bulldog, inwardly he knew the true military vulnerability and the weakness of his own political position. However, Britain was still intact, had the wealthiest empire man had ever witnessed, so could in theory fund an extended conflict; a fact that would be worthless if Germany was to invade and conquer in the spring of 1941. Essentially, the whole future and direction of the war was as yet undecided, and Germany was about to take a massive leap into the dark. A leap that Churchill already knew about. It almost appears that Hitler had yet to decide on his next step. He seriously courted Russia in November 1940 without success whilst at the same time sounding out Britain.

Chapter 11: Tancred Borenius

It is now over twenty years since we introduced the role of Tancred Borenius to the Hess affair. We still believe him to be central and yet there is much we still do not know about his role subsequent to his extraordinary trip to Geneva in January 1941. Who was he specifically representing and did anything happen following his return? We suspect that it did, and being Finnish could all make his actions deniable, should the need arise. The fact that he was given a suicide pill must surely mean that what he was imparting was deemed important to the British, the supplier of the said pill.

Chapter 12: The British Constitution

This chapter simply illustrates how a peace or treaty could be concluded outside any interference from Winston Churchill or the British Government. We have always been fascinated by the reference to Hess studying the British constitution in the spring of 1941 and now believe this chapter explains why.

Chapter 13: So, What Precisely was Rudolf Hess Doing?

This chapter merely tries to give a flavour of Hess's lifestyle during the period under review. It appears to be a mixture of official business in Berlin with party business in Munich whilst, at the same time, learning how to fly a Bf110, one of the fastest aircraft in the world. It appears to us to be inconceivable that Hitler did not know what his deputy was doing. We do not subscribe to the theory that Hess had made previous attempts at the flight before 10 May. The plane was only made ready following radio trials on 6 May.

Chapter 14: The Zeileis Institute

It would be easy to dismiss this chapter as an idiosyncratic aside, were it not for the fact that Pintsch, Hess's adjutant, sent his driver and security adviser to Gallspach on the night of 10 May 1941. They were arrested there the following morning. This could be a recognition that Pintsch was unsure as to Hitler's reaction to the flight and so was trying to protect his colleagues, but there again, Hess may not have told Pintsch the whole story either. There is some evidence to suggest that Hess had been to Gallspach on more than the two occasions that we have been able to prove via the Zeileis Institute.

Chapter 15: Poland

Nominally at least, the German invasion of Poland is the stated reason that Britain went to war and so logically must feature in any potential peace treaty, particularly as the government in exile was based in the United Kingdom. If only life was so simple. Britain did not really go to war because of Poland, and Hitler also believed that Britain would not go to war over Poland. However, because of the March and August 1939 treaties, Britain found herself at war in September 1939 when the said treaties were knowingly breached.

A long time ago, in 1999 we had discovered that General Sikorski had flown into Prestwick on the morning of 11 May 1941. Prestwick is no more than 25 miles from the Hess crash site. Lowland Scotland in 1941 was full of exiled Polish soldiers and the Poles themselves were typically split politically from top to bottom, with a number of anti-Sikorski officers already being interned on the Isle of Bute. President Raczkiewicz, who had also tried to sack his Prime Minister in July 1940 and in April 1941, was declaring to his pilots serving within the RAF that 'he hoped to meet them again in Poland next Easter'. How this was to be achieved he did not readily explain.

Given that it was Raczkiewicz rather than Sikorski who had the power under the recent 1935 Polish constitution to make a peace, we hope the reader can see why we started to think that Hess was actually targeting the Poles: not the British at all. Imagine the effect had an independent peace been negotiated. We were also fascinated to learn that Sikorski's principal advisor was Józef Retinger, an arch exponent of a federal Europe; something that Albrecht Haushofer had also proposed to the German Foreign Office in late 1940.

However, since our *Rudolf Hess: Truth at Last*, in 2019, we have discovered that the Poles, rather than wishing to meet Hess to talk peace, actually tried to meet him in order to kill him. We have also unearthed two important accounts of the arrival of Hess from the Polish perspective: one from Roman Battaglia in Scotland, the other from the Polish Foreign Minister. Neither, at least, appear to know why Hess had arrived.

This is still a controversial area, as it may well be that a scion of the Poles wished to murder Hess, whereas it is still possible that the old Pilsudki Poles would have been the more accommodating. This dilemma is debated later in the summing up, together with their very odd linkage to the British Royal family.

Chapter 16: Germany – Spring 1941

This is an important aspect to the affair. Seemingly, in spring 1941 Germany was unassailable and yet the cracks were beginning to show, even before Operation Barbarossa had commenced. Above all the need for a speedy victory was becoming paramount, as Hitler knew that eventually he could be 'out produced'. That in turn placed additional emphasis and pressures on new technical weaponry which might in extremis be called upon to win the war.

Chapter 17: Spain

Time had run out for Hitler. Ideally Spain would have declared war on Britain, thus placing yet more pressure on Churchill. However, Britain's wealth had again helped to bribe the Spanish generals to remain neutral, alongside the fact that the country was heartily sick of war, having only just concluded the Civil War. It does now seem likely that Samuel Hoare, the British Ambassador in Madrid, was involved in the Hess initiative and dialogue in spring 1941.

Chapter 18: Westminster, London, 7 May 1941

Had Churchill's own vote of confidence been defeated, then Hess's flight might well have become unnecessary. It is quite possible that the actual result in Churchill's favour was the determining factor to convince Hess to finally fly. Time was fast running out and an intra-governmental negotiated settlement was not going to happen. The motion and its management also begs the question as to whether Churchill was intending to 'draw fire' so as to establish just how politically secure he really was.

Chapter 19: The Flight and its Character

The more we have studied the flight, the more we believe its character to be the most important aspect. Most importantly, because we can prove how there had to be British involvement in its planning; not necessarily its implementation, as we do not think Hess was physically 'guided in' in (he did not need to be), given the previous meticulous planning that is now self-evident.

Our other major contribution in this area is the discovery that there was no auxiliary oil tank fitted to the Hess plane fuselage. That meant that a landing in Germany was necessary to prevent an act of utter recklessness later on. This en route landing ties in nicely with the pilot's notes given to us by Peter Padfield and the Lennoxlove radio map that still hangs in the Duke of Hamilton's home to this day.

What is absolutely sure is that Hess did not intend to crash in Eaglesham or anywhere else. As soon as he came under the control of the Churchillian Home Guard in Eaglesham, his mission had failed and the character of the mission was such that lifetime imprisonment now beckoned to preserve the fact.

Chapters 20 and 21: Britain and Germany, 10–13 May 1941

These chapters draw on witness accounts of the actions of others closely involved in the Hess affair, both in Germany and Britain. What becomes clear is that Hitler did not lose his cool until he knew the mission had failed. Thereafter came the acting masterclass, mostly for the benefit of Stalin and his own Reichsleiters.

In Britain, there certainly was not a governmental control centre, as seen in the Bin Laden execution some seventy years later. Instead, all the major politicians were spread far and wide. The Churchill government were not expecting Hess that night, at least.

However, non-governmentally the same cannot be said. On 10 May 1941, Lowland Scotland was literally full of the obvious candidates for an Anglo-German accord, including the Duke of Buccleuch (Drumlanrig), the Duke and Duchess of Hamilton (Turnhouse), General Sir Ian Hamilton (Blair Drummond) the Duke of Bedford (Cairnsmore), and on 10 May 10, we have discovered, they were joined by Montagu Norman, the Governor of the Bank of England (and no fan of Churchill) at Dawych, his sister's married home, the Duke and Duchess of Gloucester (presumably staying with the Duchesses' brother at Drumlanrig) and the Duke of Kent, somewhat inexplicably reviewing ships in Scapa Flow, dressed as a Rear Admiral.

We cautiously use the word 'inexplicably', because at the time the Duke was nominally, at least, a member of the RAF and his job was to inspect airfields, which he had been doing in the first few days of May 1941. Previously, he had been in the navy and had been appointed a Rear Admiral, but certainly during spring 1941 his role was clear: an officer in the RAF.

We also have the vexed issue of why Viscount Alanbrooke was despatched to the Orkneys on 13 May. It has taken us more than twenty years to ascertain where the Duke of Kent was located on the night of 10 May 1941, hence our heightened suspicion of the movements of Alanbrooke. If the Duke was merely inspecting ships in Scapa Flow, why on earth not just say so? We will debate this apparent obfuscation in due course.

Unfortunately, there is also the similar obfuscation by the Duke of Hamilton and Hector MacLean at RAF Ayr, which also will be debated further.

Chapter 22: Push and Pull

This summary chapter merely describes the forces at play in Hess making the decision to fly to Scotland.

Chapter 23: The Poles and Their Somewhat Odd Assassination Attempt

This whole area should be treated with caution. The simple explanation to the attempt is that the Poles wanted Hess dead so as to prevent any further peace negotiations taking place, with the fear of Poland being left under German control or influence.

However, the involvement of Alfgar Hesketh-Prichard raises further particular issues, especially as he was, or shortly was to become, a member of the SOE. Moreover, was he and his would-be assassins acting on behalf of a united Polish government in exile, or just a part of the Polish government in exile? Were they even being sub-contracted to (or by) the SOE?

Chapter 24: Thereafter and Nuremberg

As regards the Hess affair, the Nuremberg Trials were notable for what was not uncovered. Despite a massive Allied legal operation, with detailed interrogations, affidavits and interviews, we learned virtually nothing as to why Hess had flown to Scotland in 1941. Given that his life was certainly at threat, one might have thought that the details of the mission would have been discussed in open forum, but instead nothing. Initially Hess feigned amnesia and then having admitted as much, said very little else that made sense. The tactic succeeded. Hess survived, along with the secret as to why he had really flown.

Chapter 25: Carl Burckhardt Tries to Clear his Name

There is little doubt that Carl Burckhardt saw an opportunity in 1941 to act as a mediator in what was about to become a worldwide conflict. However, there were a few issues. First, whilst he knew the major players (and was having an affair with the wife of the British Minister of Information) he was at the same time employed by the International Red Cross, an organisation that was founded on the principle of political non-involvement, and secondly, he had (unknowingly at the time) backed the wrong horse, being largely pro-German. In 1946 this was not seen as being wise, particularly as he was then running for the presidency of the International Red Cross. Consequently, this chapter deals with his efforts to re-write history, which largely failed.

Chapter 26: A Possible Common Denominator?

This chapter makes the case that there was one person who appears to be the common denominator in the various facets of the Hess affair: HRH the Duke of Kent.

Chapter 27: Albrecht Haushofer – British Agent?

James Douglas-Hamilton's 1971 *Motive for a Mission* first made the case that Albrecht Haushofer was instrumental in Rudolf Hess making his May 1941 flight. We have merely questioned his true allegiances. Clearly he was anti-Hitler but was he knowingly conveying false information to the Deputy Führer? This is now virtually impossible to answer, but would have become very obvious, very quickly had Hess managed to land his Bf110 intact in Scotland.

Chapter 28: Parlamentär

This chapter debates the legal definition of a Parlamentär and explains how Hitler's initial communique effectively ended any prospect of Hess being able to rely upon the definition once under British control. We also look at the continued claims that Hess had the protection of King George VI.

Chapter 29: William Spelman Pilcher, Kenneth de Courcy and James Lonsdale-Bryans

In this chapter we de-bunk some of the wilder stories concerning Pilcher, de Courcy and Lonsdale-Bryans.

Chapter 30: Spandau

This is an unsatisfactory chapter in that it is currently impossible to say with any degree of certainty whether Hess was murdered in August 1987. The British pathologist said not; the German pathologist hired by the family thought that the wounds 'were consistent with strangulation, not suspension'. A score draw.

What is for sure is that Hess is dead (even though that is not officially confirmed, as the British subsequently withdrew the original death certificate) and if the death was murder, the policy of not allowing Hess the opportunity to explain his actions was upheld throughout his entire forty-seven-year captivity. It would also be virtually unique for a modern Western state to admit to a political assassination and so that fact alone might justify the official retention/destruction of certain Hess papers.

However, whether Hess was not murdered and instead committed suicide, the outcome remains essentially the same. He was silenced from 1941 to 1987.

So. We have now presented the major evidence to the reader and hopefully have drawn out the salient points from our recent research. Do we now have sufficient evidence to support the premise raised by the title of this book?

In order to answer that basic question, we now summarise what we believe happened and why.

EXPLANATION PART ONE: UP TO 15 MARCH 1941

1. Rudolf Hess was both practical and pragmatic. He understood the risk of a protracted two-front war and earnestly tried to prevent it. He was completely sane and rational. He knew of the atrocities taking place in Poland and knew of the Commando Order that was about to precede Barbarossa. He knew and thoroughly understood the immense risk (and its possible dire implications) of the action that Hitler was contemplating and about to commence. He wanted to de-risk that action.
2. Throughout the mid- to late 1930s Hess was in receipt of detailed and quality British political intelligence. It is now clear that this was emanating from Dr Gerl in the Allgäu and Kurt Jahnke through the services of Gulla Pfeffer, then based and operating in central London. Additionally, Hess still had the enduring friendship of Karl Haushofer, his old university professor and his son, Albrecht, who was then based in Berlin, working for von Ribbentrop.
3. The full extent and effectiveness of these information channels has been previously unknown, but it now appears that amongst others, Lloyd George, Stanley Baldwin, Lady Elizabeth Percy and Stewart Blacker were all patients/visitors to the clinic in the Allgäu.
4. All the visitors were saying the same thing. Britain did not want a war, but Hitler was the problem. No one could trust him. A line in the sand had to be drawn.
5. At the onset of the war in September 1939, Hess then lost two of his

best channels of information. Gulla Pfeffer was interned in London and visits to the Allgäu by the British great and good were no longer physically possible.

6. Consequently, Hess had returned to the Haushofers in August 1940 with the aim of exploring a western settlement prior to the onslaught of Barbarossa. His old friends and their English contacts were now the best/only sources of reliable information available to him.
7. After meeting with Karl Haushofer in late August 1940, Hess approved the sending of a letter to a pre-war friend of Martha Haushofer, Mrs Mary Violet Roberts, who lived in Cambridge, England.
8. Through a misunderstanding, deliberate or otherwise, the letter was duly intercepted by British Intelligence. The interception made clear that Albrecht Haushofer was attempting to contact the Duke of Hamilton, a pre-war friend, with a view to meeting 'at the outskirts of Europe'.
9. The letter was duly intercepted in early November 1940 and copies sent to MI5, MI6 and SOE.
10. At the same time, British Intelligence was re-arranging itself at the onset of the war, following the disasters of Venlo and the loss of its Passport Office system of intelligence collection.
11. Part of the re-arranging spawned an intra-service committee, the W Board, whose specific role was to distribute 'disinformation' to the enemy. It was accountable to no-one, being a creation of the intelligence bodies themselves. It boasted a potent mix of intelligence and practical service-based abilities and soon spawned the XX committee to deal with the day to day management of turned agents. The members of the W Board continue to appear throughout the Hess affair in one guise or another.
12. It appears no direct answer was sent in response to the Haushofer letter. In early November 1940, Hess was bemoaning that no reply had been received.
13. MI5 and MI6 were making a dog's dinner of deciding how to respond. First, they could not identify Mrs Roberts and then the relevant file appears to have gone missing.
14. However, it is our contention that by that time Claude Dansey had

the file and knew exactly what was going on. He then specifically recruited Tancred Borenius and briefed him to go to Geneva, ostensibly to deliver one-time pads to the British Embassy. This is precisely what the Borenius family had told Harris in the late 1990s.

15. At the same time, it seems that it was also arranged for Borenius to meet Carl Burckhardt, an ambitious and senior member of the International Red Cross. Pre-war he was well known in London and somehow managed to find time to conduct an affair with the wife of the British Minister of Information, Duff Cooper. We now know for sure that Borenius and Burckhardt had previously met in London in October 1939, so were acquainted to each other.
16. Consequently, and duly armed with a suicide pill, Borenius left London in mid-January 1941. He flew to Portugal and then caught trains via Vichy France to Geneva, where he again met Burckhardt at the end of January 1941.
17. Burckhardt then duly reported the conversation he had with Borenius to Ulrich von Hassell (who was also in Geneva at around the same time as Borenius). He in turn passed on the information to Albrecht Haushofer, a fellow member of the nascent anti-Nazi resistance and adviser to Rudolf Hess. Burckhardt may well have passed on the clear message that Borenius brought to others, but if so, there are no records extant.
18. The message was clear. Britain still wanted a peace 'but for not much longer'. Borenius was back in London by mid-March 1941. The message was clever, playing on the very extant German fears.
19. What is currently far from clear is who Borenius was representing whilst talking to Burckhardt. According to the London-based Polish Relief Fund, of which he was secretary, he was noted as being away on 'Finnish diplomatic business'. We also know that he was facilitated in his travels by MI6, and we also know that von Hassell thought that Borenius might be representing an 'Englische stellen', which is best translated as 'an English body' – (note not the English government).

And so there we are. In terms of understanding, this is roughly where the authors of this book were in 2015 when we published our *Treachery and Deception*. However, we have subsequently conducted further work and now feel confident enough to continue and develop our analysis.

EXPLANATION PART TWO: 15 MARCH 1941 OR THEREABOUTS – THE BIGGER PICTURE

It was now mid-March 1941 and Tancred Borenius was back in London. Wladyslaw Sikorski and Józef Retinger were about to leave for the US, but not before meeting Borenius.

The pre-escalation war inexorably continued. In Germany rationing was becoming more stringent. The stakes and risks were about to get much, much higher and far more obvious. Rudolf Hess continued to practise flying his recently acquired Bf110. The Luftwaffe continued to target British ports, with Liverpool, Glasgow and Portsmouth all being badly damaged. The awful continental winter weather was slowly lifting, making wanton destruction that much easier and convenient for all concerned. The phrase that warfare is an extension of diplomacy was being played out across Europe with its attendant terrifying consequences.

Militarily, in Europe there was a very subtle movement from west to east. German units were slowly being moved away from France and into Poland, where the railway system was also being upgraded and airfields quietly constructed. Eventually there would still be forty-nine German divisions remaining, deemed necessary to protect Hitler's western boundaries, divisions that could have been decisive if they too had been used against Russia. However, to the world at large, Russia and Germany were still economic partners, although Stalin had cannily still not committed to join Germany in the 'liquidation of the British Empire', as had been offered to Foreign Minister Molotov in Berlin in November 1940.

Bletchley Park in Buckinghamshire, England had picked up the sure radio signs of the preparatory action and now had the task of ascertaining if this was for real or merely a plausible bluff, prior perhaps to a British invasion attempt. They decided it was no bluff and the information was disguised and imparted to Stalin, who seemingly ignored it. However, it appears from our recent research that he too was moving men and machines, but this time from east to west. He knew precisely what was happening physically, but also chose not to act in an obvious manner, or be seen guilty of provocation.

To date there has been no written record of any further interaction between the main protagonists in the lead up to the Hess flight, thus allowing the likes of Sir Richard Evans to make his conclusions. However, just because there is no public record, no doubt neatly catalogued and archived, does not necessarily mean there was no such action. For instance, at the time of writing it is 8.00pm and I have just eaten my supper of sausages and mash. There is certainly no written record of that fact and yet my stomach and waistline both know of and can likely demonstrate the effects of the meal. However, Sir Richard would conclude that without a catalogued, authenticated record, no such supper was partaken and anyone who suggests to the counter is obviously a dangerous sausage conspiracy theorist.[3]

This poor analogy is probably the crux of the affair. Up to around 15 March we know exactly the timings of the various meetings and initiatives. Albrecht Haushofer recorded the late autumn of 1940 meticulously, part through self-justification, part through the need for family protection. Borenius's actions are similarly recorded, via von Hassell. Yet, as the tempo increased and the pressures really came to a head, there were only sporadic mentions of what was actually happening, usually from the papers of associates rather than the main players themselves. Haushofer was chasing around Europe all spring, and yet by contrast to his previous meticulous autumnal recording there is nothing, or at least nothing that has yet seen the light of an open archive. If it requires files of letters to record the posting of a letter to Lisbon, just imagine what might have been written when dealing with Burckhardt, Sweden and quite possibly Samuel Hoare (!). Is it perhaps the case that Haushofer deliberately did not record his spring 1941 meetings in the same manner as those in the previous autumn? If so, why might that be? What was he trying to obscure and hide, and from whom and why?

We know from Ernst Bohle's 1945/6 Nuremberg interviews that he had finished drafting the Hess treaty by early January 1941.

We also know that Albrecht Haushofer was in neutral Sweden in early February 1941. To our knowledge there is no extant record of what he was doing there. He completely failed to mention the journey when accounting for his actions to Hitler on 12 May 1941.

These facts raise further questions and makes us wonder if we have even accurately assessed the timings of the key stages of the affair. Was the mission perhaps further advanced than previously thought?

If one accepts that Rudolf Hess was acting rationally by flying to Scotland in May 1941, then it is very unlikely that he would have flown anywhere in order to try and instigate, negotiate and finalise a settlement. To conclude a settlement, quite possibly, but surely not negotiate one from scratch?

If one studies the timings of a previous Nazi treaty, the one now known as the Molotov-Ribbentrop Pact of August 1939, that certainly did not happen without a period of intense courting before the details were initially debated and the protagonists met in person to sign the treaty.

The biography of Von Ribbentrop, *Hitler's Diplomat* by John Weitz makes it is clear that whilst signed (initially, at least) in August 1939, the signatures were the culmination of a number of months' diplomatic activity, starting with debates around the issue of trade in March 1939. Geo-politics then came into play in May 1939, with von Ribbentrop telling Molotov, 'Even if Germany and Poland went to war, Russia's special interests could be taken into consideration.'

This self-serving process eventually led to von Ribbentrop's momentous airflight to Moscow, via Königsberg in East Prussia on 23 August 1939. The deal itself still was not yet concluded and von Ribbentrop had to telephone Berlin on a few occasions for his Führer's approval of particular issues. Famously, part of the treaty was intended to remain secret, condemning the Baltic States to Russian domination for the following fifty years.

If one now compares the above process with the Hess mission of May 1941, one can see there are naturally distinct similarities in methodology. A period of initial flirtation. Intermediaries became involved (Schnurre and von der Schulenburg in 1939; Borenius and Haushofer in 1940/41) and then an invitation was issued from one party to another to physically meet. The invitation would of course have to give the necessary details regarding travel, times of arrival and eventual destination, etc.

By way of hypothetical comparison, imagine the situation if, in say, May 1939 von Ribbentrop had turned up 'Hess like', supposedly unannounced in Moscow and had demanded to meet Molotov or some other named Russian politician? The politician would most likely have been shot in similar manner to Tukhachevsky in 1937 and von Ribbentrop interned at the least. Hitler in denial mode would have said that von Ribbentrop had stolen the aircraft and was most probably mad. Does this perhaps sound at all familiar? It does make us wonder if Hess had gained some form of misplaced confidence from the Molotov-Ribbentrop Pact. If von Ribbentrop could pull off such a coup, then why couldn't he? The process does appear somewhat similar in outline.

The second important issue that arises from the Molotov-Ribbentrop Pact is that part of the treaty which remained secret. It was only at Nuremberg that the secret protocol was discovered and perhaps, ironically, passed to Rudolf Hess's second attorney, Alfred Seidl. Apart from the negotiators, the part dealing with the Baltic states was unknown for six years until inadvertently discovered and leaked.

The need for secrecy?

Clearly the need for secrecy applied to Hess in just the same way as the earlier secret protocol. Surely, here was never going to be an international announcement that Germany and Britain had just signed a peace treaty, or more likely 'a secret treaty of mutual non-aggression'? A wholly secret, non-governmental-driven deal, demanding British non-aggression and a removal of Churchill, in exchange for German non-invasion? Earlier in our research we studied if George VI even had the capability to make such an announcement to the British nation, even assuming he had wanted to. (He did have the capability and Windsor Castle had recently installed the necessary BBC radio equipment.)

This, we now assert, is why Hess had told his wife that he was not sure when he would be back. Presumably, it is also why he took two pairs of underpants with him (one pair, neatly ironed, currently resides in the IWM archives). He did not know how long the details of the concluding negotiations might take and, above all else, he needed to preserve both his and the proposed treaty's secrecy. That was why his flight was so well planned, to maximise the chance of the flight succeeding and the subsequent 'actions' also remaining secret. The awkward and not altogether unlikely alternative was what of course happened; a catastrophic crash and near immediate, uncontrolled full exposure, followed by the USA, Russia and sundry other Allies wondering (or guessing) what exactly was happening. No wonder that Churchill, 'Had anxious inquiries from a dozen countries, and reports of enemy propaganda in a score of countries, all turning upon the point whether His Majesty's present Government is to be dismissed from power or not.'[4]

Moreover, it is the need for secrecy that renders Dungavel a frankly ridiculous notion as a potential landing strip. Even if Hess managed to have landed 'secretly' at Dungavel without killing himself, the strip was certainly not long enough to facilitate him ever taking off from it – if that was ever the intention.

Whilst contemplating the secret nature of the flight, it is surely for reasons of secrecy that Hess was dressed as a Hauptmann in the Luftwaffe, rather than the Stellvertreter of Nazi Germany, and why he duly proceeded to give a false name on capture. It is also why the flight was described as a solo initiative and endeavour, whereas it was of course no such thing. Hess clearly had landed en route to prevent the danger of running out of oil mid-flight. He was also using the state-of-the-art Luftwaffe Elektra navigation system. So, this is where the story becomes even more interesting.

If one accepts that Hess was on a secret mission and the outcome of the mission would remain secret, then much becomes clear. It explains why there are no records extant as to the flirtations and necessary exchanges that would be necessary between the parties, because that would inform subsequent history and Sir Richard Evans, that Britain and Germany were engaged in serious peace negotiations, real or illusory, in the spring of 1941; a fact that would perhaps be hard to bear given the known subsequent history. It is almost certain that those peace negotiations, again real or illusory, were not being carried out by the British Government, or in the name of the British Government. Lastly, the role of the International Red Cross would also come under detailed scrutiny, particularly given its stated non-political and non- partisan position.

It also explains much about the later behaviour of some of the protagonists. We now suspect that some of those involved thought they were really in pursuit of an actual peace and were thoroughly engaged and committed in such a process. Dansey and the W Board were simply using some convenient, duly qualified and willing people, whatever their true motivations, to prevent an invasion and quite possibly, if needs must, come to an understanding of sorts with the Fascists.

The reader at this junction may well be thinking, this is all very well Harris and Wilbourn, but on one hand you are saying there is no record of negotiation post-March 1941 and yet you are now saying that you believe this to be the case. What specific evidence do you have?

EXPLANATION PART THREE: THE EVIDENCE OF CONTINUED NEGOTIATIONS

In response to the very fair question above, we now list the evidence that we believe indicates that the Hess flight, even in its inconclusive and failed state, demonstrates that there had indeed been the necessary pre-flight negotiations and the suggested flight destination being sent to Germany.

1. We know for sure that the Hess 'treaty' was complete by mid-January 1941. We have assumed previously that this was the same document

that was found in the 'wee burn' following the crash on 10 May. It may, however, of course be the case that Borenius had already brought a copy of the document back with him in February 1941 and his trip to Burckhardt had been instigated by the Germans rather than the British. The timings and the two men's relationship are debated later in this chapter. The document in the 'wee burn' may quite possibly be the treaty that was about to be concluded and signed. (The fact that it was temporarily lost and not physically attached to Hess also indicates that what happened at Eaglesham was certainly not what was meant to have happened. It is careless in the extreme to lose a secret international peace treaty in a Scottish ditch.)

2. In November 1940, Martha Haushofer had noted that there was no reply from the 'Lisbon letter'. On a practical level, this is not surprising given that it was only censored on 1 November 1940, but on the assumption that there was no response, would Hess really have done nothing politically until sending Albrecht Haushofer to Geneva in late April 1941 (nearly 6 months later)? Of course not. It was leaving it far too late to achieve anything meaningful, especially as Barbarossa was originally scheduled for 15 May. Had Hess/Haushofer already prompted Burckhardt to invite the 'person well known and respected in London'?
3. Conversely, the major British objective from late 1940 to late 1941 was above all to prevent an invasion; the outcome of which in military terms was very uncertain. We have learned that as a consequence to this overriding fact, all intelligence operations were defensive by their very nature and requirement. The sending of an envoy to Geneva would certainly satisfy the intelligence brief, especially one offering 'peace, but not for much longer'. We of course now know that Borenius, at the time, was essentially in the pay of MI6.
4. Over the years there have been rumours of forged documents and forged replies to the Hamilton letter. We have absolutely no proof of any of this at all, save to say that the British certainly had the knowledge and necessary nous to pull off such a ruse. Messrs. Delmer and Howe were already in Woburn, with their pencils ready and sharpened. The source for this information primarily comes from the memoirs of František Moravec, the Chief of Intelligence for the Czech government in exile. He was also the Czech liaison

officer with the SOE and being based near to Woburn, he was at least well placed to at least visit Woburn, if indeed this was the source of the documentation. We also note that Sefton Delmer was stopped from going to Scotland to identify Hess (source: Robert Bruce Lockhart diaries) and wonder why this might be. Ivone Kirkpatrick was eventually sent. A second source of corroboration came from Edvard Beneš, Moravec's president, though we wonder if any such correspondence was in response to the Borenius initiative rather than the Hamilton letter of 23 September 1940?

5. In a similar vein, if one believes that there was communication passing between the parties prior to the flight, there must have been a means of transmission of that information. Moreover, and introducing yet another tricky hurdle, a means of communication that had to be seen to be non-governmental by the Germans. In this connection we can offer few alternatives; Gerl and Pfeffer were both out of commission from September 1939 and so the Haushofers' expertise and contacts had been brought back into play.
6. We also have the known pre-war RAF channel of Winterbotham–de Ropp–Rosenberg and Hess to consider. There is currently absolutely nothing known about de Ropp post-1939, save that he was recorded as moving to Switzerland and visiting Berlin from time to time. Again, just because we know nothing of this channel's activity does not mean that there was none. We also note that aeronautical credibility is a necessary component to the flight. More anon.
7. After the war, Sir Owen Morshead (1893–1977), the Royal Archivist, and Anthony Blunt were dispatched to Germany post-haste to recover documents sensitive to the British royal family. They quickly descended on the properties of the Princes of Hessen, though the subject matter would be unlikely to just be that pertaining to the Hess affair (the Duke of Windsor and the Duke of Kent must also be contenders). The somewhat flimsy excuse given was that the recovery was for documents pertaining to the Princess Victoria, the eldest daughter of Queen Victoria. Morshead was a friend of Queen Mary. We have also recently discovered an archive that may well demonstrate a linkage between Blunt and Borenius. Spring 1941 is often given as the start of Blunt's activity with Soviet Intelligence.

In other words, to quote the sausage and mash analogy once again, the means of communication had certainly existed and there are some hints as to its use, but in fairness to Sir Richard Evans, there is as yet, no external, neatly recorded, third-party record of such exchange of information. Nor would we expect there to be, given the obvious need for secrecy as to all matters Hess and what he was trying to achieve.

However.

Further evidence of prior communication, gained by reference to the flight

In 2012 we started studying the nature and character of the flight. We did this to learn more of wartime aviation and also to discover what precisely was possible and not possible given the strictures of 1941 aviation.

By adopting this approach, we also believe that we have discovered further clues to suggest the British had been advising and communicating to Hess certain aspects of his flight.

We list these as follows, as this is obviously an important and controversial area:

8. By supposedly targeting the Duke of Hamilton, Hess had discovered the only serving member of the aristocracy who a) was a pre-war supporter of Germany and had travelled widely throughout the country prior to the war, b) was in control of a section of British airspace and, c) was well known, liked and trusted by Albrecht Haushofer. Otherwise, how on earth did Hess know where Hamilton could be found? What if Hess had turned up at Dungavel on the off-chance, only to discover that the Duke had been previously posted to London, or perhaps more likely wherever his beloved 602 Squadron was stationed? How would Hess have got home? Are we really to believe that Hess would have flown to Britain, not knowing where and who he was to meet? Given the detailed planning that was conducted in every other aspect of the flight, that notion is surely nonsense.
9. Similarly, where precisely was Hess heading? It clearly was not Dungavel as that would have been a suicide mission (and we know, thanks to the ROC, that Hess wisely chose to overfly the area at 4000 ft). For reasons that are now well known, we believe that Hess had been told to land at RAF Dundonald, northeast of Ayr. Once on the ground

Hess could of course be taken anywhere. Quite possibly even Dungavel House, but that would be by motorcar rather than air. Other authors, such as Roy Conyers Nesbit, Georges van Acker and Peter Padfield, have also sensibly discounted Dungavel as a landing strip, so we are not alone in making this assertion.

Dungavel House was sold by the Hamilton family after the war to the Coal Board and the family moved to Lennoxlove House, near Haddington. Thereafter, the house was converted into an immigration centre. We have therefore found it difficult to find any accounts about what happened at the house on the night in question. We do know that the local Home Guard were detailed to attend the house, but currently have no idea as to why. We also know for sure that the Duke of Hamilton was not in residence that night.

10. We believe that he map that resides at Lennoxlove House, Haddington proves that Dungavel was not the target. There is a myriad of markings on the two road maps (that have been glued together), but those that are not either heights of hills or radio frequencies are the centre of circles whose circumferences all converge on Dundonald. In other words, at various points on the map (and hence Hess's route) he not unnaturally wanted to know how far he was from his target. Dundonald is the only point that is vectored by all circles (please see the diagram on p. 525). By contrast, Dungavel House *is not* marked on the map, nor is any landing ground nearby. Glengavel Reservoir, adjacent to Dungavel House, is marked, simply because it is a clear and obvious landmark in all light conditions. It was also on the Hess flight route, en route to Dundonald. We have also squabbled with the Hamilton family over the existence of a further map that is described by Roy Conyers Nesbit and was also previously detailed on the Lennoxlove website. Claiming to 'cover an area to the north' of the other maps, this mysterious third map has now disappeared from the website and its existence has been denied by the Estate. Conyers Nesbit correctly stated that 'it is not on display'.

11. We are very content that Hess was more than capable of finding the Scottish lowland coast without any information from the British whatsoever. Nor did he need any assistance through the air defences as by choosing the route he did there were actually very few air defences to avoid. This again is not a coincidence, especially as a recent re-reading of Hector MacLean's account of the Second World War describes the

precise manoeuvre that Hess performed on approaching the British mainland. By dropping altitude rapidly, he managed to confuse the Chain Home radar system in a well-known manoeuvre that was nicknamed by the RAF as the 'Ogo Pogo', a reference to a mythical bird, 'one that may have once existed'. As Hector later stated, 'The truth of the matter is that the system was designed to deal with easily detected mass raids for which it worked well. Sneak raiders and reconnaissance hostiles were much more difficult to find, although we managed to bag a few.'

12. The next clue again involves Hector in person. On 10 May 1941, Hector was at Rosemount House, just outside Prestwick, which doubled as the operations room for RAF Ayr. We know that at 22.34 hours he chose to launch Messrs Cuddie and Hodge in their Defiant T.4040.

We have also learned that he gave them a very precise instruction: 'Zero 9 degrees, climb to 2000 feet and dive and buster.'

This is actually quite extraordinary. We have learned of this instruction, not from Hector's book, (he chose to not mention it at all), but instead from a letter that Peter Padfield had received in 1991 from Squadron Leader R.G. (Tim)Woodman DFC, DSO. Woodman had been tasked with conducting a review of the affair by the RAF and had interviewed the main protagonists post-event. A later interview with Cuddie in a Canadian newspaper also fails to mention the very specific instruction.

The instructions, if accurately carried out, placed the Defiant literally at the end of Dundonald Airfield. At 22.34, when the instruction was given, the Bf110 was somewhere in the middle of Lowland Scotland and could well have been heading anywhere. Clydeside may well have been a more obvious bet… and yet, no. Hector MacLean placed the plane over RAF Dundonald, and then chose to say nothing further about the matter.

Of further relevance is the fact that MacLean, by his own admission, had other planes up in the sky, 'Fortunately, we had two Defiants, fully armed airborne practicing with their AI. I told them to orbit Kilmarnock which seemed to lie in the path of the hostile.'

This is really most odd. How did he know that (the two other Defiants do not appear in the ORB)?

Moreover, RAF Ayr was joined telephonically to RAF Turnhouse as it was the lead station in that sector. We now wonder if the order to 'dive and buster'

Dundonald had come from Turnhouse in the knowledge that it was now far too dark to attempt a landing at a base that had no lighting? Consequently, had the RAF hierarchy decided to shoot down the Bf110 so as to prevent the debacle unfolding in the exact manner as that which transpired?

We are afraid that this part of the flight is perhaps the most obvious indication of prior knowledge. Sadly, Hector MacLean died in 2007 and we do wonder if he knew a lot more about the true events of that night than later recounted in his biography of that period. He perhaps ironically concluded the Hess chapter of his book by stating, 'Should there still be an unrevealed secret the British people and particularly those of us who spent six years of our young lives containing the aspirations of German tyranny, have a right to know it.'

Hmm.

13. The next clue comes from James Leasors' Rudolf Hess: The Uninvited Envoy of 1962. This is a good book and Leasor, who was being sponsored by Lord Beaverbrook, his employer, took the time and trouble to interview those protagonists still alive. The 14th Duke of Hamilton was acknowledged for his help, which we take to be an interview. He was also the only person so acknowledged who has detailed aeronautical knowledge of Lowland Scotland as far as we are aware.

On page 19, Leasor opens his book with the usual account of the flight and then makes the revelation that, 'He [Hess] did not know, as he flew back over the coast, picking up the railway lines that glittered like two silver snakes in the moonlight … that he was following the daily routine of British RAF pilots under instruction; they would leave Irvine airbase (Dundonald) near Prestwick, fly north to Renfrew, then south east to Dungavel and, using the hill as a landmark turn south-east for their base.'

This account can only have come from the Duke. Leasor would not otherwise have been aware, and the Duke of course was a world-famous airman and former chief of the 602 City of Glasgow squadron. In short, had the Duke just explained to James Leasor the precise route that Hess had followed?

A study of the geography would suggest that was indeed the case. Somewhat confusingly, there are two Dungavel hills. The obvious one is near Dungavel house at 1,302 ft, adjacent to Glengavel Reservoir (which is clearly marked on the Hess flight map). The other, however, is further away in the Tinto hills, near to Wiston. This is, however, adjacent to the marking of 58 km on the Hess map. Not surprisingly, perhaps, from there it is precisely 58 km to Dundonald.

So, it seems to us that Hess was trying to take advantage of the knowledge that the RAF student pilots had been sharing – find Dungavel house, then the Dungavel to Kilmarnock railway and having followed to Kilmarnock, bear left and the adjacent railway (to Troon) will place you directly onto the Dundonald airstrip (58 km from the marker of the 'other' Dungavel Hill).

This does all seem to fit, very precisely, except for one major problem. When Hess arrived in the area it was dark, he was late and Dundonald did not have lights. So, Hess logically flew on and crossed the coast at West Kilbride. In anticipation of a landing, he was now virtually at sea level and already in a great deal of trouble. We know this from the ROC records at West Kilbride and our much later visits to the ROC post site near the cemetery at the top of the village.

The point here is that it appears to us that the Duke of Hamilton in the early 1960s had described the precise route that Hess had followed twenty years earlier.

It is at this point that the ROC post at Irvine would have been in the 'box seats' watching the spectacle unfold. Based on the top of the Blue Billy Bing (an old spoil heap), they would surely have seen what happened next, when Hess then chose to almost double-back on himself, when coming inland from the Clyde. Needless to say, these records have yet to see the light of day, unfortunately more likely destroyed when the ROC was stood down in 1995.

We make the above point as we have recently obtained two reports of Hess flying through the Barrage balloons at Ardeer and it would be interesting to know if this action had contributed to the eventual crash, or whether he was being pursued in earnest by Cuddie and Hodge.

14. Following on from the above, we should make three further obvious points that seem to have been overlooked previously:

- Why did the Duke of Hamilton choose to get involved at all, if he truly knew nothing?
- Similarly, why did the Duke fly to Churchill to explain what was going on?
- And thirdly, why was he stripped of his command?

The available details to date do not really help the Duke. First, there is the important discrepancy between his and the Duchess's account of the early morning of 11 May 1941. According to the Duke, he first met Hess in Maryhill Prison at 10.00am on 11 May 11. However, the Duchess, when writing to Peter Padfield, stated that her husband had left their lodging, Millburn Towers, in the early hours of 11 May and did not return until the late afternoon, prior to flying to London. Consequently, there has been understandable speculation as to what the Duke was really doing.

Secondly, if the Duke was not involved, why did he fly anywhere? His job was Station Commander at RAF Turnhouse, so whilst the Hess flight crossed the airspace for which he was responsible, that was it. The nominal head of the RAF in 13 Group was J.O. (Jock) Andrews, not the Duke of Hamilton. Andrews was based at Ouston.

And thirdly, Mark Peel in The Patriotic Duke is quick to make the point that the he was promoted to Group Leader on 31 May 1941, after spending most of the latter part of May in London on account of Herr R. Hess. However, as Sandy Johnstone succinctly comments in his *Spitfire into War*, 'Douglo did not resume command of Turnhouse'.

Instead, he took command of the Air Training Corps in Scotland. Peel naturally cites examples of what a splendid job he made of the task, but surely, in the midst of a war, to lose command of an active station in favour of essentially a non-combatant role must make some form of statement?

We should say that the Hamilton family has always been most courteous to us (although they did deny us access to their muniments) and James Douglas-Hamilton politely deals with our various requests from time to time. We should also say that we have no doubt that we, too, would have held the duke's many achievements in complete awe, and it is wholly clear that virtually all who served with him held him in very high regard indeed.

But…

It may well be the case that in part he did not really help himself. His September 1939 letter to *The Times* could easily be misconstrued and he did not comment (nor was allowed to comment) publicly on the affair, although he was apparently planning to write a book on the subject just before he died in 1973. Moreover, the government did not really help him, with various ministers (and Churchill) stating that he and Hess had met before 1939. He was also prevented from going to the US in 1945 by a government obviously anxious to retain the control of the Hess affair. At Nuremberg it was stated that he had met Hess before the war.

Consequently, we now believe that the Duke of Hamilton was wholly aware of the Hess mission and had earlier contributed intelligence to enable the flight to be made – not though to the MI5 initiative but another, more advanced operation. That is why he played his later role.

He did not allow the Bf110 through Scottish airspace as that was not necessary, but someone would have to have told Hess where to go and target, and Hamilton is, we fear, the most likely individual with the almost unique skill-set and knowledge necessary. We are also very interested in the Duchess's trips to the Allgäu pre-war. Later on, the duke was always quick to sue for libel, but we now wonder if the defendants had actually got the right person? Not the duke, perhaps, but the Duchess?

> 15. The next piece of information that again appears to indicate foreknowledge of the Hess flight relates to the excellent research performed by Tony Marczan and Andrew Rosthorn in the 1990s. This concerns the Czech RAF squadron then at RAF Aldergrove in Northern Ireland and the radio command to pilot officer Felix Baumann to not shoot down a Bf110.

Initially, we should say that we are not wholly convinced that the plane concerned was the Hess plane. There are some discrepancies in the details, not least that (according to the ROC) it at no time crossed into Northern Irish airspace, but what is wholly accurate is the account of a party on the Irish base that night 10 May 1941 to celebrate the announcement of a bar to a DFC being awarded to the Squadron leader, J.W. Simpson.

Whilst the party was in full swing ('cocktails, supper and dancing. It was a riot'), an Avro Anson landed at the base with high-ranking officers on board, who then told the two Czech pilots to keep their mouths shut regarding the command that had just been issued to them. The report places the arrival of the plane after dark, and presumably, if it were truly the Hess plane, it would have to be after 23.07 hours, when the Bf110 had come down over Eaglesham.

Needless to say, the necessary detail is not recorded. The arrival of the Anson and its departure from somewhere else is not recorded (little concerning the RAF involvement is) and so we are back into the dangerous territory. Sir Richard Evans would say that there was no Anson as it is not recorded properly, but we know from elsewhere (Marczan and Rosthorn) and other accounts that there was an Anson.

Given the proximity of Aldergrove and Northern Ireland to the scene of the Hess crash, we do wonder if the high ranking officers had just fled the scene, cognisant of the catastrophe unfolding across the North Channel, though that of course, is complete conjecture. Certainly, the Anson could not have travelled from too far away, else otherwise the party-goers and the two Czech pilots would have already dispersed and presumably be recorded as being found in bed at diverse locations.

So, we hope the reader can understand our methodology here. Rather than speculate as to how the communication to Hess was being made, we have instead chosen to try and illustrate through our analysis of the flight itself and its aftermath that it does appear that the RAF/RAF intelligence had supplied details to at least facilitate the flight in its planning stage. Nothing more, save the fact that Hess attempted the feat means that he in turn had used the information imparted to him.

So, how was Hess being reached?

As previously recorded, our detailed analysis of events had come to a grinding halt somewhere around 15 March 1941. Up until that time we know pretty well the precise whereabouts and actions of the key players. Hess was training for the flight and modifying his plane now the awful winter weather had lifted. The Duke of Hamilton was in Turnhouse on operational duty, though having enjoyed ten days' leave on 26 January 1941 and again in March whilst he was dealing with the request to attend the Air Ministry with a view to formulating a very unlikely reply to the Haushofer letter from the previous autumn .Albrecht Haushofer was in Berlin, having been to Stockholm in early February. Tancred Borenius was back in London reporting to the committee of the Polish Relief Fund about his recent trip and Wladyslaw Sikorski was about to leave for the US.

Let us consider the routes of communication already known to us:

- **Overt Government to Government:** We discount this completely as Ribbentrop had alienated most of the Nazi leaders, and the British government had made its position consistently and very eloquently clear. Hitler's last speech to the German people prior to the Hess flight (on 4 May 1941) was a direct attack on Churchill, 'All my endeavours to come to an understanding with Britain were wrecked by the determination of a small clique which, whether from motives of hate or for the sake of material gain, rejected every German proposal for an understanding due to their resolve, which they never concealed, to resort to war, whatever happened. The man behind this fanatical and diabolical plan to bring about war at whatever cost was Mr. Churchill. His associates were the men who now form the British Government.' This verbal attack being just three days before the self-imposed vote of confidence in Churchill in the House of Commons.

- **Opponents of the incumbent government:** In this connection it is probably quicker, shorter and thereby easier to list the friends of the Churchill government. Bizarrely, one could nearly make the case that it was the Labour Party who was keeping the Churchillian rump of the Tory party in power. The politics were extremely odd here. Churchill had supplanted the Tory hero Chamberlain and so was hated by most within the party. Moreover, the incumbent Churchill government had never won a general election; the last being in 1935 when Stanley Baldwin triumphed. We would also include the royal family in this category, for a variety of reasons: Churchill's support for Edward VIII, a natural affinity for the Germanic (although not necessarily the Nazis) and in some cases a sneaking respect for what Hitler had achieved since the wild days of 1919/20. There are records of the Duke of Kent writing to the Princes of Hessen and Prince Paul of Yugoslavia in 1940/41, so clearly there were still channels of communication open at that level. We would also include Samuel Hoare and Lord Halifax in this category, although Andrew Roberts makes the case that whilst Halifax would have preferred a negotiated settlement, it was never to be at any cost.[5] Hoare may well have been different. Both had been moved well away from Whitehall.
- **Haushofer:** As has already been demonstrated Albrecht Haushofer was rightly concerned about being implicated in any 'off piste' peace negotiations being promoted by Rudolf Hess, or anyone else. His writing and diligent recording make that clear. However, we do know that he was in receipt of intelligence from Carl Burckhardt following his January 1941 meeting with Borenius.
- **Gerl–Calthrop:** We suspect that this route of information, which pre-war seemed surprisingly prolific, would have dried up at the start of conflict. Mrs Calthrop presumably returned to London (or Cumbria)

for the duration. Franz Gerl was later mooted by Rudolf Hess as a potential German Foreign Minister when he was busily planning a Fourth Reich in Spandau in the late 1940s.

- **Pfeffer/Fletcher/Jahnke:** This is more difficult, in that Fletcher was being watched by MI5 well after Gulla Pfeffer had been interned on the Isle of Man in late 1939. We have also discovered that Fletcher appears to have somehow travelled to the Balkans in 1941, whereupon he was laid low with the early stages of the TB that would eventually kill him. This channel still requires further research, but it does appear to concentrate on the passing of various Foreign Office documentation and not the type of information necessary for the non-governmental initiative that Hess was seeking to pursue.
- **Borenius:** Despite having discovered the role of Tancred Borenius in the story in the late 1990s, just like Albrecht Haushofer, nothing is known of the actions of the Finnish art historian/diplomat in the period from March to May 1941. We have recounted his sad demise, but in the critical period of our review – nothing. This, of course, may well be the case, his involvement may have ceased on his return to London, but we would suggest it would be extraordinary if that were to have happened. Presumably, given he was briefed by Claude Dansey prior to departure, there would be at the very least a similar de-brief on return (and the return of the unused suicide pill?). We very much doubt that this wholly deniable gentleman with royal credentials played no further role. We do know that he continued to attend the meetings of the Anglo-Polish Relief Fund from March onwards, as his attendance was duly minuted in the record book.
- **RAF intelligence/Alfred Rosenberg/Wilhelm de Ropp:** We currently know absolutely nothing, save that de Ropp apparently had moved to Switzerland (from central Berlin) and Rosenberg was asked to Munich to share lunch with Rudolf Hess immediately prior to him flying on 10 May 1941. We should also say that the recently unearthed Rosenberg diaries provide no specific clues, save to illustrate the extraordinary closeness of the Luftwaffe and RAF in the mid-1930s and the role of the Duke of Kent as the unofficial intelligence officer to the King. The silence is deafening.
- **Governments in exile:** It is easy to dismiss the role of the various governments that were sheltering from the storm in Britain. Each

had a specific relationship with Germany, and we had seriously considered whether Hess was actually seeking to split the Poles (and the Allies) further asunder by an offer of peace. Similarly, Chips Channon was reported as fearing that Britain would shortly be going to war with France (16 May 1941). In short, it appears to us that the final allegiances of the major players were still in sufficient doubt to make a Hess-type initiative very viable. If there was no doubt as to the eventual outcome, there would be no need to fly anywhere.

We trust we have made our point. There were, of course, channels of communication still open outside the control, or apparent control, of the British Government. They in turn had to remain secret, so as to preserve the secrecy of the operation. We have also highlighted the areas that indicate to us that Hess was being helped and encouraged in his mission and logically, surely, he had to have that reassurance? Why fly anywhere if he was to be simply incarcerated (or quite possibly shot) on arrival? Is this the reason for the rumoured Canadian Bearer bonds that Hess had stuffed down his shirt?[6] Was he ready to buy his way out of any potential trouble?

So, if the reader is content to agree with our contention that Hess was certainly in receipt of intelligence advising him of proposed outcome, location and destination, let us go one stage further (and this is the really contentious part of the book, Sir Richard).

---

1 Guy Liddell Diaries, Entry for May 18th 1941.

2 See Chapter 30 – Colonel Eugene Bird.

3 We should also make the second obvious comment that records of any such actions may simply have been destroyed to prevent their subsequent discovery.

4 *Hansard*, 27 January 1942.

5 Andrew Roberts, *The Holy Fox: The Life of Lord Halifax*, Weidenfeld & Nicolson, London, 1991.

6 Please see Helen Fry, *Spymaster*, where she quotes a MI6 report detailing $140,000 of Bearer Bonds.

CHAPTER 32

CONCLUSIONS – 15 MARCH 1941 ONWARDS AND THE KILLER QUESTION: COUP OR LURE?

We have used 15 March 1941 as a 'waymarker' in the Hess affair. Up until that date the movements and actions of the key players are reasonably well known and recorded. By contrast, after 15 March little is recorded, though that does not infer inaction – just the fact that there are few extant records available.

Consequently, we need to consider and debate the various possibilities and assess them accordingly, rather than simply concluding that there were no such actions and Hess simply stole an aircraft and under a delusion flew to the enemy.

What was Rudolf Hess being told and when and by whom?

In order to give Hess the necessary confidence to fly to Scotland on 10 May 10 1941, logically, he must have been given some information that imparted at least the chance of a favourable outcome. Else, why fly anywhere, unless truly mad (which he was not)?

We know that pre-war, the Gerl/Calthrop/Jahnke channels were in operation together with the far more direct RAF /Winterbotham /de Ropp/ Rosenberg route to the leading Nazis.

We also know the Haushofers were imparting, and being imparted with, high-grade political intelligence both prior to and during the period under review. Albrecht Haushofer and the Duke of Hamilton were undoubtedly close friends, and the Duchess of Hamilton was a client/contact of Dr Gerl, whatever that meant in practice.

We know that Borenius had again repeated the prospect of a peace in late January 1941. Hess knew this fact by 10 March 1941, at the very latest. We suspect that Borenius had also gone beyond the von Hassell report of the conversation, even though that was pretty all encompassing. It is surely unlikely that an emissary such as Borenius would have relayed that a peace was possible, here were the acceptable terms (but not with Hitler) and then left on the next train? There must surely have been indications or even instructions as to what a proposed next step might be?

The linkages between Borenius and the exiled Polish community are also fascinating. Despite being a Finnish national, he became the secretary of the Anglo-Polish Relief Fund which in late 1939 listed Lord Derwent and Nina, Countess Granville[1] as its joint Presidents. Lord Derwent then conveniently moved to Switzerland as honorary attaché to David Kelly, the newly appointed ambassador. As Kelly later described the appointment, 'Before I left, I was approached by Lord Derwent, who offered to go with me as Honorary Attaché…'[2]

Consequently, when Borenius travelled to Switzerland in January 1941, it is quite possible that he would have met his former fellow office holder from the Polish Relief Fund, though there is no document in the public archives we have trawled that shows that to be the case. Whilst common friendship is not proof of anything, at the least it must make any potential communication easier.

It now appears to us that the next step/reassurance/reinforcement came from Spain. Samuel Hoare, the British Ambassador, was brilliantly well connected and had been politically exiled in Spain, ostensibly to keep them out of the war; a feat he achieved by literally buying British influence with hard cash. However, he too had extensive intelligence experience and also knew all the key aeronautical participants through his stints as minister at the Air Ministry in the 1930s.

As has been recounted in Chapter 17, it was Hoare who had arranged for the acquisition of the British Embassy literally next door to the home of the German Ambassador von Stohrer, on the Avenue Generalissimo Franco. It should also be noted that Albrecht Haushofer had a former student, Heinrich Stahmer, working at the German Embassy. In 1959 Stahmer claimed that Hess had met Samuel Hoare and Lord Halifax in Madrid. However, this we find very difficult to believe as a) there was not really time, and b) Lord Halifax, according to his diaries, was in the US, having a difficult start as the British Ambassador. On 19–21 April, the usual weekend that is cited for the said meeting, the Halifaxes were guests of the Fisher family just outside Baltimore. From there they travelled to Kansas.[3]

However, we do not easily discount the potential role that Hoare may have played in the affair. Brilliantly connected, twice the Minister of Aviation, a foreign secretary and an intelligence operator in revolutionary Russia, he certainly had the necessary credentials and contacts to facilitate an exchange of information. Real or imaginary. He was also a 'scorned man' in the context of the British wartime Cabinet.

A perusal of the vast Templewood papers in the University of Cambridge library reveals some obvious gaps in the sequence of transmissions between London and Madrid in the period under review. As J.A. Cross records in Hoare's political biography, 'The wartime British embassy in Madrid was a vital point of personal and intelligence contact with occupied Europe.'

Quite.

So far, we have the following key dates:

17 January Borenius leaves England for Geneva, via Portugal and Vichy France

20 January and 23 January The Duke of Hamilton meets the Duke of Kent at Prestwick

26 January – 4 February The Duke of Hamilton is on leave

30 (?) January Borenius meets Burckhardt in Geneva

30 January Burckhardt meets von Hassell in Geneva and reports on Borenius (per the von Hassell diary)

The last entry is particularly interesting in that Ulrich von Hassell had met Carl Burckhardt on his return from Paris where he had delivered a lecture and attended a Rodin and Manet exhibition. He was en route to Arosa, Switzerland, to visit his wife and son at the Hotel Isla. It was whilst he was in Paris that he had been again contacted by 'the Doctor' – James Lonsdale-Bryans, the amateur British diplomat who was in Lisbon at the time and had met von Hassell in Arosa the previous spring (see Chapter 29).

Carl Burckhardt describes the Borenius meeting to von Hassell as being 'very recent'. One is tempted to wonder if the Borenius and Burckhardt meetings were even on the same day, 30 January 1941? Von Hassell states that he was to be in Arosa 'until Saturday 1st February'. This would not have given him much time at all to get to Arosa and spend time with his wife and son.

2 February – 5 February Haushofer travels to Sweden

21 February to 24 February Haushofer with Hess in Munich

5 March Hoare meets Prince Hohenlohe in Madrid

8 March – 17 March The Duke of Hamilton on leave

10 March Haushofer meets von Hassell in Berlin

12 March Borenius back in London

13 March Borenius dines with Cazalet and Sikorski
14 March Italian report of the Hoare/Hohenlohe Madrid meeting

Clearly much is going on and the above dates are only those that have yet surfaced. We know in addition that the Duke of Kent was regularly meeting Sikorski throughout, prior to his departure to the US in late March. We also know that Prince Hohenlohe had regularly been trying to promote a peace throughout the late autumn of 1940; first, via Kelly in Switzerland and now he was continuing the same strategy in his newly adopted country of Spain in the early new year of 1941.

What is also interesting are the contrasting reports of such meetings. Sir Samuel Hoare reported in his autobiography that he had told Hohenlohe on 5 March, 'My staff and I made it clear beyond a doubt that the British government would have nothing to do with any peace negotiations and sooner or later the British people would undoubtedly win the war.'

The Italian report of the same meeting was somewhat different: 'Hoare stated that the position of the British government could not remain secure; Churchill could no longer rely on a majority and sooner or later he, Hoare would be called back to London to take over the government with the precise task of concluding a compromise peace.'

And here comes the dilemma. Both reported statements could personally be quite honourable, if Hoare was deliberately giving misinformation to the enemy. The key question remains as to whether he was skilfully engaged in buying time so as to avert the invasion of Britain as well as Spain, nominally a component of his self-professed 'special mission'? By alluding to an internal regime change, was Hoare essentially saying, 'Don't invade, Churchill will go, and you will get a more pliable alternative'? Alternatively, did he truly mean what he was reported as saying? What agenda was he truly following? More than eighty years later, this is virtually impossible to discern without other evidence. Making the ascertainment of true allegiance all the more difficult was the fact that Hoare was also as stated, a 'scorned man'.

So, yet again, the coup or lure question.

Thereafter, until the end of April, there is currently little recorded activity. We know:

15–17 March Hoare travels to Lisbon to meet the US envoy Donovan
18 March Borenius lunches with Sikorski and Cazalet

24 March Sikorski leaves for the USA on HMS Revenge
Mid-April Hoare travels to Gibraltar
9 April Von Hassell is in Berlin and meets Albrecht Haushofer and Popitz
12 April – 15 April Haushofer with Hess in Berlin
25 April The Duke of Hamilton is interviewed by T.A. Robertson
26 April Hess meets the Haushofers at his Munich home
27 April Haushofer travels to Geneva
28 April Haushofer meets Burckhardt (and others) in Geneva
29 April Haushofer travels to Lausanne and then to Arosa

Presumably, as a result of the Hess/Haushofer meeting on 15 April, Martha Haushofer records in her diaries that some 'remarkable news' had been received by Hess and the Haushofers. Let us now consider what this might be:

- The Italian report of the Hoare/Hohenlohe meeting perhaps, or
- Another communication giving fresh hope and more plausible detail (but quite possibly just buying yet more time).

The likelihood would favour the latter, we suspect, and so would ask the reader to consider the same issue. We currently have no evidence to support what that communication or the 'remarkable news' might be.

Haushofer in Geneva, 28 April 1941

We would now like to concentrate on the lead-up to the flight and, in particular, the Haushofer/Burckhardt meeting in Geneva on 28 April 1941. The reader will remember that this was ostensibly the first recorded German reaction to the Borenius mission in late January 1941. This we do not believe for an instant.

Rudolf Hess had given specific permission for the Haushofer trip to Geneva, according to the Haushofer report to Hitler of 12 May 12.. Hess also met with Albrecht on 26 April, so was appearing to give the meeting a degree of priority.

We also know that Haushofer knew of the Borenius approach much earlier; by 10 March 10 at the very latest when he attended a Berlin meeting of the anti-Hitler resistance at the house of Johannes Popitz. This meeting is well documented in the von Hassell diaries.

We now need to look very carefully at the role of C.J. Burckhardt and what meetings he was present at during the period under review.

Given that the initial impetus for the negotiation for peace had come from Hess in August 1940, in early 1941 a Finnish-born member of British high society had taken a completely deniable message to Carl Burckhardt in Switzerland, saying just the same thing. Borenius had been briefed by Claude Dansey prior to departure. This was not a coincidence.

Burckhardt, as the middleman (an intermediary, as Hess would describe him), seems to have passed on the message to both the anti-Hitler resistance (von Hassell and Haushofer) and almost simultaneously delivered the message to the Deputy Führer of Nazi Germany (again via Haushofer, but this time in his – Haushofer's – other capacity as a diplomatic expert for the Nazi Government).

We do not think that much disputable. We have listed three independent sources of evidence to support the above facts (the Borenius family, Haushofer's report to Hitler of 12 May 1941 and the von Hassell diaries).

The dilemma comes when trying to then decide the true motives. We could easily now make a case that Tancred Borenius was being sent on behalf of the British royal family (the 'British officials'/*stellen*: he knew most of them), to sound out the possibility of a negotiated settlement with Nazi Germany (as the real enemy of royalty anywhere was always Communist Russia), using the W Board and RAF communication channels through and to Switzerland. (The W Board was, of course, helping the royal family, not the government). Hess eventually flew to seal the deal and provide the necessary credibility for the insurgents. On his arrival in Scotland, the Dukes of Hamilton, Gloucester and Kent would contact the King (with Hess in the background as support) and the King (willingly or not) would either blackmail or depose Churchill constitutionally. A secret compromise treaty would then be made, and the British elite would have saved their skins, dogs and acres – at least for the time being. Job done.

Alternatively, and dare we say, far more simply, Hess would be taken to meet the recently arrived Sikorski and the Polish Army who would then be promised the restoration of Poland, thus ending their terrible slaughter. That outcome may well have also caused chaos in Scotland (it very nearly did anyway) and may have allowed President Raczkiewicz his wish to go home 'before next Easter'. The Duke of Kent may well have been allowed the Polish throne as an added sign of Nazi sincerity. This is why we have been trying to find the diary of the Polish 309 Squadron, then based at Renfrew airfield. Hess lands at Dundonald and is then flown by Polish courier Lysander to Gask and then onto Moncreiffe House, the Polish HQ.

However, somewhat inconveniently, what we do know for sure is that Hess had got lost, crashed to earth and fell literally into the hands of the British Government (i.e. Churchillian) agencies of the Home Guard, police and army. Very close to success perhaps, but in reality, a crushing failure. He did not meet who he was supposed to meet. His carefully planned non-governmental mission had now turned into a very public British and German governmental news damage limitation management event. This was all deemed far too sensitive for public consumption for obvious reasons, and so Churchill kept a 'lid' on the affair in exchange for the undying loyalty ever after from those involved in the proceedings. So, quickly divert press attention from what had just happened to stories of the plucky ploughman with his pitchfork, move the Scottish crown jewels, just in case, and place the leading contenders under house arrest. Send Alanbrooke to the Orkneys to recover that troublemaker and ringleader Prince George…

Sensational stuff!

However.

Now please read the previous paragraphs in exactly the same way, but instead this time insert, and then read, 'but it was all a W Board/MI6/RAF intelligence illusion' at the very end. In other words, the British had successfully deceived the Germans (who in the meanwhile had run out of time to invade Britain) and so Hess, Parsifal like (and depressed), chose to go and see if that was really the case. That is why 'he dared', as it said on his gravestone (before it was removed from the Friedhof Wunsiedel). Not daring in the sense of a physical and technical challenge, although of course it was, but daring in that he flew to go and try and find the answer, find the real truth before Barbarossa was unleashed. When 'push really came to shove', with whom would Britain really side? In that respect it could be said that he actually succeeded, in that Britain certainly did not declare a truce or peace in May 1941. Indeed, the Bismarck was sunk at the end of the month, thus making very clear probable allegiances, however difficult politically. When Hitler finally gave the command to invade Russia on 21 June 1941, he was in little doubt as to Britain's position (however unpalatable to many Britons). At least the Hess flight had told him that.

Consequently, we have scoured Europe for twenty-five years in an attempt to locate a viable, plausible means of communication, seemingly out of British governmental control, between Rudolf Hess and a party of convincing 'British Officials' (*stellen*) as Ulrich von Hassell had described them, who were presumably prepared to take action to unseat, assassinate or blackmail Winston Churchill and force a compromise treaty.

The means to deliver relatively detailed information in a timely manner then becomes of vital import, whether in fact the message so delivered is real or illusory. We now believe we have discovered the relevant channel of communication and so would now wish to insert that knowledge into our precise interpretation of the events from 31 August 1940 to 10 May 1941, whilst also drawing on the information that we have already presented in the previous chapters.

Albrecht Haushofer and the initial approach

The extent and accepted role of Albrecht Haushofer in the Hess affair must also now be under severe scrutiny and doubt. The September 1940 letter sequence was actually a very well-documented farce, as the letter should never have reached England, let alone Mrs Roberts in Cambridge or the Duke of Hamilton at the House of Lords in London. There was seemingly a fundamental failure of understanding the Thomas Cook Postal system, to the extent that it is now obvious why Albrecht was able to give Hess the impression that Mrs Roberts was residing in Lisbon. Whether this was a wholly genuine mistake we would seriously doubt. It would appear to us that the letter, having undergone censorship, received special treatment, as according to the MI5 files, Thomas Cook in London had even addressed the letter revealing Mrs Roberts's Cambridge address! A more typical fate would have been a Lisbon wastepaper bin.

This sequence is now quite clear to us. However, why MI5 then spent a month trying to ascertain who Mrs Roberts was and precisely where she lived is beyond us, unless they were deliberately being kept in the dark by those who had already recognised the importance of the letter and from where it had come.

In any event, it was certainly the impetus for the British response.

The British response

The British response was not to send any reply to the Haushofer letter as, clearly, they could not, even if they wanted to. To have responded to a letter that should not have been delivered would have been folly. Instead, they recruited, around Christmas 1940, the services of Tancred Borenius, the then fifty-six-year-old art historian. On the face of it, a very odd choice of agent, but given the unique circumstances, there could really have been no one any better qualified.

Being a Finnish national and a part-time diplomat, Borenius could travel more easily than a Briton and also have a viable alibi in that he was recognised as Finland's 'Man in London'. He was well known to Gustav Mannerheim and so had good diplomatic credentials when travelling to Geneva in January 1941. Moreover, we now know for sure that Borenius already knew Carl Jacob Burckhardt through his Anglo-Polish Relief Fund contacts. It is also conceivable, but again as yet unproven, that he may even have known the Haushofers, this time through his earlier university and academic contacts. We have now learned that after Geneva he was to travel to Italy, to meet, we presume, Bernard Berenson, his friend and famous art historian, and, we have discovered, also an MI6 agent.[4]

As far as the 'coup or lure' dilemma is concerned, we must also consider the timings. Was Borenius approached by the royals/officials at all? Did Dansey merely discover that Borenius was travelling on Finnish Government business and ask that he deliver the code book? Which came first? Clearly, we currently have no way of finding out. The royals may quite possibly play no part in this at all. Perhaps the W Board get Borenius to Geneva and then he goes 'off piste' when talking later to Burckhardt. However, we do know through von Hassell that Borenius was giving the usual stock version of what terms might or might not be acceptable. He was also ramping up the pressure by ending with the 'peace, but not for much longer' comment, presumably coinciding with the growing and increasingly visible entente between the US and Britain.

We also question the cyanide pill. If Dansey gave it to Borenius as described, then surely it would not be necessary if he was just passing a code book? Surely the pill was to stop Borenius telling what he knew of peace and who was offering it, were he to be captured and imprisoned? (Quite possibly even by the Churchill government if one is happy with the 'coup' line of thought.) Given that he was also a Finnish diplomat, we do feel that this is evidence that Dansey had impressed on Borenius the need to protect what he either knew or had been told. Clearly, given the need for the suicide pill, it was extremely sensitive.

Either way, the fact that Borenius was travelling to Geneva to meet Carl Jacob Burckhardt had to be initially communicated from London to Geneva in such a way that a viable meeting could be held. If communication was not effective, how would Burckhardt, for example, have known to be in Geneva at the appointed date and hour? We only ask this obvious question because at no time has the later reciprocal issue as to how Hess was supposed to have known that the Duke of Hamilton might be at home at Dungavel on 10 May 1941 been satisfactorily addressed. The notion that Hess might fly 900 miles or so on the chance that Hamilton, a serving RAF officer, might just happen to be at home upon his arrival, is simply nonsense.

Arranging both meetings clearly needed a viable means of communication.

We gained the first clue for how this might be achieved by re-reading Albrecht Haushofer's memorandum to Adolf Hitler that he prepared on 12 May 1941. Haushofer wrote, 'Burckhardt stated that he was willing to act as go-between in this manner: it would simply be communicated to England through an entirely safe channel…'

So, the question appeared to us to slightly move and narrow, as to how Burckhardt, a member of the International Red Cross Committee, could communicate through an 'entirely safe channel' to England.

In order to try and find out, we duly wrote to the International Red Cross in Geneva. They were very helpful, and we reproduce their reply below as we think this reply very important indeed.

> *Dear Sir,*
>
> *We thank you for your message.*
>
> *Generally, the parcels were delivered by train or by ship (at the end of war, trucks were also used, especially in Germany). When arrived at destination, the authorities were in charge of assuming the transports to the final destination. Following your scenario, from Geneva, the transport will be made by train, and, in your example, this train will reach a port (for instance Genoa) where the parcels will be transferred on ships directed to the United Kingdom. But we are not sure that this scenario happened, due to the continental blockade imposed by the Allied,*
>
> *The ICRC didn't own any machine for secure communication. For really confidential documents, it used the Swiss diplomatic case.*
>
> *We hope that this information will be useful, and we remain,*
>
> *Yours sincerely*

This reply, dated 3 September 2015, potentially explains the channel of communication that was used to eventually facilitate the Hess mission of 10 May 1941.

We had asked the question as to how the International Red Cross might communicate with its offices and branches in the various countries in which it operated . The first paragraph describes what we already knew; the route via neutral countries. Early on, we had even wondered if the IRC had used the commercial version of the Enigma machines, but it appears not. Instead, as can be seen above, it used the Swiss diplomatic case, 'for really confidential documents'.

The reason this is so important is simply that it allowed communication from Burckhardt to groupings other than governments. It allowed, for instance, Burckhardt to securely communicate with, say, Tancred Borenius, once back in London, this time using his capacity as a Finnish Diplomat: (Burckhardt (IRC) to Swiss Consul (Geneva) to Swiss Consul (London) to Borenius (Finnish 'Consul').

In other words, it allowed for the Hess–Haushofer–Burckhardt–Borenius–'British officials' channel of communication to operate securely (at least theoretically) well outside British government/Churchillian control. *It therefore makes communications pertaining to a non-governmental coup, or the illusion of a coup, a possibility.*

It would be quite excusable for the reader at this juncture to exclaim, 'Here we go again, Harris and Wilbourn – no proof, just speculation'. We can almost hear the groan from a certain knighted professor. Normally, we would frown and then reluctantly agree – but no longer. It was this precise route in reverse that Hess used, later on, whilst in British captivity. J.R. Rees, in *The Case of Rudolf Hess*, gives details how the letters that Hess and Ilse wrote to each other were relayed via the Swiss Envoy.

Obviously, when used in reverse, the British censor was engaged before any release to the Swiss for delivery, but this is to us at least proof that the means and system existed and was being used as described in our 2015 letter from the IRC in Geneva.

So, we are content to believe that Tancred Borenius sent warning to Carl Burckhardt that he was intending to travel to Geneva in late January 1941 and would like to meet him. Given the desperate need to pass the 'one time message code book', it would appear likely that Dansey had helped the plan as a ruse to deliver the vital code book (which, as we know was disguised as a novel in this instance). It may well be that Borenius had used a normal means of communication, such as that employed by Mrs Roberts when writing to Martha Haushofer in the July of 1940 to initially arrange the meeting. It is, however, much more likely that Borenius, making use of his Finnish

Diplomatic status, would have availed himself of the diplomatic channel through the diplomatic bag. Presumably that belonging to Finland, if indeed their London representative possessed such an item.

This is precisely why Tancred Borenius was so ideal. If necessary or desirable, he could distance himself from the British when convenient, by playing the Finnish card. It is, however, very much the case that this was a British operation funded by British Intelligence and overseen by Claude Dansey. The use of perceived foreign intermediaries has been used subsequently, such as Alexander Haig in the early days of the Falkland conflict, some forty years later.

Did Churchill know? Probably not at the onset, for on one level why would he, or why should he? At that stage probably the main objective was not to promulgate a European peace, it was probably to just smuggle the vital code book so that British Government (London) could communicate securely to British Government (Switzerland). If nothing else, that was the excuse. That type of delivery mission would not normally require any formal ministerial approval but could certainly be used as the rationale to send the rotund art historian halfway around Europe to Geneva.

At that point the Borenius mission seems reasonably straightforward to us. He was acting as a delivery boy for MI6/W Board – essentially a 'bag man'.

What then becomes far more difficult is the part of the trip when Borenius went to meet Carl Jacob Burckhardt, who we now know was known to Borenius, the two men having met in London in October 1939. First, it would appear to us that he did not obviously need to visit Burckhardt. If he was merely delivering code books, then why go at all, unless this was giving the pretex, or the excuse for the trip, so as to eliminate suspicion. (Alternatively, it may well be the case that the code book was the excuse for the more serious peace negotiations.) The 'condition of Prisoners of War' was the usual excuse trotted out by those wishing to speak to Burckhardt (the British Government made the same justification in November 1941; Ulrich von Hassell also had done so in March 1941). However, we know that Borenius wished to talk about much more that POWs when he made his trip. Presumably it is because of what he was going to say, rather than what he was to deliver, that Borenius was given the cyanide capsule. Von Hassell detailed more of what was said, but again, given his precarious position in Nazi society, it is unlikely that even he recorded the entirety of the Borenius discourse, simply for fear of undeniable association if ever the diaries were to be discovered.

The diary record starts, 'Professor Borenius, who has lived in London for many years, came to him[Burckhardt] to explain, apparently at the behest of British officials, that a reasonable peace could still be concluded. He has very intimate connections with the Royal House (principally the Queen)…'

The diary then continues to detail what Borenius thought might be acceptable and unacceptable.

However, and this is certainly the crux of the Hess affair, was this real or was this an illusion, a plausible deception? Did Borenius speak for other, 'British officials' or was the whole charade just that? Was it no more than an illusion to buy time, especially given that the British had a good idea by late January 1941 that Barbarossa was to take place later that spring?

Options and alternatives

Given the importance of the issue, as it certainly would explain the post-war reticence to discuss the affair, we think it relevant at this stage to consider the consequences and various alternatives.

1. **Borenius was a true representative of an anti-Churchill, pro-peace grouping backed by the British Secret Services**

Pro

- There is no debate that Borenius was certainly well-connected enough to provide a suitable cover, were the above to be the case. He knew or acted for Queen Mary, the Duke and Duchess of Kent, the Lascelles family and much of the upper echelons of British society – precisely the people who wished for a negotiated settlement.
- Borenius's Finnish background would give him the ability to travel and communicate throughout Europe, espousing such aims and goals. We know he was briefed by Claude Dansey. His natural affinity to Finland would also favour an Anglo-German settlement.
- We also know that Borenius had met Cazalet and Sikorski, prior to their trip to the US. Sikorski, we are sure, would have known that Borenius had gone to Switzerland and, indeed, Borenius had reported back to him after the trip. In other words, at the very least, Sikorski must have been suspicious as to the true British motives. No wonder Sikorski was in such a rush to return. Had he even pledged Polish Army support to any coup attempt in exchange for a restoration of his homeland?
- Through Burckhardt there was the available means of relatively quick

and theoretically secure communication using the Swiss Embassy if required. Borenius lived reasonably close to the Swiss Legation (then in Bryanston Square) at 28 Kensington Gate. At least theoretically, intra-continental, secure communication was possible through the diplomatic bag.

- Borenius would also have favoured a British/German peace, as his natural affinity was of course anti-Bolshevik, on account of his Finnish heritage, as evidenced by his sister's plight during the Winter War.
- We now know that Borenius had met with Burckhardt in London in late 1939. The two men knew each other prior to the 1941 trip and meeting.
- There was no doubt that those with much to lose favoured a peace settlement rather than run the risk of a Nazi invasion, or worse still a Russian invasion. Those with much to lose were closely connected to British Secret Services, e.g. the Duke of Buccleuch's 'sprog' at Eton was Stuart Menzies the wartime Head of MI6. MI6 was not pro-Churchill at the onset of the war. Churchill had wanted a 'Navy man' rather than Menzies, as replacement for Admiral Sinclair who had died in November 1939.
- Churchill was still not liked by much of his own political party, let alone the opposition. A viable opposition was only to be expected. Is this why Churchill deliberately made the debate on 6/7 May 1941 one of confidence?
- The continued doubt as to the location of the key players does make us wonder what was actually going on. The British Establishment is still being secretive about things that it does not need to be secretive about, unless…
- If a coup attempt was underway, however misguided, that fact alone would certainly justify the subsequent cover-up that appears to have taken place, in terms of making sure that Hess was never in a position to be able to reveal the truth. All the other protagonists were either dead or had been effectively neutralised by the time of Nuremberg.
- Churchill's stance was decidedly anti-peace, as any indication of weakness would put into jeopardy his sole strategy of Anglo-Americanism. Therefore, it seems unlikely that he would have run the risk or sanctioned such a high-risk strategy, real or illusory. It may, of course, simply be the case that he was not told. He certainly does not appear to have known of the intended arrival.

- According to Prof. Keith Jeffery, there is no mention of the Hess affair being an MI6 operation. This would infer to us that either a) it was not an MI6 operation and instead it really was essentially a British Coup attempt, orchestrated at a 'higher level' than MI6, such as the W Board, or b) MI6 had disowned it as one of its own operations, instead treating it as a Finnish diplomatic initiative or some such nonsense, or c) they were just lying and had destroyed all the evidence.
- When Hess was captured, Churchill placed him under the control of MI6. At Mytchett he was looked after by Messrs Foley, Kendrick and Arnold Baker. Was this because MI6 operatives had been working to get Hess to fly? (Conversely it could be simply that MI6 under Kendrick had developed a sophisticated listening/bugging system and they wished to take advantage of the same.)
- Until 2010 Tancred Borenius was no more than a footnote in the von Hassell diary. He has not been acknowledged or recognised in any way. Had he been instrumental in helping prevent a German invasion attempt by portraying a viable alternative strategy, then surely, he would have been recognised in some manner? Instead, nothing, which makes us wonder if his actions were not those with which the Churchillian government approved.

Against

- MI6 or the W Board (and/or the royals) would be running an operation directly against government policy. The Secret Service would be essentially operating outside government guidelines and policy. However, this does seem to be exactly what Duško Popov implies in his memoirs.
- The omission may well have been simple misinformation, but in that case why is there no mention in the MI6 files, according to Keith Jeffery? Was it not deemed an MI6 operation because MI6 officers such as Dansey were acting outside of, or beyond, their authority, or was Dansey choosing to wear a W Board hat?
- To our minds, such a plot, if real, displays supreme arrogance on behalf of the potential participators. True, Churchill was disliked by much of the Tory Party, but in the country his popularity never was lower than 75 per cent. In other words, if there really was a coup in the offing, we doubt that it would have succeeded in practice, as the

British public may well have sided with Churchill rather than the plutocracy and/or the monarchy. The days of deference and blind obedience were subsiding, and we do not believe that such a coup (which constitutionally did not need any German interference as a catalyst) would have succeeded either. That opinion, however, does not mean of course that such an attempt may not have been made. A British civil war would also be a good outcome for the Hess flight.

- The only way we can see such a coup succeeding would be if Churchill were to be assassinated, threatened or blackmailed, and there is currently no evidence of such an occurrence in the period in question (apart from the parliamentary vote of confidence). A political vacuum would have been created that Hess may well have been pleased to have flown into, complete with his Ernst Bohle-drafted solution, that may well have been in Britain since late January.
- If such a coup was to have taken place, but failed because Hess crashed and was captured, one might think that the participators would then have suffered a horrible fate, unless the British Government wished to hide the true rationale behind the flight. To summarise the key players later fates:

Hess – incarcerated, completely silenced, died 1987
Menzies – honoured, died 1967
Dansey – honoured, died 1948
Borenius – not honoured, died in asylum 1948
Sikorski – died in air crash 1943
Duke of Kent – died in air crash 1942
Burckhardt – died of natural causes 1974
Hamilton – died of natural causes 1973
Albrecht Haushofer – shot 1945
Karl and Martha Haushofer – suicide 1946
Walter Thurnheer (Swiss legation, London, 1940/41) – died 1945.

The reader must come to their own conclusion as to whether any correlation exists.

2. Borenius was being used by the British Secret Services to foster an illusion of peace – nothing more

Pro

- Duško Popov alludes to this strategy being adopted by the double agents in the spring of 1941.
- Borenius was briefed by Dansey, so we know the Secret Services were involved in some capacity.
- The strategy, if so employed, was a wholly defensive one, exactly as described by Sir Michael Howard as being employed. It follows as a counter to what the JIC was predicting in spring 1941.
- The means were available to communicate in an authentic, plausible manner.
- Borenius would have been willing to tell the message, as it coincided with his 'Finnish position'.
- As described above, Borenius was an entirely suitable candidate as the go-between.
- It is precisely what intelligence agencies are paid to do.
- When Hess arrived, he was placed in the care of MI6, and it ended up with his spare underpants as a trophy(!). Was this because it had succeeded in its task of buying time through false peace negotiations?

Against

- Keith Jeffery denies MI6 involvement in the Hess affair, but this could be simply a) a truth that is not yet able to be revealed, or b) the relevant papers were destroyed, or c) Dansey was acting with his 'W Board hat on'.
- It was a high-risk strategy as far as UK/US relations were concerned, should it ever become public knowledge.
- Given that Churchill knew that a German invasion of Britain was unlikely through his use of Ultra intelligence, was such a high-risk strategy likely or even needed?

Again, we find neither option conclusive, nor indeed exclusive of each other. The complication is that the truth may well be an amalgamation of the two possibilities, that is, an attempt to maintain a channel of communication into the early stages of coup attempt that eventually morphed into an intelligence lure, that morphed into Hess flying to Scotland.

To explore the possibilities further, a more detailed timescale may be useful, though this remains strictly hypothetical:

16/17 January Borenius leaves London for Geneva.

Late January 1941 Borenius is recorded as being in Geneva (Von Hassell). *Takes British message of peace offer.*

Late January 1941 Haushofer is in Stockholm. *Takes German terms for peace.*

21–24 February 1941 Haushofer meets Hess in Berlin. *Composes reply?*

10 March 1941 Von Hassell records meeting Haushofer in Berlin at Popitz's.

16 March 1941 Borenius back in London. *Receives message – sends reply.*

12–15 April 1941 Haushofer meets Hess in Berlin. *Receives message – sends reply?*

28 April 1941 Haushofer with Burckhardt (and others) in Geneva. *Receives detailed message.*

End of April Haushofer meets Ilse von Hassell in Arosa. *Receives/passes message.*

5 May 1941 Haushofer with Hess in Augsburg. *Reports to Hess.*

Mid-May 1941 Haushofer was to meet Burckhardt, who meanwhile was to have contacted the British.[5] (Obviously, this meeting never took place.)

Clearly, the above interpretation is very much subject for debate, but we do know that the entries of January 1941 (Geneva meeting) and 5 May (Hess with Haushofer in Augsburg) are absolutely correct and fully documented. Von Hassell is quite explicit in describing Borenius's January journey and also the fact that following the 28 April meeting in Geneva, Burckhardt was to have contacted the British, again through his secure channel.

So, the real debate is what happened between the end of January and 5 May 1941, a period of some twelve weeks. Our suggested interpretation above shows that reciprocal messages were possible, certainly through the Swiss diplomatic bag and, moreover, the basic question remains – what on earth were Hess and Haushofer doing if they were not replying to the Borenius initiative? One can only discuss matters for so long, and what was Haushofer doing chasing around Sweden, Switzerland and Germany in the period under review?

It does appear to us that it is very likely that Haushofer/Hess were quite aware of the Borenius mission far, far sooner than has been previously intimated. Von Hassell would suggest that Haushofer knew by 10 March, at the latest, but it would appear more likely to us that the Hess/Haushofer meeting of 21–24 February in Berlin was specifically to formulate a reply to the Borenius initiative, which was certainly exactly the right message at the right time as far as Hess was concerned. Burckhardt was well known to other leading Nazis: Heydrich, Himmler and Von Ribbentrop in particular, so it may well be that he had communicated with them too.

We would also record that in early April 1941 there was a Red Cross mission to London by Marcel Junod and Lucie Odier, two senior officers of the Red Cross Geneva. The precise dates are uncertain, but there was a Foreign Office report to Churchill, FO916/112, dated 7 April 1941, so presumably the actual visit was shortly before that date. This information may well, of course, be completely irrelevant, but it does provide another possible means of ''secure communication' between Burckhardt and the so called 'British officials', as outlined in the Haushofer 12 May report.

There is some other, though circumstantial, evidence to support our belief of an earlier series of communications. The Soviet Secret Service, through the Czech government in exile, suspected that British Intelligence had participated in the sending of forged messages, supposedly from the Duke of Hamilton.[6]

In 1991, the Soviet *Military History Journal* reported that the fake correspondence had invented a 'Scottish revolutionary movement', something that correlates with Tancred Borenius's own Jacobite sympathies.[7] Apparently, Hess was to bring the prospect of German military assistance to Scotland to promote a broad-based revolution. Quite how this was to cater for the resident Polish Army, if at all, was not clarified. It could well be the case that Hess had decided to fly, almost irrespective of what he was being told and how likely the outcome.

However, this Soviet report makes a lot of sense, given the 'gap' in activity, but not as a result of the 23 September 1940 letter. We now strongly believe that any forgeries came as a result of the Borenius trip to Geneva in January 1941 and they were being transmitted between Britain and Germany back and forth, through the Swiss diplomatic service and Tancred Borenius.

We would also draw attention to the fact that as the apparent climax approached, the frequency of the communication not unnaturally quickened in pace, as the need for detail and agreement became more pressing. Hess was being slowly drawn into the web – along with Adolf Hitler, his Führer and the consummate geo-political gambler.

Did Hitler know?

Adolf Hitler knew both of the intended flight and gave it his full blessing. As far as he was concerned, it was certainly a chance worth taking if it resulted in a Western peace. His reaction to the flight as detailed in Chapter 18 is important. Until he knew for sure of the crash and the failure of the mission, his reaction was measured. It was only when he knew Hess had failed that he became more hysterical, as indeed the altered circumstances then demanded. He had to disown Hess and his part in the flight for fear of alerting Stalin to its true intentions. The telephone calls to Göring and Udet were all part of the charade; no more than a smokescreen should all not go well. Realistically, Adolf Galland, who was given the task of shooting down Hess, never stood a chance of so doing. He knew that, Göring knew that, as indeed did Hitler.

Hitler was also quite naturally distraught on a personal level. He had lost one of his earliest supporters and colleagues and no one was ever allowed to get as close to him again – certainly not Bormann, the so-called replacement. There are quotes ascribed to Hitler stating that effectively Hess bored him, essentially as a civilian, perhaps again not unnaturally in a time of war, but Hess had held an almost unique position and relationship with Hitler and the other leaders knew that and so were only too pleased to pour their scorn. Indeed, in 1941, the NSDAP had been around for twenty or so years and the next generation of Nazis were starting to seek to stake their claim to the positions of power. Heydrich, at around this time has been cited as referring to Hitler as 'the Old Man' and so it is clear that the removal of one of the incumbents of a top position, for whatever reason, was no bad thing as far as the up-and-coming adherents were concerned.

Without doubt, sufficient smoke was raised in 1941 to have created enough uncertainty to last to the present day. However, a careful scrutiny of the available facts makes it clear that Hitler knew of the scheme and even altered his Reichstag speech of 4 May as a direct result of Karl Haushofer's interventions the previous evening in Munich. Hess's later protestations that Hitler knew nothing of the mission can be seen in the same light as his lies about the state of his mind, his flight path and any other information he wished to hide or disguise.

The Duke of Hamilton

We now have doubt about Hamilton's loyalties to the 1941 government, although not those to the Crown. We have already highlighted the potential legal position of any persons who could be seen to be acting against the interests of the Crown (see Chapter 12).

We believe that it was the use of Hamilton's name and aeronautical knowledge, in the necessary communications passing between January–May 1941, that actually enabled Hess to fly and gave it sufficient justification and promise of success. We can only presume and hope that James Douglas-Hamilton has adopted the stance towards the Hess story that he has in order to hide the true extent of Secret Service involvement.

There is no doubt that prior to the outbreak of war Hamilton was deeply involved in Anglo-German relations at a very high level or 'plane', indeed. *Double Standards* records his attendance at an Anglo-German Foreign Office summit in June 1939, and his letter to *The Times* after the outbreak of the war is essentially an appeal to Albrecht Haushofer to do something. Whether through self-interest, a hatred of Communism or a genuine sympathy towards Nazi Germany, there is absolutely no doubt as to where the Duke of Hamilton stood prior to 3 September 1939. In just the same way, one could also cite the Duke of Buccleuch, the Duke of Bedford and much of the British plutocracy, as Haushofer chose to describe them.

Even more controversially, included within the above definition must also be included some or all of the then royal family, no more exemplified by the personage of Queen Mary, who as we have seen was strongly linked to Tancred Borenius, the messenger sent to Geneva to talk peace. It now appears from the latest release of the Channon diaries (2021) that she had asked for copies of all Anglo-German communications during the period under review.

The Duke of Hamilton, however, was uniquely qualified to be used in any scam/ruse/illusion/coup, simply because he uniquely had some degree of control over Scottish airspace – again a vital component of the Hess affair. Apart from being the Premier Duke in Scotland, essentially the King's representative when in absentia, he was the Station Commander of RAF Turnhouse, which in turn controlled much of western Scottish airspace, as RAF Ayr, Prestwick and Dundonald were at least nominally under its direct jurisdiction. Consequently, it all became possible – theoretical or illusional, perhaps, but possible nevertheless.

Equally, for those supporting the 'treachery' argument, the Duke of Hamilton and the Duke of Kent were well acquainted with Loel Guinness, the millionaire member of the banking family who at the time was Station

Commander at RAF Ayr. Guinness lived in what is now the luxurious Lochgreen House Hotel, close by to Rosemount House, the control centre of the base.

Chapter 19 makes it clear that Hamilton acted as a man with some knowledge, but not a complete knowledge, might do on hearing of Hess's arrival on 10 May 1941.

We now suspect that he had been approached by two branches of the British Secret Services. The first, MI5, well documented its various approaches in letter form that do indeed form part of its published archive (see Chapter 6). This is not surprising, as that clearly demonstrates that MI5 was unaware of the operation – a conclusion also reached by a reading of Guy Liddell's diaries and MI5's subsequent panic policing, as evidenced by the re-hiding of the Scottish crown jewels and the house arrest of sundry other dukes and marquesses, such as Buccleuch and Tavistock. For further details of these understandable post-event responses, we would refer you to our *Rudolf Hess: The British Illusion of Peace*.

More pertinently, however, we now strongly suggest that Hamilton had been engaged in another, quite separate and far more secret operation that had been going on in London since late November 1940. That is why Cuddie and Hodge were told to target the runway at Dundonald. The RAF and Hamilton knew that Hess was coming that evening, as a very small number of participants had effectively invited him there, through the messages and detail sent from Britain from March to 5 May 1941. Messages which, if ostensibly from Hamilton, could actually be quite detailed in aeronautical terms, thus providing yet more plausibility. We hope that the reader can see our justification in the above statement by reason of the subsequent actions of those involved.

Consequently, if correct, it explains why James Douglas-Hamilton is so vague about his father's whereabouts during the night of 10/11 May 1941. The Duke knew that it was likely that it was indeed Hess who had landed; hence his palpable anxiety when being told that 'he was being asked for'. What he did not know for sure was whether it really was Hess or a plausible double, designed to make fools of the British. That is why he had to find out for certain, leaving the Duchess in her bed and eventually flying to Ditchley. Having seen Hess, he knew it was the Deputy Führer and that is why Churchill felt so sure to release the British communique before Ivone Kirkpatrick had even got close to seeing Hess. Quite what Kirkpatrick must have thought when the British communique was released before he had even got to Buchanan Castle is thankfully not recorded.

It is for exactly this same reason that Churchill was able to tell his Downing Street staff that Hess had landed, thus giving explanation to the infamous Colville, 'Has anybody arrived?' construction. Once Hamilton knew that it was Hess, he arranged for Churchill to be told, who probably knew, we would suspect, from around 4.00am on 11 May, thus giving him plenty of time to order a room from Nancy Tree for the Duke of Hamilton later on the morning of 11 May. He knew where the Duke would be staying that evening well before the Duke himself knew.

The other obvious question is, 'Why did the Duke get involved at all?'

Particularly, if he was not involved, as James Douglas-Hamilton states. A very fair question, given that the hierarchy would dictate that Hamilton certainly should not have been involved. If anyone, it should have been J.O. Andrews who leapt in his Hurricane rather than the Station Commander of RAF Turnhouse. Andrews was head of 13 Group, not Hamilton. So why did Hamilton have to fly anywhere? Especially if he was not involved?

The answer must surely be identification and possible further explanation. We now believe that Hamilton was aware of what had been relayed to Germany (as he had provided the information), but no more than that, as it certainly was not a sure outcome. It is likely that he had provided the information to the W Board, most likely in the personage of Archie Boyle. Consequently, when Hess arrived late and was not killed on arrival, the British had to deal with the worst of all scenarios: a leading Nazi wandering around in Scotland and moreover, even worse, the press had soon learned of the identity of the leading Nazi.

Consequently, Hamilton's role was twofold: first, to provide confirmation of identity, and the second to appraise Churchill of the specific details of the event so as to allow news management to take place. As we have seen, the British initially disagreed as to how the affair might be played out in news management terms, ever fearful of playing to the American isolationists. The worst outcome would be if the British had been taken in by a Hess lookalike and the real plutocratic feelings had surfaced mistakenly by consequence. America may well have turned away.

That is why Hamilton flew to Northolt on 11 May 1941 – principally to provide evidence of identification. However, the 'Nazi prostitute had thrown his arms around Hamilton's neck and wouldn't let go'.[8]

Winston Spencer Churchill

The interesting question surrounding Winston Churchill's involvement in the Hess affair is not *did* he know, but rather *when* did he know?

Upon inspection of the facts, it would now appear to us that the climax to the Hess affair unexpectedly morphed out of the pressing requirement to get a British 'one time' pad to the MI6 station in Switzerland. Consequently, there would be no more reason to inform the Prime Minister of Great Britain of that requirement any more than, say, the need to ensure there was sufficient aviation fuel at RAF bases to ensure their planes could operate effectively. Both objectives were vital, but neither really required Prime Ministerial approval. They were just logistical, operational needs that were taken for granted.

It was only when perhaps unanticipated responses were being received that those in positions of responsibility may have seen fit to cover their own positions by informing those higher up the food chain.

If the Harris/Wilbourn supposition is correct, then the first person one might think to be in that position was Tancred Borenius, by reason of the receipt of a message in response to his travels to Geneva. The response would have to have been received by Borenius after mid-March 1941, as this is when we know he was back in situ at the Polish Relief Fund in London. As far as we can determine, he remained in the UK thereafter, even though it was nominally at war with Finland after June 1941.

Let us for an instance imagine that to be the case. Borenius had travelled to Geneva, returned to Britain, safe and happy in the knowledge that he had not had to use his cyanide pill and probably still more safe in the knowledge that he was considerably better off than he had been prior to his departure. Spying had paid far better than wartime art history.

What would his attitude have become were he to then have learned of the receipt of a letter at the Swiss Legation in Bryanston Square, marked for his attention? We have no doubt that in the first instance he would have collected the letter and read it. A wholly natural response.

The key is really what happened then. Did he forward it to a 'British official' such as Hamilton, or did he revert to his original engager and send it to Claude Dansey? We suspect the latter, but even if he sent it on to the Duke of Hamilton, we feel sure that Hamilton, in turn, would have returned it to London, most likely to the Air Ministry. It may well be pertinent to record that the Duke was on leave from Turnhouse from 8–17 March.

Peter Padfield comments that this period of leave was 'in response to

Stammers' letter'. This may indeed be the case, but equally it could well be that at that time Hamilton became aware – or at least becomes suspicious – of the fact that his name and knowledge was being used in another parallel intelligence operation, that operating on a 'higher plane'. During this period, Hamilton is also reported as meeting Eustace Percy (1887–1958), his wife's uncle and a senior Conservative MP. However, and above all, it does not take ten days' leave to deal with a letter. We suspect Hamilton was taking specific advice from Eustace Percy about how to deal with the Secret Services, particularly with the Treason Acts in mind.

We should also comment that British Intelligence had instigated an operation entitled 'TRIPLEX', yet again a play on words in a similar vein to the XX committee. TRIPLEX involved placing agents in various foreign embassies and legations, with the express intention of intercepting diplomatic bags and post, so it may well be that MI6 already knew that Burckhardt was passing enticing correspondence through the Swiss diplomatic bag to Britain and vice versa.

So, by whatever means, whether via Borenius, Hamilton or TRIPLEX, we remain confident that Dansey was quite aware of any subsequent communication trail passing between Geneva, Stockholm, Madrid and London, and may well have instigated the same.

The next question is therefore how far up the reporting system did this information go? Dansey was the Deputy of MI6, second only to Stuart Menzies in terms of responsibility. However, this would appear not to be an MI6 operation in the strict sense. As we have already learned from our 2010 challenge to Prof. Jeffery, there are no MI6 files specifically concerning the Hess mission. We now believe the W Board to be the more likely candidate.

Consequently, it should be considered as to whether Dansey was acting 'wearing another hat'. We have seen in Chapter 8 that Menzies was also quite capable of running agents independently in the early days of double-cross and it is quite conceivable that Dansey was doing the same with Borenius, perhaps reporting to Menzies and through the W Board, perhaps not.

Indeed, in the spring of 1941 it is fair to comment that British Intelligence appeared to consist of a number of rival organisations each 'doing their own thing'. Indeed, Dansey complained to Menzies on 1 May 1941 that, 'SO2 – lives and grows at an astonishing rate, seemingly without any governing factor as far as finance goes, and that whether we like it or not they do become in a sense competitors.'

It may well be the case that the sense of competition to which Dansey refers is used to justify him 'keeping Borenius to himself' in the same way as Menzies had treated Popov over Christmas 1940. However, the need for detailed Aeronautical Intelligence and liaison would render this unlikely, making W Board cooperation with Archie Boyle and the RAF the more likely.

Consequently, by the middle of March 1941 we are now sure that Dansey and Borenius would be aware that Haushofer and Burckhardt had engaged in a process. However, given its still fledgling nature and the fact that it had a high probability of being stillborn, we do not believe that Churchill would have been made aware of the mission at that time. Had he been told at this time he would probably have killed it off straightaway, as his whole war strategy would be at risk. That is the real problem when deception goes wrong – it makes the intended actions the more obvious. Equally, it should also be said that if a coup was truly being planned, Churchill would certainly not be told.

There are currently no files to our knowledge that reveal any prior knowledge of the Hess flight by Churchill and so whilst that situation persists, a coup does remain a possibility.

However, it also appears likely to us that in making the parliamentary debate on 6/7 May a confidence motion, Churchill may well have been actively participating in the affair himself. We know that specific choice of action was very much Churchill's, albeit cleverly phrased in a manner unlikely to not succeed, as detailed in Chapter 17. We now also wonder whether Beaverbrook's resignation on 30 April 1941 was a truly independent action or part of an illusion designed to give further credence by 'British officials' to those watching and listening carefully in Bavaria, Madrid, Berlin and Geneva.

There is, however, a distinct possibility that Churchill knew nothing about the affair at all until the plane crash and that is why he was reported as being 'in a raging temper' on 14 May 14 in London.[9] He had just survived a coup attempt, through no more than the good fortune that Hess had got lost in the dark and crashed.

The fact of the matter is that the content of the messages was by that time almost irrelevant, the Germans were being exactly what they wished to hear and were now seeing physical, verifiable independent confirmation by way of the events unfolding, exactly as they had previously been told and had hoped would be happening. There was certainly no need to invade, even if there had ever been any such intention. Britain was about to implode and concede. All that was perhaps required was a little more political pressure.

Consequently, Adolf Hitler altered his Reichstag speech on 4 May to include the personal attack on Churchill. The message was very much the case of 'get rid of Churchill and we can come to an arrangement'.

That was why the parliamentary debate of 6/7 May was central to the affair. Had Churchill not made it into a confidence motion, then it is quite likely that the opposition would have damaged Churchill more than in fact happened. However, by phrasing the debate in the way he did, Churchill essentially made the act of voting against him one of treachery, not necessarily against him, but against the nation. Not surprisingly, only three MPs saw fit to act in this manner.

We now believe that it was this parliamentary debate and its failure to remove Churchill that was to act as the sub-conscious signal for Hess to fly. We have often thought that were there really a coup in the offing, it certainly did not require any German or Hess intervention. There was already a constitutional method that could have facilitated an overthrow of Churchill at any time, as long as the King agreed to participate by proroguing Parliament. The only time we believe that a Hess flight into the unknown may have worked or had an impact was in the immediate aftermath of a vote that had made Churchill's position untenable. Would that gesture have then given the King sufficient political credibility to exercise his reserve powers and dispense with Churchill? For sure, a political vacuum would be the consequence and Hess's sudden physical presence a sure statement of German (though not Hitler) credibility.

As it was, Churchill had won a decisive victory and was ready to fight another day.

It is at this stage that we now believe Hess may have acted irrationally for the only time in the entire process. We strongly suspect that although Hess realised that the main opportunity had passed him by, he now *decided to fly anyway*. That decision was a personal one, based largely on his own unhappiness and the private circumstances described earlier in the book. This was why Hitler, Haushofer and the British were surprised when he flew; they had all assumed that the idea of the British flight had died with the parliamentary defeat of the 'British officials'.

Thereafter, Churchill acted precisely as a rational leader might do. The first priority was to establish that the German pilot was truly Rudolf Hess.

This was achieved and communicated to Churchill by the early hours of Sunday 11 May. The next issue was how to react publicly, and in this area there was dissension between Churchill and the Foreign Office. Thankfully, the Foreign Office won the debate and Churchill was wise enough to listen to the argument that the best approach was to say nothing and keep the public guessing – an approach that has worked to the present day. Churchill then knew exactly what had happened, but the secret that could not be revealed was the fact that Britain, not Germany, had actually instigated the final stages of the Hess affair. The next process became the necessary cover-up.

It now appears that the British Secret Service was also operating contrary to British Government foreign policy in making the Borenius approach in the spring of 1941. This, too, would simply add more weight to those already unhappy with the autocratic and independent abilities of the various secret sections and their component parts to do what they wanted, when they wanted.

All the above reasons would be more than enough to ensure that those who knew had to keep their silence. It might certainly explain the post-war treatment of Hess and Borenius. They could not be allowed to speak and tell of their role, nor what they had been told and knew. Previously, we have also speculated that the reason for the silence was the potential participation of the royal family in the Hess affair. This may indeed still be the case, but not in an active sense (though that, too, is possible), but more likely in the sense that their names were being used as participators when the earlier communications were passing between London and Geneva. We suspect that royal involvement may have been limited to the knowledge that if Churchill had lost on 7 May 1941, the King would have acted.

Richard Wilbourn has also made the point that magicians do not like to reveal the secrets of their illusions, and perhaps the British Secret Service are of the same mentality.

Germany

The German position is perhaps initially easier to read and understand. Hess and Hitler had far more to gain than lose by trying to maintain a secret dialogue with 'British officials' during the spring of 1941, but only if the dialogue eventually produced a result. That was why they reacted positively to the news of the Borenius mission to Geneva, as it was precisely what they had hoped for as a result of their strategy of aerial bombardment over the winter of 1940/41.

Not unnaturally, they saw it as an affirmation that their strategy was beginning to work.

So, of course they would choose to engage.

However, in utilising the services of Albrecht Haushofer, Rudolf Hess had not chosen particularly well, though as we have seen he had little choice. Simultaneously, Haushofer was also engaging in the process with a separate agenda of his own, that of a leading anti-Hitler activist, on the face of it a wholly incompatible objective. Haushofer was also engaged with a Spanish channel, through a former student of his, Herbert Stahmer. Both channels were inferring the same thing – Britain wished to engage in negotiations. He had also been to Stockholm in early February, presumably following a similar agenda.

Rudolf Hess had been wholly aware of Hitler's military wish to go eastwards, virtually from the day the Western peace was signed in Compiègne. He had, of course, known of Hitler's political desire for the same objective since the days of Landsberg Prison. So, he had consulted his friend, Karl Haushofer, in August 1940 and had used his son Albrecht to write the letter of 23 September. Shortly afterwards he had rediscovered his interest in aviation and had started to dictate draft peace terms to Ernst Bohle in his Berlin flat. The relationship between Hess and Albrecht Haushofer was far less personal than between Albrecht's father, Karl, and Hess. However, not all share Hess's view, even of Karl Haushofer, with Ulrich von Hassell stating, 'I like the man as little as I did before, full of himself…'[10]

Clearly, Hess was considering the formative stages of the May 1941 mission well before Christmas 1940. However, three things were then holding him back:

1. He needed to be able to be sure that he could make the flight independently to be able to portray it as a solo mission and thus deniable. In order to be sure of that ability he then typically 'over engineered' his plane to incorporate the latest Luftwaffe navigational system, the ELEKTRA. This process also required detailed training and operational experience.
2. The weather was awful in the early weeks of 1941
3. He had yet to complete the peace document. Bohle, under interrogation in 1945, stated that it was finally completed in early January.[11] Consequently, it was only after the Borenius mission in late January that the impetus really started to build. The required logistics

> were slowly being put into place and the political need for settlement was growing by the day.

Thereafter, throughout the spring of 1941, Hess slowly gained confidence in the Bf110, 'werk nummer' 3869. He regularly met Albrecht Haushofer, usually in Berlin. The plan was coming together, but the need was becoming more immediate. Hess had attended a conference in late March in Berlin specifically dealing with the resettlement of Germans in the eastern provinces, once obtained. There was no doubt that Hitler would go east, it was just a question of when.

At the end of April 1941, Haushofer travelled to Geneva to meet Carl Burckhardt. This meeting appears to have been organised by Ilse von Hassell, the wife of Ulrich, who had previously met Burckhardt in Zurich. She was a member of the Tirpitz family and was well connected in her own stead. At the time she was staying in Switzerland, at Arosa, looking after a sick son. Paul Stauffer, in *Sechs furchtbare Jahre*,[12] makes the case that it was Ilse von Hassell that had made the preliminary arrangements, making it clear that that Haushofer was making his way to Geneva, essentially 'wearing two hats'.

One 'hat' was that of a representative of the Hitler resistance, the other was that of an emissary of Rudolf Hess. Logically, it must be the case that it was Hess that effectively authorised the trip and that it was the Hess mission that allowed it to take place. Haushofer stated that Hess had 'decided I should go', in his memorandum to Hitler on 12 May 1941. Wolf Hess goes further, stating that it was Hitler who had approved the journey.[13]

The meeting itself is clearly of fundamental importance, given what happened twelve days later. It is, we suggest, clearly a nonsense to suggest that this was the initial reaction to the Borenius meeting of late January 1941 and that nothing had happened in the meanwhile. Hess simply did not have that luxury. He knew that a Russian invasion was originally planned for mid-May 1941 and that time was running out. His plane was nearly ready, and we strongly suspect from the timeline described above that those communications had been passing through the Red Cross throughout the spring of 1941 and this meeting was one to confirm precise detail – not talk in principles.

In stark contrast to the series of memorandums and notes that the Haushofer Hess meetings produced the previous September, the April/May 1941 meetings have to date yielded no such detailed record. In fact, virtually no record at all. The only reaction to the meetings come first from Albrecht's mother, whose diary records that the meeting had,

> 3 May 1941 'nicht von vornherein gescheitert' (not failed from the onset)

and

> 5 May 1941 'nicht voellig fruchtlos verlaufen' (does not extend to being completely fruitless)

and thirdly, Karl Haushofer had spoken to Erika Mann, a journalist, and told her that a meeting in Madrid was in the process of being arranged as a result of the meeting.

Lastly, Ulrich von Hassell records that his wife Ilse had also had a long conversation with Carl Burckhardt in Zurich *before* the meeting and with Albrecht Haushofer *after* the meeting. He records that Britain still wanted peace on a rational basis, but (1) not with our present leaders and (2) perhaps not much longer.

Albrecht Haushofer makes no such detailed comment in his 12 May 1941 report to Hitler, nor does he mention von Hassell's role. Instead, he naturally describes the trip in terms of the Hess mission and states that Burckhardt had simply said that he would be willing to act as a go-between.

These facts are reasonably well known and appear in most works on Rudolf Hess. However, we believe they now require further analysis.

We have little doubt that Carl Burckhardt was looking to broker a peace between Germany and Britain. At the time he appears to be pro-German, as we assume he anticipated a German victory. There are some telling signs that this was the case in his behaviour when reporting for the Red Cross about conditions in German concentration camps in the late 1930s. No doubt the wish for Swiss neutrality and the absolute need for impartiality as far as the International Red Cross was concerned would also have played some part in his reckoning.

However, it is difficult to see precisely what message Haushofer brought to Geneva from the anti-Hitler resistance that had not been relayed already by Ilse von Hassell. Further proof of conviction, certainly, but there was really nothing new to say. The fact of the matter was that whilst Hitler was winning, there really was little impetus to dislodge him, by those that could and heaven help those that tried and failed, or even tried and succeeded without a viable mass alternative. In May 1941 there certainly was no viable mass alternative. Consequently, we can see little scope for Haushofer with his anti-Hitler 'hat' on, though we suspect that it was this part of the conversation that Martha and Karl Haushofer were referring to, both in their diary and interview with Erika Mann.

The fascinating part of this process is to consider what progress was made when Albrecht Haushofer then put on his 'Hess hat'. We now suspect that this part of the conversation was far more developed, and the late January 1941 meeting had spawned further communication throughout the spring. We repeat again, it would not take until 28 April to respond to the Borenius meeting, almost exactly three months earlier.

The meeting places. Hotel Isla (Arosa)

Consequently, we now suspect that it was this meeting which gave Hess the details of where to head for and what might happen when he arrived.

What proof is there for the above statement, probably the most controversial in this book? None, but nor would we expect there to be. However, we can check the timings.

Hotel Drei Mohren, Augsburg

28 April Haushofer meets Burckhardt in Geneva. Then he travels to Arosa (either late on 28 or 29 April) and meets Ilse von Hassell, presumably at the Hotel Isla. Arosa is some 250 miles from Geneva and would take a day to get there by rail. Haushofer is also recorded as meeting Hans Heinrich Noebel (1921–2016), another former student of his, in Lausanne, en route to Arosa, thus taking yet more precious time. It appears that the two men shared a meal and Haushofer was pleased with how things had gone. Noebel was at the University of Geneva on sabbatical for a term.[14] It is also reported that Haushofer had said that he had attended a number of meetings – that is to say, not just with Burckhardt.

29 April En route to Arosa (presumably train)

30 April Arosa

1 May Travel to parents' house at Pahl (presumably train)

2 May At Pahl

3 May Martha Haushofer makes her first diary entry. It is therefore a reasonably safe assumption that from Arosa, Albrecht had called in at Hartschimmelhof to visit his parents.

5 May Albrecht is called to Augsburg, to the Hotel Drei Mohren. Meets Hess for lunch. Hess had arrived early in the morning, following a train journey from Berlin the previous evening. Clearly the subject for discussion had to be the Geneva meeting.

We can therefore see no reason for a meeting with Haushofer (wearing his Hess 'hat'), unless it was to give him or tell him something. The Borenius mission had been debated ad nauseam within both the Haushofer/Hess camp and the Haushofer/Popitz/resistance camp. They had known the contents of Borenius's meeting for literally months.

The last piece of the jigsaw was for Hess to gather Hitler's approval for the most dramatic act of the war that was about to take place, even though it is quite simply inconceivable in a police state that Hess's aeronautical activities were not already widely known about.

There are various reports that Hess and Hitler met for four hours, around the time of the Reichstag speech on 4 May. Peter Padfield places the meeting after the speech, but this is not possible, as Hess was on the Munich train that night which left at 10.05pm. The Reichstag session commenced at 6.00pm, so there was no time for protracted conversation after the speech. It seems much more likely that the detailed meeting was held in the Chancellery in the afternoon of 4 May, where there was sufficient time.

This is important, because it places the Hitler/Hess meeting before the Hess/Haushofer meeting. In other words, it appears to us that Hess went into the meeting with Hitler without full possession of all the relevant facts. That is why the reports of the meeting all revolve around principles, 'Does the Führer still believe in an Anglo-German alliance, etc,' rather than focusing on specific details. We suspect the specific details came the following day in Augsburg – where, when and at what time?

And, yet, here comes the rub. The messenger, Albrecht Haushofer, we are quite convinced, gave Hess the final instructions in the Hotel Drei Mohren. Instructions convincing enough to make Hess fly. It was probably a low standard of proof that was required, but we are now far from convinced that Haushofer actually believed what he was being told, *or perhaps even made up some of the details himself.* This is the crux of the affair. When the climax was being approached, the stakes being increased, the deadline ever closer, was Rudolf Hess being actively deceived by Albrecht Haushofer? It now seems very likely to us that he was, albeit with the connivance and 'support' of the

British Secret Service. This is where the boundaries between anti-Hitler resistance and the Hess mission become very blurred indeed.

Chapter 25 deals with the pertinent question as to whether Albrecht Haushofer was a British agent. We believe we are the first authors to pose the question, but it is obviously not the first occasion that the question has been raised. Wolf Hess, in his 1984 book, raised the issue of the relationship between Karl and Albrecht Haushofer and indeed stated: 'It appears that towards the end of his life the father began to doubt whether his son had always acted correctly in the Hess affair…'

He recorded that in the winter of 1944 Karl Haushofer wrote, 'That Albrecht had perhaps toyed with the fate of well-meaning people … which worries me much more than it did him.'[15]

We have already made the case that the younger Haushofer had acted very strangely throughout the affair, and it is in the period from 28 April to 5 May that he had the opportunity to directly affect events. Given the potential importance of the events it does seem most odd to us that he detoured to both Lausanne and then Arosa on his way back to the Munich area. Arosa, in particular, was well out of his way, and it has to be initially assumed that he went to discuss the Burckhardt meeting with Ilse von Hassell. Ilse von Hassell was born Ilse von Tirpitz, daughter of the First World War German Groβ Admiral, after whom the Kriegsmarine had also named their largest ship in 1939.

She was, in fact, in Arosa, staying at the Hotel Isla, to nurse her son, Wolf Ulrich, born in 1913. It appears that she had been in Switzerland for some time, as Ulrich von Hassell's diaries record earlier visits to Arosa in June 1940 and perhaps more notably in February 1940.

In February 1940, Ulrich von Hassell had been staying at the Hotel Isla, when he met James Lonsdale-Bryans, yet another amateur diplomat, this time British. This meeting was held prior to the western invasion in May that year and was therefore whilst Chamberlain was still in power. Lonsdale-Bryans was given permission to travel to Arosa, via Rome, by Lord Halifax and was sponsored by Lord Brocket to the tune of £200. John Costello also tells this story well in Appendix 3 to his *Ten Days that Saved the West*.[16]

Later in the war Walter Schellenberg, the head of the Foreign Section of the RHSA, met General Guisan, the Head of the Swiss Army, and travelled to Arosa, this time using the Swiss Skiing Championship as a camouflage.

This all just seems very odd to us. We do not understand why Albrecht

Haushofer should go so far out of his way to travel to Arosa, which is certainly not easy to get to and would involve extensive rail and road travel. It is 425 km from Geneva. There is no main trunk road nearby. Von Hassell earlier describes travelling there by 'car to St Margarethen'. Thereafter there is a two-and-a-half-hour train journey. Arosa is the terminus of the tortuous, single track, 16-mile metre gauge Arosabahn branch of the Rhaetian railway. We have yet to visit the resort, but it just looks unnecessarily difficult.

Hence, we are suspicious that there had to be other notable persons at Arosa in and around 29/30 April 1941 to justify the trip. Ilse von Hassell was apparently a very formidable character in her own right, particularly given her pedigree. She and her sister were even educated at Cheltenham Ladies College. But would Albrecht really have made that trek just to see Ilse, the wife of a potential resistance member, however formidable? It just seems very unlikely to us, but may of course be just that.

The von Hassell diary on 10 April 1941 is also a little unclear, as he refers to 'my visitor Bryans in Arosa'. It is not clear to us whether this in in the past or current tense. We suspect the past tense, as Lonsdale-Bryans details his return to England in mid-March 1941. We also have learned that Bill de Ropp, the pre-war aviation expert and member of Air Intelligence, had moved to Montreux at the start of the war. Another potential visitor perhaps? Naturally, we have contacted the Hotel Isla, but no guestbooks survive from that time.

The possibilities are endless. Had Lonsdale-Bryans or de Ropp brought details and plans for Haushofer to pass on? We may never know, for sure, but we do know that Hess had flown with detailed aeronautical information concerning the Scottish Lowlands.

Moreover, fuelling our suspicion about Arosa still further is the fact also recorded in Ulrich von Hassell's diaries that after at least fifteen months' convalescence, on 16 May 1941 Ilse von Hassell and their son, who was soon to sit his doctorate, returned home to Germany. They lived at Ebenhausen, just outside Munich. One is tempted to suspect that their presence in Switzerland was in part extended, simply to provide a convenient cover for various meetings being carried on in the neutral country.

We then next record Albrecht Haushofer as being in Augsburg, on 5 May. The two men met at the Hotel Drei Mohren. Given that Hess had been in Berlin on much of 3 and 4 May, this probably represents the earliest the two men could practically meet face to face. (Hess was in Augsburg on 1 May at the Messerschmitt works, whilst presumably Haushofer was either in Geneva, Arosa or still in transit.) This seems to us to be the critical meeting of the whole affair.

Haushofer came to the exclusive hotel from Geneva, via the seemingly odd meeting in Arosa. Hess came fresh from the meeting with Adolf Hitler the previous day. He had effectively obtained the sanction that Hitler still desired a Western peace with Britain. He now hoped that Haushofer would bring him the necessary details as to how that might be achieved.

And this is the crux of the matter. Precisely what was he told by Albrecht Haushofer?

Haushofer was clearly prepared to lie. He lied to Hitler on 12 May by not mentioning the detour to Arosa at all. This was a gamble in that he could have easily been tailed whilst in Switzerland. Did he also lie to Hess and impart false hope and information that encouraged Hess to fly?

Equally, he may just have told Hess the truth as he knew it, and Hess could see that he was not going to be able to influence the course of events prior to Barbarossa if the current rate of progress, as just reported, continued. Erika Mann later reported that Hess flew out of a sense of frustration, depression and disappointment. This may well, of course, also have been the case.

Our proposal in this regard is actually a compound of the above. We believe Hess had to know where to fly to at the very least. He had to have time to have marked-up his flight map and learn and compute the various ELEKTRA settings pertaining thereto. From where did he get this information? Either from Burckhardt or via Arosa, both via Haushofer. He was probably also told of the possibility of a meeting in Spain. In short, he could have been told virtually anything, because by this time we suspect he had already made up his mind. He may even have suspected that what Albrecht was telling him was not the complete story. There was not an automatic, mutual trust between the two men as in the same way as there was between Hess and Karl Haushofer.

Haushofer would have known this too. When the flight did eventually take place, Haushofer was not expecting it. Hence, 'the winged Parsifal comment'. Therefore, it appears likely that Haushofer had either tried to dissuade Hess or there was not enough information at the time to judge the likelihood of success, or Haushofer fed Hess deliberate disinformation on the basis that he did not want the flight to succeed, even if it was possible. Presumably a viable Western peace would bolster Hitler's position and prestige once again. Precisely what the 'resistance' did not want.

This is the key moment in the Hess affair. We suspect that Haushofer gave some detail, enough to encourage Hess still further, who probably by now would have flown, even knowing that it was a potential suicide mission. If the Haushofer report of 12 May is believable in any way, it also gave sufficient justification to Adolf Hitler that his deputy's mission was well founded and not just an act of treachery.

5 May 1941 was a Monday, and we know that by the end of the week Haushofer was back in Berlin. We have also discovered the fascinating evidence that attached to Hess's letter to Hitler was one from Karl Haushofer, praising the virtue of the mission, so we can only presume that either Albrecht gave his father's letter to Hess on 5 May or that Hess met his professor later in the week, either on 7 or 9 May. We know that Albrecht called in on his parents, as it is recorded in his mother's diary.

Either way, after the Augsburg lunch, Hess departed to the Haunstetten airfield to test the newly installed ELEKTRA radio guidance system. It is not recorded that the two men ever met again.

It is also most strange that we can find no later evidence of the two men ever corresponding. Hess wrote to Karl Haushofer – Ilse Hess published some of the letters in *Prisoner of Peace*. But Albrecht – nothing. We do not think it too speculative to suggest that this was for a reason. The reason being that Hess, too, had worked out that Haushofer had not been telling the truth, when briefing him; we suspect on 5 May.

The obvious subject for misleading was aeronautical. Did Haushofer suggest Dungavel, knowing that to attempt to land was a death trap? Or was the arrival of the Boulton Paul Defiant over the end of Dundonald runway a sign to Hess that he had been betrayed and deceived? Either way, the two men's subsequent estrangement speaks volumes to us. It could be, of course, that the British censor just prevented any correspondence from passing, for fear of what it might reveal, but as has been disclosed already, the modern Hess family is still suspicious of Albrecht Haushofer. Quite rightly so, in our opinion.

Basic timing

At a fundamental level the Hess affair descended into farce because Hess crashed and did not reach his intended target. However, one could also argue that Hess failed because the basic timing that his task required was not yet prescient. In the early days of the 2022 Russian invasion of Ukraine, various peace meetings were held, but all failed. They failed because the timing of the meetings was such that the two opponents were not yet prepared to deal; Russia because she had not yet obtained what she wished to obtain and Ukraine because she did not consider herself so defeated that she had to concede. Eventually, no doubt, there will be enough brutality and killing and occupation for both sides to come to some form of settlement, though at the time of writing this point is difficult to forecast.

The position in 1941 was identical, save that Germany also had the additional impediment of the knowledge that she was about to embark on the largest invasion ever mounted by man and so really needed to conclude a deal before its commencement. Moreover, and unbeknown to it, the British government and opponent also realised that to be the case. A very good card to hold.

In short, the basic timing of the Hess affair was flawed in that it was never based on a defeated enemy; it was based on a battered enemy, an enemy near breaking point, but one not yet cowed sufficiently to have to come to the peace table. Consequently, the German timing was fundamentally flawed in that it had run out of time and was trying to engineer a solution before it had completed the job, *because it felt it had to*, rather than having an absolute ascendancy and superiority.

However, the additional difficulty with the Hess affair is that Hess did not think he was dealing with the government of the enemy at all, but a non-governmental body (*stellen*) who would depose or coerce the government, making use of an unusual, though typically British, constitutional device. This just made his task the more difficult, though not impossible.

Hitler's reactions

As has already been stated, we are clear that Hitler knew of the flight and had sanctioned it. If one dissects the various reports, it become clear that the hysterical reactions only started once it looked as if the mission had failed. Up until that time he was sensibly taking soundings as to its likelihood of success from an aeronautical viewpoint. Again, we suspect that he already knew Hess was likely to succeed in aviation terms and was merely trying to work out when it might be possible to ascertain the fact for sure from the possible timing of the receipt of confirmatory information. (Hess had arranged for such a telegram to be delivered to his aunt in Zurich.)

Thereafter, once it was clear the mission had failed, Hess became disposable, persona non grata, and the mission deniable. When the Gauleiters were duly assembled on 15 May, it is notable that Ernst Bohle, head of the Auslands Organisation, complained that this was the only time he had been asked to attend such a meeting.[17] Presumably so that Hitler could then stage-manage his theatrical rebuke for helping Hess with his peace document. The very same terms that Hess had discussed with Hitler on 4 May. Hypocrisy clearly ruled the day, but it had to, so as to distance Hitler from Hess and his mission.

The reaction that, to date has not yet been recorded, is that of Hitler and Hess to Churchill's Common's victory of 7 May. This, we feel, may have been the 'final straw' as far as Hess was concerned. If the British politicians would not do his job for him, he would have to fly.

Final Conclusions – nearly

And that was it. Hess got into his Bf110 and flew to Scotland, taking off between 5.45 to 6.15pm, depending upon whose report one reads. It is generally agreed that he crashed some five hours later at around 11.09pm.

The last public pronouncement he made was his rather rambling eulogy to Adolf Hitler at Nuremberg, five years later. Thereafter silence. Complete silence, despite the best efforts of his family to later try and secure a release, and Messrs Bird and Zwar's attempts to publish some memoirs.

On one level one could make the bland statement that the Allies merely carried out the sentence that had been handed down at Nuremberg in 1946. Life meant life. There was, and is, no secret to preserve, they were just doing their job in carrying out the sentence. This may, of course, be the case.

However, were it to be the case and it was as simple as that, surely the subsequent treatment meted out seems simply inhumane? At the most generous it was not a consistent treatment, or indeed more arguably, even a consistent sentence by comparison to the other Nuremberg defendants.

The obvious comment must be that by his treatment Rudolf Hess was silenced deliberately, and even murdered, as his family have alleged. But to what end? What on earth can justify the treatment Rudolf Hess received from 1941 to 1987?

The following reasons have been mooted:

- At the end of the First World War there was a widespread suspicion that Germany had not been beaten on the battlefield, but had instead lost the war by the by the duplicitous civilians, Jews and the almost supernatural powers of British Intelligence. The so-called stab in the back. The NSDAP often played on these suspicions as a later justification for its own actions and policies. Indeed, it is an oft-cited reason for Hitler's apparent dislike of secret intelligence services. Consequently, if the Hess affair was yet another intelligence sting, there was the risk that yet again the stab in the back theory might well resurface in later, post-Second World War years.

- There is an argument that Hess was proven correct by subsequent events. In 1945, at the end of the war, Britain was bankrupt and instead of an aggressive Germany there was now the latent threat of Soviet Russia that would eventually manifest itself for the remainder of the century (and now beyond). Yes, Britain had helped to defeat Fascism and all that it entailed, but it was America who had taken the economic spoils and Russia those geographical. Britain eventually came to lose her empire.
- The Allied wish to retain a foothold in Berlin. After May 1945, Germany and Berlin were divided into individual Allied zones: US, French, Russian and British. Spandau Prison was in the British zone of west Berlin. Consequently, the need to provide, on a rotational basis, a guard for the seven prisoners in Spandau gave the Allies a justification for maintaining a modest military presence in the centre of the former German capital. We do not give this theory too much credence. The airlift of 1948–9 amply demonstrated the Allied resolve to maintain a presence in Berlin. That was nothing to do with Rudolf Hess, but rather the desire to maintain a Western presence.
- Anglo-Russian relations. The figure of 20 million has been used as the best estimate of Russian dead through the period 1939–45. Therefore, the argument runs that Russian relations could be damaged, even after more than seventy years if it was shown that Britain was talking peace in 1941 to the extent that enabled Hitler to garner confidence sufficient to launch Barbarossa. A supreme act of self-preservation by the British. Superficially, this is an attractive argument in that it is essentially true. Stalin suspected the involvement of the British Secret Service and even taunted Churchill that his NKVD did not tell him everything that they did. It is quite possible that he knew the truth through the likes of Kim Philby, who were becoming active at around the time of the flight. The Russians at Nuremberg certainly saw Hess

in terms of trying to arrange a peace to facilitate Russian annihilation being that much easier. However, we feel the argument flounders on the basis that Hitler, we are quite sure, was going to attack Russia, irrespective of Britain's position. Britain was technically unbeaten, but equally she was effectively neutralised. In June 1941, Hitler embarked on a two-front war, to be sure, but the western front was virtually benign. Britain was on the ropes, still wholly defensive in strategy and so, we would suggest, Hitler was not truly fighting a two-front war at that time. He was quite aware for the need for a quick victory in the east – his December 1940 Führer Order stressed the point. Otherwise, the latent western front would literally explode in his face, as indeed it eventually did. It is well known that Stalin was pressing Churchill for the commencement of the second front, as he wanted action as well as munitions. What would have been his reaction if he learned that the man who was now his ally had presided over peace negotiations just a month before the German invasion?

- Given that there are still a vast number of Russian survivors of the Great Patriotic War, all of whom have memories of the immense suffering of that period, perhaps Hess was kept quiet out of simple respect for the dead. If the truth came out in the post-war period, perhaps Communism would have appeared somewhat more straightforward than the duplicitous West, and provide some form of encouragement. Indeed, given the recent Russian resurgence, this may still be the case and was perhaps what John Scarlett was referring to when he made the comment in 2010 that 'secrets which still prejudice relations with other nations would have to remain secret.'
- We have learned from from Keith Jeffery that the MI6 archives make it clear that the Hess affair was not an MI6 operation make us question whether the 'big secret' is that it signalled a failed coup attempt on behalf of the rump of Chamberlain supporters, the British Secret Service and the British plutocracy, with much to lose in terms of property and possession. Hence the title of this book.
- Indeed, the list of potential participants can be extended almost indefinitely to include the various members of the British royal family and even exiled kings. Again, superficially it is an attractive argument for the reasons given earlier in this chapter. It is almost too convincing, we believe, to be credible, but we have no doubt whatsoever that if

Hess, aged ninety-three, had been released into the West Germany of the 1980s only to declare that he had been invited over by King George VI and the Duke of Kent in 1941, the Germans would have seen the affair and his imprisonment very differently.

In the late 1980s the scandalous behaviour of the Duke of Windsor was coming under detailed scrutiny and various offspring of the Queen and Duke of Edinburgh were all going through trying times. Whether one could say that it could have threatened the future of the monarchy we are not sure, but it certainly would not have enhanced it.

In 1941, the King and Queen were not yet particularly popular, so imagine the impact if Hess was able to tell how he had been invited over as a 'Parlamentär' to talk peace. It is unlikely the British population, then suffering the heaviest bombing of the war, would be that charitable. Throw in the growth and strength of the Labour movement as evidenced in July 1945, and anything could have been possible.

- In this connection, it must also be relevant to consider the position of the substantial Polish Army that was firmly rooted in Lowland Scotland. What would their reaction be to a Hess offer of peace that included a restoration of Poland, in part or in whole? Clearly this would not satisfy British ambitions, but might it satisfy the Poles, particularly if it brought an end to the slaughter in their homeland? How could they bring their wish to bear? This would certainly explain the mad panic to find the peace document that Hess brought with him on the morning of Sunday 11 May. This idea, whilst far-fetched, does explain why Hess flew to Scotland. He was offering a separate peace, as he knew full well that Churchill would never cede, but the Poles might. What might happen if the Poles wanted peace, but the British did not? Throw in the throne for Prince George in Poland and anything could be possible. Does this explain Sikorski's mad rush back to Scotland and then his week-long isolation at Moncreiffe House when the Hess mission failed?
- The Duke of Kent's role is also fascinating. On the one hand, the trip to the Orkneys could be seen as no more than an official visit, in just the same way as his more usual RAF duties at that time. However, if so, why not say so? It is not mentioned in the official RAF/AIR file alongside the Duke's other engagements.

Moreover, the Duke was dressed as a Rear Admiral whilst making his visit. At the time he was second in rank only to Vice Admiral

Hugh Binney, who was in Naval Command of the Orkneys and Shetland Islands. In the absence of any further evidence, we will leave the reader to ascertain the possibilities. In theory at least, he was under naval control and command.

- Anglo-US relations. In a similar manner to Anglo-Russian relations, Churchill's principal strategy in May 1941 was to 'draw in' America. This was by way of highlighting German threats, both militarily and economically. Again, imagine the impact were it to become known in 1941 that Hess had effectively been invited to talk peace. This would have handed the American isolationists the necessary evidence of worthlessness on a plate.

We trust the above reasons have been sufficiently well explained in the first thirty chapters of the book. We now come to the 'killer question'.

The killer question – coup or lure?

So, Rudolf Hess was both deceived and deceitful. He was deceived by the British. He was deceived by Albrecht Haushofer, who at the very least was promoting the cause of the German resistance to Hitler. In turn, Hess also deceived Adolf Hitler by his ready acceptance to grasp at a straw that perhaps was never there. This is the real debate concerning the Hess affair that extends to this day. Was it truly a British coup attempt, or just a lure, an illusion of something that never really existed, but was so convincing to the German who wanted so desperately to believe?

An answer is contained in the 1946 letter to Ernest Bevin, sent by Duff Cooper, then Ambassador to France (see chapter 23). Duff Cooper comments on the role of Carl Burckhardt, 'Nor do I see that a Swiss should be much, if at all, be blamed for having been willing to lend his services to the cause of peace, however much he may have misunderstood the real facts of the situation.'

In 1941, Duff Cooper was the much-maligned British Minister of Information, so knew the truth behind the affair, as we believe did Ernest Bevin. Therefore, the key is to interpret what he thought Burckhardt was doing – at face value, surely acting as intermediary for two parties, the British and the Germans, trying to come to a negotiated settlement?

However, if this straightforward explanation is misunderstanding 'the real facts of the situation', we can only conclude that the straightforward and obvious was not actually the case. As has already been stated, our principal complaint against the coup argument is that it is based on such arrogance we do not believe it could have ever worked with Churchill still alive. He was just too popular 'in the country' for an aristocratic uprising to succeed (even though, of course, Churchill was also ostensibly an aristocrat). Moreover, no Hess/German flight was necessary to instigate such an action. It could theoretically have been implemented at any time, if that time was thought opportune.

Consequently, this line of argument appears to support the lure theory. The events were simply an intelligence ruse, albeit with certain individuals possibly believing they were engaged in a coup attempt.

So, coup or lure – our answer

However, we suspect that the issue was not that simple.

1. We have no doubt whatsoever that there was deception aplenty in the Hess affair. That is the job of the intelligence services. However, Hess was being secretive within and distrustful of the German Nazi Party. Britain, in turn, was certainly being at the very least provocative, by allowing and aiding Borenius to travel to Geneva in January 1941.

2. Thereafter it all gets much more difficult. We suspect that we will never be openly told of the high-level treachery that took place in late 1940 and early 1941. However, to our minds there are distinct signs of such action:
   - The nagging uncertainty as to the King and Queen's precise whereabouts on 10 May 1941 (see Chapter 21).
   - The conviction that Hess later showed in his belief that the King had promised him safe passage. Why, when and how did the King do this? (See Chapter 28)
   - The strange diary entry that the King made concerning the crash, inferring that Hess had missed his target by only 2 miles (see Chapter 21).
   - The continued reluctance to tell us the Duke of Kent's official, precise whereabouts on 10 May 1941. The Orkney trip was not recorded in the relevant AIR files at the National Archives (equally, that may well be because it was technically a naval responsibility) (see Chapter 21).

- The concentration of the various dukes and dignitaries in Lowland Scotland on 10 May 1941, by stark contrast to the random locations of the various government ministers (see Chapter 21).
- The apparent ignorance of the affair by Winston Churchill until the plane had crashed. His subsequent references to the 'certain circles' (see Introduction).
- The continued failure to release information and documents we know have existed (see Appendix 8 for a full list).
- The subsequent removal of the Scottish crown jewels and virtual house arrest of Buccleuch and Tavistock (see Chapter 21).
- Alanbrooke's sudden appearance on the Orkney Islands on 13 May 1941.Was this to recover the Duke of Kent for the Government? (see Chapter 21)
- The fact that Hess lied in captivity about his flight. This was to prevent accusations of Luftwaffe connivance, thus threatening the official 'flight of a madman' explanation (see Chapter 19).
- The lack of *any* released papers from Air Intelligence. Contrast that, for example, with the files, papers and later various books (and films) concerning Operation Mincemeat, Ultra and the XX committee. When wishing to portray a good outcome, the British do eventually reveal their secrets.
- No released RAF report on the incident. This is really the most damning. Deputy Führer Hess flies into Scotland, evades the air defences and yet no report from the RAF?
- No release of the RAE Farnborough report on the Bf110 plane, that we know was made. No pictures whatsoever of the cockpit of the plane.
- The subsequent removal of the Duke of Hamilton from active command. Why? (See Chapter 31)
- The Hamilton family's denial of the existence of the 'third map to the north' (see Chapter 19).
- The stage-management of the Eaglesham crash site, designed simply to foster an impression of randomness. The fiasco of the pitchfork.[18]
- The continuing question as to a second occupant of the crashed plane.[19]
- The behaviour of General Sikorski and the Poles in May 1941 (see

Chapter 23). The role, whatever it really was, of Alfgar Hesketh-Prichard.

- The fact that Sefton Delmer was prevented from going to Scotland to identify Hess. Was this because he had been instrumental in previous communications? (Source: Bruce Lockhart diaries, 14 May 1941)
- Churchill's parliamentary tactics on 7 May 1941 and 27 January 1942. Who were the 'certain circles' and were they the same as the '*Englischen stellen*' that Borenius was appearing to represent in Geneva? (See Chapter 18) If there were no 'certain circles', why mention them at all?
- The March 1941 meetings between Sikorski and the messenger Borenius (see Chapter 11).
- The fact that Tancred Borenius was not subsequently decorated or even fêted. Surely, had he really been party to preventing a German Invasion of Britain he would have received some recognition? (See Chapter 11)
- Hess's continued incarceration in Spandau, despite all other prisoners being released (see Chapter 30).
- The suspicion that Hess was murdered in 1987 to prevent his release (see Chapter 30).
- The treatment and behaviour of Hess at Nuremberg and the fact that J.R. Rees gained an OBE shortly afterwards. The stated use of potentially dangerous narcotics on the prisoner (see Chapter 24).
- The denial by MI6 historians of any involvement, when we know for sure that Dansey of MI6 was involved, though we concede, may have been wearing a 'different hat' (see Chapter 8)
- And lastly, the somewhat odd fact that it was recorded that when the Duke of Kent was buried in 1942, the King had specifically asked that no cabinet ministers should attend the funeral. Did he in some way blame the Government for his brother's death and if so, why?

We could go further but will stop at the above, save being accused of being too conspiratorial, although this is precisely the nature of the Hess affair. We do hope that we have at least highlighted the various significant aspects of the affair, which, quite frankly, renders Richard Evans's interpretation of the event as ludicrous.

The British were clearly being deceptive, but we do also suspect in-house treachery as well, directed against the incumbent Churchillian government. Treachery that was only thwarted when Hess inadvertently crashed and the whole affair dramatically unravelled.

In short, our final conclusion, reinforcing the title of this book and the relevant definitions, is that the Hess affair was certainly a *conspiracy* prior to the flight, the flight itself then became an absolute *calamity*, and a long-standing *cover-up* was implemented to hide the former.

Does the reader concur?

---

[1] (Countess Granville (1876–1955) was a Baring heiress, whose husband, Granville Leveson-Gower, the 3rd Earl Granville, had recently died. Both were close to the British royal family and the Earl was a member of the Duke of Sutherland's family. The 4th Earl had married the Queen Mother's sister, Rose, in 1916.)

[2] David Kelly, *The Ruling Few*, Hollis and Carter, London, 1952.

[3] *Lord Halifax Diaries*, University of York, England.

[4] Please see Keith Jeffery's official history of MI6. He clearly describes but does not name Berenson.

[5] *The Ulrich von Hassell Diaries*, Frontline, Barnsley, 2011 (18 May 1941).

[6] NKVD Archives, Moscow - N.450, file 20566.

[7] Voenno-istoricheskii Zhurnal, 1991, pp. 37-42.

[8] James Douglas-Hamilton, *Motive for a Mission*, Macmillan, London, 1971

[9] *Sir Alexander Cadogan Diaries*, Cassell, London, 1971 (14 May 1941).

[10] *The Ulrich von Hassell Diaries*, Frontline, Barnsley, 2011 (17 January 1941).

[11] Frank-Rutger Hausmann, *Ernst Wilhelm Bohle*, Duncker und Humblot, Berlin, 2009. This book places the end of the translation process at the rather precise date of 7 January 1941.

[12] Paul Stauffer, *Sechs furchtbare Jahre*, Neue Zürcher Zeitung, Zurich, 1998.

[13] Wolf Hess, *My Father Rudolf Hess*, WH Allen, London, 1984.

[14] This information was gleaned during a conversation between Ernst Haiger and Hans Noebel in 1987. Cited by Ulrich Schlie in *Kein Friede mit Deutschland*, Langen Muller, Munich, 1994. Noebel later became a distinguished diplomat.

[15] Wolf Hess, *My Father Rudolf Hess*, WH Allen, London, 1984.

[16] John Costello, *Ten Days that Saved the West*, Bantam Press, London, 1991.

[17] Frank-Rutger Hausmann, *Ernst Wilhelm Bohle*, Duncker und Humblot, Berlin, 2009.

[18] See Harris and Wilbourn, *Rudolf Hess: Truth at Last*, Unicorn, 2019.

[19] (FO1093/11) which mentions, 'So far nothing can be ascertained about the second occupant of the aircraft.'

APPENDICES

APPENDIX I

THE SHOOTING PARTY

This diversion has certainly been one of the most enjoyable over the past twenty-five years.

Following the publication of our *Treachery and Deception*, we were contacted by an academic, who in a previous life had been a TV producer. He wished to meet to discuss matters Hess. This led to us travelling to first London and then to Seahouses, in Northumberland to meet with Lloyd, a former fisherman, who had important information to impart.

After a pleasant lunch in the Ship Inn, Lloyd told us that he was aware of a pre-war photograph of a shooting party taken outside what is now the Beadnell Towers Hotel in Chathill. Amongst its members was Rudolf Hess.

Straightaway, we drew deep breath, simply because we could not envisage Rudolf Hess being a game-shooting man at all, with what we knew of his faith healing, homeopathy and his pursuit and love of aviation. (However, we have subsequently learned that he did own a rifle and was obviously used to handling guns as he fought as an infantryman in the First World War.)

As we asked more questions, the mystery seemed to deepen. The Beadnell Towers Hotel was at the time owned by the Allhusen family, a Danish family who had settled in Britain and made a fortune in iron, steel and shipping in the late Victorian era. Apparently, according to Lloyd, in the 1930s the house sported a large radio aerial on account of Mr Allhusen being an early radio ham.

He went on. The photograph is in possession of a former retainer of the Runciman family who previously lived nearby at Doxford Hall. Lord Runciman was packed off to Czechoslovakia in 1938 by Chamberlain and it is, of course, quite likely that he had come to know Hess. The shooting party was apparently hosted by Lord Runciman.

(Lloyd also made mention of the autonomous nature of the ICI works at Billingham at the time and questioned if the sinking of the P&O freighter SS Somali was in some way linked to early nuclear experimentation that was being shipped off to ICI India, so as to evade possible invading Germans.)

In a final coincidence, Margaret, Lord Runciman's daughter, who became famous as the first woman to fly a Spitfire, had married Douglas Fairweather, the son of the Fairweather family at Newton Mearns who were also famous aviators and most bizarrely, on 10 May 1941, the landlord of Roman Battaglia, the newly installed Polish Consul in Glasgow. Armed with this fresh information, we left for home.

On the way down the A1 we had put into place the complete 1941 conspiracy. Radio communication, political connection, German connections through Allhusen shipping, aviation. This had to be the secret. Unfortunately, at that time we had yet to see the elusive photograph, although we understand that since our visit another TV producer has been prowling the area with a cheque book to try and prise out the said image.

It is of course easy to dismiss the above as a real life 'fisherman's story' and we suspected this to be the most likely explanation. However, on 27 July 2015, we were duly shown the photograph, that in the meantime had surfaced. We believe it shows Helmut von Moltke, not Rudolf Hess, getting into a car, accompanied by an attractive younger lady and a couple who we have been told were Mr and Mrs Marshall, local landowners from the Allsteads Farm, Chathill. As to its location, it could well have been Beadnell House. But that would certainly not be a straightforward identification.

It would not be overly surprising to find that Helmut von Moltke was meeting the 'great and the good' of Northumberland in the late 1930s, including Lord Runciman. But that would hardly explain the events of 1940–41. Equally, it is interesting to note that Hess crossed the English coast almost exactly over the purported location of the photograph and that the occupants of Fa'side house in Newton Mearns, the Fairweather residence, were almost the first people asked to identify Hess after his landing in Scotland. Yet another coincidence?

APPENDIX II
THE PATRIOTIC DUKE

The Patriotic Duke by Mark Peel[1] is, we are afraid, a missed opportunity. It was published in 2014.

It is the first full-length biography of Douglas, 14th Duke of Hamilton, and it fails to clear up the detail as to whether the Duke met Hess prior to the war, but, more importantly, it also fails to clear up the mystery of the extent of the Duke's true movements on the night of 10/11 May 1941.

The Dowager Duchess of Hamilton wrote to Peter Padfield on 12 July 1992, stating that her late husband had left Turnhouse in the middle of the night (10 May) and that she did not see him thereafter until about 4.00pm the following afternoon.

By contrast, Mark Peel tells the normal, oft-repeated, story of the Duke leaving for Maryhill Barracks, Glasgow, arriving there at 10.00am on the Sunday morning. The differing versions highlight the question as to what the Duke was really doing in the early hours of 11 May 1941 and why?

Most disappointingly, when challenged by us on this specific point, James Douglas-Hamilton, the source for much information in the book, blamed the disparity on his mother's growing dementia. She had died seventeen years later. At the very least, this is unfair.

As regards the question as to whether or not Hess had met the Duke in Berlin in 1936, it appears that the two men did probably meet. Not at the official reception for Robert Vansittart, hosted by Hitler, but at a luncheon held the following day at Hess's official house on the Wilhelmstrasse. Surely Hamilton would have remembered this, if true? The National Archives file FCO 12/259 seems to deal with not whether the two men met, but whether it could be *proven* the two men met. Included within this file is the admission from a D.H.B. Gregory of the Foreign Office that on 3 July 1980, some material dated May 1941 has been withheld by the FCO and 'is not open to public inspection'.

However, this is not particularly relevant to the current debate, for there is absolutely no firm evidence that Hess had met the Duke of Hamilton between 1936 and 11 May 1941. The Haushofers, yes, certainly, but not the Duke. The Duchess however…?

So, in conclusion we still think this to have been a wasted opportunity. We continue to believe that the Duke was involved with the planning for the Hess flight, but thereafter acted out of a mixture of a sense of a misguided guilty conscience, the protection of actual Secret Service involvement and the fear of any misplaced association. The Patriotic Duke has unfortunately not helped to clear this matter up.

APPENDIX III
A DARING ADVENTURE

A Daring Venture was written by Peter Raina[2], an Oxford academic, and published in 2014. We are afraid this book completely misses the point. Raina essentially reproduces the story of the early years of Hess's captivity and his peace talks with Lord Simon on 9 June 1941 and with Lord Beaverbrook in the September of the same year.

Typical of most academic works, on one level it cannot be criticised, as no doubt the translations are accurate. We have not checked. Consequently, it becomes by enlarge a transcript, without giving any particular insight. It is also flawed in important commentary detail, for example:

> p. 4: 'It must have been 3 or 4 in the morning. Wing Commander Hamilton was fast asleep' (see above ref: *The Patriotic Duke*)
>
> p. 7: 'From 1936 onwards … Albrecht worked as a secret government envoy…' (why secret?)
>
> pp. 15 and 18: Places Mrs Roberts in Lisbon (nonsense!)
>
> p. 35: 3 May, after his Reichstag speech, Hitler had declared… (the speech was on 4 May),
> etc, etc…

However, on another level, the more serious point is that Raina has completely missed the 'cleverness' of Hess. By the time he was in front of Simon and Beaverbrook he knew he had failed and was in front of members of the 'Churchillian clique', a fact that he at least understood, even though Simon had been an appeaser in earlier years. He was not talking to the people who he had anticipated meeting at all. Consequently, he just told them what he wanted them to know, whilst understanding that his mission was not now likely to succeed. Nowhere is there any mention of Albrecht Haushofer's 1941 conversations with Burckhardt, nowhere is Hoare's Madrid role discussed.

Neither do either of these key players feature in the analysis. Instead, the Hess oration is treated at face value and then not surprisingly interpreted as the action of a stupid man. We can only sadly conclude (typified by the silly errors of detail that Raina has perpetuated) that whilst performing a useful service of recording, translating and transcribing, he has not actually added anything to the debate in toto. He too, unfortunately, appears to have been taken in by Hess. He certainly is not the first.

We should also record that any reading of the transcripts put paid to the notion that Hess was delusional. Given that his papers had been taken from him at Eaglesham, the depth of detail that Hess recalls is very impressive.

APPENDIX IV

RENÉ VOULON AND LUCHTOORLOG.NET

Since 2014 we have also attempted to ascertain which German records might have recorded the Hess Bf110 when passing over German airspace at a bearing of 335 degrees from Augsburg.

In particular, we have tried to ascertain if any operational records exist pertaining to either Lippstadt, Göttingen and Giessen airfields, potential landing strips for Hess en route to the coast. After employing a research agent, it has been ascertained that no records exist at Freiburg, the normal Bundesarchiv depository for such files. Apparently 95 per cent of Luftwaffe records were destroyed at the end of the war.

However, René Voulon and his Luchtoorlog.net website have been very helpful. René is a former Dutch Airforce Officer and in particular has studied the Flak stations established in the Low Countries following the May 1940 invasion. This organisation was administered by the Kriegsmarine. René was kind enough to send us the archives for the Den Helder flakgroup and there is no mention whatsoever of a Bf110 on 10 May 1941. This comes as no surprise whatsoever to us, as we are sure Hess crossed the coast over Wangerooge to the east. It does, however, directly contradict the 1942 flight plan (which we never believed to be true). That map places Hess directly over Den Helder, before flying over the Friesian Islands.

Equally, we are quite content that the Germans may well have been told not to record the Hess plane at all, but we felt the need to ascertain what records existed and to eliminate a possibility.

APPENDIX V

THE SECRET SCOTLAND WEBSITE

For some while the authors have participated in and read with interest the Secret Scotland website. This is a dedicated site dealing with mainly recent military history and such installations pertaining thereto in Scotland. It is a very sensible site, both well run and well moderated.

Following the release of *Rudolf Hess: A Technical Analysis* in 2014, the site administrator has dedicated a separate section of the webpage to the Hess affair, which in turn is subdivided into relevant sections – flight, aircraft, etc. We can only recommend the site to the readers of this book. We also maintain a Facebook page 'Rudolf Hess: Treachery and Deception'.

APPENDIX VI
SUBSEQUENT TIMELINE

Subsequent reaction

The main timeline concerning the various explanations and understanding of the Hess affair can be summarised as follows:

10 May 1941 Rudolf Hess parachutes from his Bf110 over Eaglesham, Scotland. He enters lifelong captivity.
13 May 1941 The *Daily Telegraph* leads with 'Death Mystery of Hitler's Deputy'. This follows the German communique the previous evening.
14 May 1941 The *Daily Telegraph* leads with 'Hess's Long Talk to British Diplomat'. This follows confirmation by the British that Hess is in Scotland.
15 May 1941 The *Daily Telegraph* leads with 'Ministers see reports on Hess'.
12 July 1941 An article is published in *Liberty*, an American magazine, claiming that Hess was lured to Britain by British Intelligence. The author is Johannes Steel, a German émigré with links to Russian intelligence.
1942 Winston Churchill, with American support now firmly crystallised into an Alliance, feel confident enough to answer a question on Hess in the House of Commons. The conversation is reproduced from *Hansard* below:

> *The Prime Minister:* 'Surely the Hon. Gentleman is not the man to be frightened of a Whip? The House of Commons, which is at present the most powerful representative Assembly in the world, must also, I am sure, will also bear in mind the effect produced abroad by all its proceeding. We have also to remember how oddly foreigners view our country and its way of doing things. *When Rudolf Hess flew over here some months ago he firmly believed that he had only to gain access to certain circles in this country for what he described as "the Churchill clique".*'
>
> **Mr. Thorne (Plaistow):** 'Where is he now?'
> **The Prime Minister:** 'Where he ought to be – *to be thrown out of power and for a Government to be set up with which Hitler could negotiate a*

magnanimous peace. The only importance attaching to the opinions of Hess is the fact that he was fresh from the atmosphere of Hitler's intimate table. But, Sir, I can assure you that since I have been back in this country I have had anxious inquiries from a dozen countries, and reports of enemy propaganda in a score of countries, all turning upon the point whether His Majesty's present Government is to be dismissed from power or not. The crux of this exchange is the extent to which the "certain circles" had been active in the affair.'

1943 An article is published in the *American Mercury*, claiming that Hess was lured to Britain by British Intelligence.[3] The source remains anonymous to this day.
1947 Hess is imprisoned in Spandau Prison, Berlin.
1947 J.R. Rees writes *The Case of Rudolf Hess*.[4] Whilst principally dealing with Hess's post-1941 mental state, it somewhat oddly includes the first flight plan, supposedly drawn by Hess in late 1941. It is this plan that most authors mistakenly refer to and try to justify.
1954 Ilse Hess writes *Prisoner of Peace*,[5] translated into English by Meyrick Booth. This book uses extracts of letters from Rudolf Hess to his wife in order to give the reader an explanation of the events. It certainly gives no answers to the major issues surrounding the flight but does give some clues that were explored in Harris and Wilbourn's *Technical Analysis*.
1962 James Leasor writes *Rudolf Hess: The Uninvited Envoy*.[6] Whilst the pretext behind the title is still worthy of debate, the work is very useful as it draws on the experiences of many actually involved in the flight who were still alive at the time the book was being researched. We understand that Leasor was a *Daily Express* journalist and as such Lord Beaverbrook, his employer, encouraged the book to be published. It introduces the connection between the Haushofer family and Rudolf Hess. Whilst we challenge the conclusion, it is one of the first books to be written independently of the families involved.
1966 Albert Speer is released from Spandau Prison. Hess is now its only prisoner.
1971 James Douglas-Hamilton writes *Motive for a Mission*.[7] This book deals in detail with the pre-war relationship between the Hamilton family and Albrecht Haushofer.
30 March 1973 The 14th Duke of Hamilton dies.
1976 Derek Wood writes *Attack Warning Red*. This history of the Royal

Observer Corps includes a detailed plan of the Hess flight over Scotland.[8] Subsequent to the disbandment of the ROC in 1995, much of the archival material on which this book drew has either been lost or destroyed.

1986 Wolf Ruediger Hess, then forty-eight years old, writes *My Father, Rudolf Hess*.[9] This book seeks to justify the action of his father, then still alive in Spandau, Berlin. He questions the role of the British Secret Service and understandably asks that his ninety-three-year-old father be released.

17 August 1987 Rudolf Hess is found dead in Spandau Prison.

1987 John Harris and Richard Wilbourn commence their enquiries.

1992 Douglas Hurd, the then Foreign Secretary, announces the release of two batches of Hess document, largely from the Foreign Office, but also WO199/3288B and DEFE1/134. Many of these papers deal with the treatment of Hess on arrival in Britain. Douglas Hurd also commented that he had kept at least one file back because it contained certain records which 'still pose a risk to national security'.[10] Interestingly, James Douglas-Hamilton writes that the files not released were withheld, 'For reasons which have nothing to do with the substance of the Hess case.' We do not wholly understand how James Douglas-Hamilton would know this.

1994 John McBlain produces *Rudolf Hess: The British Conspiracy*, a pamphlet which details the background to Mrs Roberts, the wartime intermediary between Albrecht Haushofer and the Duke of Hamilton. Mrs Roberts's nephew was an important member of SO1, the wartime black propaganda department. This was further expanded upon in 1999 in John Harris and Mei Trow's *Hess: the British Conspiracy*, which also reveals that Sikorski, the Prime Minister of the Polish government in exile, had landed at Prestwick on 11 May 1941.[11]

1995 Harris flies to Munich to discuss the Mrs Roberts findings with Wolf Hess. Hess Jr is convinced of British Secret Service involvement. With his British agent, Alfred Smith, of Northampton, he contemplates launching a legal challenge in respect of the death certificate. Harris also meets Andrea Schroder Haushofer in her Munich apartment.

24 October 2001 Wolf Hess dies in Munich and with him dies the legal challenge. Not surprisingly, the remaining Hess family have had enough of the matter and treat any approach with caution.

2001 *Double Standards* is released.[12] Whilst sensationalist in parts and nonsense in others, there was some good original research which once again brought the Hess affair to prominence, this time suggesting that Hess was to be met by the Duke of Kent at Dungavel and Hess dying with the Duke in 1942. We understand that the four co-authors of *Double Standards* received a substantial advance which may unfortunately explain some of the wilder allegations made later in their book.

2009 William Hague admits that the Hess papers are being withheld on account of National Security.

2010 Keith Jeffery is commissioned to write the official history of MI6. At its press release at Bletchley Park, Jeffery states that there are no files dealing with the Hess affair. This opinion is revised later, following enquiry by Harris and Wilbourn.

2010 John Harris writes *Rudolf Hess: The British Illusion of Peace*,[13] which, for the first time, partially outlines the role of Tancred Borenius, the Finnish art historian, in the affair. It also questions the role of the Duke of Hamilton and details the fact that the Hamilton family owned the site of RAF Prestwick. Moreover, it makes the point that if Churchill were to be forcibly removed as part of any Anglo-German peace plan, constitutionally the King would have to be involved.

2014 John Harris and Richard Wilbourn write *Rudolf Hess: A New Technical Analysis of the Hess Flight, May 1941*. This book demonstrates that the flight required a meticulous level of planning, and the failure of the Elektra Radio navigation system led to Hess running late and simply crashing in the dark. The lack of an auxiliary oil tank infers a landing in Germany en route. The Hess mission was a highly planned mission with in-built deniability.

August 2015 John Harris flies to Munich to meet the Hess family. He is told that at the time of the Wunsiedel reinternment in 2011, DNA tests were made, which prove that the gentleman in Spandau was indeed Rudolf Hess. At the same time, Harris is told that the family have undertaken expert calligraphy analysis of the so-called 1987 suicide note. It appears that whilst an accurate representation of Hess's writing, there is no allowance at all for Hess's advanced years. Bluntly, Hess, riddled with arthritis, could not have written the letter at the time it was allegedly produced. If the letter was forged, the obvious question is 'why?' Secondly, if Hess was murdered, why was it deemed so important to silence him?

May 2016 *Rudolf Hess: Treachery and Deception* is published.

December 2019 *Rudolf Hess: Truth at Last* is published.

March 2022 Peter Padfield dies, aged eighty-nine.

October 2022 *Conspiracy, Calamity and Cover-Up* is published.

APPENDIX VII
THE MISSING FILES

Apparently, according to Prof. Sir Richard Evans, a classic trait of a conspiracist is to allude to missing files or information. Unfortunately, in the Hess case there really are a number of files and documents that we know to have once existed but now are no longer in the public domain. Whilst their individual release may not supply a comprehensive explanation to the whole, they would certainly assist an interpretation. In legal terms, currently, the disclosure of evidence is far from complete.

In the hope that Sir Richard may now use his influence to obtain their release we now list our 'wish list' as follows: The list below is certainly not exclusive.

1. An official confirmation of the location of the Duke of Kent on 10 May 1941. (Despite a number of requests, this piece of information is being denied to us, with most recently a Freedom of Information request in March 2021.) If he was reviewing the fleet at Scapa Flow and its defences, then why not just say so? Access to the Royal Archives would be a privilege, but we now suspect this unlikely.
2. The location of the King and Queen on 10 May 1941. (William Shawcross places them at Windsor, which is certainly the most likely.) We have a letter from the Queen to Churchill dated 12 May, which is addressed from Windsor.
3. Hess' s explanatory letter to Hitler, as delivered by Pintsch to Hitler with a copy sent to Ilse Hess. The end of this letter is often quoted, '... if all else fails say I had gone mad'.
4. The Haushofer letter that was attached to the above letter.
5. Hitler's explanatory letter to Stalin on 13 May 1941. Whilst we have quoted the letter, from Bernd Schwipper's book, we are unaware of its current repository.
6. The RAF report into the affair.
7. Any RAF intelligence reports into the affair.
8. The RAE Farnborough report into the Hess plane. We know that David

Mitchell was sent to recover various parts from the plane. We presume it was he who removed the compass from the fuselage.

9. The Giessen and Augsburg ORBs, or their Luftwaffe equivalent.
10. Any photograph of the Hess plane cockpit. Is the omission to conceal the existence of the second occupant?
11. Hess's original pilot's notes, copies of which we know ended up with Prof. AWB Simpson).
12. Any ROC station observation reports. (These certainly existed in the 1970s when Derek Wood wrote *Attack Warning Red*.) In particular, we would like to examine Irvine, West Kilbride and Eaglesham. It now appears that there were subsequent orders given to erase the Eaglesham ROC records, which were apparently done with a 'thick greasy pencil'.[14] Consequently we have no record as to how the plane crashed, from what height or whether indeed it was being pursued by an RAF aircraft.
13. The Hess/Bohle peace proposals found in the 'wee burn' on Sunday 11 May. These have been referred to by both Bohle in his post-war interrogation and Margaret Baird (the farmer's wife) in her letter to her sister.[15]
14. MI6/MI5 files on Borenius, Gerl, Calthrop, Blacker, Semmelbauer, Maas, Sikorski, Retinger and the Duke of Hamilton. We presume these would form part of the 'PV' files.
15. The full Haushofer/Roberts correspondence from July 1940 to May 1941. To date we have only seen the copy letter of 23 September 1940 that was intercepted by the British censor.
16. The Haushofer correspondence of October 1940 to May 1941. Given that there are nearly a dozen reports in the autumn of 1940 detailing how to incorrectly send a letter to Lisbon, one could anticipate at least some documentation concerning Albrecht's spring excursions.
17. MI5 files on the Polish government in exile. (Liddell refers to a 'De Rema' being an informer.)
18. Prestwick airfield ORB. So as to confirm Sikorski's precise time of arrival.
19. Although we have now traced the Operational Record Book for the Polish 309 squadron it is obviously incomplete as few flights are recorded at all! The squadron was in process of moving to RAF Dunino, from Renfrew, but no flight details are made. For example, we know that Sikorski flew from Glasgow to Findo Gask on 11 May 1941. This is not recorded.
20. W Board meeting minutes from its inception to June 1941.

21. We also presume that Hess, or his office, kept an appointments diary. This, too, has yet to see the light of day.
22. SO1 files (1941). Some are released, some not.
23. The Civil Defence report into the crash. We know that a senior officer was despatched to the crash site, as he is often pictured amongst the wreckage. We now understand his name to be William Ferguson.
24. The letter Hess wrote to the King whilst in the Tower of London, asking for safe passage.
25. The letter Hess wrote to the King on 13 November 1941, insisting on the '*protection which had been promised me*.'

The Civil Defence inspector, identified as William Ferguson of Glasgow

---

[1] Mark Peel, *The Patriotic Duke*, Thistle, Edinburgh, 2013.
[2] Peter Raina, *A Daring Venture*, Peter Lang, Bern, 2014.
[3] We have extensively researched the publication of this article. In 1943 the *American Mercury* was owned and edited by L.E. Spivak, whose archives are held in Washington, DC. Whilst there are detailed records recording the payments made to contributing authors, in the case of the Hess article there is no such entry, simply marked 'anonymous'. Who the source was remains a mystery.
[4] J.R. Rees, *The Case of Rudolf Hess*, Heinemann, London, 1947.
[5] Ilse Hess, *Prisoner of Peace*, Briton Publishing Co., London, 1954.
[6] James Leasor, *Rudolf Hess: The Uninvited Envoy*, George Allen & Unwin Ltd, London, 1962.
[7] James Douglas-Hamilton, *Motive for Mission*, Macmillan, London, 1971.
[8] Derek Wood, *Attack Warning Red*, Macdonald and Janes, London, 1976.
[9] Wolf Hess, *My Father Rudolf Hess*, WH Allen, London, 1986.
[10] *Hansard*, Vol. 208, column 823.
[11] John McBlain, *Rudolf Hess: The British Conspiracy*, JEMA, Moulton, 1992; John Harris and Mei Trow, *Hess: The British Conspiracy*, Andre Deutsch, London, 1999.
[12] Lynn Picknett, Clive Price and Stephen Prior, *Double Standards: The Rudolf Hess Cover-Up*, Little Brown, London, 2003.
[13] John Harris, *Rudolf Hess: The British Illusion of Peace*, JEMA, Moulton, 2010.
[14] *Silverroc* magazine, the magazine of the former ROC, Summer 2015.
[15] John Harris, *BBC History* magazine, May 2001, citing the letter from Margaret Baird to her sister.

APPENDIX VIII

MAPS AND CHARTS

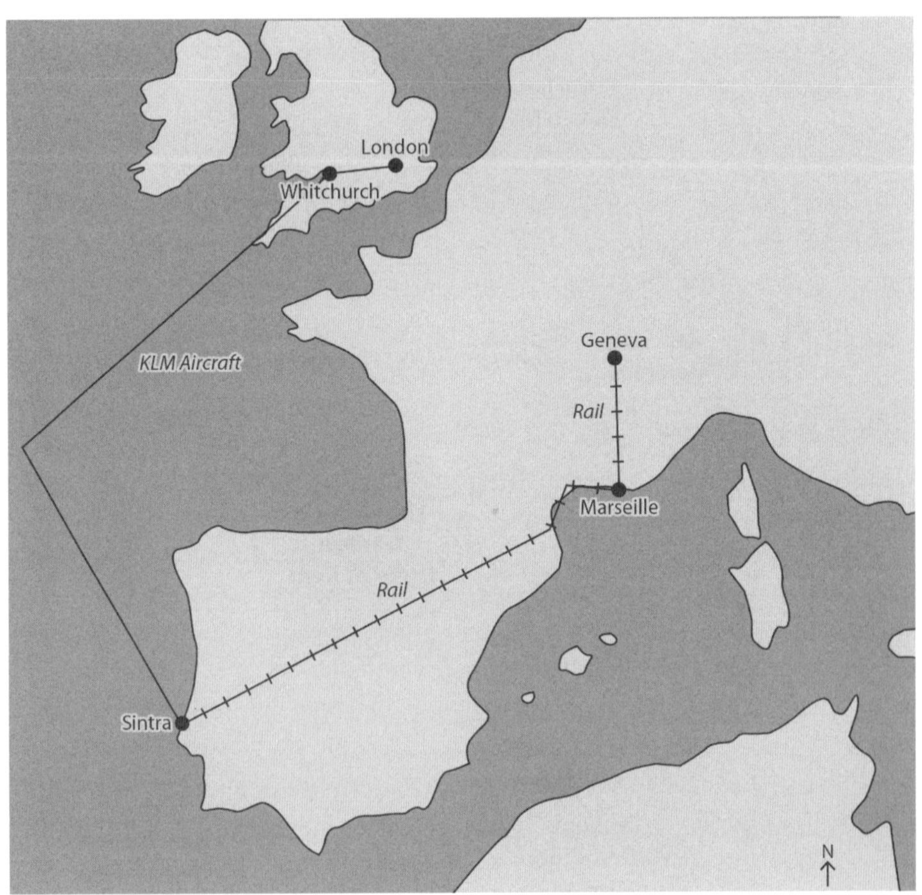

Tancred Borenius – Trip to Geneva – Spring 1941

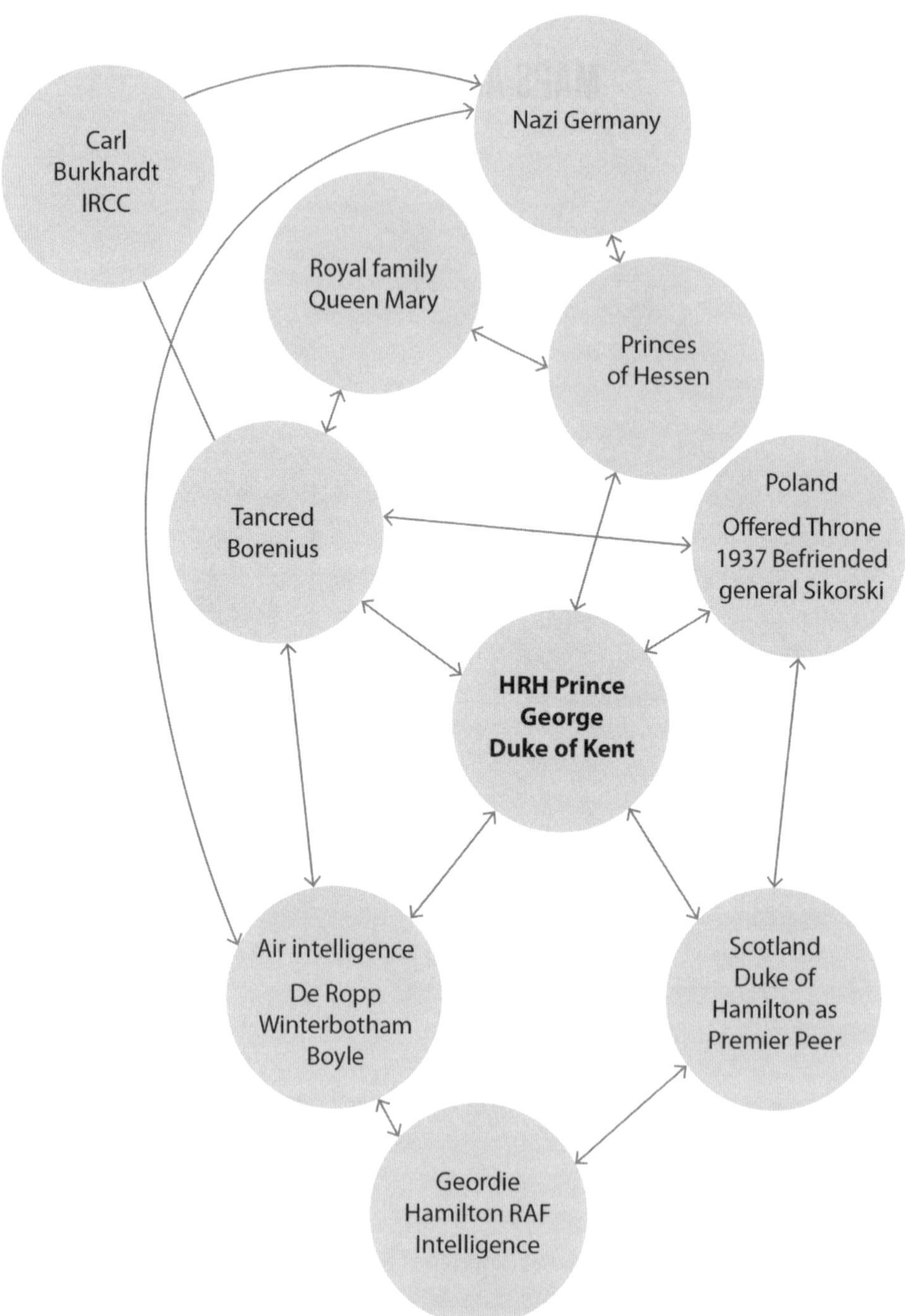

HRH Prince George – A common denominator?

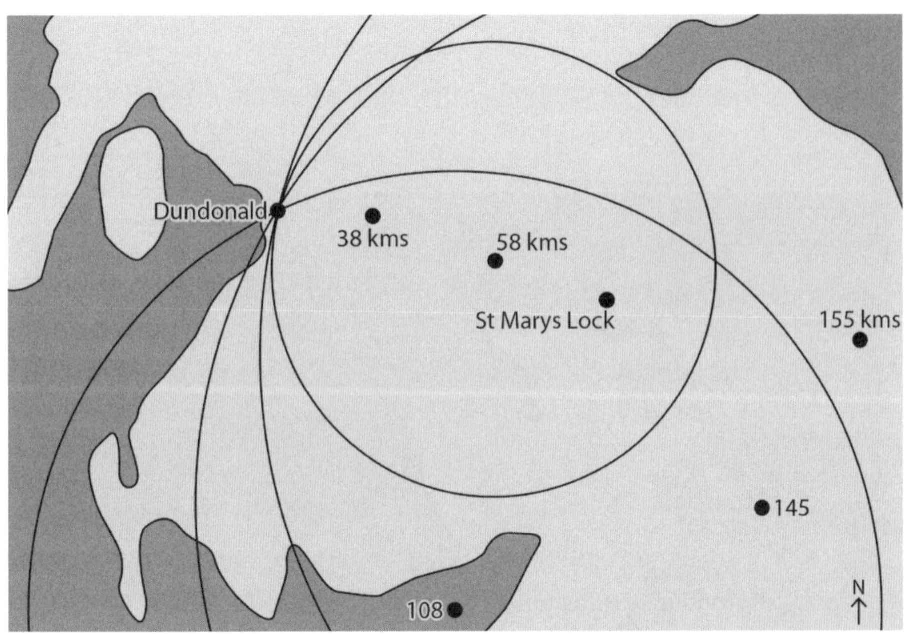

The Lennoxlove map – using the marked distances as the centre of a circle of the same radius

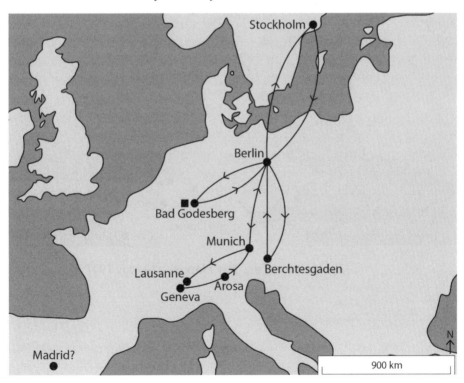

Albrecht Haushofer's travels – Spring 1941

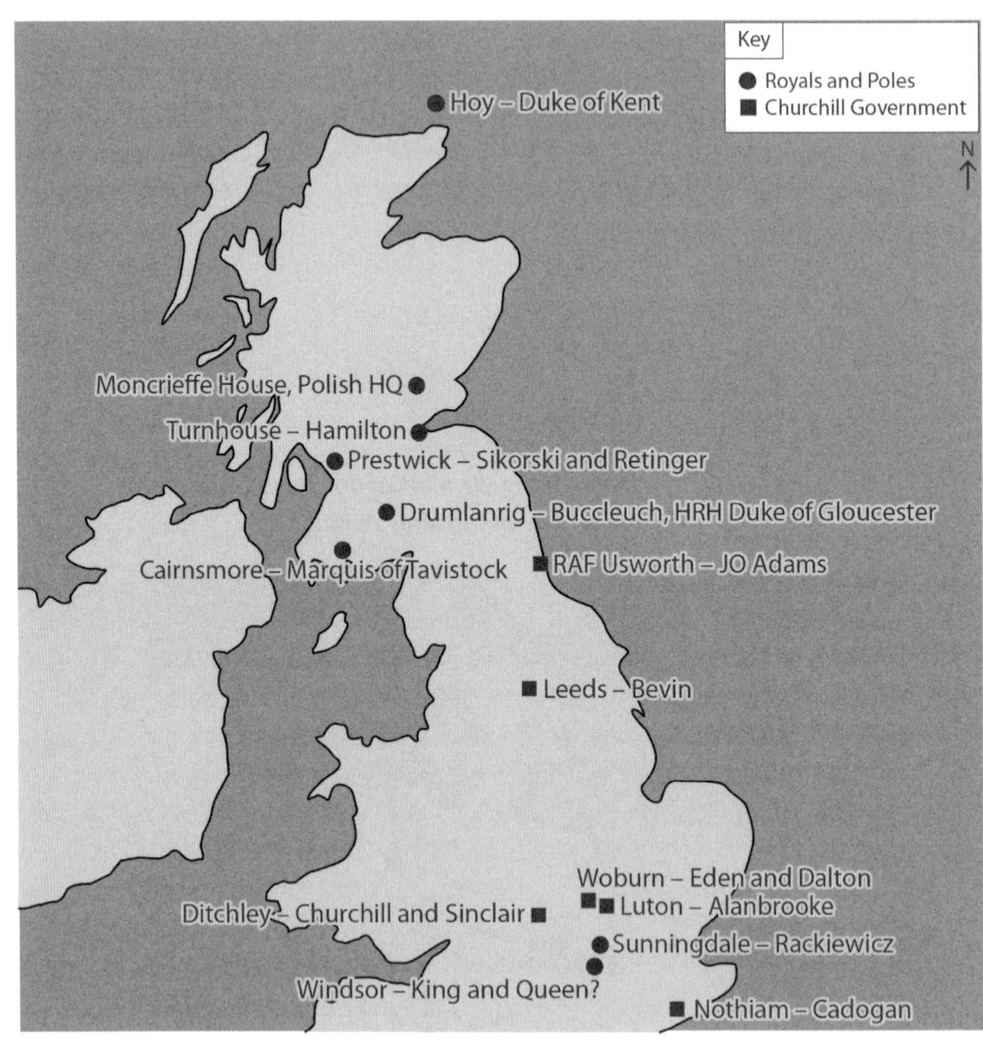

The location of the 'Key Players' – 10 May 1941

THE FLIGHT OF RUDOLF HESS

Comparison of Actual versus Flight Notes versus Hess later lies

		ACTUAL	KMS	FLIGHT NOTE PLANNED	KMS	AS LIED	KMS	
Leave Augsberg		17.45		17.45		17.45		
Arrive Borkum						19.33	675	
Arrive Giessen	290	18.30	290	18.30	290			
Leave Giessen		19.00		19.00				(Landing disguised by dog leg over Holland)
Arrive Wangerooge	370	19.58	370	19.54	370	19.58	126	(As per Hess plan – 370kms – 410kms per hour – 54 minutes)
Arrive at Nord punkt	410	20.52	410	20.54	410	20.52	410	(as per Hess plan – 410kms – 410kms per hour – 60 minutes)
North sea 'box'	410	21.52	410			21.12	410	(Hess loses his ELEKTRA)
Crosses coast	210	22.23	210	21.42	210	22.23	210	
St Mary's Loch	100		100		100		100	
58kms marker	30		30		30		30	
Dundonald	58		58	22.31	58		58	
Eaglesham	66	23.07	66			23.07	66	
			1944		1468		2085	
Time in the air		4hrs 52mins		4hrs 15mins		5hrs 24mins		
Average speed (kms per hr)		399		345		386		
Oil Consumption at 75 litres per hour (capacity 35)		30.75		26.25		41.25		
Fuel Consumption at 660 litres per hour (likely capacity 3070 litres)		2706		2310		3597		

APPENDIX IX

THE PRIVY COUNCIL

At the end of the concluding chapter we have suggested that it was most likely that an attempt was being made to remove Winston Churchill as Prime Minister on 10 May 1941 and that it was constitutionally possible to do so, without necessarily calling a General Election (a process which cannot take place in wartime).

Consequently, we are still in the research stage as to how this might practically be done and as such have concluded that constitutionally it is most likely (even though not strictly necessary) that the Privy Council would have become involved, largely so that the Monarch could not be accused of acting alone without advice.

The Privy Council is described as such:

> '**The Privy Council** (PC), officially **His Majesty's Most Honourable Privy Council**, is a formal body of advisers to the sovereign of the United Kingdom. Its membership mainly comprises senior politicians who are current or former members of either the House of Commons or the House of Lords.
>
> The Privy Council formally advises the sovereign on the exercise of the Royal Prerogative.'

It is an ancient body and essentially was created to advise the Monarch. Of possible pertinence to the Hess affair, the following were extant and living Privy Councillors in May 1941.

The Duke of Buccleuch (*)
The Duke of Gloucester (*)
The Duke of Kent (*)
The Duke of Hamilton (*)
Lord Eustace Percy
Sir John Anderson
Montagu Norman (*)

We have already ascertained that those marked (*) were in Scotland on 10 May 1941. Sir John Anderson held the role of Lord President of the Council, being responsible for presiding over the meetings. His whereabouts on 10th May 1941 have still to be ascertained.

We have also ascertained that the King had met with Sir John Anderson alone, prior to the Privy Council meeting held on Friday 9 May 1941 at Buckingham Palace, London.

The quorum for a Privy Council meeting is three. Consequently, it is quite possible that such a meeting could be convened constitutionally.

We obviously have further work to do in this regard.

APPENDIX X
TANCRED BORENIUS AND ANTHONY BLUNT

In June 2022 Harris read an article on the National Gallery website which announced that the *Burlington Magazine* had donated its archive to the National Gallery. We knew that previously it had been housed in Sea Containers House, on the South Bank in London, but had never really got on very well when visiting. The files always appeared somewhat askew during the period we were interested in, that being whilst the magazine was under the editorial control of one Tancred Borenius. We hoped that perhaps the National Gallery would catalogue the archives in a clearer manner? (Apparently, they have applied, albeit unsuccessfully to date, for a grant to do the task).

Our principal objective has always been to see if there are any clues as to the subsequent whereabouts of Tancred following his return from the Continent in spring 1941. Perhaps some routine correspondence might reveal the information we desperately require?

John Harris duly visited Trafalgar Square in late July 2022 and was in part frustrated, in part intrigued. It was explained that Tancred's papers were still in a bit of a mess and surprisingly short in supply. However, Harris was given a file which detailed the relationship of the Burlington with one Anthony Frederick Blunt (1907–83). File A2018/1/HCS.

Starting in 1943, the files document Blunt's usually successful various attempts to offer articles for publication in the *Burlington*. The earliest we could find was dated 10 January 1943 and was notable for its forced formality (Dear Dr. Borenius / Yours sincerely and Dear Major Blunt / Yours sincerely). This starkly contrasts in style to Blunt's correspondence to Ben Nicholson, a later editor.

There are, to date, no further earlier details in the National Gallery's newly acquired collection. In 1945 Tancred writes to congratulate Blunt on becoming Keeper of the Kings Pictures and typically offers him the use of 'his notes on the Royal collections'.

However, if one then looks in the *Burlington* online archive, it is clear that Blunt was a prolific contributor to the *Burlington* over a long period of time. The earliest review appears to be in July 1937 with 'L'art primitif; L'art medieval'. This appears to roughly coincide with his appointment to the directorship of the Courtauld Gallery. Essentially, Blunt was doing his job. Similarly, there are reviews from Blunt appearing in the 1970s, nearly forty years later.

However, we of course also know that simultaneously he was also acting as a Soviet spy and Miranda Carter, his biographer, places the date of his recruitment as 1937. Soon after Dunkirk he was recruited to MI5 and started passing Ultra decrypts to the Soviets. A perusal of the Guy Liddell diaries make clear that by August / September 1940 at the latest, Blunt was actively working for MI5. (24 September 1940 – 'I dined with Anthony Blunt and Guy Burgess at the Reform Club…).

Clearly, the possibilities in this regard are endless though equally and quite possibly just latent. What we can say is that it is plain that the two men (Borenius and Blunt) were well acquainted, formally or otherwise and it is quite possible given Borenius' known garrulousness that the Soviets also knew precisely what Borenius had been up to in Geneva in January 1941. Given that Blunt was openly protected by the British Monarchy from 1963 to 1979, was his knowledge of the Hess affair part of the perceived justification? Yet again, more work to be done.

BIBLIOGRAPHY

Public archives

Bundesarchiv, Berlin, Freiburg and Koblenz (Roberts, Haushofer, Hess, Leitgen)
Companies House, Cardiff (Hamilton)
Deutsches Museum, Munich (Pintsch)
East Kilbride Library, Scotland (Baird letter)
London Metropolitan Archives, Clerkenwell, London (Borenius)
National Archives, Kew, London (Various)
Oriental and Indian Office Collection, c/o British Library, London (Roberts)
Polish National Archives, Warsaw (RHSA/Zeileis)
Probate Records, York, England (Roberts and Heal)
Swiss National Archives, Berne (Hess family papers)
United States National Archives, College Park, Maryland (Haushofer)
Wiltshire County Records, Chippenham, Wiltshire (Borenius)

Other collections

Berlin Science Museum (Extant Bf110 exhibit)
Burlington Magazine, April 1941
Cambridge University Library, Cambridge (Roberts)
Churchill College, Cambridge (Churchill, Cadogan, Colville)
Ditchley Park, Enstone, Oxfordshire (Churchill)
Eton College, Windsor (Cazalet)
Gonville and Caius College, Cambridge (Roberts)
Hickleton Papers. University of York, (Halifax)
House of Commons Library, London (Ref. 7 May 1941)
International Red Cross Museum, Geneva (Burckhardt, Borenius)
Imperial War Museum, Duxford (Hess plane fuselage and engine)
Imperial War Museum London
Mannerheim Museum, Helsinki (Borenius)
Kevin Mount report on Hess crash, courtesy of Andrew Rosthorn
Munich Science Museum, DB601 exhibit
National Army Museum, Chelsea, London (Roberts)
Polish Institute and Sikorski Museum, conference papers, November 2003
Postal Museum, Finsbury, London (Roberts)
Private Secretary to the Duke of Kent

Royal Archives, Windsor (HRH King George VI and HRH the Duke of Kent)
Formerly RAF East Fortune, Scotland, Hess plane engine
RAF Stafford, various parts of the Hess plane
RAF Henlow, radio navigation
RAF Museum, Hendon, Air Historical Branch and extant Bf110
ROC Museum, Winchester, ROC records
Rudolf Hess Gesellschaft,ev – Dokumentation Nr.1 - 1989
Sheffield University Library (A.W.B. Simpson)
Sikorski Institute, London (General Sikorski)
Stanford University, California (Haushofer)
Templewood papers, Cambridge University Library (Hoare)
Tim Woodman papers, courtesy of Peter Padfield
United States Holocaust Memorial Museum, Washington, DC (Rosenberg)
University of Basle Library, Switzerland (Burckhardt)

Interviews

Arthur Bauer, Diemen, Holland, 2012
Lars Borenius, telephone, 1999
Persis Bower, by email, 2021
Gordon Corera, London, 2015
John Costello, London, 1994
Glynn Gowans, London, 2015
Richard Griffiths, London, 1994
Trevor Hearing, Northampton and London, 2015
W.R. Hess, Munich, 1996
W. Hess, Munich, 2015
Margaret Morrell, Turnberry, 2015
Peter Padfield, various
Wolfgang Perr, Gallspach, Austria, 2015
Pilcher family, London, 2020/21
Andrew Rosthorn and Spike Hodbod, Lancashire, 2015, 2020, 2021
Andrea Schroder-Haushofer, Munich, 1996
Bernd Schwipper, Mecklenburg, 2017
Alfred Smith, Northampton 2001
Andrew Stewart-Roberts, London, 1993
Nigel West, London, 2011
Martin Zeileis, Gallspach, 2015

PUBLISHED WORKS

ADAIR – Sir Allan, *A Guards General*, Hamish Hamilton, London, 1987
AFTER THE BATTLE, *Rudolf Hess* – Nr.58, London, 1987
AIR MINISTRY – *Atlantic Bridge*, HMSO, London, 1945
AIR MINISTRY – *We speak from the Air*, HMSO, London, 1942
ASTLEY, Joan Bright, *The Inner Circle*, Little Brown, Toronto, 1971
ALLEN, Martin – *The Hitler/Hess Deception*, Harper Collins, London, 2003
BAKER, David – *Adolf Galland*, Windrow & Green, London, 1996
BARNES J. AND BARNES P. – *Nazis in Pre-War London*, Brighton, 2005
BASFORD, Elisabeth – *Princess Mary*, The History Press, Stroud, 2021
BAUMBACH, Werner –*Broken Swastika*, Robert Hale, London, 1976
BBC History Magazine – *Harris article on Hess crash*, May 2001
BEEDLE, James – *43 (F) Squadron*, Beaumont Aviation, London, 1985
BERENSON, Bernard – *Rumour and Reflection*, Constable, London, 1952
BERNADOTTE, Folke – *Instead of Arms*, Hodder & Stoughton, London, 1949
BISKUPSKI, M.B.B. – *War and Diplomacy in East and West*, Routledge, Abingdon, 2017
BIRD, Eugene – *The Loneliest Man in the World*, Sphere, London, 1976
BLACKSTONE, *William – Commentaries on the Laws of England*, Clarendon Press, Oxford, 1758
BLOOM, Ursula – *The House of Kent*, Robert Hale, London, 1969
BOGDANOR, Victor – *The British Constitution in the Twentieth Century*, The British Academy, Oxford, 2005
BORENIUS, TANCRED – *Field Marshal Mannerheim*, Hutchinson, London, 1940
BOLITHO, Hector – *A Penguin in the Eyrie*, Hutchinson, London, 1955
BOYLE, Andrew – *The Climate of Treason*, Hutchinson, London, 1979
BOYLE, Andrew – *Montagu Norman*, Cassell, London, 1967
BRADFORD, Sarah – *George VI*, Penguin, London, 2002
BRAUNSCHWEIG, *Pierre – Secret Channel to Berlin*, Casemate, Philadelphia, PA, 2004
BREITMAN, Richard – *Official Secrets*, Penguin, London, 1998
BREITMAN, Richard – *The Architect of Genocide*, Pimlico, London, 2004
BRENDON, Piers – *The Dark Valley*, Jonathan Cape, London, 2000

BRETTINGHAM, Laurie – *Beam Benders*, Earl Shilton, Midlands, 1997
BRON, Barwa – *Wojsko Polskie*, Interpress, Warsaw, 1984
BROOKE, Alan – *The War Diaries*, Weidenfeld & Nicolson, London, 2001
BROWN, Malcolm and MEEHAN, Patricia – *Scapa Flow*, Pan, London, 1968
BRUCE LOCKHART, R.H. – *Memoirs of a British Agent*, Pan, London, 2002
BURCKHARDT, Carl J. – *Meine Danziger Mission*, Callwey, Munich, 1960
BULLOCK, Alan – *The Life and Times of Ernest Bevin*, Heinemann, London, 1967
CADBURY, Deborah – *Princes at War: The British Royal Family's Private Battle in the Second World War*, Bloomsbury, London, 2015
CARTER, Miranda – *Anthony Blunt*, Pan, London, 2001
CAVE BROWN, Anthony – *'C', Macmillan*, New York, 1987
CHANNON, Henry – *The Diaries of Sir Henry Channon*, Phoenix, London, 1996
CHANNON, Henry – *The Diaries 1938–1943*, Hutchinson, London, 2021
CHARMLEY, John – *Duff Cooper*, Weidenfeld & Nicolson, London, 1986
CHARNDLER, Andrew – *George Bell, Bishop of Chichester*, Eerdmans, Grand Rapids, MI, 2016
CHISHOLM AND DAVIE – *Beaverbrook, A Life*, Hutchinson, London, 2002
CHURCHILL, Winston – *The Second World War (vol. 5)*, Cassell, London, 1964
CHURCHILL, Winston – *Great Contemporaries*, Reprint Society, London, 1941
CIANO'S DIARY 1937–1943 – Phoenix Press, London, 2002
CIECHANOWSKI, Jan – *Defeat in Victory*, Doubleday and Company, New York, 1947
COLVILLE, John – *The Churchillians*, Weidenfeld & Nicolson, London, 1981
COLVIN, Ian – *Chief of Intelligence*, Gollancz, London, 1951
COSTELLO, John – *Ten Days that Saved the West*, Bantam Press, London, 1991
CROSS, Colin – *Life with Lloyd George*, Macmillan, London ,1975
CROSS, J.A. – *Sir Samuel Hoare, A political biography*, Jonathan Cape, London, 1977
CROSS, Robin – *Fallen Eagle*, Caxton, London, 2000
DAHLERUS, Birger – *Der Letze Versuch*, Nymphenburger, Munich, 1948
DALTON, Hugh – *The Political Diary of Hugh Dalton*, Jonathan Cape, London, 1986
DAVIDSON, Basil – *Special Operations Europe*, Readers Union, Newton Abbott, 1982

DEACON, Richard – *The British Secret Service*, Grafton, London, 1991
DE COURCY, Kenneth – *Review of World Affairs, Volume 111*, self-published, London, 1942
DE GROOT, Gerard – *The Life of Archibald Sinclair*, Hurst, London, 1993
DELMER, Sefton – *The Black Boomerang*, Secker and Warburg, London, 1962
DIETRICH, Otto – *The Hitler I Knew*, Skyhorse, New York, 2010
DILKS, David – *Sir Alexander Cadogan Diaries*, Cassell, London, 1971
DOBINSON, Colin – *AA Command*, English Heritage/Methuen, London, 2001
DORNEY, Richard – *An Active Service*, Helion and Company, Solihull, 2006
DORPALEN, Andreas – *The World of General Haushofer*, Farrar and Rinehart, New York, 1942
DOUGLAS-HAMILTON – *Alasdair, Lord of the Skies*, Lulu, 2011
DOUGLAS-HAMILTON – *Motive for a Mission: The Story Behind Hess's Flight to Britain*, Macmillan, London, 1971
DOUGLAS-HAMILTON, James – *The Truth About Rudolf Hess*, Mainstream, Edinburgh, 1993
DREXEL BIDDLE, A.J. – *Poland and the Coming of the Second World War*, Ohio State University, OH, 1976
DUFF COOPER – *Old Men Forget*, Readers Union, London, 1955
DUGGAN, John – *Herr Hempel 1937–1945*, Irish Academic Press, Dublin, 2003
EARL OF BIRKENHEAD – *Halifax*, Hamish Hamilton, London, 1965
EDWARDS, Anne – *Matriach*, Hodder & Stoughton, London, 1984
ENGEL, Gerhard – *At the Heart of the Reich: The Secret Diary of Hitler's Army Adjutant*, Greenhill Books, London, 2005
ENTWISTLE, Charles – U*ndercover Addresses of World War II*, Chavril Press, Perth, 1992
EVANS, Trevor – *Bevin*, George Allen & Unwin, London, 1946
FALCONER, Jonathan – *RAF Fighter Airfields of World War 2*, Allan, Surrey, 1993
FARAGO, Ladislas – *The Game of Foxes*, Hodder & Stoughton, London, 1971
FELLOWES, P.F.M. – *First Over Everest,* Bodley Head, London, 1935
FEST, Joachim – *Plotting Hitler's Death*, Weidenfeld and Nicolson, London, 1996
FLEMING, Peter – *Invasion 1940*, Hart-Davis, London, 1957

FLEMING, Peter – *The Flying Visit*, Jonathan Cape, London, 1940
FOOT MRD – *MI9*, Book Club, London, 1979
FORBES, Patrick – *The Grenadier Guards in the War 1939–45*, N&M Press, 1948
FRAYN TURNER, John – *The Battle of Britain*, BCA, London, 1999
FRY, Helen – *Spymaster*, Yale, London, 2021
GAMES, Stephen – *Pevsner*, Continuum, New York, 2010
GERRARD, Craig – *The Foreign Office and Finland 1938–1940*, Frank Cass, Abington, 2005
GEYDYE, G.E. – *Fallen Bastions*, Left Book Club, London, 1939
GLENDENNING, Raymond – *Just a Word in Your Ear*, Stanley Paul, London, 1953
GNAUCK, Gerhard – *Polen Verstehen*, Klett-Cotta, Stuttgart, 2018
GODA, Norman J.W. – *Tales from Spandau*, Cambridge University Press, New York, 2007
GOEBBELS, Joseph – *The Goebbels Diaries*, Hamish Hamilton, London, 1948.
GOEBBELS, Joseph – *The Goebbels Diaries 1939–41*, Hamish Hamilton, 1982
GOLDENSOHN, Leon – T*he Nuremberg Interviews*, Pimlico, London, 2006
GOODMAN, Michael –*The Official History of the Joint Intelligence Committee*, Routledge, Abingdon, 2014
GREIG, Geordie – *The King Maker*, Hodder & Stoughton, London, 2011
GRETZYNGIER, Robert – *Poles in Defence of Britain*, Grub Street, London, 2001
GRIFFITHS, Richard – *Fellow Travellers of the Right*, Constable, London, 1980
GRIFFITHS, Richard – *Patriotism Perverted*, Constable, London, 1988
GROSSMITH, F.T. – *The Cross and the Swastika*, H.E. Walter Limited, Worthing, 1984
HAIGER, Ernst – *Albrecht Haushofer,* Ernst-Freiberger, Berlin, 2008
HALDER WAR DIARY – *Presidio*, Novarta, 1988
HALIFAX, Earl of – *The Fullness of Days*, Collins, London, 1957
HAMILTON, Sir Ian – *The Commander*, Hollis and Carter, London, 1957
HAMMOND, Reginald – *Northern Scotland*, Ward Lock, London, 1980
HARRIES, Susie – *Nikolaus Pevsner: The Life*, Chatto & Windus, London, 2011
HARRIS, John and TROW, Mei – *Hess: The British Conspiracy*, Andre Deutsch, London, 1999

HARRIS, John and WILBOURN, Richard – *Rudolf Hess: A New Technical Analysis of the Hess Flight, May 1941*, The History Press, Stroud, 2014

HARRIS, John – *Rudolf Hess: The British Illusion of Peace*, JEMA, Moulton, 2010

HART- DAVIS, Duff – *Peter Fleming*, Jonathan Cape, London, 1975

HASTINGS, Max – *All Hell Let Loose*, Harper, London, 2011

HAUSHOFER, Albrecht – *Moabit Sonnets*, Norton, Toronto, 1978

HAUSMANN, Frank-Rutger – *Ernst Wilhelm Bohle*, Duncker und Humblot, Berlin, 2009

HAYWARD, James – *Myths and Legends of the Second World War*, Sutton, 2004

HAYWARD, James – *Hitler's Spy*, Simon and Schuster, London, 2012

HEINZELMANN, Martin – *Gottingen im Luftkrieg*, Verlad die Werkstatt, Gottingen, 2003

HENDERSON Diana – *The Lion and the Eagle*, Cualann Press, Dunfermline, 2001

HENDERSON, Sir Neville – *Failure of a Mission*, Hodder & Stoughton, London, 1940

HERWIG, Holger H. – *The Demon of Geopolitics*, Rowman and Littlefield, London, 2016

HESS, Ilse – *Prisoner of Peace*, Druffel Verlag, Germany, 1954

HESS, Rudolf – *Germany and Peace*, private publication

HESS, Wolf – *My Father Rudolf Hess*, WH Allen, London, 1986

HICKMAN, Tom – *Churchill's Bodyguard*, Headline, London, 2005

HINKS, Roger – *The Gymnasium of the Mind*, Michael Russell, Salisbury, 1984

HINSLEY, F.H. and STRIPP, Alan – *Code Breakers*, Oxford University Press, Oxford, 1994

HITLER'S TABLE TALK – Phoenix, London, 2002

HMSO – *Roof over Britain*, HMSO, London, 1943

HOARE, Philip – *Serious Pleasures*, Penguin, London, 1990

HOARE, Samuel – *Ambassador on Special Mission*, Collins, London, 1946

HOFFMAN, Peter – *The History of the German Resistance 1933–45*, MIT Press, Cambridge, MA, 1977

HOLTER, Alfred – *Dreissig Jahre Gallspach*, Leitner & Co, Wels, 1956

HOME, Lord – *The Way the Wind Blows*, Collins, London, 1976

HOWARD, Michael – *Strategic Deception in the Second World War*, Norton, New York 1995

HOWE, Ellic – *The Black Game*, Queen Anne Press, London, 1982
HRH The Duke of Windsor – *A King's Story*, Cassell, London, 1952
HUDSONS HISTORIC HOUSES AND GARDENS – Heritage House, Ketteringham, 2009
HUTCHINSON – *British German and Italian Aircraft*, Hutchinson, London 1941
HUTTER, Clemens – *Hitlers Obersalzberg*, Verlag Berchtesgadener Anzeiger, Berchtesgaden, 1996
IMPERIAL WAR MUSEUM – *Sonderfahndungsliste GB*, reprinted London, 1989
IRVING, David – *Accident*, William Kimber, London, 1967
IRVING, David – *Hitler's War 1930–1942*, Papermac, London, 1988
IRVING, David – *Hess: The Missing Years 1941–1945*, Focal Point, Windsor, 2010
IRVING, David – *The Virus House*, Focal Point, Windsor, 2010
ISMAY, H.L. – *Memoirs*, Heinemann, London, 1960
JEBB, Gladwyn – *The Memoirs of Lord Gladwyn*, Weybridge and Tally, New York, 1972
JENKINS, Roy – *Churchill*, Macmillan, London, 2001
JEFFERY, Keith – *MI6: The History of the Secret Intelligence Service 1909–1949*, Bloomsbury, London, 2010
JERROLD, Walter – *Lord Roberts of Kandahar*, Partridge & Co., London, 1901
JONES, R.V. – *Most Secret War*, Coronet, London, 1978
JONES, THOMAS – *A Diary with Letters, 1931–1950*, Oxford University Press, 1954
JUNGE, Traudl – *Downfall*, Phoenix, London, 2002
KÄPPNER, Joachim – 1941, *Der Angriff Auf Die Ganz Welt*, Rowohlt, Berlin, 2016
KASPAR – *Teach Yourself Air Navigation*, EUP, London, 1942
KEIR, D.L. – *The Constitutional History of Modern Britain 1485–1937*, A&C Black, London, 1938
KELLY, David – *The Ruling Few*, Hollis and Carter, London, 1952
KERSHAW, Ian – *Hitler 1889–1936*, Allen Lane, London, 1998
KILZER, Louis – *Churchill's Deception*, Simon & Schuster, New York, 2004
KIRKPATRICK, Ivone – *The Inner Circle*, Macmillan, London, 1959
KIRSZAK, Jerzy – *General Kazimierz Sosnkowski (1885–1969)*, Instytut Pamieci Narodowej, Warsaw, 2012

KOCHANSKI, Halik – *The Eagle Unbowed*, Penguin, London, 2012
LAMB, Richard – *Churchill as War Leader*, Bloomsbury, London, 1993
LANGBEHN, Claus – *Das Spiel des Verteidigers*, Lukas Verlag, Berlin, 2014
LANE, Thomas and WOLANSKI, Marian – *Poland and European Integration*, Palgrave, Basingstoke, 2009
LAWLOR, Sheila – *Churchill and the Politics of War*, Cambridge University Press, 1994
LEASOR, James – *Rudolf Hess: The Uninvited Envoy*, Allen and Unwin, London, 1962
LECKIE, Ross – *Scipio*, Abacus, London, 1999
LEE, Celia – *Jean, Lady Hamilton*, Celia Lee, 2001
LEE, John – *A Soldier's Life*, Pan, London, 2000
LEWIN, Ronald – *Ultra Goes to War*, Hutchinson, London, 1978
LEWIS, Stanley – *Military Map Reading*, Wheaton & Co, Exeter, 1941
LIBERTY MAGAZINE – July 12th 1941, *Hess' plan to divide the World with England*
LOGUE, Mark – *The King's Speech*, Quercus, London, 2010
LONDONDERRY, Marquis of – *Wings of Destiny*, Macmillan, London, 1943
LONSDALE-BRYANS, James – *The Curve of Fate*, Andrew Dakers, London, 1941
LONSDALE-BRYANS, James – *Blind Victory: Secret Communications, Halifax–Hassell*, Skeffington and Son Limited, London, 1951
LUFTWAFFE – *BF110 g-2 Flugzeug*, Handbuch, Germany, 1943
MACKINDER, H.J. – *The Rhine*, Chatto & Windus, London, 1908
MACMILLAN, Margaret – *Peacemakers*, John Murray, London, 2002
MACLEAN, Hector – *Fighters in Defence: Memories of the Glasgow Squadron*, Squadron Prints, Glasgow, 1999
MAISKY, Ivan – *Journey into the Past*, Hutchinson, London, 1962
MALINOWSKI, B. – *The Story of a Marriage*, Routledge, London, 1995
MARKS, Leo – *Between Silk and Cyanide*, Harper Collins, London, 1998
MASTERMAN, J.C. – *The Double Cross System*, History Book Club, London, 1972
MAXWELL, General – *Pribbles and Prabbles*, Skeffington and Son, London, 1906
MAZOWER, Mark – *Hitler's Empire*, Penguin, London, 2009
MCBLAIN, John – *Rudolf Hess: The British Conspiracy*, JEMA, Moulton, 1992

McCORMICK Donald – *The Life of Ian Fleming*, Peter Owen, London, 1993
McGINTY, Stephen – *Camp Z*, Quercus, London, 2011
McINTYRE, Dougal – *Prestwick's Pioneer*, Woodfield, Bognor Regis, 2004
MIDDLEMASS, Keith and BARNES, John – *Baldwin*, Weidenfeld & Nicolson, London, 1969
MILLER, Russell – *Codename Tricycle*, Pimlico, London, 2005
MISCH, Rochus – *J'etais garde du corps d'Hitler*, Le Cherche midi, Paris, 2006
MOLLOY, E. – *Aeroplane Radio Equipment*, Chemical publishing, New York, 1941
MONDEY, David – *Axis Aircraft of World War 2*, Chancellor, London, 1996
MOOREHEAD, Caroline – *Dunant's Dream*, Harper Collins, London, 1998
MORAVEC, Frantisek – *Master of Spies*, Doubleday, New York, 1975
MUNICH DOCUMENTATION CENTRE – *Munich and National Socialism*, Munich, 2015
MYERSCOUGH, W. – *Air Navigation Simply Explained*, Pitmans, Bath (undated)
NESBIT, Roy Conyers and VAN ACKER, Georges – T*he Flight of Rudolf Hess*, Sutton, Stroud, 1999
NORWICH, J.J. – *The Duff Cooper Diaries*, Phoenix, London, 2005
NOWAK, Jan – *Courier from Warsaw*, Wayne State Press, Detroit, 1982
ORLOW, Dietrich – *The Nazi Party 1919–1945: A Complete History*, Enigma, New York, 2008
OSBORN, Patrick – *Operation Pike*, Greenwood Press, Westport, 2000
OVERY, Richard – *Bomber Command*, Harper Collins, London, 1997
OVERY, Richard – *The Battle*, Penguin, London, 2000
OWEN, James – *Nuremberg: Evil on Trial*, Headline, London, 2006
PADFIELD, Peter – *Hess: The Führer's Disciple*, Cassell & Co., London, 2001
PADFIELD, Peter – *Himmler*, Macmillan, London, 1990
PADFIELD, Peter – *Hess, Hitler and Churchill: The Real Turning Point of the Second World War*, Icon, London, 2013
PALMER,DEAN – *Tea with Hitler*, The History Press ,Cheltenham, 2022
PAUL, Wolfgang – *Herman Goering*, Arms and Armour, London, 1998
PEARSON, John – *The Life of Ian Fleming*, Jonathan Cape, London, 1966
PEEL, Mark – *The Patriotic Duke*, Thistle, London, 2013
PETROPOULOS, Jonathan – *Royals and the Reich*, Oxford University Press, Oxford, 2006
PHILBY, Kim – *My Silent War*, Macgibbon & Kee, London, 1968

PICKNETT, Lynn, PRINCE, Clive and PRIOR Stephen – *Double Standards*, Little Brown, London, 2003

PICKNETT, Lynn, PRINCE, Clive and PRIOR Stephen – *War of the Windsors*, Mainstream, London, 2003

PIDGEON, Geoffrey – *The Secret Wireless War*, Arundel Books, Richmond, 2003

PLESHAKOV, Constantine – *Stalin's Folly*, Weidenfeld & Nicolson, London, 2005

POGONOWSKI, Iwo – *Poland, Hippocrene*, New York, 2000

POLISH MINISTRY OF INFORMATION – *The German New Order*, Hutchinson, London, 1942

POMIAN, John – *Joseph Retinger*, Sussex University Press, 1972

POPE, Ernest – *Munich Playground*, WH Allen, London, 1942.

POPOV, Duško – *Spy/Counterspy*, Grosset and Dunlap, New York, 1974

PRATT, George – *The Scottish Red Cross*, Jackson, Glasgow, 1952

PRICE Alfred – *The Luftwaffe Data Book*, Greenhill, London, 1997

PYE, Michael – *The King Over the Water*, Hutchinson, London, 1981

RACZYNSKI, Edward – *W Sojuszniczym Londynie*, II wydanie, London, 1974

RAINA, Peter – *A Daring Venture*, Peter Lang, Bern, 2014

READ, Anthony and FISHER, David – *Colonel Z*, Hodder & Stoughton, London, 1984

READ, Anthony – *The Devil's Disciples*, Pimlico, London, 2004

REES, John – *The Case of Rudolf Hess*, Heinemann, London, 1947

REES, John – *Mental Health and the Offender*, Clarke Hall Lecture, 1947

REICHMINISTER der LUFTFAHRT – *BF110 Flugzeug*, Handbuch, Berlin, 1943

RETINGER, J.H. – *All about Poland*, Minerva, London, 1940

RHODES-JAMES, Robert – *Victor Cazalet*, Hamish Hamilton, London, 1976

RICHARDSON, Dickie – *Man is Not Lost*, Airlife, Shrewsbury, 1997

RICHARDS, Denis – *Portal of Hungerford*, Heinemann, London, 1977

ROBERTS, Andrew – *Eminent Churchillians*, Phoenix, London, 1994

ROBERTS, Mrs Ernest Stewart – *Sherbourne, Oxford and Cambridge*, Martin Hopkinson, London, 1934

ROHWER, J. and HUMMELCHEN, G. – *The War at Sea*, Ian Allen, London, 1974

ROMERA, E. – *Atlas Historyczny Polski*, PPWK, Warsaw, 1998

ROSE, Norman – *The Cliveden Set*, Jonathan Cape, London, 2000
RUSSELL, John – *A Silver Plated Spoon*, Cassell, London, 1959
SARKAR, Dilip – *Guards VC*, Ramrod- Malvern, 1999
SATTLER, Peter W. – *Giessen, Stadt im Wandel 1933–2007*, Sutton Verlag, Erfurt, 2008
SCHLIE, Ulrich – *Kein Friede mit Deutschland*, Langen Muller, Munich, 1994
SCHMIDT, Rainer – *Botengang Eines Toren?*, Econ, Düsseldorf, 1997
SCHELLENBERG, Walter – *Hitler's Secret Service: Memoirs*, Pyramid, New York, 1958
SCHWARZWALLER, Wulf – *Rudolf Hess: The Deputy*, Quartet, London, 1988
SCHWIPPER, Bernd – *Deutschland in Visier Stalins*, Druffel & vowinckel, Gilching, 2016
SCOTT, Lord George – *Lucy Walter: Wife or Mistress*, Harrap, London 1947
SEIDL, Alfred – *Der verweigerte Friede*, Universitas, Munich, 1985
SHACKLADY, Edward – *B24 Liberator*, Cerberus, Bristol, 2002
SHAWCROSS, William – *Queen Elizabeth: The Queen Mother*, MacMillan, London, 2009
SHENKAR, Joan – *Truly Wilde*, Virago, London, 2000
SHENNAN, Andrew – *De Gaulle*, Longman, London 1993
SHIRER, William – *The Rise and Fall of the Third Reich*, Mandarin, London, 1991
SHUKMAN, Harold – *Stalin*, Sutton, Stroud, 1999
SISMAN, Adam – *Hugh Trevor-Roper*, Phoenix, London, 2011
SMITH, Alfred – *Rudolf Hess and Germany's Reluctant War*, Book Guild, Lewes, 2001
SPEER, Albert – *Inside the Third Reich*, Phoenix, London, 2001
SMITH, Michael – *Foley, The Spy who Saved 10,000 Jews*, Hodder & Stoughton, London, 1999
STACHURA, Peter – *Poland in the Twentieth Century*, Macmillan, London, 1999
STAFFORD, David – *Flight from Reality*, Pimlico, London, 2002
STANLEY LEWIS, W. – *Military Map Reading*, Wheaton, Exeter, 1941
STAUFFER, Paul, – *Sechs furchtbare Jahre*, Neue Zürcher Zeitung, Zurich, 1998
STETTLER, M. – *Kuratorium C.J. Burckhardt*, Des Schriftlichen Nacklasses, Basle University, 1978

STEPHENS, Mark – *Ernest Bevin*, TGWU, London, 1981
SWORD, Keith – *Sikorski: Soldier and Statesman*, Orbis, London, 1990
TAYLOR, A.J.P. – *The Origins of the Second World War*, Penguin, London, 1991
TAYLOR, Les – *Luftwaffe over Scotland*, Whittles, Dunbeath, 2010
TENNANT, Peter – *Touchlines of War*, University of Hull Press, 1992
TERRY, Sarah – *Poland's Place in Europe*, Princeton University Press, Princeton, NJ, 1993
THOMAS, Hugh – *The Murder of Rudolf Hess*, Hodder & Stoughton, London, 1979
THOMPSON, *Carlos* – *The Assassination of Winston Churchill*, Smythe, Gerrards Cross, 1969
THOMPSON, J. – *The Charterhall Story*, Air Research, Surrey, 2004
TREE, Ronald – *When the Moon was High*, Macmillan, London, 1975
TURNER, John – *The Battle of Britain*, BCA, London, 1998
URBACH, Karina – *Go-Betweens for Hitler*, Oxford, 2015
VAN ISHOVEN, Armand – *The Fall of an Eagle*, William Kimber, London, 1979
VAN ISHOVEN, Armand – *Udet*, Paul Neff Verlag, Berlin, 1977
VAN ISHOVEN, Armand – *Messerschmitt*, Gentry, London, 1975
VASCO, J. and CORNWELL, P. – *Zerstorer*, JAC Publications, Norwich, 1995
VON HASSELL, Ulrich – *The Von Hassell Diaries 1938–1944*, Hamish Hamilton, London, 1948
VON HASSELL, Ulrich – *The Ulrich von Hassell Diaries*, Frontline, Barnsley, 2011
VON HEINTZE, Ian – *War Chronicles of Jerzy Dobiecki*, Winged Hussar, New Jersey, 2018
VON LANG, Jochen – *Bormann*, Random House, London, 1979
WALLER, John H. – *The Unseen War*, Random House, New York, 1996
WAKEFIELD, Ken – *Somewhere in the West Country*, Crecy, Wilmslow, 1997
WARWICK, Christopher – *George and Marina: Duke and Duchess of Kent*, Albert Bridge, 2014
WASZAK, Leon – *Agreement in Principle*, Peter Lang, New York
WAYNE, Helena (ed.) – *The Story of a Marriage, Vol. 2*, Routledge, London and New York, 1995
WEBSTER, Jason – *The Spy with 29 names*, Chatto & Windus, London, 2014

WEITZ, John – *Hitler's Diplomat*, Weidenfeld & Nicolson, London, 1992
WEITZ, John – *Hitlers Banker*, Warner, London, 1999
WELCHMAN, Gordon – T*he Hut 6 Story: Breaking the Enigma Codes*, M&M Baldwin, Shropshire, 2018
WELSH, Ian – *Prestwick in the 1940s*, Kyle Libraries, Ayr, 1992
WEST, Nigel – *MI6*, Weidenfeld & Nicolson, London, 1983
WEST, Nigel – *The Guy Liddell Diaries*, Vol. 1 1939–1942, Routledge, Abingdon, 2005
WHEELER-HOLOHAN, V. – *The History of the Kings Messengers*, Grayson, London, 1935
WHEELER-BENNETT, John W. – *King George VI*, Macmillan, London, 1958
WHEELER-BENNETT, John W. – *John Anderson – Viscount Waverley*, Macmillan, London 1962
WHITE, L. and HUSSEY, W. – *Government*, Cambridge University Press, London, 1966
WHITING, Audrey – *The Kents*, Hutchinson, London, 1985
WHITING, Charles – *Heydrich*, Leo Cooper, Barnsley, 1999
WILMOT, Chester – *The Struggle for Europe*, Collins, London, 1952
WITTMAN, Robert and KINNEY, David – T*he Devil's Diary*, William Collins, London, 2016
WINTERBOTHAM, Fred – *Secret and Personal*, William Kimber, London, 1969
WOOD, Derek – *Attack Warning Red*, Macdonald and Janes, London, 1976
WYLLIE, James – *Nazi Wives*, The History Press, Stroud, 2019
YOUNG, G.M. – *Baldwin*, Rupert Hart-Davis, London, 1952
ZIEGLER, Philip – *Diana Cooper*, Hamish Hamilton, London, 1981
ZIEGLER Philip – *King Edward VII*, Collins, London, 1990
ZWAR, Desmond – *Talking to Rudolf Hess*, The History Press, Stroud, 2010